SOCIOPHONETICS

Also by Erik R. Thomas

AN ACOUSTIC ANALYSIS OF VOWEL VARIATION IN NEW WORLD ENGLISH

THE DEVELOPMENT OF AFRICAN AMERICAN ENGLISH (*with Walt Wolfram*)

AFRICAN AMERICAN ENGLISH SPEAKERS AND THEIR PARTICIPATION IN LOCAL SOUND CHANGES: A COMPARATIVE STUDY (*ed. with Malcah Yaeger-Dror*)

Sociophonetics

An Introduction

Erik R. Thomas

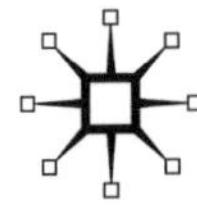

First published 2011 by
PALGRAVE MACMILLAN

Palgrave Macmillan in the UK is an imprint of Macmillan Publishers Limited, registered in England, company number 785998, of Houndmills, Basingstoke, Hampshire RG21 6XS.

Palgrave Macmillan in the US is a division of St Martin's Press LLC, 175 Fifth Avenue, New York, NY 10010.

Palgrave Macmillan is the global academic imprint of the above companies and has companies and representatives throughout the world.

Palgrave® and Macmillan® are registered trademarks in the United States, the United Kingdom, Europe and other countries.

ISBN 978–0–230–22455–1 hardback
ISBN 978–0–230–22456–8 paperback

This book is printed on paper suitable for recycling and made from fully managed and sustained forest sources. Logging, pulping and manufacturing processes are expected to conform to the environmental regulations of the country of origin.

A catalogue record for this book is available from the British Library.

A catalog record for this book is available from the Library of Congress.

10 9 8 7 6 5 4 3 2 1
20 19 18 17 16 15 14 13 12 11

Printed and bound in Great Britain by
CPI Antony Rowe, Chippenham and Eastbourne

To my four mentors

Guy Bailey

Ronald R. Butters

Robert D. King

Walt Wolfram

Without any one of them, I wouldn't be here to write this book.

Brief Contents

Contents

Preface

This introduction to sociolinguistics grew out of my long interest in the interface between sociolinguistics and phonetics. There's never been a time when I didn't see the two as supremely compatible and intertwined. This interrelationship holds on numerous levels, from the most concrete to the most abstract. I find it unfortunate that sociophonetics is too often seen as merely methodological. Its theoretical aspects, discussed in the latter chapters of this book leading up to the lateral transfer model in Chapter 12, can help sociolinguistics to become more integrated into linguistics as a whole, and indeed to be seen as central, as it should be.

This book is intended for students in both sociolinguistics and phonetics. Both groups can use this as a guide to phonetic techniques and to some theoretical issues that affect both fields. It's designed differently from any previous phonetics or sociolinguistics textbook. Most of all, though, I hope that it aids both groups in seeing how interrelated their fields are.

The approach I take in this book is that there's no one right method for performing an analysis. Instead, there are usually several ways, each with its advantages and disadvantages. It's better to make an informed decision among different techniques than to stick blindly with one. Moreover, the equipment and programs used to conduct analyses should be largely interchangeable. Hence, the methods presented in this book can be implemented using a variety of analysis tools. Nevertheless, to create the figures and to extract data for some of the tables, I relied primarily on Praat, version 5.1.04 (Boersma and Weenink 2009), for acoustic analysis, and Origin™, version 6.1, for plotting. Figure 7.10 is a screenshot.

Many of the spectrograms and other acoustic analyses are of my voice or of my daughter's. These recordings were made with a Marantz Portable Cassette Recorder PMD222, using a Sony F-V200 omnidirectional microphone, and were recorded in a soundproof booth (or sometimes in a quiet room) and digitized later at a sampling rate of 44.1 kHz with lowpass filtering at 20 kHz. Some of the recordings of North Carolinians were also made in a soundproof booth but were recorded digitally with a sampling rate of 22.05 kHz and lowpass filtering at 10 kHz. The remaining acoustic analyses were based on field recordings, usually made with a Marantz Portable Cassette Recorder PMD222 and a Sony F-V200 omnidirectional microphone. They were digitized at a sampling rate of 44.1 kHz with lowpass filtering at 20 kHz.

A number of people provided assistance in the production of this book, and I owe them considerable thanks. Tyler S. Kendall created the website in which the downloadable soundfiles used for the practice exercises are stored. He did most of the work in developing the program on which the demonstrations of vowel normalization techniques in Chapter 5 were run. He also created Figure 6.1 and the prototypes for Figures 6.2 and 6.3 for me. I thank my daughter, Jane Thomas, for her cooperation and patience as I recorded her voice in a number of sessions in the soundproof booth. I couldn't ask for a nicer daughter. Warren Maguire provided me with recordings of speakers from Newcastle-upon-Tyne, England, and Northern Ireland. Margaret Maclagan, Jaclyn Ocumpaugh and Walt Wolfram provided other recordings. My mother, Mary C. Thomas, was instrumental in contacting the speakers from Ohio. Robert Bayley, Richard Cantu, Belinda Schouten and especially Yolanda Treviño provided me with access to the speakers from southern Texas. I thank all of the anonymous speakers whose voices are featured in various figures in this book for their cooperation. James Hillenbrand and Laura Colantoni helpfully and promptly answered a number of queries I sent them. Robin Dodsworth provided helpful advice on statistics and sociological analyses. Other key assistance was provided by Josh Rector and Charlotte Vaughn. Three anonymous referees provided useful advice that I incorporated into this book. The editorial staff at Palgrave Macmillan, particularly Kitty van Boxel, Kate Haines, Keith Povey and Felicity Noble, have been a pleasure to work with. Walt Wolfram provided constant moral support throughout the whole project. Finally, I especially thank my wife, Barbara Hunter, for her emotional support and encouragement and for her tolerance of the long, often late hours and preoccupation that this project led me into.

ERIK R. THOMAS

The Place of Sociophonetics

1

1.1 A youthful field

Sociophonetics has seemingly burst upon the linguistic scene in recent years. In the mid-1990s, the term *sociophonetics* was virtually unknown, used occasionally in phonetics but otherwise unrecognized. Foulkes and Docherty (2006) date its first use to a study of Québec French by Deschaies-Lafontaine (1974), but it was seldom used for the following 20 years. Now the term is heard widely in both sociolinguistic and phonetic circles. It has become a staple at conferences in both fields and even draws attention in phonology.

Sociophonetics, in its rapid growth, has expanded in various directions and hence hasn't been as easy to define as it might seem. Most basically, it is the interface of sociolinguistics and phonetics. Its phonetic aspects are usually limited to practices of modern phonetics, including acoustic and articulatory analysis and speech perception experiments. That circumscription excludes traditional impressionistic phonetic transcription, though some authorities might include it. The scope of sociolinguistic topics that it covers includes any kind of variation – stylistic, geographical, social class-based, gender-based, generational, ethnic and social clique-based. It also encompasses applications in fields such as language contact and forensic linguistics. That definition may seem broad enough to please everybody, but concepts of what sociophonetics is still differ a lot. Phoneticians tend to view it as comprising phonetic studies that involve any kind of dialectal variation, but not necessarily examining social aspects of language. Sociolinguists, conversely, often see it as including any sociolinguistic studies that utilize modern phonetic techniques, particularly acoustic analysis or speech perception experiments, but they don't consider any of the theoretical issues of concern to phoneticians to be essential to it. Furthermore, many people from both fields often view sociophonetics as a methodological construct, whereas others recognize a theoretical side to it as well. Within sociolinguistics it has become identified with the study of vowel shifting, though this represents only one corner in a roomful of possibilities.

Such different viewpoints on definition are the mark of a field that is just emerging. As widespread as sociophonetics is becoming, though, the time has come for the field to begin to define itself. Among the aims of this book are those of tying together the various strands – sociolinguistic and phonetic, methodological and theoretical – and of expanding the purview of the field by showing readers the range of possible issues that sociophonetics can address. Most of all, I'd like readers to see why the research aims of sociolinguistics and phonetics aren't as disparate as they seem and how they actually converge on the goal of understanding the cognitive and diachronic aspects of language.

1.2 What is sociophonetics?

So what's sociophonetics all about? To begin with, it's intrinsically empirical. Its theoretical aims are closely linked to its empirical methods. That is, it views language as something that must be observed to be understood, and it generally holds that hypotheses should be accompanied by data collection. Phonetics is the aspect of language that is most easily observed because it can be physically measured in sundry ways, and sociophonetics takes phonetics as an entry point into language. Yet sociophonetics also views variation and change as the most fundamental of properties of language. Speakers adjust to their environment by adjusting their phonetics. Phonetic properties provide speakers with more parameters to vary than other realms of language (with the possible exception of lexicon, but most lexical variables appear infrequently in speech). Hence sociophonetics holds that an understanding of the cognitive forces underlying speech cannot be based on a notion of language as static. Instead, it has to be based on a perspective of language as inherently unstable, allowing speakers to adapt and accommodate to social situations in which they find themselves.

Docherty et al. (1997) discuss the tension between two well-known approaches to linguistic research. One, the 'top-down' approach, begins with a theory developed by the researcher based on a small amount of data. The theory is intended to provide an elegant means of accounting for the data. The other approach, 'bottom-up', starts with a survey that yields a large amount of data, after which researchers construct a hypothesis that best matches the data. The hypothesis isn't always perfectly elegant because large corpora of data almost always produce a few loose ends that seem to fit no pattern, especially where human behaviour is concerned. Formal fields of linguistics, including phonology, have customarily favoured top-down designs, though in recent years the laboratory phonology movement has emphasized more bottom-up approaches. Sociolinguists, on the other hand, have privileged bottom-up procedures because of their emphasis on fieldwork, survey designs and interviewing techniques. Docherty et al. (1997) take, as an example of the value of bottom-up approaches, one variable, the glottalization of voiceless stops in the English of Tyneside in northern England. Previous studies had formulated hypotheses about the distribution and phonological specification of glottalization using a top-down perspective. Docherty et al., however, showed that a survey of Tyneside English produced data that contradicted the expectations of the top-down hypotheses. Furthermore, it yielded other unexpected results.

For example, glottalization was disfavoured in Tyneside English before pauses, a configuration at odds with patterns found in other dialects.

Like sociolinguists, experimental phoneticians prefer 'bottom-up', empirical routes to hypotheses. The two groups differ on methodological priorities, however. Sociolinguists usually place a high priority on defining the community that they're studying. The 'speech community' circumscribes a sociolinguistic study, and the history and social structure of the community under study factor heavily into both the hypotheses being tested and the findings. Phoneticians are seldom concerned about speech communities except in the broadest terms – e.g. speakers from a particular nation who speak the same language. Sociolinguists tend to be far more concerned than phoneticians with sampling techniques. They place a lot of emphasis on finding 'typical' or 'representative' speakers and with population sampling techniques as a whole. Even though they rarely attempt random samples and often rely on convenience sampling, they frequently construct stratified samples in which the possible combinations of social classes, age groups, sexes, ethnic groups and other factors are represented. At other times, they target specific groups, such as members of a social clique or of a minority group. Phoneticians sometimes target particular groups, such as bilinguals with a particular L1 and L2 (where L1 is 'first language' and L2 is 'second language') or speakers with hearing impairments, but most of the time they don't concern themselves with population sampling. Their subjects are frequently whatever students or colleagues they can persuade to take part in their studies. On the other hand, phoneticians often try to get large amounts of data from individual subjects, which reduces potential random errors. Sociolinguists, who like to get larger samples of subjects, often aren't as concerned with getting large samples of data from individual subjects, except when they target stylistic variation.

Another key difference is that sociolinguists aim for naturalness in speech samples, while phoneticians aim for experimental control. That is, sociolinguists value speech samples that are closest to conversations in everyday encounters. They attempt to minimize the 'observer's paradox' or 'Hawthorne effect', the fact that subjects' behaviour changes when they know that they are being observed. This isn't to say that sociolinguists always obtain natural conversations – in fact, interview-style conversation is probably most common, and they often elicit read speech – but speaking style is a critical issue for them. Phoneticians, conversely, value replicability most highly. When conducting an experiment, it's important to them to control for as many factors as possible, both to isolate the factors that are under study and to make the study repeatable to see whether the same result is obtained. Hence, most of the time they use read speech that has been recorded in a laboratory when they study speech production, or they conduct laboratory experiments to study speech perception. The sociolinguistic need to capture naturalistic situations can preclude replication of studies. At the same time, phoneticians' need for controlled experimentation tends to preclude naturalness. The empirical challenge of sociophonetics is to take the methodological concerns of both traditions seriously.

While the empirical practices of sociophonetics require the balancing of sociolinguistic and phonetic priorities, the research questions that it addresses must be related to the larger aims of linguistics as a whole. Linguistics, over its history, has been concerned primarily with two questions. Each of these questions has been modified from its earlier form over the years. The first question is how and why language changes. Linguistics has traditionally focused more on the intricacies of sound change than on other types of linguistic changes. It was the subject of the first great controversy in linguistics, the dispute over the Neogrammarian Hypothesis during the 1870s and 1880s. The Neogrammarian Hypothesis stated that sound changes were exceptionless and that they could be conditioned only by phonetic factors (Osthoff and Brugmann 1967). The main objections to it over the past century have come from the question of whether sound changes can be conditioned by morphology and syntax and from adherents of 'lexical diffusion', the notion that sound changes spread through the lexicon word by word (see Wang 1977). Another development came with the advent of phonetics, when it became clear that sounds are not discrete entities but grade into each other. If anything, this development made it easier to see how sounds could change. During the twentieth century, the study of linguistic change gradually shifted towards examining language contact instead of just genetic developments as scholars such as Uriel Weinreich (1953) drew attention to the importance of contact. The major shift in the question of how and why language changes, however, was associated with Labovian sociolinguistics. Labov (1975) popularized 'the use of the present to understand the past' in linguistic change. This approach is an instantiation of the uniformitarian principle, a widely recognized principle used in biology, geology, physics and other sciences, which asserts that processes observable today are the same processes that have always operated. As it applies to linguistic change, it involves examining how linguistic innovations originate and are propagated within speech communities. In effect, the study of how linguistic change occurs has been equated in part with sociolinguistics. Yet the aim of sociolinguistics is to study how and why language *varies*. The result, and a productive result it has been, is that variation is seen as inseparable from change and vice versa. Thus, this first major question in linguistics can be reformulated as: how and why does language vary and change?

The other major concern of linguistics is that of how language is structured. This question, formulated in terms of language as an abstract object, was essentially the prime concern of Saussure, the American Structuralists and the Prague School. Language had to be objectified because of the rudimentary state of knowledge at that time about the neural structures underlying language. Bloomfield (1933: 34–6), for example, describes what was then known about aphasias, but otherwise avoids discussion of the brain. Bloomfield was, by his own account, opposed to a 'mentalistic' approach to language, but by that he didn't mean that the psychological organization of language was unimportant. Instead, he argued against any 'non-physical factor' (Ibid.:32) governing language. At any rate, the neurological basis of linguistics was too little-known in his day for him to address it in any depth. Hence he and other structuralists concerned themselves with, as their name suggests, structural aspects of language, especially in phonology and morphology. Across the Atlantic, the Prague School Linguists didn't ignore the neurological basis of language.

Roman Jakobson, for example, wrote extensively about aphasias, beginning as early as 1941 (Jakobson 1962). However, they were also largely confined to discussing linguistic structures, not neural substrates of language.

The shift, though, came with Chomsky, who put the 'mind' and/or brain at the front and centre. As is well known, he has maintained that there is a special cognitive module predisposed to language. The rest of linguistics came to agree with him that the human brain is predisposed to language, and today the main point of contention is the extent of the innate components of language. The fact that this question has become so important reflects how Chomsky shifted the second major issue in linguistics. Chomsky (1965: 4) contended that 'in the technical sense, linguistic theory is mentalistic, since it is concerned with discovering a mental reality underlying actual behavior'. This mental reality was his concept of *competence*. Discovering what competence consists of became and has remained a primary focus of linguistics. More recently, Chomsky (1988: 3) formulated what he considered to be the major questions for linguistics, and the first two deal directly with the cognitive substrate of language:

1. What is the system of knowledge? What is in the mind/brain of the speaker of English or Spanish or Japanese?
2. How does this system of knowledge arise in the mind/brain?

While not all linguists attack the problem of the mental/neural organization of language the same way that Chomsky does, and not all share Chomsky's views of how language is represented psychologically, virtually all linguists now agree that understanding the mental/neural organization of language is a fundamental aim of linguistics and a large part of the field is devoted to studying it. This second general issue in linguistics has, then, been shifted from how is language structured? to how is language structured in the mind/brain?

The two great concerns of linguistics seem disparate, but there are links between them. The most obvious link is that any change or variation in a linguistic characteristic necessarily entails a change or variation in the internalized grammar. Hence, the study of linguistic variation is also the study of neurolinguistic variation. In addition, though, language variation and change can offer other cues into the grammatical and neurological structure of language. Linguistic changes may reflect grammatical parameters: for example, sound changes normally involve one sound changing into a similar sound. Proposed derivations in phonological theories frequently follow historical processes closely, famously (or notoriously, depending on one's point of view) the derivations involving long/short vowel alternations in English in Chomsky and Halle (1968). Variation, whether intraspeaker, intralinguistic or interlinguistic, may show that certain linguistic factors are internalized and aren't automatic consequences of the linguistic processing system or the articulators. Kingston and Diehl (1994) illustrate that fact in discussing cross-linguistic differences in the phonetic cues used to effect the [±voice] phonological feature. Finally, variation can indicate that particular facets of language not otherwise considered part of the grammar are internalized in some way. Hymes (1974: 174 ff.), for example, proposed that linguistic competence shouldn't just encompass referential aspects of language, but should also contain the pragmatic knowledge a speaker has about what variants mean socially and how to use them for stylistic purposes.

The division between linguists who study variation and change in language and those who study structure and neural substrates is sometimes broken down into a division between 'functional linguistics' and 'structural linguistics'. Functional linguistics examines not just variation and change but everything that Ferdinand de Saussure (1983) had dubbed *parole*, that is, the social uses of language. Structural linguistics has its roots in Saussure's concept of *langue*, the grammatical system of language, though it now operates through the lens of Chomsky's *competence*, which has superseded *langue* and which, unlike *langue*, is seen as speaker-internal. The functional/structural division has been recognized widely within linguistics. For example, Hymes (1974) devotes a chapter to the division, and an entire two-volume compendium (Darnell et al. 1999) has appeared with the division as its theme. Under this classification, the generative fields – phonology, morphology, syntax and semantics – as well as neurolinguistics, much of language acquisition study and certain aspects of phonetics, are structural. Sociolinguistics, historical linguistics, pragmatics, anthropological linguistics and many areas within phonetics are functional.

I find this structural/functional division rather unfortunate. First, the grammatical basis of language has not proved as isolatable as is often assumed in structural linguistics. Chomsky (1980) divided the human language capacity into three 'mental organs': the grammar, the conceptual system (lexicon and semantics) and pragmatic competence. The last of the three, as Hymes (1974) argues at length, is a key concern of sociolinguistics. Neuroscience, however, has not found these functions easy to separate within the brain. They may well be too highly interconnected to untangle. Current understandings that brain function is as network oriented as modular make one wonder whether we should be trying to isolate the different linguistic capacities. The relationship between phonology/phonetics and pragmatic competence is likely to be especially close because so many phonetic and phonological variables in any language show stylistic variation. In English, for example, the present participial and gerundive suffix is [ɪn] in less formal styles and [ɪŋ] in more formal ones; rising final intonational contours may signal deference; and coarticulation between vowels and approximants is strongly influenced by rate of speech, which in turn is affected by the social setting. Phonetics and sociolinguistics, and hence sociophonetics, can thereby have quite a lot to contribute to what has been the domain of structural linguistics.

Second, fields classified as functional, including both sociolinguistics and phonetics, are the seat of considerable research relevant to language structure. The phonetic details that phoneticians concern themselves with and the lectal and stylistic variants that sociolinguists deal with thus take on new meaning. They are vital to understanding phonological competence.

The functional versus structural issue has been a concern not just in linguistics as a whole but within sociolinguistics too. Hymes (1974) divides sociolinguistics into three areas of interest. The first, which he calls 'the social as well as the linguistic', he identifies as real-world applications of sociolinguistics, such as in education and law. The other two are theoretical in nature. The second area, 'socially realistic linguistics', is essentially Labovian or quantitative sociolinguistics, and he (1974: 196) identifies it with the traditional linguistic concerns of 'the nature of linguistic rules, the nature of sound change'. The third area, 'socially constituted linguistics', is, he says (ibid.), 'concerned with social as well as referential meaning'. I would assert that the second area is the basic focus of sociophonetics. Although in linguistics as a whole the functional versus structural opposition, I think, obscures aspects of linguistic organization, within sociolinguistics it takes on distinctly different connotations. The structural outlook maintains language as the focus of study, and, when Hymes speaks of what he recognizes as a second area of sociolinguistics, 'the nature of linguistic rules, the nature of sound change', he is speaking of the two basic concerns of linguistics, respectively: how language is structured (whether in the mind/brain or not) and why language varies and changes. On the other hand, the functional outlook, represented by Hymes's 'socially constituted linguistics', places its focus on social meaning. That is, discovering language is no longer the final aim, but instead language, as an index of social meaning, becomes a way of discovering social function. Hence Hymes's third area of sociolinguistics addresses a question that is, in its essence, sociological. Trudgill (1978) makes a similar point in noting that some studies labelled as sociolinguistics address sociological questions, some address purely linguistic questions, and some lie on the border. Sociophonetic methods can offer linguistic sociologists useful tools for determining how language indexes social meaning. In fact, Chapter 11 will touch on some ways sociophonetic methods can do so, and specific applications will appear in the text and practice exercises of Chapters 4–7 as well. However, it's unfortunate that the field of sociology has never developed a linguistic branch. Where can linguistic sociologists go? In addition to the ethnography of speaking, there is Joshua Fishman's sociology of language movement and the *International Journal of the Sociology of Language*, but most of its contributors aren't in sociology departments. Linguistic sociologists are forced either to melt into linguistic anthropology or to try to fit into linguistics. The incongruity hinders and diminishes their labour and insights, which address an essential aspect of human life.

More recently, Eckert (2005) has taken up the status of functional approaches within sociolinguistics. Eckert, as demonstrated by her previous work (e.g. Eckert 1989a), resides partly in the Hymesian tradition of focusing on social meaning. From her perspective, she sees variationist work as representing three waves. The first wave, typified by Labov's (1966) survey of the Lower East Side of Manhattan, examined correlations between linguistic variation and broad demographic characteristics. The second wave, exemplified by Milroy's (1980) study of Belfast, took an ethnographic approach, examining, for example, how linguistic variation is correlated with an individual's engagement in local community networks. The third wave, according to Eckert, focuses on stylistic variation and how speakers use it to project different identities. Sociophonetics takes stylistic variation seriously. In contrast to the characterization of formal linguistics as treating styles 'solely as successive modifications of an ordinary grammar' (Hymes 1974: 177), sociophonetics treats styles as integral parts of how language is internalized. It also recognizes the intertwined nature of linguistic variation and social meaning. However, it offers an alternative to having the discovery of social function as the ultimate goal of variation studies. Instead of focusing on how language variation and the construction of speaking styles are a means of constructing social meaning, sociophonetics addresses how speaking styles, with their inherent social meanings, are a path to understanding how language is structured. It thereby views social meaning as a crucial aspect of the cognition of language. Some recent sociophonetic papers illustrate this focus. For instance, Foulkes and Docherty (2006) discuss how language variation can inform Exemplar Theory, a new and controversial conception of how language acquisition and the cognitive organization of language take place. Similarly, Purnell et al. (2005b) explore the plasticity of a phonological contrast by examining changes in the cues used to produce the voicing contrast across four generations of residents of a German–American community in Wisconsin.

The notion that sociolinguistics can provide clues to how language is internalized is by no means new. During the heyday of generative phonology, sociolinguists developed variable rules that represented the ordering of constraints on phonological variables (e.g. Labov 1969; Cedergren and Sankoff 1974). The rules were construed as reflecting internalized processes that governed the occurrence of variants. In the years since the popularity of variable rules has waned, other papers relating sociolinguistic findings to the structure of internalized grammar have appeared sporadically. Some of these efforts are framed in terms of more recent phonological theories, such as Optimality Theory (Nagy and Reynolds 1997). Optimality Theory holds that phonologies of languages differ in the importance that each places on various competing constraints. Other efforts aren't tied to a particular phonological theory. For example, Labov (e.g. Labov 1994) has proposed a phonological feature [±peripheral] to account for why, over time, long or tense vowels tend to be made higher in the mouth and short or lax vowels lower in the mouth. Sociophonetics represents the continuation of the movement to relate language variation to the cognitive structure of language. As such, it is also the continuation of the side of sociolinguistics that is focused on the two traditional questions of linguistics: how language is structured in the mind/brain and how/why language varies and changes. Moreover, no subfield of linguistics is better positioned to show how those two questions are interrelated.

1.3 History of sociophonetics

Sociophonetics began before the name was apparently coined in 1974. This precedence holds even if we exclude studies that used only impressionistic transcription, since, as I mentioned earlier, *sociophonetics* is usually used to denote approaches using more modern phonetic techniques. Within sociolinguistics, the genesis of sociophonetics is, basically, Labov, Yaeger and Steiner (1972), though even earlier Labov (1963) made limited use of acoustic data. Labov et al. (1972) ushered into sociolinguistics the use of acoustic analysis for studying vowel variation. Their primary aim was to determine the principles governing vowel shifting. The equipment available in those days was a lot less user-friendly than the equipment we have today. They had to print out large numbers of spectrograms and measure the formants by hand from the printed spectrograms. Today, spectrographic software and linear predictive coding (LPC) (Atal and Hanauer 1971) have made measurement of formants, the main parameters of vowels, paperless and much faster. However, reliance on vowel formant measurements and on plots showing the first two formants has remained standard for studying vowel variation.

Labov and his students at the University of Pennsylvania were nearly the only sociolinguists to use acoustic analysis of vowels in dialectal studies for two decades. Besides Labov et al. (1972), Hindle (1980), Labov (1980, 1991), Ash (1988) and Veatch (1991) represent works by Labov's research team during this earlier stage. Among the few outsiders to conduct acoustic research on dialects of English were Habick (1980), Maclagan (1982) and Godinez (1984). The situation changed during the 1990s, however, as numerous researchers beyond the University of Pennsylvania adopted spectrographic methods for vowel analysis. Most of these studies – e.g. Thomas and Bailey (1992); Esling and Warkentyne (1993); Ito and Preston (1998); Fought (1999); Wolfram et al. (1999); Fridland (2000, 2003); and Thomas (2001) – have been conducted in North America. However, a growing number – e.g. McClure (1995); Cox (1999); Watt and Tillotson (2001); Fabricius (2002); Deterding (2003); Torgersen and Kerswill (2004); and Sharbawi (2006), in addition to Maclagan's (1982) previous study of Australian English – have taken place elsewhere and analysed varieties of English from other parts of the world. The flowering of acoustic analysis of vowel variation represents an encouraging democratization of sociophonetics. However, acoustic vowel variation work has barely spread beyond analysis of English. Among the few exceptions are studies of Dutch vowel variation by van Heuven et al. (2002), Adank et al. (2007) and Jacobi et al. (2007).

Within phonetics, sociophonetics hasn't had as clear of a beginning as in sociolinguistics. Over the years, occasional studies appeared that utilized dialectal or other variations, e.g. Fourakis and Port (1986), Henton (1988) and Munro et al. (1999), but sociophonetics was usually neglected. Foulkes and Docherty (1999: 22) asserted that phoneticians were 'treating variation as a nuisance', as something that represented an obstacle to isolating other factors that they were interested in. Now, though, it's clear that phoneticians are taking notice of variation. This interest is most obviously reflected at phonetics conferences. The International Congress of Phonetic Sciences now regularly holds sessions devoted to sociophonetics. Meetings of the Acoustical Society of America usually have a number of sociophonetic presentations and occasionally a session, and even the International Congress on Speech and Language Processing has a few papers involving variation. Laboratory phonology has followed suit: the 9th Conference on Laboratory Phonology, held in 2004, had as its theme 'Change in Phonology' (see Cole and Hualde 2007).

Acoustic studies of variation in elements of language besides vowels have proceeded at a far slower pace. Docherty and Foulkes (1999) and Purnell et al. (2005a) both bemoan the shortage of acoustic studies of consonantal variation, though both provide fine examples of how to approach this acoustically. Both demonstrate that acoustic analysis can reveal details of consonantal variation that are difficult or impossible to gauge using impressionistic analysis. Nevertheless, because sociolinguists have generally considered impressionistic analysis adequate – not to mention quicker – they have held fast to it and no sustained tradition of acoustic analysis of consonants has developed. Perhaps that will change.

The treatment of prosodic variation has been something of a joint effort among sociolinguists, phoneticians and phonologists. Acoustic studies of intonational variation got off to a slow start, since impressionistic transcription of intonation was the rule for decades. The development of the Tone and Break Index (ToBI) transcription system (Beckman and Hirschberg 1994) encouraged greater use of acoustic methods, mainly pitch tracking; even though it's an impressionistic transcription system, implementing it involves reference to pitch tracks. Work on intonational variation employing pitch tracks, generally relying on ToBI or similar systems, has expanded in recent years, and much of the work has occurred in Europe (e.g. Gussenhoven and van der Vliet 1999; Grabe et al. 2000; Selting 2003). Another aspect of prosody – prosodic rhythm – has also attracted attention recently. Prosodic rhythm is conventionally regarded as the degree of syllable-timing versus stress-timing that a language exhibits. A number of dialectal studies of prosodic rhythm, using new methods of quantitative, acoustic-based analysis, have appeared (e.g. Low et al. 2000; Deterding 2001; Thomas and Carter 2006). Other aspects of prosody, such as lexical tones and stress realization, have received less sustained attention.

Studies of speech perception as it relates to language variation have proceeded in fits and starts, but on a wide variety of research issues. Studies of dialect identification go back at least as far as Dickens and Sawyer (1952), and some of the recent studies, such as Bezooijen and Gooskens (1999) and Clopper and Pisoni (2007), have become quite sophisticated in both phonetic techniques and statistical analyses. Studies of attitudes towards different forms of speech also have a long history, as exemplified by the matched-guise experiment in Lambert et al. (1960). Synthetic manipulation of stimuli, introduced by Brown et al. (1972), has provided a means of controlling stimuli in attitude experiments. The perception of segments that are phonologically merged for some speakers but not for others has drawn some attention (e.g. Labov et al. 1991). Various other issues, such as the intelligibility of dialectal variants of segments (e.g. Labov and Ash 1997), have also been addressed in different experiments. Sociophonetic study of perception has lacked a specific focus but has figured prominently in the development of sociophonetics. See Thomas (2002b) for a detailed discussion of the history of socioperceptual studies.

1.4 Plan of this book

This book is designed to give you two kinds of information. One is specific information on how to analyse speech sounds and conduct experiments. It is intended for anyone who's beginning to conduct phonetic research or who has experience in one type of phonetic research but would like to expand his or her areas of work. It helps to have an introductory phonetics course first, but I've written it so that you can plunge into phonetic analysis with little more than an introduction to linguistics course and perhaps a general sociolinguistics class. For many people, it's easier to learn through experience with analysis than through listening to lectures.

The other kind of information is a more abstract one about sociophonetics. We've just discussed what sociophonetics is and how it came about. In the last few chapters, we'll return to theoretical issues and discuss some that sociophonetics addresses. The chapters vary considerably in length. Some eyebrows may be raised at the length variation, but I feel it's more important for the chapters to cover topics of equal rank than for them to have a uniform length.

Before you start the subsequent chapters, you should make sure you're familiar with how to formulate and test a hypothesis. You can do exploratory and some kinds of descriptive work without a hypothesis, but most of the analyses you'll do will depend on hypothesis testing. The general procedure is shown in Figure 1.1. First, you have to figure out what you want to show in your experiment. Then you decide what your dependent variable is – normally the linguistic variable – and what the independent variable(s) are – that is, whatever factors, linguistic, social or other – that might influence the dependent variables. Next, you decide on a hypothesis. For example, you may wish to hypothesize that short durations cause vowel undershoot or that listeners can distinguish speakers from a certain region. The *null hypothesis* is the opposite

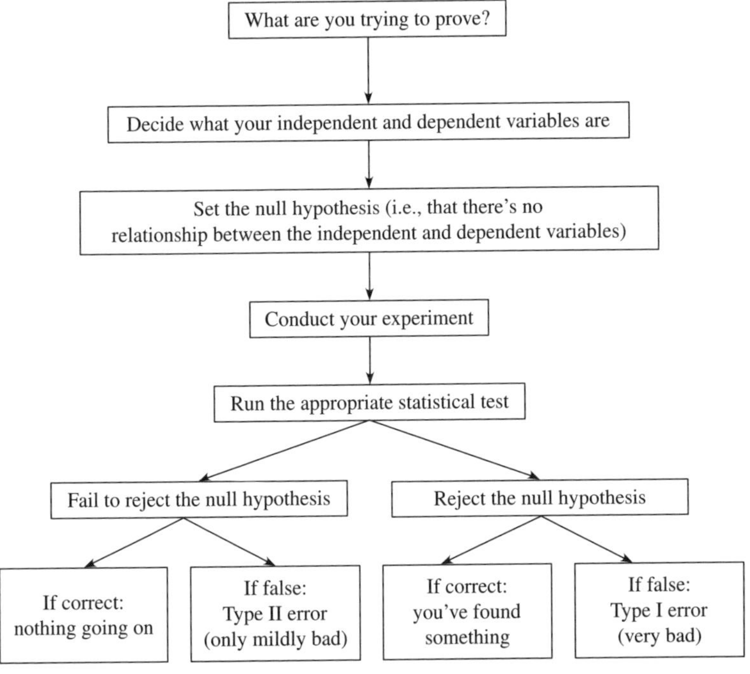

Figure 1.1 Steps in hypothesis testing.

of your hypothesis. That is, the null hypothesis states that there's no correlation between the independent and dependent variables at all. After you run your experiment and apply the right kind of statistical analysis to it, your results will either reject or not reject the null hypothesis. If the results don't reject the null hypothesis, it might mean that there's no relationship between the independent and dependent variables. However, it might mean that you didn't have enough data or the right kind of data to reject the null hypothesis, which is called a Type II or β error. If the results reject the null hypothesis, it probably means that there's a correlation between the independent and dependent variables, which is what you want. However, it's possible that there's no correlation but that, by chance, the data you have were skewed enough that they fooled the statistical test into indicating that there was. This situation is called a Type I or α error. Type I errors are considered more damaging than Type II errors. Statistical tests are designed to tell you what the chances are that their results are erroneous. They tell you this through the p (probability) value. A p value of .05 means that there's a 5 per cent chance of erroneous results, and a p value of .01 means that there's only a 1 per cent chance. In linguistics, the standard for reporting the results is $p < .05$.

I might add, though, that the statistical test is only as good as your data sample. You have to make sure that your sample is representative of the population you are studying. For some things, such as samples of phonetic data from a single speaker, the sampling isn't always an issue, though it can be insofar as speaking style is concerned. When samples of people are involved, though, ensuring that the sample is representative is crucial. Sampling is touched on a little in Chapter 11. Sometimes, usually when you're studying a small group such as a social clique, you can get data from the entire population, in which case you aren't sampling at all. Otherwise you have to sample. Kalton (1983) provides a taxonomy of sampling techniques. *Random samples* are ideal for sociological research, but they're difficult to get and they usually necessitate short interviews that preclude many kinds of linguistic research. Few linguistic studies, e.g. Bailey et al. (1993), have used them. A simple random sample involves one sample of the entire population, while a *stratified* random sample involves separate samples of different groups within the population. *Quota samples*, in which a certain number of people who meet each of various combinations of features are interviewed, have been used for some linguistic studies, such as Wolfram (1969). For a quota sample, the number of subjects with each combination may or may not represent the proportion of such people in the whole population. *Judgement samples* resemble quota samples, but the researcher chooses subjects deemed representative of their respective groups. *Convenience samples* are the most commonly taken kind in linguistics, but the least desirable for statistical comparison. A convenience sample is one that includes whatever people you were able to access. When you use a convenience sample, you assume, overtly or implicitly, that your sample isn't skewed in a way that compromises your findings. As you can imagine, that assumption isn't always safe. Nevertheless, if you're studying speech production, convenience sampling often lets you get longer interviews because these samples are acquired in less impersonal ways, such as through social networks, than quota or random samples are. With longer interviews, you'll probably be getting a more representative sample of the subject's speech than you would with the short interviews that random sampling usually involves.

I've organized this book in a somewhat modular fashion. The next two chapters discuss speech production and speech perception, respectively, and how to study them. Quite a bit of knowledge about acoustics is needed for each one, so Chapter 2 begins with a general overview of what you'll need to know about acoustics. Many techniques of acoustic analysis are covered in this chapter, rather than in later ones, because they apply to more than one kind of variable. Chapter 3 discusses techniques and experimental designs that are useful in sociophonetics for studying speech perception. The following four chapters discuss the different kinds of variables: consonants, vowels, prosody and voice quality. These have not had equal attention from sociophoneticians; vowels have attracted by far the most research. Besides showing you how past approaches work – especially in vowel study – I want to introduce you to other techniques that are useful for the lesser-studied variables and even some new techniques for vowel study. I hope that the imbalance in attention researchers have given to different kinds of variables can be evened out in the future. Most of the techniques discussed in Chapters 4–7 relate to speech production, but once you understand them it shouldn't be hard to see how you can adapt the information to experiments targeting speech perception.

The final five chapters take on a more abstract bent. In Chapter 8 I argue for the necessity of taking a broad view of variation by combining different kinds of phonetic variables in analyses, both in production and in perception. Chapter 9 brings us around to cognitive processing related to phonetics and phonology. Sociophonetics can address this issue in a number of ways, and, as I've indicated earlier, cognitive processing of language should be one of the primary aims of sociophonetics. We'll explore what sociolinguistic 'knowledge' is and how sociophonetics can be used to test the recently formulated Exemplar Theory, which relates especially strongly to phonology. Chapter 10 discusses theories of sound change. The origin, or actuation, of sound changes has vexed linguists for two centuries, and we'll examine some of the different ideas scholars have proposed to account for it. Sociophonetics has revolutionized the way sound change is examined, though the focus has been almost entirely on vowel shifting. Different approaches apply to shifting and to phonological restructurings (mergers and splits). Sociophonetics has also tied sound change study unalterably to sociological factors. Chapter 11 addresses in more detail how sociological constructs such as communities of practice and the role of individual identity as opposed to group identity figure into sociophonetic analysis. Like Chapter 9, it addresses cognitive encoding, this time of sociolinguistic 'knowledge'. Finally, Chapter 12 asserts that the traditional Lamarckian and Darwinian approach to language change and cognition is inappropriate. A new model called lateral transfer with origins in molecular studies of biological evolution works better, ties the sociolinguistic, phonetic and cognitive threads of sociophonetics together, and thrusts sociolinguistics to the centre of linguistic theory.

I've chosen to restrict this book to linguistic issues in sociophonetics. Certain other topics that are important in sociophonetic practice are omitted for various reasons. For one, I won't discuss recording or analysis equipment in any detail, and with rare exceptions I'll avoid discussing any particular model of equipment. Equipment changes constantly and discussion of particular models quickly becomes outdated. Discussion of how to evaluate equipment and the ways that equipment can vary would require another book the length of this one to cover adequately. All I'll say here is that you should treat equipment as a serious issue in its own right and that you should pay careful attention to the specifications for any equipment that you procure. Keep in mind that the make and model of equipment is only one factor – wear and tear make a difference, and equipment cleanliness can, too. Not only that, but the environmental conditions in which you make recordings or conduct perception experiments can affect your results. Whenever possible, use the same equipment for all recordings or trials in a single study. The main equipment issues you need to attend to in conducting a recorded interview or a perception experiment are schematized in Figure 1.2. You can test your equipment in various ways. For example, you can test the frequency fidelity of a microphone or recorder with a method as simple as sounding a tuning fork or playing a tone into it. A commonly used method of comparing the amplitude characteristics of different equipment is to play the same recording into it and then to examine power spectra of the sound recorded by the equipment. Analogous methods can be employed to test earphones used for perception experiments. Don't get too obsessed with equipment, though.

Another issue that I won't delve into in any depth is statistical analysis. A limited number of statistical procedures will take care of most of your needs. Some of the most useful and widely used tests are outlined in Table 1.1. Like evaluation of equipment, statistical procedures deserve a book-length treatment

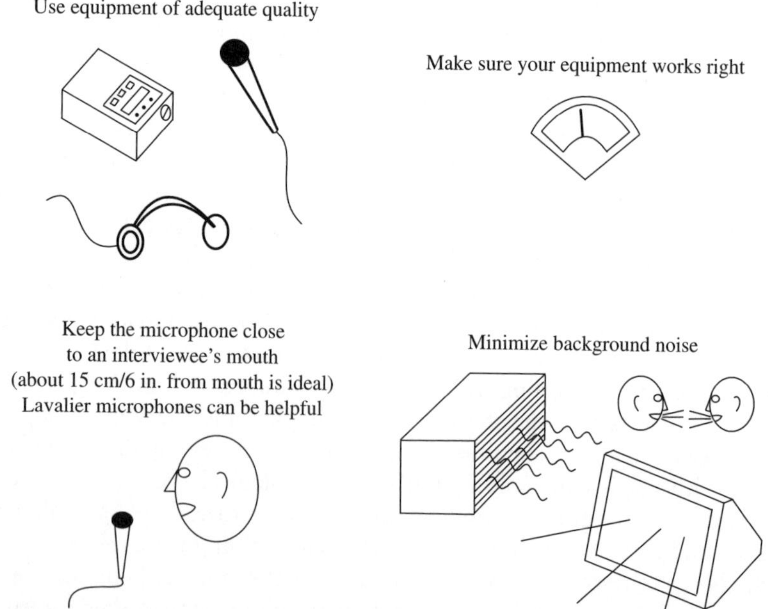

Figure 1.2 Primary equipment issues in conducting sociophonetic research.

Table 1.1 Some statistical procedures commonly used in sociophonetics.

Statistical procedure	*Use*
t-test	Testing whether sample means of two populations of continuous data are different or not (there have to be two distinct groups).
ANOVA (analysis of variance; a member of the family of tests called general linear models (GLM))	Testing whether sample means of two or more populations of continuous data are different or not; independent variables can be continuous or discrete; tells you if one differs, but doesn't tell you which one.
Post hoc tests, e.g. Tukey's *W*	After you run ANOVA, post hoc tests can show which populations differ from each other.
MANOVA (multivariate analysis of variance)	Similar to ANOVA, but used with two or more dependent variables.
Mixed models	Similar to ANOVA, but a random variable can be included.
Confidence intervals	Provides estimates of how likely it is that a sample mean matches the actual population mean, e.g. 95 or 99%; confidence intervals from different populations can be compared for overlap.
Principal components	Shows overall similarity of different individuals or groups across multiple variables.
χ^2	Used for countable data; it will tell you whether the actual distribution varies from the expected distribution, but it won't tell you which particular cell(s) differ – a post hoc test is necessary for that.
Linear regression	Used to show the relationship between two or more continuous variables; associated ANOVA shows whether they're correlated with each other, and other procedures can show the relative strength of independent variables.
Logistic regression	Used to show the relationship between two or more discrete variables.
Intraclass correlation	Used to determine the degree of difference between paired sets of data (e.g. for a reliability test).
Dendrogram	Shows relative similarity of different sets of data using a branching tree-like structure.
Multidimensional scaling	Shows relative similarity of different sets of data.
Box-and-whiskers plot (boxplot)	Provides a visual display of data distribution and reveals outliers.

themselves. In fact, several statistics textbooks designed specifically for linguistics have appeared recently: see Rietveld and van Hout (2005), Johnson (2008), Baayen (2008) and Gries (2009). Rietveld and van Hout focus on the use of ANOVA, or General Linear Models. Baayen and Gries discuss how to conduct analyses using the statistical program *R*. Johnson aims to provide a more general overview. Even these linguistically oriented statistics guides may not tell you everything you need to know for your own project. If you're using SAS™ or SPSS™ for analyses, you can often find help online. Frequently a more general statistics textbook, or one designed for social sciences, may be useful. A statistical counselling service, if your university provides it, can be invaluable.

Impressionistic phonetic transcription is excluded for reasons given earlier. It certainly has a long tradition in linguistics in general and in dialectology and sociolinguistics in particular. The International Phonetic Alphabet (IPA), of course, is the standard for phonetic transcription. Thorough discussions of IPA symbols and use of the IPA are found in the *Handbook of the International Phonetic Association* (International Phonetic Association 1999) and in Ladefoged (2001). I assume that you'll have some familiarity with the IPA and with the basic descriptions of consonants and vowels before you begin this book.

EXERCISES

1. Name several ways information on language variation can demonstrate links between variation/change in language and the organization of language in the mind/brain.
2. What are some of the ways that sociophonetic studies can meet the methodological requirements of both sociolinguistics and phonetics, especially in terms of replicability, getting naturalistic data and defining the speech community?
3. What is the status of functional and structural approaches to linguistics in general and sociolinguistics in particular? Do you agree or disagree with the perspective presented in this chapter?

FURTHER READING

Docherty, Gerard J., Paul Foulkes, James Milroy, Leslie Milroy and David Walshaw. 1997. Descriptive adequacy in phonology: a variationist perspective. *Journal of Linguistics* 33:275–310.

Foulkes, Paul and Gerard J. Docherty. 2006. The social life of phonetics and phonology. *Journal of Phonetics* 34:409–38.

Production

2

2.1 Production versus perception

Phoneticians generally divide phonetics into speech production and speech perception. Production, as you'd guess, has to do with how speakers make speech sounds, while perception has to do with how listeners process speech sounds that they hear. The means of studying production and perception differ sharply, making it logical to split phonetics instruction along the line between production and perception. Hence this chapter is devoted to introducing the basic techniques used for speech production, while Chapter 3 will cover techniques for speech perception. In both chapters there is an orientation towards methods that are useful for exploring language variation. Some techniques that are useful for only one type of sound, such as analysis of frication spectra, are discussed in later chapters.

Phonetics is sometimes split along different lines, into a three-way division among articulation, acoustics and audition. I've chosen to follow the two-way production/perception taxonomy instead because it matches up better with the way sociophonetic studies are conducted. Articulatory analyses are relatively rare in sociophonetic studies, largely because most desired information about articulation (with a few notable exceptions) can be addressed through acoustic analysis. Not only that, but the main methods of studying speech articulation directly – e.g. X-ray microbeams, magnetic resonance imaging (MRI) and devices such as electropalatographs – are poorly suited for field research. However, we'll cover several of these methods briefly in this chapter, since they can be useful for laboratory studies.

2.2 Basic acoustic and signal-processing concepts

The main tool for analysing speech production is spectrographic analysis. Spectrographic analysis gives you a visual representation of sound. This section will cover the basic terminology of acoustics and signal processing quickly. The items discussed here are also the ones that you'll need to mention when you describe the methods for acoustic studies that you conduct. The coverage here isn't intended to go into great depth. For more detail, consult a regular phonetics textbook or a longer manual. Stevens (1998) offers an exhaustive treatment. Johnson (2003) is more concise and quite good, and other fine explanations of various elements of what I'll cover can be found in Lieberman and Blumstein (1988), Kent and Read (2002), Hewlett and Beck (2006), and Reetz and Jongman (2009).

Units of measurement

Acoustic signals have three basic dimensions. One is *time*, which is displayed in seconds (s) or milliseconds (ms). Another is *frequency*, which is measured in *hertz* (*Hz*). Older literature often refers to hertz as *cycles per second* (*cps*), which gives you a clue about what the term *hertz* means. A cycle is the period in which a sound wave goes through its pattern before repeating it. We'll see how that works shortly. The final dimension of sound is *amplitude*. The official unit of measure for amplitude is the *pascal*. Most of the time, though, you'll see amplitude measured in *decibels* (*dB*).

Decibels are a different kind of unit from what you're used to because there's no set standard for what a decibel is. In descriptions of amplitude that you read in popular publications, the 0 dB point is conventionally set to the lower threshold of human hearing – or actually the lower threshold of hearing for a young person with no injury or impairment to his or her hearing – for a tone with a frequency of 1000 Hz. Note that the dB figures you see in such publications are positive numbers. On the other hand, electronic equipment sets the reference point in other ways. Recording devices often set the 0 dB mark at the maximum level that the device can handle, so you'll see negative dB numbers listed on the recorder. Acoustic analysis software generally sets the 0 dB point to the lowest level that can be digitized, so once again the dB numbers will be positive. The decibel scale is logarithmic, not linear, unlike time and frequency. Human perception of amplitude is logarithmic, too, so the dB scale roughly reflects how our hearing works.

Sound waves

The simplest kind of sound is a pure tone – a tone at a single frequency. The waveform for this sound is represented as a sine wave, as shown in Figure 2.1. The length of the period, from start to finish, for the sine wave determines its frequency. To calculate the frequency, you measure the length of the period in milliseconds and divide it into 1000 (or measure it in seconds and divide it into 1). For example, if the period is 5 ms, the frequency of the wave is 200 Hz because $1000 \div 5 = 200$. Figure 2.2 shows sine waves with different frequencies. The representation of a waveform as a sine wave actually refers to the movement of air molecules as they transmit the sound. When a noise is created, the air molecules are perturbed. They alternately move closer together – called *compression* – and farther apart – called *rarefaction*. The bands of compressed and rarefied air molecules spread outward from the sound's point of origin, like the waves produced when you drop a rock into a pond but in three dimensions.

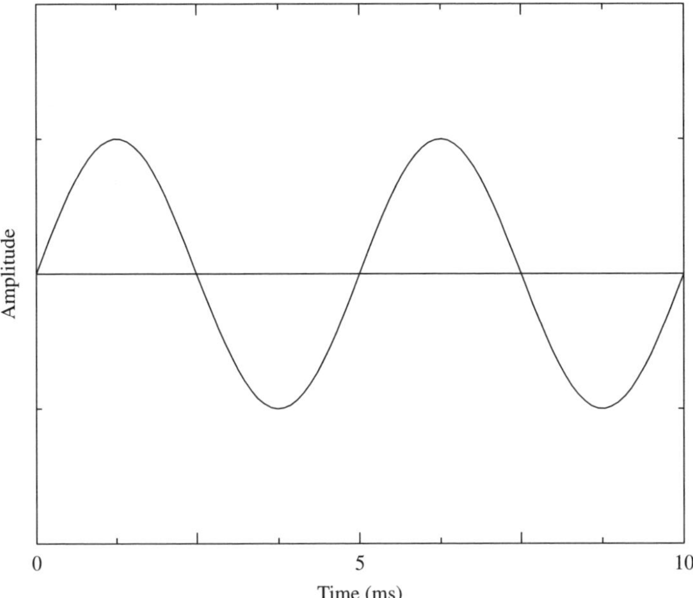

Figure 2.1 A sine waveform representing a pure tone.

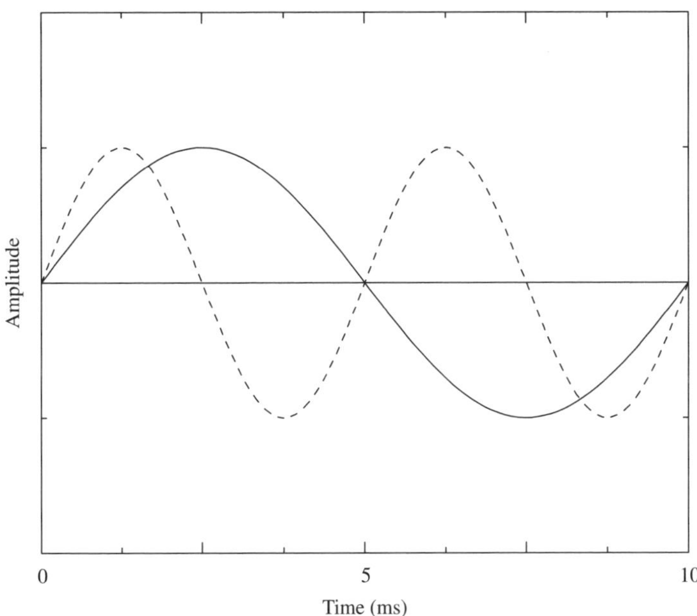

Figure 2.2 Two sine waveforms, one with a wavelength twice that of the other.

Note that compression and rarefaction are connected with how fast the air molecules move. There is an inverse relationship between the amount of compression/rarefaction and the speed the molecules are moving. It works like a playground swing. The neutral point of the swing is when the swing is hanging straight down. When somebody is swinging, though, the swing moves back and forth, crossing that neutral point. As the swing gets closer to its most forward position, it slows down until it stops and reverses direction. Then it speeds up until it crosses the neutral point, and after that it gradually slows down until it reaches its most backward position. Air molecules transmitting a sound do the same thing. They slow down as they're compressed until they stop and begin to move farther apart. They move fastest when they're at their neutral position, and then slow down again as they become rarefied. Whereas gravity causes the swing to slow down, in sound transmission the slowing is caused by molecules bumping into each other.

Amplitude is represented by how far the peaks in the sine wave get from the neutral position. For a soft sound, the air molecules don't get compressed and rarefied very much, whereas for a loud sound they do. This difference is represented by the sine waves in Figure 2.3. The two waves have the same frequency but differ in amplitude.

Most sounds are not tones that can be represented by a single sine wave. They show more complicated waveforms and are called *complex waves*. An example is shown in Figure 2.4. However, any complex wave can be decomposed into a series of simple waves by a process called *Fourier analysis*. The waveform shown as a solid line in Figure 2.4, for example, can be broken down into the two waves shown with dashed lines, one with a frequency twice that of the other. You could also say that the two simple waves add up to make the complex wave. Note that actual speech consists of a lot more than just two components.

When Jean Baptiste Joseph Fourier first proposed the theory that any complex wave can be broken down into simple waves, he stipulated that it applied

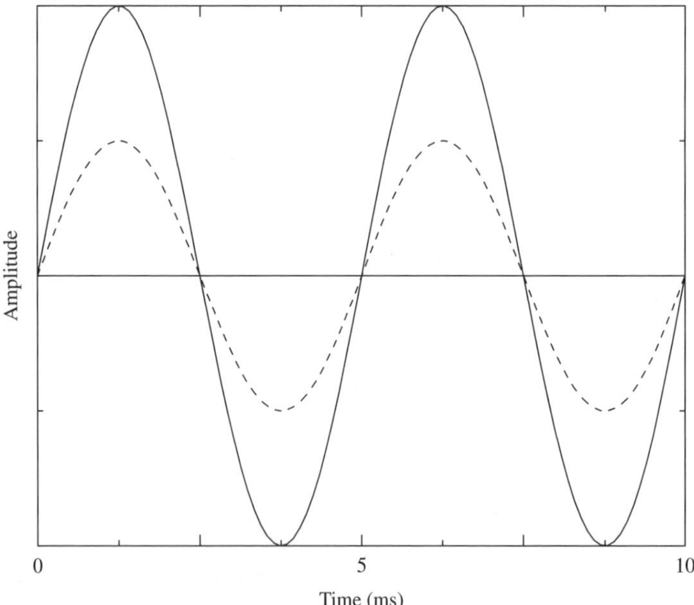

Figure 2.3 Two sine waveforms with same frequency but different amplitudes.

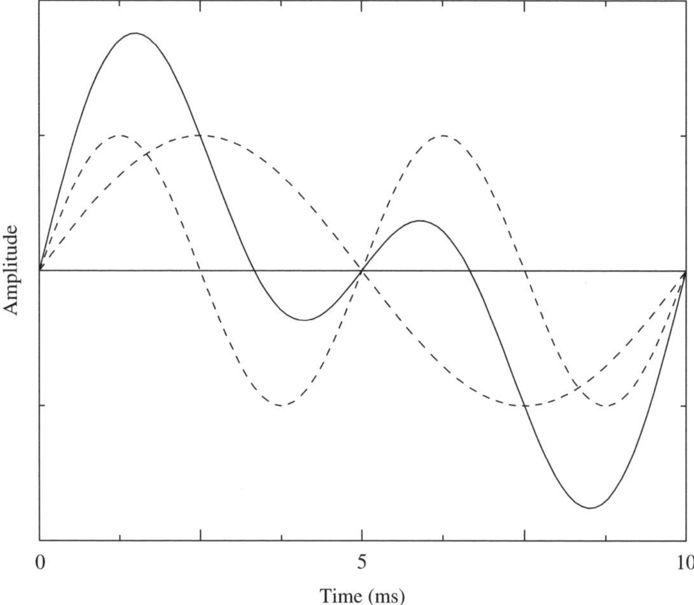

Figure 2.4 A complex waveform (sold line) and its component waveforms (dashed lines).

only to continuous sounds. However, in real life sounds are never indefinitely continuous. Because of that, *discrete Fourier transforms* (*DFT*) were developed. They operate by analysing only a *window* – a short segment of time – within the sound signal. The window may or may not be attenuated at each end, depending on which of various *windowing* methods is used for creating it. In addition, a special type of DFT, called the *fast Fourier transform* (*FFT*), was developed for digital computers. FFT works on digital computers because the number of points that are analysed has to be a power of two – i.e. 2, 4, 8, 16, 32, 64, 128, 256, 512, 1024, etc. As the name suggests, FFT is a lot faster than other methods of Fourier analysis.

Figure 2.5 illustrates the stages in Fourier analysis of speech. From the original signal, as in Figure 2.5(a), simple waves are extracted, starting with the lowest-frequency components. The result is a series of simple waves, as in 2.5(b). The frequency and amplitude of each wave is measured. Figure 2.5(c) gives an idealization of a spectrum of the component waves, though in real life windowing yields spectra with humps, as in 2.5(d). For voicing in speech, all the component waves – the *harmonics* – have to be at multiples of the lowest component, which is the *fundamental frequency* (F_0). The reason is that the length of the lowest wave corresponds to the time between vocal fold vibrations. Any wave with zero-crossing points at the same places as F_0 will 'fit' between the vocal pulses. All multiples of F_0 match that description.

Waves can differ in another way besides frequency and amplitude. They can also differ in *phase*. Phase involves the location of starting points for waveforms relative to each other. For example, Figure 2.6 shows two waveforms that have

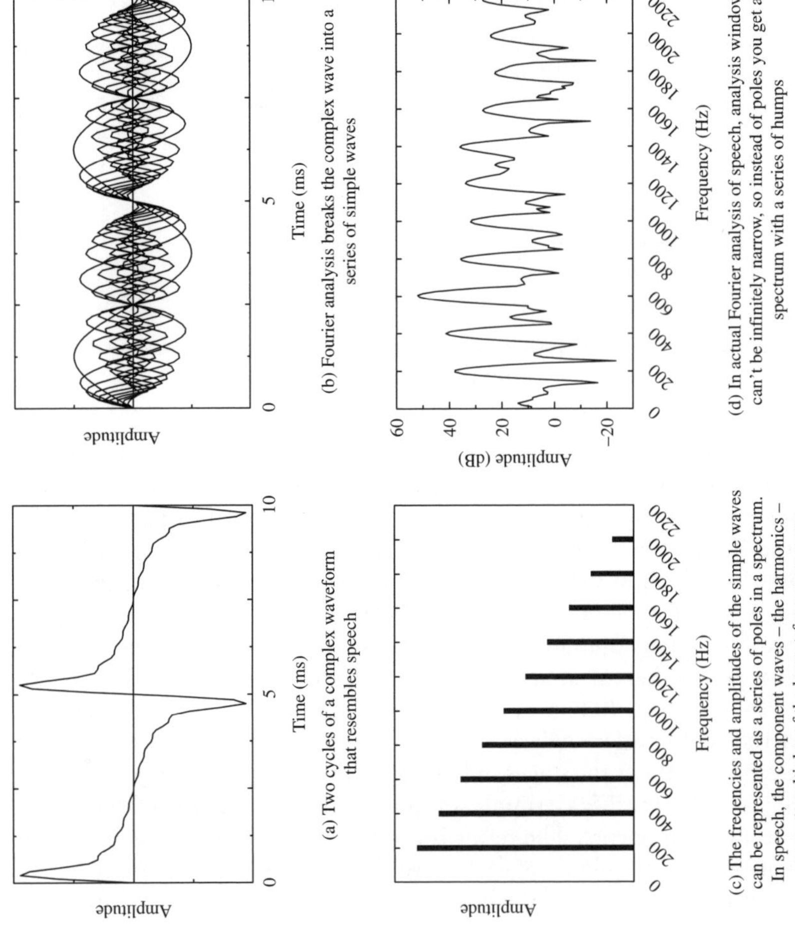

Amplitude
0
5
10
Time (ms)
(a) Two cycles of a complex waveform that resembles speech
Amplitude
0
5
10
Time (ms)
(b) Fourier analysis breaks the complex wave into a series of simple waves
Amplitude
0
200
400
600
800
1000
1200
1400
1600
1800
2000
2200
Frequency (Hz)
(c) The freqencies and amplitudes of the simple waves can be represented as a series of poles in a spectrum. In speech, the component waves – the harmonics – come at multiples of the lowest-frequency wave
Amplitude (dB)
60
40
20
0
−20
0
200
400
600
800
1000
1200
1400
1600
1800
2000
2200
Frequency (Hz)
(d) In actual Fourier analysis of speech, analysis windows can't be infinitely narrow, so instead of poles you get a spectrum with a series of humps

Figure 2.5 Steps in Fourier analysis.

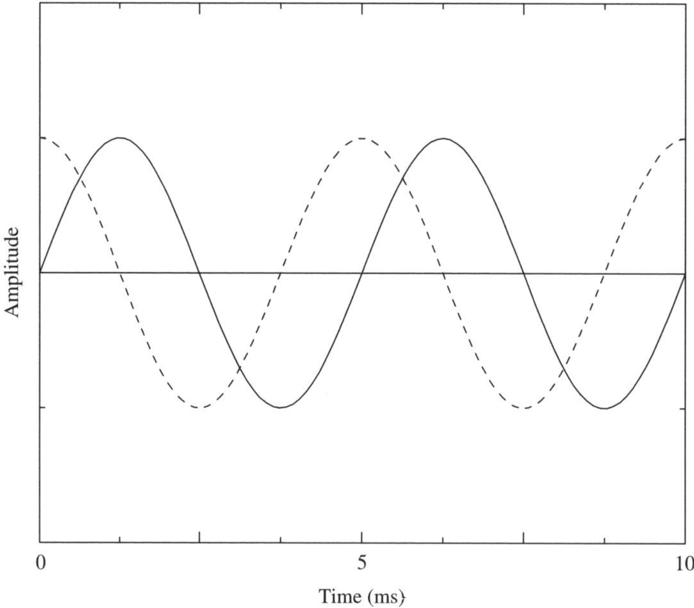

Figure 2.6 Two waveforms with the same frequency and amplitude but different phases.

the same frequency and amplitude but are out of phase with each other. Phase generally doesn't make much difference for speech sounds, with one major exception: when two sounds are in opposite phase, as in Figure 2.7. When that happens, the two sounds cancel each other out and the result is silence. Sounds in opposite phase are important for nasality, for which the oral cavity produces resonances that cancel out a resonance of the nasal cavity (for an oral consonant) or a nasal resonance cancels out an oral resonance (for a nasal vowel). These are called *antiformats* or *zeroes*. A similar phenomenon happens with laterals, for which the tongue is aligned so that it creates side-by-side cavities.

Sound signals come in two basic types: periodic and aperiodic. A *periodic* signal is one with a repeating pattern – i.e. a waveform. Bird song and the sounds of musical instruments in the wind and string groups are examples of periodic signals. In human speech, voicing, as with vowels and voiced consonants, is almost periodic. It is not perfectly periodic because the vocal fold vibration isn't repeated exactly, but it is close. An *aperiodic* signal is one in which the pattern doesn't repeat. Aperiodic signals themselves fall into two categories. A sustained aperiodic signal is called *noise*. (No, it isn't very creative, but that's the official term.) The sound of wind blowing through trees or of a fan blowing or static on a television that isn't tuned in to a channel are all noise. In speech, noise occurs in frication and aspiration. You can certainly hear the staticky quality of frication when you say a sustained [sːː] sound. An aperiodic signal that isn't sustained is called a *transient*. Transients are sudden, sharp noises. Think of the sound of a knock on a door or a gunshot or what this book would sound like if you dropped it on the floor. Transients in speech

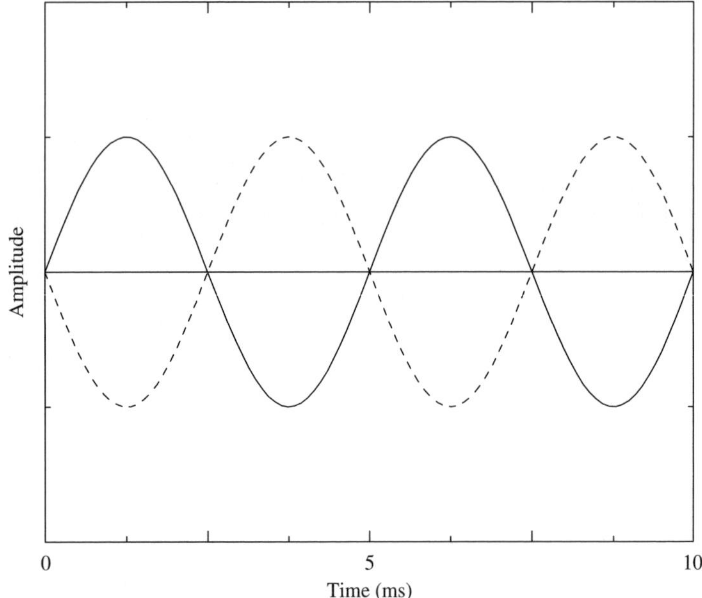

Figure 2.7 Two waveforms with the same frequency and amplitude but opposite phases – when combined, the result is silence.

are best known in one situation: when a speaker lets go of the closure for a stop consonant, there is a small pop called the *burst* when the air behind the occlusion rushes forward and hits the air in front of the occlusion. This stop burst is a transient. Transients also appear in the click sounds of the San languages of southern Africa.

Digitization

Sounds are recorded in two formats: *analogue* and *digital*. Analogue recordings, such as on cassette tapes and other older media, record a continuous signal. Their disadvantage is that they can't be copied exactly and the signal degrades over too many generations of copying. Moreover, analogue recordings aren't compatible with computers.

Computers require signals to be digitized. These days, digital recorders do this step for you, but there are digitizers and computer programs that can digitize analogue recordings. Here's how digitization works. I'm going to explain the process backwards because the reasons for the earlier steps are easier to understand this way. Digitization involves *sampling* the sound signal at intervals. That is, at each interval the energy in the waveform is measured, as shown in Figure 2.8. The result is a series of discrete measurements; some information is lost because the sampling measures the waveform at points instead of continuously. The loss is called quantization error. However, continuous measurements would produce an infinite amount of data. Sampling at points makes the amount of data manageable. The measurements are then converted

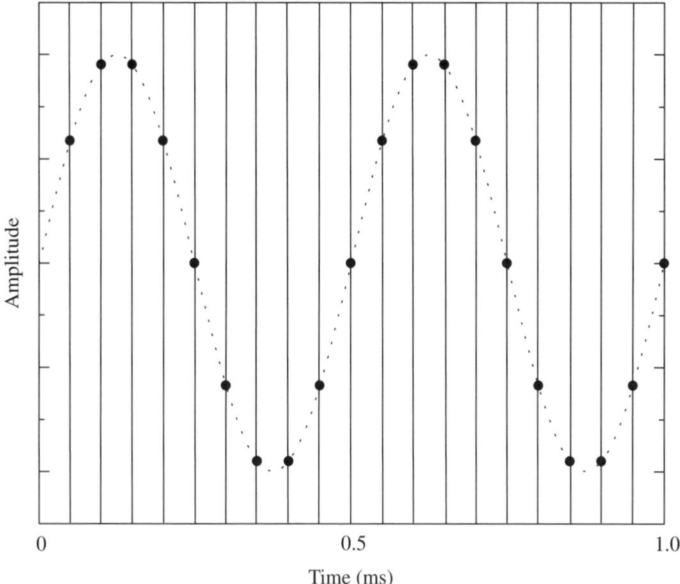

Figure 2.8 Sampling of a waveform. The waveform is measured at points represented by each vertical line. Regions of the waveform in between measurement points are not sampled – all the computer can see are the measured points – so a small amount of error, called quantization error, is introduced by the sampling procedure.

to base two (digital) numbers that a computer can process. The digitizing device has a limit to how many possible amplitude values it can read. The limit depends on the number of digital bits devoted to it, which is usually 16: hence, the number of possible amplitude values is 2^{16}, or 65,536, and this is called 16-bit resolution. Once the computer processes the numbers, the digitized signal can be copied exactly so that the signal doesn't degrade any more.

The next thing to figure out is how often to take the samples. This is called the *sampling rate.* The sampling rate becomes an issue because, if you don't have enough samples, the computer will misinterpret the signal and tell you that there's a frequency that isn't actually there. This misinterpretation is called *aliasing.* Figure 2.9 shows how aliasing happens. If the sampling rate's too low, you'll get samples where the dots are on the figure. The computer just connects the dots and extrapolates a waveform that fits them, which, in this example, didn't exist in the original signal. To prevent aliasing, your sampling rate has to be at least twice the frequency of the highest-frequency component of the signal. Or, to put it another way, the highest-frequency component of the signal can be no higher than half the sampling rate. The frequency that is half the sampling rate is called the *Nyquist frequency.* For recording music, a sampling rate of 44.1 kilohertz (kHz) is most commonly used, so that the Nyquist frequency is 22.05 kHz. However, for recording voices, a sampling rate of 22.05 kHz is adequate because voices don't contain any perceptually important components over 11 kHz.

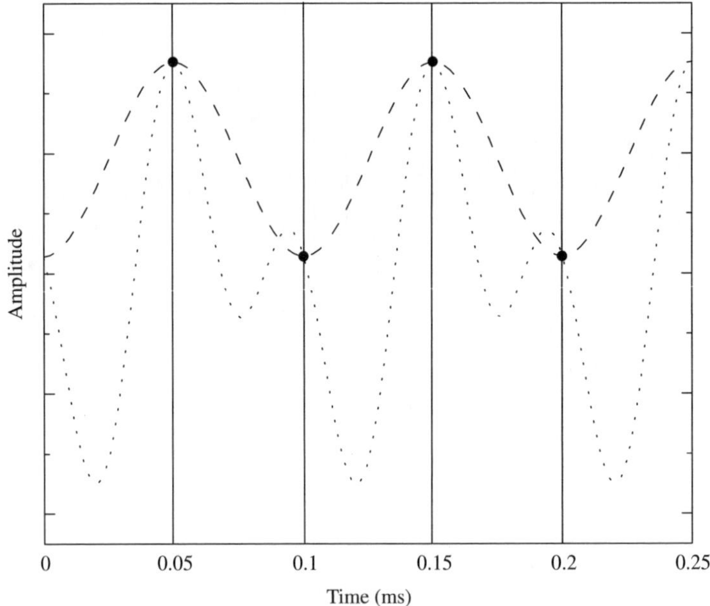

Figure 2.9 Aliasing creates the phony waveform frequency, shown as a dashed line, because the sampling rate here (20 kHz, a hypothetical value) is too low for the signal being analysed. The vertical lines represent the sampling times and the dark circles represent the sampled points. A computer extrapolates the simplest possible function from the sampled points. The dotted line represents the real waveform that's being sampled improperly.

You might notice that there's a problem with what I've just said. It's fine to sample a signal at, say, 22.05 kHz if the signal doesn't have any components over 11 kHz. The problem, though, is that any natural recording environment will have components with frequencies greater than the Nyquist frequency. What the recording device has to do, then, is to *filter* the signal to eliminate any components with higher frequencies. Filtering has to be done before sampling. This kind of filtering is called *lowpass filtering* because it 'passes' lower frequencies through and cuts out ('stops' or 'rejects') higher frequencies. Unfortunately, it's impossible to construct a perfect filter that will pass all sound up to a specific frequency and eliminate all sound above that frequency. There is always a transition zone with any filter. Because of that, the filtering has to be set somewhat below the Nyquist frequency. For example, with a 44.1 kHz sampling rate, you might set the filter at 18 or 20 kHz.

For recordings of speech, something else has to be done to the signal. In raw speech signals, the low-frequency components of the signal have much greater amplitude than the higher-frequency components. If the signal's left the way it is, you won't be able to analyse higher-frequency components because they won't reach the *mark level* for visual representations of the sound. The mark level is the lowest frequency that appears in the visual representation. The solution to this problem is another kind of filtering called *pre-emphasis.*

Pre-emphasis increases the amplitude by 6 dB per octave above a certain frequency; however, the full 6 dB usually isn't added – instead a proportion of it, such as 0.90, called the *factor*, is added (Kent and Read 2002:63–4; Johnson 2003:41). Pre-emphasis can be applied to the analogue signal before lowpass filtering or to the digitized signal.

Digitization, then, involves three steps. The steps can be ordered in two different ways. In one order, pre-emphasis of the signal comes first, with lowpass filtering second. The actual digitization, which consists of sampling the signal at a particular sampling rate, comes third. Digitization occurs with amplitude resolution at the digitizing device's bit rate and with a specified type of windowing. The other possible order is lowpass filtering first, digitization second, and pre-emphasis third.

Visual representations

The most basic visual representation of sound is an *oscillogram* or *waveform*. A waveform is the familiar representation of a sound wave. An example is shown in Figure 2.10.

The other kinds of visual representations, and the ones that you use for most acoustic analyses, are power spectra and spectrograms. In a *power spectrum*, frequency in Hz is shown on the x-axis and amplitude in dB on the y-axis, as in Figure 2.11. Time isn't shown on a spectrum because a spectrum is a snapshot – a

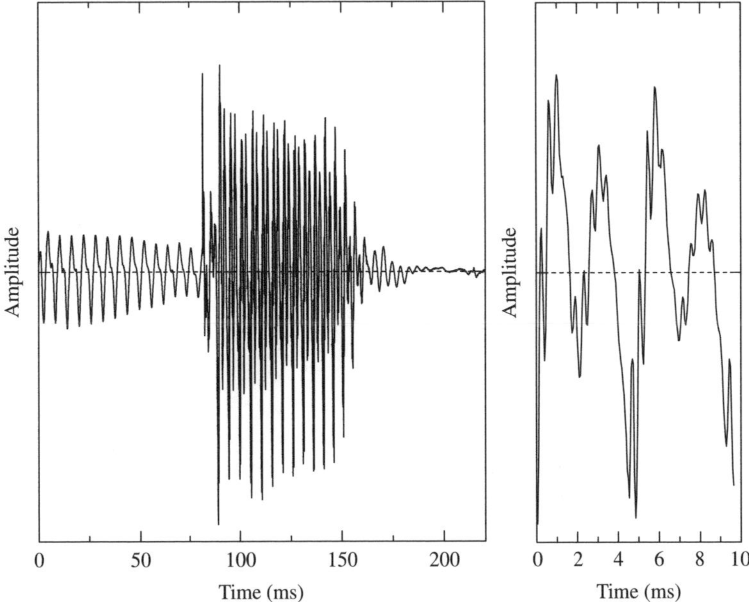

Figure 2.10 The left panel shows an oscillogram, or waveform, of the syllable [bɪg], uttered by an African American female from North Carolina. Fine details of the waves aren't visible. The visible wave-like fluctuations are the vocal fold vibrations. The right panel shows a detail of two vocal fold vibrations near the end of the vowel.

picture of a single moment of time. A spectrogram consists of a series of consecutive spectra turned on their sides and lined up. On a spectrogram, as in Figure 2.12, time is shown on the x-axis, frequency is shown on the y-axis and amplitude is indicated by the darkness of the items within the spectrogram.

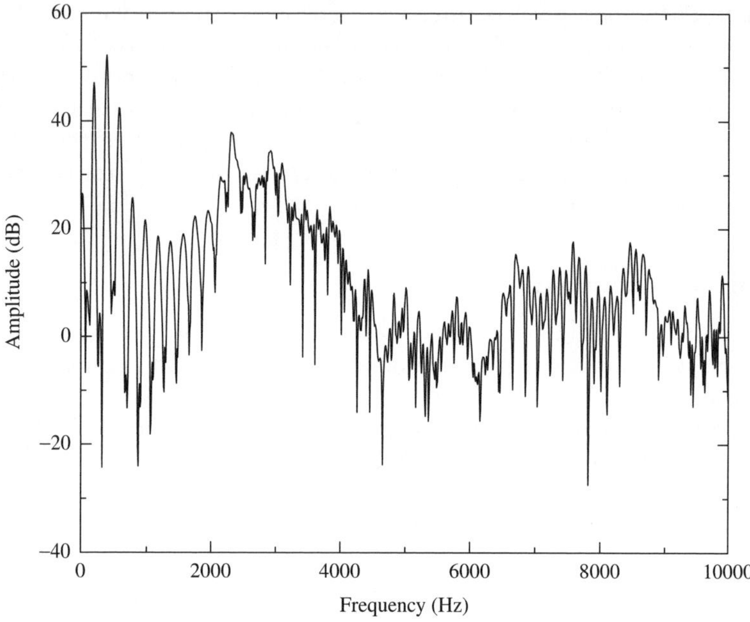

Figure 2.11 A narrowband power spectrum of a point at the centre of the vowel from Figure 2.10.

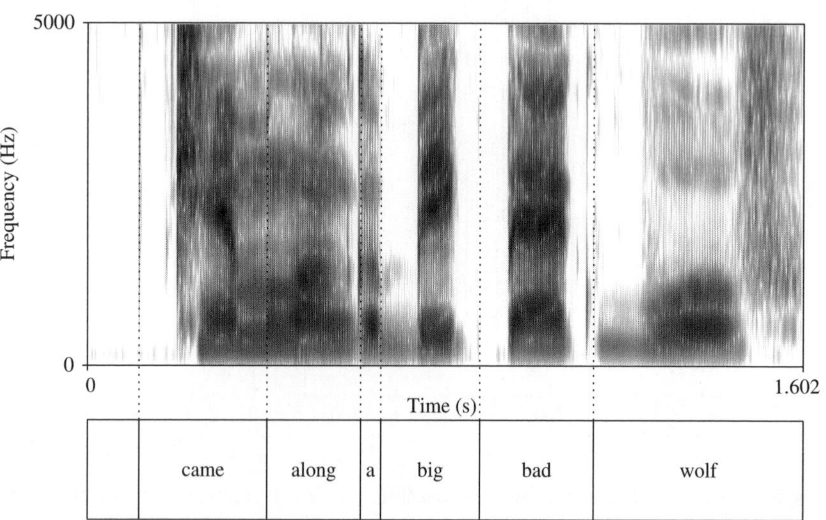

Figure 2.12 A wideband spectrogram of some running speech that includes the syllable from Figure 2.10. The utterance is 'came along a big, bad wolf'.

Back in the old days, spectra and spectrograms were generated by a machine called a *spectrograph*. The spectrograph was encased in a big, clumsy box and it printed spectrograms on special, expensive paper – not conducive to university budgets today – onto which the image was burned with a stylus. Around the early 1990s, spectrographs were superseded by spectrographic software. Current software is significantly faster, more user-friendly and more versatile than spectrographs were. It even makes better-looking spectrograms than the old equipment.

The settings of spectrograms and spectra can be varied, depending on what you want to examine. The viewing range, for example, can be adjusted easily. Spectrographic programs designed for speech may set the default viewing range for 0 to 5 kHz, which usually works well for human voices (though not for music or bird song for example, which involve higher frequencies) but may need to be adjusted upward for sibilants or for some children's voices. Another crucial setting is the *window length*. Short window lengths, such as 5 ms, give you good time resolution but poor frequency resolution. The result is a *wideband* spectrogram. The poor frequency resolution of wideband spectrograms can be advantageous because it makes the resonances of vowels more obvious, and the superior time resolution makes it easy to see such features as vocal fold vibrations and transients: see Figure 2.13. A long window length, such as 50 ms, gives you poor time resolution but good frequency resolution. The output is called a *narrowband* spectrogram.[1] Narrowband spectrograms make it easy to discern the individual harmonics of the vocal fold vibrations, as in Figure 2.14, and thus can be useful for prosodic analysis.

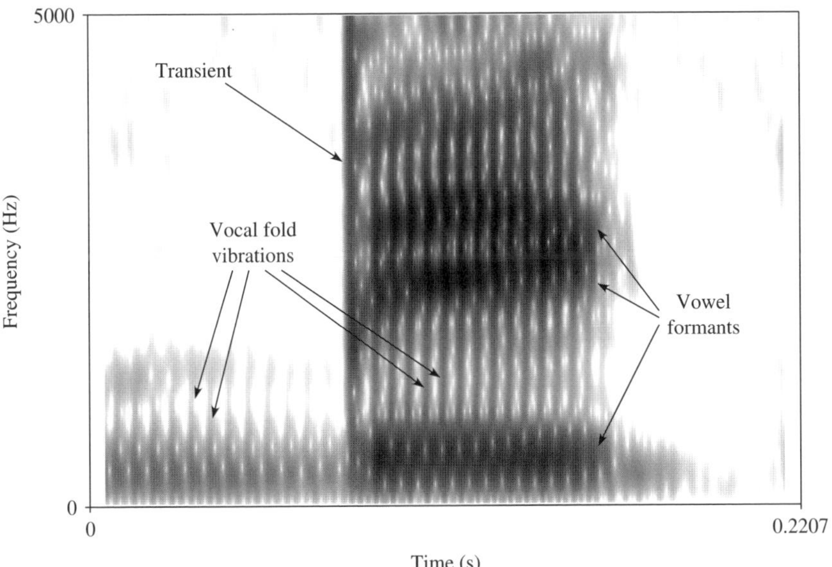

Figure 2.13 A wideband spectrogram of the same spoken syllable as in Figure 2.10. Note how the vowel formants, vocal fold vibrations and a transient are all readily discernible.

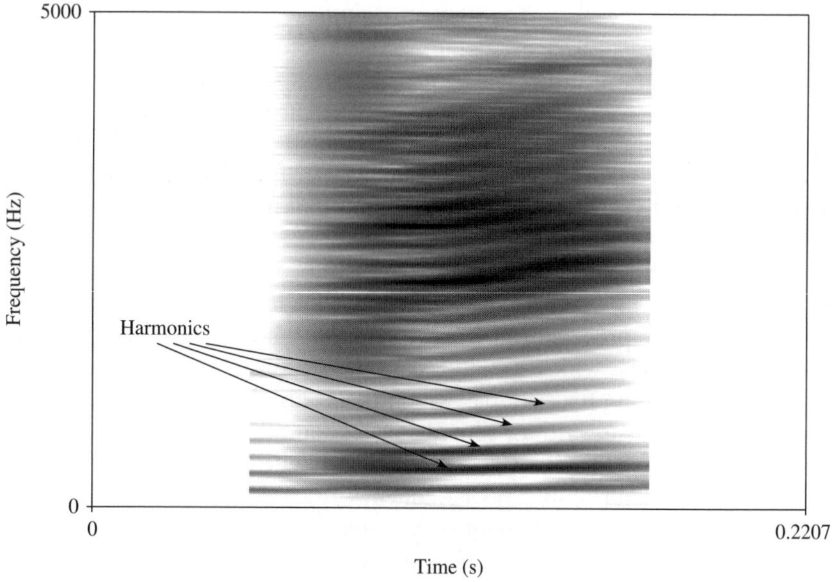

Figure 2.14 A narrowband spectrogram of the same spoken syllable as in Figures 2.10 and 2.13. Note how the harmonics are readily discernible, but formants and the transient are less so, with the vocal fold vibrations being completely obscured. The different window size shrinks the amount of time shown.

2.3 The source-filter theory

Human speech production is thought of in terms of the *source-filter theory*. This theory appeared during the nineteenth century (Lieberman and Blumstein 1988:1), well before the advent of modern phonetics. It models speech production as consisting of two parts. The first part is the source of the sound. In human speech, the source is most often the vibration of the vocal folds in the larynx. However, for fricatives the source is turbulence caused by the airstream passing rapidly through a narrow constriction and, often, hitting an obstruction as well, such as the front teeth for [s]. For stop bursts and clicks, the source is the contact of suddenly released air with inert air. The second part of the model is how the sound is modified, through filtering, after it is produced. What I'll say about the filtering applies to both consonants and vowels, but we'll discuss it in terms of vowels here and then come back to the consonants in Chapter 4.

The fundamental frequency

The fundamental frequency is the rate at which the vocal folds vibrate – that is, the number of times the vocal folds clap together per second. This is abbreviated as either F_0 or f_0, depending on an author's preference. The sound is created because the airstream from the lungs is interrupted when the vocal folds come together before bursting through, hitting the downstream air. You hear

F_0 as the pitch of the speaker's voice. In singing, the vocalist's F_0 goes up for high notes and down for low notes. It goes up and down less dramatically during speech. Men generally have modal F_0 values in the range of 90 to 140 Hz, women's modal F_0 values tend to be in the range of 170 to 220 Hz, and young children's modal F_0 values are even higher. Many speakers' modal values fall outside those ranges, though, and any speaker with a normal voice can vary his or her F_0 well beyond the modal ranges.

If F_0 were the only sound produced by the vocal folds, speech would sound quite different than it does, more like a low-frequency hum. However, F_0 is accompanied by a series of other tones called *harmonics*. The fundamental frequency is the lowest harmonic, or H1, but the other harmonics appear at multiples of F_0, called H2, H3, etc. Thus, if F_0 (H1) has a frequency of 180 Hz, H2 will be at 360 Hz, H3 at 540 Hz, and so on. As you move up the series of harmonics, their amplitude gradually falls off. A schematized spectrum, with harmonics represented as vertical lines (poles), is shown in Figure 2.15. This represents what a voice (in this example, most likely a female voice) would sound like if there were no oral cavity.

The mouth as a filter

Of course, there *is* an oral cavity downstream from the vocal folds, and this is where the filter part of the source-filter theory comes in. The oral cavity is

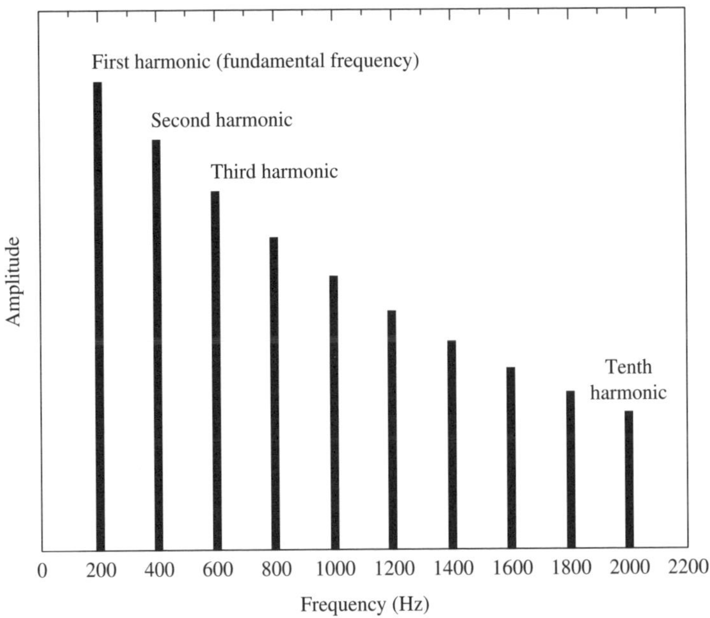

Figure 2.15 A schematized spectrum, with harmonics represented as vertical lines, of a vocal signal with no filter. In this example, the fundamental frequency (F_0) is 200 Hz (a modal value for an adult female speaker), so the harmonics come at multiples of 200.

viewed as one or more tubes. Each tube has certain frequencies that it favours. Sounds from the source that fall at or near these frequencies are passed. Other frequencies are *damped* – that is, their amplitudes are reduced. This represents a type of filtering. We saw lowpass filtering before, but a cavity in the oral tract serves as a *bandpass filter*. With a bandpass filter, frequencies within the band are passed and those lower or higher than the band are stopped. Figure 2.16 shows what the spectrum from Figure 2.15 might look like after being filtered to produce a schwa vowel.

Which frequencies a cavity passes or stops depend on (a) its length, (b) whether it's closed or not at the end, and (c) whether it has any constrictions or flares out at one end. As for the length, the longer a cavity is, the lower the frequencies that it passes will be. Wind instruments work similarly. A shorter instrument, such as a flute or piccolo, will produce a higher-frequency resonance, while a longer one, such as a clarinet or an oboe, will produce a lower-frequency resonance. The main difference is that in speech the sound *source* is not the tube (it is the vocal fold vibration), whereas for a wind instrument, the sound source is the air turbulence within the tube. Whistling operates like a wind instrument. When you whistle, the tube is the space between the ridge of your tongue and your lips. You move the highest point of your tongue forward, shortening the tube, to whistle a higher note, and you move it backward, lengthening the tube, to whistle a lower note.

The next important variable in tubes is whether they're open at one end or closed at both ends. Tubes that are open at one end occur with unrounded

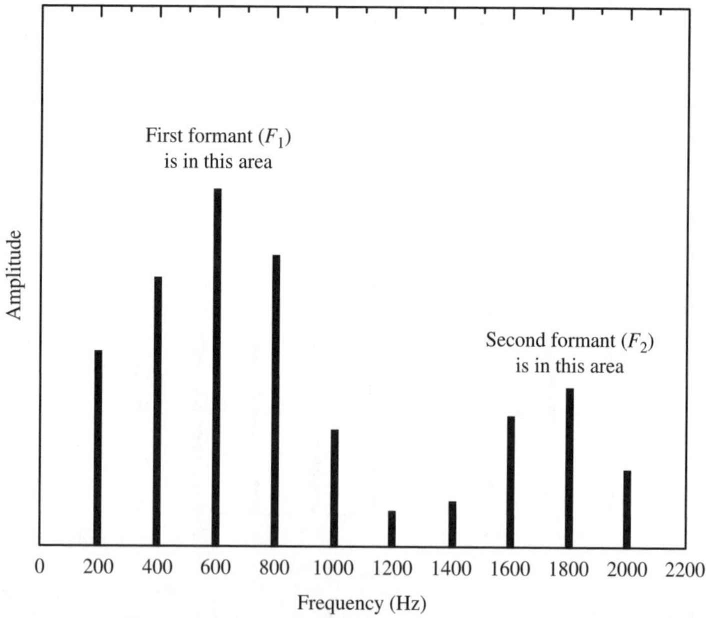

Figure 2.16 The spectrum shown in Figure 2.15 after filtering appropriate for the schwa of an adult female speaker. The high regions in the spectrum are the resonances, or formants, of the filter.

vowels. For a schwa, there is one long tube between the larynx and the opening of the mouth. For other unrounded vowels, the space between the tongue ridge and the mouth opening (called the *front cavity*) constitutes such a tube. For low back vowels, the space behind the tongue consists of a tube open at one end, too. The reason is that the tongue root moves backward for a low back vowel, constricting the pharynx, so that it makes a narrow tube that opens into the wider cavity in front of the tongue. Figure 2.17 schematically illustrates the occurrence of tubes open at one end for a few vowels.

The favoured resonances, or *formants,* of a tube depend on the patterns of compression and rarefaction of air molecules. Recall that 'compression' means that the air molecules are under high pressure but are moving more slowly, 'rarefaction' means they're under low pressure but are also moving slowly, and 'equilibrium' means that they're under medium (atmospheric) pressure but are moving quickly. In a resonating cavity, a *node* is located where there's equilibrium and an *antinode* is located where there's the most compression or rarefaction. For a tube open at one end, the favoured resonance has to have a node at its open end because the air outside the tube is at atmospheric pressure. That is, the best situation is where the air at the open end of the tube and the air outside have the same pressure. That means that an antinode has to be at the other – closed – end. An infinite number of resonances fit that description. The lowest one, which becomes the first formant (F_1) for that tube, has a cycle four times the length of the tube. The wave starts with compression at the closed end, travels to the open end, then reflects off the outside air as rarefaction for the return trip to the closed end, where it then reflects off the closed end, switches back to compression when it reflects off the open end, and goes back to the closed end as compression – four trips across the tube. The switches between

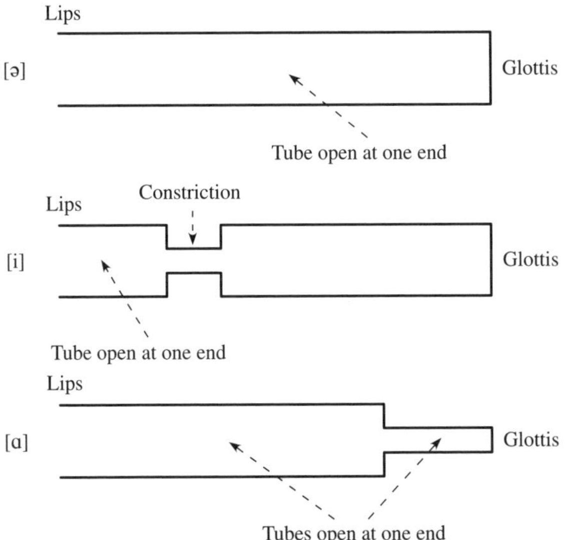

Figure 2.17 Examples of tubes open at one end among some vowels.

compression and rarefaction at the open end happen because the pressure there has to match that of the outside air, and the switch makes that happen because compression and rarefaction cancel each other out, thereby equalling atmospheric pressure. The next resonance that has an antinode at the closed end and a node at the open end is one for which the tube is three-fourths of the cycle, as shown in Figure 2.18. This becomes the second formant (F_2). After that, you get one for which the tube is five-fourths of the cycle. The frequencies keep going up as the cycles get shorter. The formula for resonances of a tube open at one end is

$$F_n = (2n - 1)c/4L$$

where F is the formant, n is the formant number (F_1, F_2, etc.), c is the speed of sound (~34,300 cm/s, give or take some depending on altitude, temperature and humidity), and L is the tube length. Note that the resonance goes down as the length goes up.

If the tube is closed at both ends, things are different. Tubes closed at both ends occur with rounded vowels, for which the front cavity becomes closed at each end. When the tongue makes a constriction, such as for consonants or for mid and high vowels, the space between the larynx and the tongue constriction (called the *back cavity*) becomes a tube closed at both ends. Figure 2.19 schematically illustrates the occurrence of tubes closed at both ends for a few vowels.

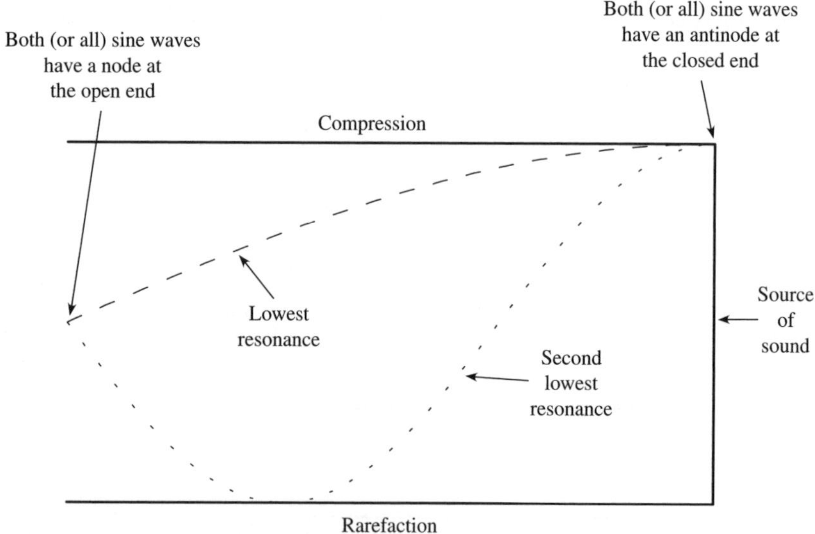

Figure 2.18 Resonances of a tube open at one end and closed at the other. The sine waves represent the two lowest resonances of the tube. For each waveform, deviations from zero (i.e. midway between the top and bottom of the diagram) represent compression or rarefaction of air molecules.

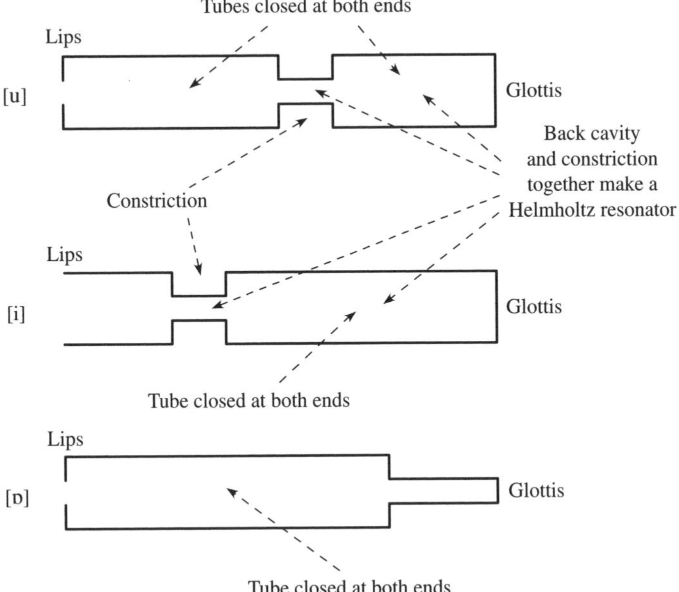

Figure 2.19 Examples of tubes closed at both ends among some vowels. Helmholtz resonators are also indicated. The back cavity is actually proportionately longer than shown here.

For this kind of tube, there's no switch from compression to rarefaction or vice versa at the end of the tube. The band of compression starts at the near end of the tube, travels across the tube, reflects off the far end, and returns to the near end. While the compression is travelling to the far end, rarefaction sets in at the near end. Then, after the compression wave reflects off the far end and comes back to the near end, the rarefaction moves to the far end. In between, the alternating bands of compression and rarefaction cancel out, so you get a node in the middle. Any resonance that has antinodes at both ends of the tube will fit. The two lowest resonances for a tube closed at both ends are shown in Figure 2.20. The formula for a tube closed at both ends is

$$F_n = nc/2L$$

where, again, F is the formant, n is the formant number, c is the speed of sound, and L is the tube length. Like a tube open at one end, lengthening the tube lowers the resonance frequency.

The last variable has to do with constrictions and flaring in a tube. It relates to something called *perturbation theory.* A constriction gives air molecules less room to move around, meaning that they can reach maximum pressure faster. If the constriction is at an antinode, it will speed up the wave, increasing its frequency. However, constriction also slows molecule movement, so if the constriction's at a node – where the movement's supposed to be fastest – it will slow

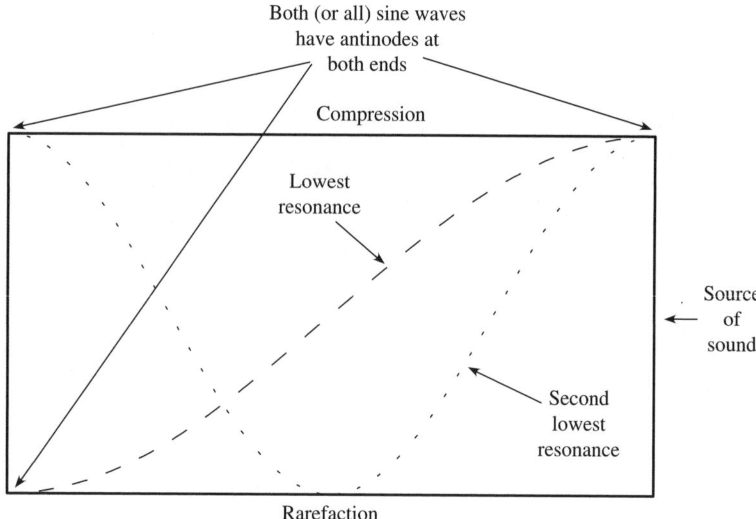

Figure 2.20 Resonances of a tube closed at both ends. The sine waves represent the two lowest resonances of the tube.

the wave down, decreasing its frequency. Flaring at one end of a tube does the opposite, giving molecules more room to move around but also speeding them up. This model explains the pattern for the mid-front vowel [e] well. When you say [e], your mouth is essentially a tube open at the front but with the tongue making a partial constriction about two-thirds of the way between the larynx and the lips. The first resonance doesn't have either a node or an antinode there, so it isn't affected much. The second resonance has an antinode there, though, so its frequency is increased. The result is a vowel with a first resonance (formant) at a medium value but a second resonance at a high value, and that's what [e] has.

There's one other factor to explain in resonances. High vowels show a low F_1. This is accounted for by another kind of tube called a *Helmholtz resonator*. This is a jug-shaped cavity – one consisting of a large body and a narrow neck. The tone you get when you blow on the top of a jug or bottle is due to this resonance. For a high vowel, the body of the Helmholtz resonator is the back cavity and the neck is the constriction made by the tongue. Unlike the other tube models, the cross-sectional area of the body and neck are part of the formula for the resonance, which is

$$F=(c/2\pi)\sqrt{(A_n)/(V_b L_n)}$$

where c is the speed of sound, A_n is the cross-sectional area of the neck, V_b is the area of the body (cross-sectional area times the length), and L_n is the length of the neck. For a Helmholtz resonator, increasing the area of the neck raises the resonance frequency, giving you a higher F_1. Increasing the area or length of the body or the length of the neck, though, lowers the resonance, yielding a lower F_1. Two examples were shown in Figure 2.19.

2.4 Measuring the fundamental frequency

The most prominent role of the fundamental frequency, or F_0, is in prosody, particularly intonation, tone and word stress. However, F_0 affects other realms of phonetics as well. It is involved as a secondary cue in some consonant contrasts: F_0 falls whenever glottalization occurs, and otherwise voiced consonants decrease F_0 while voiceless consonants increase it. It also serves a secondary role in certain vowel contrasts. For instance, high vowels tend on average to show higher F_0 than lower vowels. It even appears in voice quality. Overall F_0 is in itself a voice quality feature, and some voice qualities, notably creaky and hoarse voicing and falsetto, involve dramatic modifications of F_0. As you can see, the functions of F_0 are ubiquitous.

In this section, we'll cover different methods that are used to measure F_0. There's one other method, *cepstral analysis*, that we won't cover here. Cepstral analysis operates by making a spectrum of the logarithm of a power spectrum. It's the most accurate method of measuring F_0 in pristine recordings, but it's adversely affected by any noise in the signal and thus isn't useful for measuring F_0 in most sociophonetic applications. However, it's useful for gauging certain voice quality features, so we'll take it up in Chapter 7.

Autocorrelation

The most commonly used method of estimating F_0 today is *autocorrelation*, usually displayed as *autocorrelation pitch tracks*. In autocorrelation, the waveform of a speech signal is compared with itself. Or rather it is compared with a delayed ('lagged') version of itself. In a waveform of running speech, one *pitch period* – the period of a single vocal fold vibration – looks pretty much like the next pitch period. For autocorrelation, the signal is lagged until the waveform matches up optimally with the unlagged version. When this happens, it's normally because successive pitch periods are matched – after all, they're the segments of a waveform that are most likely to look like each other. F_0 is calculated from the length of time between the matched pitch periods with the formula 1000 ms ÷ length of time in ms = F_0 in Hz. A series of these measurements is strung together to make a pitch track, as in Figure 2.21.

Autocorrelation is quick, efficient and easy to use. However, you have to watch it like a hawk because it's prone to errors. Breathy and whispered speech are difficult to analyse, as you'd expect, because their aperiodic components are so prominent. Background noise in the signal can cause problems, too. However, even when the signal lacks such noise, two kinds of errors are common: *pitch-halving* and *pitch-doubling*. Pitch-halving occurs when the autocorrelation mistakes two pitch periods for a single period. Pitch-doubling occurs when it mistakes half a pitch period for a whole period. Often, these errors occur because the autocorrelation settings are wrong. Analysis programs allow you to specify the range of frequencies in which F_0 estimates can fall. If the actual F_0 lies outside the specified range, you'll get a bad reading. For example, you might be analysing a female voice and have the lower limit of the range set at 100 Hz. However, when the speaker shows some glottalization, her F_0 will

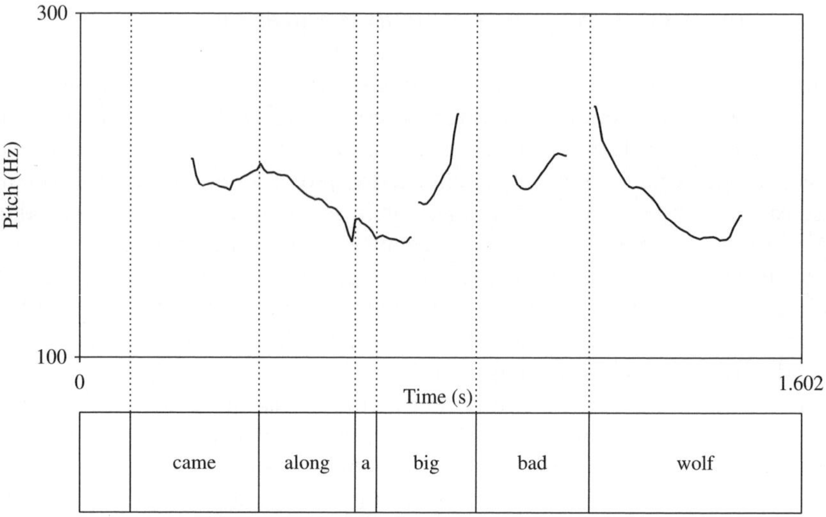

Figure 2.21 An autocorrelation pitch track of the utterance featured in Figure 2.12. Note that the scale is from 100 to 300 Hz.

dip well below 100 Hz. You'll end up with crazy F_0 readings. To fix the problem, adjust the pitch range setting.

There are ways to tell if you have faulty F_0 readings. One is to compare the reading with what the signal sounds like impressionistically. For example, if the F_0 reading is 93 Hz but the recording of that segment sounds like an ordinary female voice with no creakiness, something's wrong – probably pitch-halving. On the other hand, a reading of 93 Hz shouldn't raise much suspicion if the speaker's an adult male. Another way to check for bad readings is to scan the pitch track for sudden jumps and falls. Such sudden changes are normal when a speaker breaks into and out of creaky voicing, such as for glottalized segments. Otherwise, though, abrupt changes in an F_0 track indicate faulty readings. If the sudden jump or fall isn't accompanied by a change in spacing between glottal pulses, the pitch track is erroneous. You should adjust the pitch range setting until the autocorrelation gives you the right readings.

Measuring F_0 from narrowband spectra and spectrograms

Sometimes, no matter what you do, you can't get usable readings with autocorrelation. Often, you'll need a pitch track of a whole utterance and autocorrelation will give you a spotty, interrupted track. This problem is common with field recordings. When it happens, narrowband spectra and spectrograms provide useful backup methods.

If you need a reading for a particular time point, make a power spectrum at that point. Then, on the spectrum, look for the *harmonics*. Harmonics appear as peaks in a narrowband spectrum. To calculate F_0, count up to the fifth

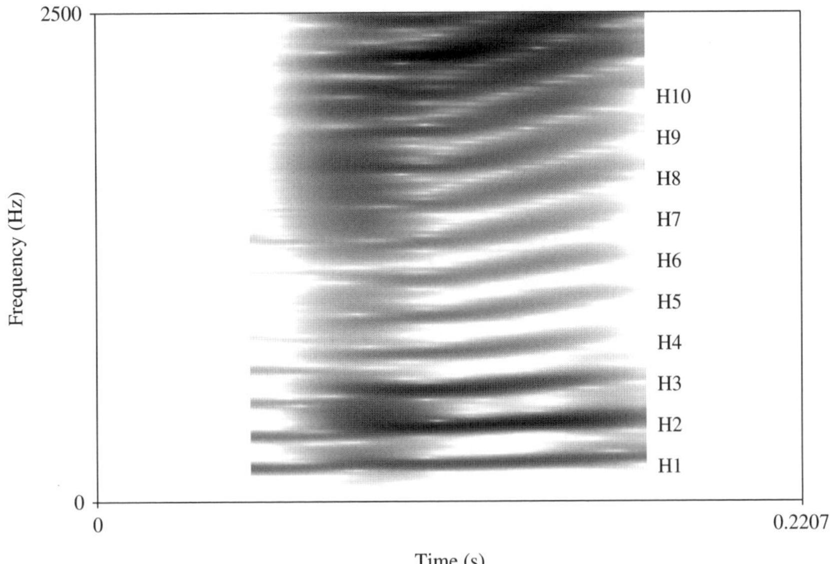

Figure 2.22 Estimation of F_0 from the harmonics on a narrowband spectrogram of the syllable featured in Figure 2.10. The harmonics are numbered. The tenth harmonic shows a contour, rising from approximately 1,880 Hz to about 2,160 Hz, so F_0 rises from 1,880/10 or 188 Hz to 2,160/10 or 216 Hz.

harmonic and divide by five, or count to the tenth harmonic and divide by ten, or count to whatever harmonic is easily visible. Figure 2.22 shows an example. Just be careful not to confuse background noise with the harmonics. Note that harmonics will appear at even intervals – any peak that's not at one of those intervals is extraneous noise.

If you need to know F_0 contours over a period of time, as a pitch track would give you, make a narrowband spectrogram. Set the viewing range so that its maximum is somewhere in the range of 400 to 800 Hz. That way, only the lowest harmonics are visible, and you can really see how they curve up and down. An example is shown in Figure 2.23.

Measuring F_0 from vibrations per unit of time

If all else fails, there's one other method you can try. You might resort to this method for highly creaky speech. You'll need a wideband spectrogram so that you can see where the individual glottal pulses are and a waveform to accompany it. Find the glottal pulses on the spectrogram and then, on the waveform, measure the span of time from the peak of one glottal pulse to the peak of any other glottal pulse. Count the number of glottal pulses in that span of time, with the starting point counting as the zeroth peak. Then use the formula $F_0 = 1000 \times$ (number of pulses / span of time in ms) or F_0 = number of pulses / span of time in s. An example is shown in Figure 2.24.

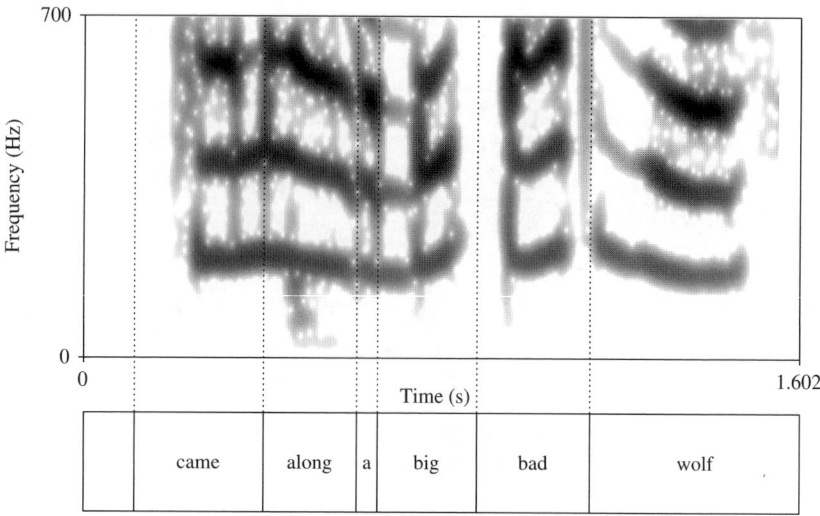

Figure 2.23 F_0 contours are readily visible in a narrowband spectrogram with a low-frequency viewing range (0 to 700 Hz in this case). Here, you can easily follow the three lowest harmonics. This method can be useful when autocorrelation pitch tracking fails.

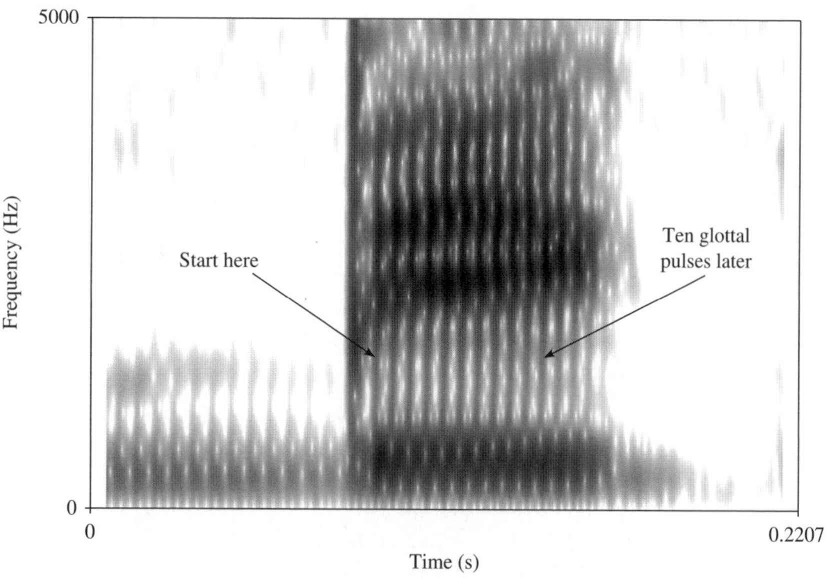

Figure 2.24 Estimation of F_0 as number of glottal pulses per unit of time. The starting point is at 0.089 s from the beginning of the spectrogram, and the tenth glottal pulse after that is at 0.141 s. The difference between the two points is 0.052 s (52 ms). Thus F_0 is 1000 × (10/52 ms) or 10/0.052 s, which comes to 192 Hz.

2.5 Measuring formants

Since Labov et al. (1972) demonstrated its usefulness for studying vowel shifting, formant analysis has been the most commonly performed type of acoustic analysis in sociophonetics. Because it's so much associated with vowel analysis, one might expect discussion of formant measurement to appear in Chapter 5. Formants aren't just properties of vowels, though. They're critical for consonants as well. Consonant place of articulation is indexed by the formant patterns of the transitions between a consonant and neighbouring vowels. Many of the approximants look like vowels on spectrograms, with full-fledged formant structures. Formants also appear in aspiration and frication, and to an extent in bursts. Hence, formant measurement is just as much a part of consonantal analysis as it is part of vocalic analysis. Formant analysis plays a marginal role in prosodic analysis in that vowel reduction is related to stress patterns. It interfaces with voice quality, too, such as for nasality. Formant analysis is covered here because its applications are so general.

A few words of caution about formant measurement are in order. First, although acoustic measurement is useful for a wide range of vowel analyses, it's not necessary for all studies. For some studies, impressionistic transcription is quite adequate. Second, bear in mind that any measurement of a formant is an estimate – it isn't really possible to determine a formant value exactly. In addition, not every variation visible in a spectrogram is relevant for lectal variation. Missing the forest for the trees is easy to do. Furthermore, you have to be careful not to take faulty measurements. The following sections will show you how to analyse consonant transitions and vowels acoustically and how to avoid pitfalls that result in bad measurements.

Linear predictive coding (LPC)

Today, software programs that estimate centre frequencies of formants nearly always do so by means of a process called *linear predictive coding*, or *LPC*. LPC became the standard tool for estimating formant frequencies after the influential publications of Atal and Hanauer (1971) and Markel and Gray (1976). Most acoustic software packages available today will show LPC readings in the form of *formant tracks*, that is, series of marks that are superimposed across the spectrogram in wavy lines where the formants are. Of course, if you perform LPC in conjunction with a power spectrum, you'll see a quite different display – a series of pointed peaks with rounded valleys between them distributed across the frequency scale of the spectrum, with the peaks representing formant readings. This kind of display is called an *LPC spectrum*. Various figures in the succeeding sections illustrate these displays.

Mechanism of LPC

The basic purpose of LPC is to separate the source and filter components of a human voice. It operates by taking samples of the acoustic signal, weighting them and determining frequencies at which the amplitudes are generally greatest. The weightings are called *linear prediction coefficients.* Often, the names *poles* or *filter order* appear instead of *coefficients.* The number of coefficients, or number of poles, or filter order are all effectively equivalent. See Markel and Gray (1976) for details on how the coefficients are obtained. The samples are collected via analysis frames whose lengths either are fixed or vary with the pitch periods. LPC is ordinarily designated 'all-pole', meaning that it can't measure antiformants.

For LPC, there are two variables to specify. First is the analysis range. Some software programs set the default upper limit of the analysis range at 5,000 or 5,500 Hz, which is ordinarily adequate because the important formants have frequencies lower than that for normal adult speakers. The second variable is the number of coefficients. This is related to how many formants you expect to see. There is one coefficient for each formant and one for each formant bandwidth, so there are at least twice as many coefficients as formants. However, a couple of extra coefficients are often needed to ensure that you get enough formant readings. Thus, for example, if you expect to find five formants within the analysis range, then the number of coefficients will be at least ten and perhaps twelve. Some software packages, such as Praat, now circumvent specification of coefficients altogether and have users specify the number of formants instead. Figure 2.25 shows an FFT power spectrum with an LPC spectrum superimposed on it. In this example, the peaks of both the FFT spectrum and the LPC spectrum line up well, leaving no doubt about what the formant frequencies are. At times, though, things aren't quite so easy.

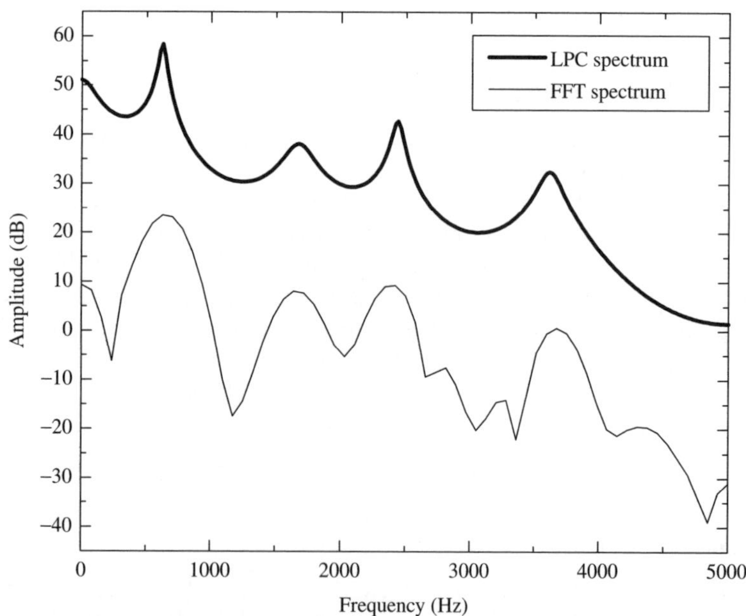

Figure 2.25 A wideband FFT power spectrum with a superimposed LPC spectrum. These spectra represent analyses of an utterance of the word ***bet***.

Adjusting LPC Coefficients

As the above discussion implies, the number of coefficients (or number of formants) can vary. Software packages will let you adjust the number of coefficients or formants if you need to, and you shouldn't hesitate to do so if necessary. In fact, you should probably expect to adjust the number of coefficients or formants constantly in order to get the most accurate formant frequencies for every token you measure. Ten or twelve coefficients (which equals five formants) in an analysis range of 5,000 Hz work well for consonant transitions and non-nasalized vowels of a typical adult male speaker. However, for nasalized vowels, there will be both oral and nasal resonances, and hence more formants, so you'll need to increase the number of coefficients. Conversely, speakers with smaller mouths than adult males, i.e. women and especially children, will generally have fewer formants within the analysis range, so you'll need to lower the number of coefficients or increase the analysis range for them. Other factors can enter the picture, too, and give you more reasons to fiddle with the number of coefficients. What happens is that, if you specify too few coefficients, formants may not be recognized by LPC or two formants that are close to each other may be read as a single formant. On the other hand, if you specify too many coefficients, you'll get 'false formants', that is, formant values where there's no formant at all. Figures 2.26–28 show spectrograms of the same utterance with LPC formant tracks superimposed – the first diagram with too few coefficients, the next one with too many, and the last one with the appropriate number. When this situation arises, make sure you're like Goldilocks and choose the one that's just right.

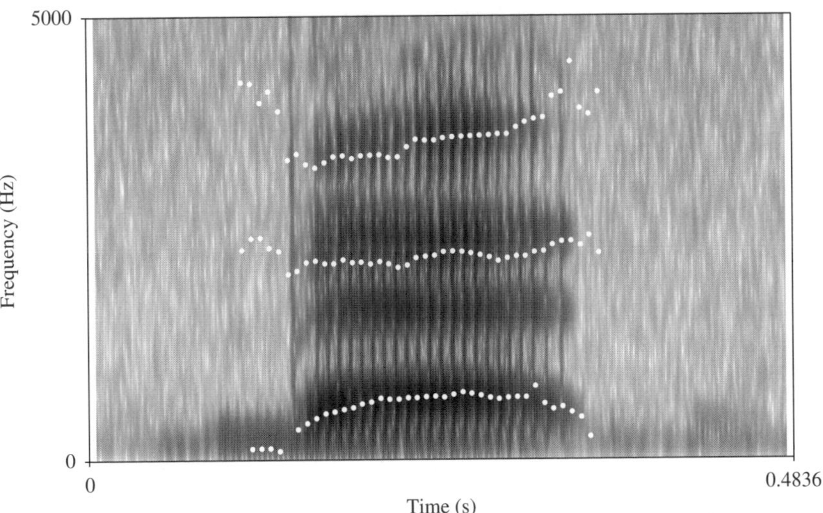

Figure 2.26 Spectrogram of ***bet*** with an LPC formant track with too few coefficients. Note that a formant track is like a series of LPC spectra (as shown in Figure 2.25) stood on their sides and lined up side-by-side. The white dots shown here correspond to peaks in the LPC spectra.

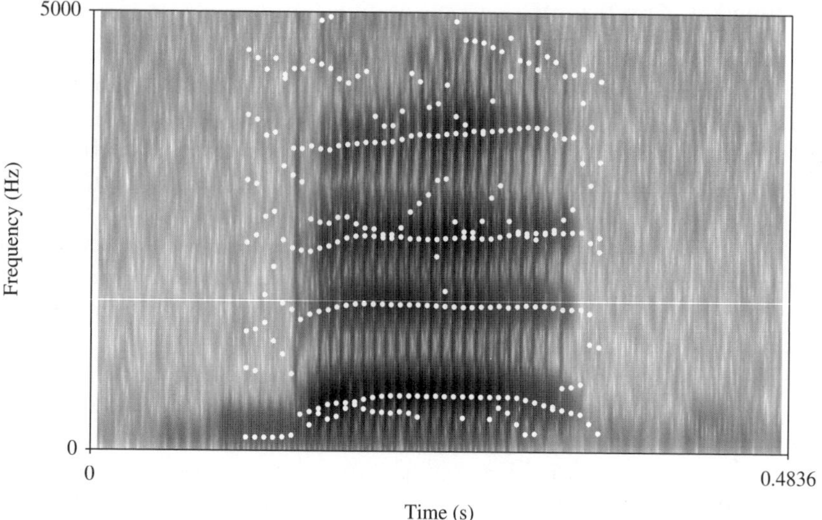

Figure 2.27 Spectrogram of *bet* with a formant track with too many coefficients.

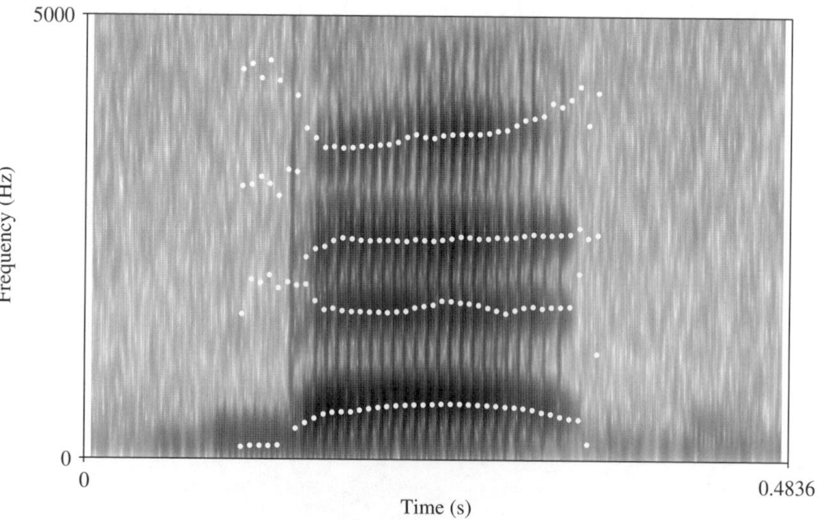

Figure 2.28 Spectrogram of *bet* with a formant track with the appropriate number of coefficients.

Other formant estimation methods

Formant estimation wasn't as easy before LPC programs became widely available. Several older methods were used to estimate formant frequencies. I'll describe three here. All of them, but particularly measurement of spectrograms and estimation from harmonic frequencies, seem less precise than LPC. LPC programs churn out formant readings on the order of 1 Hz or less – often many decimal places beyond 1 Hz. Such precision is misleading and illusory. We've already noted how formant estimates can be affected dramatically by simply adjusting the number of LPC coefficients. As you can see, there's considerable arbitrariness in pinpointing formant frequencies. There simply are limits to how closely you can estimate a formant frequency. Even measuring a formant to the nearest Hz may be suspect. This lack of precision is especially acute for the field recordings that are necessary for sociolinguistic research because even soft background noise or any distance between a speaker and the microphone will make formant frequencies harder to determine exactly. The upshot is that the older, pre-LPC methods really aren't that bad.

Measurement of spectrograms

One older method of estimating formant values is to measure wideband spectrograms. On a printed spectrogram, the centre (on the frequency axis) of the dark zone representing the formant is measured with a ruler. Analogous measurement can be done with spectrograms on a computer monitor. This method is rather crude and should be used only for exploratory work.

Estimation from wideband FFT spectra

Another method is to use wideband FFT power spectra. A curve can be fitted to the spectrum, and the peaks represent the formant values. Figure 2.29 shows a series of peaks, each representing a formant.

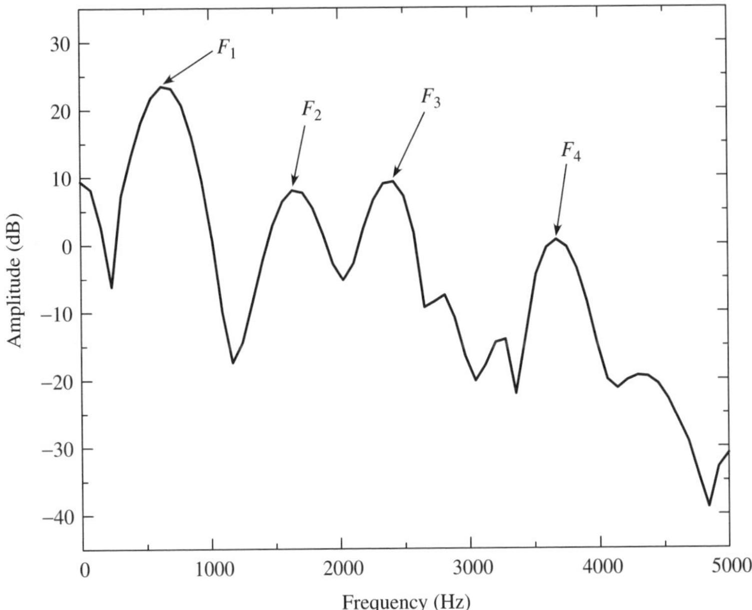

Figure 2.29 Use of a wideband FFT power spectrum to estimate formant values. The peaks in the spectrum correspond to formants. The peaks of the four formants occur at about 635 Hz, 1,645 Hz, 2,405 Hz and 3,675 Hz. The peak at 4,310 Hz may represent a fifth formant.

Estimation from narrowband FFT spectra

A third alternative method also involves FFT spectra. In this case, though, narrowband power spectra are used instead of wideband spectra. Here you examine the peaks representing the harmonics. If one harmonic in the vicinity of the formant clearly has higher amplitude than neighbouring harmonics, take the frequency of that harmonic as the estimate of the formant value. If, on the other hand, there are two neighbouring harmonics that have roughly similar high amplitudes, take a frequency halfway between them as the estimate of the formant value. Labov et al. (1972) used this method effectively for their groundbreaking study of vowel shifting. They added one rule, that if there are three harmonics of roughly equal amplitude in the vicinity of a formant, the frequency of the middle harmonic is taken as the formant estimate. Figure 2.30 illustrates this method. In this spectrum, F_1, F_2 and F_3 each show a single high-amplitude harmonic, while F_4 shows two harmonics of similar amplitude in its vicinity. Several important studies from the early days of acoustic phonetics, such as the oft-cited Peterson and Barney (1952) paper on vowel formant values, used a variation of this method.

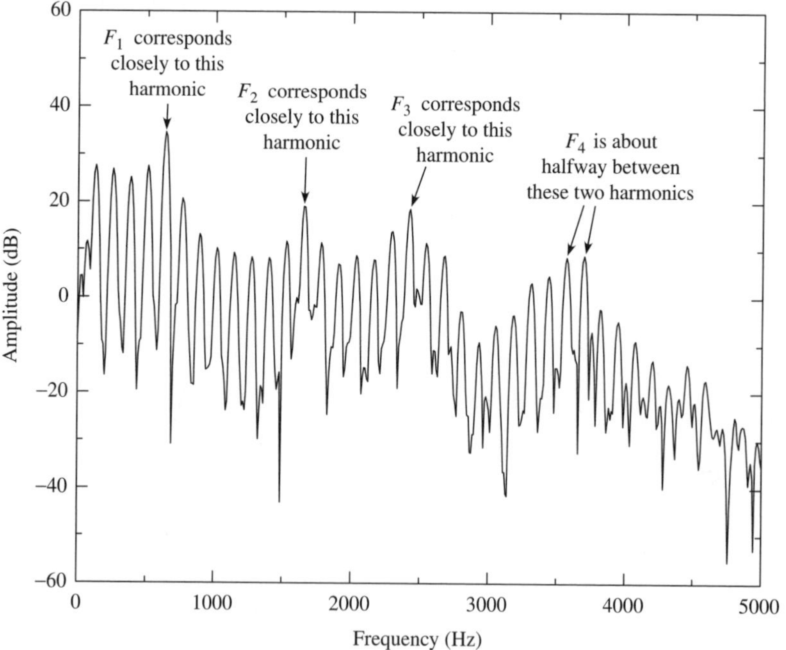

Figure 2.30 Estimation of formant values using harmonic values in a narrowband FFT power spectrum. For F_1, F_2 and F_3, the formant peak coincides closely with a harmonic, so the frequency of the harmonic can be taken as the estimate of the formant value (635 Hz, 1,652 Hz and 2,422 Hz, respectively). For F_4, the formant peak straddles two harmonics (with frequencies of 3,564 Hz and 3,692 Hz), so the formant can be estimated as a value halfway between the frequencies of the two harmonics (3628 Hz).

Bandwidth

Formants have other properties besides their centre frequency. They have *bandwidths*. The bandwidth of a formant is usually given as the width of the formant 3 dB lower than the amplitude of its peak (Johnson 2003:17). Figure 2.31 gives an idealization of how formants with the same centre frequency but different bandwidths compare to each other.

Bandwidth has an effect on your perception of a sound. A speech sound with large ('wide') bandwidths would sound muffled, as if you had heard it through a wall. Large bandwidths can also create the impression of nasality if there are many formants – in fact, more formants than usual and large bandwidths are the hallmark of nasalized sounds. If, on the other hand, the bandwidths are too narrow – this wouldn't happen with a real voice, but it's an issue for speech synthesis – the voice will have a tinny, artificial quality.

Reliability testing

It's all too easy to obtain faulty formant readings. However, there are ways of ensuring that you have accurate readings. Reliability testing can occur at two stages of your project. The first stage is while you're taking the measurements for the first time. You should always follow reliability safeguards during this stage. The second stage is after you've taken the measurements, when you look over them and you or someone else can redo some of them.

Checking for false formant readings

There are several safeguards to use while you take formant measurements using LPC. You should *always* use these safeguards whenever you estimate formant

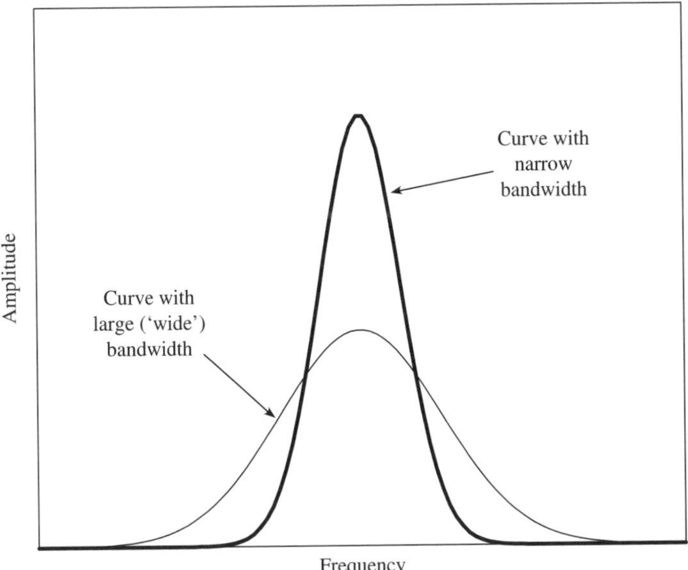

Figure 2.31 Normal curves representing idealized power spectra of formants with the same centre frequency but different bandwidths.

values with LPC – or any other method, for that matter. If it appears that you've obtained a bad reading, adjust the number of LPC coefficients and measure it again. For some tokens, you may have to adjust the number of LPC coefficients several times before you find a number that works. Also check to make sure that you're measuring the right time point. Sometimes you may find yourself measuring the wrong point because spectrograms can mislead you into marking the onset or offset in the wrong spot. For these reasons, always take LPC readings with a grain of salt. You should check each of the following four items.

Checking LPC readings against spectrograms

The first and most obvious thing to check is whether the LPC readings match up with what you see on the spectrogram. Formants appear as broad, dark zones on wideband spectrograms. If you don't see a formant reading where the spectrogram shows a formant, or if you see a formant reading where there's no formant on the spectrogram, something's wrong. One exception, however, is that sometimes a formant's amplitude doesn't reach the mark level of the spectrogram but still registers in the LPC analysis.

Comparison with impressionistic phonetics

It helps to have a good ear for vowel quality. Being able to recognize by ear how high or low a vowel is, or how back or front it is, can be a powerful aid in checking formant readings. For example, if a particular token of the KIT vowel shows unusually low F_2 values, you can isolate it by marking it off or highlighting it in the spectrogram and then listen to it. If it sounds rather central, then the LPC reading of an unusually low F_2 is probably correct. Various factors, particularly coarticulation, undershoot and dialectal variation, can result in odd-looking formant values.

Knowing where the formants 'should' be

Another effective way to check formant readings is to know where to expect them to be. For example, for any labial or any strongly back vowel, F_1 and F_2 will be close to each other. Similarly, for dorsal consonants and for high front and (to a lesser extent) mid-front vowels, F_2 and F_3 will be close together and both will have a relatively high frequency. For the [ɹ] of English and [ɹ]-coloured vowels, F_2 and F_3 will also be close together, but at a significantly lower frequency than for dorsals or high front vowels. Nasal vowels show more formants than oral vowels. All vowels and approximants have their own distinctive formant patterns. As a rule:

- high vowels show low F_1 and low vowels show high F_1;
- front vowels show high F_2 and back vowels show low F_2;
- lip rounding lowers (some) formant values.

Keep in mind that all the formant values will be shifted proportionately higher for speakers with smaller mouth sizes, i.e. women and children. If the LPC readings you obtain don't match up with what you'd expect for a particular consonant or vowel, and if you listen to the segment and it doesn't sound at all unusual when you isolate it, then the formant readings are probably incorrect. Go back and adjust the number of LPC coefficients.

Predicting effects of coarticulation and duration

Finally, you should understand how coarticulation will affect formant values. Consonant transition values can appear to vary a lot depending on the neighbouring vowel. However, coarticulation is no less important for measurements of vowels. The fact that each token of a vowel phoneme that you measure will show slightly different formant values is nothing to worry about. Adjacent segments always overlap, and formants are warped in sundry ways in those overlapping areas.

It's imperative to know what formant-warping effects to expect in any coarticulation situation. We'll discuss the transition patterns of various consonants in Chapter 4, and you should refer to section 4.1 for more detail on them. For now, the rule of thumb is that labial consonants lower F_2 and F_3 of neighbouring vowels, dorsal consonants raise F_2 and often lower F_3, and coronal consonants raise F_2 for back vowels but lower F_2 for front vowels (with subtler effects on F_3). Lip rounding can influence the transition patterns, most notably for dorsal consonants. All consonants except pharyngeals lower F_1 – hence, the point of maximum F_1 in a vowel is generally the point farthest from the consonants. You should expect to see these patterns reflected in the formant measurements you obtain. In fact, coarticulation is the first factor you should consider when you try to account for variations in the formant values obtained for different tokens of the same vowel phoneme. Figure 2.32 shows the words *bab* [bæb],

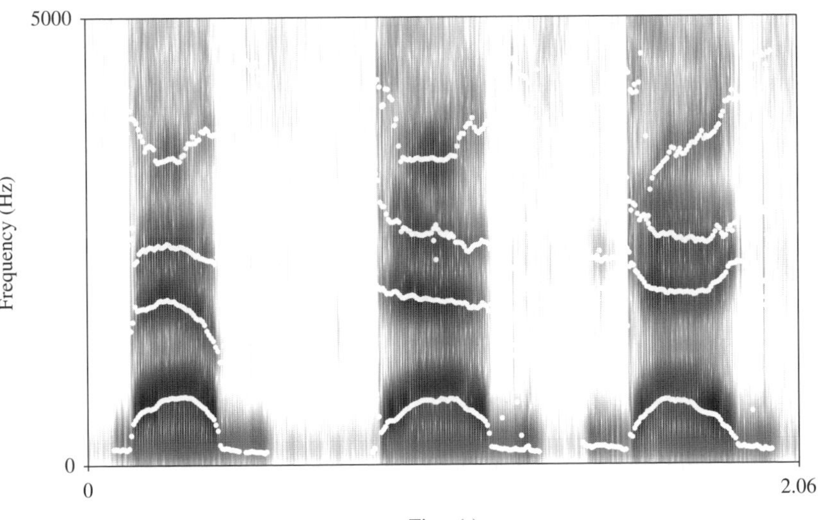

Figure 2.32 Spectrogram of *bab*, *dad* and *gag* with superimposed formant track. Note that the formant frequencies of each syllable are about the same in the centre of the vowel but differ markedly at the vowel onsets and offsets.

dad [dæd], and *gag* [gæg] with LPC formant tracks. Note how dramatically the transitions differ for each word and for each formant.

Duration interacts with coarticulation as well. If the duration of a vowel is long, only the edges of the vowels may show coarticulation. However, if a vowel's short, you'll see strong coarticulatory effects throughout the vowel. Duration generally doesn't show such obvious effects for consonants – that is, the transitions show similar patterns most of the time, largely because consonants can be compressed only so much before they become indistinct or they're elided altogether.

Reliability measures

Once you've finished your measurements, using the safeguards mentioned above, there are further reliability procedures that you can conduct. The basic element here is redoing some of the measurements. Ideally, you should choose some of the measured utterances randomly – perhaps 10 per cent, perhaps fewer, depending on the size of your corpus. Less ideally, you might select particular speakers. Then the selected utterances are remeasured, ideally by a different person from the one who took the initial measurements. The results are shown as the mean percentage difference between the values obtained originally and on the second trial. Statistical comparisons between original and remeasured values, particularly intraclass correlation, are also useful.

A twist on redoing measurements for reliability is to redo them with a different formant estimation method. That is, if you obtained them using LPC the first time, you could remeasure them using an FFT method.

One other procedure to ensure reliability is to check any outliers in the obtained measurements. Outliers can be found simply by plotting the data – e.g. on an F_1/F_2 or F_2/F_3 plot – or by using a procedure such as a box-and-whiskers plot. For the latter, determine the quartile value of the measurements (the points that divide the lowest and highest 25 per cent of the measurements from the other measurements). Then find the difference between the two quartiles, called the interquartile difference (IQR). Next, multiply the IQR by 1.5 for mild outliers and by 3.0 for extreme outliers, adding these numbers to the upper quartile and subtracting them from the lower quartile (Tukey 1977). For example, if the quartile values are 592 Hz and 672 Hz, respectively, then the IQR is 80 Hz; any values below 472 Hz or above 792 Hz would be mild outliers, and any values below 352 Hz or above 912 Hz would be extreme outliers. Finally, remeasure the outliers, especially the extreme ones.

2.6 Measuring articulation directly

Speech sounds are produced through series of articulatory gestures. A *gesture* is the movement of an individual articulator, such as the tongue tip or the lips. Direct measurement of gestures is usually a concern of phonetics and speech pathology. Occasionally, though, it can have sociolinguistic significance. For example, one of the most commonly studied variables in sociolinguistic studies of English is consonant cluster simplification, as in *best* pronounced [bɛs], with loss of the final [t]. However, Browman and Goldstein (1991) have noted that stops in such clusters, particularly coronal stops, are sometimes articulated but acoustically masked by neighbouring segments. The speaker 'intends' to produce a stop, and moves the tongue to produce it, but still leaves no audible evidence of the gesture. Hence, the match between articulation and acoustics isn't always one-to-one. For a sociolinguistically marked variable, such as consonant cluster simplification, the result is a mismatch in social indexing.

Numerous techniques are used for measuring articulation. We'll cover five briefly here and discuss a sixth, nasometry, in Chapter 7. All of these techniques are designed for laboratory use. X-rays and MRI can't be used in the field at all with current technology. Ultrasound technology has progressed to where it can now be used in the field.

Electropalatography

Electropalatography involves placing a device that looks much like an orthodontic retainer in a person's mouth. The device covers the subject's palate and is filled with electrodes. The subject is asked to say various speech sounds, and the electrodes that fire indicate where the tongue made contact with the roof of the mouth. It's used mostly to investigate consonantal articulation.

Electromyography

Electromyography (EMG) works much like electropalatography in that it involves electrodes. However, the electrodes aren't embedded in a device. Instead, they're attached directly to the skin that covers a particular muscle – e.g. on the lips or tongue – or they're implanted into the muscle. The electrodes indicate whether the muscle is active during the production of a particular sound. EMG signals can become hard to interpret when several muscles are moving at the same time.

X-ray microbeams

For X-ray studies, pellets that are opaque to X-rays are glued to various mouth parts – the surface of the tongue (usually four pellets), the lips, the gum line where it meets the upper front teeth, and the jaw – with some reference pellets outside the mouth, such as on the nose or chin. A small X-ray beam follows each pellet and the image is recorded, formerly on X-ray photographic paper but now on a computer. Current techniques are said to expose subjects to no more radiation than they receive from the environment. Images may be static pictures or moving pictures, the latter called *cineradiography*. Cineradiography allows the velocity of movement to be recorded. Purnell (2008) made use of X-ray microbeams to examine differences in the articulation of the TRAP vowel before /k/ and /g/, as in *back* and *bag*, in Wisconsin English.

MRI

Magnetic Resonance Imaging (MRI) has become popular in recent years – probably more popular than X-rays. MRI is especially useful for tracking tongue movements. The subject lies on his or her back in the MRI scanner, which produces a magnetic field that causes protons in hydrogen atoms in the subject's body to be aligned a certain way. Then a radiowave signal is applied and the effects on the protons are measured. The product is a fine-grained cross-sectional image that differentiates kinds of tissues. As Parthasarathy et al. (2007) describe, both static and cine-MRI have been developed. Cine-MRI can be combined with the magnetic 'tagging' (i.e. marking) of a plane in the tongue or other organ so that the deformation of the plane can be followed as the organ moves. This process is called tMRI, or tagged cine-MRI.

Ultrasound

Recently, Mielke et al. (2005) and Recasens and Espinosa (2005) have explored the use of ultrasound to examine tongue position during articulation. There are a variety of technical difficulties, such as the need for various filters to sharpen images and problems with missing or false readings. Nevertheless, the procedure is non-invasive and shows promise. Bauer and Parker (2008) successfully used ultrasound in the field to demonstrate that the vowel in *bag* is articulated differently from the vowels in *back* or *bake*.

2.7 Brain imaging techniques and production

Recent progress in neuro-imaging techniques has spawned interest in ways that they can be applied to various linguistic questions. Most research so far has been directed at understanding the basics of language processing. Currently, the technology allows researchers to identify regions of the brain that are activated during particular linguistic activities. Prospects for identifying specific neurons that are activated are quite dim at the moment. However, the technology is advancing rapidly. Moreover, even though there are limitations to what can be discerned in a scan, there are numerous unexplored applications for the technology that does exist, including applications in sociophonetics.

The three brain scanning techniques that have proved most useful for linguistic research are event-related potentials (ERPs), positron emission tomography (PET) and functional magnetic resonance imaging (fMRI). Each has its advantages and drawbacks. Others, including computerized axial tomography (CAT) and MRI, have been used as well (Harley 2008).

ERPs are elements of another process called electroencephalograms (EEGs). In EEGs, electrodes are attached to the scalp to measure electrical activity in the brain. ERPs are parts of the EEG signal that are time linked to particular events in the brain. They have excellent temporal resolution but poor spatial resolution. Filtering the non-ERP elements out of an EEG is difficult, and the most common method is to repeat a stimulus many times with a subject so that the repeating pattern within the EEG can be discerned. The electrical waveforms for the trials are then averaged. Deflections of the waveform indicate neural activity and are denoted according to their latency (in ms) from the stimulus and whether the deflection is positive or negative (Fabiani et al. 2007).

PET requires injection of a radioactive isotope into the subject's bloodstream (Wager et al. 2007). The PET scanner detects photons emitted when positrons created by radioactive decay collide with electrons. Depending on the isotope, blood flow in the brain, glucose uptake or neurotransmitter receptor activity, all of which indicate neural activity, can be measured. PET has moderate temporal and spatial precision, but it can be used in conjunction with ERPs.

fMRI measures the release of oxygen by haemoglobin, which increases where neurons are active. It creates a magnetic field that allows it to detect the magnetic effect on the haemoglobin. fMRIs have excellent spatial resolution but poor temporal resolution. Because fMRI is a noisy process, it's difficult to use with audio stimuli, and earphones are problematic because the metal in them interferes with the magnetic imaging (Wager et al. 2007). Hence visual stimuli are usually used in fMRI studies, which are practical for studying speech production but not for most speech perception work. The magnetic field also prevents fMRI from being used with ERPs.

An important problem for sociophonetic studies is that all of these techniques involve cumbersome equipment. For PET and fMRI, subjects have to lie on their backs with their heads inserted into the imaging machine. Needless to say, this is no way to study natural conversations. ERPs are less problematic in this regard, since the electrodes placed on the subject's scalp can be hooked to equipment while subjects are sitting up. Nevertheless, most brain scanning will be confined to laboratories for the foreseeable future.

Brain scanning techniques could address specific sociophonetic problems. One key area for sociophonetic interest would be in determining how phonological coding is linked with sociolinguistic indexing of variants. Indefrey and Levelt (2004) map out a sequence in which an utterance starts with semantic conceptualization, followed by retrieval and selection of lemmas (syntactic/semantic structures), then by phonological retrieval and finally by syllabification. The whole process takes about 600 ms. Indefrey and Levelt also note which areas in the brain are activated for each task. Phonological retrieval is associated with Wernicke's Area, while syllabification and prosody are associated with Broca's Area. Additional experiments could investigate how stylistic variation fits into the picture, what brain areas are involved with it, and whether it adds any time to the process. Such experiments could be especially informative with people who are strongly bidialectal. Another application would be to investigate how phonological variation is coded neurologically. For example, when producing a word with a variably merged phonological distinction, how differently do subjects with and without the distinction process it?

EXERCISES

1. What is the frequency of a tone whose period is 10 ms? How about a tone with a period of 15 ms? Of 8 ms?
2. What kinds of sounds (periodic or nearly periodic, noise, transients) are involved in each of the following speech sounds: [d], [k], [e], [f], [tʰ], [z], [bʱ]?
3. Describe the steps involved in digitization of a sound signal.
4. What tasks are wideband and narrowband spectrograms useful for?
5. Explain how the source-filter theory pertains to vowels and how it operates differently for fricatives.
6. Calculate the frequencies of three lowest resonances for a tube, 6 cm long, that is (a) open at one end and (b) closed at both ends.
7. Record yourself uttering any vowel or download a practice example from http://ncslaap.lib.ncsu.edu/sociophonetics/. Then measure F_0 in the centre of the vowel using (a) autocorrelation, (b) measurement from a narrowband spectrum and spectrogram, and (c) measuring from vocal fold vibrations per unit of time.
8. Using the vowel that you used for exercise 7 or another one, measure the formants in the centre of the vowel using (a) LPC, (b) a wideband FFT spectrum, and (c) a narrowband FFT spectrum.
9. How can you tell if you have faulty F_0 or formant readings? What can you do to fix the problems?

FURTHER READING

Hewlett, Nigel and Janet Mackenzie Beck. 2006. *An Introduction to the Science of Phonetics*. London: Routledge/Mahwah, NJ: Erlbaum.

Johnson, Keith. 2003. *Acoustic and Auditory Phonetics*, 2nd edn. Oxford, UK/Malden, MA: Blackwell.

Kent, Ray D. and Charles Read. 2002. *The Acoustic Analysis of Speech*, 2nd edn. Albany, NY: Thomson Learning.

Lieberman, Philip and Sheila E. Blumstein. 1988. *Speech Physiology, Speech Perception, and Acoustic Phonetics*. Cambridge, UK/New York: Cambridge University Press.

Reetz, Henning and Allard Jongman. 2009. *Phonetics: Transcription, Production, Acoustics, and Perception*. Blackwell Textbooks in Linguistics 22. Oxford, UK/Malden, MA: Blackwell.

Perception

3

3.1 Approaching speech perception

When most sociolinguists – for that matter, most linguists in general – think about studying language, they first think of the production of speech. The other side of the coin, speech perception, isn't what tends to come to mind right away. This bias is reflected in the way phonetics is taught in introductory linguistics classes, where speech sounds are defined in terms of articulation and perception is hardly, if at all, mentioned. Not surprisingly, sociophonetic studies fall disproportionately on the production side of the fence.

What is surprising, however, is that sociophonetic studies of perception have in fact thrived, albeit somewhat out of the limelight. Certain topics, such as the perception of phonological mergers, the auditory discrimination of different groups of speakers and subjective reactions to certain kinds of voices, have attracted sustained attention from sociophoneticians and have yielded extensive lists of publications. Other topics have garnered only sporadic attention, and many others none at all. They all deserve attention, and they offer inroads for sociolinguists to address cognitive issues. You shouldn't think that those of us who study language variation are merely taking theories and methods from perceptual phonetics and applying them to variation. Language variation has a great deal to contribute to what we know about speech perception, too. Socio-perceptual study is a wide-open field with numerous opportunities for researchers.

The study of perception seems intimidating at first. Once you understand how to approach it, though, you'll see that it isn't so daunting after all. In this chapter, we'll start by discussing some basic perceptual properties of the human auditory system and how they affect sociophonetic studies. Then we'll discuss what kinds of socio-perceptual experiments can be conducted and how to set them up. One practical difference between studies of production and of perception concerns which stage of the project most of the work lies in. When you're studying production, the hardest work comes after you've interviewed subjects, when you're analysing the interviews. With perception, though, the hard work comes before you interact with your subjects, when you're designing and assembling the experiment. After discussing perception experiments, we'll briefly look ahead to what brain scans may contribute to socio-perceptual inquiry in the future.

3.2 Auditory transformation

Before we get into how to set up and conduct perception experiments, we should discuss how the human auditory system processes speech sounds. Our auditory systems don't hear speech sounds – or other sounds, for that matter – exactly the same way as they reach our ears. Instead, both frequency and amplitude are shaped in specific ways. The effects on frequency are particularly important, both for perception experiments and for other issues that we'll take up in later chapters. At the heart of the shaping of frequency is the cochlea.

The cochlea

The *cochlea* is a coiled, snail-shaped organ inside the inner ear in which sound vibrations are transferred to neural signals, which are then sent to the auditory cortex within the brain. Sound vibrations are transmitted from the eardrum via the ear ossicles (the 'hammer', 'anvil' and 'stirrup') to the cochlea. Within the cochlea is a tissue called the *basilar membrane* that runs along its length. Different parts of the basilar membrane vibrate most strongly when stimulated by particular ranges of frequencies. When a section of the membrane vibrates, it stimulates hair cells that cause nerves to fire. The part of the basilar membrane sensitive to the lowest frequencies is at its broad end, while the area sensitive to the highest frequencies is at its narrow end. Generally, the lower end of audition is approximately 20–25 Hz. The upper end varies according to the speaker. Young children with no damage to their hearing can normally hear sounds with frequencies close to 20 kHz. This upper limit declines with age, however, on average more quickly for males than for females, and especially if a subject has been exposed to noisy environments over a long period.

One important aspect of the cochlea is that it isn't sensitive in a linear way to amplitude or frequency. For both amplitude and frequency, the sensitivity is more or less logarithmic. First, it is far more sensitive to amplitude differences at low amplitudes than at high ones. Second, it is a lot more sensitive to frequency differences at low frequencies than at high ones. Third, its sensitivity to amplitude interacts with frequency in a complex way, with the result that it is more sensitive to amplitude differences at some frequencies than at others. The way people perceive amplitude, taking into account the differential sensitivity, is called *loudness*. Similarly, the way people perceive frequency is called *pitch*. Table 3.1 shows the corresponding physical and perceptual terms and units of measurement.

The differential sensitivity that makes pitch distinct from raw frequency is especially important for speech. It affects the way people perceive vowels and

Table 3.1 Terminology and units of measurement for physical and perceptual scales.

	Physical		*Perceptual*	
	Name	*Units of measurement*	*Name*	*Units of measurement*
Wavelength	Frequency	Hertz (Hz)	Pitch	mel Bark ERB [semitone]
Wave excursion	Amplitude	Pascal (Pa) Decibel (dB)	Loudness	Sone (see Chapter 6)

consonants and hence the number of phonological contrasts that a language can have. Four scales – the mel, Bark, ERB and semitone scales – are widely used to represent pitch, as opposed to frequency.

The mel scale

The mel scale was an early attempt to set the auditory representation of frequency in a formulaic way. It was based on how subjects divided series of simple tones into what sounded like equal intervals. The formula for the mel scale, following Traunmüller (1997), is

$$m = 1127 \ln (1 + Hz / 700)$$

where m is the value of a tone in mel. Figure 3.1 plots the transformation.

The Bark scale

The *Bark*, or *critical band rate*, scale was designed as an improvement on the mel scale. Whereas the mel scale was based on subjects' judgements about equal pitch differences, the Bark scale was based on the interaction of frequency and loudness. Two pure tones with frequencies very close together will sound no louder than a single tone to listeners. When the frequencies of the tones are spaced farther and farther apart, though, at a certain point the two tones begin sounding louder to subjects, and this point is called the critical band width (Zwicker et al. 1957). The critical band rate differs according to frequency, and it is usually referred to in Bark units. Two formulas for Bark have been in common use. One, developed by Zwicker and Terhardt (1980), is

$$Z = 13 \arctan (0.76 [f]) + 3.5 \arctan (f / 7.5)^2$$

where Z is the value of a sound in Bark and f is the frequency of the sound in kHz. The two additive parts are needed to make the formula approximate the

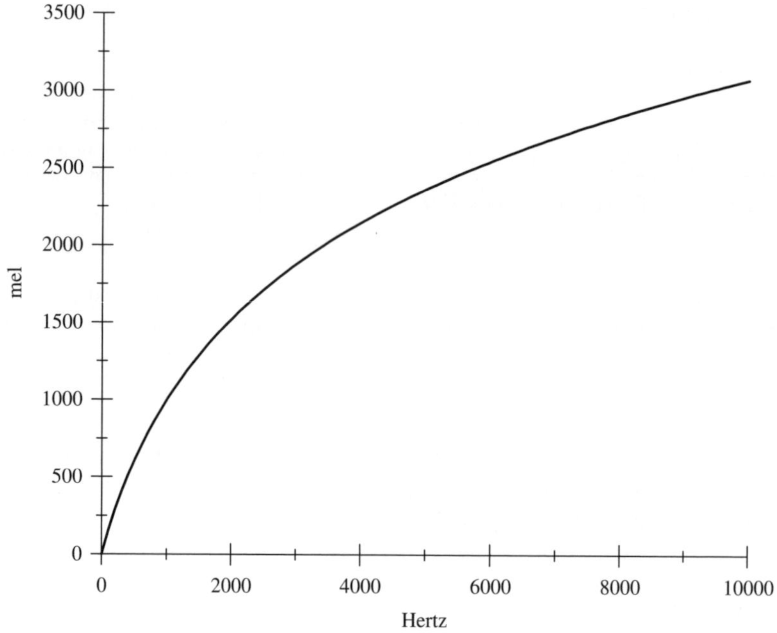

Figure 3.1 Relationship of the Hertz scale to the mel scale.

critical band rate at different parts of the frequency scale. A newer formula developed by Traunmüller (1990) is

$$Z = [26.81 / (1 + 1960/f)] - 0.53$$

where f is the frequency of a sound in hertz (not kHz, as with the Zwicker and Terhardt formula). Figure 3.2 plots the transformation. Traunmüller reports that his formula is more accurate than the older Zwicker and Terhardt. However, he had to provide correction formulas for frequencies under 2 Bark (approximately 200 Hz) and over 20.1 Bark (approximately 6,550 Hz), as follows:

$$\text{if } Z < 2 \text{ Bark: } Z' = Z + 0.15\,(2 - Z)$$

$$\text{if } Z > 20.1 \text{ Bark: } Z' = Z + 0.22\,(Z - 20.1)$$

The mel and Bark scales have proved most useful for transformations of formant values, either for vowel quality or for consonantal properties. In perception experiments, it is sometimes useful to speak in terms of one of these perceptual scales instead of in terms of the physical hertz scale.

The ERB scale

Whereas mel and Bark are used mainly for study of formants, the *equivalent rectangular bandwidth rate* (*ERB*) *scale* has proved most useful for transformations of F_0. The reason is that, while ERB and Bark are proportional to each

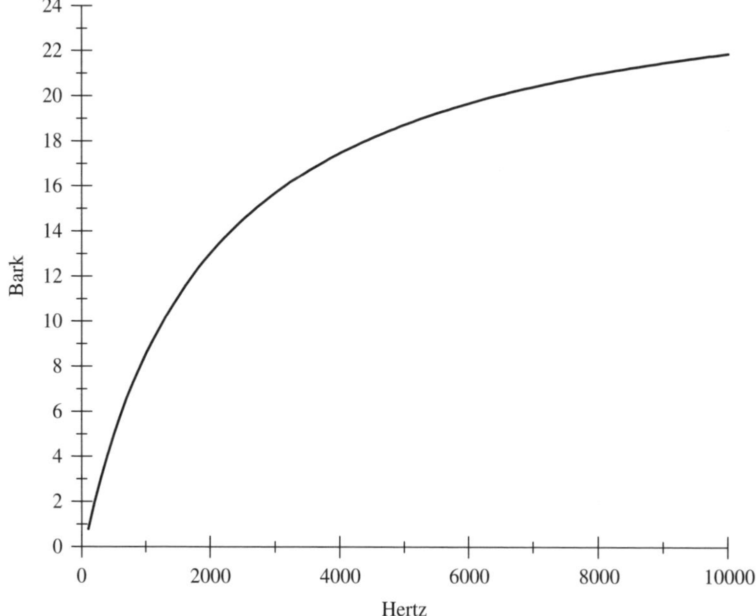

Figure 3.2 Relationship of the Hertz scale to the Bark scale. The Bark transformation here uses the Traunmüller (1990) formula.

other above 500 Hz, ERB provides better resolution below 500 Hz. The ERB scale could certainly be used for formant study, though the Bark scale is used for historical reasons. Studies of F_0 variation that require a numerical transformation – as for intonational studies – should, however, use the ERB scale. Different formulas have been developed for ERB, just as for Bark. A widely used formula is that of Greenwood (1961):

$$\text{ERB} = 16.7 \log_{10} (0.006046f + 1)$$

where f is the frequency of a sound in hertz. Figure 3.3 plots the transformation.

The semitone scale

The semitone scale is different from the other scales. First, it's not, strictly speaking, a perceptual scale, though it has been used by phoneticians for a long time, especially as a transformation of F_0. Second, and more importantly, it can be used only to express the difference between two sounds, not to describe a single sound.

Semitones are based on the musical scale. An *octave* is any doubling of frequency. For example, a 200 Hz sound is one octave higher than a 100 Hz sound, and a 900 Hz sound is one octave higher than a 450 Hz sound. A *semitone* is one-twelfth of an octave. Semitones correspond to each note on a

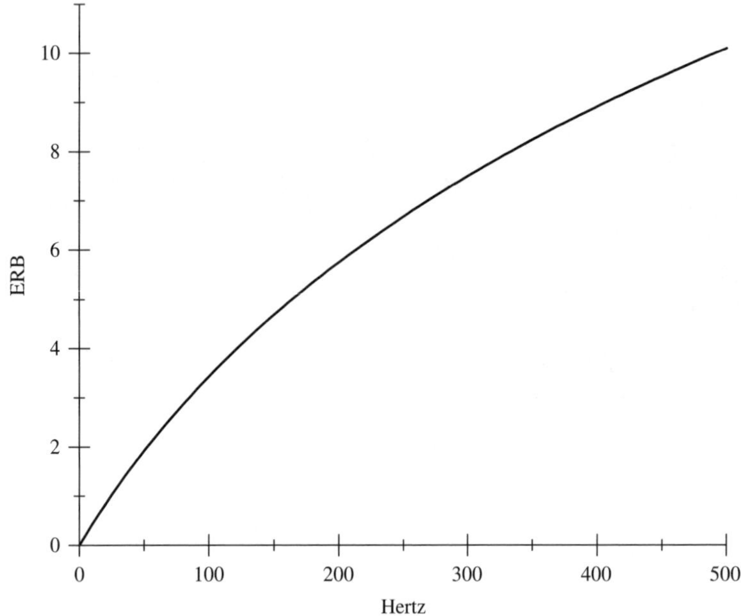

Figure 3.3 Relationship of the Hertz scale to the ERB scale. Hertz values are shown only up to 500 Hz because the main use of ERB is for transformations of F_0.

musical scale, including the sharps. The formula for converting Hz to semitones (from Hewlett and Beck 2006:124) is:

$$\text{Semitones} = 3.863 \times \log_{10} (\text{higher sound in Hz / lower sound in Hz})$$

Uses of perceptual scales

The mel, Bark, ERB and semitone transformations have several uses. One has to do with the perception experiments that we'll cover later in this chapter. For some experiments, stimuli need to be created so that they fall at even intervals in frequency. But what kind of frequency should you use – the physical measure of Hz or a perceptual scale such as Mel, Bark or ERB? Sometimes the difference isn't crucial and you can get by with using intervals in Hz. However, it may be important for your experiment to correspond to human perceptual abilities closely, and in that case you should calibrate your stimuli on a perceptual scale.

We'll see other uses of perceptual scales in succeeding chapters. For vowel formants and for formants in consonantal transitions or frication noise, perceptual scales can give you a better picture of what people actually hear than the physical Hz scale can. Thus, it may at times be useful to plot measurements on a perceptual scale. Some normalization techniques involve conversion to a perceptual scale. For example, when comparing intonational contours of different speakers, you may need to convert from Hz to ERB in order to normalize the changes in frequency of F_0 among the different speakers.

3.3 Perception experiments

When you're studying anything in speech production, you analyse speech directly by auditory transcription of some sort, by conducting acoustic measurements or sometimes by measuring articulation. You can't measure speech perception in such direct ways, however. You may want to determine whether a subject can recognize a phonological distinction that is undergoing a merger. You may want to learn how listeners tell speakers of particular dialects or members of ethnic groups apart by ear. You may wish to find out what range of intonational contours or segmental realizations sound 'natural' or even recognizable to a certain group of people, or how different groups categorize certain sounds differently. For all of these research issues, you can't simply turn on a machine and ascertain answers by measuring the output. Instead, you need to set up experiments with appropriate subjects and see how those subjects react when confronted with auditory stimuli.

One thing that's important in perception experiments is that whatever factors you test should be related to factors present in speech production. You need to have some knowledge of how the variable is correlated with production in the group(s) you're examining or what range of variation the variable(s) show. Usually, you should know this information ahead of time. However, especially if you're using stimuli that aren't synthetically modified, you can perform measurements on the stimuli themselves and then correlate the measurements with the results of the perception experiment.

There are several steps involved in a perception experiment. First, you need to decide what sort of task your subjects should perform. Next you need to figure out what to use as a basis for your stimuli. Then you should determine whether to apply any treatments to the stimuli and, if so, do this. After that, you put the stimuli together to make the experimental recording. Finally, you need to find appropriate subjects to participate in the experiment and present it to them. After that you apply the appropriate statistical analyses. Don't forget that you'll need to report the make and model of each piece of equipment you use when you write the methods section of your study.

For more in-depth reviews of studies, see Thomas (2002b), which focuses on sociolinguistic studies, and Komatsu (2007), which concentrates on prosodic experiments.

Identification tasks

Tasks that subjects are asked to perform essentially fall into two types: identification tasks and discrimination tasks. In an identification task, subjects assign a label to each stimulus they hear. Identification tasks can be further divided in two ways. They may be open-ended tasks or forced-choice tasks, and they may involve identification of linguistic features or features of the speaker (or something intermediate). Each of these divisions is described below.

Open-ended tasks

In an *open-ended* task, subjects aren't given a list of possible answers. Instead, they're instructed to write out an answer. For example, subjects might be instructed to listen to a stimulus and then write down what word they thought they heard. In another experiment, subjects might hear a voice and write down what job they think the speaker is suited for. Open-ended response sheets are useful for some kinds of experiments, such as gating experiments (see pp. 73–4) and experiments testing the confusability of dialectal variants of sounds. Their main drawback is that they generate a wide variety of responses that then have to be classified in some way.

One sort of open-ended experiment involves creating a *confusion matrix.* This design can be applied to any segmental or prosodic variable for which subjects are able to classify stimuli into linguistic categories. The classic confusion matrix study is Miller and Nicely (1955), which compared 16 English consonants in a /Cɑ/ frame. In this sort of experiment, subjects are presented with stimuli and are asked to identify each stimulus – e.g. by writing down what they think they hear. Actually, you can handle this step either open-endedly, allowing subjects to write down anything, or as a forced choice in which you give subjects a list of possible answers to circle. The responses are classified according to the variables under study. For example, if vowels are the object of study, any identification of a word with vowel X as vowel Y is put in the identified-as-vowel-Y category, regardless of any misidentifications of consonants in the word. Then a table is created, with the actual sounds listed in rows and the identifications listed in columns. A hypothetical matrix is shown in Table 3.2. Normally, correct identifications outnumber misidentifications, but you can influence subjects' identifications by using any of the various experimental treatments discussed below. Once you've created the table, you use the number of correct identifications and misidentifications to calculate a similarity index for any two sounds included in the experiment. For two sounds X and Y, the formula (from Johnson 2003:68) is:

$$\text{Similarity index for X and Y} = (p_{XY} + p_{YX}) \;/\; (p_{XX} + p_{YY})$$

where p_{XY} is the proportion of sound X stimuli identified as sound Y, p_{YX} is the proportion of sound Y stimuli identified as sound X, p_{XX} is the proportion of sound X stimuli identified as sound X, and p_{YY} is the proportion of sound Y stimuli identified as sound Y. When you have the similarity index, you can then calculate the perceptual similarity of sounds X and Y as the negative natural logarithm (ln) of the similarity index. As Johnson (2003) notes, you can map the perceptual similarity of several sounds on a graph by connecting them with lines whose lengths correspond to these calculated perceptual similarities. This technique could be useful for comparing how speakers of different dialects perceive sounds differently. One caveat is that perceptual similarity is

Table 3.2 A hypothetical confusion matrix. Note the asymmetry in which sound d is heard as sound e more often than sound e was heard as sound d.

	Responses by listeners				
Sound that was played	*Sound a*	*Sound b*	*Sound c*	*Sound d*	*Sound e*
Sound a	47	2	0	1	0
Sound b	7	32	5	4	2
Sound c	0	1	41	7	1
Sound d	0	3	4	26	17
Sound e	0	4	1	8	37

often asymmetrical: i.e. sound X is misidentified as sound Y more often than sound Y is misidentified as sound X.

Another type of open-ended experiment is *free classification*. In a free classification experiment, subjects listen to the stimuli and then put them into groups based on how similar they are to each other. For this kind of experiment, subjects ordinarily need to be able to hear a stimulus as many times as they like. However, the researcher has flexibility in one important respect: subjects may be allowed to create as many categories as they like or may be instructed to create a set number of categories. Having an indeterminate number of categories may result in too many large or small groupings, but having a set number may result in unnatural groupings if the stimuli don't correspond to that number of groups in a subject's perception. One successful use of free classification has been for determining the perceptual similarity of regional dialects. For example, Clopper (2008) applied free classification to classification of American dialect samples, asking subjects to classify the samples into six groups. The results were then subjected to a dendrogram-construction program and to multidimensional scaling, both of which showed how perceptually similar the stimuli and the dialects they represented were.

Free classification can provide a holistic way of examining the similarity of dialects. A more conventional analysis of production, in contrast, would necessarily focus on particular variables and could miss other variables that are salient to listeners. There are some pitfalls as well, though. One is that subjects could focus on a few stereotypically marked variables instead of paying attention to the speech as a whole. Another is that F_0 and various other factors make male and female voices sound different in an immediately recognizable way. Hence, subjects may make sex the primary classificatory factor unless they're instructed not to or unless male and female voices are considered in separate experiments. Other physiological differences that result in different voice qualities among speakers could confound the results as well.

A special type of open-ended identification experiment used to test for mergers is a *commutation* experiment. In a commutation experiment, utterances of words that form minimal pairs (for the merged or nearly merged sounds) are recorded from the speech of local dialect speakers. As Labov (1994:356) notes, the usual method is to have the speaker read a list of words in randomized order. Some of the words will be those that form the minimal pairs. Then listeners from the same dialect are presented with the recorded words one at a time and are asked to identify the word (usually open-endedly, though they could be given words to choose from). If a listener's accuracy rate is close to 100 per cent, then it's clear that the speaker distinguishes the sounds in question and the listener recognizes the distinction. If the accuracy rate is close to 50 per cent, which would represent randomness, then either the speaker, the listener or both have merged the two sounds. An accuracy rate close to 0 per cent would be bizarre, but if it occurred it would indicate that the listener recognizes the distinction in a way opposite to that of how the speaker produces it. Results of several commutation experiments are discussed in Labov (1994).

Forced-choice tasks

In a *forced-choice* experiment, subjects are given a list of possible responses, from which they choose (usually) one. Most perception experiments use a forced-choice design. They may involve identification of linguistic categories, identification of characteristics of speakers or ratings of intelligibility.

Identification of linguistic categories

Fairly diverse approaches have been taken in experiments that ask subjects about linguistic categories. One strategy is to present subjects with stimuli that lie along an acoustic continuum between two or more phonemes and ask them to name which phoneme each stimulus sounds most like. Two studies that used this method are Willis (1972) and Janson (1983). Willis found significant differences in phoneme boundary placement between subjects from Buffalo, New York, and those from an adjacent community in Canada. Janson, similarly, found a generational difference in the placement of a phoneme boundary in Stockholm Swedish. A caution about interpreting the results is that, in some cases, subjects' responses can be influenced by stereotypes of the different realizations. Perceptual boundaries can also shift depending on expectations about the speaker – for instance, for male versus female speakers. Of course, such influences can be important findings in themselves, and for that reason it may be useful to compare the perception of phoneme boundaries with production by the subjects. Figure 3.4 depicts a hypothetical situation in which a perceptual boundary differed for two lects, resulting in different crossover points.

Stimuli can be varied along more than one dimension as well. This design is suitable for investigating the relative importance of several cues for a particular phonological contrast. Most phonological contrasts depend on multiple phonetic cues, and the cues commonly participate in what are called *trading relations*. In a trading relation, when one cue is absent, another one is strengthened (in production) or given greater importance (in perception) as compensation (e.g. Repp 1982; Parker et al. 1986). Cross-linguistic and cross-dialectal variation in which cues are emphasized or present at all is common. An example is a study I conducted comparing the cues two groups of subjects, Mexican Americans and Anglos, used to distinguish /d/ and /t/ in codas after a diphthong (Thomas 2000). I varied the length of the preceding diphthong, the realization of the diphthong glide and the length of voicing during the stop

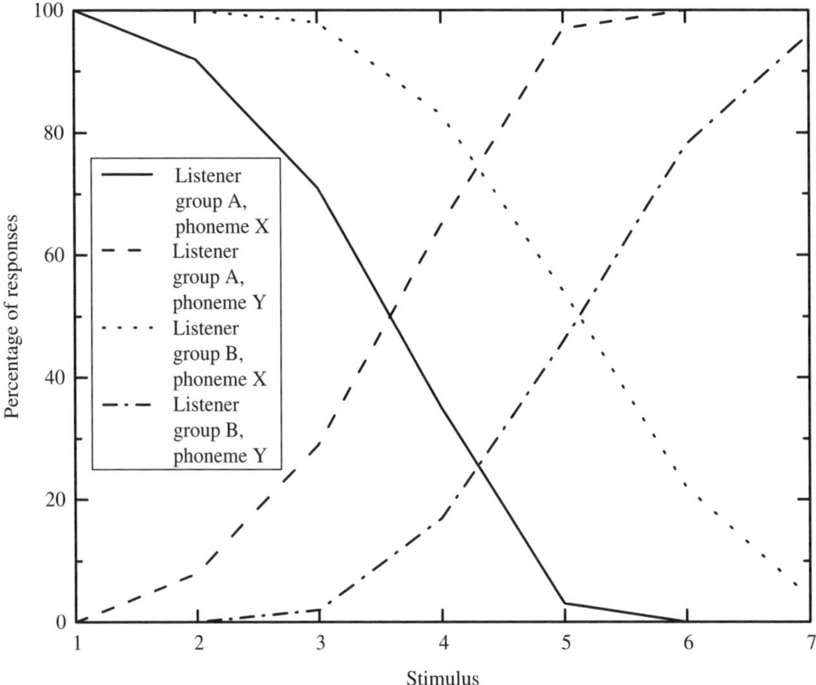

Figure 3.4 A model of how different perceptual boundaries would create different crossover points in a perception experiment involving identification of categories. For listener group A, the crossover occurs between stimuli 3 and 4, but for listener group B, the crossover occurs between stimuli 5 and 6.

closure along continua. The two ethnic groups did, in fact, differ in their reliance on specific cues.

A different design involves playing dialectal variants to subjects – either from their own dialect or a different one – and asking them to identify the word or the sound in each stimulus. This kind of experiment can be conducted in an open-ended or a forced-choice format. For example, Traill et al. (1995) used this design to investigate how confusable vowels undergoing a diachronic shift in South African English could be. They played South African utterances of individual words to British listeners and gave them three choices for each stimulus. Not surprisingly, words with shifted vowels were often misidentified. This design is relatively easy to construct.

Among the most intriguing identification experiments are those that involve what's become known as the *McGurk Effect*. The McGurk Effect comes about when subjects are exposed to conflicting visual and audio stimuli and report hearing something different from what they actually heard. In the original study by McGurk and McDonald (1976), subjects who saw a video of a speaker saying [ga] or [ka] and heard a voice saying [ba] or [pa] most often reported that they heard [da] or [ta], respectively. Numerous possible variables could be tested for the McGurk Effect. Strand (1999) and Johnson et al. (1999), for example, tested how listeners' perceptions of the same audio stimulus changed depending on whether video stimulus of a male or a female speaker accompanied the audio. Use of conflicting audio and video of speakers from different ethnicities or social classes – the latter perhaps conjured by use of different clothing or scenery in the video – may well reveal stereotypes about language. Hay et al. (2006) investigated perception of the NEAR/SQUARE merger in New Zealand by pairing utterances with photographs of people of different ages or in different clothes.[1]

There's another way in which conflicting information presented to subjects can reveal stereotyping. Before subjects answer questions about stimuli, they can be told false information about the speakers whose voices make up the stimuli (though you should give them the correct information after the experiment is over!). An example is Niedzielski (1999). Subjects who were Michigan natives were told that a speaker was either from Detroit or from Canada. The speaker was actually from Detroit. The subjects heard stimuli with the MOUTH vowel and were asked to match them with resynthesized tokens. The experiment tested whether subjects would match the stimuli with different sounds depending on what they'd been told, which, in fact, they did.

Judging quality of stimuli

In a test of *category goodness*, subjects rate how realistic a stimulus sounds or how close it is to their own speech. Although, as we'll see, scalar ratings of the speakers themselves are used extensively in socio-perceptual experiments, such ratings of the linguistic forms are relatively rare. An example is in Peeters (1991), who varied the relative lengths of the onset steady state, transition and offset steady state of diphthongs and compared the goodness ratings for each stimulus given by speakers of different Germanic languages and dialects of German.

Identification of characteristics of speakers

Scores of socio-perceptual experiments have involved asking subjects to identify some characteristic of the speaker. The characteristics can be either a demographic factor such as ethnicity or geographic origin, or a psychological factor such as a personality trait. Subjects may be given only two choices, less commonly three or more, from a list, or they may be asked to rate the speaker on a scale. Another option is to give subjects choices but to ask them how sure they are for each rating.

Experiments in which subjects identify a demographic factor ordinarily give subjects a list of choices. For nearly all experiments on ethnic identification, only two choices are given. The preference for a binary design probably stems from the fact that most ethnic identification experiments have focused on distinguishing African Americans from European Americans (see Thomas and Reaser 2004 for a review). However, in studies involving identification of geographical regions, subjects are generally given a list of locales from which to choose or are asked to name the provenance of the voice open-endedly. In a few cases, however, scales have been employed. Munro et al. (1999) had subjects rate speakers based on how Canadian or how Alabamian they sounded, and Preston (1993) had subjects order voices on a north–south transect.

Demographic factors have usually been either ethnicity or geographic origin, but social class has been rated occasionally and other factors could be used.

The real stronghold of scalar rating has been in experiments on psychological ratings of speakers. These studies may be called *subjective reaction* studies. In these studies, subjects listen to stimuli and then rate the speaker in each stimulus for various personality or other traits, such as friendliness, trustworthiness, toughness and intelligence. The scale may be 5 point, 7 point, 10 point or the like. The classic study of this sort is the *matched-guise* experiment of Lambert et al. (1960), in which stimuli consisted of bilinguals speaking French and English (in different stimuli) and subjects from Quebec rated each stimulus on various scales. A matched-guise experiment is one in which the same speaker produces different stimuli using different languages or accents. The aim of Lambert et al. (1960) was to determine whether listeners would rate the same speaker differently on intelligence and personality, depending on what language the speaker was using – and they did. Further information on how to construct matched-guise experiments, and not just with bilingual speakers, is found in Ball and Giles (1988). Only a subset of subjective reaction studies uses the matched-guise design. Furthermore, determining stereotypes associated with different languages is only one use of psychological ratings of speakers. For example, Frazer (1987) had subjects rate the prestige of accents from different parts of Illinois by asking subjects to answer, for each voice, 'Would you be proud if a friend or member of your family spoke this way?'.

By far the majority of experiments on identification of characteristics of speakers have utilized unmodified recordings of speakers. A fair number have used stimuli subjected to some of the synthetic treatments discussed below, however. In studies of ethnic and geographical variation, unmodified recordings are sufficient to determine whether listeners can identify the ethnicity or geographical origin of a speaker. To figure out *how* listeners tell the difference, though, you have to impose treatments on the stimuli. Stimuli can be chosen so that certain variables are present or absent, making it possible to show whether subjects need to access those features to make identifications. Some variables can't be selected so easily, and synthetic manipulation is necessary to treat them. Synthetic manipulation has been used successfully in studies on identification of regional dialects (e.g. Bezooijen and Gooskens 1999), on identification of ethnicity (e.g. Thomas et al. 2010) and even on psychological ratings of speakers (e.g. Brown et al. 1974).

Rating intelligibility or divergence

At least one type of identification straddles the line between identification of linguistic categories and identification of characteristics of speakers. This type is the rating of intelligibility or linguistic divergence. For example, subjects may be presented with recordings of speakers of various dialects of a language and asked to rate subjectively how 'divergent' each sample is. Divergent from what?, you might ask. You have to decide what the basis of comparison should be. A national standard is one possibility: Bezooijen and Gooskens (1999) used standard Netherlands Dutch and standard British English as the bases for comparison when they asked subjects to rate the degree of divergence of various dialects of Dutch and English. A different option would be to have subjects rate the divergence from their own speech.

Another approach is to test the intelligibility of different varieties to listeners. To test intelligibility, you may have subjects translate a word or sentence they hear into their own dialect or into the standard dialect and then compute the proportion of mistakes. Bezooijen and Berg (1999) used this method for dialects of Dutch. Tang and van Heuven (2008) did so for different varieties of Chinese; in their experiment, they had subjects name the semantic category of individual words and translate entire sentences, though for the sentences they based the measure only on the accuracy of translation of the final word. Intelligibility is inherently subjective, and thus there are multiple ways to rate it, as these studies show.

Discrimination tasks

In contrast to identification tasks, *discrimination* tasks require subjects to try to tell stimuli apart. They're most useful for studying phonological mergers and for examining how listeners distinguish phonological categories that aren't necessarily merging. They've been used primarily for segmental distinctions but could easily be adapted to prosodic distinctions.

Same or different?

The most commonly used discrimination task in socio-perceptual experiments is to present subjects with two stimuli and ask them some question about whether the two sound the same or different. This design is often used to test for mergers. The question doesn't have to be literally whether the stimuli sound the same or not; in fact, that question may give misleading answers, since subjects may notice slight differences that have no semantic significance. For testing mergers, other questions may be more effective. Subjects can be asked instead whether stimuli represent the same word, belong to the same sound category, or rhyme.

Stimuli in these experiments often are taken from spoken utterances, usually from reading wordlists. Stimuli could be taken from spontaneous speech, but the difficulty with spontaneous speech is that it's hard to find minimal pairs. A different option is to generate a continuum of synthetic or synthetically modified stimuli, play tokens that are adjacent on the continuum to subjects, and then ask them whether the members of each pair are distinct.

Mergers certainly aren't the only possible object of same/different experiments. They can also be used to determine whether different subjects recognize a distinction in different ways. The simplest experiment of this type would be to adapt the phoneme boundary experiments, described earlier, to a same/different design. Stimuli that are adjacent on a continuum can be presented to subjects. The subjects should then be asked if the members of each pair belong to the same category in order to see whether different speakers locate the phoneme boundary in different places. A more complex experiment would test more than one phonetic cue at the same time: this experiment would determine whether different groups of listeners rely on different cues to identify a phonological distinction. A hypothetical example is that speakers of one dialect might distinguish final voiced and voiceless stops mainly by the length of the preceding vowel, while speakers of another dialect might place more importance on properties of the stop release.

Oddball detection and ABX

Oddball detection involves presenting subjects with three or more stimuli and asking them which two are most alike – or which one is most unlike the others. An *ABX* experiment is similar. In ABX, subjects are given two reference signals (A and B) and asked which one a stimulus (X) is closer to or the same as. One use of these experiments would be in constructing similarity matrices. For example, subjects could be presented with samples of different dialects, three at a time, and each time would be asked to name which two sound most alike. The results could then be fed into a dendrogram construction program, much like what was discussed earlier for free classification. Similarly, speakers within a single community, such as a sample of adolescents from one town, could be analysed in this way. The resulting groupings of speakers could provide insights into how individuals group together linguistically.

The method could potentially be applied to categorization of phones as well. It could be used to determine perceptual boundaries between phonemes. Conversely, it could be used as an alternative to a goodness rating in ascertaining what listeners consider an acceptable range of variation for a sound.

Judgement versus functional testing

So far we've mainly discussed tasks that involve asking subjects to name something. This design works for many experiments. However, it has one big disadvantage: it draws on subjects' conscious knowledge, either of social characteristics of speakers or of the language itself. Language in general, and phonetic cues in particular, are subconscious faculties. Sometimes asking people for their judgements or opinions doesn't really tap into what they actually 'know'.

An alternative is to set up a *functional testing* experiment. In such an experiment, subjects are asked to do something based on stimuli they hear, not just to give an answer. An example was the 'coach test' in Labov et al. (1991). Labov et al. were investigating a phonological merger. With mergers, subjects often give erroneous answers when asked whether they say particular words the same or differently or when asked whether a particular stimulus represents one sound or the other. They do so because they honestly don't know consciously, and they may also be misled by spelling or simply not understand how to perform the task. In the coach test, control subjects and subjects from Philadelphia, where words such as *ferry* and *furry* are merged or nearly merged, listened to a story about a coach in which the crux of the story depended on an ambiguity involving a minimal pair. Subjects heard the story first with one member of the minimal pair and then with the other. They were asked questions each time to determine how they interpreted the story and hence whether they could distinguish the words in the minimal pair.

Designing a functional testing experiment requires ingenuity. In some cases, though, it is the only way to extract what listeners subconsciously 'know' about language. Besides testing mergers, it could be used to examine subjects' stereotypical attitudes about certain groups, to determine how native-like particular stimuli sound, or to investigate the meanings associated with intonational contours.

Choice of stimuli before modification

One critical decision you'll need to make is what stimuli to use. Obviously, the stimuli should contain the variables you want to test and should be uttered by speakers with the right demographic specifications. However, there are other criteria as well. Most of these apply primarily to stimuli that are based on real human voices, as opposed to machine-generated stimuli.

First, should you use read or spontaneous speech? This question rests on whether you need the content to be tightly controlled and whether reading will compromise some aspects of speech. If you need stimuli with exactly the same content, then clearly you need read speech. Probably the majority of sociophonetic experiments and the vast majority of those in phonetics and speech pathology involve stimuli that are tightly controlled for content. However, some aspects of prosody are affected by reading (Swerts et al. 1996), and people also tend to avoid stigmatized variants when reading, so spontaneous speech may be preferable for experiments involving such variables.

Second, how long should the stimuli be? Length of stimuli depends on the experiment. Some experiments involve stimuli consisting of one word or even less, others involve sentence-length utterances, and a few involve longer passages.

Third, where should the stimuli be recorded? Phoneticians and speech pathologists prefer to use speech that was recorded in a soundproof booth. Such recordings are easier to modify synthetically than recordings made in environments with background noise. If your stimuli involve read speech, you may be able to record them in a soundproof booth. However, for sociophonetic purposes, some experiments require stimuli that are recorded in more natural sociolinguistic situations. Conversations are difficult to carry on in a soundproof booth, and many speech acts are impossible to conduct there. Not only that, but the voices you need may be of people whom you can access only in the field. Hence, you can't always record your stimuli in a perfect acoustic environment. When you need to use field recordings for stimuli, check to make sure that background noise is minimal and that the speaker's voice is recorded clearly.

Experimental treatments

Lots of experiments require some sort of treatment to be applied to the stimuli. In experiments testing whether subjects can distinguish regional or ethnic dialects, for example, untreated stimuli consist merely of samples of speech taken directly from members of the groups being compared. Such samples can tell you only whether listeners can distinguish the groups. They can't tell you *how* the listeners distinguished them. To figure that out, you need a way to treat the stimuli so that some have a certain variant and others lack it, or so that the stimuli feature a range of states for that variant. There are three basic means of treating stimuli. One is to choose speech samples that contain or lack the variants you're interested in. A second is to have an impersonator produce the stimuli. A third is to apply experimental treatments to the stimuli electronically.

One caution should be offered here. Experimental treatments are often the only way to tell how listeners go about a particular perceptual task. However, the experimental treatment can induce them to pay more attention to a particular cue than they would in an ordinary conversational situation. As a result, what your results may actually tell you isn't that listeners *do* use that cue in real-life situations, but instead that they *can* use it if necessary. Additional experiments may be needed to determine which cues are most important.

Pre-selection of stimuli

There are numerous types of speech perception experiments in which impersonation or artificial modification of the stimuli is unnecessary. In these experiments, stimuli are preselected to contain the variables being tested. If you're conducting an intelligibility experiment, you almost certainly shouldn't modify the stimuli because what you're testing is how understandable a dialect is and any modification would compromise the results. You wouldn't want to modify stimuli in a dialect categorization experiment for essentially the same reason.

There are also experiments in which you can apply treatments just by the way you select the samples to use as stimuli. If, for example, you're testing variants that can be elicited by reading or from spontaneous speech – e.g. intonational contours associated with questions or a vowel variant for which individuals don't show stylistic variation – you won't necessarily need to modify your stimuli. What you do is to pick some samples that have the variable and some samples that lack it altogether. Then you can test whether the presence of the variable makes a difference in listeners' responses. There's one experimental drawback to beware of. With this method, you can't completely eliminate the possibility of spuriousness because there might be some other variant in the stimuli that's influencing the listeners' responses.

Impersonators

Human impersonators have been used occasionally in experiments. The matched-guise design discussed earlier, in effect, uses impersonators because the same speakers produce the different stimuli – even if the bilingual speakers aren't really impersonating anybody because they're producing what for them may be natural speech. Impersonation in the strict sense has been utilized in experiments. In Purnell et al. (1999), a single speaker produced three ethnic guises. Addington (1968) employed a more complex design in which four trained impersonators read a passage using combinations of seven voice qualities, three speaking rates and three degrees of F_0 variation, yielding 252 ($4 \times 7 \times 3 \times 3$) total samples of speech.

Impersonation hasn't been used often except in matched-guise experiments. One difficulty is that speakers with special training or talents are needed to produce the stimuli. Another problem is that the impersonators may inadvertently vary features besides the desired ones. A third problem is that the impersonators can't vary factors such as speaking rate and F_0 variance at perfectly even intervals, and even intervals are needed for some kinds of statistical analysis.

Electronic modification

The two big advantages of electronic modification are that they allow you to modify a single cue without modifying others and that they allow you to modify cues in a precise, quantifiable way. A wide range of treatments can be applied to stimuli electronically. In fact, practically any aspect of a speech signal used for a stimulus can be modified. The succeeding sections describe the most common treatments, how to apply them and what kinds of experiments each one is useful for. The list is not intended to be exhaustive. Some modifications of acoustic signals are performed with a synthesizer, while others aren't. In general, modifications of vowel formant frequencies and bandwidths, of consonantal qualities, and of F_0, as well as temporal compression, require a synthesizer. Other treatments, such as adding noise, filtering, temporal truncation (as with gating) and resplicing are performed by other means – you don't need a synthesizer for them.

Numerous types of synthesizers have been developed; see Carlson and Grandström (1997) and Lemmetty (1999) for fuller discussions. Some years ago, they could be divided into those that generated speech electronically from typed commands and those that modified recordings of real voices. Today, though, the two functions have been integrated in synthesis packages that are useful for speech perception research. That is, a synthetic signal can be generated entirely from scratch by means of computational commands or it can be modelled from a real voice and then modified. In both cases, the signal is based on the source-filter model of human speech: a 'source', analogous to vocal fold vibrations, is created and then several filters that imitate the effects of filters in the oral tract are applied. This method can be applied to synthesize both vowels and consonants. In sociophonetic experiments, you'll nearly always model stimuli on real voices. Stimuli modelled from human voices will sound more realistic because of the myriad of subtle factors in voices that are hard to program from scratch. Synthesis from scratch is useful only occasionally in sociophonetic experiments – in creating stimuli along an acoustic continuum, perhaps. The main applications of generating signals from scratch are non-experimental, such as prosthetic devices for laryngectomy patients and reading devices for blind people.

One older method that is still in use is the *pitch synchronous overlap add method* (*PSOLA*). This is used for modification of F_0 and duration and can't be applied to segmental quality. It operates by reconfiguring vocal pulses synthetically.

Untreated and resynthesized control stimuli

Whenever an experiment involves synthetic modification of stimuli, the experimenter should ask whether the synthesis degraded the stimuli enough to affect the experiment. In some cases, the degradation may be minimal and not an important factor. For instance, F_0 is easily modified with a synthesizer and the resulting stimuli usually sound quite realistic. However, when unmodified control stimuli are also used in the experiment, the difference between modified and unmodified signals is ordinarily detectable. To counteract this difference, it may be desirable to *resynthesize* the control stimuli.

In resynthesis, the control stimuli are simply fed into the synthesizer and the synthesized model of them is created, but no other modification – such as changing durations, F_0 or formant values – is applied. The processed signals are then used as the control stimuli. Hence, if the other stimuli sound a bit tinny or staticky, so will the control stimuli. It's up to the researcher to decide whether this step is necessary.

Splicing

In certain cases, you may wish to modify synthetically only part of a stimulus. Preferably you should resynthesize the whole stimulus, including the parts that aren't otherwise modified. If there's some reason not to do that, however, you'll need to splice the unmodified and modified parts together. Splicing introduces a problem of its own: transience. Unless you're careful, an audible pop or crackle will result where you spliced the signal together. The best way to avoid this is to start and end the signals that you're splicing together at zero-crossing points in their waveforms. A zero-crossing point is a timepoint where the waveform crosses the line of zero amplitude.

Gating

One treatment that can be applied to stimuli is *gating*. In a gating experiment, subjects first hear and react to a tiny bit of the acoustic signal – perhaps part of one syllable – and then longer and longer parts of the same signal are played and their reactions are recorded each time. The full signal might be a complete word, a phrase or a full sentence. In such experiments, you should expect the accuracy level to rise as the length of the stimuli increases. An example of an utterance subjected to gating is shown in Figure 3.5.

Gating is useful for determining whether certain sounds are confusable with other sounds. For example, Labov and Ash (1997) used gating to determine how well listeners from Birmingham, Alabama, Philadelphia and Chicago could understand vowel realizations from their own dialect and from the dialects of the two other cities. In their experiment, they first played single words to subjects, then phrases, and then entire sentences. While Labov and Ash were interested in the recognizability of stressed vowels, numerous other phonetic factors may also be tested this way. Gating experiments can easily be used to examine the amount of confusion created by unstressed vowels, deletions of consonants, different intonational contours, varying stress patterns and tonal contrasts, and the like.

Addition of noise or babble

Another technique that's used widely in phonetic studies of speech perception is the addition of noise of various types to the signal. While phoneticians and speech pathologists commonly use this method to study hearing deficiencies,

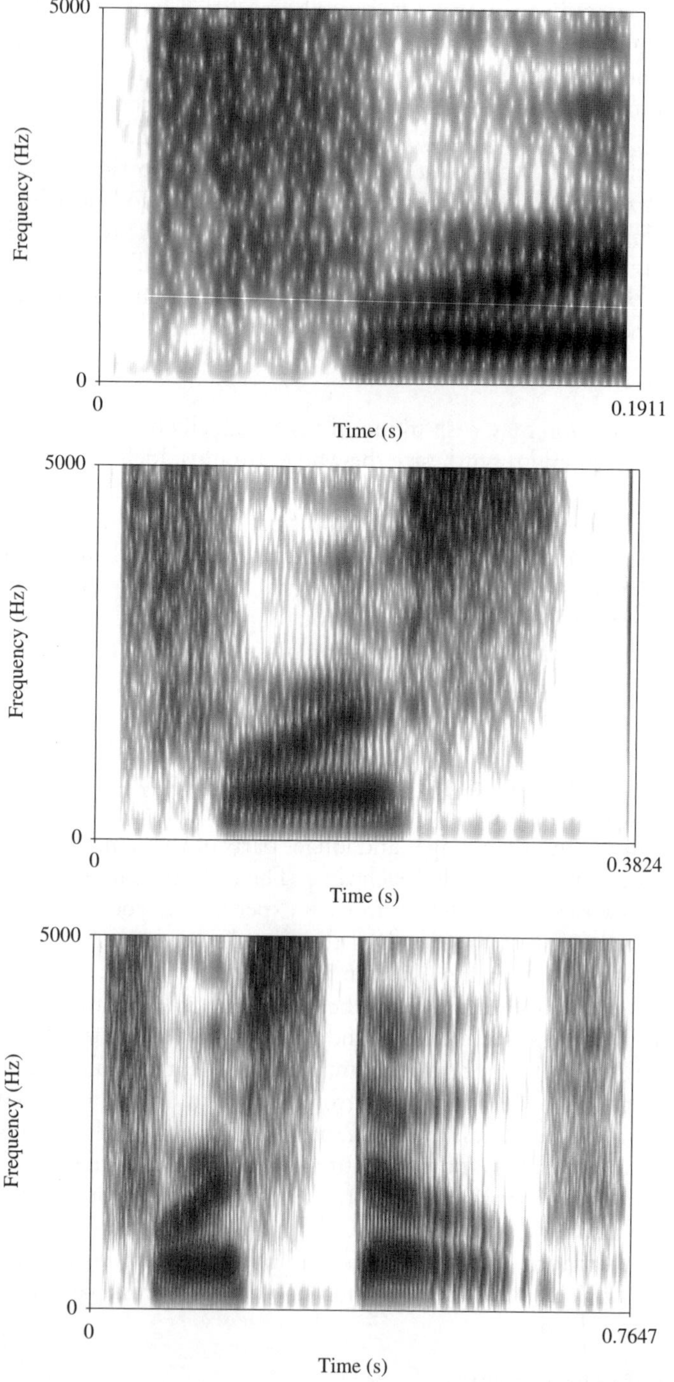

Figure 3.5 Spectrograms of a signal subjected to three levels of gating. The utterance is 'for a stove'.

it ought to be useful for sociophonetic studies as well. After all, conversations don't normally occur in the perfectly quiet environments that we often simulate in speech perception experiments. Instead, we carry on conversations in places with all kinds of noises that can distract us and mask our speech, with echoes and with other people talking in the background.

Nevertheless, it's important to be able to regulate the noise in an experiment. Hence, several ways of adding noise to signals have been developed. One commonly used method is to add *white noise* or *pink noise* to the stimuli. White noise is aperiodic noise at all frequencies, while pink noise is aperiodic noise only at lower frequencies – e.g. those important for speech sounds. Figure 3.6 shows spectrograms of a signal with and without the addition of white noise at 80 dB. Another kind of noise is *speech-shaped noise*. Speech-shaped noise is noise with amplitudes at different frequencies to match those of natural speech, derived from long-term average spectra (see pp. 107–9) of speech. A third method is to add *babble*. Babble is jumbled human voices. It's used to simulate conditions in a crowded room where everyone is talking and the background conversations make it harder to understand one's interlocutor. Speech-shaped noise and babble have the advantage of simulating a more natural situation than white (or pink) noise does. Both can be downloaded from various online sources. Yet another method is to add *echo* to the stimuli, which involves repeating each stimulus in a way that mimics the echo in a room.

There are various ways to introduce noise to a signal. One is to add the noise constantly, as in Figure 3.6. Another is to interrupt the speech signal periodically – say, zeroing out every other half-second of the signal or certain segments: – and replace the zeroed portions with noise. When noise is introduced, it doesn't have to be added at a constant rate. It can also be *modulated*: fixed so that its amplitude varies cyclically.

Filtering

A method that can be effective for eliminating certain elements of speech is *filtering*. As we saw in Chapter 2, any signal undergoing digitization has to be *lowpass filtered* to eliminate aliasing. That is, frequencies above the specified point are deleted and those below that point are kept ('passed'). Whereas the lowpass filtering that occurs during digitization is at quite a high frequency – e.g. at 20 kHz if a sampling rate of 44 kHz is used – much lower lowpass filtering is used for perception experiments. Lowpass filtering can be set so that it preserves the fundamental frequency but eliminates vowel formants, say, at 300 to 400 Hz. This procedure is useful if you want to focus subjects' attention on F_0. A narrowband spectrogram of a signal that's been lowpass filtered at 350 Hz is shown in Figure 3.7. You can also lowpass filter the signal so that it preserves F_1 but eliminates (for the most part) higher formants by setting the filtering somewhere in the range of 700 to 900 Hz. One difficulty with lowpass filtering is that, depending on how low it is set, it may be difficult or impossible for subjects to understand what they're hearing, which can affect their responses adversely. For that reason, you may wish to consider providing subjects with the text of the stimuli they will listen to.

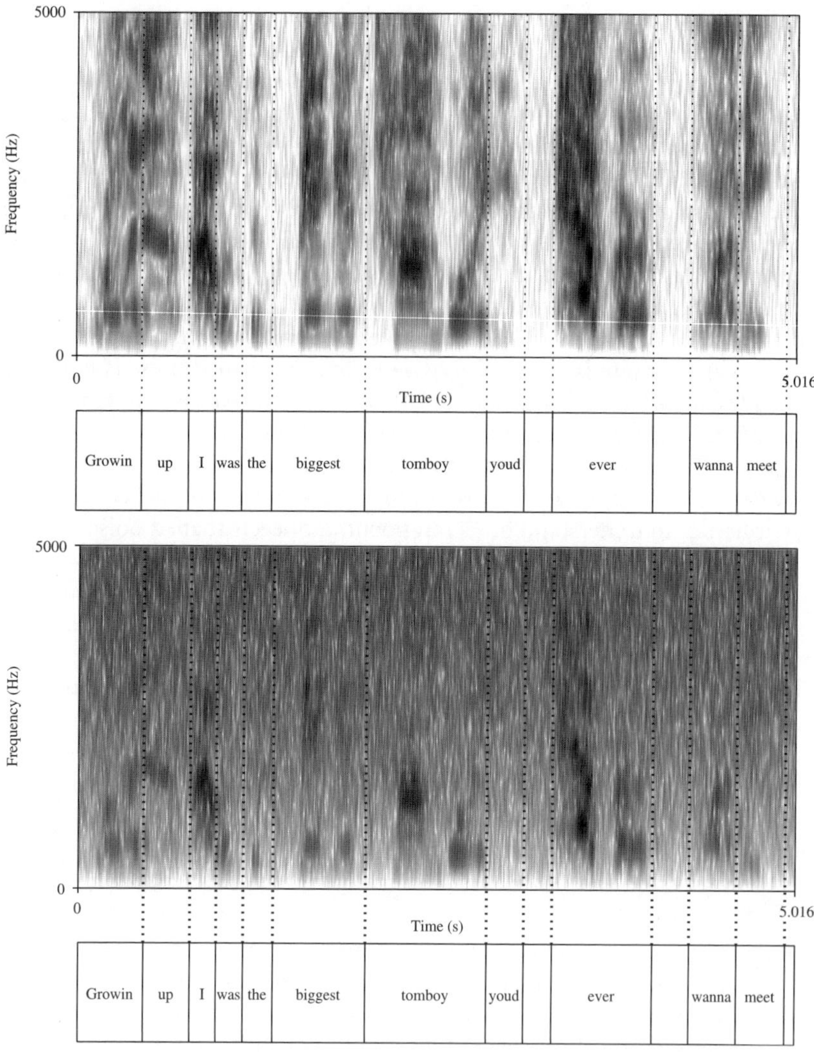

Figure 3.6 Spectrograms of a signal, spoken by an African American female from North Carolina, without (top spectrogram) and with (lower spectrogram) addition of white noise. The utterance is 'Growin' up, I was the biggest tomboy you'd ever wanna meet.'

Highpass filtering does the opposite of lowpass filtering: it retains parts of the signal above the specified frequency and deletes parts of the signal below that point. An example wideband spectrogram of a signal highpass filtered at 2,000 Hz is shown in Figure 3.8. Highpass filtering is useful if you want to focus attention on higher formants – e.g. you can focus attention on F_2 by deleting F_1 if you highpass filter at, say, 800 Hz. Nevertheless, highpass filtering can't eliminate F_0-dependent information. Listeners can still interpret F_0 and its movements because the vocal fold vibrations are still evident in a highpass filtered signal.

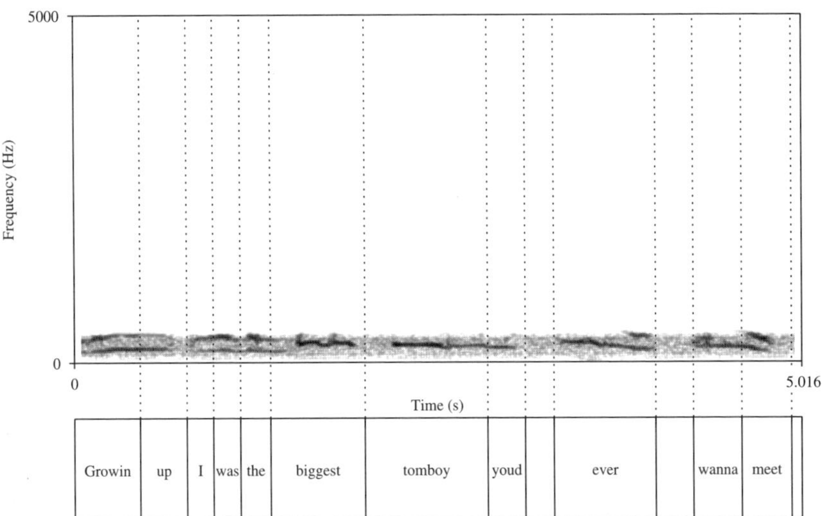

Figure 3.7 Narrowband spectrogram of the same signal as in Figure 3.6, but lowpass filtered at 350 Hz.

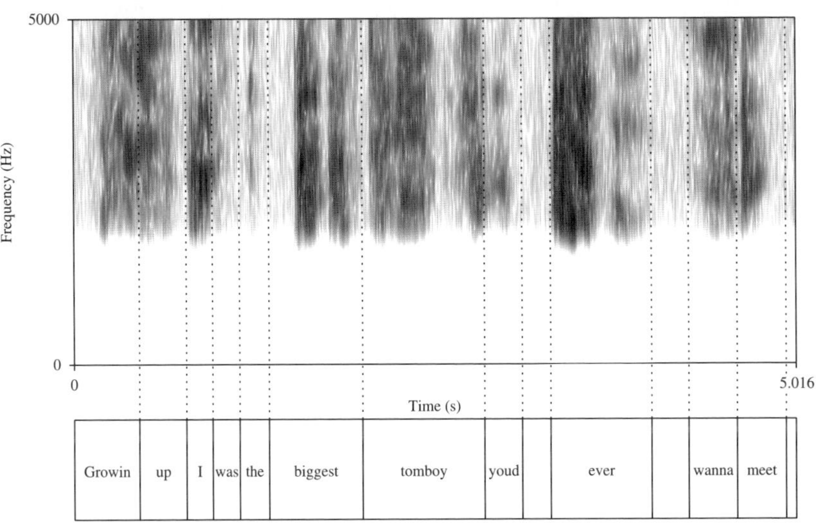

Figure 3.8 Wideband spectrogram of the same signal as in Figures 3.6–3.7, but highpass filtered at 2,000 Hz.

Two other kinds of filtering are *bandpass filtering* and *band zeroing*. Bandpass filtering involves using a lowpass and a highpass filter simultaneously so that only frequencies between two specified points are retained. Band zeroing is the opposite – frequencies between two specified points are deleted. Bandpass filtering could be used to focus attention more narrowly than highpass filtering, e.g. on a single formant, a single type of consonant transition or a narrow part of consonant releases. Band zeroing can be used to eliminate information from a single formant while retaining other formants.

A special kind of filtering is *inverse LPC filtering*. This is used for experiments targeting prosody and voice quality, e.g. Komatsu et al. (2002). This involves LPC, which we covered in Chapter 2. LPC is commonly used in speech synthesizers that model the signal after a real voice. An LPC synthesizer is supposed to separate a voice signal into source and filter components. LPC finds the peaks in the spectrum and models them and then the synthesizer subtracts them from the signal. The remaining part, called the *residual signal*, ideally represents what the voice would sound like without the filtering of the oral track. The process is schematized in Figure 3.9. The residual signal is the part used for experiments on prosody and voice quality. The filtering works when the sound quality of the original signal is impeccable, but with lower-quality recordings it tends to leave some filter components in the residual signal.

An example of a dialectal comparison that employed filtering was Bush (1967), which used both lowpass and highpass filtering to assess whether listeners needed prosodic information to distinguish British, American and Indian English.

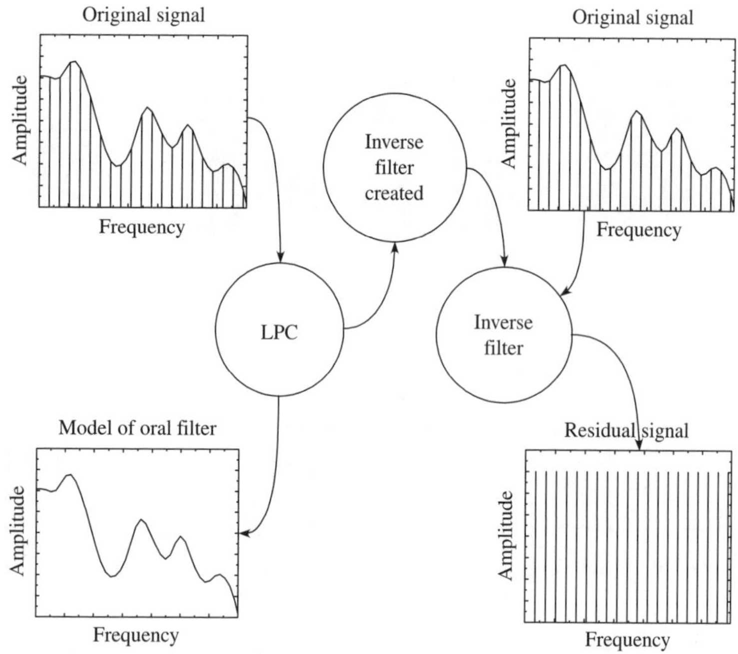

Figure 3.9 Steps involved in inverse LPC filtering. Vertical lines in the original and residual signals represent the harmonics. In this example, the residual signal has a flat spectrum, but the more realistic pattern in which the amplitude decreases as the frequency of the harmonics increases can be attained by applying pre-emphasis to the original signal before subjecting it to LPC.

Modifications of F_0

Several techniques involve modification of F_0. These methods are used to eliminate cues based on F_0 or to alter them in order to mislead listeners. F_0 is the most important cue for tone and intonation and is important for certain consonantal contrasts (particularly voicing contrasts) and for word stress as well. In many languages, such as most of the Romance languages, F_0 is the primary cue for word stress. Altering F_0, then, can be used in experiments investigating F_0-dependent aspects of speech.

Modifications of F_0 have been used to test whether F_0-related factors, especially intonation, serve as identifying features for certain groups. That is, in the experiment, subjects are presented with F_0-altered stimuli and control stimuli and are tested to see whether the lack of F_0 information impairs their ability to distinguish the groups. Similar techniques could be used to investigate such factors as tonal contrasts or the meanings encoded by intonation.

One experimental technique is to present subjects with signals that increase and decrease in frequency to mimic F_0 patterns, including timing and amplitude. One way is to use simple *sine wave stimuli*. Another is to create a *voice train*, which synthetically mimics vocal pulses and sounds buzz-like. Subjects may be asked to identify demographic or personality features of a speaker with that F_0 pattern or to discern meanings from the contours. Because the words are usually indecipherable, you may need to provide subjects with a script. These methods haven't proved as useful for sociophonetic work on F_0 as the next two techniques.

A particularly effective technique is *monotonization*. Monotonization means setting F_0 to a constant value. You might use monotonal stimuli when you want to eliminate information that's encoded in F_0. That is, monotonization will eliminate most information about intonation and tone and some information about word stress. Because intonation and especially stress also involve amplitude and timing factors, monotonization will not completely obliterate them. However, it'll certainly hamper listeners' ability to access intonation. For more complete removal of intonation and stress cues, monotonization can be used together with modification of amplitude and timing. Monotonization is a relatively simple operation for most speech synthesizers. In experiments, it yields consistent results that are usually easy to interpret.

Other alterations of F_0 can be effective as well. One such procedure is *control of F_0 contours*. Most often, controlling for F_0 contours amounts to substituting the F_0 contours of one speaker for those of another. One way to go about such substitution is to use the contours of a single speaker for all of the stimuli, even if the stimuli were taken from the speech of many people. Another way is to swap the F_0 contours of different speakers, so that speaker A has speaker B's F_0 pattern and speaker B has speaker A's F_0 pattern. I've found F_0 swapping to be effective in experiments on what auditory cues listeners use to distinguish African Americans from European Americans. It's useful when you want to produce stimuli with contradictory cues, since F_0 (and any other cues you've swapped) will come from one speaker and the remaining cues from another speaker.

Yet another technique that's been used in experiments is numerical manipulation of F_0. Along with monotonization, it's one of the easiest transformations to perform with a synthesizer. Adding and subtracting to F_0 is a quite straightforward procedure. Synthesis packages usually allow you to add or subtract in Hz. You are required to make some calculations if you want to change the F_0 by ERB or semitones. Multiplication by a factor greater than 1 will raise F_0, and multiplication by any number between 0 and 1 will lower F_0. Figure 3.10 shows a signal with a superimposed pitch track, first unmodified and then with the pitch multiplied by 0.5.

One use of this method is to disguise the sex of speakers. It doesn't yield a perfect 'sex change' because other cues, particularly formant values, also

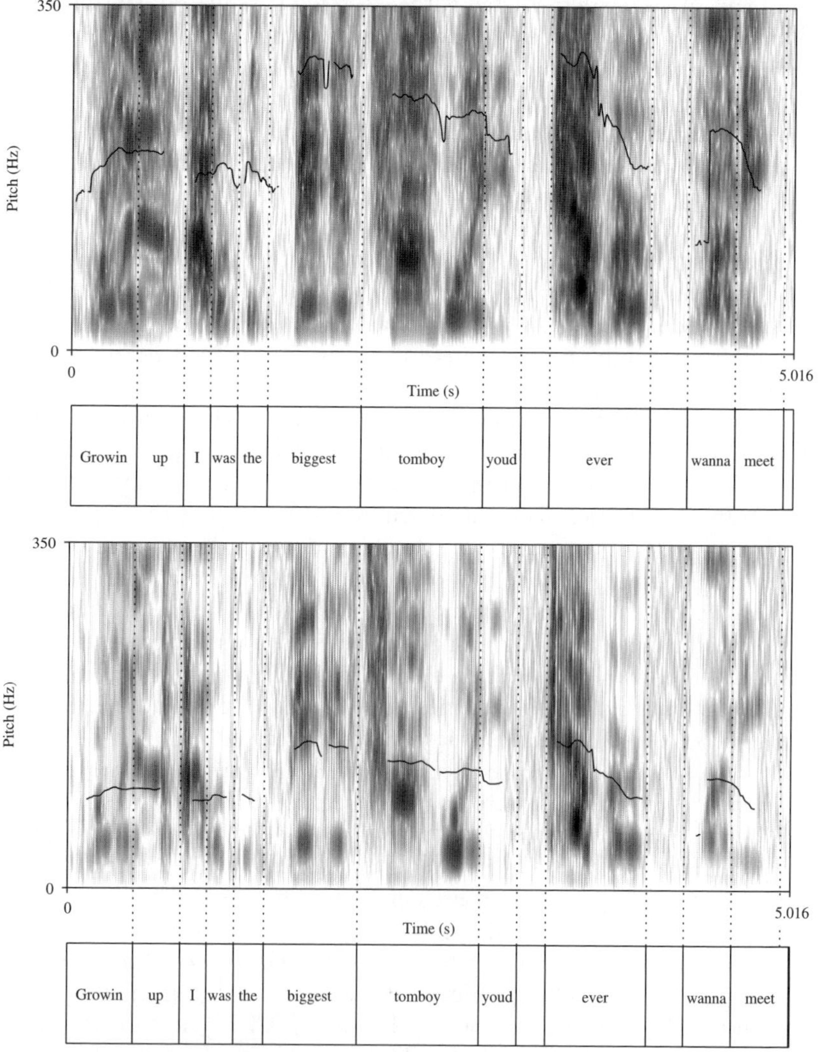

Figure 3.10 Wideband spectrograms with pitch tracks of the same signal as in Figures 3.6–3.8, first unmodified and then with F_0 halved. The scale on the y-axis pertains to the pitch tracks, not the spectrograms.

index male versus female voices. However, the results can be improved when F_0 multiplication is performed in conjunction with modification of formant values. Testing impressions of gender identity is another possible use of F_0 levels. However, relatively high or low F_0 may be associated with factors other than gender as well. Walton and Orlikoff (1994) found lower F_0 levels to be associated with African American males and relatively higher F_0 levels with European American males. Experiments could certainly test for such associations.

Modification of formant values

Because formant values are important for distinguishing both vowels and consonants, modification of formants can be highly useful for perception experiments. Unfortunately, formant modification is one of the more difficult synthetic operations; sometimes the results are satisfactory and sometimes they aren't. Some voices don't lend themselves well to formant modification, so if you use this treatment you may need to have some backup voices handy in case you encounter problems.

Arrays of stimuli – i.e. stimuli modified so that they form series – are generally used in two ways. The more common application is to create a one-dimensional continuum of stimuli. Formant values of each stimulus are set at intervals along a continuum. The continuum might be in Hz or in Bark or another perceptual scale. Subjects are then asked to identify the phoneme to which each stimulus belongs. For sociolinguistic uses, a researcher uses two or more groups of subjects and compares their responses. The two groups may place the boundaries between phonemes at different points along the continuum. This was the method used by Willis (1972) and Janson (1983), who, as noted earlier, looked at geographical and generational differences, respectively, in phoneme boundaries.

Less commonly, two- or multi-dimensional arrays of stimuli can be created. Using more than one dimension is useful for gauging phoneme boundaries. Another use is in experiments rating the goodness of stimuli, as in the Peeters (1991) cross-linguistic study of diphthong realizations mentioned earlier.

Alterations of formants in stimuli that are not in arrays – usually stimuli longer than one word – are used for different kinds of experiments. Such experiments might involve identification of demographic features of the speakers or testing whether the semantic content of the stimuli is still decipherable. These alterations are ordinarily applied in two ways. One sort is to set all formants at the same value. For vowels, a 'neutral value', i.e. schwa, is customary. There's no reason that some other value couldn't be used, however, except perhaps that it may require greater adjustments of consonant transitions to make the stimuli sound right. Setting all vowels to a single quality serves to eliminate vowel quality as a cue in stimuli, thereby forcing subjects to focus on other cues to decipher the signal. For consonants, the formant transitions could be set so that they all have the same sort of locus. For example, the transitions could be adjusted so that all the consonants sound coronal. In that case, consonantal place of articulation would be removed as a cue.

The other common use of formant modification is to examine the effects of the realization of a single vowel or consonant. Here, a particular vowel or a particular consonant transition is adjusted instead of all of them. This method can be used to determine whether a certain dialectal variant is salient or to determine how much a sound can vary before it sounds unnatural. Graff et al. (1986) modified the F_2 of individual vowels in test sentences and found that the modifications affected listeners' identifications of the speakers' ethnicity; in Philadelphia, where they conducted the experiment, different realizations of those vowels characterize African Americans and European Americans.

Bandwidth modification

Large formant bandwidths are associated with muffled voices, voices at some distance away, and nasality, while narrow bandwidths are associated with the opposite qualities. Nasal voice quality can be simulated using a combination of more formants than occur with oral vowels and large bandwidths on those formants. The formant values, of course, have to be calibrated to correspond to the values of natural nasal vowel formants.

Temporal modification

Compression and *prolongation* of entire stimuli are easy to do with most synthesis packages. The main use of speeding up or slowing down sentence-length stimuli has been to study stereotypes of speakers – e.g. whether listeners associate slow speech with low intelligence or rapid speech with low trustworthiness.

Prolongation of particular parts of a signal, such as a particular sound, can have other uses. Most importantly, it can be used to test whether segmental length serves as a cue to the identification of segments, and, if so, where the boundaries are between different phonemes. Compression and/or *truncation* of parts of the signal can be used in conjunction with prolongation. Length is crucial for some distinctions, such as phonological voicing of consonants – which in most languages with the distinction involves the lengths of both the particular consonant token and the preceding vowel – and phonological length, both of long versus short vowels and of geminate versus non-geminate consonants. Experiments examining cross-dialectal treatment of length can expose differences in whether length is used as a cue for a distinction, how phonemic boundaries are realized if length is a cue and even if there is a phonological contrast at all.

Other temporal modifications involve making syllable-by-syllable changes to durations in order to apply the tempo from one dialect or accent onto another. This operation is difficult to perform unless you have speakers of both varieties reading the same sentences or passages. In that case, you can fit the syllable or segmental durations of one speaker onto the speech of another speaker.

Modifying spectral tilt

Spectral tilt involves how rapidly the amplitude of harmonics decreases from the lowest-frequency harmonics to higher-frequency ones. It's commonly used to gauge to the degree of breathiness in a sample of speech. Breathy voicing involves a relatively rapid decrease in amplitude. Thus, the lowest harmonics show much greater amplitudes than higher harmonics. Modal and creaky voicing show less stark differences in amplitude between the lowest and other harmonics.

Because pre-emphasis of the signal has the opposite effect from breathy voicing, this and its opposite, de-emphasis, can be used to simulate lesser and greater degrees of breathiness, respectively. Both can be performed synthetically. Unfortunately, the effect isn't perfect because high-frequency aperiodic noise also characterizes breathiness.

Resplicing

The signals used for stimuli can be cut at random points, with the order of the spliced pieces then scrambled and the pieces *respliced* in random order. The aim of this procedure is to focus subjects' attention on the voice quality in the stimuli, since they can't understand the content. Bezooijen (1988) used it as one treatment in an experiment to test what phonetic cues Dutch listeners accessed to judge the personality of speakers.

Backward playing

Playing signals backward has been used to focus subjects' attention on factors such as voice quality and F_0 variation (Lass et al. 1978). It does so because it makes segmental variants unrecognizable. This method's usefulness is limited, however. Subjects experience difficulty performing perceptual tasks if they can't understand what words they're hearing, and most people can't understand backward-played signals.

Assembling experimental recordings

The actual assembly of the experimental recording is a straightforward process. All it involves is concatenating the stimuli together in the right order, with appropriate pauses (silent periods) between stimuli. It's helpful if the stimuli start and begin at zero-crossing points so you avoid transience between the pauses and the stimuli. Another trick you can use to minimize transience is to attenuate the signal near the boundary between modified and unmodified sections.

However, there are a few other things you need to consider before you assemble the recording. How long should the pauses be? How do you make sure subjects know which stimulus they're responding to? What if you need to keep subjects from figuring out what the purpose of the experiment is? How long can the trials be? Another issue that may not come to mind immediately is that subjects often need to listen to a few stimuli before their senses become attuned to what they're supposed to listen for in the stimuli. You need to address all of these issues before you put the recording together.

Pauses between stimuli

You should have some sort of pause between each stimulus. The pause helps subjects know when the end of each stimulus is. It also gives them time to mark their responses on the answer form. Be sure that the pauses are long enough that subjects can formulate and mark their answers but not so long that subjects get impatient with the experiment.

Another thing you should consider is providing a reference point after a certain number of stimuli. That is, it's helpful if a voice on the experimental recording announces 'Set One', 'Set Two' and so forth (or 'Group One', 'Part One', etc.) at intervals. A beep or other such noise can also suffice. With long stimuli, you may need an announcement before each stimulus. If the reference points aren't there, subjects can get lost while they're filling out the answer form. The last thing you want is a subject marking their response to, say, stimulus no. 34 in the space for stimulus no. 33.

Distractor stimuli

In some experiments, it can skew the results if subjects figure out what the experiment is testing. If that's the case, you should intersperse stimuli that test the variable with *distractor stimuli*. A distractor stimulus is one that doesn't have the variable you're testing in it. It is there to throw subjects off, so that they can't discern the purpose of the experiment, or even to mislead them into thinking that the purpose is something different from what it is. Often you'll need more distractor stimuli than test stimuli. Distractor stimuli aren't needed if the purpose of the experiment is so opaque that subjects won't figure it out anyway or if it doesn't matter whether subjects know what the experiment is testing.

Acclimatization to the experimental task

Subjects often take some time to get a sense of what they're listening for in stimuli. Hence their responses for stimuli at the beginning of the experiment may differ from those in the rest of the experiment and, if there are correct and incorrect answers, may be less accurate than later stimuli. These stimuli should be excluded from the analysis. When you write about the experiment, you should note how many stimuli from the beginning of the experimental recording you excluded.

Length of experimental trials

Subjects can't concentrate on a task indefinitely. The length of trials should depend on the difficulty of the task. If subjects have only to identify stimuli as one of two or three choices, the trials can last as long as 10 to 15 minutes. On the other hand, if subjects have to rate speakers on several personality scales or have to rate their certainty about responses, the trials should be significantly shorter. A new trial may begin after subjects have a chance to rest – a minute or two for simple tasks, longer (even several days) for complex ones.

Presentation to subjects

Once you've assembled the experimental recording, you need to find subjects to administer the experiment to and you need to decide how to administer it to them. There are several issues here to consider and a variety of options to choose from.

Choosing and screening subjects

Naturally, you need to find subjects with the right demographic characteristics for your experiment. For many experiments, the demographics aren't critical, and in those cases it's usually easiest to employ students in university classes. Students may find the experience more worthwhile if the experiment can be tied in with lessons in the course. However, for some experiments you need subjects from a particular region, community, ethnic group, age group and so forth. Such a restriction is necessary if you're comparing perception by different groups.

If you have the proper equipment, you may wish to test subjects' hearing to make sure that it's normal. Most sociolinguists don't have the equipment to screen subjects' hearing, though. A practical substitute is to ask subjects on the questionnaire whether they've ever been diagnosed with any kind of hearing impairment and, if so, to describe it. Generally, you'll need to exclude data from subjects with hearing problems unless, of course, your experiment targets people with impaired hearing.

Familiarization

Sometimes, a task is unusually complicated and requires that the subjects undergo special training. For example, a task might require subjects to recognize certain intonational contours or to be able to name all the vowels of a language such as English with many vowels, or it might be something that involves several steps. If so, you'll need to provide practice exercises for your subjects so that they become proficient with the task or with the skills they'll need to perform the task. The amount of time required for familiarization varies with the task. Depending on how complicated the training is, familiarization exercises may be completed immediately before the experiment or days ahead of time.

Presentation format

Most of the time, presentation involves playing the experimental recording to subjects, who then mark responses to the different stimuli. Sometimes, however, special formats are required. In an experiment involving functional testing, it may be necessary to act out a scene for subjects. Another kind of format is one that combines audio stimuli with visual stimuli, such as when testing the McGurk Effect.

Experimental setting

The prototypical setting for a speech perception experiment is a laboratory where subjects can listen to the stimuli through earphones. This design works well if your subjects are university students. If subjects take the experiment one at a time, all you have to do is to bring them into the lab and start the experiment. If many students take part in the experiment at the same time, a laboratory with numerous listening stations equipped with earphones may work well. Universities normally have such rooms for foreign language classes and you can usually get permission to use them for an experiment.

For sociophonetic projects, you may need subjects who fit a certain demographic description. Finding such subjects often means running the experiment in the field. If you aren't conducting your experiment at a university, you'll probably have only two choices as to how to conduct it: either run the experiment on subjects one at a time using earphones or forgo the use of earphones. Lack of earphones, of course, introduces some potentially undesirable factors, such as background noise, echoes and the fact that subjects will be different distances and directions from the loudspeaker. To counteract these problems, find the quietest setting you can for the experiment and try to position the loudspeaker so that there's as little variation as possible in the distance of subjects from it. As for the direction, although low-frequency sounds travel about as well in all directions, high-frequency sounds travel better forward than sideways. Fortunately, this issue is unlikely to pose a problem unless sibilants are the focus of your experiment. Be sure to set the volume of the loudspeaker so that everyone can hear it comfortably. Take note of the general listening conditions in the setting, including any audible echo.

Use of earphones and volume control

If you use earphones, it's crucial to make sure that the volume is set so that all subjects can hear the stimuli comfortably. In fact, when possible you should allow subjects to adjust the volume themselves. Earphones, like other equipment, are affected by age, wear and cleanliness, and each one may be different. If all subjects use the same pair of earphones, you may not have any further concerns unless some mechanical malfunction occurs. However, in a room with listening stations, not all of the stations may operate equally well and too often some are completely inoperative, so be sure that all of your subjects can hear a signal adequately before the experiment begins.

Response forms

In a few experiments, the researcher records responses from subjects. In most, though, the subjects record their responses on some sort of response form. The traditional, low-tech way is to provide paper response sheets. These are easy to make and don't require access to electronic scoring programs, which not everyone has. However, the responses have to be tallied by hand, which is time-consuming. Another option is to have subjects fill in answers on a form that is then scanned and scored electronically. This method requires access to equipment that can score the sheets, which many universities provide. The new, and perhaps most convenient, way is to have subjects take the test on a computer.

The response forms should have spaces for subjects to fill in or circle in all of their responses. In addition, you should remember to provide subjects with spaces for the demographic information about them that you'll need – e.g. their age or year of birth, sex, places they've lived and ethnicity. You may want to ask them about their experience with other languages, and you should certainly have a space for them to report whether they have any hearing impairment. Individual experiments can require numerous other sorts of questions. Be sure to consider carefully what information you'll need because you can't ask for it after the experiment is over.

Timing responses

Timing of responses in perception experiments is common in phonetics, but has been almost absent from socio-perceptual research. That's not to say that it couldn't be useful, though. Timing is often an effective way of measuring how sure subjects are of their responses. When answers come automatically to subjects, their response times are normally short, whereas if they have to stop and think about the answer, their response times will be longer. Timing responses could be used in a wide variety of socio-perceptual experiments. For example, in identification experiments, voices that are most typical of their regional dialect, ethnic group and so on should be easy for subjects to label and thus would induce short response times. In an experiment testing a phonological merger, longer response times could be interpreted as uncertainty about whether the sounds are merged or distinct. An example of the use of response timing is in Guenter (2000). Guenter asked subjects to assign the vowels in individual words to lists of other words that each had a particular vowel. He timed their responses to see whether they had difficulty with any of the words, which happened for vowels before /r/, /l/ and /ŋ/. He interpreted this result as evidence that vowels before /r/, /l/ and /ŋ/ are undergoing phonological splits from vowels in other contexts.

Response timing can be used to test mergers as well. For such an experiment, pairs of words are played to subjects and the subjects mark whether the second word is a real word. When the second word, called the *probe*, is real, the first word, called the *prime*, may or may not be semantically related to it. Response times should be faster when the prime and probe are semantically related than when they aren't. When a merger has happened, a wider range of stimuli will sound semantically related than when the merger hasn't happened. Rae and Warren (2002) used this method to test whether New Zealand subjects merged the NEAR and SQUARE vowels. The two merge to a vowel that sounds like the pre-merger NEAR class. Hence, listeners with the merger had faster response times for pairs such as *sit/cheer* than listeners without the merger because the stimulus sounded like *sit/chair* to them.

It's necessary to score experiments involving response times on a computer. One consideration is when to start the clock. This isn't a problem with visual stimuli, such as written words that are presented – the timing starts as soon as the visual prompt appears. However, if auditory stimuli are presented, you have to decide whether to start the clock at the beginning of each auditory stimulus or at the end. If the stimuli vary in length, it may be better to start the clock when the stimulus stops, but if subjects are allowed to respond before the stimulus stops, you'll need to start the clock at the beginning of the stimulus.

3.4 Brain imaging techniques and perception

We discussed the basic types of brain scanning equipment that are available currently in Chapter 2. The same kinds of scans useful for studying speech production can be applied to examining speech perception. One potential application is in dialect intelligibility experiments. Certain ERP patterns, for example, have been linked with semantic incongruities, and it seems likely that a similar effect would occur when a listener encounters a dialectal pronunciation that's unintelligible or difficult to understand. Other uses are in discrimination tasks – in which distinct brain activity patterns can appear depending on whether stimuli are alike or different – and in measurements of category goodness – in which stronger activity patterns may appear for stimuli that are poorer matches for a category.

Additional applications involve the localization of neural activity. Neuroimaging of the effects of dialectally unfamiliar and atypical phonetic forms could shed light on how the brain processes acoustic properties of speech sounds. Kutas et al. (2007) discuss some evidence that speech perception may be less localized on the left hemisphere of the brain than speech production and that perception of prosody, in particular, may be processed on the right hemisphere. Brain scans of subjects hearing dialectal variations in intonation could provide new insights into where and how the brain processes prosody.

Neuroimaging has not yet arrived as a sociophonetic method. However, it appears to hold a lot of potential. The continual improvements to imaging technology, the variety of applications to language variation and the potential contributions of language variation to neurolinguistics could make it an important strain of socio-perceptual research in the future.

EXERCISES

1. Using the formulas provided, convert each of the following Hz values to mel, Bark and ERB: 100 Hz, 150 Hz, 200 Hz, 500 Hz, 1,000 Hz, 2,000 Hz and 3,500 Hz.
2. What are the various ways that researchers can study phonological mergers perceptually?
3. Imagine that a particular ethnic group showed distinctive patterns in intonation, tempo, realizations of certain vowels and lack of aspiration on voiceless stops. How would you design a perception experiment to test which of these variables were salient to listeners? If more than one were salient, how would you test which was most salient?
4. Design an experiment to test whether speakers of two dialects differ in what pronunciations of particular vowels they consider to be most like their own. How would you test whether their ratings matched up with their actual pronunciations?
5. How would you test whether listeners from a dialect with substrate influence and a dialect without substrate influence use vowel length and consonant length the same way?
6. Design an experiment testing the intelligibility of different dialects in quiet versus noisy environments. How would you incorporate response timing into the experiment?

EXERCISES

7. Using appropriate equipment, subject a short (< 5 seconds) signal to the following treatments: lowpass filtering at 350 ms; gating; monotonization; multiplying F_0 by 1.5; and prolongation. You can download some practice signals from http://ncslaap.lib.ncsu.edu/sociophonetics/.
8. Create a practice experimental recording. Include prompts and silent periods of appropriate length.

FURTHER READING

Denes, Peter B. and Elliot N. Pinson. 1963. *The Speech Chain: The Physics and Biology of Spoken Language.* Baltimore: Waverly Press. See especially Chapter 6, 'Nerves, brain, and the speech chain'.

Janson, Tore. 1986. Sound change in perception: an experiment. In John J. Ohala and Jeri J. Jaeger (eds), *Experimental Phonology.* Orlando: Academic Press, 253–60.

Labov, William and Sharon Ash. 1997. Understanding Birmingham. In Cynthia Bernstein, Thomas Nunnally and Robin Sabino (eds), *Language Variety in the South Revisited.* Tuscaloosa/London: University of Alabama Press, 508–73.

Labov, William, Mark Karen and Corey Miller. 1991. Near-mergers and the suspension of phonemic contrast. *Language Variation and Change* 3:33–74.

Lambert, W.E., R.C. Hodgsen, R.D. Gardner and S. Fillenbaum. 1960. Evaluational reaction to spoken language. *Journal of Abnormal and Social Psychology* 60:44–51.

McGurk, Harry and John McDonald. 1976. Hearing lips and seeing voices. *Nature* 264:746–8.

Thomas, Erik R. 2002. Sociophonetic applications of speech perception experiments. *American Speech* 77:115–47.

Traunmüller, Hartmut. 1997. Auditory scales of frequency representation. http://www2.ling.su.se/staff/hartmut/bark.htm. Contains concise descriptions of various auditory scales and provides mathematical formulas to convert to them from Hz.

Consonants

4

4.1 Lots of attention, but...

Consonantal variation has received extensive attention from sociolinguists working on English, Spanish, Arabic and other languages. Consonantal studies have formed the foundation for much of sociolinguistics. For example, Cedergren's (1973) study of spirantization (mutation to a fricative) of /r/ and lenition (weakening) of /tʃ/ to [ʃ] in Panama City Spanish was instrumental in the development of variable rules (Cedergren and Sankoff 1974) and of the use of generational differences to examine diachronic change. Several consonantal variables were crucial in developing the study of African American Vernacular English (e.g. Labov et al. 1968; Wolfram 1969). Studies of /t/ glottalization and other consonantal variables have helped to establish sociolinguistics in Great Britain (e.g. Trudgill 1974b; Macauley 1977).

Nearly all of this work, however, has involved impressionistic transcription. Sociolinguists have mostly been content with auditory coding of consonants. It's assumed that auditory coding is accurate enough and faster than acoustic or articulatory methods. However, a few voices of protest have emerged, notably Docherty and Foulkes (1999) and Purnell et al. (2005a). They note that some aspects of consonantal variation are subtle and difficult to transcribe by ear, yet still socially important. Hence there's a need for more instrumental work on consonantal variation. This chapter will show you how to analyse consonantal variation acoustically.

4.2 Manner of articulation

Consonantal acoustics often aren't very straightforward. However, one of the easier aspects of consonants to get a grip on is the manner of articulation. This is commonly divided into the categories of *stops*, *fricatives* and *approximants*. Stops are further divided into *oral stops* (or plosives), which are usually just called stops, and *nasal stops*, commonly referred to as just '*nasals*'. A stop and a fricative pronounced in quick succession, such as [tʃ], make an *affricate*.

Approximants are divided in various ways, such as *semivowels* ([w], [j], etc.) versus *liquids* ([l], [r], etc.) or *lateral approximants* such as [l] versus *central approximants*.

Acoustically, (oral) stops are the easiest group to recognize because they have a silent period, the stop closure or 'stop gap', during which airflow through the mouth is shut off. For a voiceless stop, the closure looks like a blank period on a spectrogram. For a voiced stop (if it truly has vocal pulsing in it – the pulsing may be absent in some languages, such as English), you'll see a band of murmur at the bottom of the spectrogram. Stops also show a transient, the *stop burst*, marking the point where the speaker let go of the stop closure and the air that was building up behind it – e.g. behind the tongue tip for [t] or [d], or behind the lips for [p] or [b] – was released. A burst sounds like a soft pop if you isolate it, and it looks like a vertical line on a spectrogram. Figure 4.1 shows a wideband spectrogram of the sequences [əpə] and [əbə]. You can see the blank space for the silent stop closure clearly in the [əpə] utterance and the murmur in the [əbə] utterance. In both utterances, a burst is visible.

Nasals are a little different. What makes a nasal stop different from an oral stop is that the passageway to the nose – the nasopharyngeal port – is open, so (a) the nasal cavity contributes resonances and (b) airflow through the nose occurs. On a spectrogram of a nasal, you'll usually see a murmur at the bottom and an assortment of formants at different frequencies. The formants are made by both the oral cavity and the nasal cavity, and the oral cavity produces some antiformants as well. The exact pattern of formants depends on the place of articulation of the nasal (e.g. [m] versus [n]) as well as on the condition of

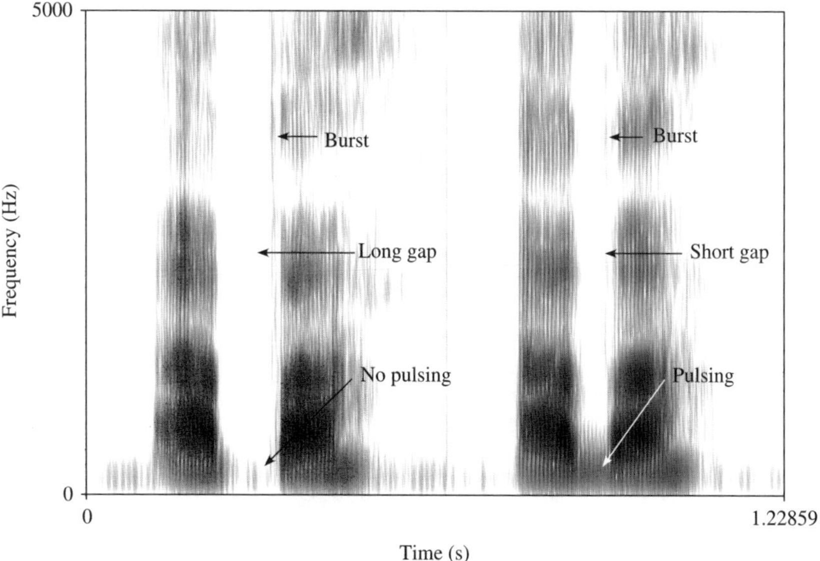

Figure 4.1 Wideband spectrogram of [əpə] and [əbə]. Note the appearance of the stop closures, or stop gaps – a blank space for [p], and a somewhat shorter, mostly blank space with a low-frequency murmur for [b]. Note the bursts as well.

sinuses in the nasal cavity. That's why nasals can sound like oral stops when your nose is stuffed up – the sinuses are swollen and the resonating spaces are reduced. Airflow through the nose has an effect on the acoustics, too. The stop bursts are often hard to see or absent altogether. The reason for that is that, with air flowing out of the nose, air pressure can't build up as easily behind the constriction. Figure 4.2 shows a spectrogram of the utterance [əmə]. Note the generally murky appearance of the stop closure due to the formants and the absence of an obvious burst.

Fricatives also lack bursts, for the same reason – airflow isn't completely cut off. However, fricatives have another component, aperiodic sound called *frication noise.* This ordinarily has two sources. One source is the turbulence created when air rushes through the narrow constriction, such as the tiny space between your front teeth and your lower lip when you say [f]. The other source is the noise produced when that air hits an obstacle downstream. For [f], the obstacle is the upper lip and for [s] or [ʃ] it's the front teeth. Not all fricatives have a clearly defined downstream obstacle – for the bilabial fricatives [ɸ] and [β], there's nothing for the airstream to hit, and for the velar fricatives [x] and [ɣ] and the palatal fricatives [ç] and [ʝ], the airstream scatters and hits the whole palate. Frication noise usually lasts a long time for sibilant fricatives such as [s], [ʃ] and [ʂ] and their voiced counterparts [z], [ʒ] and [ʐ], but it's shorter for other fricatives. It's also longer for voiceless fricatives than for voiced fricatives. Figure 4.3 shows a spectrogram of [əfə] and [əvə]. Note that the frication noise is clearer for a voiceless fricative than for a voiced fricative.

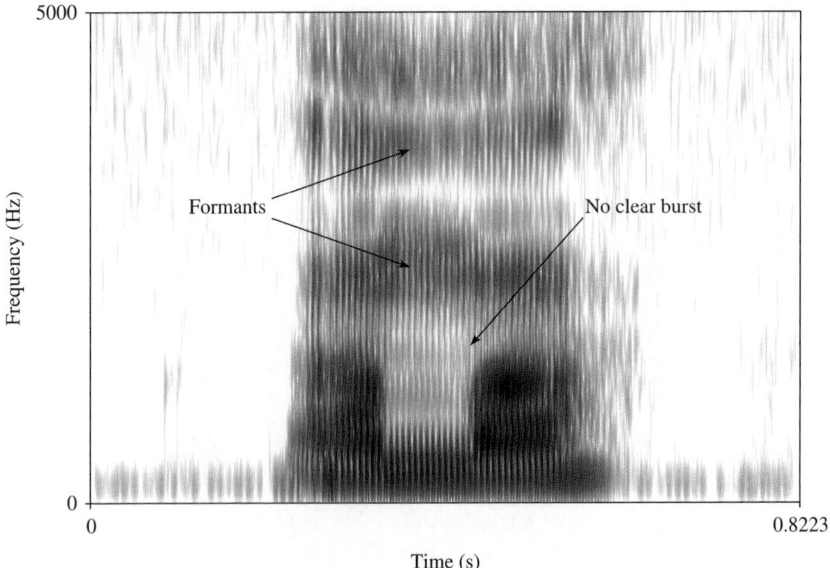

Figure 4.2 Spectrogram of [əmə]. Some formant structure is visible, but there's no clearly defined burst.

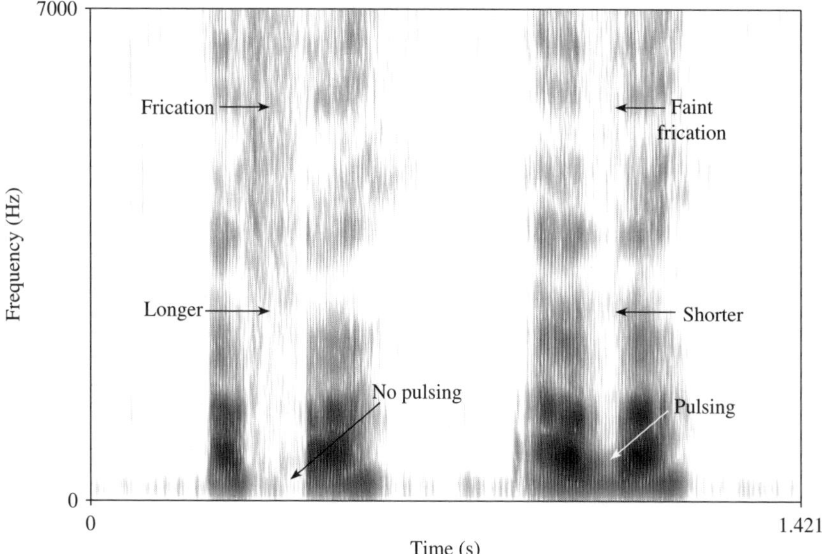

Figure 4.3 Spectrogram of [əfə] and [əvə]. Note the frication noise, which is more obvious for [f]. [f] also averages longer in duration than [v].

An affricate looks pretty much like what you'd expect, since it's a stop and fricative in quick succession. You see a stop closure followed by frication noise. Figure 4.4 shows a spectrogram of [ə.pfə] and [ə.bvə]. The frication noise differs in one respect from the frication noise of a simple fricative. It's strongest, and therefore darkest in a spectrogram, near its beginning. In an ordinary fricative, the amplitude rises more gradually.

Many of the approximants look like vowels in spectrograms. They may show clearly visible formants just like vowels. [w], [j] and [ɹ] do, for example. Taps and trills such as [ɾ], [r] and [ʀ], which are often separated as a subgroup of approximants, exhibit vibratory patterns. Some approximants can be hard to tell from voiced fricatives, and there's really no clear delineation between them – they grade into each other. Figure 4.5 shows a spectrogram of [əwə] and [ərə]. You can see that there isn't a discernible boundary between [w] and the neighbouring vowels. The tongue vibrations for the trilled [r] are obvious. Laterals, which form a subtype of approximants, and rhotics such as [r], which form a heterogeneous group, show a lot of variation and get their own sections later on.

Example variables involving manner of articulation

With the guidelines given above, you should know what to look for in any variable you encounter that involves manner of articulation. Naturally, we can't cover every possible variable in all the world's languages and dialects in detail here – you have to apply the guidelines to figure out how to analyse a new variable. Nevertheless, we'll go through a few examples of commonly studied variables. For a comprehensive discussion of articulatory and acoustic features

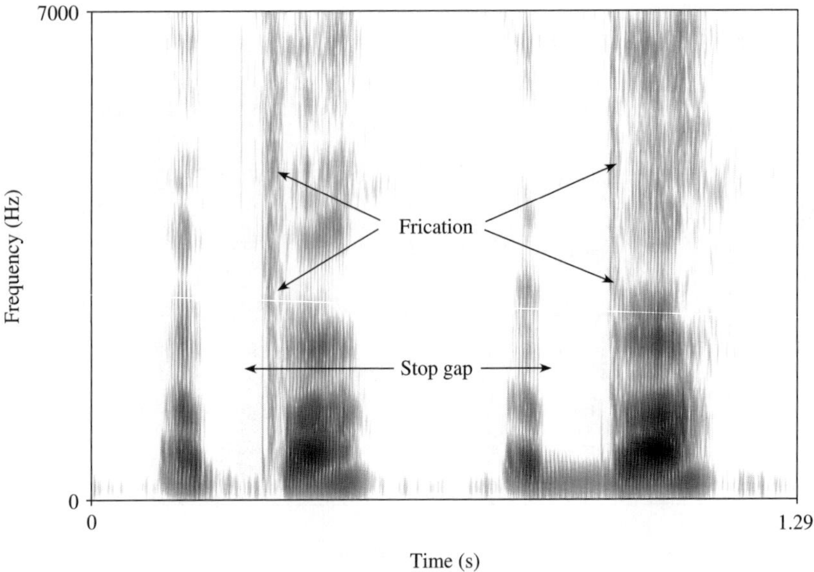

Figure 4.4 Spectrogram of [ə.pfə] and [ə.bvə]. Both a stop gap and frication noise are present for each affricate. Note how the frication shows its greatest amplitude near its beginning.

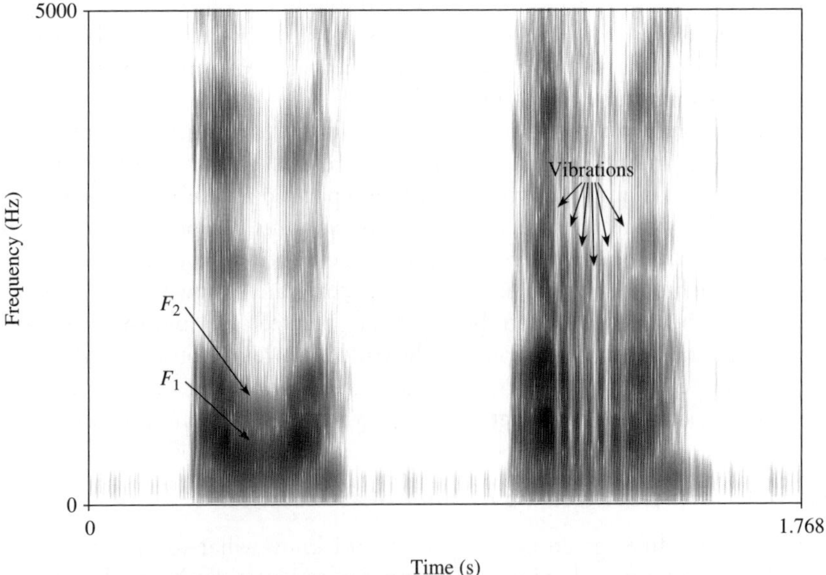

Figure 4.5 Spectrogram of [əwə] and [ərə]. F_1 and F_2 run seamlessly through the [əwə] utterance. The vibratory pattern stands out for [ərə].

of the known consonantal sounds throughout the world, see Ladefoged and Maddieson (1996).

Interdental fricatives versus stops

Interdental fricatives occur sporadically in the world's languages, and they're often unstable when they do occur, as in English. One common process they undergo is stopping. That is, [θ] may become dental [t̪] or alveolar [t] and [ð] may become [d̪] or [d]. This process is especially common when there's a linguistic substrate, such as Irish for Irish English or Spanish for Mexican American English. For initial and medial tokens, look for a burst, as in Figure 4.6, which indicates a stop. Lack of a burst signifies a fricative. For phrase-final tokens, look for frication noise.

The easiest way to quantify stopping is simply to count the number of stopped tokens out of the total. Basing discrimination on the presence or absence of the burst makes the binary division possible. You should count word-initial and medial tokens separately. Phrase-final tokens also have to be considered separately because they aren't discriminated by bursts. Tokens with a preceding coronal stop are best omitted.

Weakening of stops

In Spanish and Portuguese, the voiced stops /b/, /d/, and /g/ are weakened when they fall after a vowel. Thus Spanish *abogado* (lawyer) is pronounced [aβo'ɣaðo], not [abo'gado]. It's hard to tell whether the resulting sounds are voiced fricatives or approximants, and phoneticians disagree about that. They're definitely not stops, though. Figure 4.7 shows an utterance of *pagaban* by a Spanish speaker from southern Texas. Note that the /g/ and /b/ don't

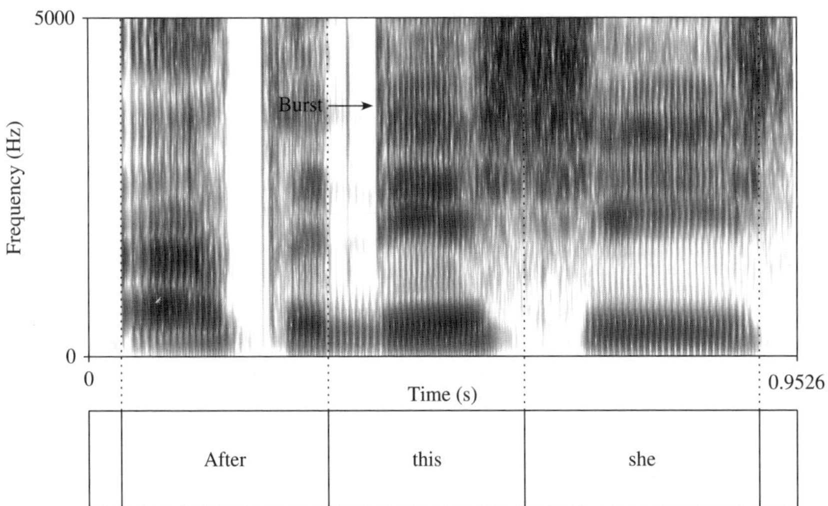

Figure 4.6 An utterance of *this* produced as [dɪs], with a stop, by an African American speaker from North Carolina in the string *After this she*. Note the burst.

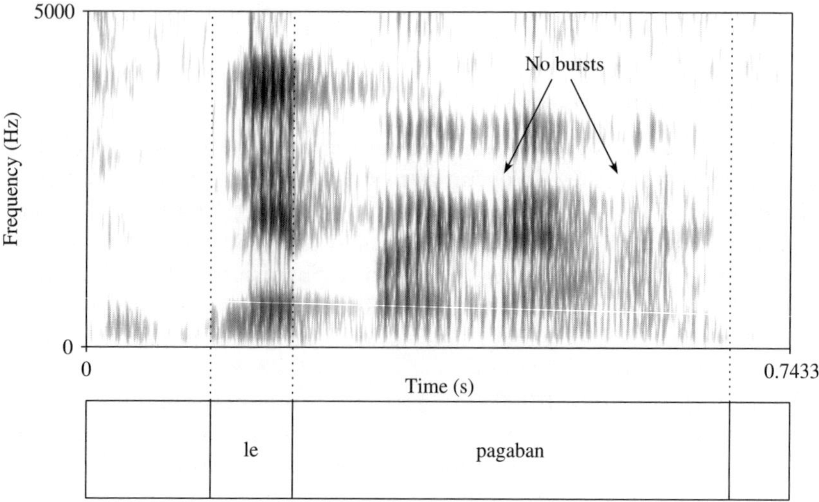

Figure 4.7 The Spanish phrase *le pagaban* 'they paid him', uttered in conversation by a Mexican American male from southern Texas. Note the absence of bursts for /g/=[ɣ] and /b/=[β].

show bursts and the formants continue through them. Spanish and Portuguese speakers with an indigenous language substrate may produce the weakening inconsistently. The weakening should be watched for among speakers of other languages with a Spanish or Portuguese substrate.

A similar weakening affects the alveolar stops /t/, /d/ and /n/ and the sequence /nt/ in North American and Australian English when they fall between two vowels or a vowel and /r/ and the preceding syllable has stronger stress than the following syllable. This is the well-known tapping or flapping process. Thus [ɾ] appears in *batty*, *party*, *redder*, and [ɾ̃] in *Tina*, *Santa*. An example of *out of* with a tap is shown in Figure 4.8. The diagnostic features are the lack of a burst, the continuation (usually) of vocal fold vibrations through the tap, and especially the short duration, usually around 25 ms. Australians are said to be less consistent about tapping than North Americans, other English speakers produce taps occasionally, and sometimes they're elided altogether.

Affrication of stops

Stops can sometimes be mutated to affricates. For example, in Quebec French /t/ and /d/ appear before high front vowels as [ts] and [dz], respectively (Dumas 1987:1–3), and several stop consonants can be affricated in Scouse, the dialect of Liverpool, England. Historically, this process is widely known for its effects on High German: Proto-Germanic *p, *t and *k became [pf], [ts] and [kx] during the transition to Old High German. Sangster (2001) investigated affrication of /t/ and /d/ in Liverpool by measuring the duration of the frication noise after the stop closure and comparing it to the duration of the stop closure. Her concern wasn't distinguishing affricated /t/ and /d/ from aspirated forms, but instead distinguishing them from /s/ and /z/. She compared the percentage

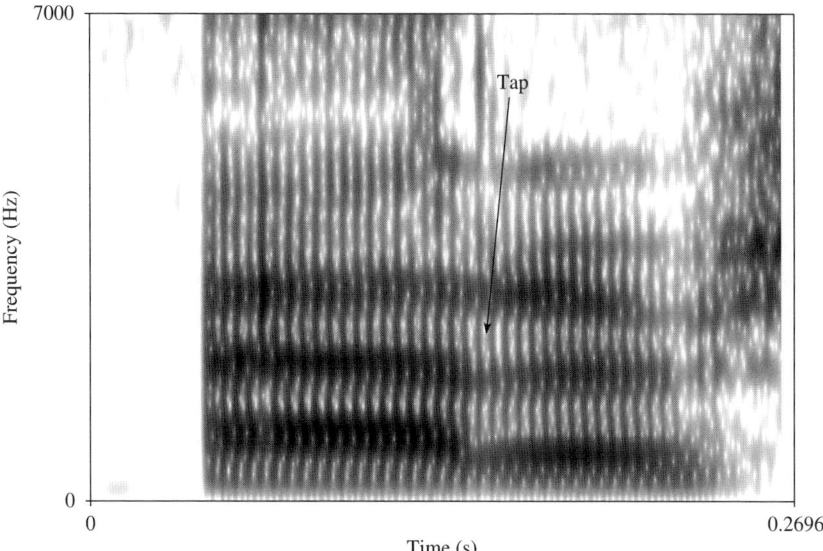

Figure 4.8 An utterance of *out of* with a tapped /t/, spoken by an adult female from North Carolina. The tap is visible as a lower-amplitude area between the two vowels. There is no burst, and the tap is quite short in duration (~17 ms).

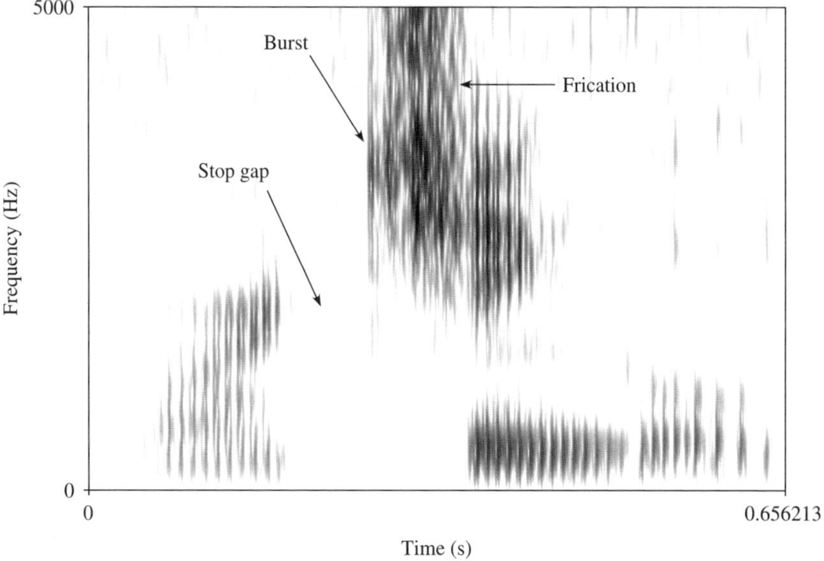

Figure 4.9 Spectrogram of an utterance of *or shingle* with an affricated /ʃ/, produced as [tʃ], in *shingle*. Spoken in conversation by a Mexican American male from southern Texas.

of frication noise out of the total duration of closure and stop, which would be close to 100 per cent for /s/ and /z/ but lower for an affricate. In some contexts, /t/ and /d/ could lose their stop closure entirely and become fricatives.

Affricates versus fricatives

Sometimes variation occurs between affricates and fricatives. An example is Panama City Spanish, in which Cedergren (1973) found that Spanish /tʃ/, as in *ocho* /ˈotʃo/ 'eight', was commonly weakened to [ʃ]. Another example is that speakers whose L1 is Spanish often have difficulty distinguishing English /tʃ/ from /ʃ/ and may produce [tʃ] where standard English has [ʃ]. An example, produced by a Mexican American, is shown in Figure 4.9. Note the stop closure before the frication noise, indicating an affricate pronunciation. It's best to limit analysis to cases that aren't preceded by a stop. For a sequence such as *what she*, it would be unclear whether the stop closure belonged solely to the /t/ in *what* or to both the /t/ of *what* and to an affricated pronunciation of the /ʃ/ in *she*.

4.3 Place of articulation: transitions

Some kinds of consonantal variation involve the place of articulation of a consonant. For example, variation between apical (alveolar) and dorsal (uvular) /r/ in continental European languages has to do with the place of articulation. The most important correlates of place of articulation are formants, or resonances, which were introduced in Chapter 2. You may be used to thinking of formants in terms of vowels, but they're crucial for consonants too. These resonances are manifested in different ways, especially for fricatives. We'll start with properties of the *transitions*, the short but vitally important periods on the borders between consonants and vowels.

Back in section 2.5, we touched on transitions a little. There we were mainly concerned with what effects consonants have on vowels. Now we'll look at transitions from the perspective of the consonants. Figure 4.10 shows the same spectrogram of the words *bab* [bæb], *dad* [dæd] and *gag* [gæg] as in Figure 2.32. Look again at the differences in the transitions. Each consonant has its own transition pattern. The differences in transition patterns work for variation within a consonantal phoneme, too. When a consonant shows variation in its place of articulation, you can gauge the difference by examining the transitions. However, it's not as simple as just looking at the formant values of the transition, as you might do for vowels. For consonants, you have to take into account what vowel's next to the consonant and sometimes the slope of the formant in the transition.

The transition patterns are created by the front and back cavities in the mouth, as we discussed in Chapter 2. Wherever the constriction is – the palate, velum or uvula for dorsal consonants, the alveolar ridge or teeth for a coronal one, and so forth – the space between the glottis and the constriction becomes the back cavity and the space from the constriction to the lips becomes the front cavity. For a bilabial consonant, there's no front cavity at all. The back cavity

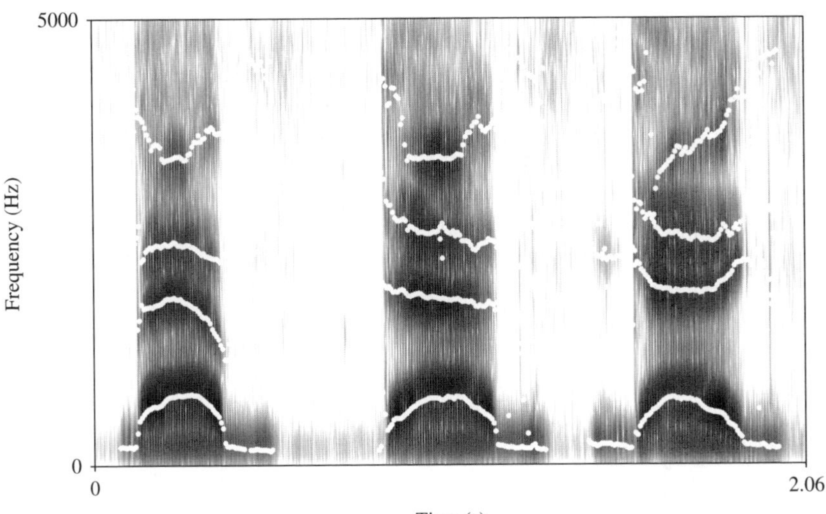

Figure 4.10 Spectrogram of the words *bab* [bæb], *dad* [dæd] and *gag* [gæg] with a superimposed LPC formant track. Observe the differing transitions for each consonantal sound.

is modelled as a tube closed at both ends, with the glottis and the constriction forming the ends. The front cavity is ordinarily modelled as a tube open at one end. When a consonant has rounding as a secondary articulation, as with [kʷ], the front cavity becomes closed at both ends. Certain other consonants with more than one constriction, such as the 'bunched' [ɹ] (which has pharyngeal and dorsal constrictions) also have two tubes closed at both ends.

Consonants with one constriction and two cavities – one closed at both ends and one open at the front – are reasonably straightforward. Basically, you can expect each of the two cavities to have its own set of resonances. For a pharyngeal consonant, the back cavity is short and the front cavity is long, but as the constriction moves forward in the mouth, the back cavity gets longer and the front cavity gets shorter. Simple enough, isn't it? As you'd expect, longer cavities make lower-frequency resonances (formants) and shorter cavities make higher-frequency resonances. Of course, each cavity also has an infinite number of resonances at higher frequencies. Figure 4.11, modelled after a nomogram in Stevens (1998:145), shows how this works for somebody with a 16-cm oral cavity, a possible length for an adult male. The x-axis tells you how far the constriction is from the glottis – i.e. how long the back cavity is. The front cavity is simply 16 minus the length of the back cavity. The curved lines are the resonances from each cavity: solid for back cavity resonances and dashed for front cavity ones. Since the back cavity's closed at both ends, we use the formula $F_n = nc/2L$ to get the resonances for it. For the front cavity, we use the formula for a tube open at one end, $F_n = (2n–1)c/4L$.

Whichever resonance is lowest, regardless of whether it comes from the back cavity or the front cavity, is labelled F_1. The next highest formant is called F_2, and so on. Where the lines meet, we say that the formants switch their

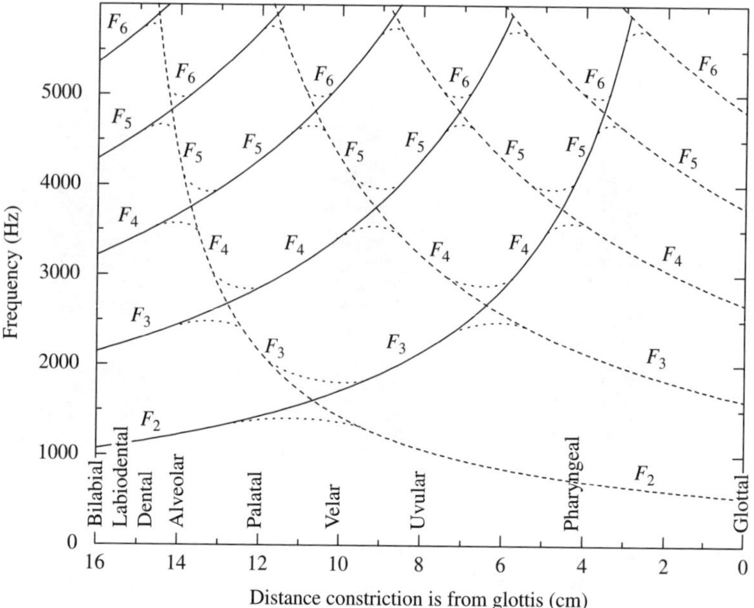

Figure 4.11 A nomogram showing how front and back cavity resonance frequencies change depending on the distance of the constriction from the glottis. Coupling effects and locations of certain places of articulation are shown. For retroflex (not shown), the expanded space under the tongue lowers F_3 additionally. Modelled, with modifications, from Stevens (1998). See text for F_1.

affiliation. For example, F_2 might be a front cavity resonance if the constriction's a little behind a certain point, and a back cavity resonance if the constriction's a little to the front.

You'll notice that the lowest resonance on Figure 4.11 is labelled as F_2, not F_1. Why? The reason is that there's a lower resonance, not shown, created because the back cavity and the constriction together make a Helmholtz resonator. One other thing you'll notice on Figure 4.11 is the dotted lines where resonances meet. Wherever formants switch affiliation, the resonances undergo coupling. That is, the cavities become partially merged and their resonances are affected so that they're more like where the dotted lines indicate.

Looking back at Figure 4.10, you can see that [b] reduces F_2 and F_3 values, [ɟ] (the palatal allophone of /g/) raises F_2 and F_3, and it's not clear whether [d] raises or lowers F_2 or F_3. This is what happens when an [æ] vowel falls next to a bilabial, palatal or alveolar consonant, respectively. The effects differ for each consonantal place of articulation, including others not shown in Figure 4.10. The effects also differ depending on the vowel. Some effects are consistent – bilabial consonants rather dependably lower F_2 and F_3, and velars show the 'velar pinch' in which F_2 and F_3 converge. Alveolars and other coronal consonants, however, vary more. Next to a front vowel, an alveolar or dental consonant will lower F_2, but next to a back vowel, it'll raise F_2. In addition, the transitions can be longer or shorter, depending on how much vocal fold vibration the consonant exhibits and how much coarticulation there is between the consonant and the vowel.

Once you know the transition patterns, you'll know what to look for if there's social or stylistic variation in consonantal place of articulation. Table 4.1 shows the general patterns for the first three formants for each of the common places of articulation.

To quantify variation, you need to measure formant values at two places:

1. the onset of the vowel (for a CV transition) or offset (for VC);
2. somewhere farther into the vowel, either (a) a set distance from the onset or offset (e.g. 25 ms, 35ms, 50 ms) or (b) a fraction of the duration through the vowel (most commonly one-half, i.e. at the vowel's midpoint) or (c) at the point where the vowel reaches its maximum F_1 value, maximum or minimum F_2 value, or a steady state.

An example spectrogram showing where to take measurements appears in Figure 4.12. Once you have formant measurements at both locations, you plot values against each other for each relevant formant. You have a choice in what you plot. One method is to plot measurement 2, the one from within the vowel, against the subtracted value: measurement 2 minus measurement 1. To achieve approximate normalization of speakers with different mouth sizes, it is helpful to convert the formant values from hertz to a perceptual scale such as Bark first. Examples of this kind of plot for CV sequences are shown in Figure 4.13 for both me, an adult male, and my daughter, aged ten, when she uttered the words. Her vocal tract is about 3 cm shorter than mine. Figure 4.13 shows

Table 4.1 Generalized effects of different consonantal places of articulation on the first three formants, observable in vowel transitions.

Place of articulation	*General effect on:*		
	F_1	F_2	F_3
Bilabial	Lowered	Lowered	Lowered
Labiodental	Lowered	Lowered	Lowered
Dental	Lowered	Raised next to back rounded vowels, lowered next to front vowels	Slightly raised except next to high front vowels
Alveolar	Lowered	Raised next to central and back vowels, lowered next to mid and high front vowels	Slightly raised except next to high front vowels
Retroflex	Lowered	Raised next to back vowels, lowered next to front vowels	Strongly lowered
Palato-alveolar	Lowered	Raised	Raised
Palatal	Lowered	Strongly raised	Slightly raised
Velar	Lowered	Raised	Lowered
Uvular	Lowered?	Lowered	Slightly lowered
Pharyngeal	Raised	Strongly lowered	Strongly lowered

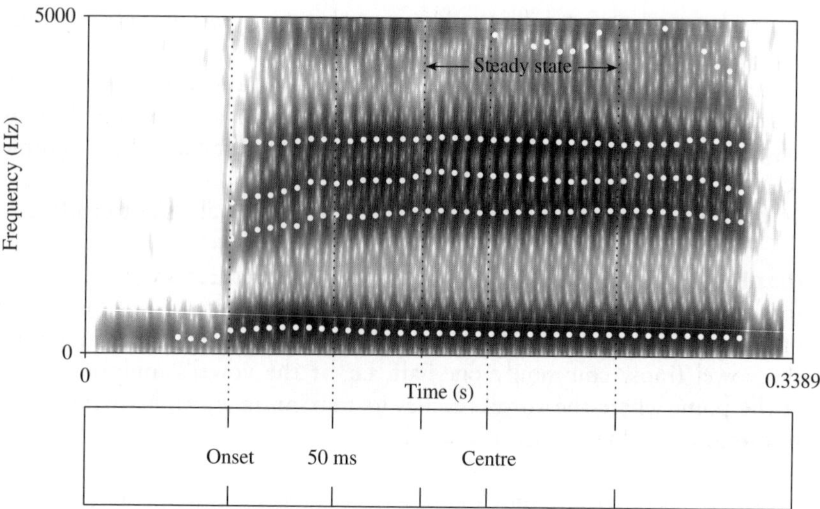

Figure 4.12 Spectrogram showing some possible locations at which to take measurements for analysing transition patterns: the onset, a point 50 ms after the onset, the centre of the vowel, and the steady-state region for F_1 and F_2. The beginning and end of the steady state are indicated by the arrows. An LPC formant track is superimposed.

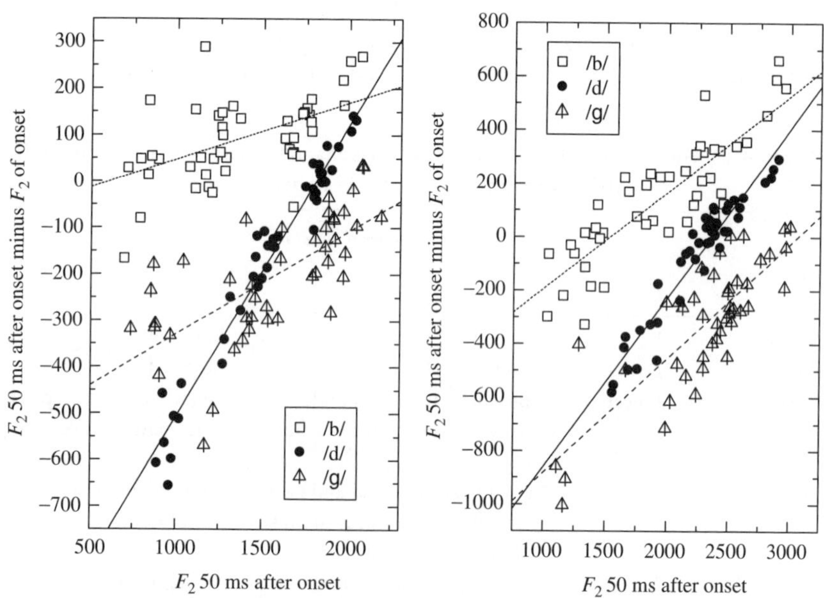

Figure 4.13 One method of plotting transition measurements: the vowel-internal formant frequency against the difference between vowel-internal and onset frequencies. Graphs are shown for adult male (left) and ten-year-old girl (right) values. Regression lines are given for each consonant. Differences in the relative positions of each line in the two graphs represent lectal variations.

F_2, but you can plot F_3 or other formants the same way. Then you compare results for the consonant you're interested in. You can compute the slope and/or y-intercept of a regression line through the measurements, or you may compare the means of two or more clouds of values.

The other way to plot the measurements is to forget about the subtraction and just plot measurement 2 against measurement 1. Again, you can compute the slope and y-intercept of the regression line for each consonant or cloud of values, as shown in Figure 4.14, or you can compare the means of clouds. Results are generally better for CV sequences than for VC sequences. Regression line formulas computed this way have a special name: *locus equations*. Sussman et al. (1993) compare five languages and show how the 'same' consonant can show locus equations with different slopes and y-intercepts in different languages, apparently depending on the amount of consonant/vowel coarticulation that typifies it in each language. This procedure could just as easily be applied to dialectal or stylistic variation.

Locus equations have some history associated with them. The notion of a *locus* was described by Delattre et al. (1955) as an abstract point at which all exemplars of a formant for a particular place of articulation would meet. For example, F_2 rises from the onset to the vowel steady state in a [di] syllable,

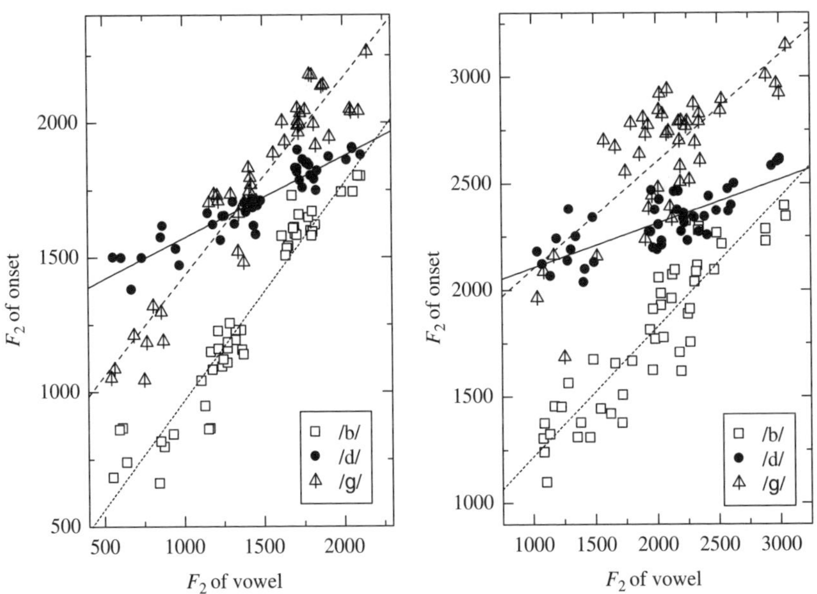

Figure 4.14 Another method of plotting transition measurements: the vowel-internal formant frequency against the onset frequency. The regression line is shown, and its formula is called a *locus equation*. Graphs are shown for adult male (left) and ten-year-old girl (right) values. The vowel-internal measurement is taken where F_1 and/or F_2 reaches a minimum or maximum frequency or is in a steady state, following Sussman et al. (1991). The differing positions of the /g/ line relative to the other two lines represent a lectal variation.

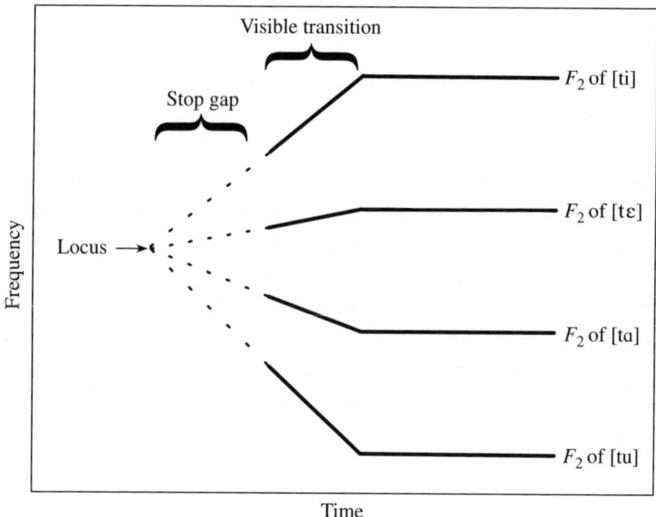

Figure 4.15 The now-discredited notion of a locus. The transitions before different vowels were thought to converge at a point called a *locus*. In fact, they don't all converge at any single point.

but it falls from the onset to the steady state in a [du] syllable. The concept is illustrated in Figure 4.15. However, later research showed that loci don't really exist – there isn't any point where all transitional values of a formant meet (see Sussman et al. 1991 for a review). Since then, locus equations have been proposed, with some controversy, as cognitive mechanisms that listeners use to distinguish consonants.

Example variables involving transition parameters

Interdental vs labiodental fricatives

An important variable in English, especially in England, is that between interdental and labiodental fricatives. In affected dialects, *north* may be pronounced [nɔːf] and *feather* may be pronounced ['fɛvə]. This variation can be described in terms of transitions because labiodental sounds lower F_2 values, while interdental sounds raise them. One method of distinguishing [θ] from [f] and [ð] from [v] would be to calculate a locus equation for the analysed consonants. What you would expect is that the vowel onset (or offset) would be higher in hertz for interdentals than for labiodentals, but that the difference would be greater for back vowels than for front vowels. Thus interdentals should show a higher y-intercept but a lower slope than labiodentals. Another method would be to construct a similar equation, but this time showing the difference – in hertz or, better yet, in Bark – between F_2 at the centre of the vowel and at the vowel onset or offset. The numbers won't be the same for all vowels. For high to mid-front vowels, they will both be negative. For back, rounded vowels, they will be positive next to an interdental and close to zero next to a labiodental. Figure 4.16 shows some examples.

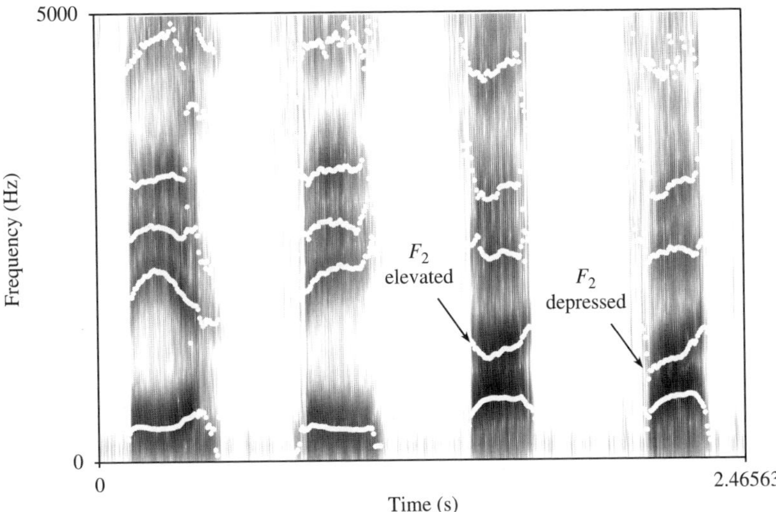

Figure 4.16 A comparison of transitions for [θ] and [f] in the words *Thea, fee, thought* and *fought*. Although the transitions are nearly identical before [i], [θ] raises F_2 before [ɑ], while [f] lowers it.

Dental, alveolar and retroflex obstruents

Different languages vary in the exact placement of their coronal consonants and some, especially in India, contrast more than one coronal place. As a result, variation within a language can occur, particularly when language contact is involved. For example, speakers of languages such as Hindi with dental and retroflex stops often use one of those articulations in producing English /t/, /d/ and /n/ instead of the alveolar articulation.

Coronal obstruents all have quite similar transition properties. Retroflex obstruents can be distinguished most easily by their F_3 patterns. Retroflex consonants pull the F_3 frequency downward, while dental and alveolar consonants are apt to pull F_3 upward slightly. In a locus equation for F_3, this difference would be reflected in a lower y-intercept for the retroflex forms.

Dental and alveolar consonants are highly similar. Generally, alveolars tend to show a stronger upward pull on F_2 than dentals. The difference is slight, however. F_3 may differ similarly. Figure 4.17 shows an example of voiced retroflex, alveolar and dental stops in an [ə_ə] context.

Incidentally, Jongman et al. (1985) suggested a completely different method of distinguishing dental and alveolar stops. They divided the amplitude of the onset of the following vowel by the amplitude of the burst. Alveolars usually had a ratio under five and dentals a ratio over five. This threshold worked quite well for Malayalam, which contrasts dental and alveolar stops, but far less well for languages that don't contrast them.

Alveolar/dental vs velar nasals

Transitions don't always distinguish consonants when it seems that they should. Variation between [n] and [ŋ] is well-known in English for the participial/gerundive suffix *-ing* and the pronominals *something* and *nothing*. Moreover,

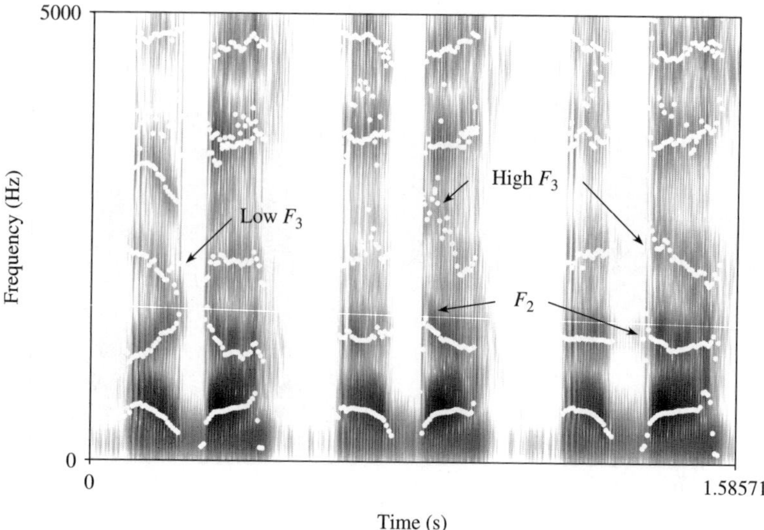

Figure 4.17 Spectrogram of [əɖə], [əd̪ə] and [ədə], in that order. The retroflex [ɖ] is easily distinguished by its lowering effect on F_3. The alveolar [d] shows a stronger upward pull on F_2 than dental [d̪].

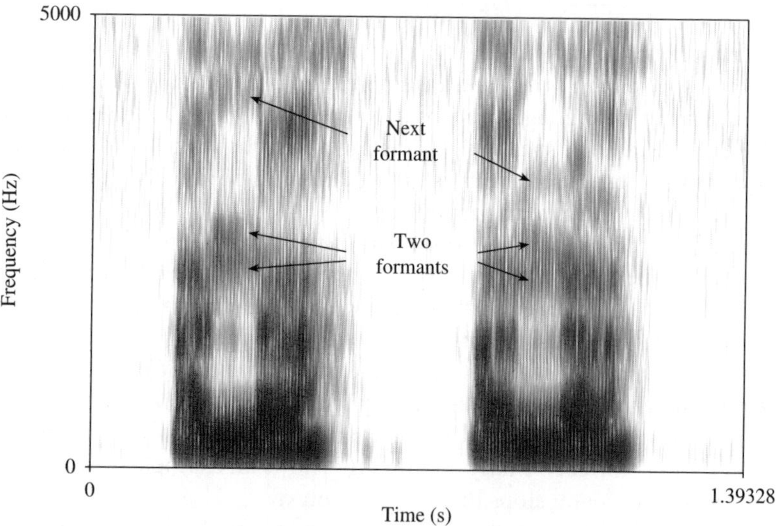

Figure 4.18 Spectrogram of [ənə] and [əŋə]. Both nasals show two formants at approximately the frequency of F_3 for the vowels. However, the next formant is much higher for the alveolar [n] than for the velar [ŋ].

phonological alternations between the two aren't uncommon in other languages (e.g. Japanese) and sound changes between them are frequent. You would expect that [n] and [ŋ] could be readily distinguished by their formant transition patterns. Actually, though, their transitions are almost identical. As the comparison of [ənə] and [əŋə] in Figure 4.18 shows, you have to look at the formants within the closure. They both show two formants close together at about the level of F_3 of the surrounding vowels. The next-higher formant is the crucial one – it is a lot higher for [n] than for [ŋ].

4.4 Place of articulation: frication and burst spectra

Hughes and Halle (1956) demonstrated the usefulness of power spectra of frication noise for distinguishing the quality of fricatives. In the years since then, phoneticians have created several variations on that basic method. Unfortunately for sociophoneticians, most of the research has concentrated on ways of discriminating the contrasting fricatives of a few languages, mainly English. That won't help you much when you need a fine-grained analysis to gauge subphonemic variation or when you're working on fricatives such as [x] and [χ] that Modern English lacks. Frication noise analysis is a wide-open field. Your best bet is to test out the methods described below until you find one that works for the variable you're studying.

Methods of analysing spectra

The most basic component of many methods is creating power spectra of the frication noise. You can't just make one spectrum, though, because frication noise is quite irregular and no one spectrum will be representative of the noise as a whole. What you need is a way to average the noise across different time points. The method used to do so is called an *average spectrum*. It works much like a spectrogram in that it consists of a series of overlapping FFT analysis windows that are applied to the signal. You just have to make sure that the beginning of the first analysis window is lined up with the onset of the frication noise and the end of the last window is lined up with the offset of the noise. With most analysis packages, you do that by setting the cursors to highlight the portion of the signal between the onset and offset of the noise. Spectral averaging is often used for long stretches of speech – hence the name *long-term average spectrum* (LTAS) – but the LTAS technique can also be applied to short segments of a signal, such as one fricative. What makes spectral averaging different from a spectrogram is that it retains the dimensions of a power spectrum – frequency on the x-axis and amplitude on the y-axis. The amplitudes are averaged across all the analysis windows. An example is shown in Figure 4.19.

Spectral peak location

Once you have your average spectrum of the fricative, the fun begins. A simple and easy method is to determine what Jongman et al. (2000) call the *spectral peak location*. This is merely the frequency in the spectrum with the highest amplitude. For a single person, and in the absence of lip rounding, laminal alveolar [s] will have a higher-frequency peak than palatal [ç], which in turn will have a higher-frequency peak than post-alveolar [ʃ] and retroflex [ʂ]. Peaks for [ʃ] and [ʂ] occur at nearly the same frequencies. In Figure 4.20, which shows the Mandarin affricates [tʂ] and [tç], the highest peaks are at 3,978 Hz for [ʂ]

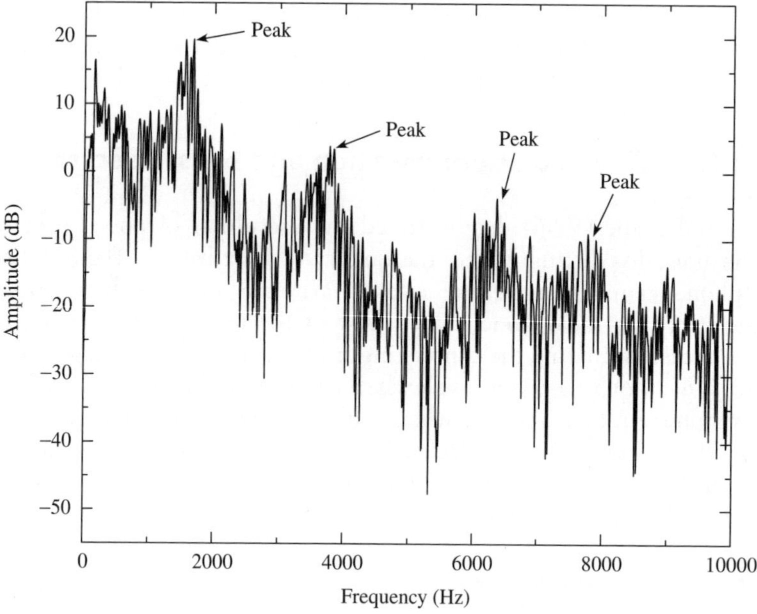

Figure 4.19 An unsmoothed average spectrum for the fricative [x]. Note the presence of peaks in the spectrum.

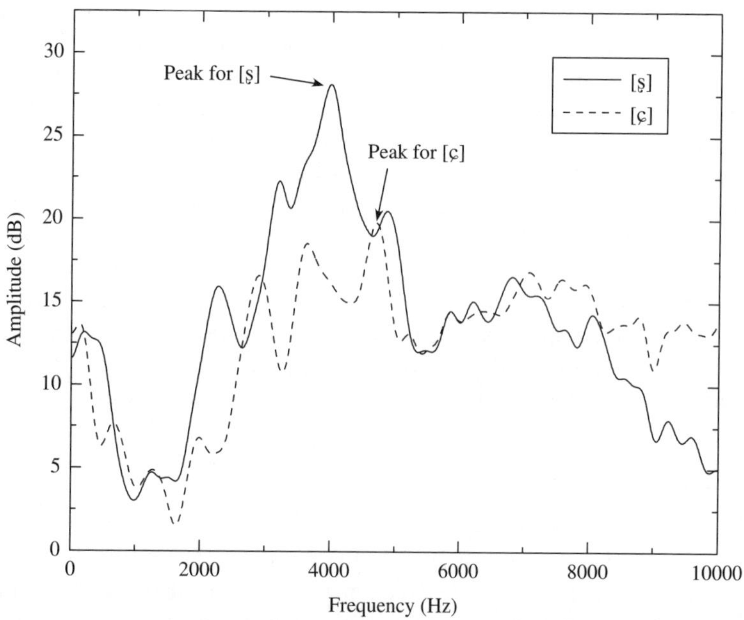

Figure 4.20 Smoothed average spectra for the frication in the Mandarin affricates [tʂ] (in *chīfàn* 'meal, food') and [tɕ] (in *qǐng* 'to treat'). The highest-amplitude peak for [ʂ] has a lower frequency than the highest-amplitude peak for [ɕ]. The speaker was an adult female.

and at 4,699 Hz for [ç]. Keep in mind that the spectral peak location is more effective for sibilants, which usually have clearly defined peaks, than for non-sibilants, whose spectra may appear rather flat. Another issue is that a speaker's vocal tract length affects peak locations. As you can see in Figure 4.21, the [ʃ] peak for my daughter (at age ten) is nearly as high in frequency as my [s] peak. You may need to normalize values for different speakers.

Sometimes you need to find a peak in a fricative spectrum, but not necessarily the highest one. Like vowels, frication noise may show formants within it. Usually, you can follow these formants into a neighbouring vowel. In the spectrogram of the utterance [əxə] in Figure 4.22, note how you can follow F_2 and some higher formants from the first vowel through the fricative to the second vowel. For some analyses, you may need to find the fricative formant that is associated with F_2 or F_3 or even higher formants in a neighbouring vowel. One use is to find the frequency of the formant. To do so, you measure the frequency of the correct peak in the spectrum.

Spectral moments

A different way of analysing average spectra of fricative noise has been used by Forrest et al. (1988) and several subsequent authors. With this method, instead of peak frequencies, the *spectral moments* are computed. For this kind of analysis, you first need to delimit minimum and maximum frequencies to be included. The maximum value is usually set to around 10 or 11 kHz, which can correspond to the lowpass filtering of the signal if the sampling rate is

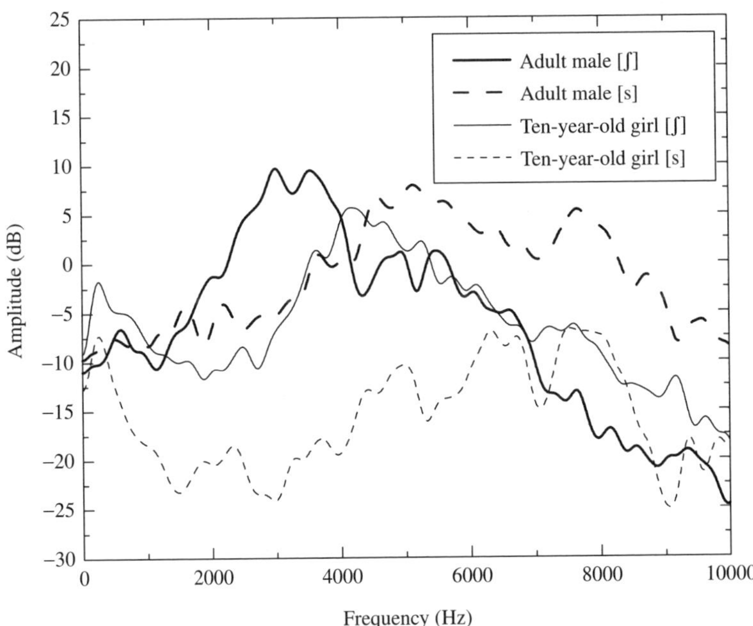

Figure 4.21 Smoothed average spectra for fricatives of an adult male and a ten-year-old girl

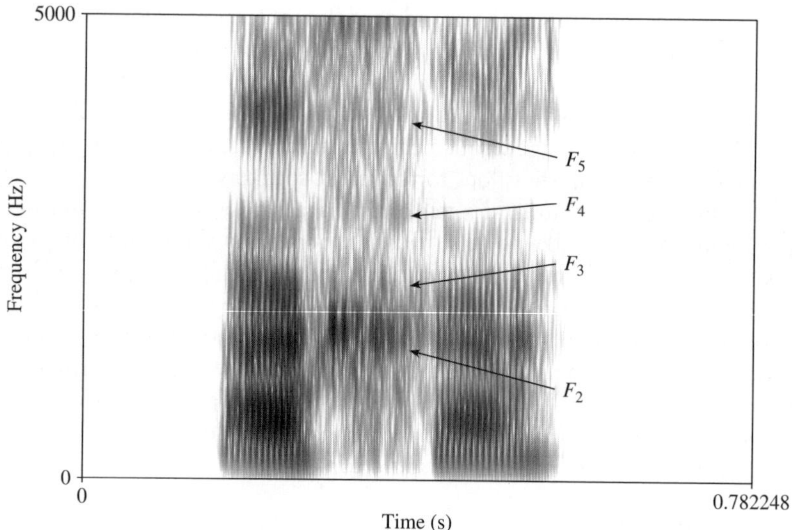

Figure 4.22 Spectrogram of [əxə]. Note how F_2 and higher formants can be tracked from the first vowel through the fricative to the second vowel. F_2 and F_3 are nearly coalesced in the frication.

22 kHz. Values over 10 kHz are regarded as unimportant to audition. The minimum value is commonly 0 Hz, but if you wish to exclude vocal pulsing or reduce ambient noise, you may set it at 500 or even 1,000 Hz. The frequencies can be analysed in hertz or Bark.

There are four spectral moments. Moment 1 is the mean frequency of the spectrum. It is computed by multiplying each frequency sample by its spectral energy, summing those products and dividing that number by the sum of the energies of the samples. [s], with more high-frequency energy, normally has a higher mean frequency than [ʃ]. Similarly, [ç] has a higher mean frequency than [x] or [χ]. Moment 2 is the variance of the spectrum. It tells you the range of energy in the spectrum. Fricatives with energy that's relatively concentrated at certain ranges of frequencies, such as [s] and [ʃ], will have lower variance than fricatives with more distributed energy and flatter spectra, such as [θ] and [f]. [ʂ] can be distinguished from [ʃ] because its energy is even more concentrated than that of [ʃ]. Moment 3 is the skewness, which tells you about the *spectral tilt*. This has to do with how fast the amount of energy falls off as frequency increases. When the peak of the spectrum has a relatively low frequency, the skewness will be positive and the spectral tilt greater, and when the peak has a relatively high frequency, the skewness will be negative and the spectral tilt lesser. Thus the skewness of [ʃ], with a fairly low-frequency peak, will be greater than that of [s], which has a higher-frequency peak. Likewise, [x] should have greater skewness than [ç]. Moment 4 is the kurtosis, which indicates the peakedness of the spectrum. Jongman et al. (2000) found [s] and [z] to have generally greater kurtosis than the other fricatives of English.

The A_d, S_p and S'_p parameters

Jesus and Shadle (2002) developed other metrics for frication spectra to study Portuguese fricatives. First, they devised a parameter *F*, which represents, for each fricative place of articulation, the peak amplitude value that is associated with the front cavity – in other words, the one associated with F_2 of the neighbouring vowel(s). Then they averaged all the *F* values for all of their subjects to create a parameter $\bar{F}$ for each place of articulation. Their next parameter was the dynamic amplitude or A_d. A_d is the difference in amplitude between the maximum and minimum amplitudes, with the following restrictions: the maximum has to lie between 500 Hz and 20 kHz, and the minimum has to lie between 0 and 2 kHz. The last two parameters are regression slopes. One, called S_p, is the slope of the spectrum between $\bar{F}$ and 20 kHz. The other, S'_p, is the slope of the spectrum between 500 Hz and $\bar{F}$. Figure 4.23 illustrates these parameters with a spectrum. $\bar{F}$ serves to normalize the values across speakers. You'll have to decide for yourself whether you need $\bar{F}$ or if *F* by itself is adequate as the cut-off point for S_p and S'_p. Note that Jesus and Shadle had an equal number of male and female speakers – your sample may not. The longer vocal tracts of men will lower *F*, which you'd expect to push S_p lower and S'_p higher, but they found an effect only for S'_p. An increase in amplitude, such as with sibilants, will affect the measures by increasing A_d, which decreases S_p and raises S'_p. Voicing causes an increase in S'_p because of the low-frequency energy of vocal pulsing. Finally, the longer the back cavity

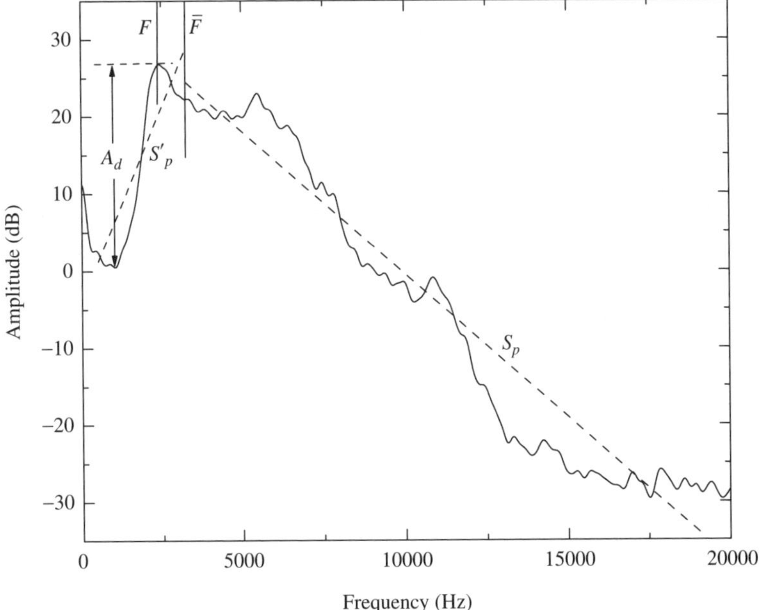

Figure 4.23 The F, $\bar{F}$, A_d, S_p and S'_p parameters in a smoothed spectrum of the fricative [ʃ], following the method of Jesus and Shadle (2002). $\bar{F}$ is simulated.

Table 4.2 Observed patterns for the parameters F, A_d, S_p and S'_p, based on Jesus and Shadle (2002).

Effect of:	*Parameter*			
	F	A_d	S_p	S'_p
increasing vocal tract length (e.g. by sex of speaker)	Lowered	No change	No change	Sometimes raised
raising amplitude (e.g. for sibilants)	No change	Slightly raised	Lowered	Sometimes raised
voicing	No change	Variable effects	No change	Lowered
increasing length of back cavity	Lowered	Slightly lowered	No change	Usually lowered

is, the lower F becomes, and as F decreases, the slope value represented by S'_p decreases. These effects are shown in Table 4.2, based on results in Jesus and Shadle (2002: 449).

Uses of amplitude and duration

Amplitude is sometimes used as a way of distinguishing fricatives. For the most part, overall amplitude is mainly useful for distinguishing sibilants, which have high amplitude, from non-sibilants, which have lower amplitude. Another use of amplitude, described by Jongman et al. (2000) and Maniwa et al. (2009), is called the *frequency-specific relative amplitude.* First, a discrete Fourier transform, or DFT, is taken at the onset of the vowel after the fricative. In the resulting spectrum, F_3 is located if the fricative is /s/, /z/, /ʃ/ or /ʒ/, and F_5 if the fricative is /f/, /v/, /θ/ or /ð/. The amplitude of the selected formant is measured in dB. Then a spectrum is taken at the centre of the fricative and the amplitude is measured at the same frequency as that for the vowel onset. The amplitude at the vowel onset is subtracted from the amplitude at the centre of the fricative. This difference is the relative amplitude. Jongman et al. (2000) found that the relative amplitude was greatest (least negative) for /ʃ/ and /ʒ/, followed by /f/ and /v/ and then by /θ/ and /ð/. Lowest of all were /s/ and /z/.

Duration of frication noise also has some limited use. Voiceless fricatives average much longer than voiced fricatives. Sibilants tend to be a little longer than non-sibilants (Jongman et al. 2000).

Stop burst spectra

Stop bursts, like fricatives, can be analysed using spectra. A simple method is to create a power spectrum of the burst, averaged over its short duration, and measure the frequencies of the peaks. Cho and McQueen (2005:132) went further and computed Moment 1, the mean or centroid value, of bursts. They limited their analysis to frequencies between 1,000 and 10,000 Hz.

Example variables involving analysis of noise spectra

Laminal and apical [s]

There is more to [s] than just that it's a voiceless alveolar fricative. There are a number of ways to articulate [s]. Dental articulations are possible. However, even for alveolar articulations, there are two basic variants. The kind usually heard in English and many other languages is the *laminal* [s], in which the sides of the tongue are curled up, cup-like, to make the constriction. The other type is the *apical* [s], in which the tongue tip, not the sides, makes the constriction. This also holds for the voiced counterpart [z].

Stuart-Smith (2007) described variation between laminal and apical [s] in the English of Glasgow, Scotland. Apical [s] has a lower-frequency peak than laminal [s], and Stuart-Smith exploited this property. She used both the spectral moments analysis, mainly Moments 1 and 2 (the spectral mean or centroid and the variance), and one of the slope metrics from Jesus and Shadle (2002), S'_p. She did not normalize for vocal tract length, though this was not necessary. Male and female values fell into separate groups, as you'd expect with their different tract lengths, with one exception. Young working-class females showed values within the range of the men's values, not within those of the other females' values. The lower-frequency peak of apical [s] was the reason – young working-class females were the only group who used it, but they used it consistently.

Dorsal fricatives

Among dorsal fricatives, it's relatively common for palatal [ç] and velar [x] to function allophonically, as in German. [x] and uvular [χ] may also grade into each other in some languages. The spectra of these fricatives differ measurably, though. Metrics such as spectral moments or the parameters developed by Jesus and Shadle (2002) could certainly be applied to dorsal fricatives. One difficulty with applying those methods to dorsal fricatives is that dorsal fricatives show several peaks, each representing a formant, and the highest-amplitude peak isn't always the same formant. Fortunately, the well-defined formant structure of dorsal fricatives permits a different method. F_2 is the formant that's most diagnostic of place of articulation for these fricatives, so you can base your analysis on F_2 values. F_2 corresponds to the front-cavity resonance in this region. The formants can usually be tracked from neighbouring vowels, which provides a check to make sure you have the right spectral peak. Table 4.3 shows measurements of the F_2 peak for my voice. F_2 is a lot higher for [ç] than for the other two. [x] is noticeably higher than [χ], but there is overlap when you take lip rounding into consideration. Of course, speakers with different-sized vocal tracts will have different resonance frequencies, so you need some way to normalize for mouth size. To do that, normalize the fricatives against the speaker's vowels. You can use one of the vowel-external normalization methods covered in Chapter 5 – Lobanov, Nearey, or Watt and Fabricius – and scale the fricative F_2 against the centroid value from the normalization. The Bark-difference normalization method may also work for distinguishing uvular fricatives from

Table 4.3 F_2-related peak frequencies for voiceless dorsal fricatives uttered by the author. For each place of articulation, values are lowered considerably by lip rounding. Note that values for a female or child speaker would be shifted upward.

Vocalic context	[ç]	[x]	[χ]
i_i	3,066	1,684	1,296
ə_ə	2,918	1,548	1,127
a_a	2,933	1,593	1,127
u_u	2,072	963	772
ɔ_ɔ	2,206	974	731

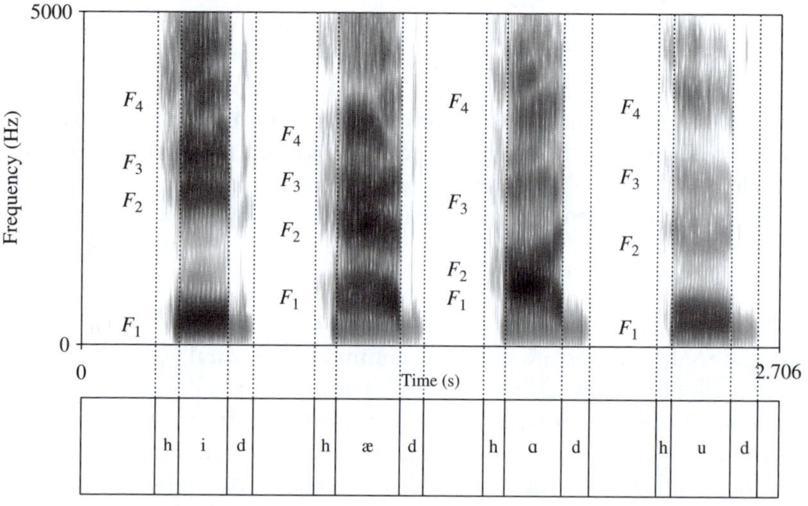

Figure 4.24 [h] in the words *heed, had, hod* and *who'd*. Note how the formant pattern for each vowel is anticipated in the aspiration for [h].

velar and palatal fricatives because uvulars have high F_3 values, while velars and palatals have low F_3 values. To use it, you'd need to measure the frequency of F_3 of the fricative, convert both F_2 and F_3 to Bark, and compute the difference.

[h] or aspiration and voiceless fricatives

[h] is fricative-like and, though lacking the narrow constriction that characterizes canonical fricatives, alternates with voiceless fricatives in some languages. In Old English, for example, [x] and [h] functioned allophonically, and in some varieties of Spanish today, particularly in the Caribbean, /s/ is commonly realized as [h]. Acoustically, the most readily apparent difference is in formant structure. [h] exhibits the formants of nearby vowels, as if it were a voiceless vowel, as in Figure 4.24. The main factor that can change spectral peak values of canonical fricatives is lip rounding, which will lower the peak value.

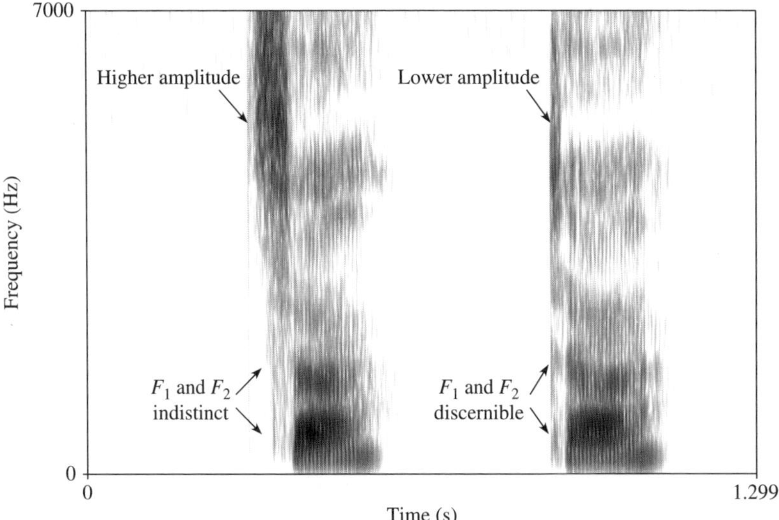

Figure 4.25 Spectrogram of [tsə] (left) and [tʰə] (right). F_1 and F_2 are recognizable in the aspiration for [tʰə], but not in the frication for [tsə]. The frication also shows a higher amplitude than the aspiration, but this difference applies only to sibilants such as [s].

Otherwise, a given speaker will show fairly stable peak values for each canonical fricative, at least if the fricative is long enough to get beyond the transition zone.

The same diagnostic features can be used to distinguish affricated stops from aspirated stops. As we've already seen, affrication of certain stops appears in Quebec French and Liverpool English. Aspiration, like [h], shows formant patterns of the following vowel, while fricatives show their own specific spectral patterns. For example, [s] shows only high-frequency formants. A comparison of [ts] and [tʰ] is shown in Figure 4.25. Note that a hybrid form [tsʰ], in which the noise shifts from alveolar frication to aspiration through its course, is also possible.

4.5 Place of articulation: direct measurement of articulation

Devices that measure articulation directly have found their most extensive application in the study of consonants. In fact, nearly all of the techniques mentioned in Chapter 2 – X-rays, MRI, ultrasound and electropalatography – have been used to study the articulation of consonants. Consonants cover a wide range of articulatory strategies, and these techniques have been indispensable in figuring some of them out. Moreover, in a few cases such as bunched and retroflex /r/, differing articulations produce nearly identical acoustic patterns, and it has taken articulatory measurements to differentiate them.

Articulatory measurements have been particularly important for understanding laterals and rhotics. However, they can be used for dialectal variation in the place of articulation of other sounds. Purnell (2008) turned to X-ray microbeams after acoustic analyses revealed coarticulatory patterns for /g/ and /k/ in Wisconsin English that were difficult to explain. The X-rays showed that /g/ was produced with a more anterior articulation than /k/ and with lip protrusion that /k/ lacked.

4.6 Voice onset time

Voice Onset Time (VOT) is a property of stop consonants. As defined by Lisker and Abramson (1964), it represents the interval of time, measured in ms, between the stop burst and the onset of vocal fold pulsing. The vocal fold pulsing may start well before the burst, as with the /b, d, g/ of Spanish. It may start just after the burst, as in the /p, t, k/ of Spanish or the utterance-initial /b, d, g/ of English. Or it may start well after the burst, which happens with aspirated stops, such as initial /p, t, k/ in English. These three levels of VOT are illustrated in Figure 4.26. When the vocal pulsing starts before the burst, VOT is a negative number, and when it starts after the burst, VOT is positive. When pulsing starts before the burst, you get *lead VOT.* When pulsing begins very soon after the burst, it's called *short-lag VOT,* and when aspiration causes the pulsing to be delayed long after the burst, you get *long-lag VOT.*

VOT has received quite a bit of attention from phoneticians because it shows considerable interlanguage variability. It hasn't received much attention from

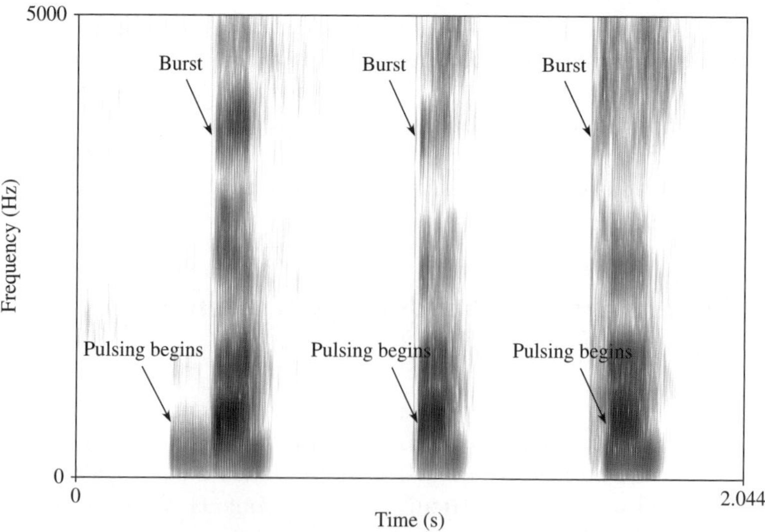

Figure 4.26 Comparison of (left to right) lead VOT in [bɐ], short-lag VOT in [pɐ] and long-lag VOT in [pʰɐ]. Observe where the burst is and where the glottal pulsing starts. VOT values for these tokens are −121 ms, 13ms and 56 ms, respectively.

sociolinguists, mainly because intralanguage social variability in VOT for particular consonants tends to be low. Intralanguage variability in VOT isn't non-existent though and can become a sociolinguistic variable, especially in language contact situations.

Measuring VOT

Measuring VOT seems pretty straightforward, but like everything else in life there are a few complications.[1] First, dorsal stops commonly show two or more bursts, as in Figure 4.27. Preferably, you should follow Cho and Ladefoged (1999), who measured VOT from the last burst. Second, where do you mark the onset of vocal fold vibrations? You would think that this would be clear, but often it's not. Breathiness or aspiration frequently make it ambiguous where the vocal pulses begin, as you can see in Figure 4.28. Klatt (1975) counted it as the point where vocal pulses begin in F_2 and higher formants. Third, for lead VOT, where is the onset of vocal pulsing if a vowel precedes the stop and the pulsing continues through the stop? Cho and McQueen (2005) used the point where the F_2 of the preceding vowel disappears, which is basically the offset of the preceding vowel. Figure 4.29 illustrates this situation. One other thing to watch out for is that long-lag VOT is ordinarily longer for dorsal stops than for coronal or labial stops, apparently for articulatory or aerodynamic reasons (Cho and Ladefoged 1999).

Social variation in VOT

As mentioned above, VOT is something to watch for in language contact situations. Numerous papers have found that L2 learners may show interference for

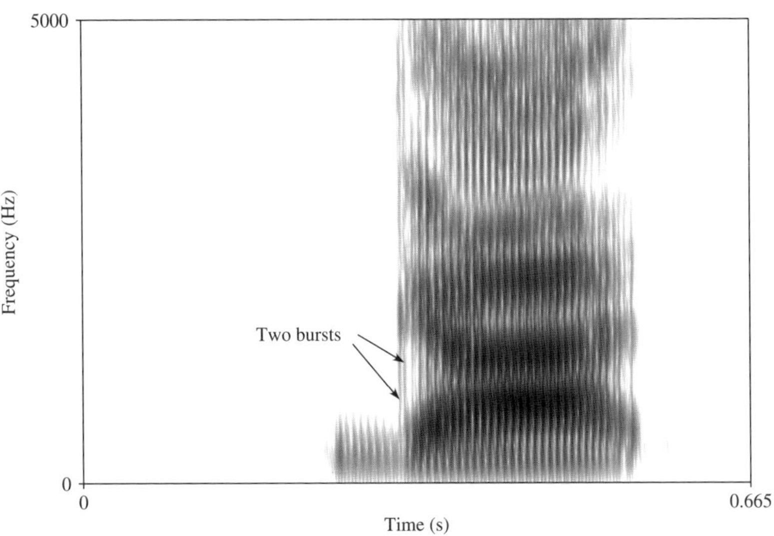

Figure 4.27 Spectrogram of *got* in which [g] has two bursts.

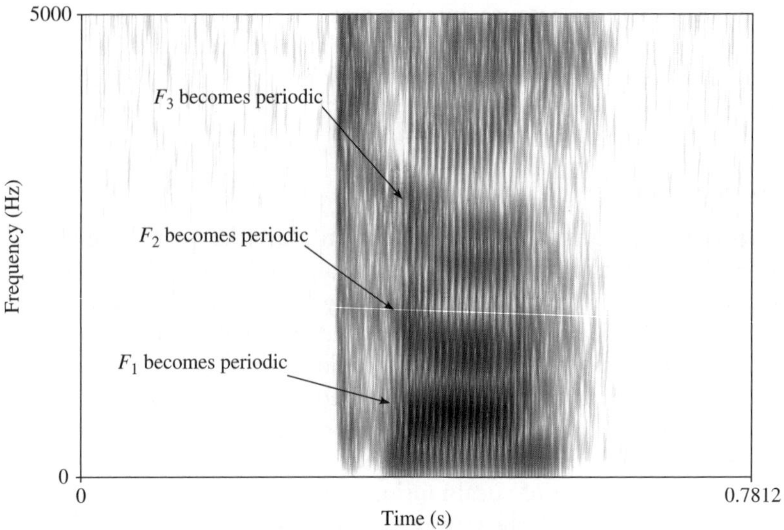

Figure 4.28 Aspiration can make it unclear exactly when glottal pulsing begins. In this spectrogram of [tʰə], F_1 shows a periodic pattern first, followed by F_2 and then F_3 on successive glottal pulses. F_3 shows some breathy pulses before it becomes periodic.

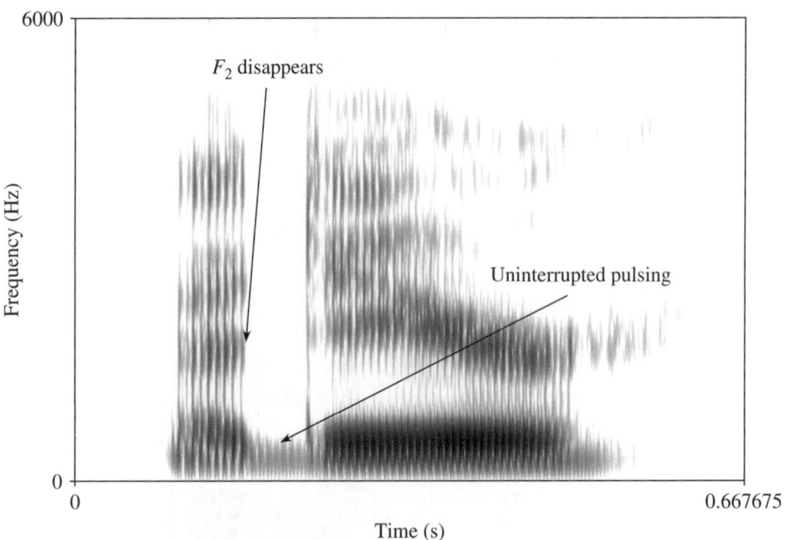

Figure 4.29 Illustration of lead VOT when the stop is preceded by a consonant in the phrase *a deer*. Counting the VOT from the point where F_2 for the preceding vowel disappears is recommended.

VOT. For example, Flege and Hillenbrand (1984) found that late learners of English (with long-lag /t/) whose first language was Spanish (with short-lag /t/) produced English initial /t/ with VOT intermediate between values appropriate for Spanish and English. Similarly, Flege (1991) found that Americans learning French and French natives living in the United States produced initial /t/ with intermediate values. Heselwood and McChrystal (1999) examined VOT in a contact situation from a sociolinguistic perspective. They studied the realization of stops in Panjabi spoken in Bradford, England. Panjabi has a three-way realization of prevoiced (i.e. lead VOT), voiceless unaspirated (short-lag VOT) and voiceless aspirated (long-lag VOT) stops. Their measurements showed that younger Panjabi speakers, probably influenced by English, were losing the prevoicing, so that the prevoiced stops of Panjabi were falling together with the voiceless unaspirated ones. See also Maclagan et al. (2009), who found that VOT for /p/, /t/ and /k/ was increasing in Maori due to increasing aspiration, undoubtedly from contact with English. Whether altered VOT values persist for several generations in substrate situations requires further research.

Language contact situations aren't the only ones in which VOT can vary. Takada and Tomimori (2006) conducted a regional survey of VOT in Japanese. Word-initial voiced stops were undergoing a change. Older speakers had strongly negative VOT values except in north-eastern Japan, where short-lag forms predominated. However, VOT values were rising among younger speakers in central and south-western Japan – i.e. the prevoicing of initial 'voiced' stops was disappearing. Scobbie (2006) reports a case from English, in the Shetland Isles. Some Shetlanders had short-lag /b/, /d/ and /g/ and long-lag /p/, /t/ and /k/, like most English speakers. Other Shetlanders, mostly with island heritages, had lead /b/, /d/ and /g/ and short-lag /p/, /t/ and /k/. As you can see, sociolinguists should keep a closer eye on VOT, even in well-studied languages whose VOT characteristics are thought to be well known.

4.7 Processes affecting coda stops

Glottalization

Glottalization is a common feature of languages. The glottal stop [ʔ] occurs widely in languages as a phonological category, and glottalization appears frequently as a secondary articulation of consonants – e.g. it is common in indigenous American languages. In some languages, such as English and German, glottalized obstruents may occur as conditioned variants. In both of those languages, glottalization is associated with voiceless stops in syllable codas, as in Figure 4.30. Glottalization can occur for ambisyllabic stops, in which the stop forms the coda of one syllable and the onset of the next, as well. The diagnostic phonetic property of glottalization is the exceptionally slow, glottal pulses that occur just before the occlusion for the obstruent. This property typifies creaky voicing, which we'll go into in some depth in Chapter 7, and in fact glottalization is essentially creaky voicing.

At the same time, a common sound change is the shift of glottalized obstruents to a glottal stop. The shift of /t/ to [ʔ] in final and intervocalic

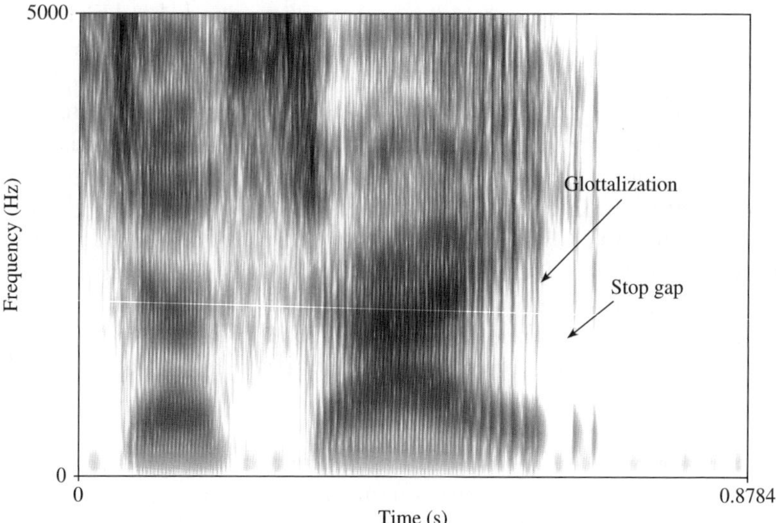

Figure 4.30 Glottalization is associated with syllable-coda voiceless stops in English, as this utterance of *right* in the phrase *just right* spoken by a European American female from North Carolina illustrates. The glottalization is manifested in the slowed glottal pulses right before the stop closure. She also shows two glottal pulses after the stop closure begins.

contests has been studied extensively in the dialects of England and Scotland by Trudgill (1974b), Macauley (1977) and numerous later authors. Actually, the process can occasionally affect /p/ and /k/ as well, but it most commonly affects /t/. The acoustics aren't as simple as you'd expect. As Docherty and Foulkes (1999) and Foulkes and Docherty (2006) have pointed out, at least three different variants occur just in Tyneside (the vicinity of Newcastle-upon-Tyne), and a fourth could be added. These variants are quite difficult to distinguish auditorily and acoustic analysis is necessary to differentiate them reliably. One is the 'glottal reinforcement' depicted in Figure 4.31. To measure it, you look for a steep drop in F_0 before the affected obstruent. The fall in F_0 can be seen in various ways. In a wideband spectrogram, you can see that the glottal pulses become more widely separated near the stop and somewhat irregular in frequency. In a narrowband spectrogram, the harmonics fall in frequency. In an autocorrelation pitch track, the F_0 measurements decrease. The obstruent – [t] in this case – is still present and is manifested as a stop closure, visible in a wideband spectrogram as a blank area just after the creaky voicing followed by a burst.

The next variant, not explicitly mentioned by Docherty and Foulkes, is a glottal stop with no other stop articulation. A comparison of a /t/ with glottal reinforcement and a pure glottal stop is shown in Figure 4.32. The blank space produced by the stop closure is present for both. What distinguishes [ʔ] from [ʔt] is the formant patterns. For a pure [ʔ], the formants remain practically level right into the [ʔ], and you can see that in Figure 4.32. When another

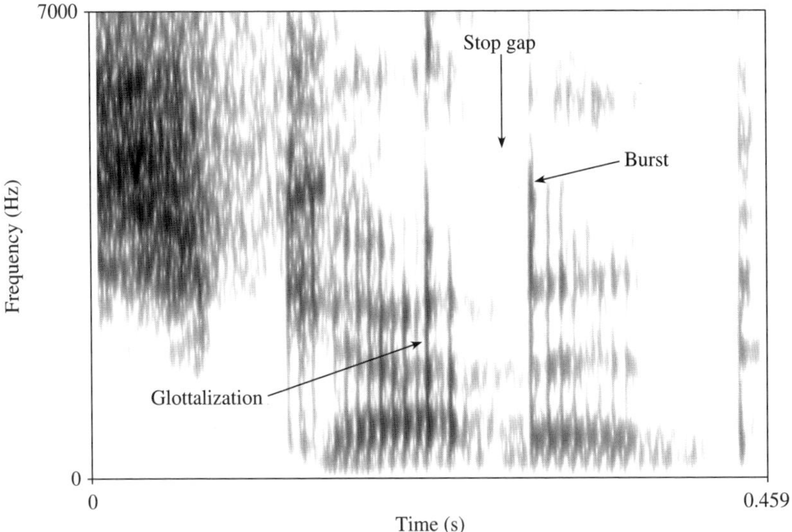

Figure 4.31 Glottal reinforcement of intervocalic [t] in *scattered* by an older male speaker from Tyneside, England. The slowed glottal pulses characteristic of glottalization and the stop gap and burst indicating a stop are all present.

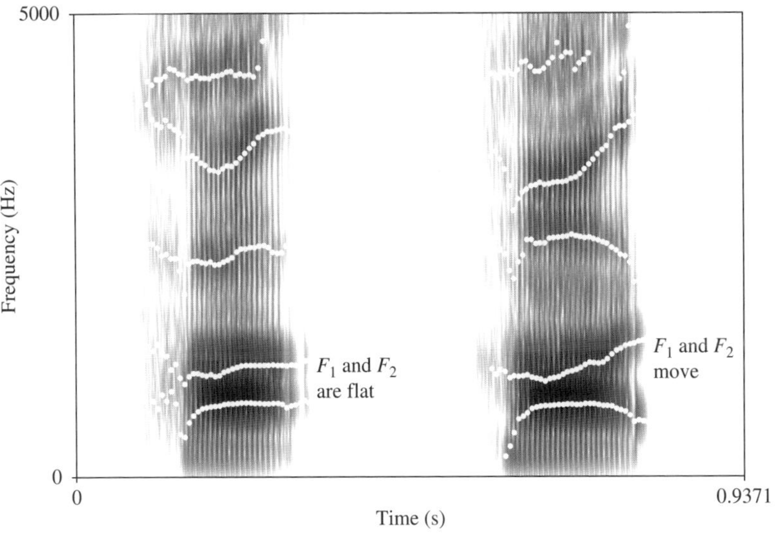

Figure 4.32 Comparison of the word *hot* pronounced as [hɑʔ] and as [hɑʔt]. Note how F_1 and F_2 show very little movement at the vowel offset for [hɑʔ] but considerable movement for [hɑʔt].

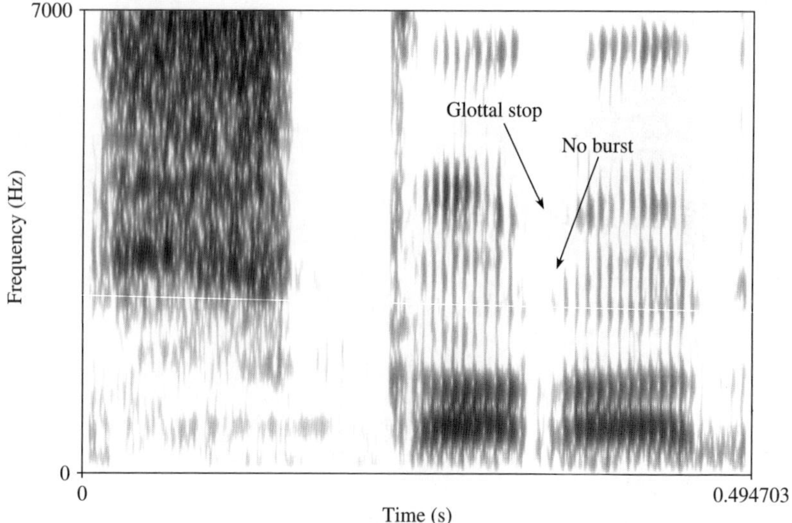

Figure 4.33 Intervocalic /t/ in *scattered*, uttered by a young male from Tyneside, England, and realized as a glottal stop. Two faint glottal pulses are visible within the glottal stop, so it isn't a complete stop. There is no burst after it.

stop is articulated, though, the formants will move in directions appropriate for the particular stop. For the [ʔt], you can see how F_1 falls and F_2 rises as they approach the stop closure. An intervocalic example from Tyneside of /t/ realized as [ʔ] is shown in Figure 4.33.

The other two variants that Docherty and Foulkes describe lack the stop closure. They are found in medial environments, ordinarily when the preceding syllable has stronger stress than the following syllable – the same context in which taps occur in American English. For these two variants, there is no blank space on the spectrogram from a stop closure. Instead, you see a period of creaky voicing in what otherwise looks like continuous vowel articulation. In one variant, more common among young Tyneside males, there is no stop release, as in Figure 4.34. In the other variant, more common among older Tyneside natives, there is a stop release at the end of the creaky period. Ladefoged and Maddieson (1996: 75) point out that intervocalic glottal stops are realized as creaky voicing with no stop closure in many languages. Quantitative measurement of these forms would focus on F_0, using the techniques mentioned above, and on amplitude.

Aspiration of coda stops

Less common in Western languages is aspiration of coda stops. Docherty and Foulkes (1999) and Foulkes and Docherty (2006) describe the presence of 'pre-aspiration' of /t/ (called 'extended frication' in the earlier paper) in Tyneside English. The stop closure is preceded by a period of aspiration or alveolar frication or both, as in Figure 4.35, and sometimes may disappear entirely.[2] Similar

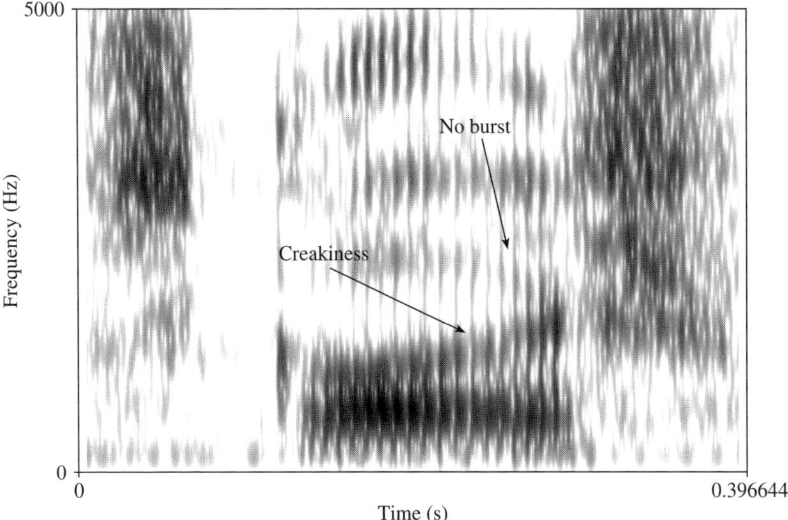

Figure 4.34 Intervocalic /t/ in *Scottish* realized as a period of creakiness without a burst or stop gap, uttered by the same young male speaker from Tyneside, England.

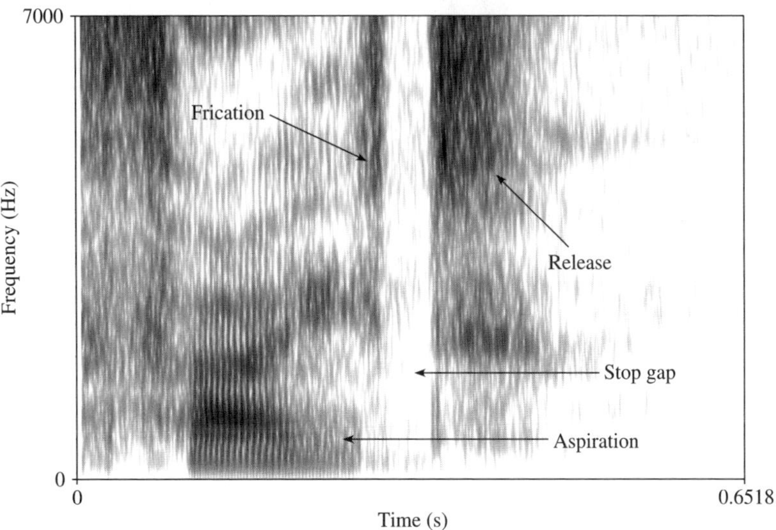

Figure 4.35 Final /t/ in *fight* realized with pre-aspiration, uttered by a female speaker from Tyneside, England. Note how the vowel first becomes breathy and then changes into frication before the stop gap, which is followed by a heavily aperiodic release.

processes are known from a few other languages, such as Faroese. For many Tyneside speakers, the pre-aspiration can be voiced throughout. The aspiration/frication may also occur for intervocalic /t/ and appear both before and after the stop gap.

Stop releases

Prepausal stops are generally described as having a release after their stop closure, as in Figure 4.36. The release consists of a stop burst and some aspiration-like noise or, for voiced stops, vocal pulsing. As data in Thomas (2000) show, though, American English is quite variable in whether the stop is released or

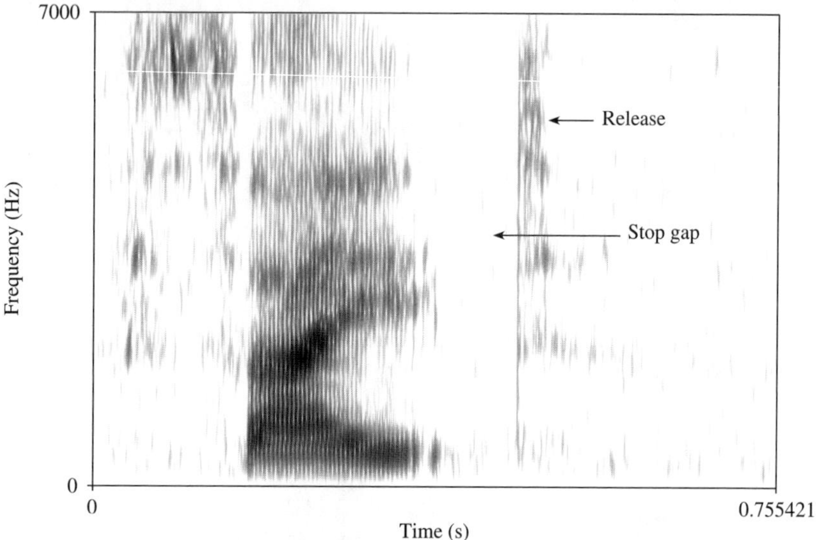

Figure 4.36 A final stop in *sight*, uttered by a young, female speaker from Johnstown, Ohio, reading a word list, realized with a release.

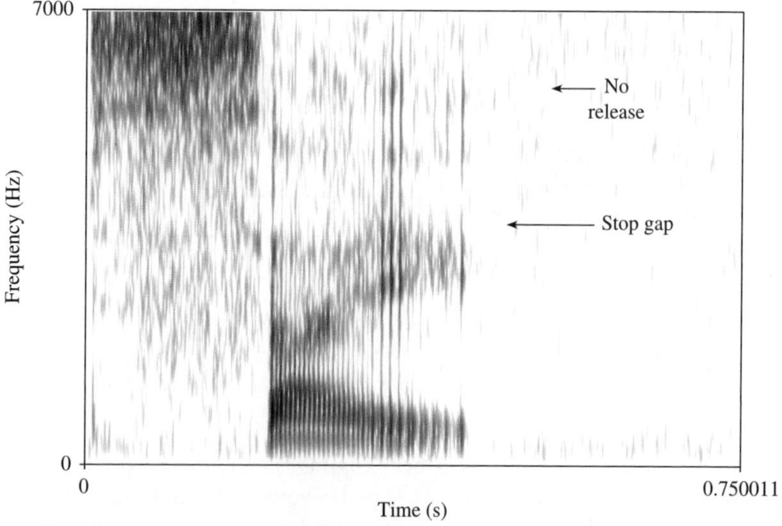

Figure 4.37 A final stop in *sight*, uttered by a different young, female speaker from Johnstown, Ohio, reading a word list, realized without a release.

not. Podesva et al. (2002: 186) suggest that releases are associated with 'education or precision'. Otherwise, this variable is almost completely ignored by sociolinguists. Ladefoged and Maddieson (1996) note that glottalization of stops may inhibit releases, and though that may explain unreleased voiceless stops, it doesn't explain unreleased voiced stops. Figure 4.37 shows an unreleased stop from a word list reading. Note the absence of a burst or other evidence of a release.

4.8 Other voicing properties

The 'voicing' feature is perhaps the most heavily studied aspect of consonants. What is known is that lots of phonetic properties are involved with it. Table 4.4 lists the common trends. Some of the different properties apparently occur together for either articulatory or perceptual reasons. For example, with a voiced obstruent, the build-up of air pressure in the mouth during glottal pulsing causes the larynx to move downward, and the resulting lengthening of the pharynx lowers the F_1 frequency of the following vowel transition. Occasionally, properties can counteract each other – for instance, glottalization can make F_0 lower before a voiceless obstruent than before a voiced obstruent in some languages, the opposite of the usual F_0 pattern. However, no single property shown in Table 4.4 seems to be essential, as various studies have shown. Instead, they often participate in trading relations (see Chapter 3). Cross-linguistic variation in cues used for voicing has spawned debate over whether [±voice] is the best phonological label or if [±spread glottis] is more appropriate for certain languages, such as English and German (see e.g. Iverson and Salmons 1995).

Table 4.4 Properties associated with 'voiced' and 'voiceless' obstruents (see e.g. Lisker 1986; Kingston and Diehl 1994; Nittrouer 2004). Note that none of these is universal.

Property	*'Voiced' (lenis or non-spread glottis)*	*'Voiceless' (fortis or spread glottis)*
Adjacent F_0 contour	Depressed	Elevated
Adjacent F_1 contour	Strongly depressed	Not depressed as much
Approach of F_1 to closure	Closer	Less close
Duration of closure	Shorter	Longer
Duration of preceding vowel	Longer	Shorter
Glottal pulsing	May be present	Absent
Intensity of burst after closure	Greater	Lesser
Associated phonation	Aspiration and glottalization less likely	Aspiration and glottalization more likely

Dialectal variations can occur regarding which cues are realized. Purnell et al. (2005b) examined coda obstruents in four generations of German–American speech in Wisconsin. The German substrate neutralizes final /t/ and /d/ to [t]. They measured the proportion of the occlusion with glottal pulsing, the duration of the preceding vowel and the ratio of the vowel duration to the stop duration. They found that speakers born before World War I showed glottal pulsing during the occlusion for voiced obstruents, but didn't show the usual length difference on preceding vowels – in fact, some speakers actually showed longer durations before voiceless obstruents. To compensate, they lengthened the voiceless obstruents. It appeared that Germans had focused on particular cues to the exclusion of others when learning English. Speakers born between the two World Wars showed a more usual American English pattern, with much longer vowel durations before voiced obstruents. Speakers born after World War II, however, showed a diminishment of the differences between voiced and voiceless obstruents. In another study, Purnell et al. (2005a) measured, besides the cues from the first study, the F_0 and F_1 contours by comparing readings at the end of the steady state and at the vowel offset. They found that Wisconsin speakers lacked the F_0 and F_1 cues that are usually reported. They also added a perception experiment, showing that listeners could usually distinguish the voiced and voiceless obstruents of Wisconsin English but not those of German. Such differences in cues used for distinctions are probably fairly common, especially in language contact situations; see Thomas (2000) for another example.

4.9 Laterals

Laterals are characterized by sideways tilting of the tongue so that it forms a side pocket. The side pocket, in turn, is responsible for high-frequency antiformants. Laterals also typically show a high F_3. The antiformant may appear among a cluster that includes F_3, F_4 and sometimes F_5. Although lateral fricatives are known from many languages, lateral approximants have received most of the attention directed at laterals and more is known about their acoustics than about those of lateral fricatives. F_2 is often the key factor in variation associated with lateral approximants.

'Clear' and 'dark' /l/

An especially oft-studied lateral variable is the variation between 'clear' [l] and 'dark' [ɫ] types. Both have a coronal articulation, either apical or laminal. The essential difference is that [ɫ] also has a second articulation. A series of papers (Recasens et al. 1995; Recasens 1996; Recasens and Espinosa 2005) has revealed new information about [ɫ] and [l]. The second articulation for [ɫ] isn't always velar, as often reported – it may also be pharyngeal. The coronal contact is usually more dentoalveolar for [ɫ] and more alveolar for [l]. Finally, the distinction between [l] and [ɫ] is gradient, not categorical (see also Sproat and Fujimura 1993). These papers also demonstrated the utility of /l/ analyses for language variation, since they examined both cross-linguistic differences and dialectal differences within Catalan: Majorcan Catalan has darker /l/ than Valencian Catalan. Similar studies found darker /l/ in Leeds than in Newcastle-upon-Tyne, England (Carter and Local 2007) and that African American English has shifted diachronically towards darker /l/ (van Hofwegen 2009).

A variety of articulatory and acoustic methods have been used to gauge this difference. Acoustically, F_2 is the key factor. It is higher for [l] and lower for [ɫ]. In fact, it is so low for [ɫ] that [ɫ] can be hard to tell from [w]. Figure 4.38 shows a comparison of [ələ] and [əɫə]. Recasens et al. (1995) used only F_2 and F_2–F_1 measurements, but the lack of normalization meant that they had to base their findings on speakers of one sex. Espy-Wilson (1992) employed a suite of measurements, including raw and Bark-transformed differences between F_1 and F_0, F_2 and F_1, F_3 and F_2, and F_4 and F_3. The Bark transformation and subtraction served to normalize interspeaker differences in vocal tract length. For [l] vs [ɫ], the Z_3–Z_2 (i.e. Bark-transformed F_3/F_2 difference) distance is the most reliable indicator. Hawkins and Nguyen (2004) applied the spectral centre-of-gravity metric, described above for frication noise. Among articulatory techniques, X-rays (Giles and Moll 1975; Sproat and Fujimura 1993), MRI (Narayanan et al. 1997) and electropalatography (Recasens and Espinosa 2005) have all been productive for determining details such as the presence of the side cavity in lateralization and the exact placement of the tongue tip.

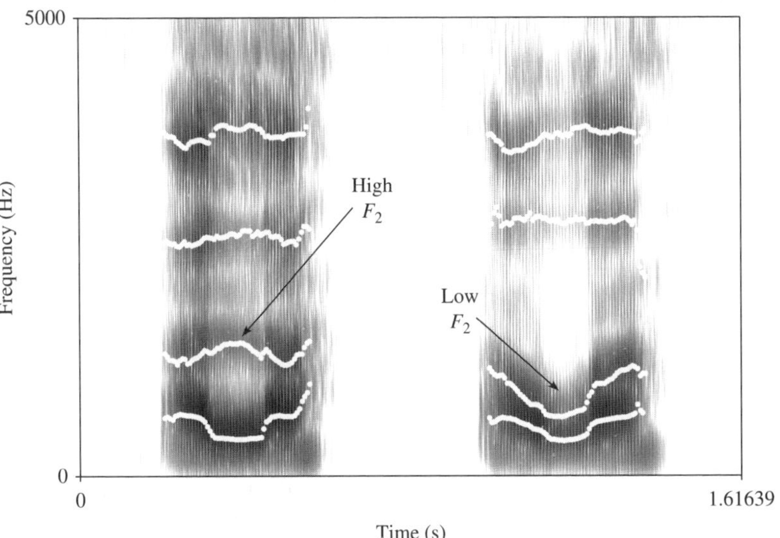

Figure 4.38 Spectrogram comparing [ələ] and [əɫə], in that order. Note how the F_2 frequency is much higher for [l] than for [ɫ].

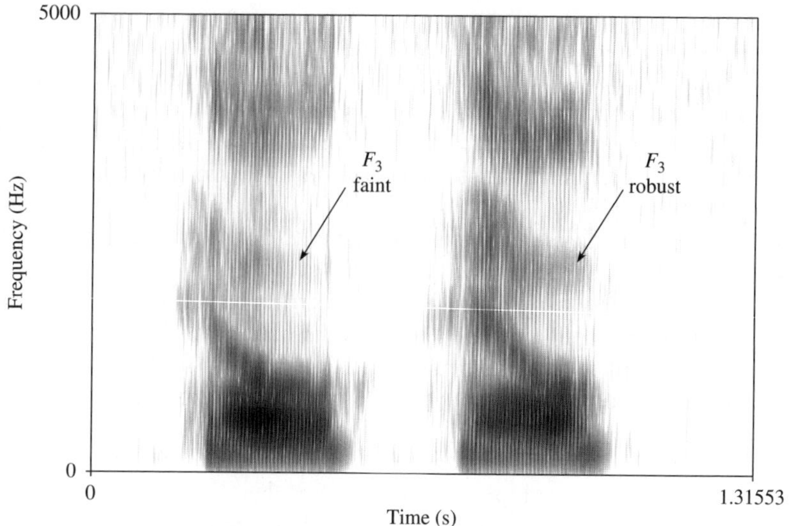

Figure 4.39 Comparison of the word *hill* produced as [hɪɫ] and, with vocalized /l/, as [hɪo]. The formant frequencies of [ɫ] and [o] are almost identical. However, F_3 has a lower amplitude for [ɫ], possibly with other faint formants near it, making the F_3 bandwidth wider for [ɫ].

Vocalization of [ɫ]

The 'dark' [ɫ] commonly shifts to or varies with back rounded vowels or [w]. This shift has occurred in Polish (Jonasson 1971) and numerous times in Romance languages (Recasens 1996) and is widespread in English today (Ohala 1974b; Thomas 2001; Gick 2002). It occurs mostly in syllable codas, though, probably because /l/ typically shows more velarization there than in onsets. Acoustically, [ɫ] is extraordinarily similar to [w~o] and difficult to distinguish on spectrograms, as Figure 4.39 shows. F_3 is fainter for [ɫ] than for [w~o], and correspondingly the F_3 bandwidth is greater for [ɫ] than for [w~o]. A nearby antiformant and two very faint adjacent formants may be the reason. Bandwidth may be the most reliable way to distinguish [ɫ] from [w~o] (Stevens and Blumstein 1994).

The palatal lateral

The palatal lateral [ʎ] has been a widespread sound in Romance languages. However, its propensity to shift to [j] has been nearly as widespread. Like [ɫ] and [w], [ʎ] and [j] are quite similar acoustically. [ʎ] shows a higher F_2 than [l] but approximately the same F_2 frequency as [j]. Colantoni (2004) reviewed various studies of [ʎ]. Collectively, they show [ʎ] exhibiting frequencies of both F_1 and F_3 varying from the same as to somewhat higher than those of [j]. Figure 4.40 shows a comparison of [əʎə] and [əjə]. The most obvious difference is that [j] shows a higher F_3 frequency than [ʎ]. Colantoni (personal communication) reported that her data corroborate the F_3 difference and show generally higher F_1 frequencies for [j] than for [ʎ] as well.

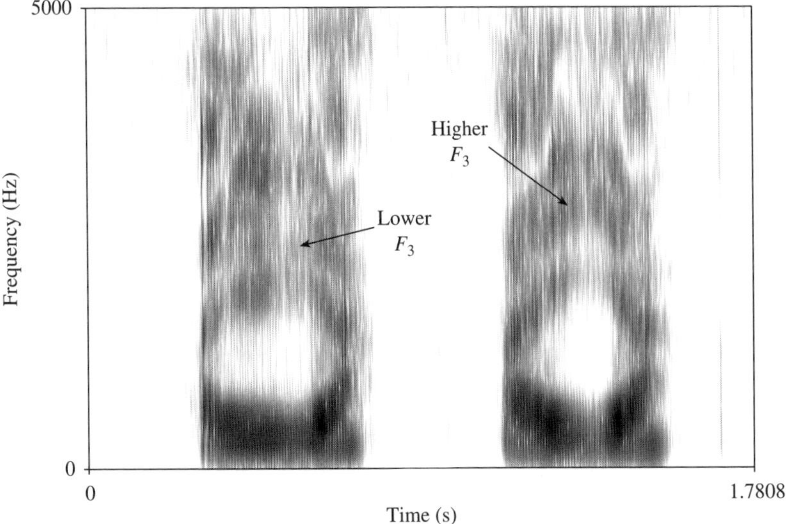

Figure 4.40 Spectrogram of [əʎə] and [əjə]. The most obvious difference is the higher F_3 frequency of [j] and the relatively low-amplitude F_3 of [ʎ], but in natural utterances [j] may tend to show a higher F_1 frequency, too.

4.10 Rhotics

The term *rhotic* is used for a collection of approximant and fricative sounds that often have little more in common than being spelled with *r* and being historically derived from an alveolar tap or trill (Ladefoged and Maddieson 1996). They may be trills, taps, approximants or fricatives. They may be produced using the tongue tip against the alveolar ridge or palate, the tongue dorsum against the uvula, or other manoeuvres such as the pharyngeal constriction typical of American English /r/. Lindau (1985) stated that there isn't any single physical property that unites rhotics. Instead, she said, they are related in steps – e.g. a uvular fricative is similar to a uvular trill, which resembles an apical trill, which shares properties with a retroflex approximant, and so on. Because rhotics are so diverse, the methods for analysing them acoustically lack overriding generalities. Hence the discussion here will move right to examples of variables.

Trills vs taps

This distinction is easy to recognize on spectrograms. Both involve bouncing one articulator off another one. The difference is that, for a tap (or flap), there is only one bounce – one vibration – while for a trill there are at least two. For alveolar taps and trills, the tongue tip vibrates against the alveolar ridge, and for uvular trills, the uvula vibrates against the tongue dorsum. Figure 4.41 illustrates the difference between an alveolar trill [r] and an alveolar tap [ɾ].

Incidentally, if you're wondering whether there's any difference between a tap and a flap, there is, technically. For a tap, the tongue tip moves backward,

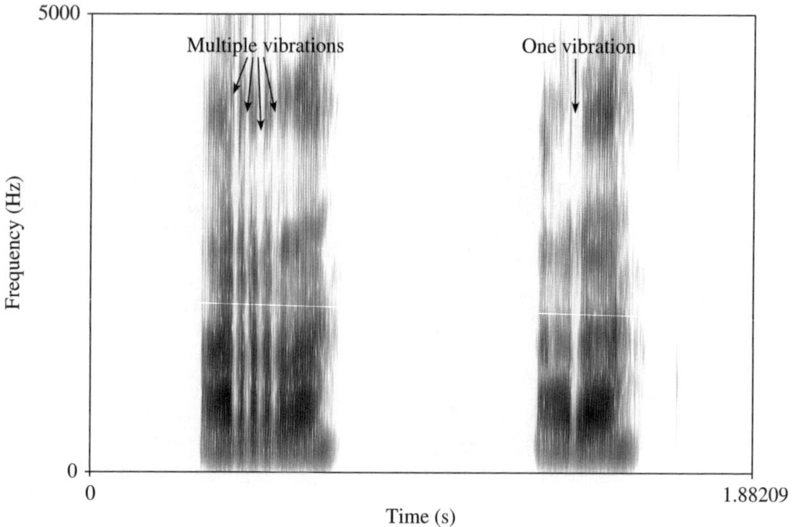

Figure 4.41 Comparison of an alveolar trill in [ərə] and an alveolar tap in [əɾə]. The trill shows several vibrations, the tap only one.

as in the /t/ in American English *potty*. For a flap, the tongue tip moves forward, as in the /t/ in American English *party* (for many speakers). The two don't sound noticeably different.

Assibilation of rhotics

In certain languages, rhotics can become sibilant fricatives. In some parts of Latin America, Spanish /rr/, as in *corre* 'run!', a trill in standard Spanish, may be produced as a voiced retroflex fricative, [ʐ]. In Turkish, prepausal /r/, as in *var* 'there is/are', is normally pronounced as a voiceless retroflex fricative, [ʂ]. An example from Turkish is shown in Figure 4.42. These forms are relatively easy to distinguish acoustically. Assibilated forms lack the vibratory patterns of trills or taps and there is some frication noise.

Uvular /r/

Uvular variants predominate as the rhotics in French, German and Danish, though apical variants can be heard in some dialects. Uvular rhotics also appear in some dialects of Norwegian (mostly in southern and western Norway), Swedish (in southern Sweden), Dutch (mostly in Limburg), in old-fashioned Northumbrian English, and as a phonologically conditioned allophone in Portuguese (in syllable onsets). Acoustically, the unifying feature of uvular sounds is their low F_2, combined with a somewhat high F_3. In contrast, apical rhotics show only a weak lowering effect on F_2 or none at all. The formant configuration can be measured at the offset of a preceding vowel or the onset of a following vowel. For uvular fricatives and non-trilled approximants, it may be measured within the uvular sound itself.

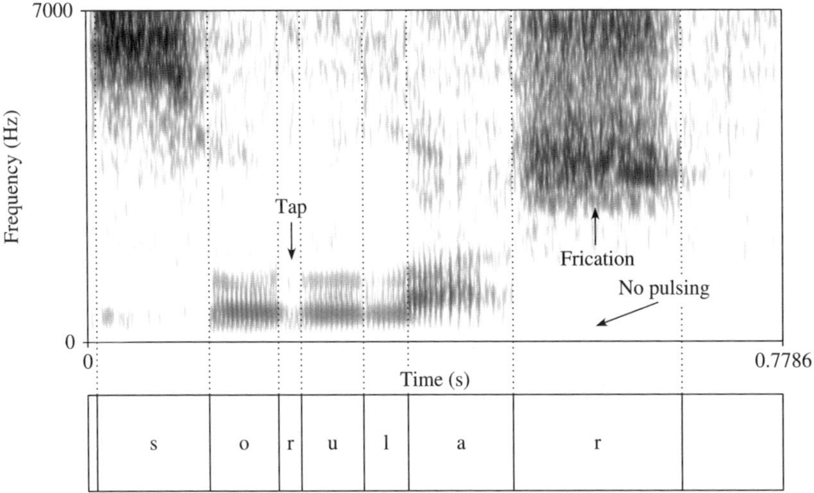

Figure 4.42 An utterance of the Turkish word *sorular* 'questions' uttered by a female native of Ankara, Turkey. She pronounced it as [ˌsɔɾɔˈɫɑʂ]. Although the intervocalic /r/ is tapped, the final /r/ is devoiced and fricated.

Not all uvular rhotics are the same. There are at least five or six different types, as well as similar vowels resulting from their vocalization. Demolin (2001) mentions four uvular forms as occurring in Belgian French: a voiced uvular trill [ʀ], a voiceless uvular trill [ʀ̥], a voiced uvular fricative [ʁ] and a voiceless uvular fricative [χ]. A fifth variant is a uvular approximant, [ʁ̞]. Wiese (2001) states that the uvular approximant is the standard German form. Presumably it may be devoiced next to a voiceless sound, and it apparently grades into velar approximants as well. Acoustically, the trills may be distinguished from the fricatives by the presence of obvious vibrations of the uvula. As with alveolar trills, the uvular vibrations appear as a series of short blank areas on a spectrogram. Voiced and voiceless forms are distinguished by the presence or absence of the low-frequency murmur caused by vocal fold vibrations. Approximants are difficult to distinguish from voiced fricatives. The main thing to focus on is whether the higher formants are periodic, for an approximant, or noisy, for a fricative. Figure 4.43 juxtaposes [əʀə] with a trill, [əʁə] with a fricative, and [əʁ̞ə] with an approximant.

Bunched-tongue and retroflex /r/

The rhotics of English have generated a great deal of controversy over the years. Although tapped [ɾ] may still be heard in Scottish and Welsh English, intervocalically as in *very* in some varieties in England, and after /θ/ as in *through* and *three* in certain dialects, other forms predominate, and they have been hard to describe. The only commonality that has been agreed on about these other forms is that they share the acoustic characteristic of a lowered F_3. Early twentieth-century discussions of the articulation of /r/ in English

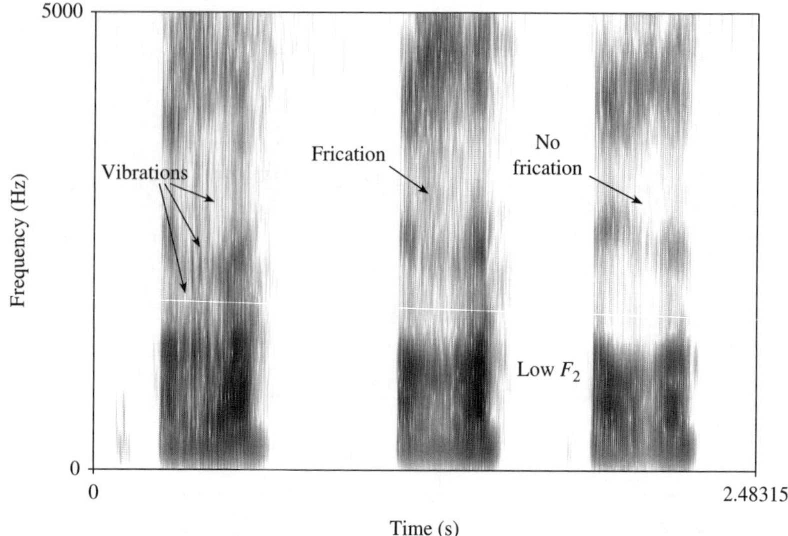

Figure 4.43 Spectrogram comparing three uvular rhotics: a trill in [əʀə], a voiced fricative in [əʁə] and an approximant in [əʁ̞ə]. The vibratory pattern readily distinguishes [ʀ]. [ʁ] is told from [ʁ̞] by the presence of some frication noise. Note the low F_2 frequency for all three uvular sounds.

variously described it as a retroflex approximant, an alveolar approximant, or a 'bunched-tongue' or 'bunched' approximant in which the body of the tongue was retracted. A milestone was Delattre and Freeman's (1968) X-ray study of /r/ by 43 Americans and three Britons. They found that different speakers didn't all articulate /r/ the same way – in fact, they listed eight different articulatory types!

Delattre and Freeman (1968) also discovered that American English /r/ exhibits more than one constriction. The articulation with the tongue tip for a retroflex or alveolar approximant or with the tongue dorsum for a bunched approximant was already known. The X-ray data revealed that there was another constriction in the pharynx. Thus the American English /r/ has three cavities: one between the glottis and the pharyngeal constriction, another between the pharyngeal and dorsal or apical constrictions, and the third in front of the dorsal or apical constriction, including the space underneath the tongue.

A third constriction is possible, too – one at the lips. Zawadzki and Kuehn (1980) noted that /r/ showed more lip protrusion in syllable onsets than in syllable nuclei or codas. My own observations suggest that this tendency is a fairly rigid rule in North American and perhaps other varieties of English. That is, the target value for onset /r/ involves lip rounding but the target value for nuclear and coda /r/ doesn't. When coda /r/ shows labial constriction, it is due to coarticulation with neighbouring sounds. The lip rounding further lowers the F_2 and F_3 of onset /r/.

Data in Delattre and Freeman (1968) suggest that most Americans make a dorsal constriction for /r/. However, it's not that simple. Westbury et al. (1998)

found that bunched and retroflex /r/ types lie on a continuum of articulation. They also noted considerable intraspeaker variation. Espy-Wilson et al. (2000) sorted the variation into three types: retroflex, tip-down bunched (the 'pure' bunched form) and a form with aspects of both, which they called tip-up bunched. It had long been thought that only articulatory techniques such as X-rays or ultrasound could differentiate these articulations. Recently, however, Zhou et al. (2008) suggested that F_4 frequency may differentiate them. They noted that F_4 was quite close to F_5 for bunched /r/ but significantly lower for retroflex /r/. Figure 4.44 compares retroflex /r/, tip-up bunched and tip-down bunched. They all exhibit a low F_3, but F_4 has a much higher frequency for the two bunched types than for the retroflex /r/. Hence, the Bark-converted F_3/F_4 distance could be used as a distinguishing metric.

Another possible way of differentiating retroflex from bunched /r/ is to examine coarticulation with a following coronal consonant. A following /s/ or /z/ should yield a clearly audible [ʂ] or [ʐ], respectively, for a retroflex variant but not for a bunched variant. This process occurs categorically in most dialects of Swedish and Norwegian: i.e., /rd/→[ɖ], /rs/→[ʂ], and so forth (Popperwell 1963, Torp 2001).

'Labiodental' /r/ in British English

A recent development in the English of England is a shift in /r/ to some sort of labial approximant (e.g. Trudgill 1988; Foulkes and Docherty 2000). It is conventionally transcribed as the labiodental approximant [ʋ] – e.g. *red* [ʋɛd] – but its exact articulation seems to vary. Docherty and Foulkes (2001) suggest

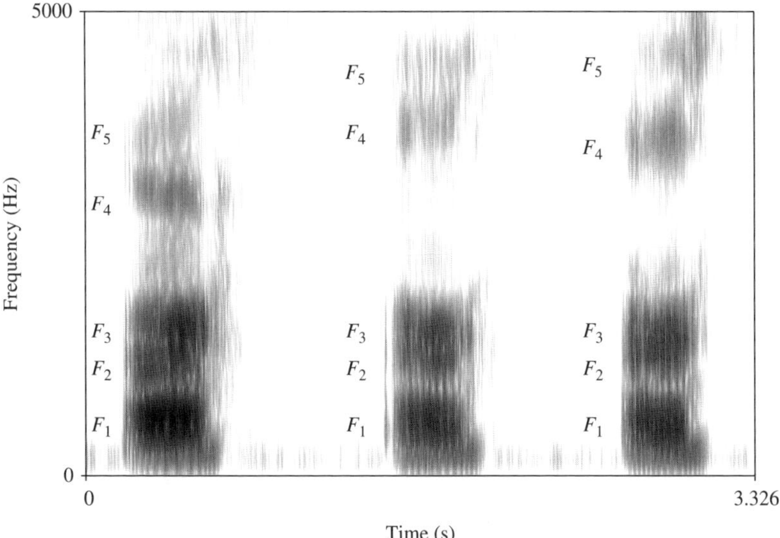

Figure 4.44 Spectrogram comparing retroflex, tip-up bunched and tip-down bunched /r/ variants, in that order. Note how F_4 has a lower frequency for the retroflex form than for the two bunched forms.

both [ʋ] and a bilabial approximant [β] as possible realizations, and there may be others. Unlike the bunched and retroflex /r/ types, its F_3 frequency isn't lowered at all (Foulkes and Docherty 2000; Docherty and Foulkes 2001). A way of distinguishing labial /r/ from bunched and retroflex types is to find a speaker's overall mean F_3 value for his or her vowels and then compare the F_3 of the /r/ token with it. Subtract the /r/ F_3 from the overall mean vowel F_3. Hagiwara (1995: 120–21) found that F_3 for /r/ was usually 60–70 per cent, though sometimes as high as 80 per cent, of the overall mean vowel F_3 for American English speakers. A labial /r/, then, shouldn't have its F_3 less than 80 per cent of the speaker's overall mean vowel F_3, and probably no less than 90 per cent. However, using a threshold value misses the point somewhat. The real strength of this quantification is that it will give you a continuous scale.

Non-rhoticity

Rhotic sounds frequently shift to vowels or disappear altogether. This process is usually limited to phrase-final and preconsonantal contexts and it is often called *non-rhoticity* or *r-lessness*. In German, for example, final and preconsonantal /r/ is usually realized as a low vowel that, by convention, is transcribed phonetically as [ɐ] – e.g. *dort* 'there' [dɔɐt]. This sort of vowel is the expected result of vocalization of a uvular /r/, which predominates in most German-speaking areas today. However, non-rhoticity is most heavily studied in English. The low F_3 of the /r/ sounds found in most dialects of English is quite salient and makes rhotic and non-rhotic variants easy to recognize. Of course, even in English there's a gradation between them. In English, a word such as *four* is realized as something close to [foɹ] in rhotic dialects and as [foə], [fɔː] or similar forms in non-rhotic dialects. The convention of writing vocalized /r/ in English as [ə] is just that – a convention. The actual quality of the vowel varies quite a bit.

Acoustically, non-rhoticity is recognized by a lack of particular qualities. Where an alveolar tap /r/ is the norm, non-rhoticity is realized as the absence of the brief blank space on a spectrogram left by the tongue tip vibration. Non-rhoticity is harder to gauge in languages with uvular /r/. Uvular approximants grade imperceptibly into [ɐ]-like vowels. Approximants tend to have lower amplitude than vowels, so a lack of a rapid dip in amplitude can indicate vocalization.

In English, F_3 is the key to gauging rhoticity. Espy-Wilson et al. (2000: 344) summarize data from several previous studies and state that, across sex, position within syllables, and other factors, mean F_3 values for American English /r/ generally fall within a range of 1,300–1,950 Hz. However, those are mean values, and, as Hagiwara (1995) noted, 'good' /r/ tokens can have noticeably higher F_3 values than that. Various speakers I've measured and who impressionistically sound rhotic show F_3 frequencies as high as 2,300 Hz for males and 2,800 Hz for females. What is important is that the F_3 has to be significantly lower than the speaker's F_3 values for non-rhotic vowels. There are a couple of ways you could distinguish rhotic and non-rhotic pronunciations in English. One is the same method described above for identifying labial /r/. That is, find the speaker's mean F_3 value for his or her vowels, measure F_3 for the /r/

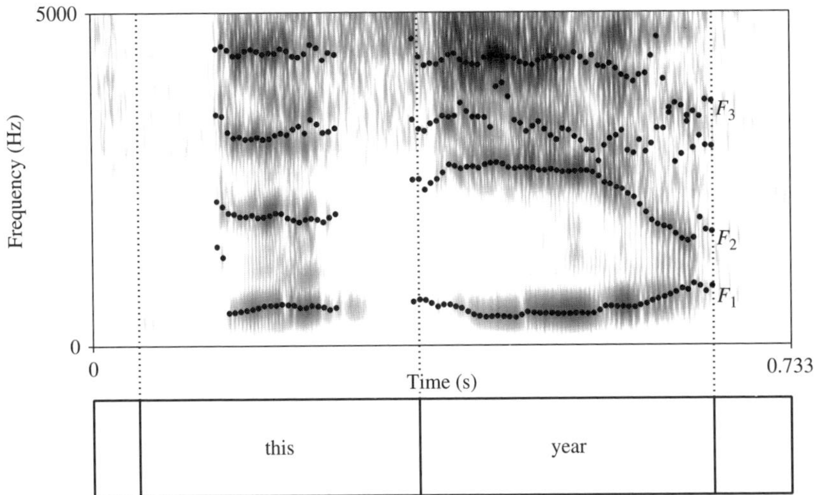

Figure 4.45 A non-rhotic exemplar of *year* in the phrase *this year*, uttered in conversation as [ˈjiə] by a female Bahamian. The schwa glide doesn't show the strong F_3 lowering effect associated with rhoticity in English: its F_3 is higher than F_3 of the vowel in *this*. Note that the superimposed LPC formant track shows some false readings below F_3 for the glide.

token, and subtract the /r/ F_3 from the overall mean vowel F_3. As noted above, Hagiwara (1995) found that 'good' rhotic tokens had values up to 80 per cent of the overall mean vowel F_3. The other method would be to convert the F_2 and F_3 of the /r/ to Bark (after which they're called Z_2 and Z_3) and then subtract Z_2 from Z_3. Data from Ocumpaugh (2001), who compared acoustic measurements against auditory rhoticity ratings by judges, suggest that the threshold of Z_3–Z_2 for rhoticity is about 3.0 Bark, but there was some overlap between tokens judged as rhotic and non-rhotic. Different listeners may have different thresholds. High front vowels also show a close approximation of F_2 and F_3, but that is not usually a problem for this method because non-rhotic dialects usually have a clear schwa-like glide for the NEAR and SQUARE vowels, and that glide is what you measure. Figure 4.45 illustrates a non-rhotic token.

4.11 Deletion of consonants

Deletion is one of the most common of sound changes, and a number of consonantal deletion processes are among the more frequently studied sociolinguistic variables. For example, the loss of /h/, as in [ɛd] 'head', is well known from studies of British English dialects. Perhaps the most heavily studied consonantal variable in American English is consonant cluster reduction, in which word-final stops in clusters are lost – e.g. [pʰæs] 'past', [tʰoɫ] 'told'. In Spanish, deletion of voiced fricatives derived from voiced stops, such as [toː~to] *todo* 'all', is quite common.

Deletion can seem deceptive. Generally, what you look for is the absence of acoustic properties of the deleted segment. A missing stop closure, for example, can be taken as a sign that the stop isn't present. Nevertheless, loss of a segment isn't necessarily categorical. Segments that are 'lost' often leave behind remnants, such as compensatory lengthening of the preceding segment, nasalization of a preceding vowel for a deleted nasal stop, or tones resulting from the F_0 patterns related to the voicing of a deleted consonant. Hence, you often have to decide how deleted a consonant has to be before it's 'deleted', or, more to the point, which articulatory gestures are essential for the consonant to be 'present'. For example, you might consider a nasal to be absent if there's no occlusion, even if the nasality is preserved on the preceding vowel. Even that criterion has a pitfall, though. When you base your judgement on acoustic data, you can't see just what's going on inside the speaker's mouth. As Browman and Goldstein (1990, 1991) point out, sounds can sometimes be camouflaged by neighbouring segments. In an example they use, the /t/ in *perfect memory*, if unreleased, can be completely camouflaged by the neighbouring [k~c] and [m] so that it leaves no detectable acoustic trace, even if the speaker's tongue tip reaches the alveolar ridge. Thus, unless you have direct articulatory evidence, you need to keep in mind that you're describing what's audible, not necessarily everything that's really going on.

EXERCISES

For the following exercises, you can download practice samples from http://ncslaap.lib.ncsu.edu/sociophonetics/.

1. Download the samples of [d̪] vs [ð], [tʰ] vs [ts], [tʃ] vs [ʃ], [n] vs [ŋ], laminal [s] vs apical [s], [l] vs [ɫ], [ɫ] vs [w], [ʎ] vs [j], [r] vs [ʀ], and bunched [ɹ] vs retroflex [ɻ], but don't listen to them! See if you can distinguish them by analysing the acoustic signals.
2. Plot locus equations for [b], [d] and [g] using your own voice. Say each sound in a variety of environments, such as [bi], [be], [bæ], [bɑ], [bo] and [bu], and then measure the vowel transitions in the way the text explains.
3. Download the adult male and child utterances of [s] and [ʃ]. Determine the peak frequency, the four spectral moments and A_d, S_p and S'_p for the fricative of each utterance. How do the adult male and child values overlap?
4. Download the practice VOT signals. Measure the VOT for each syllable-initial stop.
5. What steps would you take in figuring out how to tell the difference, acoustically, between a pair of sounds not covered in this chapter – for example, velar [k] vs uvular [q], alveolar [n] vs palatal nasal [ɲ], or lateral fricative [ɬ] vs post-alveolar [ʃ]? Hint: try producing the sounds yourself (or have a trained phonetician say them) and compare them on spectrograms.
6. If you're lucky enough to have access to ultrasound equipment, have a subject say various consonants while the ultrasound sensor is held under the subject's jaw. Practise drawing the different articulations based on the ultrasound images.

FURTHER READING

Cho, Taehong and Peter Ladefoged. 1999. Variations and universals in VOT: Evidence from 18 languages. *Journal of Phonetics* 27:207–29.

Docherty, Gerard J. and Paul Foulkes. 1999. Derby and Newcastle: Instrumental phonetics and variationist studies. In Paul Foulkes and Gerard J. Docherty (eds), *Urban Voices: Accent Studies in the British Isles*. London: Arnold, 47–71.

Ladefoged, Peter and Ian Maddieson. 1996. *The Sounds of the World's Languages*. Oxford, UK/Malden, MA: Blackwell.

Lisker, Leigh. 1986. 'Voicing' in English: A catalogue of acoustic features signaling /b/ versus /p/ in trochees. *Language and Speech* 29:3–11.

Purnell, Thomas, Joseph Salmons, Dilara Tepeli and Jennifer Mercer. 2005. Structured heterogeneity and change in laryngeal phonetics: Upper Midwestern final obstruents. *Journal of English Linguistics* 33:307–38.

Recasens, Daniel and Aina Espinosa. 2005. Articulatory, positional and coarticulatory characteristics for clear /l/ and dark /l/: Evidence from two Catalan dialects. *Journal of the International Phonetic Association* 35:1–25.

Vowels

5

5.1 Vowels in context

When dialectologists or sociolinguists study vowels, they nearly always focus on vowel quality, including height (the high/mid/low continuum), advancement (frontness/backness) and rounding. Sometimes, but far less often, they gauge vowel duration. Diphthongs typically show special constraints involving when their formants don't change values much and when they do, and the process of undershoot creates complicated patterns of its own. Here we'll discuss how to measure each of these factors. Acoustic studies of vocalic variation are better developed than those in any other realm of variation, so there's a lot to cover in this chapter.

Before we move on, a word about how vowel quality is affected by speech style is in order. We will discuss more of the particulars of style in Chapter 11. For now, let's note the observed general patterns and how they should affect your decisions about which styles to draw your tokens from. The least formal styles are best for extracting naturalistic tokens, largely because speakers take on the fewest pretensions in their least formal speech. As styles become more formal, speakers become more affected by non-local speech norms. They avoid stigmatized variants. Reading passage style, for instance, is reliable for most vowels – the tokens are usually representative of the subject's speech – but can be unreliable for variables for which a strong stigma is associated with one variant. In the most formal styles, as when speakers read minimal pairs, speakers' conscious knowledge of the language – often influenced by spelling – sometimes intrudes and skews the output further, leading them to make distinctions that they would never make in casual speech or to lose contrasts that they consistently make in casual speech. As a result, sociolinguists have long favoured casual speech as their object of study.

This practice contrasts with that of most phoneticians, who usually favour citation-form speech. Citation-form speech, whether in word lists or in carrier phrases, has two advantages of its own. For one thing, it yields more heavily stressed, longer tokens than most of those in conversational speech. As a result, the tokens in citation-form speech approximate their phonetic targets more closely than most tokens from conversational speech and hence show less coarticulation and undershoot (see section 5.9). For another, the words elicited in citation-form speech can be controlled, which is why even sociolinguists often use reading passages and minimal pairs. Controlling the words obtained can help you get comparable phonetic contexts for different vowels and can also ensure that rare vowel classes, such as the CHOICE vowel in English, are represented. The upshot is that you should consider whether it's more important in your study for your data to be naturalistic or to show less undershoot.

5.2 Duration

Duration is a natural starting point for vowel analysis. It's simpler than other vowel parameters to measure: you merely determine the distance between the *onset* of the vowel and its *offset*. The onset is the beginning of the vowel, where the transition from a preceding segment begins, and the offset is the end, where the transition to the following segment ends. The only real difficulty is in deciding what the onset and offset are.

Determination of onset and offset

Figuring out what constitutes the onset or offset can be tricky. Not only that, but you have some options on what rules you can follow here. The key is to be consistent – choose the guidelines you want to follow and then stick with them.

The easiest scenario occurs when an initial vowel follows a pause. Usually, you can equate onset of the vowel with the beginning of voicing. Keep in mind, though, that in some languages, such as German and, often, English, a glottal stop will precede an initial vowel. Glottalization is manifested as greatly slowed vocal fold vibration. In this case, you have a decision to make: you may equate the onset either with the first vocal fold vibration or with the point where the vocal fold vibration becomes faster and more regular. Figure 5.1 illustrates these options.

If the vowel whose duration you're measuring comes after a stop, you can use the burst as a reference point. Figure 5.2 shows a stop release. As for the onset of the vowel, you may place it at the beginning, in the centre or immediately after the burst, but again, be consistent about which placement you use. When the preceding stop is aspirated, as with English and German voiceless stops, the burst will occur long before the vowel commences. In this case, you should equate the onset with the beginning of voicing, as in Figure 5.3.

A preceding fricative will lack the burst. Voiceless fricatives are usually easy to deal with. Normally, you can take the beginning of voicing as the onset of the vowel after a voiceless fricative, but if you're not sure, go with where F_2 suddenly becomes clear. Voiced fricatives are not as easy because the voicing continues straight through from the fricative to the vowel. Even so, you'll normally see a point where F_2 suddenly appears, and that's what you can define as the vowel onset. Figures 5.4 and 5.5 illustrate vowels with preceding voiceless and voiced fricatives, respectively.

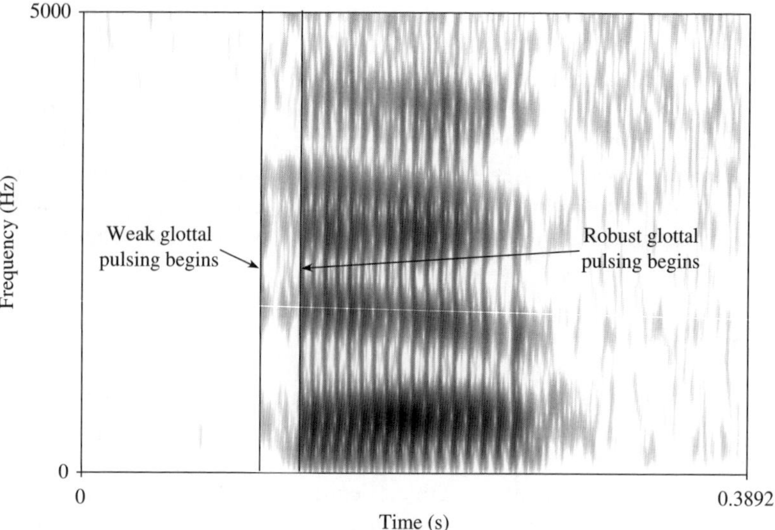

Figure 5.1 Spectrogram showing glottal stop before initial vowel in the word *if* and choices on where to start measuring the vowel. Weak glottal pulsing occurs during the glottal stop, followed by more robust glottal pulsing. The onset of either one could be treated as the vowel onset.

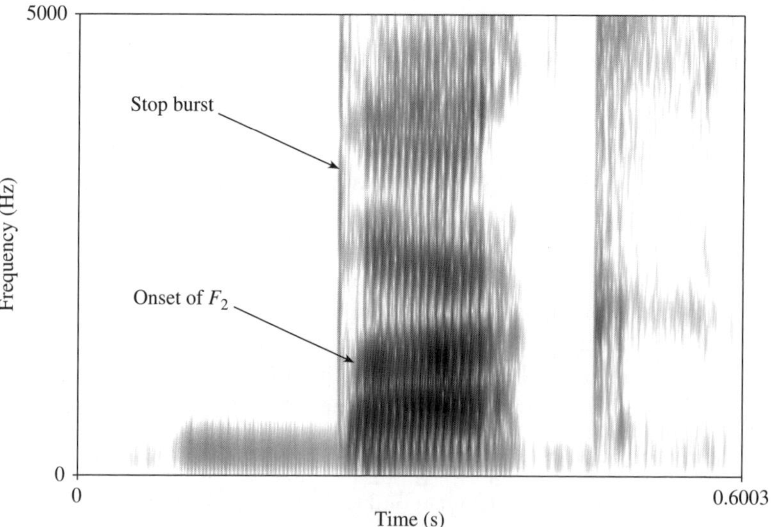

Figure 5.2 Spectrogram showing the location of a stop burst in the word *buck*. Here, the onset of the vowel can be aligned either with the burst or with the onset of glottal pulsing for F_2.

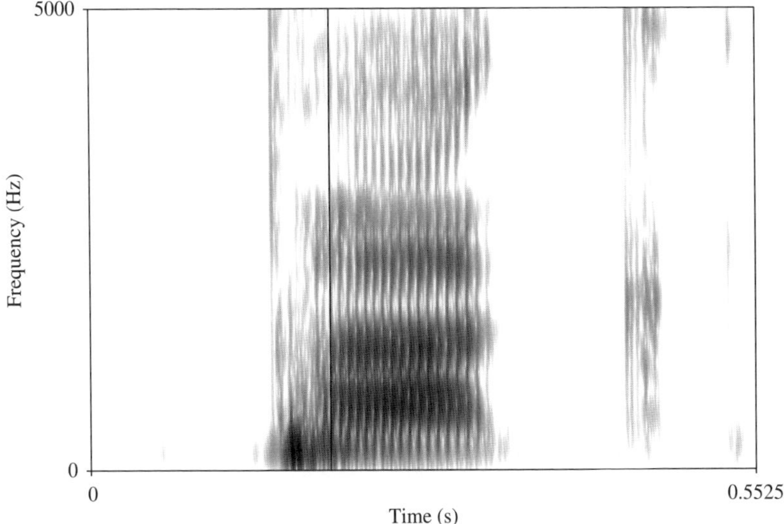

Figure 5.3 Spectrogram of the word *puck* showing where to mark the onset of a vowel when it follows an aspirated stop. Here, the onset of glottal pulsing for the vowel, indicated by the line, should be treated as the vowel onset.

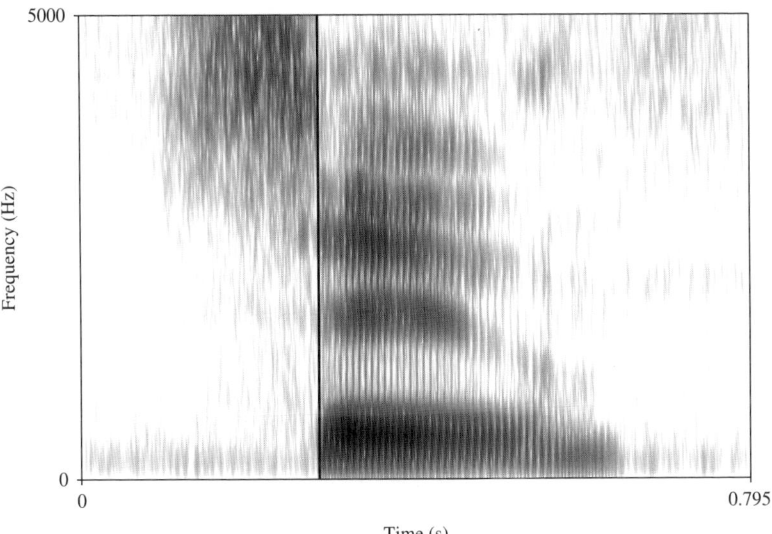

Figure 5.4 Spectrogram of a vowel with a preceding voiceless fricative in the word *sue*. The onset of vowel formants, indicated by the vertical line, should be treated as the vowel onset. In this case, the frication noise ceases at the same point.

Obstruents that follow vowels obey most of the same rules, except that bursts cannot occur there. In general, the best rule is to look for the point where F_2 seems to vanish. If the following consonant is voiceless, you can also watch for the point where voicing ceases, which will usually coincide with the point

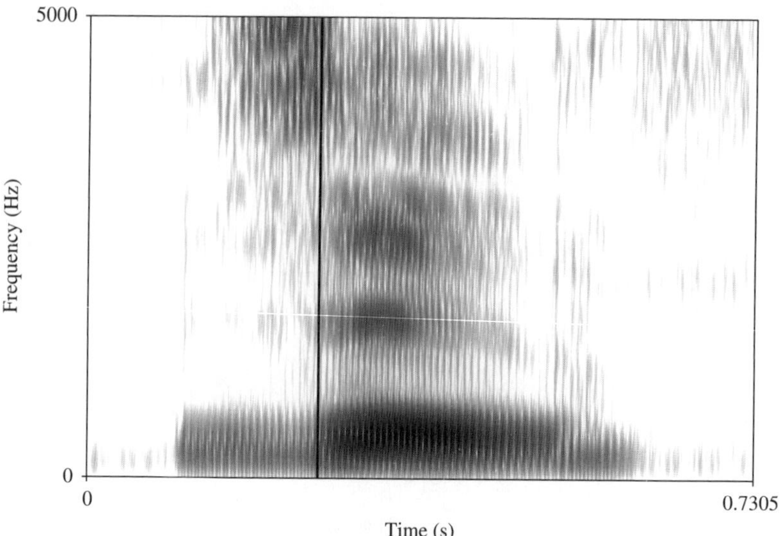

Figure 5.5 Spectrogram of a vowel with a preceding voiced fricative in the word *zoo*. The onset of glottal pulsing for vowel formants, especially F_2, should be treated as the vowel onset. In this example, that onset isn't clear-cut, but it occurs approximately where the vertical line is.

where F_2 disappears. However, voiceless consonants sometimes don't show an abrupt boundary with a preceding vowel. Instead, the vowel may gradually trail off into aspiration. The same problem crops up frequently with vowels before a pause. In these cases, you have another choice to make. One option is to look for a spot where the vocal fold vibrations become more or less unrecognizable or start looking more like the staticky pattern of aspiration than the sharper pattern usually evident with vocal fold vibrations. Often, the best way to determine this spot is by moving the cursor to different spots and listening; after a certain point, all you can hear is aspiration, and that point is where you mark the offset. The other option is to mark the offset at the end of the recognizable aspiration, though this point may be quite difficult to define. Figure 5.6 shows an example with both options marked.

When the neighbouring segment is an approximant, there is often (depending on which approximant it is) no clear boundary between the approximant and the vowel at all. For [w], [j] and [ɹ], there is never a clear boundary, while for trills and taps there usually is, and laterals vary. Without a clear boundary, the decision on where to demarcate the onset or offset can get pretty arbitrary. There are some options for these troublesome approximants, though. One is to follow the model of steady states and transitions discussed below in section 5.8 and identify the onset or offset either with the beginning of the transitional period between approximant and vowel or with its end. Another method that I find useful for approximants that precede vowels involves splicing off pieces of the acoustic signal. As more and more of a preceding [w], for example, is removed, the [w] eventually begins to sound like [b], and the point at which it does so can be taken as the onset. Similarly, a preceding [ɹ] will

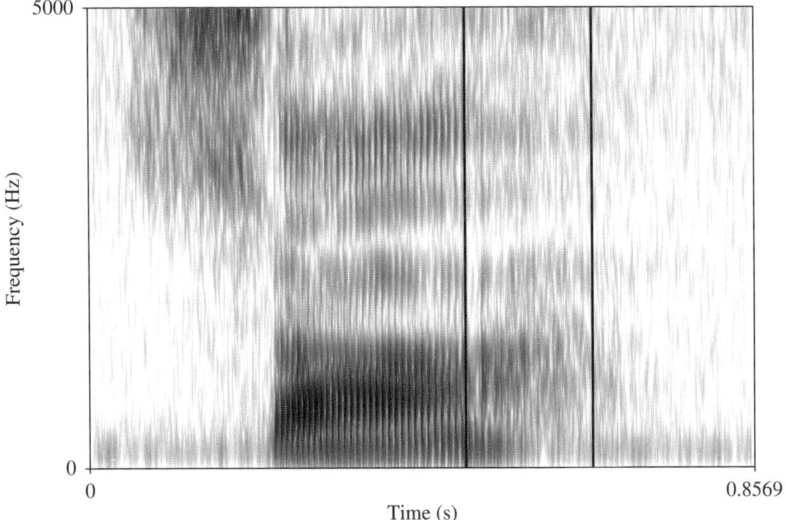

Figure 5.6 Spectrogram of vowel before a pause, trailing off into aspiration, in the word *saw*. The first line indicates where the glottal pulses become breathy. The second line indicates where the formants become indistinct. Either timepoint could be treated as the offset of the vowel.

begin to sound something like [b] and a preceding [j] more or less like [g] at a certain point.

Contrastive length and other uses of duration

A variety of linguistic processes affect vowel duration. One factor is *contrastive length*. In languages with contrastive length, some vowels are phonologically short and others are phonologically long. This opposition is common among the world's languages but is usually subsumed within the tense/lax opposition in Germanic languages. Even in English, though, length can appear as the primary contrastive mechanism for certain vowels in some dialects. For example, in Southern Hemisphere English, the vowel in *cut* may have the same quality as the vowel in *cart* but be distinguished by length, i.e. *cut* [kʰat] vs *cart* [kʰaːt]. Similarly, I have found speakers from the Great Lakes region of the United States who distinguish *bed* and *bad* primarily by length, i.e. *bed* [bɛd] and *bad* [bɛːd].[1] When you encounter contrastive length, don't expect the long vowels to show durations twice those of short vowels. Ordinarily, long vowels show durations only about 50 per cent longer than those of short vowels, and often the difference is even less than that. Apparently, though, that's enough for listeners to recognize the distinction.

Another use of durational differences is as cues for the identities of segments. As I just mentioned, Germanic languages use duration as part of their tense/lax distinction, with 'tense' vowels longer than 'lax' vowels. Also pertaining to vowels is the fact that, on average, lower vowels show longer durations than higher vowels, probably because it takes longer to lower the jaw and/or tongue enough to produce a low vowel than it does for a high vowel. Another well-known use of duration is as a cue to whether a following consonant is phonologically voiced or voiceless (e.g. House and Fairbanks 1953; Denes 1955). Vowel durations are normally quite a bit longer before a voiced consonant than they are before a voiceless consonant, often close to 50 per cent longer. This difference is an important perceptual cue to the voicing of the following consonant. There is some evidence that its magnitude varies from language to language (Keating 1985:120–4), suggesting the possibility of cross-dialectal and sociolinguistic variation, though there is also conflicting evidence about the cross-linguistic differences (Laeufer 1992). Less well known is that vowels tend to be slightly longer before a fricative than they are before a stop (Peterson and Lehiste 1960).

Prosodic factors can affect vowel duration as well. One of the most dramatic of these is *pre-pausal lengthening*, which causes any syllable or foot immediately before a pause to be lengthened (e.g. Klatt 1987, Wightman et al. 1992). (A *foot* is a stressed syllable plus any unstressed syllables that follow it immediately.) This effect is so pervasive that it even affects music: in a stanza, the final note is almost always lengthened, and it sounds weird to our ears if it's not. Among other prosodic effects on vowel duration, stressed vowels may be longer than unstressed vowels, depending on the language. The stress effect occurs robustly in Germanic languages but quite weakly in most Romance languages. A speaker's overall rate of speech can also have quite a bit of influence on the durations of individual vowels – the faster the overall rate of speech, the shorter the durations of individual vowels will be.

Prosodic factors that influence vowel duration bring up another issue. You may need to normalize for rate of speech before you can examine contrastive or contextual vowel length. To do that, you'll need two formulas, taken from Wassink (2006). The first one creates a grand mean for each speaker:

$$\text{Grand mean} = \text{mean of (mean duration of each vowel phoneme)}$$

That is, you compute the mean duration for each vowel phoneme or class and then compute the mean of all those mean values. Then the second formula gives you the normalized duration for each vowel token:

$$\text{Normalized duration} = \text{(duration of individual token)} - \text{(grand mean)}$$

Perception of duration

Duration is readily incorporated into perception experiments. One easy method is to vary the duration of a vowel by intervals and play the resulting stimuli to listeners. Because vowels are longer before voiced consonants than before voiceless consonants in most languages – at least those that contrast consonant voicing in syllable codas – you can test to see where the point is at which subjects switch from hearing a 'voiceless' consonant to hearing a 'voiced' one. Or, in a language or dialect with contrastive length, you can use the same kind of stimuli to determine where the boundary is between a phonologically short vowel and a phonologically long one. More complicated experiments could examine words in carrier sentences where an ambiguity is possible or test to see how the overall rate of speech affects the boundaries.

5.3 Applying vowel formant analysis

Analysis of vowel quality has maintained a central role in studies of lectal variation in languages, such as most Germanic languages, that have complex vowel inventories and, as a result, show unstable vowel configurations. The instability, of course, is what provides the working material for all sorts of lectal cleavage within societies. In decades past, dialect geographers relied on narrow impressionistic transcription to determine distributions of variables. Sociolinguists adopted impressionistic transcription as well, though they usually avoided the level of transcription detail that dialect geographers employed. However, acoustic analysis of vowels has become more and more widespread over the past few decades even though it is more time-consuming than impressionistic analysis. Its advantage is that it eliminates much (though not all) of the subjectivity and interpractitioner variability that pervades impressionistic analysis and that the editors of dialect atlases struggled with. We covered how to perform formant analysis in Chapter 2. Now we'll look at how it relates to vowels that you analyse.

Relationship of formants to vowel quality

Vowel height, vowel advancement and rounding are all reflected in vowel formant values. With height and advancement, the relationship with formant values is quite straightforward. Height is inversely proportional to the value of F_1, so that high vowels have low F_1 values and low vowels have high F_1 values. Advancement is directly proportional to F_2 value, so that vowels more to the front have higher F_2 values, while vowels more to the back have lower F_2 values. For rounding, the relationship is less straightforward. In general, rounding lowers formant values, but it doesn't lower all formants to the same degree, and its effects vary according to the height and, especially, the advancement of the vowel. The general rule of thumb is that, for back vowels, rounding mainly lowers F_1 and F_2, while for front vowels, rounding mainly lowers F_2 and F_3. Thus, a comparison of [i] and [y] – the high front unrounded and rounded vowels, respectively – shows that they have practically the same F_1 value, but that [y] shows lower F_2 and F_3 values than [i]. Conversely, [ɑ] and [ɒ], the two low back vowels, have similar F_3 values, but the rounded [ɒ] shows lower F_1 and F_2 values than the unrounded [ɑ]. Table 5.1 and the F_1/F_2 plot in Figure 5.7 show mean values of the 'Cardinal Vowels', as uttered by their creator, the British phonetician Daniel Jones, that I measured from an old recording.[2] The Cardinal Vowel system was an attempt to standardize impressionistic transcription to make it more useful

Table 5.1 Formant values of the Cardinal Vowels, as uttered by Daniel Jones.

Cardinal Vowel number	*Vowel symbol*	*Number of tokens*	*Mean F_1*	*Mean F_2*	*Mean F_3*
1	[i]	7	266	2581	3627
2	[e]	7	376	2213	2652
3	[ɛ]	7	588	1910	2328
4	[a]	7	929	1688	2354
5	[ɑ]	7	650	940	2472
6	[ɔ]	7	522	932	2180
7	[o]	7	354	724	2348
8	[u]	7	248	490	2512
9	[y]	5	289	2231	2747
10	[ø]	5	353	1946	2375
11	[œ]	5	554	1549	2158
12	[ɶ]	5	722	1227	2180
13	[ɒ]	5	582	769	2150
14	[ʌ]	5	542	1145	2273
15	[ɤ]	5	469	1153	2282
16	[ɯ]	5	337	1275	2180
17	[ɨ]	4	312	2078	2544
18	[ʉ]	4	285	1487	2066

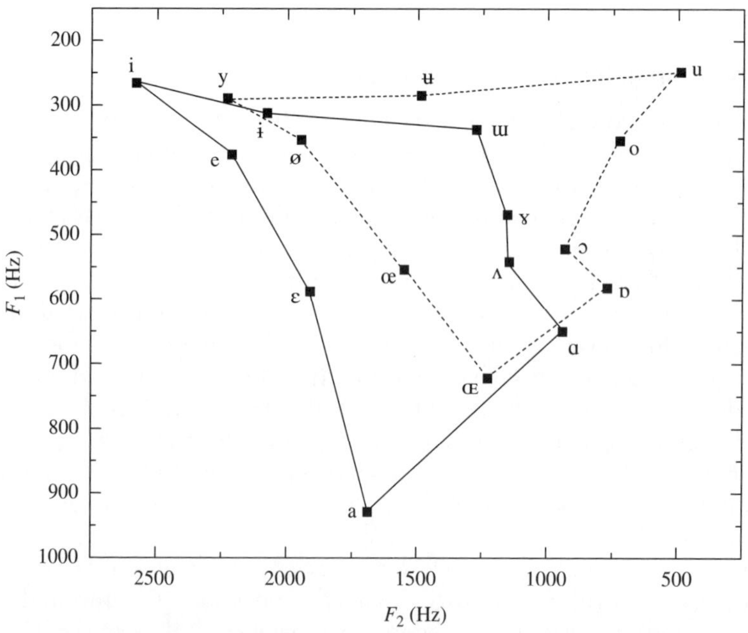

Figure 5.7 Formant plot of the Cardinal Vowels, as spoken by Daniel Jones. Each point represents the mean of several utterances. Solid lines connect unrounded vowels, and dashed lines connect rounded vowels.

for interlanguage comparisons (see Jones 1966). The vowels occur in pairs consisting of a rounded and an unrounded vowel. In the plot, unrounded vowels are connected by solid lines and rounded vowels by dashed lines. Note how rounding affects formant values differently, depending on the height and advancement of the vowels. For measurements of vowels of specific languages, see Kent and Read (2002:105–24), who list data from several studies of American English vowels as well as studies of the vowels of British English and nine other languages.

What about the tense/lax distinction, you may be asking? Tenseness is crucial in English and other Germanic languages. There is also a similar phenomenon that goes under the names of *advanced tongue root* (*ATR*) and *expanded* that is common in languages of western and eastern Africa and perhaps sporadically elsewhere. Let's consider tenseness first. The name *tenseness* is not especially helpful in understanding what's going on. It's based on the questionable notion that 'tense' vowels show more muscular tension than 'lax' vowels, but muscular tension won't help you a bit when you're trying to measure acoustic signals or conducting a perception experiment. In Germanic languages, tenseness is manifested in several ways, as listed here:

1. Tense vowels are, on average, longer than lax vowels, often by a considerable degree (Peterson and Lehiste 1960).
2. Tense vowels appear in more peripheral positions than lax vowels in the vowel envelope. (The *vowel envelope* is simply the space that all the vowels together cover when their formant values are plotted.) Certain articulatory manoeuvres yield these differences in formant values. Most importantly, for tense vowels, the tongue root is often pushed forward a little, widening the pharynx, and the tongue ridge is normally closer to the roof of the mouth than for each corresponding lax vowel (Lindau 1978).
3. On average, tense vowels are breathier, lax vowels creakier.
4. At least in most dialects of English and Dutch, tense vowels are more diphthongal than lax vowels. This difference doesn't apply to German, most dialects of Scandinavian languages or even some varieties of English, such as Scottish English.

As you can see, tenseness isn't a straightforward concept. Instead, it's mostly a phonological construct, and the factors listed above all serve as perceptual cues, often in trading relations, that listeners can utilize to tell tense vowels from lax vowels. The next plot shows mean values of some of the vowels for a female speaker of American English from Oregon (Figure 5.8). The keywords used as names for the vowels are those developed by Wells (1982); FLEECE, for example, refers to the vowel in words such as *fleece, see, eat* and *need*. Arrows denote the gliding of diphthongs from nucleus to glide, and the '=' sign is used for classes that are merged for this speaker. Some additional keywords that Wells didn't propose are added where necessary. Note that the tense vowels FLEECE, FACE and GOOSE appear around the margins of this speaker's vowel envelope, while the lax counterparts to those vowels, KIT, DRESS and FOOT, respectively, appear

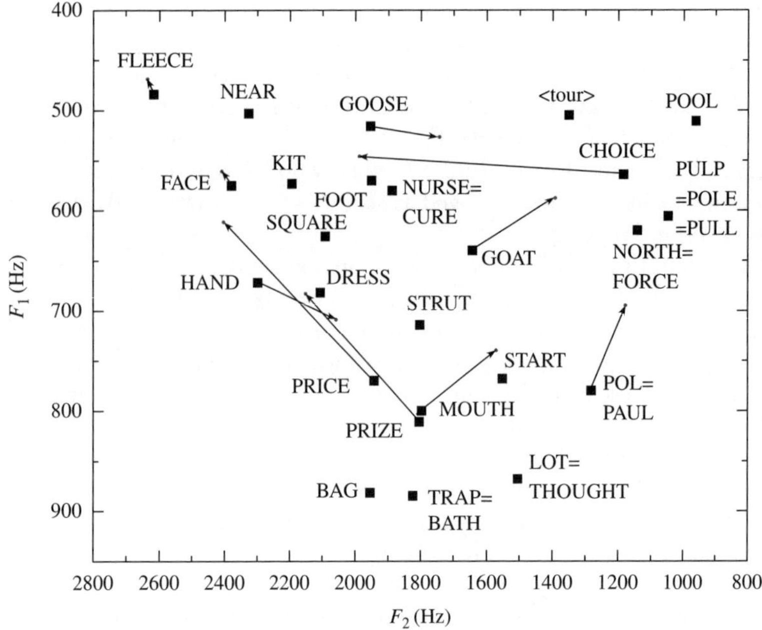

Figure 5.8 Formant plot of the vowel inventory of a female from Oregon. Each point represents the mean of numerous measurements. Arrows more or less the gliding of diphthongs.

in more interior positions. The tense vowel GOAT has an interior position, but it still forms part of a ring, together with FLEECE, FACE and GOOSE, around STRUT and the other three lax vowels. Furthermore, FACE and GOAT are more or less diphthongal.[3]

The ATR feature is simpler than Germanic-style tenseness. Languages with ATR have their vowels ordered in contrastive pairs. The tense vowels involve moving the root of the tongue forwards and often lowering the larynx, thereby expanding the width and volume of the pharynx, while the lax vowels involve the opposite – moving the root of the tongue backwards and raising the larynx, thereby reducing the width and volume of the pharynx. The tense vowels show lower F_2 and dramatically lower F_1 values than their corresponding lax vowels because of the differences in pharyngeal dimensions (Lindau 1978). Whether ATR left any substrate influence on Caribbean creoles or African American English is an intriguing question, albeit one that would be quite difficult to prove or disprove.

Vowel duration and coarticulation

Vowel duration interacts with coarticulation with neighbouring segments. Vowels that are especially long show a period of transition from the preceding segment, followed by a long *steady state* in which the formants change little and show canonical values for that particular vowel, followed by a period of transition to the following segment. When vowels are shortened, however – whether from a faster rate of speech, weaker stress, being followed by a voiceless consonant, or other factors – the steady state is what suffers the most. If the vowel is short enough, that steady state may be truncated out of existence. In that case, the transitions are all that are left and they may even overlap with each other. Hence coarticulatory effects on formant values appear to be magnified for vowels of short duration. The result can be some highly uncanonical formant values, especially if both neighbouring segments have the same effect on a particular formant. For example, in American English, the word *got* is often pronounced so rapidly in conversational speech that its formant values match those of [æ] or [ɛ] better than those of the expected [ɑ]. The reason is that both the preceding [g] and the following [t] induce a raising of F_2. Figure 5.9 compares slow and fast utterances of *got*. Note the presence of the steady state in the long version and its absence in the fast version, and how much the formant tracks differ for F_1 and F_2.

One additional note about coarticulation is that both preceding segments and following segments show noticeable coarticulatory effects. Influence from a preceding segment is called *perseveratory coarticulation*, while influence from a following segment is called *anticipatory coarticulation*. Anticipatory effects seem to result in phonologized vowel variations more often than perseveratory effects, and they get more attention in sociolinguistic studies, so you might expect anticipatory coarticulation to be more prominent than perseveratory. Generally speaking, however, you will be hard-pressed to find any consistent differences in the degree of influence they have on vowel formants.

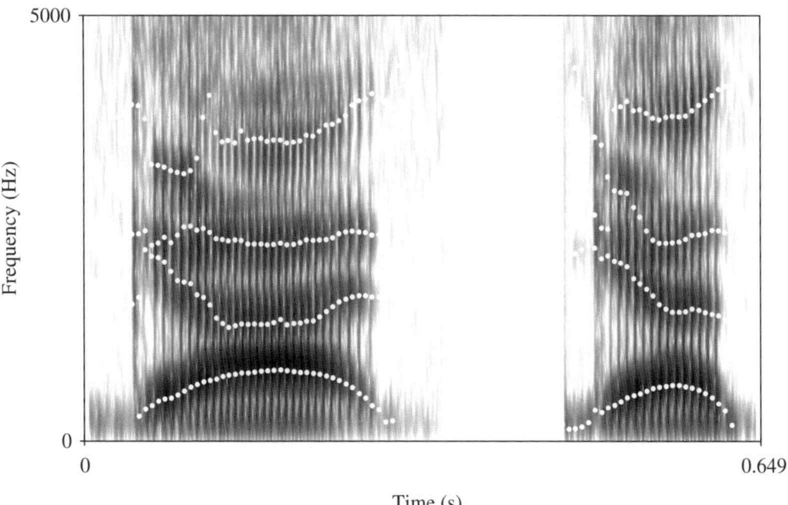

Figure 5.9 Spectrogram of slow and fast utterances of *got*. Note how F_1 and F_2 approach each other much more closely in the slow utterance than in the fast utterance.

5.4 Points to measure

We have covered how to read formants, but we still need to decide where – i.e. at what timepoint(s) – to take the measurements. There are several approaches. Each one has its uses, so the choice depends on which one is appropriate for your study. The most basic decision concerns how many timepoints you measure for each vowel. Depending on what you're trying to demonstrate in your study, you may measure as few as one timepoint or an indeterminately large number between the onset and offset of the vowel. Of course, there is a continuum between those extremes, but here I'll divide the approaches into those that measure only a small number (one to a few) and those that measure a large number at even intervals.

Measurement of nuclei and glides

Studies that involve mapping numerous vowels are ordinarily limited to obtaining only one or two, or at most three or four, measurements of each vowel. There are two reasons for this. First, different vowel tokens are readily comparable if there are only one or a few points to compare. With a larger number of points, however, the formant measurements can wander in seemingly erratic directions through the course of a vowel, making comparisons between tokens difficult. Second, plots showing many tokens are far more readable if the tokens are represented by only one or two points of measurement.

Points of maximum and minimum formant values

One popular method of deciding where to take a vowel measurement is to take it at a point at which one or more formants change direction. For example, Labov et al. (1972) took measurements at points at which F_1 reached a maximum value within a vowel. This method has certain advantages. Most importantly, it captures vowels where they show the least coarticulation with neighbouring segments (provided that one of these segments isn't a vowel that's lower than the vowel being measured, but that situation occurs infrequently). It works best when only one timepoint is measured for a particular vowel. Figure 5.10 illustrates where a measurement would be taken with this method.

This technique is more difficult to implement when more than one timepoint is desired, as with diphthongs. With any vowel, including a diphthong, there can be only one point of maximum F_1, yet you might need measurements representing both the nucleus and the glide. As an example, for a diphthong with a value of [ai], the point of maximum F_1 will correspond to the nucleus. However, what about the glide? Here you could use the point of maximum F_2, but there are still two problems. First, using a point of maximum F_2 for the glide will work only for diphthongs with a fronting glide. It won't work for diphthongs such as [au] or [ie], for which F_2 falls through the course of the diphthong. Second, if the following segment is a dorsal consonant such as [k], F_2 will continue to rise throughout the transition to the dorsal and the point of maximum F_2 will be the offset of the diphthong. In that situation, you're not really measuring the glide: you're measuring the consonant transition.

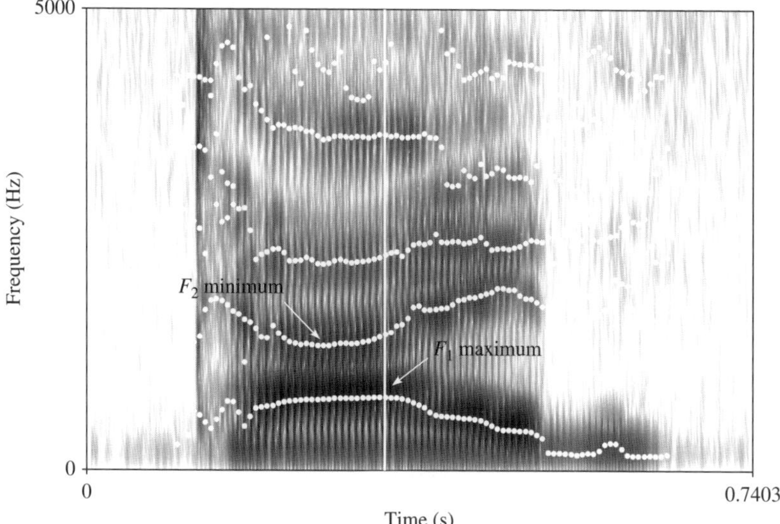

Figure 5.10 Spectrogram of the utterance of *tide* with a vertical line at the point of maximum F_1, a possible choice for measurement of the nucleus. Note that, in this utterance, the point of maximum F_1 doesn't coincide with the point of minimum F_2, which falls earlier.

Specified distances from onset or offset

A solution to the dilemma of how to measure diphthongs is to take measurements at some specified distance after the onset and before the offset. You'll have to decide what the ideal distance is in order to use this method. If you use a distance that's too short, the measurements that you obtain will lie within the transitions to or from neighbouring segments and thus will show too much coarticulatory influence. Conversely, if you choose a distance that's too long, you'll have to exclude tokens with short durations, which will skew the results. For instance, if you choose 50 ms as the distance, you won't be able to use tokens with durations less than 100 ms – if you do, your glide timepoint will fall before your nucleus timepoint! Many diphthong tokens, especially of narrow diphthongs such as [ei] and [ou], show durations less than 100 ms. I find distances in the range of 25–35 ms to be optimal. Figure 5.11 shows how a specified distance of 35 ms from onset and offset is implemented.

Incidentally, in some analyses you may need to measure formants at the onset and offset themselves (see sections 4.3 and 5.9). That counts as a specified distance from onset and offset, even though it's a distance of 0 ms.

Percentages of vowel duration from onset or offset

One other method is similar to using a specified distance. Instead of a set number of ms, however, this method uses timepoints at certain percentages of the distance from onset to offset. For example, some researchers take a measurement 30 per cent of the way through the vowel for the nucleus and 70 per cent through for the glide. Another option would be to take measurements 25, 50

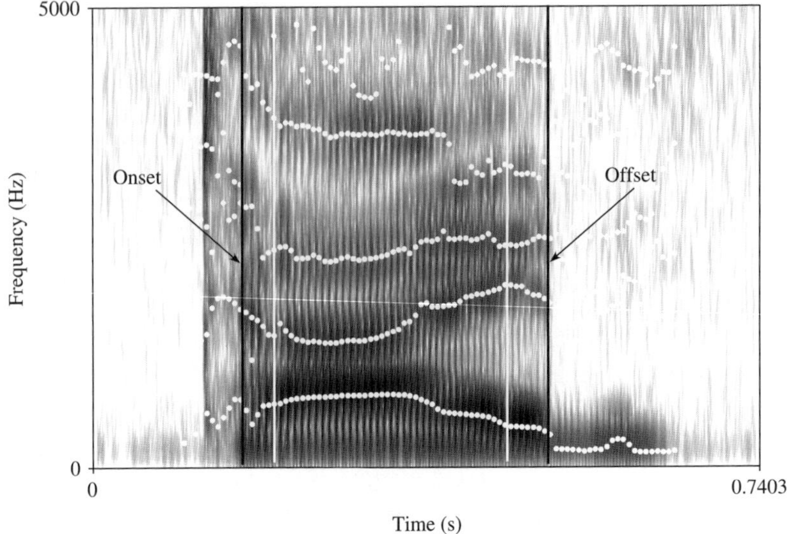

Figure 5.11 Spectrogram of the same utterance of *tide* as in Figure 5.10. The onset and offset are marked by black vertical lines, and points 35 ms after the onset and 35 ms before the offset by white vertical lines. The latter two points are possible locations to use for the nucleus and glide. See the text for other possible measurement points.

and 75 per cent of the way through the vowel. Any number of other options would be possible. Use of a specified percentage eliminates the problem of not being able to measure tokens with especially short durations. However, there is a tradeoff. The amount of coarticulation with neighbouring segments that is reflected in the measurements can vary tremendously from one token to another because the length (in ms) from onset and from offset will vary depending on the length of the entire vowel.

The percentage approach can be used as well when only one measurement is desired, as for a monophthong. In this case, the single measurement is simply taken 50 per cent of the way through the course of the vowel, i.e. at the exact midpoint of the vowel. This practice avoids any subjectivity associated with deciding where the point of maximum F_1 is.

Measurement of trajectory

Sometimes, when the analysis requires a closer examination of the trajectories of individual vowel tokens, an analysis of many timepoints is desirable. There are various uses for trajectory analyses. One, discussed later in section 5.7, is to demarcate steady-states in a diphthong. Another is to determine whether a diphthong shows curvature through its course (usually in F_1/F_2 space), such as a convex or concave pattern or even an S-curve. A third use is to examine the total amount of formant movement: trajectory analyses will give you longer distances and, sometimes, differ in other ways from vector analyses that involve only a starting and ending point. Yet another is for examining triphthongs – e.g. for the [æɛɔ] triphthong common in southern U.S. dialects in the MOUTH class – determining where different tokens show a change in trajectory and how dramatic the change is. There are two methods of determining where to take readings, and they correspond to the methods described above for taking measurements at fewer timepoints.

Intervals of specified distances

One method is to take measurements every so many ms, such as at 10-ms intervals. With this option, you are assured that the readings won't get too close together or too far apart among tokens of varying durations. However, different tokens will be difficult to compare with each other because they will have different numbers of measured timepoints. Figure 5.12 shows an example of the trajectory of the diphthong in the word *tide* with measurements taken every 10 ms.

Fractions of vowel duration

The other technique is to take readings at fractions or percentages of the distance through the course of the vowel. The advantages and drawbacks are the opposite of those of using intervals of specified distances. That is, measurements of different tokens will be readily comparable with each other, e.g. for

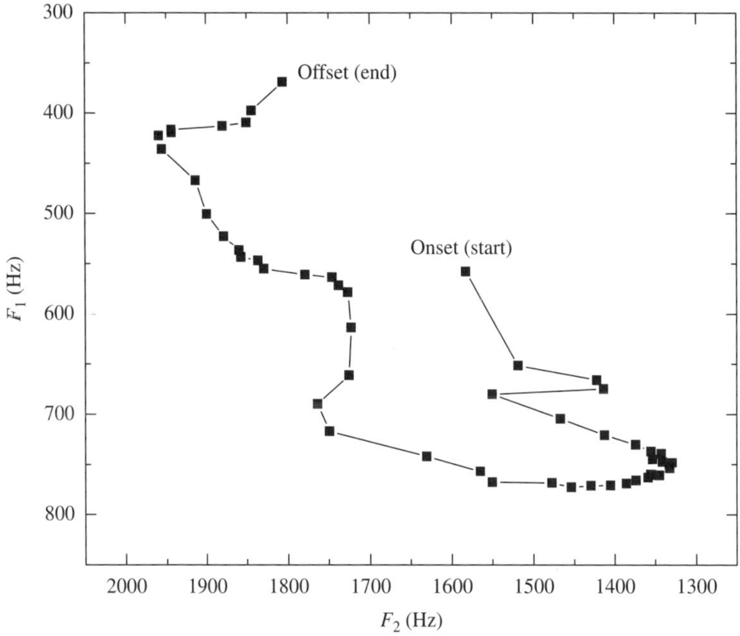

Figure 5.12 Vowel trajectory for the same token of the word *tide* as in Figures 5.10–11. The clustering of measurement points at the lower right coincides with the nuclear steady-state, and the movement from there to the upper right represents the glide. The dynamics near the onset and offset differ greatly from those between the nucleus and glide.

statistical analyses, because they will have the same number of measured time-points. However, the length of the intervals between measurements will vary considerably.

5.5 Plotting vowel formant measurements

This section focuses mainly on how to plot vowel data. However, before we move on to plotting techniques, here are some deliberately brief suggestions on plotting software. Numerous packages are available that can be used for plotting vowel formant data. Currently, several are in wide use, though the inventory will change as the years go by. Plotnik, developed by sociolinguists at the University of Pennsylvania, is quite popular and was developed specifically for studies of vowel variation. It is, however, designed around the research interests and theoretical stances of William Labov and his students and isn't always ideal for every other kind of vowel analysis, and it's inappropriate for most non-vocalic variables. Some spreadsheet-oriented and statistical packages, such as Excel™ and R™, offer plotting capabilities. Because plotting isn't the primary aim of those packages, the plotting capabilities often suffer, though they've improved. There are also commercially available packages designed specifically for plotting, such as Origin™. While they weren't created for vowel analysis per se, they offer users maximum flexibility for what can be plotted. They also provide the most options and greatest ease for aesthetic improvement of plots.

Most of the time, researchers plot F_1 on the x-axis and F_2 on the y-axis. The reason is that vowel height and vowel advancement are the factors of greatest interest. The $F_2 - F_1$ distance can be substituted for the F_2 dimension, and indeed Ladefoged (2001) advocated this practice. In addition, though, other dimensions can be depicted on graphs. F_3, for example, can be usefully plotted against F_2. Furthermore, three-dimensional graphs, with, say, F_1, F_2 and F_3, or F_1, F_2 and vowel duration, as the three axes, can also be advantageous at times.

Researchers sometimes desire to depict a speaker's vowel inventory as a series of subsystems. This device can be useful when you want to illustrate how chain shifts of vowels operate. For example, tense and lax vowels may be shown as different subsystems; or monophthongs, front-gliding diphthongs and back-gliding diphthongs can be portrayed differently. The easiest way to do that is to show members of the different subsystems with different symbols. At times, even individual words may be of interest and can be labelled; Labov (1994) often labelled individual words.

Individual tokens

Individual vowel tokens are frequently the objects that are plotted. Much of William Labov's work (e.g. Labov et al. 1972, 2006; Labov 1994, 2001) has utilized this method as the primary means of presentation. It has the advantage of bringing readers closer to the data: readers can see exactly what the readings for the individual tokens were and judge for themselves whether the author's generalizations about them are justified. The disadvantage is that the plots quickly become cluttered and less readable as more data are added. Authors can counteract this problem by using different symbols or colours for different categories of data, e.g. for different phonemes, as Labov et al. (2006) did. Another solution is to draw ellipses around the tokens representing each category, as in Labov et al. (1972). The basic method for drawing an ellipse is to run a principal components analysis on the tokens for the given vowel and then to set the radii of the ellipse at two standard deviations from the mean value along axes oriented with the principal components.

Display of individual tokens is adequate when only a single timepoint is included for each vowel, as in Figure 5.13, which shows the vowels of a Mexican American woman from southern Texas. It is also the only appropriate type of display for some analyses of individual tokens. For example, Figure 5.14 below shows the nuclei and glides of tokens of the FACE vowel for the same speaker. Her nuclei and glides form partially separate clouds, demonstrating that this speaker mostly produces FACE as a diphthong. Lines connecting nuclei with their respective glides can provide more information. The technique of showing individual tokens is hard to implement when data from more than one timepoint of vowel tokens are shown for many different vowels. Even when data from only single timepoints are shown, readers can find swarms of tokens difficult to interpret.

Mean values

A different way to plot data is to give mean values. I've used this method quite a lot, e.g. in Thomas (2001). The use of mean values produces plots that are more readable than plots that show every token. It especially makes it easier to show

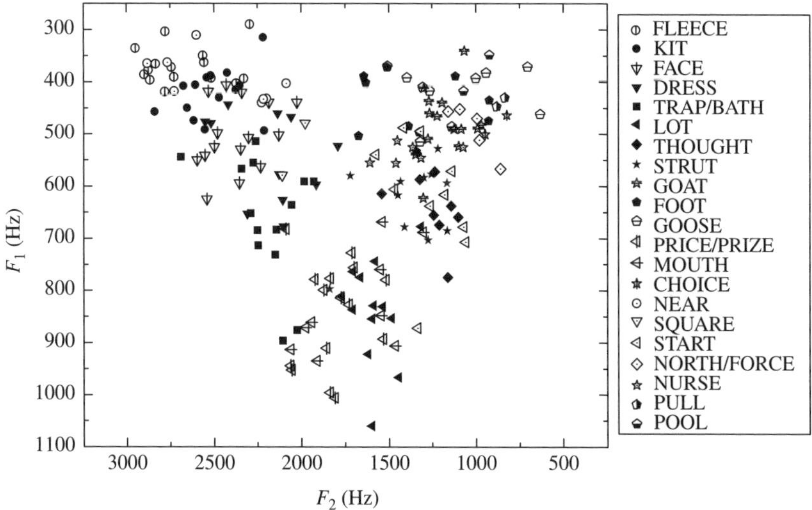

Figure 5.13 Formant plot of individual vowel nuclei tokens for a Mexican American female from southern Texas.

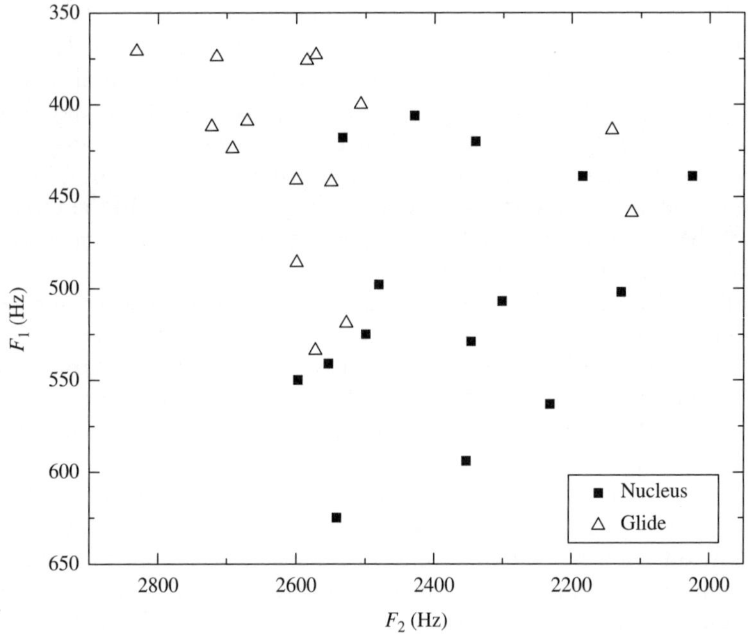

Figure 5.14 Formant plot of FACE nuclei and glides for the same speaker as in Figure 5.13. Although there are a few outliers, for the most part the glides show lower F_1s and higher F_2s than the nuclei, indicating that the target is a diphthongal pronunciation.

the gliding of diphthongs in a way that is clearly legible. Another advantage is that it makes it easier to see the relative positions of different vowel classes or phonemes because readers see a single point for each class and don't have to make guesses about clouds of data points. Of course, there are drawbacks as well. Mean values by themselves can't show how much spread there is to the data. Bars showing standard deviations can be added to the plots to indicate the degree of spread, though, of course, they can clutter the plot, making it harder to read. If the mean values involve any sort of interpretation, such as dividing phonemes into phonetic contexts, the interpretation relies heavily on the researcher's good judgement and, without the individual tokens, readers essentially have to take the researcher's word that the interpretation is appropriate. Most damaging are the occasional cases when a vowel shows a bimodal distribution. In such instances, you are best advised to show two mean values, but it is easy for bimodality to escape your notice. Figures 5.15 and 5.16 show F_1/F_2 plots of the mean values of the vowels of the same speaker as in the last two plots. Figure 5.15 shows just the mean values, with arrows indicating the gliding of diphthongs, and Figure 5.16 adds whiskers denoting the standard deviations for each mean value.

Displays of mean values are preferable when diphthongal movement is compared over a speaker's entire vowel inventory. They are also the most readable means of showing relative positions of vowels, which can be particularly useful for studies of vowel shifting. In addition, mean values are the display of choice

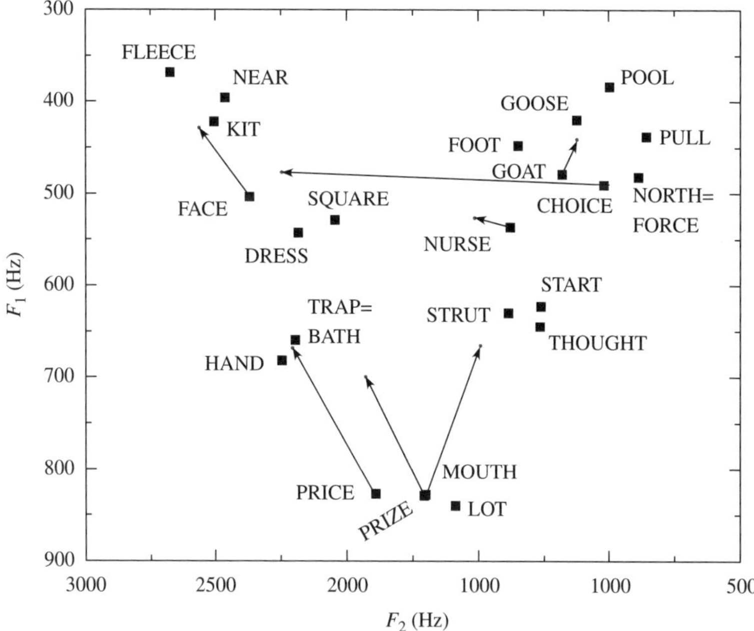

Figure 5.15 Formant plot of the mean values of the vowels of the same speaker as in Figures 5.13–14. Arrows indicate the gliding of diphthongs.

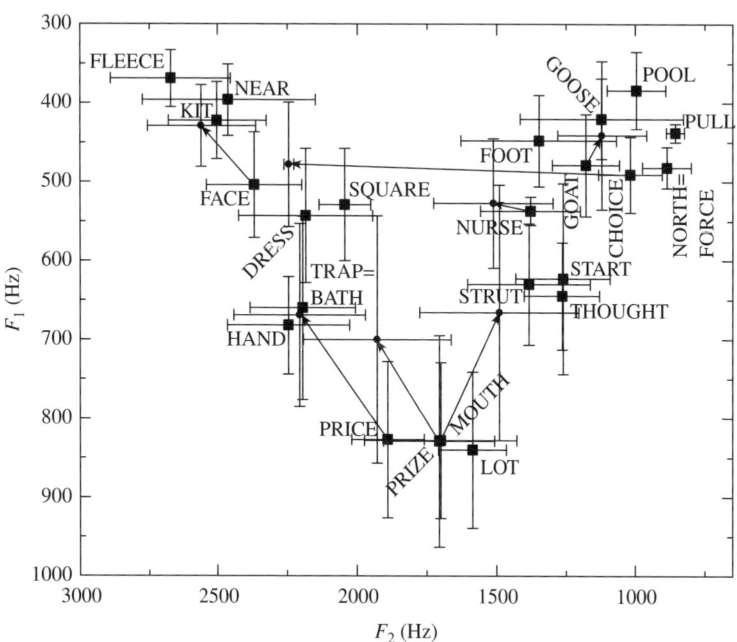

Figure 5.16 Formant plot of the mean values of the vowels of the same speaker as in Figures 5.13–15, with whiskers added to indicate standard deviations. Nuclei are indicated with large squares and glides with small circles.

for comparisons of the vowels of different speakers. The latter often involve some sort of vowel normalization, which is discussed in section 5.6 below.

Plotting in perceptual units

A variation on plotting is to use perceptual units such as Bark or mels as the unit for the axes. The results reflect what listeners are actually hearing better than plots with hertz as the unit for the axes. Figure 5.17 compares hertz and Bark values of the means of the Spanish vowels uttered by the same speaker as in the last few plots. Note how the vowels are slightly more evenly spaced in the Bark plot than in the hertz plot.

Limiting contexts to be included

One problem that crops up with vowel formant analyses, no matter which plotting method is chosen, is that some tokens show such strong coarticulation with neighbouring segments that their formant values differ wildly from those of other tokens of the same vowel class or phoneme. Some researchers would contend that this phenomenon is not a problem at all. One argument they make is that such atypical tokens may actually be inducing or 'leading' sound changes. There is no question that atypical tokens can be the harbingers of *conditioned* sound changes. However, in spite of assertions to the contrary, there is no incontrovertible evidence that atypical tokens can in some way cause *unconditioned* shifts of the vowel as a whole in their direction. Hence, atypical tokens should often be viewed as a problem, especially when vowel shifting

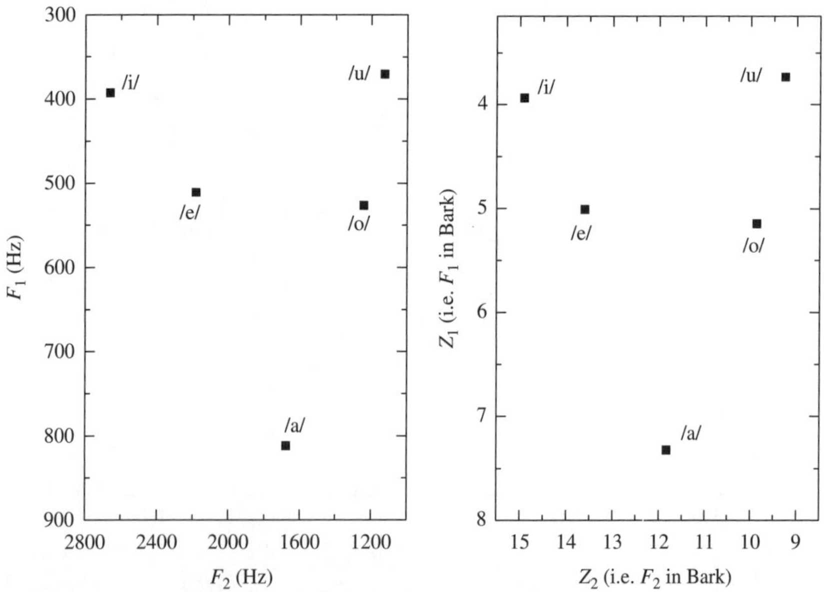

Figure 5.17 Comparison of mean values of Spanish vowels in hertz and Bark for the same speaker as in Figures 5.13–16.

per se isn't the object of the study. If, for example, a study aims to demonstrate that two groups within a community differ for some vowel variable, atypical tokens can skew the results and compromise the whole study.

Three approaches have been utilized to counteract this problem. One is bootstrapping, in which all the measured tokens of a vowel are taken as a population, numerous samples of that population of tokens are taken, and then the means of each sample are plotted. Veatch (1991) applied this method in his comparison of different vowel configurations in English, but in general it hasn't caught on widely among sociophoneticians. A second approach is the statistician's standby of eliminating outliers. A method is adopted for defining what constitutes an outlier – for example, any token that isn't among the 95 per cent closest, based either on Euclidian distance[4] or on a principal components analysis, to the mean value of the vowel class. Then any tokens so classified as outliers are excluded. A third method, one that takes linguistic factors into consideration, is to exclude tokens on the basis of phonetic context. That is, vowels in phonetic contexts that produce the greatest perturbations of formant values are excluded. The most likely contexts to be eliminated are those in which a vowel appears next to an approximant, another vowel or a nasal, but other environments, such as vowels before [g], can be added. A variation on that approach is to plot vowels in such contexts separately from other tokens, and this method is helpful when conditioned sound changes are under way. For example, in many varieties of English, vowels undergo backing or fail to undergo fronting before /l/, and it is instructive to create special pre-/l/ categories on plots (as in some of the previous figures in this chapter).

How many tokens are needed?

There is no simple answer to the question of how many tokens are needed for an analysis. Limiting factors are the number of tokens available in the recording and the researcher's available time to measure them. For studies in which speakers' entire vowel inventories are mapped, some authorities recommend measuring at least 20 tokens of each vowel. However, I've found that measuring as few as seven to ten is adequate if atypical or outlier tokens are excluded, as described above. Excluding such tokens prevents serious skewing of the mean value. For some classes that are infrequent – in English, they include the CHOICE diphthong and some of the pre-/r/ and pre-/l/ classes – you probably won't find even that many in the average interview and you'll have to make do with however many you have.

Analyses that involve more intensive examinations of a single vowel class/phoneme require more tokens. Sometimes, 50 or more tokens are required. Analyses involving linear or curvilinear regression, such as those examining undershoot and coarticulation that I'll describe later in section 5.9, tend to require the most tokens. On the other hand, certain other analyses of individual vowels require far fewer data. For example, fewer than 20 tokens were necessary to demonstrate that the speaker in Figure 5.14 showed consistent upgliding for her FACE vowel.

5.6 Vowel normalization

Because formants are resonances of the various cavities within the vocal tract, they differ depending on the overall length of a speaker's vocal tract. Different speakers have different-sized mouths. Young children, naturally, have the shortest vocal tracts, and each of their formants, correspondingly, has a relatively high frequency. Adult males have the longest vocal tracts, the lengths of which are augmented by the fact that a male's larynx undergoes lowering during puberty. Figure 5.18 illustrates this difference, showing my voice and my daughter's (when she was eight years old) saying the word *bee*. Listeners perceive both utterances as [bi], yet the visible formants fall at quite different frequencies. F_1 appears near the bottom in both utterances, but slightly higher for my daughter. In my utterance, F_2, F_3 and F_4 are clustered near the middle of the frequency range and F_5 appears at the top. In my daughter's, F_2, F_3 and F_4 appear clustered – and poorly differentiated because of her high F_0 – at the top of the spectrogram, and F_5 is out of view. Vowel normalization techniques have been developed as a means of making the differing formant values of various speakers comparable. Vowel normalization is often necessary for meaningful linguistic and sociolinguistic comparisons when you're examining the vowel realizations of different speakers acoustically.

Aims and limitations of normalization

Before you do any normalization, you should understand why you're doing it. Disner (1980) and Thomas (2002a) list four general goals of a normalization technique. Not all techniques meet all of these goals. What you need to know

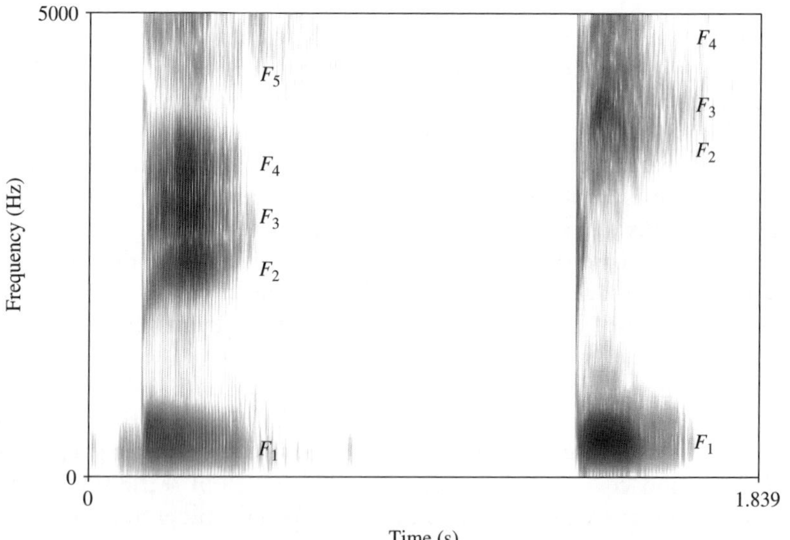

Figure 5.18 Spectrogram comparing *bee* utterances by an adult male and an eight-year-old girl.

is which of these goals are relevant for your own study. Then you can choose a technique accordingly. The four goals are:

1. eliminating variation caused by physiological differences among speakers (i.e. differences in vocal tract lengths);
2. preserving sociolinguistic/dialectal/cross-linguistic differences in vowel quality;
3. preserving phonological distinctions among vowels;
4. modelling the cognitive processes that allow human listeners to normalize vowels uttered by different speakers.

Most phoneticians who work with vowel normalization focus on the fourth goal. For example, the extensive review of normalization in Rosner and Pickering (1994) treats goal 4 as *the* purpose of normalization. They never even entertain the notion that there could be any other use for normalization. In a further twist, some phonetic researchers have recently suggested that listeners don't actually normalize vowels at all, and that comprehension of the vowels of different speakers operates by other means (Pisoni 1997). However, the majority opinion is still that listeners do normalize, and Rosner and Pickering (1994) conclude that F_1 and F_2 are by far the most important, with F_3 occasionally important and F_0, in spite of suggestions by some other researchers, not important at all. In addition, a few phoneticians have suggested that *dynamic* portions of vowels – i.e. the transitional sections where formant values are changing – may be more important than steady-state vowels (e.g. Nearey and Assmann 1986; Strange 1989).

For researchers who focus on language variation, however, goal 4 isn't particularly important in the majority of studies. Sociolinguists have traditionally focused more on ascertaining why language varies and changes. As I noted in Chapter 1 and as I'll argue in more depth in later chapters, language variationists shouldn't cede the study of cognitive processing to other linguists. Hence, goal 4 should have some relevance to sociolinguists. Nevertheless, it is dispensable for many sociolinguistic studies. Even when sociolinguists are interested in cognitive processing, such as in determining how social indexing of linguistic variants is cognitively tied to language processing, there is seldom much reason to address the cognitive instantiation of vowel normalization.

Goal 3, that of preserving phonological contrasts, quite often isn't a concern, either. In a language such as Spanish, for which vowels lack length or tenseness distinctions and for which the diphthongs aren't phonemic, we'd expect vowel normalization to meet goal 3. However, in languages with contrastive length or contrastive tenseness, such as Germanic languages, many vowel contrasts are maintained by factors other than steady-state formant values; so when analysing such languages we shouldn't expect vowel normalization to meet goal 3.

In studies of language variation, the first two goals are usually paramount. In these kinds of studies, an effective vowel normalization technique is one that filters out physiological differences (goal 1) but leaves sociolinguistic differences intact (goal 2). Hence, a normalization technique that some phoneticians might reject could serve the needs of a sociolinguistic study perfectly well. The criteria sociolinguists use for evaluating a normalization technique, then, should differ from those used by researchers who aren't concerned with language variation.

Comparisons against reference vowels

One method that is sometimes used in variationist studies is to compare the vowel or vowels that exhibit the variation that's being studied against another vowel or vowels that are thought to be stable in the dialect or community in question. For example, a study might compare F_1 and F_2 values of some vowel against those of an [i] vowel, such as the FLEECE vowel in English. This method is easy to use and requires no complicated mathematical transformations: all you need is a ratio of the formant value of the stable vowel against that of the varying vowel. There are some serious disadvantages to this method, however. First, there's no guarantee that the supposedly stable vowel really is stable. Second, male and female voices aren't scaled exactly the same way, in part because the lower larynges of adult males cause the relative lengths of the front and back cavities of adult males to differ from those of females (or of boys). Hence, the ratios may be skewed for male vs female speakers.

A variation of this method is to compute relative formant values of two vowels that are both undergoing change. This method can be used if the two vowels are moving towards or away from each other. For example, in studies of vowel shifting in American English, relative F_1 and F_2 values of the nuclei of the FACE and DRESS vowels have been compared for Southern dialects, in which the two vowels may switch positions. The method has also been used in conjunction with other, more formal normalization methods. Labov et al. (2006), for instance, use such a method to gauge the relative positions of the LOT and DRESS vowels in the Great Lakes region of the United States, where LOT is fronted and DRESS is backed. The drawback of this method is that it can't indicate whether one vowel is shifting, the other vowel is, or both are.

Vowel-intrinsic vs vowel-extrinsic normalization

Vowel normalization techniques fall into two general groups: *vowel-intrinsic* and *vowel-extrinsic*. In a vowel-intrinsic method, all the information used for the normalization formula can be found within a single vowel token. These methods use various combinations of formant values (F_1, F_2, usually F_3, and occasionally F_4), F_0 (the fundamental frequency) or even formant bandwidths or amplitudes. Vowel-extrinsic methods, on the other hand, compare formant values of different vowels spoken by a given individual.

Five useful reviews of normalization techniques are Hindle (1978), Disner (1980), Miller (1989), Adank et al. (2004) and Clopper (2009). They put varying weights on the four goals of normalization stated above. Hindle (1978) preferred vowel-extrinsic methods, particularly a now widely used formula developed by Nearey (1977). Disner (1980) discussed goal 2 at length, noting that different languages appear to use the periphery of the vowel envelope in different ways, and found that vowel-extrinsic methods weren't especially effective at capturing such differences, even though they performed well in other ways. Miller (1989) provided some useful history on vowel-intrinsic methods. Adank et al. (2004) evaluated how well different formulas matched impressionistic transcriptions and came down solidly in favour of vowel-extrinsic methods, especially those by Lobonov (1971) and Nearey (1977). However, their experiment had a built-in bias, since, of the supposed 'vowel-intrinsic' methods they tested, only one – that of Syrdal and Gopal (1986) – was really a vowel normalization technique. The others, such as conversion of hertz to Bark or mels, were simply transformations of hertz to scales that reflect auditory treatment of pitch. Clopper (2009) also found that the best techniques for reducing variance due to physiological differences were vowel extrinsic, though she noted some disadvantages of vowel-extrinsic methods as well.

You may test your vowel data with several normalization methods by accessing the website http://ncslaap.lib.ncsu.edu/tools/ and clicking on NORM. Special spreadsheets are provided for you to enter your data into.

Vowel-intrinsic methods

Vowel-intrinsic methods rely on information that can be obtained from a single vowel, without reference to other vowels or vowel classes. The most widely known vowel-intrinsic method is one suggested by Syrdal and Gopal (1986), though there are various others, e.g. by Iri (1959) and Bladon et al. (1984). Syrdal and Gopal proposed using two dimensions. Both of them involve computing differences between Bark-converted values (Z). To model advancement, they used either $Z_3 - Z_2$ or $Z_2 - Z_1$ (i.e. Bark-converted F_3 minus Bark-converted F_2 or Bark-converted F_2 minus Bark-converted F_1). To model height, they used $Z_1 - Z_0$ (Bark-converted F_1 minus Bark-converted F_0). They included Z_0 because, all other things being equal, F_0 tends to be higher for high vowels than for low vowels, thus minimizing the distance between F_0 and F_1 for high vowels and maximizing it for low vowels.

Unfortunately, however, all other things are seldom equal. Intonation, tone and consonantal influences affect F_0, as does creakiness. Those processes can be circumvented be various means, but another factor, the effects of ageing on F_0, can't, at least not speaker and vowel intrinsically. As a result, I prefer to substitute $Z_3 - Z_1$ for $Z_1 - Z_0$ to normalize height. However, I usually retain $Z_3 - Z_2$ for advancement. The 'Bark difference' method included in the NORM website noted above uses $Z_3 - Z_1$ for height and $Z_3 - Z_2$ for advancement. Figures 5.19 and 5.20 show the vowels of two speakers from central Ohio who have nearly the same dialect. Figure 5.19 shows their vowels superimposed with no normalization and Figure 5.20 shows them superimposed with Bark difference normalization performed. As can be seen, the normalization is effective at reducing interspeaker differences that are due to physiological differences.

One point I should add is that I find the $Z_2 - Z_1$ distance used alone to be adequate for gauging vowel variation that lies entirely along the continuum from [i] to [ɑ]. On this continuum, F_1 and F_2 become closer together as vowels approach [ɑ], thus rendering the $Z_2 - Z_1$ distance smaller, while the opposite

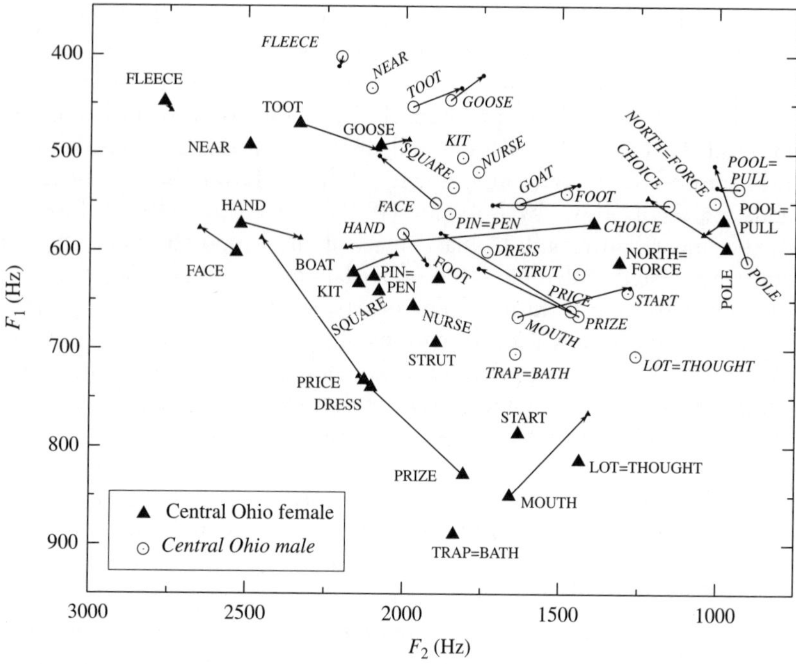

Figure 5.19 Mean values in raw hertz of the vowels of a male and a female from central Ohio.

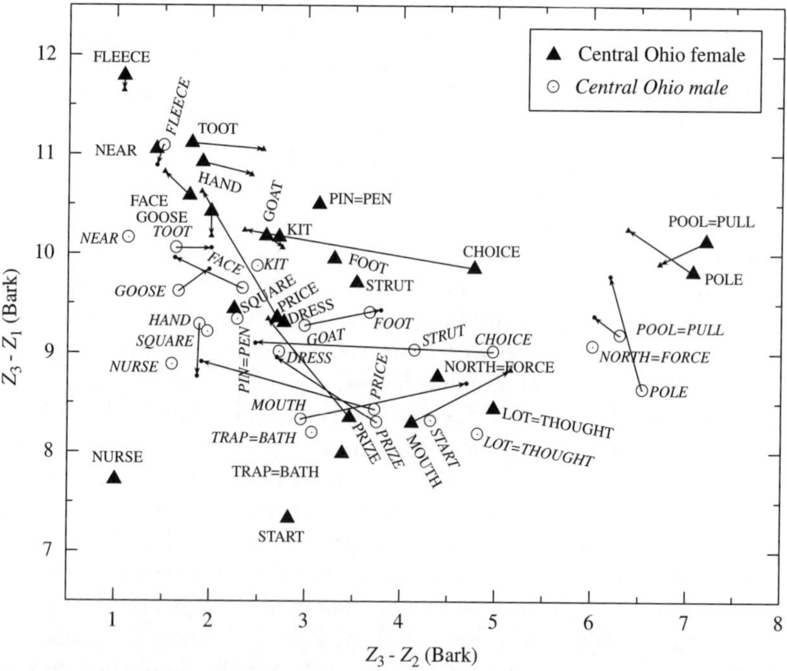

Figure 5.20 Mean values of the vowels of a male and a female from central Ohio normalized with the Bark-difference technique, a vowel-intrinsic method.

holds as vowels approach [i]. The $Z_2 - Z_1$ transformation is useful, e.g. for determining the degree of fronting of LOT or raising of TRAP/BATH or lowering of FACE in English, or the degree of lowering of the nucleus of the /ɛi/ diphthong of Dutch.

Vowel-intrinsic normalization techniques offer their own pros and cons. An important practical advantage is that they don't require measurement of all vowels for all speakers to be included in a study. Conversely, vowel-extrinsic methods work optimally when the entire vowel system is measured. This advantage can be crucial if a study is to include many speakers and the researcher lacks the time or financial resources to measure all the vowels for all subjects acoustically.

Another advantage of vowel-intrinsic methods is that they're immune to differences in the phonological inventories of dialects or languages. That is, they can't be skewed by comparison of systems with different vowels, e.g. a language that has front rounded vowels and one that doesn't. In many communities in the southern United States, where whites show much more fronting of GOOSE and GOAT than African Americans do, vowel-extrinsic methods would skew the results in an interethnic comparison.

The most important disadvantage of vowel-intrinsic methods is that they are heavily dependent on either F_0 or F_3. The difficulties that F_0 presents are discussed above. F_3 can frustrate researchers as well. On archival recordings made with early recording devices and on some modern field recordings, F_3 may be indistinct and hence difficult or impossible to measure accurately. Furthermore, rhoticized vowels, with their low F_3, aren't comparable to other vowels and have to be considered separately from the rest of the vowel inventory; note how the pre-/r/ vowels appear in unpredictable locations in Figure 5.20. Unusual speaker-specific F_3 characteristics, which might result from a physiological peculiarity in the speaker's mouth dimensions or nasality in the speaker's voice, can also skew a vowel-intrinsic method.

Vowel-intrinsic normalization methods often distort the overall shape of the vowel configuration. In the normalized vowel plot shown in Figure 5.20, for example, high front unrounded vowels appear to be stretched higher than other high vowels because F_3 is higher for them than for any other vowels. Other distortions may be more apparent than real, though. Researchers often prefer to see a 'pretty' vowel plot, which is to say that they like a figure that resembles a plot of unnormalized F_1/F_2 values. Vowel-intrinsic methods employ transformations that compare formants in some way, though, and the result is a plot with a differently shaped vowel envelope from that of an unnormalized F_1/F_2 plot. However, this preference is itself a bias because most of us are accustomed to looking at F_1/F_2 plots. If, on the other hand, we ordinarily used hertz-difference formant plots – recall Peter Ladefoged's preference for $F_2 - F_1$ to represent advancement – then the overall shape of the vowel envelopes produced by vowel-intrinsic normalization might not seem so strange and unfamiliar.

Vowel-extrinsic methods

Vowel-extrinsic normalization techniques rely on information from a range of vowels spoken by the same person. They ordinarily don't require information on F_3 or F_0; F_1 and F_2 are usually all you need to use them. However, they can't operate with data from a single vowel. Although, technically, they can be used with as few as two vowels, they work more effectively as more vowels are added and most effectively when a speaker's entire vowel system is included. Hence, they can be labour intensive. With regard to human speech perception, the evidence as to whether vowel-intrinsic or vowel-extrinsic normalization reflects human perceptual processes is mixed. Although some work has shown that listeners can understand single, isolated vowels from an unfamiliar speaker (Verbrugge et al. 1976), which would suggest a vowel-intrinsic mechanism, it is also true that listeners' understanding improves as they hear more tokens from a speaker's voice, which suggests a vowel-extrinsic mechanism. Perhaps the best answer is that listeners are flexible and can employ both modes.

Quite a number of vowel-extrinsic normalization techniques have been proposed. I will discuss three here. These three are among the most effective techniques, but they are also relatively straightforward to use. The first two, the Lobanov and Nearey techniques, are quite similar to each other in that they involve computing some sort of grand mean for all values of a particular formant by a speaker. The Watt and Fabricius method, in contrast, uses a centroid value computed from the extreme points of a speaker's vowel envelope.

First is the Lobanov (1971) technique. For it, the formula is

$$F_{n[V]n} = (F_{n[V]} - MEAN_n)/S_n$$

where $F_{n[V]n}$ is the normalized value for $F_{n[V]}$ (i.e. for formant n of vowel V). $MEAN_n$ is the mean value for formant n for the speaker in question and S_n is the standard deviation for the speaker's formant n. The two central Ohio speakers featured in Figures 5.19 and 5.20 are shown normalized with the Lobanov method in Figure 5.21.

Second is a technique developed by Nearey (1977). This method is actually only one of two methods that Terrance Nearey developed in his doctoral dissertation, but it is by far the more widely used – and, apparently, for good reason, as Nearey himself, as well as Adank et al. (2004), found it to be superior. It is vowel extrinsic and in general is rather similar to the Lobanov formula, though its formula differs. The formula is

$$F^*_{n[V]} = \text{antilog}(\log(F_{n[V]}) - MEAN_{\log})$$

where $F^*_{n[V]}$ is the normalized value for $F_{n[V]}$, formant n of vowel V, and $MEAN_{\log}$ is the log-mean of all F_1s and F_2s for the speaker in question. See p. 170 for Labov et al.'s (2006) modification of Nearey's method. The two central Ohioans are normalized with the Nearey method in Figure 5.22.

Finally, we consider a method developed recently by Watt and Fabricius (2002). This technique is vowel extrinsic, but unlike the Lobanov and Nearey methods, the centroid or grand mean value that it uses to calculate normalized values is based on points that represent the corners of the vowel envelope: one for the high front corner, one for the high back corner and one for the bottom corner. Some other normalization techniques, e.g. the method of Gerstman (1968), have used similar frameworks. For the Watt and Fabricius method, the

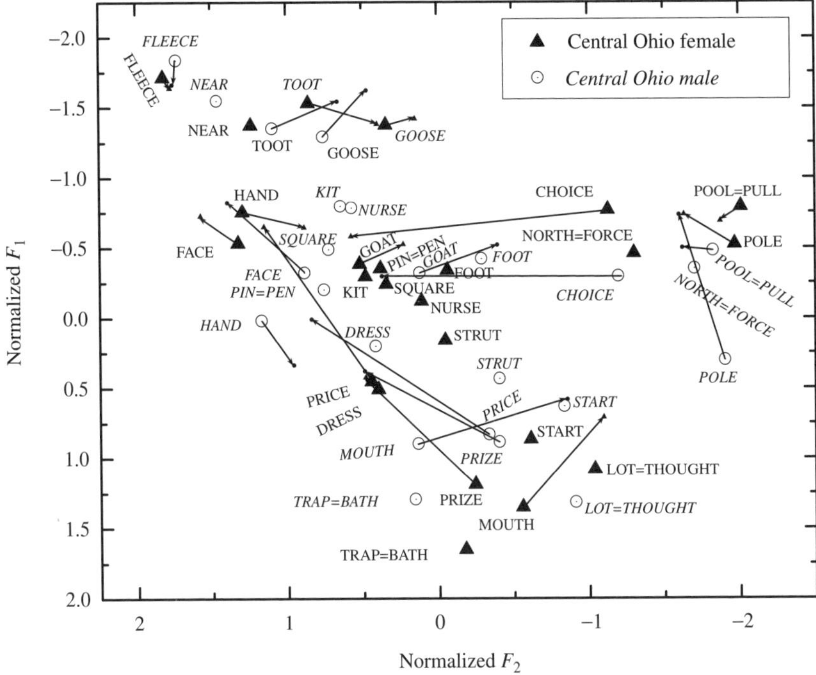

Figure 5.21 Mean values of the vowels of a male and a female from central Ohio normalized with the Lobanov technique, a vowel-extrinsic method.

mean F_1 and F_2 of the vowel that lies farthest in the high front corner of the envelope, usually the FLEECE vowel in English, are used as the minimum F_1 and maximum F_2 values. The minimum F_1 value is also used as the minimum F_2 value, so that it represents the high back corner of the envelope. Finally, the mean F_1 of whichever vowel is lowest is used as the maximum F_1 value, and together with that vowel's mean F_2, or the mean of the minimum and maximum F_2 values, it forms the bottom reference point for the vowel system. For F_1 and F_2, centroid values that Watt and Fabricius call *S transforms* are computed according to the following formulas, where *i*, *u* and *a* represent the high front, high back and bottom corners of the vowel envelope, respectively:

$$S(F_1) = (i_{F1} + a_{F1} + u_{F1})/3$$
$$S(F_2) = (i_{F2} + a_{F2} + u_{F2})/3$$

Normalized values are then computed by dividing each vowel's mean F_1 and F_2 by the appropriate S transform.[5] Figure 5.23 shows the two central Ohioans normalized with the Watt and Fabricius method.

Vowel-extrinsic methods make attractive and easily readable plots that resemble F_1/F_2 formant plots. They do an excellent job of factoring out physiologically-caused differences in formant values while retaining sociolinguistic differences. Moreover, Adank et al. (2004) found that the Lobanov and Nearey methods performed better than other techniques they tested on several

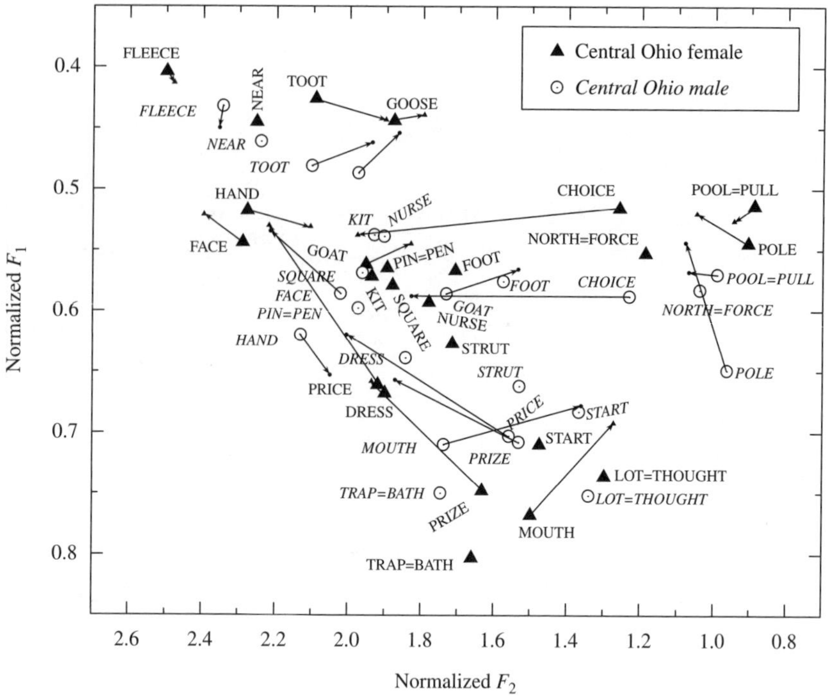

Figure 5.22 Mean values of the vowels of a male and a female from central Ohio normalized with the Nearey technique, a vowel-extrinsic method.

measures. Lobanov was best, though only slightly better than Nearey, in a discriminant analysis of Dutch vowels. The two were tied in reducing physiological variation. Nearey fared slightly better than Lobanov at preserving sociolinguistic variation. Disner (1980), however, who compared data from several languages, found that Lobanov was somewhat poorer than Nearey at reducing scatter in vowel measurements. She also noted that all of the vowel-extrinsic methods performed poorly at retaining 'linguistic validity' – i.e. at preserving subtle language-specific differences in analogous vowels.

Vowel-extrinsic methods have two main disadvantages. First, they work optimally when all the vowels of speakers' vowel systems are included. When some vowels are excluded, vowel-extrinsic methods will yield skewed normalized values. This issue, of course, is a problem for researchers with tight time or budgetary constraints.

The other disadvantage of vowel-extrinsic methods is that they may be impaired when different dialects or languages that show different vowel systems are compared. For example, the two central Ohioans featured in Figures 5.19–23 show considerable fronting of the GOOSE and GOAT vowels, which causes the whole vowel system to be weighted towards front vowels. When this dialect is normalized together with another dialect that lacks this fronting, the normalized values for the central Ohioans are shifted slightly to the right (i.e. all the vowels are represented as slightly more backed than they should be). The effect is amplified when the other dialect is one with the vowels weighted

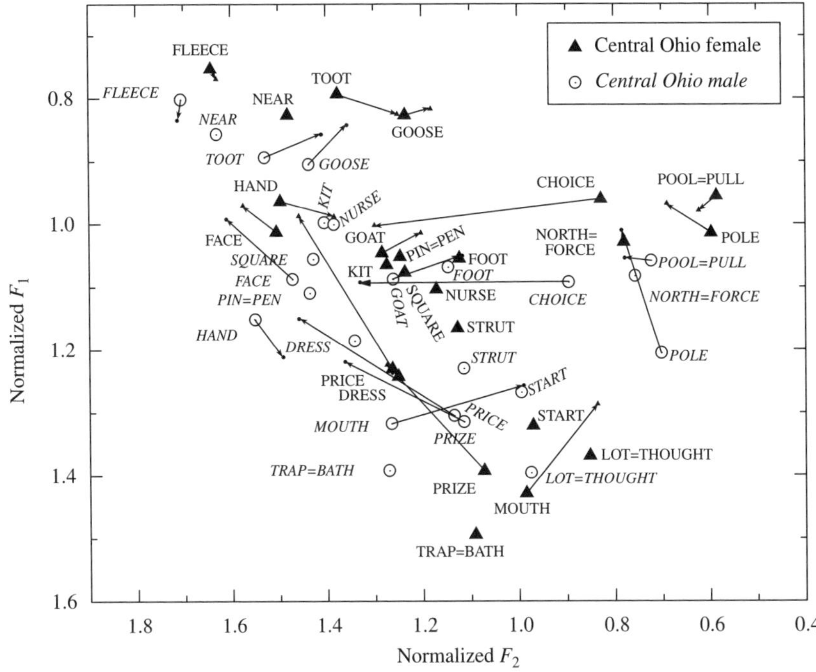

Figure 5.23 Mean values of the vowels of a male and a female from central Ohio normalized with the Watt and Fabricius technique, a vowel-extrinsic method.

towards the back. Figure 5.24 compares the male central Ohioan with a male from County Tyrone, Northern Ireland, using the Nearey method.[6] In the Tyrone dialect, the KIT vowel is strongly lowered and retracted, the STRUT vowel is backed, and the GOAT vowel is quite back, all of which weight the vowel system towards the back. The result is that the entire vowel envelope for the Ohioan appears to be shifted moderately to the right in the plot compared to that of the Northern Ireland speaker.

Another instantiation of the weighting problem has to do with the bottom corner of the vowel envelope, but it affects only the Watt and Fabricius method. Some dialects and languages have an [a] vowel that occupies this corner, while others don't but instead have a low front [æ] vowel and a low back [ɑ] vowel located across from each other. Because the Watt and Fabricius technique calculates the bottom of the normalized vowel space according to the position of the lowest vowel, the overall vowel space can be skewed depending on how the bottom corner is occupied. In contrast, grand-mean and vowel-intrinsic methods, by their nature, can't be skewed by the way the vowel configuration is weighted.

Speaker-intrinsic vs speaker-extrinsic normalization

An additional distinction is between *speaker-intrinsic* and *speaker-extrinsic* methods of normalization. Speaker-intrinsic methods normalize based on data from a single speaker's vowels. Speaker-extrinsic methods factor more than one speaker's vowels into the formula.

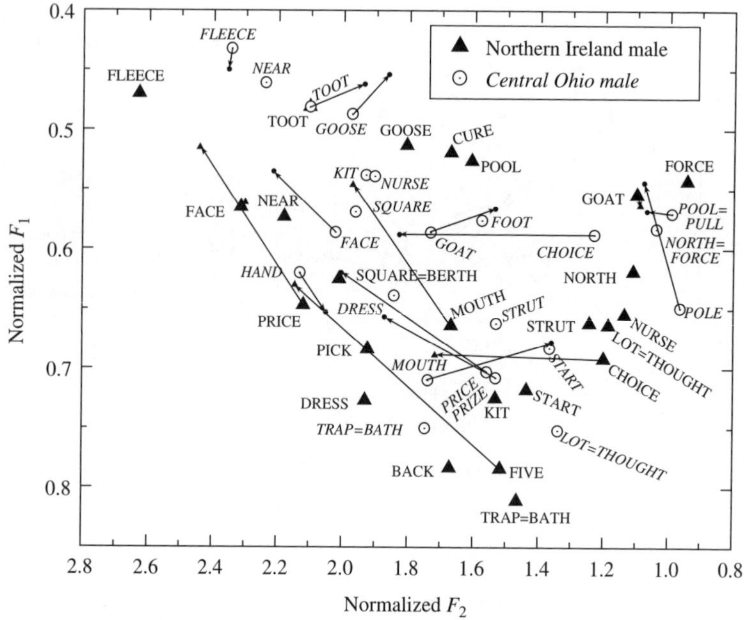

Figure 5.24 Mean values of the vowels of male speakers from central Ohio and Northern Ireland normalized with the Nearey method.

Speaker-intrinsic methods

All of the methods covered so far have been speaker intrinsic. In fact, most normalization methods that have been developed are designed for speaker-intrinsic use. Their design is simpler than that of a speaker-extrinsic method because there is only one layer of normalization in the formula.

Speaker-extrinsic methods

It is possible to design a normalization technique so that it uses data from more than one speaker – often many more – to compute a grand mean. This design adds a second layer of computation onto the normalization formula. One such method is the one used by Labov et al. (2006), which is actually a modification of Nearey's. While it also uses a log-mean method to normalize the formant values, the primary difference is that it computes a single grand mean for all speakers included in the study. As I noted earlier, vowel-extrinsic methods are more effective when more vowels are included, and similarly, speaker-extrinsic methods work better with more speakers. Labov et al., in fact, stated that their formula worked best with at least 345 speakers.

Scaling of normalized values

Another consideration is whether to *scale* the normalized values or not. Most normalization formulas yield numbers that don't resemble the hertz values from which they were derived, and many people find it hard to visualize how those numbers relate to vowel quality. Scaling is an attempt to solve that problem. It involves converting any speaker's normalized formant values to scales that correspond to a range of hertz values found in unnormalized vowels. For example, scales of 250 to 750 Hz for F_1 and 850 to 2250 Hz for F_2 have been applied to normalized values generated by the Gerstman (1968) normalization technique (Disner 1980). The method used by Labov et al. (2006) computes a *scaling factor* for each individual that is applied to the normalized values, also yielding figures that look like ordinary hertz values for each speaker.

5.7 Interactions between vowel variation and voice quality

In Chapter 7, we will cover methods for analysing voice quality. The main focus there is voice quality in its own right. However, voice quality can also be used as a means of manifesting vowel contrasts. In some cases, such contrasts may also have sociolinguistic meaning, especially when the means of making these contrasts is in flux. Here we briefly discuss two voice quality features that interact with vowel contrastiveness: phonation and nasality. Refer to Chapter 7 for the specific techniques for measuring these voice quality features.

Phonation

Phonation is known to serve as a contrastive feature of vowels in some languages. It was noted in section 5.3 that phonation plays an accessory role in the tense/lax distinction in English. However, there is some evidence that it is capable of taking over the primary role. In a series of papers, Marianna Di Paolo and Alice Faber (Di Paolo and Faber 1990; Di Paolo 1992; Faber 1992; Faber and Di Paolo 1995) presented evidence that certain vowel distinctions that are no longer maintained in Utah English through differences in formant values may be realized through differences in phonation. They focused on breathiness in citation-form speech. Little other work has been conducted on phonation-based distinctions in Western languages or on their sociolinguistic instantiations.

Nasalization

The fact that languages such as French, Hindi and Cherokee have contrastively nasal vowels is so well known that it hardly bears repeating. Nasalization may exhibit dialectal differences in its incidence in such languages. That is, some dialects may show a nasal vowel for a certain vowel class, and other dialects may show an oral vowel for the same class, or the lexical makeup of the nasal and oral classes may differ across dialects. Furthermore, in languages such as English that lack contrastive nasalization, it is possible that nasalization is stronger for some vowels than for other vowels and thus plays a secondary role in identification of the vowel. Low vowels, for example, may show some passive nasalization (Johnson 2003) that higher vowels lack. Any such variation in nasalization could easily take on sociolinguistic functions.

5.8 Steady-state patterns

Diphthongs, which have two targets – one for the nucleus and one for the glide – correspondingly involve more variables than monophthongs. A monophthong can show at most one steady state. A diphthong, however, may show two steady states. As a result, diphthongs can exhibit up to three transitions: one between the preceding segment and the nucleus, one between the nucleus and the glide, and one between the glide and the following segment. The possibilities are multiplied for triphthongs.

Nevertheless, not all diphthongs show all the possible steady states and transitions. As we will see in section 5.9, truncation of a diphthong results in the disappearance of one or both steady states. In addition, however, certain diphthongs intrinsically lack one of the steady states that they could potentially show. Lehiste and Peterson (1961) noted that, in American English, PRICE/PRIZE and MOUTH ordinarily show two steady states. However, they also found that FACE shows only one, corresponding to the glide, and GOAT likewise shows only one, but it corresponds to the nucleus. In Thomas (2000), I found a richer situation for PRICE/PRIZE. This diphthong often shows two steady states and can do so in any consonantal context. However, if only one steady state was present, it corresponded to the glide for PRICE (i.e. before voiceless consonants) but to the nucleus for PRIZE (i.e. before voiced consonants). Furthermore, my own observations suggest that the FACE diphthong may show a single steady state corresponding to the nucleus if the vowel is word-final, as in *day*. These examples from American English are allophonic. Conversely, Vincent van Heuven (personal communication) has found that the difference can be contrastive in Dutch. Dutch /ɛi/, normally spelled <ij> but now usually pronounced [aiː], shows only a glide steady state, while Dutch /aːj/, spelled <aaj> and pronounced [aːi], shows only a nuclear steady state. Peeters (1991) found considerable differences in the steady-state patterns favoured for different phonemes in different Germanic languages. Figure 5.25 shows the pair *aid/day*, illustrating an instance in which the diphthong in each word shows only one steady state but which is different for the two words: the part of the diphthong where the formants are most stable is near the end for *aid* but near the beginning for *day*.

Steady states can be hard to quantify because the boundary between a steady state and a transition is quite often unclear. One way to find steady states is to measure the change of a formant value from one timepoint to another across the trajectory of a diphthong. Steady states (or relatively steady states) will appear as regions of stability, with formant differences between timepoints close to zero, while transitions will show rates of change farther from zero. Once these values are obtained, they can be compared across tokens, across phonemes or phonetic contexts, or across speakers or speaker groups. Figure 5.26 shows such an analysis for a token of the [ai] diphthong in *tide*. An obvious steady

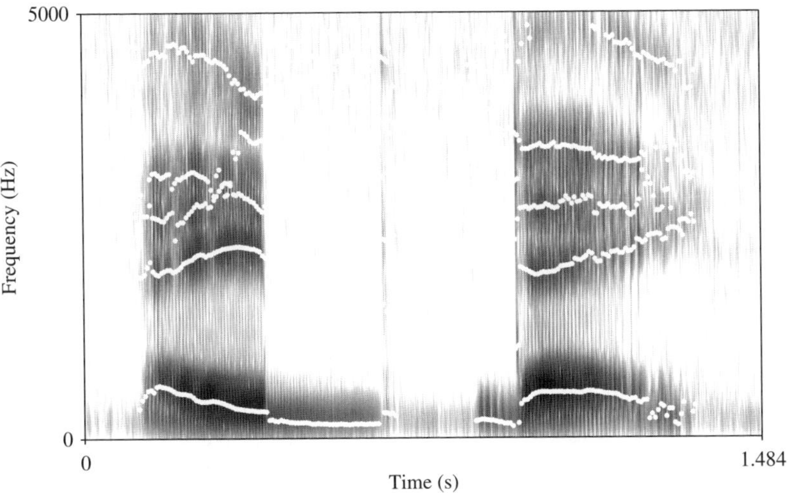

Figure 5.25 Spectrogram of the word pair *aid/day* illustrating differences in steady-state patterns. For *aid*, on the left, F_1 and F_2 are flatter towards the end than towards the beginning, but for *day*, on the right, F_1 and F_2 are flatter towards the beginning than towards the end.

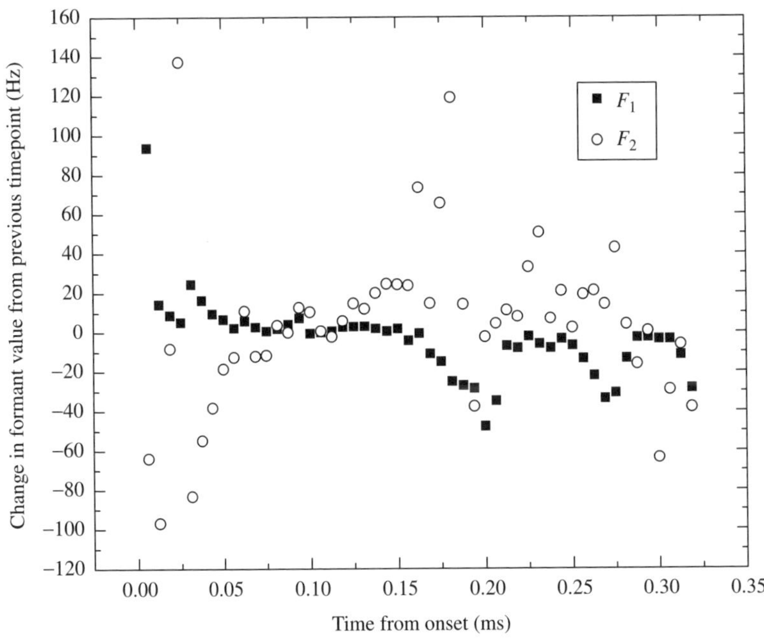

Figure 5.26 Plot of timepoint vs degree of change in formant values for an [ai] diphthong.

state, for which both F_1 and F_2 are quite stable, appears in the first half of the diphthong.

5.9 Undershoot

Most observers consider vowels to have 'phonetic targets', that is articulatory or acoustic points that they would reach if there were no neuromuscular factors holding them back. Leaving aside the issues of how neuromuscular commands operate, the basic idea is that a vowel (or a consonant or F_0 contour, for that matter) does not always attain the position that the speaker 'intends' because factors such as lack of time or effort expended to reach that position prevent it from doing so. This failure to reach a phonetic target is called *undershoot*.

Undershoot is often regarded as a purely mechanical process. When Lindblom (1963) first examined undershoot, he proposed that it was due entirely to the rate of speech. It is unclear whether he actually believed that himself, but publishing a study in which a testable hypothesis was applied to a phonetic process helped to propel phonetics into a status as an experimental science. Subsequently, numerous studies have shown that undershoot is not so mechanical and is not controlled entirely by the rate of speech. For one thing, several papers have found that the degree of stress may matter at least as much as the rate of speech (e.g. Engstrand 1988; van Son and Pols 1990). For another, additional studies have found that the degree of undershoot is language-specific and speaker-specific (e.g. Delattre 1969; Flege 1988), which in turn suggests that dialectal differences could exist and that sociolinguistic meaning could be attached to the degree of undershoot that a speaker exhibits. And why not? Doesn't it seem intuitive that some speakers could use careful articulation to project a certain identity, while other speakers could use lax articulation to project a different identity? I presented some evidence in Thomas (2002a) that speakers may project individual identity by this means. Further exploration would undoubtedly reveal other instances of undershoot indexing social identities or speaking styles. We will see in section 9.4 how variation in undershoot may reflect cognitive differences as well.

Undershoot, assimilation, truncation and reduction

Undershoot subsumes the phenomena known as assimilation, truncation and, in part, vowel reduction. *Assimilation*, a widely known term in linguistics, simply means that one sound becomes more like a neighbouring sound. This is a consequence of coarticulation, but whereas coarticulation refers to the overlapping properties of speech sounds, assimilation implies that one of the neighbouring sounds could be affected more than the other (though it doesn't exclude the possibility that both sounds could be affected equally). Naturally, the degree of coarticulation increases as the speech rate increases or the degree of stress decreases because the articulators have less time to move from one position to another (for a faster speech rate) or less energy is expended to make them move there (for decreased stress).

Truncation means that part of a sound is cut off. Once again, when truncation occurs, the usual suspects are quicker speech rate and less stress. Truncation is most easily observed for diphthongs. For diphthongs, a steady state that is present under favourable circumstances may disappear with fast speech rates or weakening of stress. That is, the diphthong has been truncated with the loss of one or both of its steady states and all that's left may be a transition.

A process often viewed as the opposite of truncation is *compression*, in which all the components of a sound remain but are squeezed into a shorter time frame. Compression is sometimes observed for intonational contours, as we'll see in Chapter 6. Some speakers do seem to compress diphthongs instead of truncating them. However, such speakers still preserve the transitions at the expense of the steady states. They just show more rapid formant dynamics during the transitions. Even for them, there's a limit to the speed of formant movement because it's difficult or impossible to move the articulators any faster.

Another term often associated with undershoot is *vowel reduction*. This basically refers to vowels becoming more schwa-like, i.e. less peripheral and hence less differentiated from each other. However, *vowel reduction* has been used in two distinct senses. One refers to a phonological alternation between schwa and a full vowel, as occurs in the verbal and nominal forms of the word *rebel*: in the verb, the first syllable has schwa and the second syllable has a full vowel, yielding /rə'bɛl/, while the noun shows the opposite pattern, yielding /'rɛbəl/. The other sense of vowel reduction is a phonetic process wherein vowels can become relatively more central as duration or stress decreases. This phonetic process is a form of undershoot.

Measuring and displaying undershoot

Undershoot can be gauged by measuring a few key factors. Vowel reduction is the simplest aspect of undershoot to measure and is useful for monophthongal vowels. The simplest investigation of reduction requires only measurements of the vowel formants at some point (such as the midpoint of the vowel or the point of maximum F_1) and the duration of the vowel. Truncation of diphthongs can be handled much like reduction because it is also more or less unidirectional – that is the end of the diphthong becomes more like the beginning if the glide is truncated, and the opposite happens if the nucleus is truncated. Investigating assimilation is more complicated because, whereas reduction assumes that undershoot will mutate a vowel in the direction of schwa, with assimilation the vowel can be changed in numerous ways, depending on the qualities of neighbouring segments.

Plotting formant readings against token durations

Showing vowel duration on one axis (normally the x-axis) of a two-dimensional graph and formant readings on the other axis is the simplest and, generally, most effective means of examining either phonetic vowel reduction or truncation of diphthongs. The axis (usually the y-axis) on which formant values are shown can be used for a single formant or, as Lindblom (1963) employed it, more than one formant. Of course, formant values can be shown in hertz, in a plain logarithmic scale, or in one of the perceptual scales. When you perform this kind of comparison, most often you will want to fit a regression line to the data. The least complicated sort of regression is linear regression, and depending on what you want to demonstrate, it may be all you need. The slope and y-intercept can be quite useful, especially for testing whether the patterning of two sets of data – such as allophones of a vowel phoneme, tokens from different speaking styles, or (for a language such as Spanish) presence or absence of lexical stress – is statistically the same or different. However, undershoot distributions are normally asymptotic, not purely linear, with the asymptote being the target value of the vowel. Hence, you may need to perform a more complicated curve-fitting or moving-average operation instead.

The following two graphs show two examples of undershoot distributions. Both show linear regression lines instead of anything more complex. The first one, Figure 5.27, shows the duration of /a/ against the F_1 at the midpoint of /a/ for the Spanish of the woman from southern Texas whose voice was featured in several earlier figures. This graph exhibits the simplest sort of display. It can be seen that the F_1 value is lower (and the vowel, thus, higher) when the vowel has a shorter duration. The regression line shows a decided slope. The second graph, Figure 5.28, shows several items. The speaker here is a man from St John's, Newfoundland, and the graph plots his PRICE/PRIZE glides. Both F_1 and F_2 are shown on the y-axis, which is logarithmic. This graph examines whether the glides differ in quality depending on whether they precede a voiceless obstruent or a voiced obstruent. Because vowels are shorter before voiceless consonants than before voiced ones, it is conceivable that any

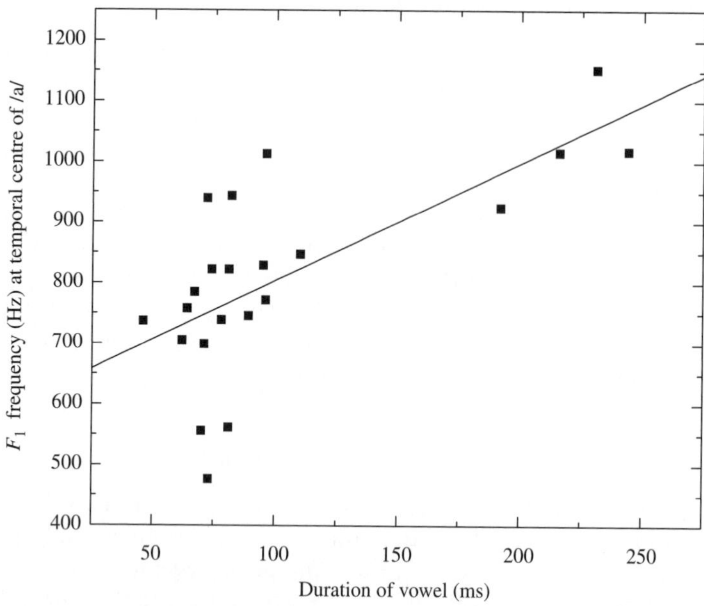

Figure 5.27 Plot with regression line comparing duration with F_1 for tokens of /a/ for Spanish spoken by the same speaker as in Figures 5.13–17

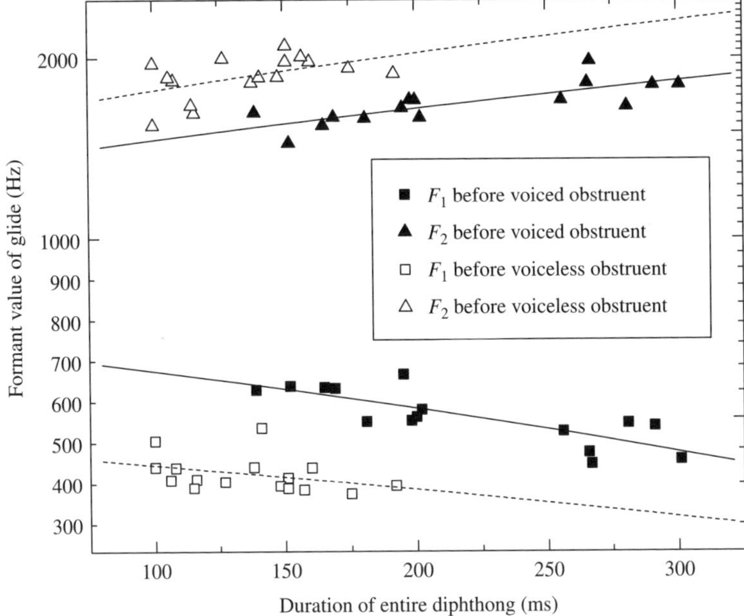

Figure 5.28 Plot with regression lines for duration of diphthong vs glide formant values for PRICE/PRIZE words uttered by a speaker from Newfoundland

observed difference in the glides could be an artefact of the difference in durations. In this example, however, the regression lines show that the differences in the glides are not due to the differences in duration. Tokens before voiceless obstruents have lower F_1 values and higher F_2 values than tokens before voiced obstruents with similar durations.

A method for filtering out coarticulation

Coarticulation seems more difficult to deal with than reduction and truncation, but in fact all we really need to do for it is to build on the methods used for reduction and truncation. A simple way to gauge the degree of coarticulatory influence on a token is to measure the formant values at the onset or offset of the vowel and then compare them with the formant values of the nucleus and/or glide. A formant value at the nucleus can be subtracted from that at the onset or offset. This method works especially well for F_2 because it is most strongly influenced by the place of articulation of neighbouring segments. F_1 is more strongly influenced by other factors, such as nasality, which aren't as linear. For the $F_{2onset} - F_{2nucleus}$, $F_{2offset} - F_{2nucleus}$ or $F_{2offset} - F_{2glide}$ metrics, labial consonants will ordinarily produce negative values and dorsal consonants will most often produce positive values. Figure 5.29 shows data from the FACE vowels of a white female from a rural part of North Carolina, with F_2 of the nucleus plotted against $F_{2onset} - F_{2nucleus}$. The nucleus was defined here as the point 35 ms from the onset. Although there's a great deal of scatter in the data, the general pattern, as indicated by the regression line, is that the two dimensions

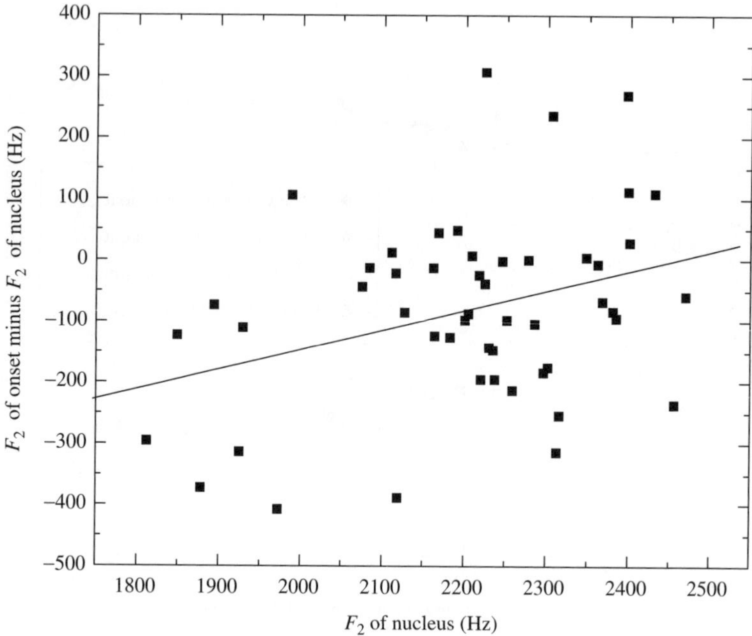

Figure 5.29 Plot of nuclear F_2 vs $F_{2onset}-F_{2nucleus}$ value for FACE nuclei of a European American female from rural North Carolina.

are correlated. That is, preceding consonants do indeed influence the nuclear values – consonants with high F_2 values generally raise F_2 of the nucleus, while consonants with low F_2 values usually lower F_2 of the nucleus.

In a multivariate analysis, the $F_{2onset} - F_{2nucleus}$ value could be used as an independent variable and thus could be used to tease the effects of coarticulation apart from those of other factors, such as speaking style/register or stress level. In this way you could use the $F_{2onset} - F_{2nucleus}$ value, which will cover both positive and negative values, as an independent variable representing the consonantal (or other) context. Figure 5.30 shows a spectrogram with the onset and a point 35 ms later (treated as the nucleus) marked.

Adjustments are needed to analyse coarticulatory effects when the nucleus isn't defined as a constant distance from the onset or the glide isn't defined as a constant distance from the offset. As you recall from section 5.3, there are two other methods of deciding where to take measurements besides set distances from the onset or offset: measuring at a point at which a certain formant reaches a maximum or minimum value (most commonly, the point of maximum F_1) or measuring a certain fraction of the distance between the onset and the offset, such as one-quarter or halfway. If you choose the method of measuring at a formant maximum or minimum, the distance from the onset or offset will vary unpredictably. For that reason, your best bet with that method is to take a measurement a set number of ms before (or after) the point where the formant minimum or maximum was. From that point on, you can treat the data in much the same way as you would with the method used for Figures 5.29 and 5.30. Note that, for vowels with long steady states, the values of these

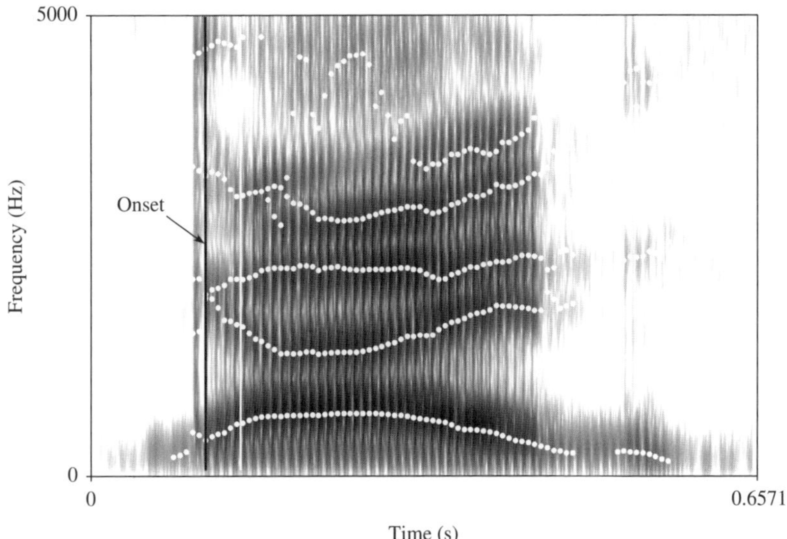

Figure 5.30 Spectrogram of an utterance of the word *guide*. The onset is marked with a black line and the point 35 ms after the onset marked with a white line. The difference in the frequency of F_1, F_2 or F_3 between the two points could be used to examine coarticulation.

metrics will be close to zero, reflecting the minimal effect of coarticulation on such tokens. Vowels without steady states will tend to show values that are strongly negative or positive, reflecting their greater degree of coarticulation. You can see why if you look back at Figure 5.9. The spectrogram in Figure 5.31 shows how this method could be used for a diphthong.

On the other hand, if you use a fractional distance, you'll need three variables: the value of the given formant at the fractional distance (i.e. the nucleus or glide), the value of that formant at the onset (or offset), and the duration of the vowel. What will happen is that, as the duration of the vowel becomes longer, the values of the nucleus and/or glide will approach their target value. The formant value of the nucleus/glide is the dependent variable, while the formant value at the onset/offset and the vowel duration are the independent variables. A plot of vowel duration vs nuclear value for a given formant will yield a fan-shaped distribution, with broad scattering of formant values at short durations and little scattering at long durations. Figure 5.32, which plots the LOT/THOUGHT vowels for a woman from Wooster, Ohio (she has the two classes merged), shows such a pattern. Note how the tokens with durations over 300 ms converge on a narrow range of hertz values.

Perceptual compensation for undershoot

Listeners seem to be able to normalize for undershoot effects most of the time. They are able to correct for coarticulatory assimilation and for vowel reduction, sometimes even overcompensating (Lindblom and Studdert-Kennedy 1967).

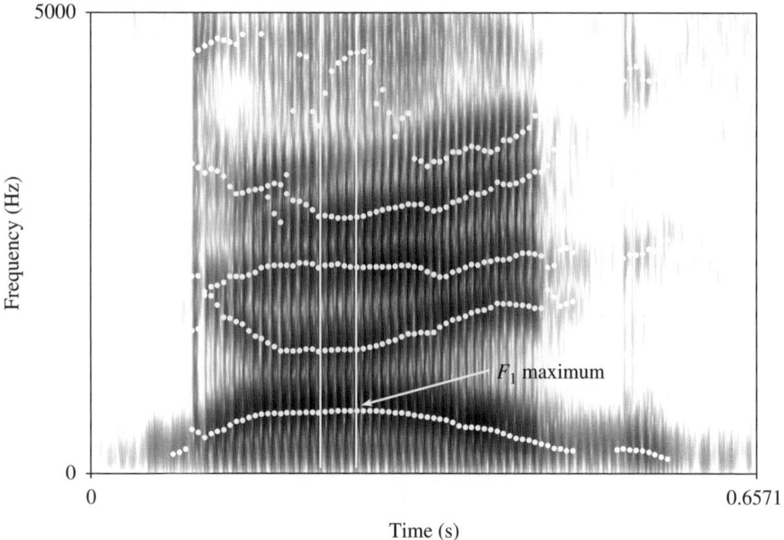

Figure 5.31 Spectrogram of the word *guide* with the point of maximum F_1 (661 Hz) and the point 35 ms earlier marked with lines.

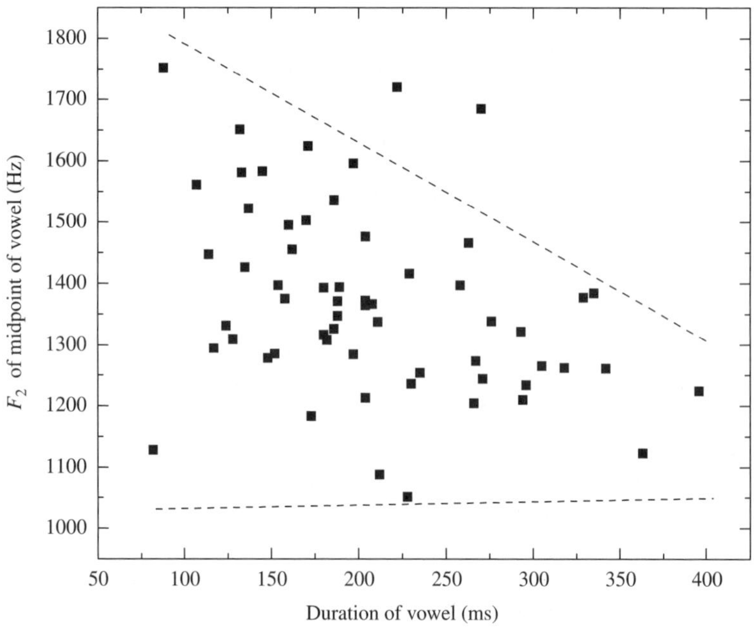

Figure 5.32 Plot of vowel duration vs nuclear values for LOT=THOUGHT vowel for a woman from Ohio. Note how most of the data points lie between the dashed lines, giving the points a fan-shaped distribution.

Ohala (1989) dubbed the mechanisms that listeners use to do this as 'corrective rules'. You could construct an experiment like that of Lindblom and Studdert-Kennedy yourself with a synthesizer. They examined perception of [ʊ] and [I] vowels in [wVw] and [jVj] contexts and found that the perceptual boundary between the two vowels differed by the context. Listeners heard [ʊ] for a greater range of stimuli in the [jVj] context than in the [wVw] context. In your follow-up experiment, you might test different segmental contexts, perhaps with different vowels, and perhaps adding in various sociolinguistic factors by for example comparing different listener groups.

Role of undershoot in conditioned vowel shifts

Sometimes, as Ohala (1989, 1993a) has noted, the 'corrective rules' that listeners use to normalize contextual effects appear to break down. Most of the time, the result is only momentary confusion by the listener. However, under certain circumstances, a sound change can result, and a class of sound changes is attributed to undershoot. When coarticulation is involved, the result is an assimilatory sound change or, less often, a dissimilatory change. A large fraction of conditioned sound changes are due to coarticulatory processes. Phonetic vowel reduction can lead to phonological vowel reduction – for example, the vowels in *was*, *what* and *of* have all shifted from the LOT class to the STRUT class in most varieties of American English, largely because all three words are destressed much of the time, making the vowels more schwa-like, with schwa becoming generalized to the stressed forms. We'll explore the influence of undershoot on sound change more in Chapter 10.

EXERCISES

For the following exercises, you can download practice samples from http://ncslaap.lib.ncsu.edu/sociophonetics/.

1. Measure the durations of many tokens of two vowels for a given speaker. You can download examples. Which vowel has a longer duration, on average? How are the durational differences and the amount of scatter in the data affected if you control for phrase-final lengthening and the voicing of the following segment?
2. Record yourself saying a vowel, such as [ɛ], first in a normal voice and then as nasally as you can; or download some practice examples. Try to measure the formants in the two utterances using LPC. How well do the LPC formant estimates match up with the formants that you can see on the spectrogram? Does LPC fare better with one than with the other? Now change the number of LPC coefficients until the utterance that initially had the poorer match comes out accurately. Do you end up with any false formants?
3. Record yourself saying the following words, first in a normal voice and second in a yawning voice: *heed, hid, hayed, head, had, hod, hawed, HUD, hoed, hood, who'd, heard* and *hold*. If you can't record your own voice, download

EXERCISES

practice examples. Measure the first three formants for each word. Then plot the first two formants for each word in a graph, denoting the normal and yawning tokens with different symbols or different colours. How do the normal and yawning vowels differ from each other? What do you think the reason is for the difference?

4. If you have access to vowel data for two different speakers, preferably a male and a female (recordings are available for you to download), go to the website http://ncslaap.lib.ncsu.edu/tools/ and normalize the datasets using the various normalization methods available there.
5. Measure the onset, midpoint, offset and duration for 50 tokens of some vowel for a single speaker, either one you have recorded yourself or one downloaded. (You'll need to choose a frequently occurring vowel to find that many tokens unless you design a special reading task for the speaker.) For F_1, plot duration against the midpoint of the vowel and perform a linear regression analysis. Does any clear pattern emerge? (It will probably be more obvious if you choose a low vowel.) For F_2, plot the midpoint value against the difference between onset and midpoint or the difference between offset and midpoint. How clearly does a fan shape emerge for the data? (It may depend on how much variation the tokens show in their durations.)
6. Measure the duration and formant values of either the nucleus or the glide of at least 25 tokens of a particular diphthong for a single speaker, again either one you have recorded yourself or one downloaded. Plot the duration against F_1 or F_2 and perform a linear regression. How linear is the resulting pattern? Does the pattern look like assimilation to the other part of the diphthong or does it look random?
7. How might difference in the degree of undershoot take on social meanings? What social meanings could they index, both for interspeaker variation and for stylistic variation?
8. Using a speech synthesizer, create a continuum of vowels from [i] to [a] in some consonantal context, such as /hVd/ or /bVt/. See Ohala and Feder (1994) for a model. Vary F_1 and F_2 by even steps in hertz values (or, if you're really daring, in Bark). Scramble the order of the stimuli, assemble them into a test recording and try playing them to some friends, asking them to identify what word they think each stimulus is. Then compare the results. How consistent are the subjects in where their phoneme boundaries are?

FURTHER READING

Adank, Patti, Roel Smits and Roeland van Hout. 2004. A comparison of vowel normalization procedures for language variation research. *Journal of the Acoustical Society of America* 116:3099–107.

Disner, Sandra Ferrari. 1980. Evaluation of vowel normalization procedures. *Journal of the Acoustical Society of America* 67:253–61.

Kent, Ray D. and Charles Read. 2002. *The Acoustic Analysis of Speech*, 2nd edn. Albany, NY: Thomson Learning. (See Chapter 4 for mean measured values in several studies of American English vowels and for several other languages.)

Labov, William. 1991. The three dialects of English. In Penelope Eckert (ed.), *New Ways of Analyzing Sound Change*. New York: Academic, 1–44.

Labov, William. 1994. *Principles of Linguistic Change. Volume 1: Internal Factors*. Language in Society 20. Oxford, UK/Cambridge, MA: Blackwell.

Lindau, Mona. 1978. Vowel features. *Language* 54:541–63.

Lindblom, Björn. 1963. Spectrographic study of vowel reduction. *Journal of the Acoustical Society of America* 35:1773–81.

Lindblom, Björn E.F. and Michael Studdert-Kennedy. 1967. On the role of formant transitions in vowel recognition. *Journal of the Acoustical Society of America* 42:830–43.

Peterson, Gordon E. and Harold L. Barney. 1952. Control methods used in a study of the vowels. *Journal of the Acoustical Society of America* 24:175–84.

Peterson, Gordon E. and Ilse Lehiste. 1960. Duration of syllable nuclei in English. *Journal of the Acoustical Society of America* 32:693–703.

Thomas, Erik R. 2001. *An Acoustic Analysis of Vowel Variation in New World English*. Publication of the American Dialect Society 85. Durham, NC: Duke University Press.

Prosody

6

6.1 Diverse and full of opportunities

Prosody encompasses a rather disparate collection of phenomena. Generally, it is taken to mean phonological or phonetic processes that aren't part of the segmental phonology. They involve pitch (the perceptual analogue of F_0 frequency), timing of items larger than segments and/or, to some extent, loudness (realized as amplitude). They range from lexical processes such as tone and lexical stress to phenomena larger than words such as intonation. Even pauses can be considered part of prosody.

Of course, F_0 and timing also figure in some segmental distinctions. As we've seen in previous chapters, F_0 plays a supplementary role in the voicing distinction for consonants and for vowel height. The role of timing in segmental distinctions is even better known. Timing is the primary factor distinguishing contrastive length, both for vowels and for consonants, and it is involved with the voicing distinction for consonants, with stop/fricative distinctions, and for tenseness and height distinctions among vowels (high vowels tend, on average, to be shorter than low vowels). There are numerous points of contact between prosodic and segmental variation, especially regarding lexical tone. As we'll see, the distinction becomes murky when we consider prosodic rhythm as well.

Prosodic variation is underexplored. As a result, it is fertile ground for innovative work and enterprising researchers. Leaving aside tone and lexical stress, there have been two major thrusts in studies of prosodic variation. One is in prosodic rhythm. This has to do with variations in the length of syllables or of the vocalic and/or consonantal portions of different syllables. It is conventionally thought of by using the terms *stress-timing* and *syllable-timing*. Studies of variation in prosodic rhythm are incipient. To date, most of the discussion of prosodic rhythm has centred on methods of gauging it instead of applications to variation. The other thrust concerns intonation. The study of variation in intonation has developed a devoted, but rather small, following. In fact, intonational variation studies have operated at some distance from other variation studies. Most of the researchers working on it are intonation specialists. The nature of intonation has led to this insularity. In segmental phonology, the phonological primitives – the segments themselves – are mostly transparent, readily permitting phonetic and sociolinguistic studies of them. In intonation, the phonological primitives are far less transparent and are open to debate. In spite of this difficulty, studies of intonational variation have gained momentum since about 1990. Beyond prosodic rhythm and intonation, a few other topics, such as overall rate of speech and analysis of pauses, have attracted sporadic study.

6.2 Global factors

Pauses

It can be hard to think of pauses as a linguistic variable. After all, aren't they the *absence* of speech? How can they show patterning? Nevertheless, pauses serve important functions in discourse, and their length and frequency can be varied in order to convey different social meanings. Much of this variation can be linked with speaking style and register. Some of it is associated with particular groups. Different papers in Tannen and Saville-Troike (1985), for example, discuss the varying cultural norms in pausing. There is evidence for cross-linguistic differences in pause length and frequency (Grosjean 1980; Campione and Véronis 2002), and now evidence is emerging for intralinguistic differences (Kendall 2009).

Pauses include more than just silent periods in the speech signal. A pause that consists of silence is called a *silent pause*. There is another kind of pause: those that consist of hesitation markers, such as *uh* and *um* in English (see Clark and Fox Tree 2002). The latter kind of pause is called a *filled pause*. Silent pauses can result when the speaker takes a breath, stops to formulate more speech or pauses for effect. Filled pauses function similarly except that they aren't normally due to respiration.

There has been a lot of disagreement about how long a silent interval has to be before it represents a pause. The main problem is that silent intervals aren't always pauses. Many of them are due to closure of stop consonants, which also produces brief periods of silence. To exclude stop closures, there has to be a minimum value that can be counted as a pause. Kowal et al. (1975) used the very cautious minimum value of 270 ms. However, many legitimate pauses are shorter than that, and later researchers have tended to use a lower threshold. Tsao and Weismer (1997), for example, used a minimum value of 150 ms, and Mukherjee (2000) used a 200-ms threshold. Even those values appear to exclude many real pauses, though. Robb et al. (2004:6) stated that silent intervals under 50 ms are reliably due to stop closure, those over 250 ms are reliably pauses, and those in the 50–250 ms range could be either one. These figures are reasonable, so the minimum value for what you count as a pause should be no less than 50 ms and no more than 250 ms. It's up to you to decide where to set the threshold between those values, though. If you set it at a higher value, you'll exclude many legitimate pauses, but if you set it at a lower value, you run the risk of counting some stop closures as pauses. Even if there's no phonological stop at a short silent interval, there's often a glottal stop present there.

Some authors use a maximum value, such as five seconds, as well. At a certain point, a pause ceases to represent an opportunity for the speaker to plan more speech before continuing. Instead, it signals to other interlocutors that the floor is open to them.

When you analyse pauses, the easiest thing to analyse is the distribution of pause lengths. Figure 6.1 shows one way to analyse pause lengths: different demographic groups from a community in southern Texas are put into different boxplots that show the distribution of pause lengths. As a rule, this distribution is skewed. For this reason, you may want to perform a logarithmic transformation of the pause lengths to make the distribution closer to a normal distribution. Frequency of pauses can be gauged not only by noting the number of pauses per unit of time, but also by comparing the lengths of time devoted to actual speech – that is, shorter stretches of speech indicate more frequent pausing.

A special kind of pause analysis was developed by Henderson et al. (1966). They developed a type of graph in which speech is represented by a stair-step line, with speech time represented as movement of the line to the right and pause time represented as movement of the line upward. Their original application was to monologic speech, but it can be applied to dialogue, as described by Kendall (2009). The overall slope of the stair-step line, either a section of it (e.g. representing a discourse topic) or of the entire conversation, is computed. Figures 6.2 and 6.3 show 'Henderson graphs' for two conversations. In Figure 6.2, there is relatively little pausing, so the stair-step line is relatively flat. In Figure 6.3, conversely, there is more pausing, so the stair-step line shows a greater overall slope.

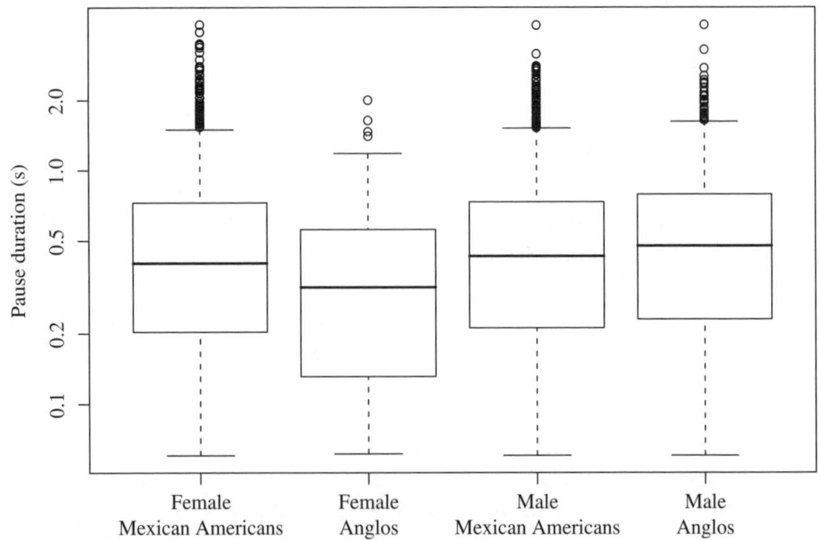

Figure 6.1 Boxplots of pause durations for speakers from a community in southern Texas.

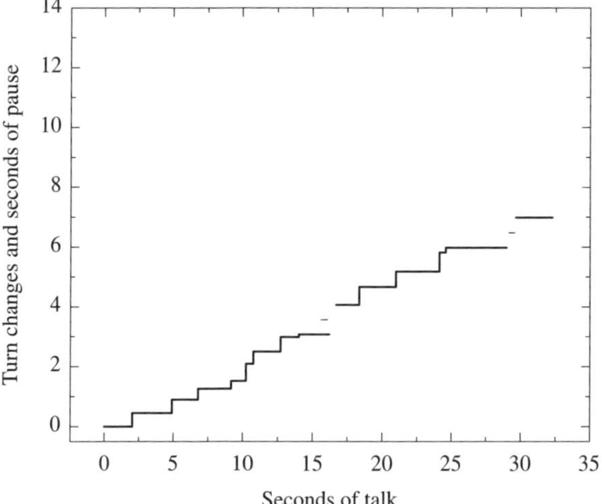

Figure 6.2 A Henderson graph, adapted for dialogue following Kendall (2009), for a conversation with relatively few turn changes and only short pauses. The interviewee's speech is shown with dark lines and the interviewer's with light lines. Data are from the North Carolina Language and Life Project archive, located at http://ncslaap.lib.ncsu.edu/ (see Kendall 2008).

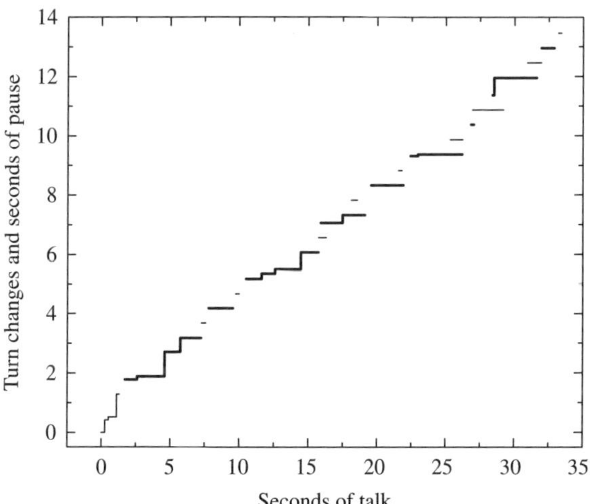

Figure 6.3 A Henderson graph for a conversation with relatively many turn changes and some longer pauses. The interviewee's speech is shown with dark lines and the interviewer's with light lines.

Rate of speech

Rate of speech has received quite a lot of attention from speech pathologists. Factors such as maturation in children and dysarthria can certainly affect speech rate (Tsao and Weismer 1997). Individual variation in speech rate has also been explored (Tsao and Weismer 1997; Kendall 2009). Can dialect affect speech rate, though? Some studies have found that it can. Robb et al. (2004) found that New Zealand English showed faster speech rates than American English or Australian English. Verhoeven et al. (2004) and Quené (2008) found faster speech rates for Netherlands Dutch than for Flemish Dutch. Other studies, such as Ray and Zahn's (1990) comparison of several American English dialects or Hewlett and Rendall's (1998) comparison of Orkney and Edinburgh English, have failed to find regional differences in speech rates. Of course, negative results don't prove that differences don't exist. In addition to regional differences, there's some evidence that gender and age differences exist and it would seem self-evident that stylistic differences in speech rate occur. In fact, Yuan et al. (2006) found that speaking rates were faster between acquainted people than between unacquainted people, both for English speakers and for Mandarin Chinese speakers.

Criteria for gauging speech rate vary. For one thing, sometimes the number of words per unit of time is counted, and sometimes the number of syllables or the number of phonemes is counted, though syllables are by far the favoured unit of measure. Counting words is problematic because words vary greatly in length. Another difference is in whether silent periods (pauses) are included in the time. Robb et al. (2004:6) note that the number of syllables divided by the amount of time, including silent periods, is called the *speaking rate*, while number of syllables per time with silent periods excluded is called the *articulation rate*. It is also possible to invert the formula so that it represents seconds per syllable, called the *average syllable duration* or *ASD* (Quené 2008).

An important alternative in measuring speech rate is to dispose of the consonantal portions of the signal and measure the durations of all the vowels. This method has been used in some studies of American English, particularly by Clopper et al. (2005) and Jacewicz et al. (2007). Both of these studies found regional differences in American English, in contrast to Ray and Zahn (1990). You have to remember, though, that with the consonants excluded, what you measure becomes something of a hybrid between rate of speech and intrinsic vowel length. In fact, Clopper et al. (2005) and a similar study of Dutch by Adank et al. (2007) both found that the regional differences in vowel duration applied only to certain vowels. Furthermore, prolongation of vowels may be limited to certain prosodic or syntactic positions.

Another consideration when measuring rate of speech is that the length of the utterance makes a big difference. The last syllable or foot before a pause is generally lengthened, so short utterances will appear to have slower rates of speech because the lengthened final portion will make up a greater fraction of the syllables. However, for very long utterances, the rate may begin to increase again (Kendall 2009). If you're comparing the rates of speech of different groups or speaking styles, you should compare utterances of similar lengths. Apparent differences in rate of speech can easily be due to differences in how often speakers pause. Nevertheless, pause length, as opposed to pause frequency, doesn't control the rate of speech but may still be related to it. Kendall (2009) found that longer pauses were correlated with slower rates of speech. This relationship may be due to planning by the speaker instead of to sociolinguistic factors, but then some kinds of social interactions induce speakers to plan their utterances more carefully.

With regard to speech style, figures given in different studies for rate of speech are often dependent upon whether spontaneous or read speech was used. Much of the research on speech rate by speech pathologists has used read speech. However, there are important differences between spontaneous and read speech that affect rate of speech. Spontaneous speech requires speakers to think on their feet, so it tends to have more pauses, both filled and unfilled. Read speech requires much less planning and the rate of speech depends in part on the speaker's reading proficiency.

6.3 Lexical prosody

Lexical aspects of prosody depend in one way or another on word structure. Jun's (2005b) typology divides prosody into prominence and the rhythmic or prosodic unit, each with a lexical and a post-lexical component. Lexical prominence involves whether a language has *lexical tones*, *lexical pitch accents* or *lexical stress*. All three may involve pitch, though stress may also involve other properties such as loudness and length. Some languages have more than one of them, while others – e.g. Korean – have none, according to Jun. Lexical rhythmic units include syllables, feet and morae. They come into play with prosodic rhythm. A language essentially bases its prosodic rhythm on only one of those units.

Lexical tone and lexical pitch accents

Lexical tonal contrasts occur in a large proportion of the world's languages. However, little sociophonetic work has occurred with lexical tone because contrastive tone doesn't occur in the European languages on which most sociophoneticians work. In a true tone language, pitch is specified for every syllable of a word. Lexical pitch accents are similar to tone, but differ in that only some syllables within words are distinguished by tones (Jun 2005b). In addition to the well-known (and non-European) case of Japanese, a few European languages – documented examples include Swedish, Norwegian, Serbo-Croatian and Basque – have lexical pitch accents. However, full-blown tone systems are pretty much unheard of among European languages. Lexical pitch accents can be studied phonetically using the same techniques as for tone, so what follows applies to them as well as to tone.

Tone is most commonly associated with languages of Africa and eastern Asia. Whereas African tone systems are relatively simple, most often consisting of only a high tone and a low tone with no intrinsic contours (*level tones* or *register tones*), Asian tone inventories tend to be complex, with both level tones and a variety of rising and falling tones (*contour tones*).

In a series of papers on Mandarin Chinese tones, Xu (e.g. 1999, 2001) and Xu and Wang (2001) found that lexical tones are tightly bound to a single syllable, which they called the *host syllable*. They also determined a number of phonetic properties of tones. You should expect to encounter these properties when you analyse tones. Among the most important properties they report are:

1. Implementation of a tone starts at the onset of its host syllable, but its effects usually last well into the following syllable. In fact, for a rising tone, the point of highest F_0 is quite often in the following syllable.
2. F_0 doesn't start off at its target value, but it gradually gets closer and closer to the target value, and it gets closest at the syllable offset. (In terms of targets, tones show undershoot much like vowels, which we saw in Chapter 5.)
3. The perseveratory effect from a preceding tone is assimilatory – e.g. a preceding low tone makes a tone lower than a preceding high tone. However, the anticipatory effect to a following tone is dissimilatory – e.g. a high tone will be higher when the next syllable has a low tone than when it has another high tone.
4. When a tone-bearing syllable is emphasized, F_0 in later syllables is lowered overall.

Some of these trends can be observed in Figure 6.4, which shows slow and fast readings by a native Mandarin speaker of the Mandarin sentence 'Wǒmén dōu dǒng, méi wèntí' ('We understand everything – no questions'). The numbers above the orthographic transcription use a commonly employed method of transcribing tone levels, with 5 highest and 1 lowest. Note how the tone is especially high for the 'dōu' syllable, which is preceded by a rising tone and followed by a low, falling tone – both of which conspire under rule 3 above to make 'dōu' higher than it would be otherwise. For the 'méi wèn' sequence,

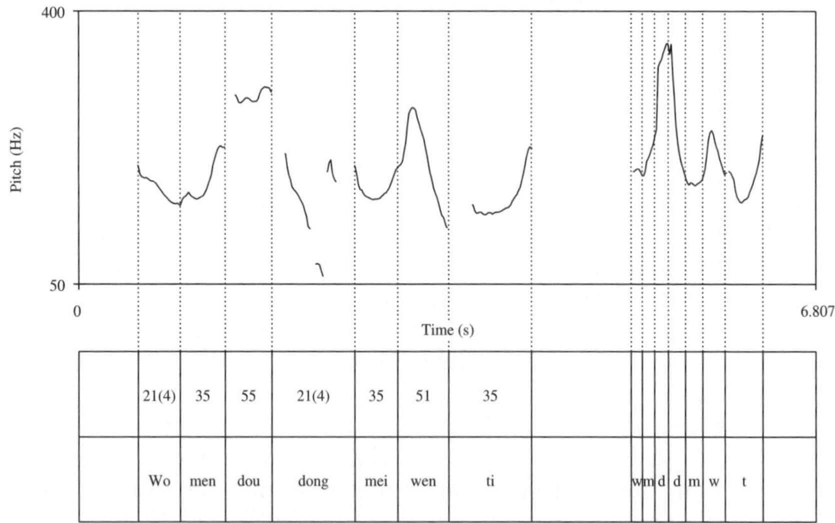

Figure 6.4 Comparison of pitch tracks for slow and fast readings of the Mandarin sentence 'Wǒmén dōu dǒng, méi wèntí.' Numbers above the Romanized orthography indicate phonological tone levels. For the fast reading, only the first consonant of the syllable is given in the orthographic tier.

the highest point isn't reached until well into the 'wèn' syllable, and in the fast reading, the lowest point for the falling tone associated with the 'wèn' syllable isn't reached until partway through the following 'tí' syllable.

In African tone languages, much of the variation centres around the locations of F_0 peaks associated with high tones. Myers (1999) used a relatively simple technique in a study of Chichewa, a tone language spoken in Malawi. He measured the amount of time between the beginning of each vowel associated with a high tone and the F_0 peak. The exact length of this time depended on the duration of the vowel. The timing relationship was linear and could be modelled by regression, but the slope differed depending on whether the tone was in the final, the penultimate or an earlier syllable within a phrase, and individual speakers showed differences in their patterning.

As you'd expect, the more complex tonal systems of eastern Asian languages, with their frequent contour tones, present more opportunities for variation. However, that also means that they're more complicated to analyse quantitatively. The main problem is that an acoustic reference point is needed before analysis can begin. Xu (1999, 2001) developed some techniques that use syllable boundaries as the reference points. He relied on two basic kinds of analyses. The first one involves normalizing time (syllable-by-syllable) and plotting it on the x-axis of a graph against F_0, which is shown on the y-axis. He used a smoothing program (see Xu 1999:105) to eliminate local perturbations of F_0, and then he averaged F_0 over many utterances. This kind of analysis lets you see how tonal contours differ in different contexts or for different speakers. An example for a Mandarin speaker is illustrated in Figure 6.5.

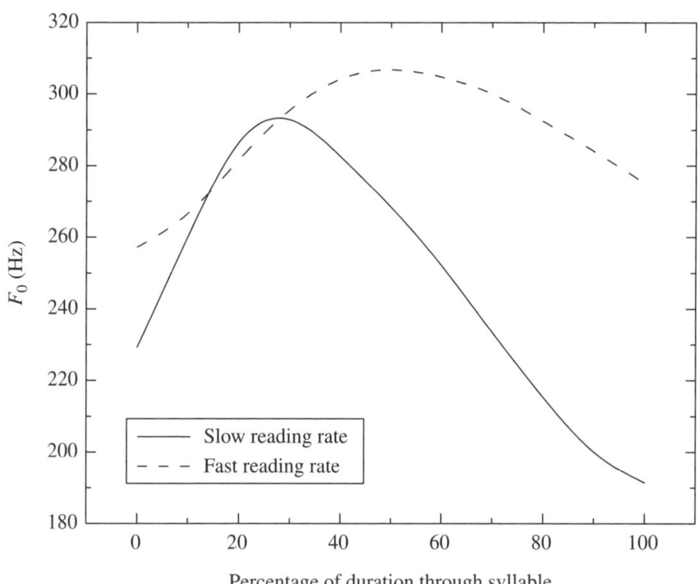

Figure 6.5 Averaged time-normalized F_0 contours for the high-falling ('fourth') tone of Mandarin uttered by a female native speaker.

Xu's other kind of analysis was similar to that of Myers (1999), but with adaptations for contour tone languages. It involves plotting (a) syllable durations on the x-axis and (b) various sorts of tonal measures on the y-axis. The syllable duration could be interpreted loosely. Xu used the distance from the onset of the host syllable to the onset of the vowel in the following syllable. If you're looking at conversational speech, in which a lot of the consonants are voiceless and have no F_0, you could substitute the duration of the host vowel for Xu's measure (Xu used syllables with sonorant consonants). The tonal measure can be different things, depending on what you want to examine. It can be the time in ms from the syllable onset to the maximum or minimum F_0, depending on whether you're looking at a rising/high tone or a falling/low tone and on whether you're examining the onset or offset of the tone. The tonal measure can also represent the distance from the syllable onset to the point of maximum F_0 velocity. For that matter, you could substitute the syllable offset for the onset if you wanted to. In this sort of analysis, different utterances aren't averaged. Instead, each one is plotted as one data point, and then a regression line for the data points is computed. Xu used this analysis to determine whether tones are aligned with syllable onsets or offsets.

Tonal analysis can certainly be applied to language variation, as shown by two recent papers, Bauer et al.'s (2003) study of Hong Kong Cantonese and Stanford's (2008) study of Sui, a language spoken in the Guizhou province in south-western China. Bauer et al. calculated normalized F_0 values using the formula

$$F_{0norm} = (F_{0i} - \bar{F}_0)/s$$

where F_{0i} is the F_0 of the individual token, $\bar{F}_0$ is the mean of all F_0 values for the speaker, and s is the standard deviation of all F_0 values for the speaker. Stanford dealt with the problem in a different way. Because Sui has a mid-level tone, he used that tone as his reference point for each speaker and gauged other tones by their deviation in semitones from the reference point. Once the reference point is determined, the realization of any token of a tone is then mapped against it. A simulation of this kind of comparison is shown in Figure 6.6. It's useful when the overall level of a tone varies. Stanford also used a different sort of reference point for a tone that shows variation in whether its contour rises and falls. For that tone, he used the onset of the tone as his reference point. A simulation of that analysis is shown in Figure 6.7.

Lexical stress

Lexical stress is so widespread among the languages of Europe that it often seems to be taken for granted by Western linguists. Stress can be realized as any combination of pitch, loudness and lengthening in a trading relation, and different languages appear to vary in the emphasis they place on each of those factors. Stressed vowels are, on average, higher-pitched, louder and longer than unstressed vowels – depending, that is, on the particular language. Kochanski et al. (2005) analysed dialects of British and Irish English and found that

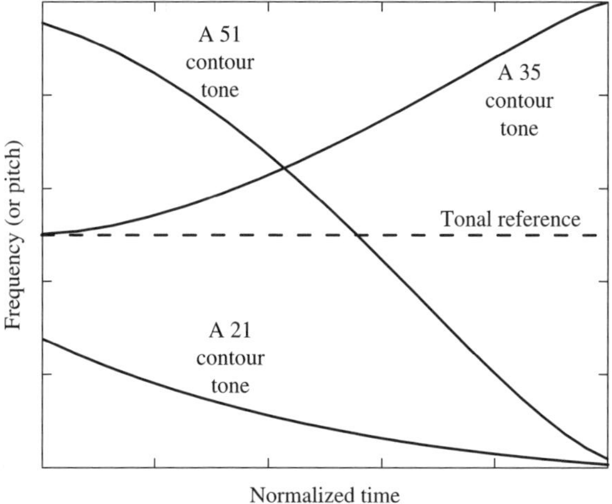

Figure 6.6 A simulation of tonal contours mapped against a tonal reference point.

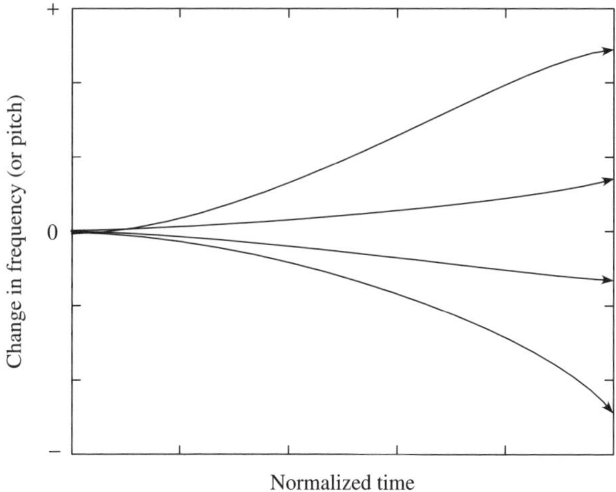

Figure 6.7 A simulation of tonal contours mapped against the tonal onset.

amplitude and duration were more correlated with stress in those dialects than pitch was. However, other languages may operate differently. Pitch seems to be more important in, e.g. Spanish. When length is correlated with stress, as in most Germanic languages, vowel reduction becomes a common consequence of destressing.

Stress can vary phonologically and phonetically. Phonological variations involve placement of stress. In English, for example, the word *object* is stressed on the first syllable if it's a noun and on the second if it's a verb. Certain words, such as *police* and *cement*, vary by dialect. Phonetic correlates include some of the same factors as for lexical tone. Beckman et al. (2002), for example, note that peak pitch alignment of stressed syllables can vary in Spanish. The generalizations that Xu (1999, 2001) noted for placement of tone-related F_0 peaks presumably pertain to stress as well. You can apply the same kinds of analyses and formulas described above for lexical tone to stress. However, you may wish to analyse amplitude instead of F_0. Doing so shouldn't be hard. For example, the procedure described above that Myers (1999) used for Chichewa tone can be applied, with the point of maximum amplitude substituted for the point of maximum F_0. Note that points of maximum amplitude don't necessarily coincide with points of maximum F_0. Not only that, but you have to remember that a stressed syllable in one part of an utterance may actually have a lower amplitude than an unstressed syllable in another part of the utterance. In that respect, amplitude resembles F_0 frequency. The most consistent tendency is for an unstressed syllable to have lower amplitude than a stressed syllable in the same foot – i.e. the immediately preceding stressed syllable, except for unstressed syllables at the beginning of an utterance, which don't belong to feet (a condition called *anacrusis*). A *foot* is a stressed syllable and all unstressed syllables until the next stressed syllable.

Although formulas are available for converting from hertz to perceptual units, as we saw in Chapter 3, the same isn't true of amplitude. The perceptual analogue to amplitude is loudness, which is generally measured in *sones*, but the dB-to-sone conversion varies according to the frequency of a sound. The only fixed conversion point is at 1 kHz, where 1 sone equals 40 dB, 2 sones equal 50 dB, 4 sones equal 60 dB, etc., if 0 dB (equal to 1/16 sone) is defined as the threshold of hearing. Of course, any speech sound covers a range of frequencies. Hence, you're better off sticking with dB. For field recordings, there may be some background noise. A common method for correcting for background noise is to sample some periods of the recording that contain no speech, average their amplitude and subtract it from the amplitude of the periods of speech that are analysed. That method works if the noise is relatively constant. Obviously, all bets are off with any sudden noises, such as slamming doors.

Prosodic rhythm

Discussion of prosodic rhythm has usually focused on the issue of stress-timing vs syllable-timing. These terms seem to have been coined by Pike (1945), though the concepts had been described earlier. The definitions of them established by Abercrombie (1967) have become widely accepted. In a language with *syllable-timing*, the length of time from one syllable to the next is relatively uniform, regardless of stress. In a language with *stress-timing*, however, the length of time from one *stressed* syllable to the next is approximately the same. Stress-timing can thus also be described as the condition in which all feet have approximately the same length. As a result, with stress-timing, syllables are shorter in feet with one or more unstressed syllables than in feet with only a stressed syllable. In Germanic languages, the unstressed syllables are especially compressed. Syllable-timing is often thought of as sounding machine-gun-like or staccato, while stress-timing is commonly described as sounding like Morse code (Lloyd James 1940). Figure 6.8 schematizes the difference. Syllable-timing is said to typify such languages as most Romance languages and Greek, while

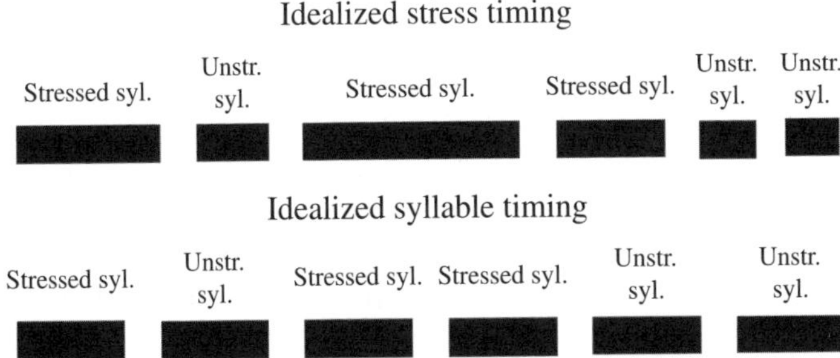

Figure 6.8 Schematized syllable durations for syllable-timing and stress-timing.

stress-timing is characteristic of, e.g., most Germanic languages. A third category, *mora-timing*, has been devised to describe the timing pattern in Japanese and other languages in which the timing is based on the number of morae.

The descriptions of the three timing types sound good, but they ran into two serious problems when acoustic measurements were first applied to timing. It turned out that syllable durations in syllable-timed languages show quite a bit of variation (Wenk and Wiolland 1982; Borzone de Manrique and Signorini 1983). That is, they're not *isochronous*. If that wasn't bad enough, it was found that durations from one stressed syllable to the next don't differ significantly between syllable- and stress-timed languages (Roach 1982; Dauer 1983). At that point, there was a lot of doubt about whether the rhythmic categories were real or not.

Even if rhythmic categories existed, though, the early findings left no reliable way to measure rhythm physically. An important breakthrough occurred when it was argued that rhythm is a gradient feature, not an absolute one (e.g. Miller 1984). This change in mindset paved the way for the development of mathematical formulas for computing the relative degree of syllable-timing or stress-timing, starting in the 1990s. In fact, now the lack of methods for measuring rhythm has been replaced by the opposite problem – there is a surplus of competing methods for measuring rhythm but no consensus as to which is best. Not everyone views rhythm as being completely continuous – Ramus (2002) argued that languages may still tend to cluster at points along continua – but mathematical approaches have come to dominate rhythm study.

Interval measures of rhythm

Cummins (2002) notes that differing definitions of rhythm have hindered the establishment of a taxonomy of rhythm types. One definition is that it consists of timing patterns caused by phonotactic phenomena. Dauer (1983) suggested that the apparent interlinguistic differences in rhythm aren't due to any intrinsic timing factors in languages but instead are consequences of the phonological structures of the languages. That is, whether a language allows syllable codas or consonant clusters, whether it possesses length contrasts for vowels, and particularly whether vowel reduction occurs could account for rhythmic variations. Formulas for prosodic rhythm based on this notion are called *interval measures*.

Ramus et al. (1999) took this approach. They defined three measures, as follows. ΔV is the standard deviation of the durations of the vocalic intervals. ΔC is the standard deviation of the durations of the consonantal intervals. %V is the percentage of the duration of an utterance made up of vocalic intervals. For example, Figure 6.9 shows a wideband spectrogram of the phrase 'and that a beanstalk would'. The sections for [æ], [ə] and so forth are the vowel intervals. The sections for [n] and [ð] together form a consonantal interval, the [ɾ] section makes another consonantal interval, and so on. Ramus et al. achieved good separation of languages by plotting ΔV against %V or by plotting ΔV against ΔC. ΔC and %V appeared to be correlated with each other, but still provided a clear separation into stress-timed, syllable-timed and mora-timed groups. That is, higher ΔC values and lower %V values are associated with stress-timing, but ΔV seems to describe something else.

A further development of Ramus et al.'s (1999) ideas was proposed by Dellwo (2006). Dellwo made a variation coefficient of Ramus et al.'s ΔC using the formula VarcoΔC = 100 x (standard deviation of consonantal interval durations) / (mean consonantal interval duration), or VarcoΔC = $100(\Delta C)/\bar{C}$. Higher VarcoΔC values are associated with stress-timing. Dellwo's interest was largely in examining how rhythm changed across different speaking rates, and he noted that, for the most part, faster speech was more syllable-timed than slower speech. White and Mattys (2007) extended Dellwo's idea to create an analogous formula for vocalic intervals: VarcoΔV = 100 x (standard deviation of vocalic interval durations) / (mean vocalic interval duration), or VarcoΔV = $100(\Delta V)/\bar{V}$. Higher VarcoΔV values are associated with stress-timing.

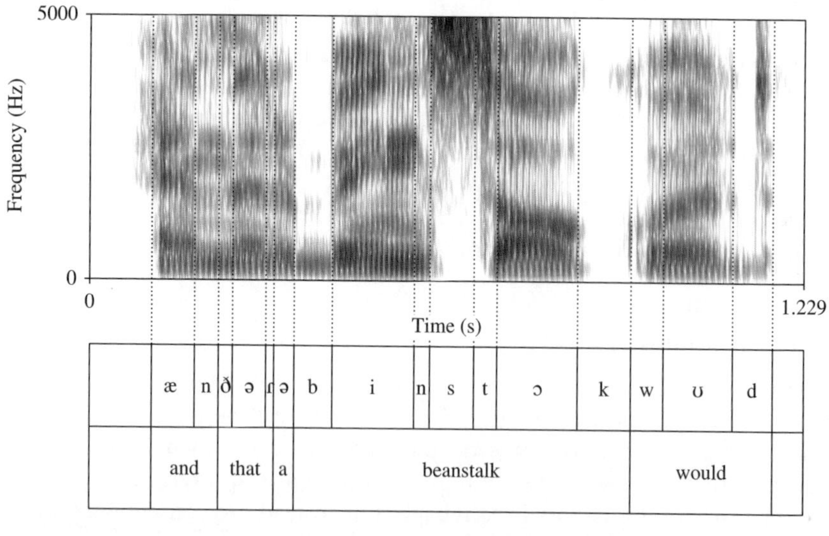

Figure 6.9 Wideband spectrogram of the phrase 'and that a beanstalk would' (taken from a spontaneous retelling of *Jack and the Beanstalk* by a North Carolinian) with each segmental interval marked.

Pairwise variability measures of rhythm

The other definition of rhythm that Cummins (2002) described is one that isn't dependent on phonotactics but is, as Cummins (2002:122) noted, 'a gradient phenomenon ... which mediates the role of syllables in determining macroscopic timing patterns'. Some evidence, such as Gut et al.'s (2002) analysis of three West African languages with different phonotactics but similar degrees of syllable-timing, has suggested that phonotactics cannot account for all aspects of rhythm. The second definition of rhythm inspired a second kind of formula for gauging prosodic rhythm: *pairwise variability measures*.

The first of these was developed by Low and Grabe (1995) and Low et al. (2000). As a test case, they compared British English, which is highly stress-timed, with Singaporean English, which is relatively more syllable-timed because of its Chinese and/or Malay substrate. Their basic method was to compare the durations of the vowels in adjacent syllables. In a syllable-timed language, the durations should mostly be pretty similar. In a stress-timed language, though, there should be greater variation in the durations. This formula, called the raw Pairwise Variability Index, or rPVI, was computed as the sum of the absolute values of the differences of durations of vowels in adjacent syllables, all divided by the total number of vowels minus one. An rPVI-C formula has been developed as an analogous measure for the consonantal portions of utterances (White and Mattys 2007).

One of the issues that confounded early attempts to quantify rhythm was variation in speech rate. Syllables will be shorter at faster speech rates than at slower ones, and if a speaker's rate of speech changes at various points during an interview, that can overshadow variations in the durations of nearby syllables. Hence, it is a good idea to find some way to normalize the speech rates. Following a suggestion by David Deterding, Low et al. (2000) solved this problem with their normalized Pairwise Variability Index (nPVI) formula. The normalization was accomplished by dividing each difference in the rPVI formula by the mean of the durations of the two vowels. The formula is thus expressed as

$$\text{nPVI} = 100 \times \left[\sum_{k=1}^{m-1} \left| \frac{d_k - d_{k+1}}{(d_k + d_{k+1})/2} \right| / (m-1) \right]$$

where m is the number of vowels in the utterance and d_k is the duration of the kth vowel.

The nPVI formula works well for Germanic languages, in which unstressed syllables are compressed much more than stressed syllables within the same foot. However, there are stress-timed languages in which the compression is more evenly distributed among syllables within a foot. Asu and Nolan (2006) discussed how to gauge the rhythm of one such language, Estonian. Their solution was to compute two rhythm metrics: the nPVI version, as described above, which is based on syllable comparisons, and a pairwise comparison of feet that they called nFPVI. The nFPVI formula is the same as that for nPVI except that d_k represents the duration of the kth foot, not the duration of a vowel. The nFPVI scores are expected to be low, since in a stress-timed language feet are supposed to be at least somewhat isochronous, and Asu and Nolan obtained that result. The difference is in the ratio of foot-based nFPVI to syllable-based nPVI. In English, where compression affects unstressed vowels disproportionately, nPVI is much higher than nFPVI. In Estonian, however, nPVI is only a little higher than nFPVI.

Low et al. (2000) used read sentences as the bases for testing their formula. The nPVI formula needed to be adapted to be usable for spontaneous speech. In Thomas and Carter (2006), nPVI was applied to conversational interview speech with a few adjustments: vowels in all prepausal feet were excluded from analysis in order to exclude phrase-final lengthening; pairwise comparisons could not cross pauses; and syllabic consonants were counted as vowels.

Deterding (2001) was also interested in analysing spontaneous speech. He developed a different formula, though, called the Variability Index, or VI, that used the durations of entire syllables, not just the vocalic part. He omitted final syllables to avoid the phrase-final lengthening effect. The resulting formula was

$$\mathrm{VI} = \frac{1}{n-2}\left[\sum_{k=1}^{n-2} |d_{k+1} - d_k|\right]$$

where d_k is the duration of the kth syllable. Like Low et al. (2000), Deterding tested the formula by comparing British and Singaporean English.

Sociophonetic uses of rhythm measurements

Debate continues among prosody specialists about the merits of the various formulas for prosodic rhythm. However, White and Mattys (2007) reported that the %V, VarcoΔV and nPVI (or nPVI-V, in their terminology) formulas provided the most consistent discrimination between languages traditionally considered stress-timed and syllable-timed. All three of these formulas are vowel-based.

The debate notwithstanding, pairwise variability measures have proved useful in some sociophonetic studies. Thus far, most of them have examined forms of English with interference or substrate effects from a more syllable-timed or mora-timed language. The studies by Low and Grabe (1995), Low et al. (2000) and Deterding (2001) on Singaporean English illustrate this tendency. Other second-language varieties of English have also been analysed. For example, Nguyen (2003) found that native speakers of Vietnamese produce English with a greater degree of syllable-timing than native English speakers, and Mochizuki-Sudo and Kiritani (1991) report the same for English spoken by native speakers of Japanese. There is also evidence that such interference features can become substrate features when groups lose their original language. White and Mattys (2007), using nPVI, %V and VarcoV, compared Welsh Valleys English, which has a Welsh substrate, and Shetland and Orkney

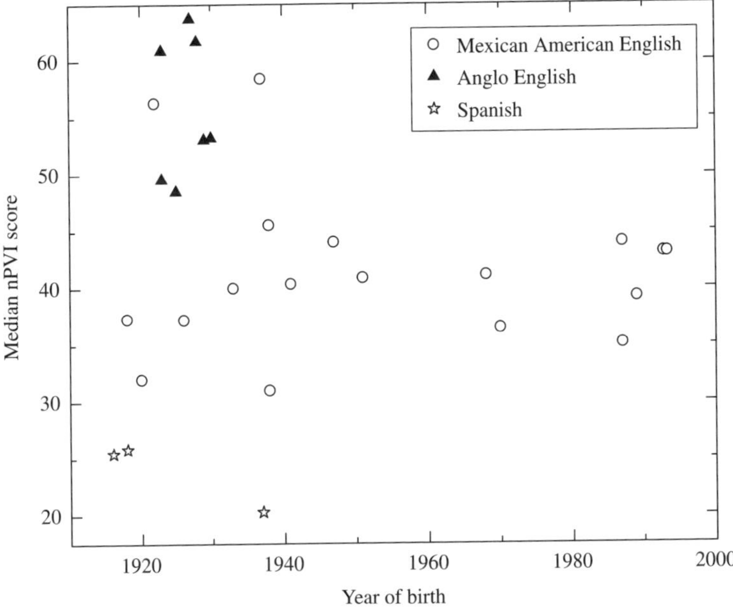

Figure 6.10 Graph of year of birth versus mean nPVI score for speakers from a community in southern Texas

English, which have a Norse substrate, with standard southern British English. They found that Welsh Valleys and Orkney varieties, at least, were more syllable-timed than standard southern British English. Thomas and Carter (2006) found that African Americans born in the mid-nineteenth century showed more syllable-timed speech than European Americans from Southern states born in that period or Southerners of either group born during the twentieth century, and used that finding to suggest that earlier African American English showed substrate influence.

Figure 6.10 illustrates how such an analysis can be applied to a community study. It features speakers from a community in southern Texas who were analysed using the nPVI method with modifications for spontaneous speech. Each symbol represents one individual. The oldest generation of Mexican Americans comprise only second-language learners of English, while the youngest generation is highly English-dominant, often with only passive knowledge of Spanish. Nonetheless, for all generations of Mexican Americans, most nPVI values are intermediate between values for Spanish and values for the Anglo contact dialect of the community. It appears that this intermediate degree of prosodic rhythm has transformed from an interference feature to a substrate feature as the new dialect of English has crystallized.

Can dialects of the same language without a linguistic substrate differ in prosodic rhythm? Once again, White and Mattys (2007) provide evidence. Besides the four dialects already mentioned, they also analysed Bristol English. It, too, turned out to be somewhat more syllable-timed than standard southern British English.

6.4 Intonation

Post-lexical prosody involves aspects of prosody that aren't dependent on word structure. The most important component of this prosody is *intonation.* Intonation, most generally, involves the use of pitch for meanings and connotations larger than individual words. It's a bewilderingly complex topic and I'm not going to try to cover it with the utmost thoroughness here – if I did, it would take up several chapters. Mainly I will try to provide some general guidelines and some methods for acoustic analysis.

Intonation, as a whole, involves two general kinds of objects. The first kind are *boundaries*, or *juncture*. These boundaries run the gamut from major ones in which the speaker resets his or her pitch after declination to boundaries between individual words. Higher-level boundaries, which delimit prosodic *phrases*, exhibit special pitch contours called *edge tones*. Lower-level boundaries, such as word boundaries, usually lack edge tones. Edge tones serve to signal addressees that a section of the discourse is completed. The second kind of intonational object is the *pitch accent*. Pitch accents are tones that are especially salient. Listeners are expected to be able to cue into the pitch accents. They are usually higher or lower in frequency than adjacent parts of the prosody. They can consist of a peak or trough or of a falling or rising contour. They usually appear in stressed syllables, but not every stressed syllable has a pitch accent. Every language and dialect has its own inventory of boundary and phrase types, edge tones and pitch accents.

Complications in studying intonational variation

Intonation is seldom included in analyses that also examine other kinds of linguistic variables. Most studies of intonational variation focus solely on intonation. Analogously, scholars who have worked on intonational variation tend to be intonation specialists. Why has intonational study become such a world unto itself? The reason is probably that the study of intonation presents a number of special problems that aren't present in other realms of language.

Transcription methods

First, there are questions about the best transcription method. While the International Phonetic Alphabet (IPA) has been the standard for transcription of segments since its development and has required only supplements and minor tinkering over the years, intonational transcription has undergone wholesale revolutions in its transcriptional notations.[1] Trager and Smith (1951) developed a system for transcription in which tones were represented as one of four pitch levels. This system was essentially a phonetic system, not a phonological one, and though it was used in numerous studies – e.g. analyses of African American English intonation by Tarone (1973) and Loman (1975) – it ultimately proved unsatisfactory. Key problems were that deciding which level a tone belonged to was too subjective and that the choice of four tones instead of some other number was subjective itself.

Another system was the 'interlinear tonetic' system described by Cruttenden (1997). This is based on the notion that movement of pitch, or contours, is what is phonologically specified, not the peaks and valleys. That is, the peaks and valleys are not seen as targets per se. It has a long tradition in the United Kingdom. In this scheme, tones are represented as filled circles, with a tail added if they show a contour, and the circles are sequenced between parallel lines that represent the upper and lower bounds of the pitch range the speaker was using. The vertical position of the circle represents its pitch.

Somewhat similar is the INSTINT (INternational Transcription System for INTonation) scheme that Hirst and Di Cristo (1998:13 ff.) propose. It also has two parallel lines representing the bounds of the pitch range used. However, tones are represented by arrows that indicate pitch relative to the preceding tone. That is, ↑ represents a higher tone, ↓ a lower one, → one at the same pitch, > a slight downstep, < a slight upstep, ⇑ movement to the upper extreme and ⇓ movement to the lower extreme. Brackets are used for boundaries of tonal units. INSTINT was intended as a phonetic transcription method that could be used for any language.

In recent years, however, autosegmental approaches to intonational transcription have gained a lot of momentum. These approaches are, for the most part, intended to be phonological, not phonetic. They rely on two important assumptions. One is that the peaks and valleys represent targets and they, not the amount of movement, are the phonological primitives. The other is that there are basically two kinds of tones, high (H) and low (L). Aside from a system called Transcription of Dutch Intonation, or ToDI (see Gussenhoven 2005), and one called the IViE (Intonational Variation in English) system developed for a study of British English dialects (Grabe 2004), the main autosegmental thrust has been the Tone and Break Index, or ToBI, system. ToBI is actually a series of related systems. It was initially designed for 'Mainstream American English', southern British English and Australian English (Beckman et al. 2005). Its phonological conception precluded its application to other languages without modification. However, it wasn't long before such modifications happened, and there are now versions of ToBI for a host of languages, such as GToBI for German or J_ToBI for Japanese: see the various papers in Jun (2005c). Beckman et al. (2005) ended up renaming their original version MAE_ToBI. I'll come back to the details of ToBI later on, but note for now that it has become the dominant paradigm for intonation and will probably remain so for the foreseeable future. However, given the past instability of intonational transcription, there's no guarantee that it'll always remain predominant.

The form-function problem

The second concern is that intonation is affected by what Foulkes and Docherty (2007:68) call the 'form-function problem'. As they explain, with segmental variables such as whether the /t/ in *better* is realized as [t] or [ʔ] or [ɾ], there is no question that the variants mean the same thing (in terms of the semantic content, that is, not sociolinguistically). On the other hand, it's not always clear that different intonational variants mean the same thing. For example, in the same sentence, with a pitch accent on the same word, whether that pitch accent shows an abruptly rising or gradually rising F_0 can result in distinct connotations.

Uncertainty about transcriptions

The third concern, and somewhat following from the form-function problem, is that transcriptions of the intonation of particular utterances are often open to question. Whereas transcribers can usually arrive at something approaching 100 per cent agreement on phonemic assignments of segments (notwithstanding issues of whether phonemes themselves exist), even experienced transcribers of intonation often disagree on the transcription of intonational notations that are assumed to be phonological. Hence, reliability testing is frequently necessary for intonational analyses. This problem is more acute for recordings of spontaneous speech than for scripted speech.

Transcription speed and quantitative analysis

Another obstacle to the study of intonational variation is that the transcription is usually painfully slow. Transcription is necessary before further acoustic analyses can take place. However, Syrdal et al. (2001) estimate that a full ToBI transcription takes 100 to 200 times the real time of the transcribed utterance. For a sociolinguistic analysis that examines trends within a population, such as a community survey, large amounts of data are necessary. The painstaking pace of transcription makes it very difficult to get enough data for a representative sample when different subgroups in the population are being compared. For example, let's say you wanted to know which subgroups show higher incidences of a certain type of pitch accent – e.g. the rising tone labelled in ToBI as L + H*. To find out, you'd have to have representative speakers from each subgroup, and then you'd need a substantial sample of pitch accents in the right kind of sentences (such as declaratives) for each speaker. That way you could compare the proportion of L + H* out of all the pitch accents each speaker produces. Intonation specialists, however, often spend hours poring over small stretches of speech, deciding how to label all of the various details of intonation. As a result, much intonation work has focused on semantic aspects of intonation because qualitative issues are all that the slow pace of analysis allows.

Similarly, work on dialectal variation has tended to concentrate on showing that different dialects show different inventories of tones. Cases in which groups differ quantitatively instead of qualitatively challenge current modes of analysis. More research needs to be devoted to finding reliable shortcuts that will permit the teasing out of quantitative differences. Syrdal et al. (2001) attempted to address the speed issue by implementing an automatic transcription program followed by manual correction of transcriptions. The results were mixed, but none of the transcribers had a real-time factor better than 80 (i.e. 80 times the actual amount of time the utterances lasted). Syrdal et al. stated that they were targeting the technique for intonation specialists and speech technologists – they didn't mention sociolinguists.

For quantitative sociolinguistic applications, other strategies will be necessary. For instance, if you want to focus on boundary tones, is it necessary to transcribe pitch accents that don't lie immediately before the boundary tone?

Or, if you're interested in pitch accents, is it necessary to identify anything more about phrasal boundaries than just the location of each boundary? The break index, a part of ToBI to be discussed below, is partially redundant with the boundary tones, and the non-redundant parts don't affect pitch accent notation much, so it would seem that the break index tier is dispensable for applications to variation.

Most intonation specialists come from a phonology background. They tend to be interested in issues such as the phonological inventories of a language or dialect. Quantitative differences don't fit well into a phonology framework, so they aren't a major concern for intonational phonologists. However, we can't paint ourselves into a corner of not being permitted to analyse a certain type of variable, especially one with as much sociolinguistic importance as intonation. We need to be able to study quantitative and not just qualitative variation in intonation. Developing faster ways to analyse intonation will facilitate that and should become a priority.

ToBI components

As Beckman et al. (2005) explain, the earliest-developed form of ToBI, MAE_ToBI, has six obligatory parts. Two are acoustic: the audio signal and an F_0 track of the signal. The other four are the autosegmental parts – that is, the tiers that the transcriber creates and associates with the audio signal. The first tier, the tonal tier, shows all the pitch accents and boundary tones, as well as lexical tones for languages that have them, and where they occur in the signal. The next tier, the orthographic tier, shows the position of each word in the signal, in ordinary orthographic spelling. Next is the break index tier, which shows a series of numbers that represent what are called *break indices* in ToBI. The break indices denote the level of each juncture in the utterance. Finally, the miscellaneous tier is designated for notes the transcriber wishes to make about disfluencies, non-linguistic utterances such as laughter and coughing, and the like. Beckman et al. encourage transcribers to add other tiers as needed.

General introductions to how to transcribe using MAE_ToBI are given in Beckman and Hirschberg (1994) and Beckman and Elam (1997). Descriptions of versions of ToBI developed for several other languages (German, Japanese, Korean, Greek, Catalan, Portuguese, Serbian, Glasgow English, Mandarin, Cantonese, Spanish and Taiwanese) and the related Transcription of Dutch Intonation (ToDI) system can be accessed through links from http://www.ling.ohio-state.edu/~tobi. Practice exercises for MAE_ToBI and a few of the other ToBI systems can also be accessed via links through that website. As I've mentioned already, ToBI systems are intended to be phonological for the most part, but it's necessary to understand the transcription system for a language before moving on to phonetic analyses of intonation.

Phrases and edge tones

In running speech, a juncture may delimit anything from words to long phrases. Prosodic units consist of the kinds of phrases for which at least the end (less commonly the beginning) is encoded in the intonation of a language. Jun (2005b) recognizes three levels of phrases. The highest-level phrase that is marked by prosody is the *Intonation(al) Phrase*, or IP. All the languages discussed by Jun are considered to have IPs. IPs show their own edge tones, called *boundary tones* and labelled as L%, H% and, in some languages, other categories. Korean, for example, has an inventory of nine IP boundary tones, such as LHLH% and HLHL%. 'Mainstream American English' has only L% and H%. Other languages, such as German and Japanese, have inventories of intermediate size. IP boundaries are most often associated with pauses, either filled or unfilled, or with prolongation of the final syllable or foot. Boundary tones normally occur only at the end of an IP. Rarely, they occur at the beginning of an IP (as, e.g., %H), but they are marked there only when there is no way the tone can be explained otherwise, such as by a nearby pitch accent. Certain languages have larger phrases that are marked by pauses or prolongation of final syllables but not by intonation.

The next highest-level phrase marked by prosody is called the *intermediate phrase*, or ip. Common locations for an ip boundary are after an interjection or discourse connective – e.g. *Oh* or *Well* in English; before conjunctions and relativizers when the orthography generally calls for a comma, as in 'Are you coming, or should I just go ahead?'; or to mark a vocative – e.g. after *John* in 'John, did you shut the door?' – if, of course, the juncture isn't strong enough to constitute an IP. Not all languages are considered to have ips. For example, the ip isn't recognized for Korean, represented by K-ToBI (Jun 2005a), and it is disputed whether Spanish, represented by Sp_ToBI, has ips (Beckman et al. 2002). (See Jun (2005b:444) for a list of which languages with extant ToBI systems have ips.)

An ip has an edge tone called a *phrase accent*. Phrase accents are denoted with -, as in H- and L- in English. Any IP boundary will also be an ip boundary in languages with ips, so the two are written together whenever an IP ends. There are, then, multiple combinations of phrase accents and boundary tones. English, with its two IP and two ip types, thus has four combinations: L-L%, L-H%, H-L% and H-H%.

For IP boundaries, the distinction between the ip component and the IP component is abstract. Acoustically and impressionistically, it is usually easier to recognize them as combinations than to distinguish the IP and ip components. The four IP boundary combinations that occur in English are generally used for different purposes. The most common is L-L%, which is the ordinary edge tone for a statement. An example is shown in Figure 6.11. H-H% is the normal edge tone for a yes/no question, as shown in Figure 6.12. The H-L% tone occurs when an IP ends in a (relatively) high, level tone, as in Figure 6.13. It is often used when a speaker is giving a list of items. Finally, L-H%, as shown in Figure 6.14, is often called a 'continuation rise' because it is used to indicate that the speaker hasn't finished talking.

Some languages have another level of phrase, lower than the ip, called the *Accentual Phrase*, or AP. This level of phrase is recognized rather sporadically among languages. Japanese and Korean are considered to have an AP level. Indo-European languages vary; the Germanic languages, Greek

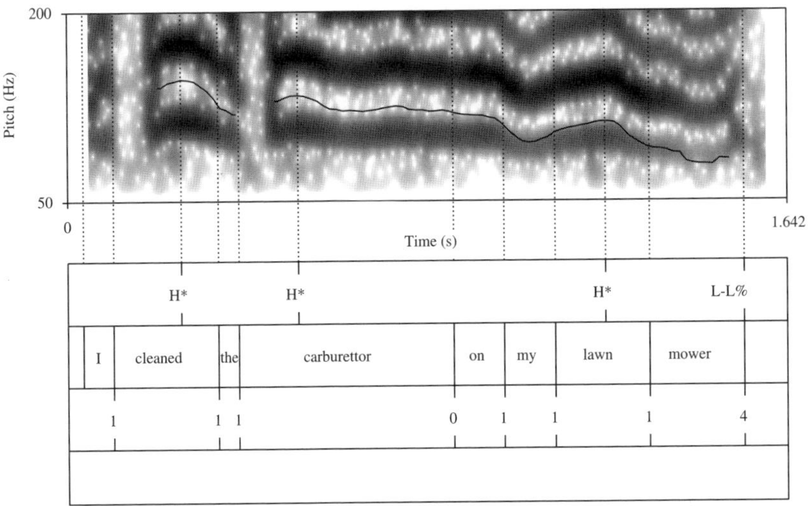

Figure 6.11 An example of an L-L% edge tone. The sentence is 'I cleaned the carburettor on my lawn mower.' The pitch track (with a range from 50 to 200 Hz), shown as the black line, is superimposed on a narrowband spectrogram with a range from 0 to 350 Hz.

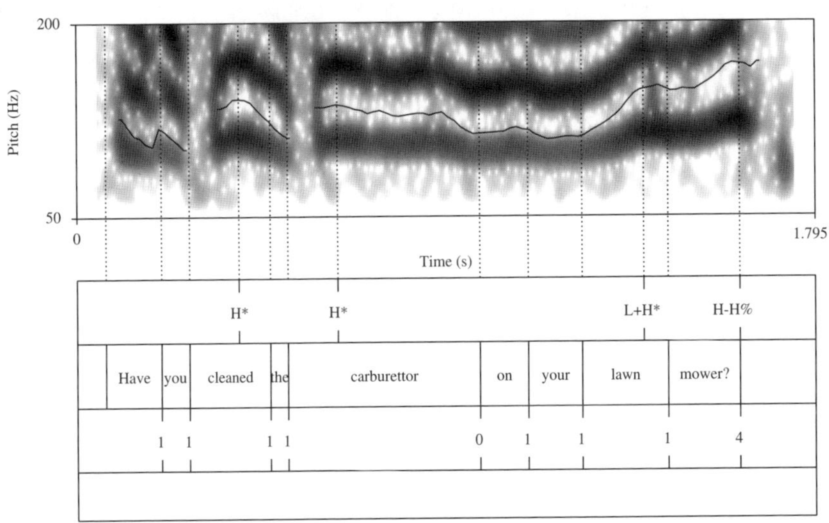

Figure 6.12 An example of an H-H% edge tone. The sentence is 'Have you cleaned the carburettor on your lawn mower?'

and most Romance languages lack it, but French, Farsi and Bengali are said to have it (Jun 2005b:444), and some forms of African American English may have it as well (Jennifer Cole, personal communication). An AP usually contains only one content word, though more than one are possible (Jun and Fougeron 2002). A potential example from African American English

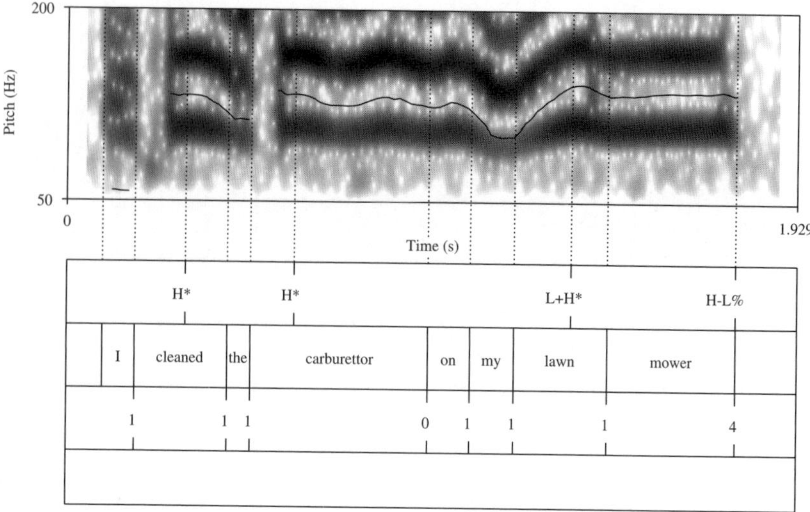

Figure 6.13 An example of an H-L% edge tone. The sentence is 'I cleaned the carburettor on my lawn mower and I changed the oil, too.'

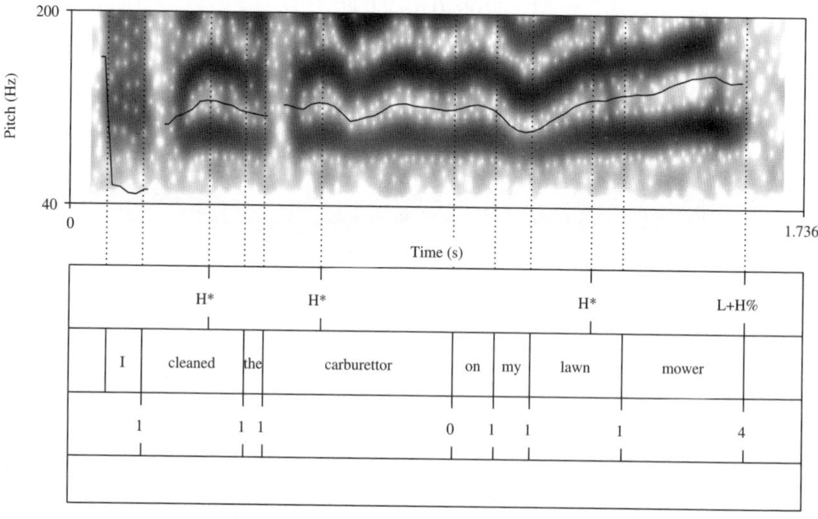

Figure 6.14 An example of an L-H% edge tone. The sentence is 'I cleaned the carburettor on my lawn mower and I changed the oil, too.'

is shown in Figure 6.15. Note how each marked section except the first one shows a noticeable peak near its beginning, even though some of the peaks are higher than others.

Break indices

Versions of ToBI for different languages have different numbers of break indices, but MAE_ToBI has five. As Beckman and Elam (1997) discuss,

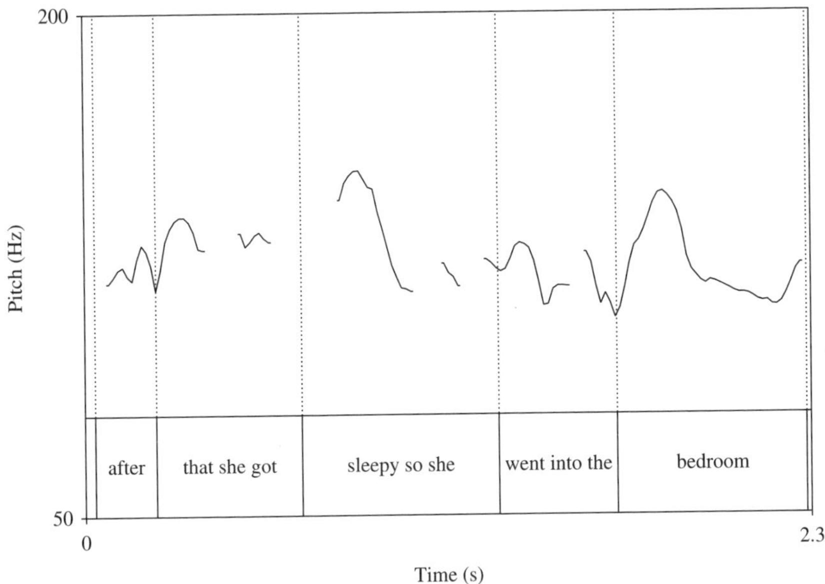

Figure 6.15 A pitch track of an utterance by an African American English speaker, with putative Accentual Phrases delineated. Note the peak on the syllable at the beginning of each phrase except the first one. The utterance is 'after that she got sleepy so she went into the bedroom', taken from a spontaneous retelling of *Goldilocks and the Three Bears*.

break index 0 is used for boundaries between words that involve cliticization or that are otherwise phonologically bound together. Break index 1 is for other word boundaries. Break index 3 is for ip boundaries, and break index 4 is for IP boundaries. The remaining break index, 2, is used for cases in which there is a mismatch between the degree of disjuncture and the presence or absence of tonal marking. Because break indices are largely redundant with boundary tones or with word boundaries, their usefulness in sociophonetics is limited.

Jun (2005b) lists break indices for several other languages with their own ToBI versions. The number of break indices varies from three, as in Cantonese, which lacks ips and APs, to five, as in English and Mandarin.

Pitch accents

Once you've located the phrasal boundaries, you can begin looking for pitch accents, assuming that you're studying a language that has them. A few languages described in ToBI so far, notably Korean and Cantonese, are not considered to have pitch accents (Jun 2005b). A pitch accent should stand out, both impressionistically and when you look at an F_0 track. It will normally be the highest or lowest point in the F_0 track in its neighbourhood. Most of the time, it will be associated with a stressed syllable, though not all stressed syllables will have pitch accents.

The versions of ToBI for different languages recognize a variety of pitch accent types. The most essential ones are H* for a high pitch accent and L* for a low pitch accent. Figures 6.16 and 6.17 illustrate H* and L* pitch accents, respectively. For H*, there is normally a rapid rise in F_0 – sometimes an abrupt jump across a consonant – that is often followed by a fall. L*, which is less common than H*, generally shows an analogous but opposite pattern.

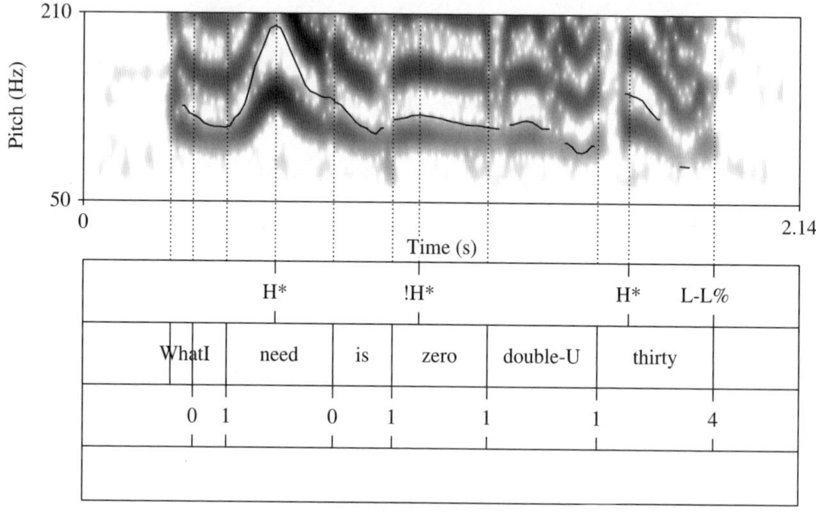

Figure 6.16 An example of an H* pitch accent. The sentence is 'What I *need* is 0W30'; note the H* on the word *need*. The pitch track (with a range from 50 to 210 Hz), represented as the black line, is superimposed on a narrowband spectrogram with a range from 0 to 350 Hz.

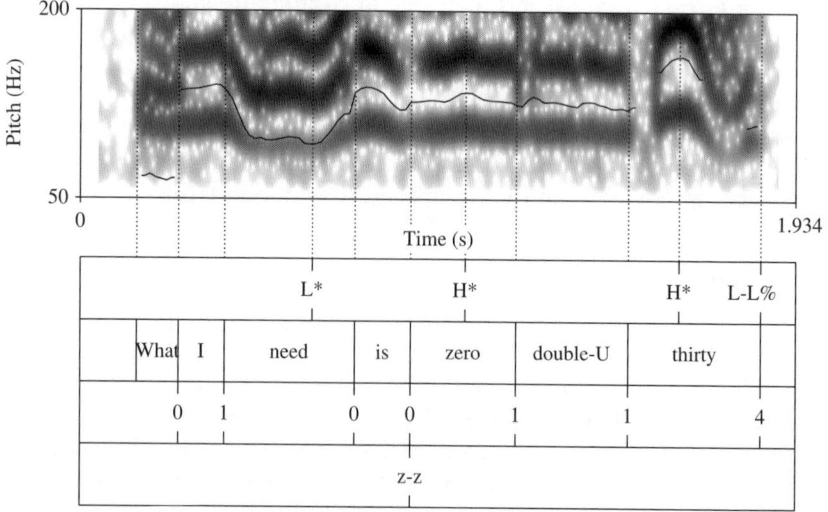

Figure 6.17 An example of an L* pitch accent. The sentence is "What I *need* is 0W30.'

Three other pitch accents are recognized in MAE_ToBI. Movement of F_0 is intrinsic to all of them. Two, L + H* and L* + H, are similar to each other. The main difference is that L + H* starts with a rise in F_0 that levels off, while L* + H, which is often called a 'scooped accent', starts with a low level tone and rises at the end. L + H* is more common in spontaneous speech. Examples are shown in Figures 6.18 and 6.19. The other pitch accent of MAE_ToBI is H + !H*. It often occurs as a high tone on an unstressed syllable followed

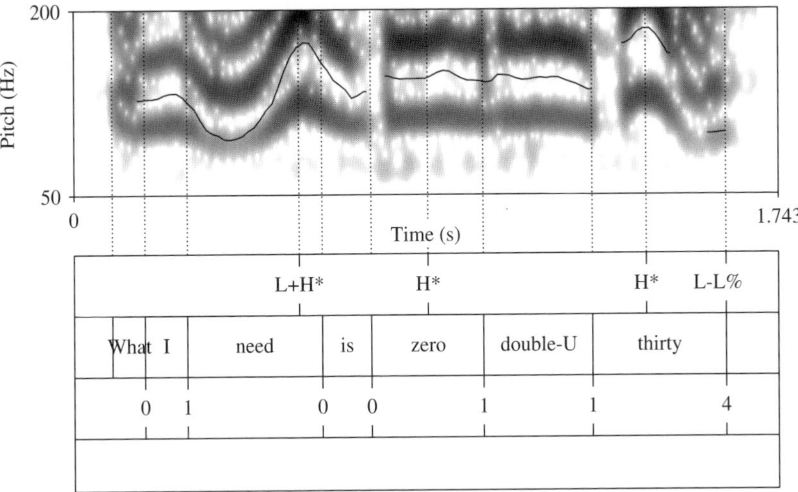

Figure 6.18 An example of an L+H* pitch accent. The sentence is 'What I *need* is 0W30.'

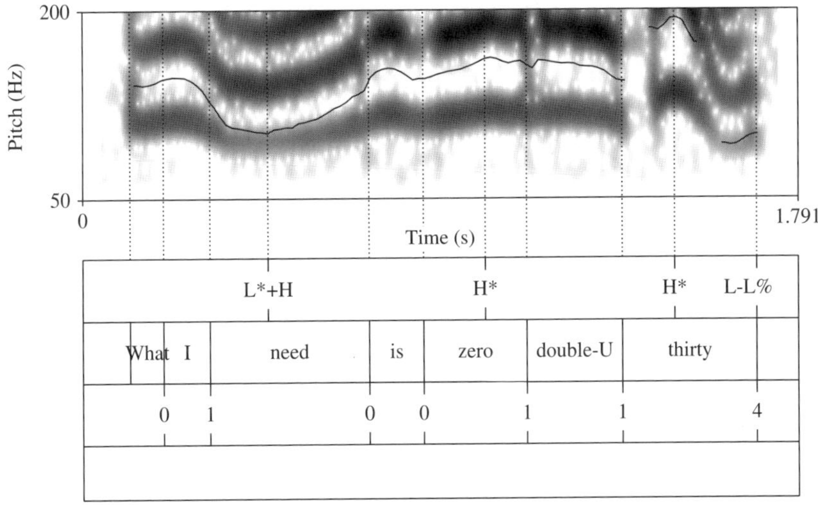

Figure 6.19 An example of an L*+H pitch accent. The sentence is 'What I *need* is 0W30.'

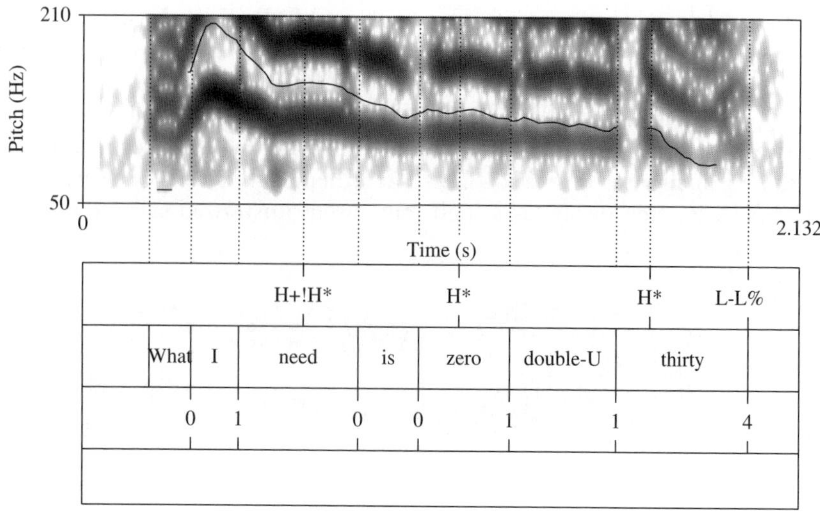

Figure 6.20 An example of an H+!H* pitch accent. The sentence is 'What *I need* is 0W30.'

by a somewhat lower tone on a stressed syllable, as in Figure 6.20, but both tones may occur within a single stressed syllable or across two stressed syllables. H + !H* may be uttered to convey annoyance or disappointment.

Versions of ToBI for other languages have their own inventories of pitch accents. For example, GToBI, the system for German, has all the pitch accents recognized for MAE_ToBI plus a H+L* pitch accent. The latter is similar to H + !H* except that it involves a fall to a low, rather than mid, tone (Grice et al. 2005a). For Spanish, Sp_ToBI recognizes H*, L* + H, L + H* and H + L* (Beckman et al. 2002). J_ToBI, for Japanese, has only H* + L, which is actually a lexical pitch accent (Venditti 2005), and for Korean, K_ToBI has no pitch accents at all (Jun 2005a). Note that, just as L + H* can contrast with L* + H, it's possible for H + L* to contrast with H* + L.

Successive pitch accents may sound noticeably different in pitch even if they're the same kind of pitch accent – e.g. both H* or both L + H*. If the second one is obviously lower than the first, you have *downstepping*. This is represented by ! placed before the second pitch accent, as in !H* or L + !H*. Sometimes, such as when a speaker is reciting a list, there can be a succession of downstepped pitch accents: e.g. H* !H* !H*. An example of downstepping is shown in Figure 6.21. MAE_ToBI has only downstepping, but systems for certain other languages recognize *upstepping*. As you'd guess, upstepping occurs when successive pitch accents go up noticeably. Upstepping is represented either as ^, as in GToBI (German), or as ¡, as in Sp_ToBI (Spanish).

Two other symbols that are used in some versions of ToBI are < and >. They are used for pitch accents that are offset from where they would be expected: < if it's earlier and > if it's later. This situation may occur, for example, when the peak of a pitch accent falls on an unstressed syllable next to the stressed syllable that the pitch accent is associated with.

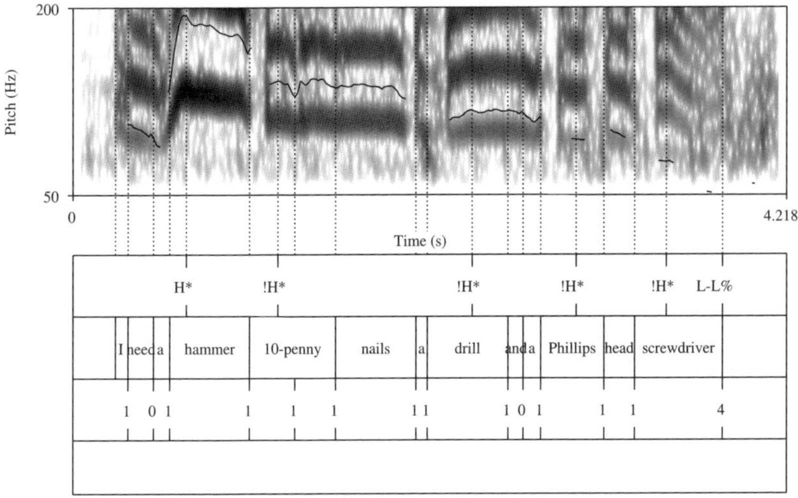

Figure 6.21 An example of a series of downstepped H* pitch accents. The sentence is 'I need a hammer, ten-penny nails, a drill, and a Phillips-head screwdriver.'

There is one final point to make here about pitch accents. The most important pitch accent within an IP is called the *nucleus*, or *nuclear accent*. In ToBI, the nucleus is always considered to be the last pitch accent in an IP.

Phonetic analyses of intonation

Quite a bit of phonetic analysis of pitch accents and edge tones has been conducted, and some useful methods have emerged. Some of these methods resemble those used for lexical tone. A good bit of the analysis has concerned what happens to the location of tones in syllables of differing durations, at different speaking rates, or across different configurations of syllables. Prieto et al. (1995) developed a method to determine where an H* pitch accent occurs within a stressed syllable. They measured several factors, among them the duration of the syllable and what they called the *peak delay*. The peak delay was the distance in ms from the onset of the syllable to the maximum F_0 value, as shown in Figure 6.22. The peak delay proved to be longest when the initial syllable of a word was stressed, and was shortest when the final syllable was stressed and an IP boundary followed.

The positioning of contour tones has received a lot of attention. An important issue that has arisen is testing whether contours are subject to *segmental anchoring* (e.g. Arvaniti et al. 1998; Ladd et al. 1999; Lickley et al. 2005). Segmental anchoring is the notion that, in a contour tone, both the L part and the H part are tied to parts of a certain syllable, generally a stressed one. It was used as evidence to support the view that targets, not contours, are the intonational primitives. This view remains controversial; see Xu (1999, 2001) for an opposing stance on lexical tones. One method used in examining segmental anchoring of a high pitch accent involves finding the maximum F_0 value associated with the

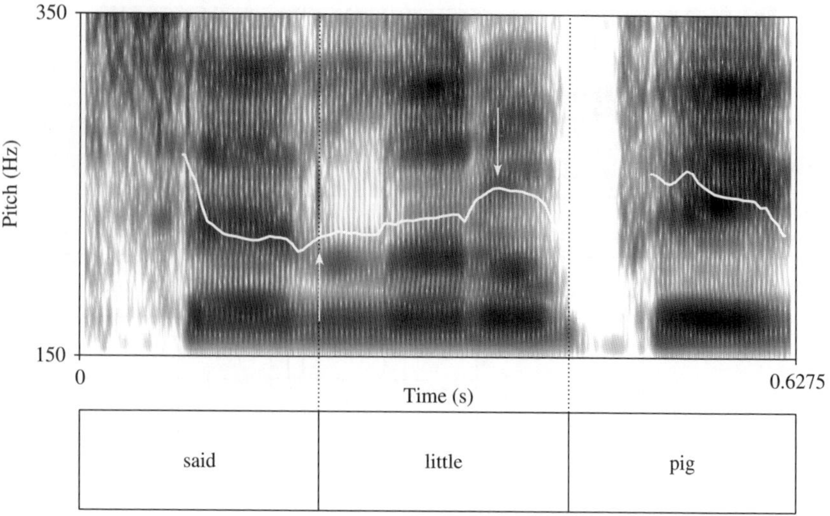

Figure 6.22 Measurement points for evaluating peak delay. The left arrow represents the onset of the syllable with which the pitch accent is associated, and the right arrow represents the maximum F_0 value – which in this example falls on the following unstressed syllable.

pitch accent and measuring the distance in ms from the maximum F_0 to the offset of the vowel in the stressed syllable with which it is associated (or, in Lickley et al. 2005, the onset of the vowel). The proportion of that distance out of the duration of the vowel can then be computed using the formula

$$\text{proportion} = [(\text{vowel offset}) - (\text{point of maximum } F_0)]/(\text{duration of vowel})$$

with all of the input values measured in ms. The proportion can then be compared with proportions computed for other pitch accents.

Another way to examine segmental anchoring is to compare the F_0 *excursion* (the change in F_0 from the immediately previous minimum point to the maximum value in the pitch accent) with the slope of F_0. The excursion is often measured in semitones or ERB instead of hertz. The slope is computed as

$$\text{slope} = (F_0 \text{ excursion})/\text{time}$$

Then pitch accents produced at slower rates of speech are compared with those produced at greater rates of speech. A change in the slope indicates segmental anchoring, while a change in F_0 excursion indicates non-anchoring. Figure 6.23 shows the various measurement points involved in segmental anchoring investigations. The above-mentioned studies on segmental anchoring used read speech, with sentences designed so that most of the consonants were sonorants, which affect F_0 less than obstruents. Subjects can be asked to read at different rates (as with Ladd et al. 1999), or the words containing the pitch accent may have different combinations of strong and weak syllables (as in Lickley et al.

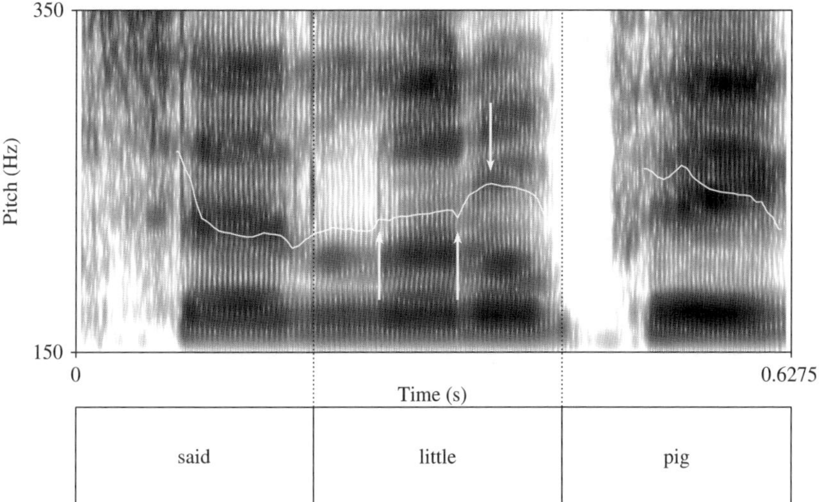

Figure 6.23 Measurement points for evaluating segmental anchoring of a pitch accent. From left to right, the measurement points are the onset of the vowel that the pitch accent is associated with, the offset of that vowel, and the point of maximum F_0.

2005). The method could be applied to spontaneous speech if syllable configuration is accounted for.

Similar methods could be applied to edge tones. These given the same ToBI label can differ significantly across languages, such as H-L%, which is level in English but shows a fall in German. Differences in edge tones could be gauged by comparing maximum or minimum F_0 values within the last syllable or last foot with the last measurable F_0 value at the end of the final syllable, as shown in Figure 6.24.

Related to the notion of segmental anchoring is the phenomenon of *tonal crowding*. This happens when two tones are close to each other, inducing one to shift away from the other. As a result, the shifted tone may not appear in the part of the stressed segment where it is to be expected. This situation may occur when two consecutive syllables are stressed, and it is common when a pitch accent occurs near an edge tone. For example, for questions in Chickasaw, Gordon (2008) found that an H* tone will shift to an earlier position when it occurs right before a L% tone. Tonal crowding is studied by measuring the same sorts of parameters as for segmental anchoring: the position of the pitch accent peak or trough relative to the onset of the stressed vowel, the length of time between the two tones, the difference in F_0 values between the two tones, and the duration of the vowel. Arvaniti et al. (1998) found that speakers may differ in how they respond to tonal crowding.

One phonetic property that is known to vary for pitch accents is whether they undergo *compression* or *truncation* when they're shortened. In compression, the entire contour is preserved, but it's squeezed into the shorter time frame. In truncation, on the other hand, the end of the contour is cut off. As a result, the same phonological contour can show different properties when

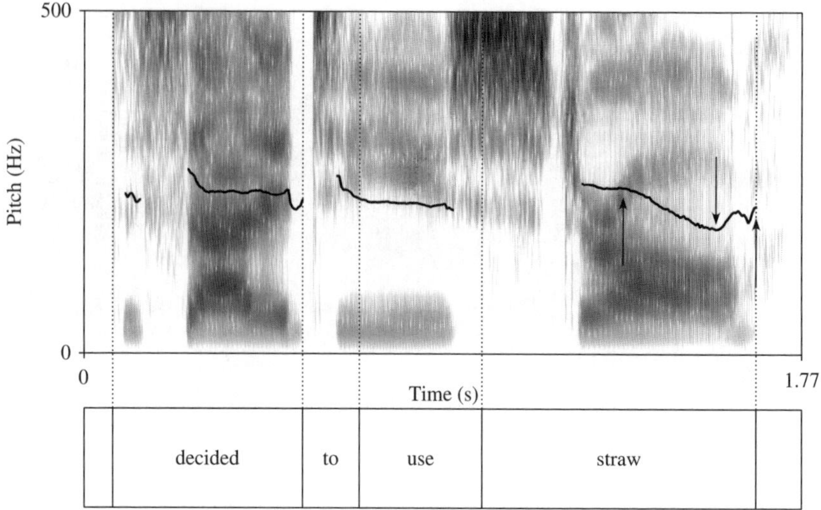

Figure 6.24 Measurement points for evaluating segmental anchoring of an edge tone. The arrows represent, from left to right, the maximum F_0 value within the last syllable, the minimum F_0 value within that syllable, and the last measurable F_0 value at the end of that syllable.

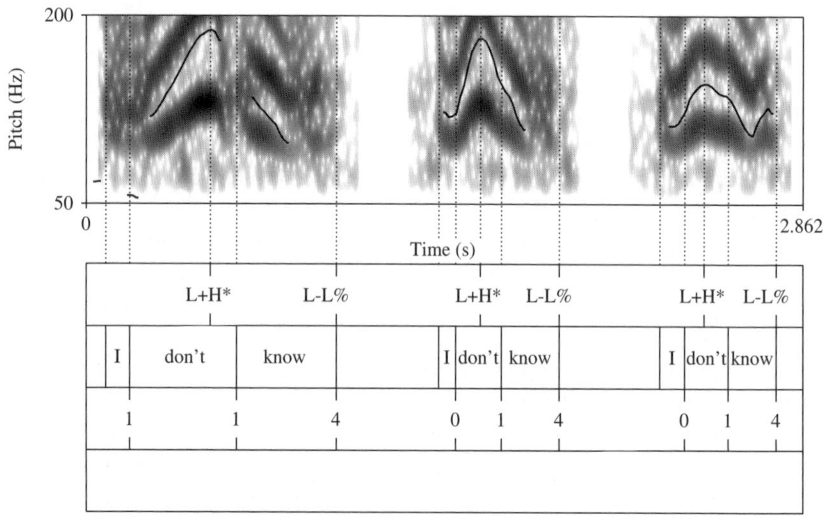

Figure 6.25 Comparison of an L+H* pitch accent in the sentence 'I don't know', realized (from left to right) fully, with compression, and with truncation.

it's shortened. A compressed contour will have basically the same range of F_0 values as one that isn't shortened, but its F_0 track will show a steeper slope. A truncated contour will have a smaller range of F_0 values compared to one that's not shortened, but it will have roughly the same slope in its F_0 track. It's also possible for shortening to involve both an increase in F_0 slope and a decrease in range of F_0 values. Grabe et al. (2000) refer to this combination as compression as well. Figure 6.25 shows a comparison of an unshortened contour, a compressed contour, and a truncated contour for the L+H* pitch accent on *don't* in the sentence 'I don't know'. Grabe (1998) compared English and German realizations of rising and falling contours, the former in exclamatory statements and the latter in yes/no questions. In the sentences they used, the contour would fall on words with a short vowel, a long vowel, and a long vowel and an unstressed syllable: *shift*, *sheaf* and *sheafer* in English and *Schiff*, *Schief* and *Shiefer* in German. They measured the duration of the word, the rate of F_0 change and the F_0 excursion. It turned out that both contours in English and rises in German underwent compression as the word became shorter, but falling contours in German underwent truncation. This method requires some adaptation for spontaneous speech. It is necessary to make sure that phonologically comparable tones are being compared. The duration of the word(s) that the contour covers varies continuously in spontaneous speech, so statistical procedures appropriate for continuous independent variables will be needed.

Dialectal variation in intonation

Dialectal variations in intonation fall into three general types. The first is a phonological difference, differences in the inventory of tones. Second is quantitative differences in the incidence of tones, which may be accompanied by changes in the meaning of the tones. Third, there are phonetic differences in the realization of tones.

Differences in tone inventories

As noted above, cross-linguistic differences in tone inventories are well-documented. Sometimes dialects of the same languages can have different pitch accent inventories, too. In Glasgow English – which may well reflect the situation across much of Scotland and Northern Ireland – the L + H* and L* + H tones aren't differentiated. Instead, they're realized as a single L*H tone that occurs with great frequency in the dialect (Mayo 1996). Discussions are ongoing about possible differences among varieties of Spanish.

As you'd expect from all the cross-linguistic differences, language contact is probably one of the ways that dialects with different tone inventories develop. Some work has addressed how this transition occurs. Queen (2001) described how Turkish Germans have taken one rising contour from German and another rising contour from Turkish and allocated them to different pragmatic purposes in Turkish German. Birkner (2004) examined how Portuguese intonation patterns affect the German spoken by German Brazilians and found that some speakers replace German patterns with Portuguese ones in their German in certain contexts. Work on other contact situations will undoubtedly uncover other configurations, making the intonation of language contact a fertile field for research.

Incidence of tones

On the whole, more work is needed on the second type of intonational variation, differences in the incidence of particular tones. One example appears in Grabe (2004:21–2), who reports differences in the incidence of various pitch accent/boundary tone combinations among dialects of the British Isles. Another example comes from Grice et al. (2005b), who compared four dialects of Italian – Neapolitan, Bari, Palermo from southern Italy and Florentine from central Italy. Although they found a few differences in tone inventories, the main differences among the dialects were in how the tones they shared were allocated to different purposes and, conversely, how the same function could employ different tones. For example, the nuclear accent for information-seeking yes/no questions bore L* + H in Neapolitan and Palermo, L + H* in Bari, and H* in Florentine.

One particular quantitative variation has received quite a bit of attention lately among students of English. This variation is called the 'high rising terminal', or HRT, and is often popularly called 'uptalk'. It involves use of H-H% boundary tones (or perhaps L-H%) in ordinary statements, not just to signal yes/no questions or continuation. This example illustrates how shifts in the commonness of tones are often linked to changes in their semantic or pragmatic function. Not only has the H-H% or L-H% tone been extended to meanings that it didn't formerly have, it's also reportedly come to be used as a politeness device (Britain 1992). HRT is most associated with New Zealand and Australian English (e.g. Guy et al. 1986), though it also seems to occur here and there in North American English; see the review of literature in Warren (2005).

Phonetic realization of tones

A moderate amount of research has been devoted to the third type: variation in the phonetic realization of particular tones. One type of variation involves the points at which tones are aligned with segments. This issue is related to the segmental anchoring problem discussed earlier. It turns out that the peaks and troughs of contour tones don't have to appear at exactly the same places in all dialects. Atterer and Ladd (2004) compared rising tones in northern and southern varieties of German. Subjects read sentences with items that would elicit rising tones. Atterer and Ladd recorded the relative timing of six points: the beginning of the consonant preceding the accented vowel, the onset of the accented vowel, the onset of the following consonant, the onset of the next vowel, the point of minimum local F_0, and the point of maximum local F_0. An example of where such measurements could be taken is shown in Figure 6.26. Both the peak and the trough were consistently aligned later in southern German than in northern German, which in turn had later alignments than what was reported in other studies for English. That is, although the minimum F_0 tended to fall before the onset of the accented vowel in both dialects, it was closer to the onset in southern German. Analogously, although the maximum F_0 generally occurred after the offset of the accented vowel in both dialects, there was a greater span of time between the offset and the F_0 maximum in southern German. The difference is schematized in Figure 6.27.

Similar findings are reported by Kügler (2004), Arvaniti and Garding (2007) and Ladd et al. (2009). Arvaniti and Garding looked at H*, L + H* and L* + H tones in California and Minnesota English. They had subjects read dialogues designed to elicit those tones. Kügler used spontaneous speech and examined

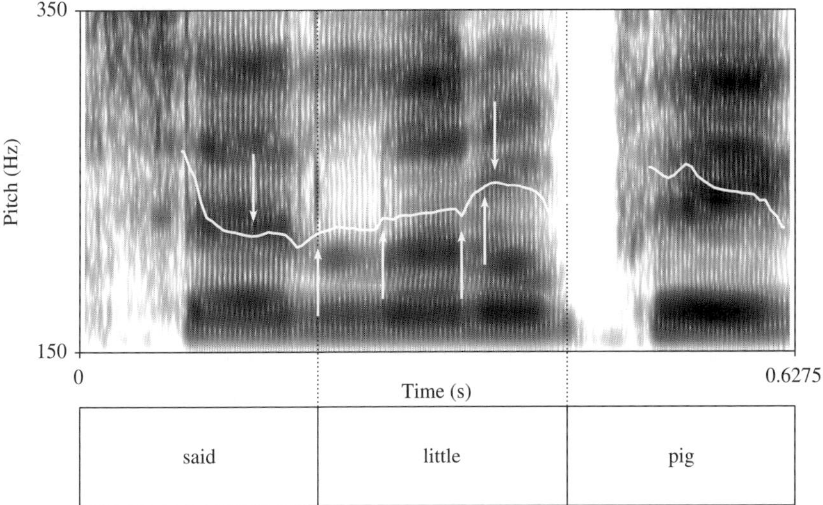

Figure 6.26 Pitch track superimposed on a spectrogram, with measurement points for evaluating trough and peak positions, following Atterer and Ladd (2004). Arrows below the pitch track indicate, from left to right, onset of consonant preceding stressed vowel, onset of stressed vowel, onset of consonant following stressed vowel, and onset of next vowel; arrows above the pitch track indicate local minimum and maximum F_0 points.

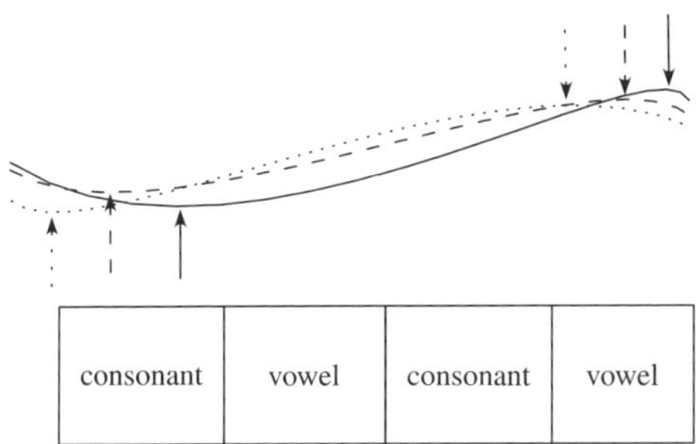

Figure 6.27 Schematized diagram showing differences in trough and peak positions for southern German (solid line), northern German (dashed line) and English (dotted line), based on Atterer and Ladd (2004). Arrows indicate positions of troughs and peaks.

realizations of the L* + H tone in nuclear pitch accents in Swabian German. Ladd et al. compared nuclear and prenuclear pitch accents in Standard Scottish English and RP (Received Pronunciation, i.e. standard English of England). All three studies measured, among other factors, the amount of time between the vowel onset and the F_0 minimum, between the F_0 maximum and the vowel offset, and between the F_0 minimum and maximum. Arvaniti and Garding demonstrated that Californians showed later alignment of the maximum F_0 in L* + H tones than Minnesotans. Kügler found that the position of the F_0 maximum shifted depending on syllable structure – the length of the vowel and whether a coda consonant was present – but it differed from patterns reported for standard German. Kügler's method of dividing words according to their syllable structure is significant because it solves a problem: how can you analyse pitch alignment in spontaneous speech? Other studies relied on carefully constructed readings. Classifying words the way Kügler did opens up spontaneous speech for analysis of pitch alignment.

Compression and truncation have been examined for cross-dialectal differences. Grabe et al. (2000) had speakers of four British English dialects read sentences that would elicit two pitch accent/boundary tone combinations (the equivalents of H* L-L% and L* H-H%, but with the latter varying by dialect) in the same three segmental environments (*sheafer*, *sheaf* and *shift*) as in Grabe (1998). Just as standard British English and standard German differed in their preference for truncation or compression, so did the dialects of English that they investigated.

6.5 Other post-lexical prosody

Intonation isn't the only post-lexical type of prosody. Declination, which is partially governed by intonational categories, is involved. *Declination* is the tendency for pitch to fall through the course of an utterance. Another feature, also partly dependent on intonation, is *pre-boundary lengthening*. This, often referred to as *pre-pausal lengthening*, is the tendency for the final syllable or foot to be prolonged before a prosodic boundary – especially a pause, whether filled or unfilled. Variation in these two factors isn't well studied, but it has potential for variation, so I'll go over some methods for studying it here.

Declination

Declination, as noted above, is the tendency of pitch to fall over the course of an utterance. After the end of the utterance, the pitch is reset to a relatively high pitch and falls over the course of the next utterance. These 'utterances' may be IPs, but they often consist of more than one IP. Declination is probably universal among the world's languages. In fact, what makes the cartoon voice of Yogi Bear so distinctive is that it violates declination – his voice rises through an utterance instead of falling. (Try saying a few sentences in a Yogi Bear voice, with a lowered larynx and rising F_0: 'Hey, Boo Boo!' 'I smell some pic-a-nic baskets!' 'I'm smarter than the average bear!')

Declination was originally conceived as a purely descriptive construct for an involuntary phenomenon of speech, but various studies have suggested that speakers do exert some control over it (Cohen et al. 1982). For example, long utterances generally show more or less the same range of F_0 values as shorter utterances. As a result the declination rate – the amount of fall in pitch per unit of time – isn't the same for long and short utterances. Pitch isn't always reset to the same point, either. Swerts et al. (1996) point out that read speech tends to show steeper declination and more dramatic resetting than spontaneous speech. Declination obviously shows stylistic variation, then. All of this evidence that speakers can control declination rate suggests that it could show dialectal or sociolectal variation as well.

Nevertheless, declination is harder to study than you'd think. The problem is that it interacts with intonational pitch accents and edge tones. It can be difficult to separate declination from downstepping of pitch accents if the latter is present. Other pitch accent patterns affect declination, too. For example, Ulbrich (2004) describes how Swiss German utterances often show pitch accents with alternating high and low tones, while utterances in the standard German of Germany tend to show a steady downward trend. As a result, Swiss German may appear to show less declination than standard German. In German and other languages, it's usually hard to pin down how much of the F_0 pattern of an utterance is due to intonation and how much is due to declination.

There are some methods for measuring the general downtrend in F_0 of an IP or utterance without extracting intonational influence from the overall declination effect. The simplest is to compute a linear regression slope, in hertz or ERB per second, for the F_0 track of the utterance. At least, it seems simple at first glance. You have to remember that, the longer the utterance, the flatter the slope of the F_0 track, because F_0 covers roughly the same range of frequencies for most utterances, long or short. Exceptionally short utterances – less than half a second – tend to show wildly varying F_0 patterns, so you should exclude them. An example analysis is shown in Figure 6.28, which compares F_0 slopes for 11 women from North Carolina. Utterances

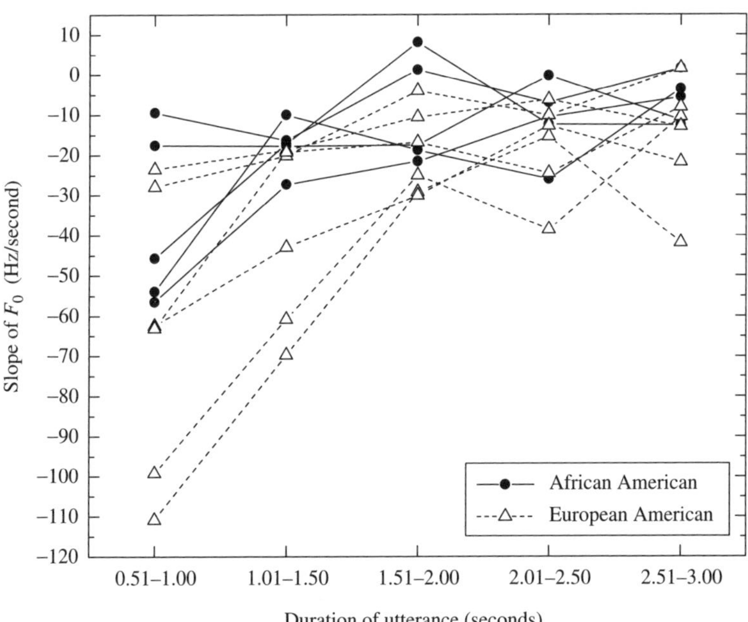

Figure 6.28 Comparison of means of F_0 downtrend slopes in utterances for 11 women from North Carolina, with utterances divided according to durational categories.

are divided into categories depending on their duration. Note that three of the European American women show more negative slopes than the other speakers for utterances between 0.5 and 2.0 s long. This sort of method can be as useful for examining intonational properties as for examining declination per se.

If you want to filter out the effects of intonation, you have to control for the placement of intonational pitch accents. To do so, you need to compare utterances that have the same number of syllables and have pitch accents in the same places in the utterance: e.g. you might look for seven-syllable declarative utterances with pitch accents on the first, fourth and sixth syllables. Unfortunately, it's hard to find many utterances in spontaneous speech that are so similar, so you'll probably have to rely on read speech for this kind of analysis.

Another method of examining declination is to focus on stressed syllables or syllables with pitch accents. Here, you measure the maximum F_0 values of each stressed or pitch accented syllable, subtract it from the maximum F_0 value for the entire utterance, and divide it by the F_0 range for the utterance. Then you compare the value for the highest stressed or pitch accented syllable with that of some point towards the end of the utterance: the maximum or minimum F_0 of the final stressed or pitch accented syllable, that of the final syllable (even if unstressed), or the last measurable F_0 value in the utterance. Converting hertz to ERB or semitones is prudent if you compare these values for different speakers.

Pre-boundary lengthening

Lengthening of the final syllable or final foot before a major prosodic boundary is widespread and perhaps universal among languages. Such boundaries may or may not have a pause after them, but the pre-boundary lengthening seems to be present consistently. Nevertheless, is it possible that languages and dialects differ in the degree of pre-pausal (or phrase-final) lengthening that they show? The topic is barely explored, but Ladd et al. (2009) found that Standard Scottish English shows less pre-pausal lengthening than RP.

Wightman et al. (1992) developed methods for examining pre-boundary lengthening. They examined lengthening at the level of the segment, while also demonstrating that it affects an entire foot, not just a single syllable (at least in English). As noted earlier, individual phonemes show intrinsic length and that has to be taken into account. Wightman et al. provided a series of formulas that filter out some of the confounding factors in pre-boundary lengthening. The first formula accounts for phoneme-intrinsic length differences. For any segment i and phoneme p:

$$d'(i) = [d(i) - \mu_p]/\sigma_p$$

where $d(i)$ is the duration of the segment and, for the duration of phoneme p, μ_p is the mean and σ_p the standard deviation. That is, you need a sufficient corpus of examples of the phoneme. Wightman et al. calculated this formula separately for every speaker.

Next, speaking rate has to be normalized. Wightman et al. did so in two steps. For a stretch of speech with little variation in speech rate, μ_p and σ_p can be scaled by a factor α. An approximation of α, which they called $\hat{\alpha}$, is calculated as

$$\hat{\alpha} = \left[\sum_{i=1}^{n} \left(d_i / \mu_p \right) \right] / n$$

where d_i is the duration of the segment and μ_p is the mean of phoneme p to which segment i belongs. Once you have this value, you can calculate the normalized mean and standard deviation as

$$\hat{\mu}_p = \hat{\alpha}\mu_p \text{ and } \hat{\sigma}_p = \hat{\alpha}\sigma_p$$

Then you apply those values of $\hat{\mu}_p$ and $\hat{\sigma}_p$ to the formula for $d'(i)$. Now, of course, 'a stretch of speech with little variation in speech rate' can be subjective, so you'll just have to judge that impressionistically.

Wightman et al. (1992) found that the amount of lengthening varied depending on the type of prosodic boundary. The stronger the boundary was, the greater the degree of lengthening was. They classified their boundaries using an early version of the ToBI system. If you examine pre-boundary lengthening, you'll need to control for boundary type. The easiest way would be to confine the analysis to instances of the strongest type of boundary, IP boundaries, that have clearly defined pauses after them.

Once you have the d_i values, you simply compare those in pre-boundary feet for different speakers. You have to take into account the number of syllables in the foot, categorizing the feet separately depending on the number of syllables they contain. If a speaker has a relatively wide difference between pre-boundary and non-pre-boundary segmental durations, the mean difference between d_i values in pre-boundary and non-pre-boundary contexts will be greater.

EXERCISES

For the following exercises, you can download practice samples from http://ncslaap.lib.ncsu.edu/sociophonetics/.

1. Create a Henderson graph for a stretch of conversational speech of between 30 seconds and a minute, either one you have recorded yourself or one downloaded. How steep is the resulting slope? How does the steepness relate to the interlocutors' involvement in the conversation?
2. Compute the speaking rate and the articulation rate for a stretch of speech uttered by a single person, again either one you have recorded yourself or one downloaded.
3. Using a tone if you have access to a lexical tone language, or a stress if you have access to a lexical stress language, make an F_0 track of the tone- or stress-bearing (host) syllable and the following syllable. Some examples

EXERCISES

are available to download. Measure the duration of the host syllable or its vowel. Then compute the position (as a proportion of the duration of the host syllable or vowel) of the point of maximum F_0. Note that the proportion will be greater than 1.0 if the maximum F_0 occurs after the end of the host syllable or vowel.

4. Make recordings of several utterances or download some. For each one, measure prosodic rhythm using (1) ΔC, %V and ΔV formulas of Ramus et al. (1999); (2) the VarcoΔC and VarcoΔV formulas of Dellwo (2006) and White and Mattys (2007); (3) the nPVI formula of Low et al. (2000), with the modifications introduced by Thomas and Carter (2006); and (4) the VI formula of Deterding (2001). For each formula, how much variation in the resulting numbers do you find among the utterances that you analyse? Are the different utterances ordered the same way by each formula?
5. Familiarize yourself with ToBI transcription through online materials or by taking a class on it. Some practice materials are also available to download. Then create a full ToBI transcription for a sample of spontaneous speech. Note how the frequent pauses found in most spontaneous speech affect the frequencies of pitch accents and edge tones.
6. Compare the peak alignment and F_0 slope of several pitch accents from a sample of speech using the formula for peak alignment:

   proportion = [(vowel offset) – (point of maximum F_0)]/(duration of vowel)

   and the formula for the F_0 slope:

   slope = (F_0 excursion)/time

7. Using the techniques of Grabe et al. (2000), examine several utterances of the same kind of pitch accent and edge tone combination (e.g. L* H-H%) in which the segmental composition differs: for example, feet with differing numbers of stressed syllables and different vowels in the stressed syllable. Compare the F_0 tracks for the various utterances. Do you find evidence for compression or truncation?
8. Compute the linear regression slope for the F_0 track of several utterances. Practice examples are available to download.

FURTHER READING

Beckman, Mary E. and Julia Hirschberg. 1994. The ToBI annotation conventions. http://www.ling.ohio-state.edu/~tobi/ame_tobi/annotation_conventions.html.

Gilles, Peter and Jörg Peters (eds). 2004. *Regional Variation in Intonation*. Linguistische Arbeiten 492. Tübingen: Max Niemeyer Verlag.

Jun, Sun-Ah (ed.). 2005. *Prosodic Typology: The Phonology of Intonation and Phrasing*. Oxford, UK: Oxford University Press.

Low, Ee Ling, Esther Grabe and Francis Nolan. 2000. Quantitative characterizations of speech rhythm: Syllable-timing in Singapore English. *Language and Speech* 43:377–401.

Ramus, Franck, Marina Nespor and Jacques Mehler. 1999. Correlates of linguistic rhythm in the speech signal. *Cognition* 73:265–92.

Xu, Yi and Q. Emily Wang. 2001. Pitch targets and their realization: Evidence from Mandarin Chinese. *Speech Communication* 33:319–37.

Voice Quality

7

7.1 The status of voice quality

Voice quality is uncharted territory in sociolinguistics. Language variationists generally regard it as a mysterious domain. For the most part, they also regard it as a non-sociolinguistic domain, an entirely physiological attribute of individual speakers and the purview of speech pathologists. The latter have, indeed, conducted most of the research on voice quality. As a result, virtually everything known about voice quality is coloured by the research aims of speech pathology.

Nevertheless, there have been a few sociolinguistic forays into voice quality. Breathy voicing is known to account for phonological distinctions in some languages, and there is some evidence that it can become a primary cue to certain phonological distinctions in particular dialects of English (e.g. Di Paolo and Faber 1990). Two studies from Scotland, in Edinburgh (Esling 1978) and Glasgow (Stuart-Smith 1999), found that particular voice quality settings characterize local dialects. Laver (1980:3–7) and Esling (2000) argued with numerous examples that voice quality settings play a role in social identity, both for regionality and for social class. Henton and Bladon (1985) found that sex-related physiological differences in voice quality were exaggerated in British English to index gender identity. Other features, including overall F_0 and nasality, have also been suggested as dialectally constrained. These findings suggest that sociolinguists and dialectologists may be writing off a whole family of variables that could serve as critical indices of social meaning. Moreover, as Henton and Bladon pointed out, in leaving voice quality to speech pathologists, sociolinguists could be allowing dialectal and sociolectal variants to be mistaken for abnormal conditions in need of therapy.

One obstacle sociolinguists and dialectologists face in investigating voice quality is that the methods of measuring it are poorly known outside of speech pathology. Even among pathologists, though, there is widespread disagreement about how to evaluate some aspects of voice quality. For example, Kreiman and Gerratt (2000) reviewed instrumental techniques for measuring roughness (or harshness) and breathiness and find wide variation in how well the techniques are correlated with traditional auditory evaluation. They then compared auditory evaluations by trained raters and found that inter-rater reliability was quite poor. Kreiman and Gerratt's conclusions about inter-rater reliability bring up another point. Although impressionistic evaluations by trained raters currently hold sway in clinical evaluations of voice quality, instrumental measurements have the advantage that they can be calibrated exactly. Generally, the goal of instrumental techniques for measuring voice quality is to find a way to simulate what trained raters do, just with greater reliability. If the raters disagree, however, what should an instrumental method measure? It's hard to determine the ideal instrumental technique when it's unclear what the technique should target.

In response, speech pathologists have developed prodigious numbers of formulas for measuring certain aspects of speech quality. For example, Buder (2000) lists 27 formulas and other procedures that had been published as of 1990 for quantifying jitter. Acoustic analysis packages generally provide one or a few formulas for computing a particular factor. It's worthwhile keeping in mind that whatever the favoured formula it may not be the only opinion.

There are quite a few factors you can measure to examine different aspects of voice quality. Each technique is appropriate for particular factors. These 'factors' are generally known as *settings*. Not surprisingly, some setting differences may be relevant for language variation and others are primarily pathological, and I have attempted to focus here on settings that can be used to study lectal variation. An important division among the various settings is that between laryngeal settings and supralaryngeal ones. Laryngeal settings include those that have to do with the configuration of the vocal folds, such as creakiness and breathiness. Supralaryngeal settings are those involving the resonating cavities above the larynx. Among them are the height of the larynx, which affects the length of the pharynx; the position of the tongue; whether the velum is raised or lowered, thus closing or opening the nasopharyngeal port (the passageway to the nasal cavity); and the configuration of the lips.

7.2 Measurement domain

Before you start measuring voice quality, you need to consider how long of a stretch of speech you're going to evaluate. The domain of a voice quality can vary widely. It may be pervasive in an individual's speech. Nasality, for instance, is often thought of as an overriding feature when it occurs as a voice quality. Overall fundamental frequency, by definition, is a mean or median value for whole utterances or longer samples of speech. On the other hand, voice quality variations can be quite localized in their occurrence. Creakiness, for example, may be confined to the last syllable or foot before a pause, and a speaker who impressionistically sounds 'creaky' may actually show slowed glottal pulses only in that context. In addition, irregularities may appear sporadically and randomly in a voice sample. Hence, when you try to measure voice quality, you should be sure that you're measuring samples of speech of appropriate length.

Another issue to consider when selecting samples to measure for voice quality is that, for the most part, voice quality applies to the *voiced* parts of the speech signal. For acoustic analysis, it is generally necessary to exclude the voiceless parts from the analysis. For F_0-related measures, it may be possible to set the analysis parameters so that voiceless sections are disregarded. Most of the time, though, you'll need to excise voiceless parts of the signal, and often even some of the voiced consonants. If you don't, those sections of the signal will affect the measurements that you get. For example, if you're using certain measures of breathiness or roughness, consonants with frication or aspiration will inflate the degree of breathiness or roughness that is reported.

7.3 Laryngeal factors

Fundamental frequency range

Speech styles, individuals and dialects may differ in how they use the possible range of F_0 values. Some use a greater or narrower fraction of the range; others use different parts of the range.

Key

Key involves the degree of F_0 variation in a speaker's voice. For certain uses, such as expressing excitement and strong emotions, speakers expand the range of F_0 in their voice, usually by increasing the upper end of their F_0 range more than by decreasing the lower end. Such variation isn't limited to emotive speech, though. Certain lects appear to use relatively wide or narrow keys as a whole. For example, in the south of the United States, many white females seem to use a wider key than African American females or males of either ethnic group.

Key can be measured by computing the variance or standard deviation of F_0 values. Before you perform this computation, F_0 values should be converted to ERB units, which cancels out, to some extent, differences in variance that are due to physiological differences.

Register

Register has to do with the average F_0. Instead of expansion of the range of F_0 values, register involves shifting of the range of values, and thus the average value, up and down. It can come into play as a stylistic difference, as an indication of different emotional states, and apparently as a dialectal difference. It is most easily gauged by calculating a speaker's mean F_0 value or their mean F_0 value in a particular speaking style or situation.

Of course, physiological differences play a large role in F_0 variation, and you will have to distinguish F_0 register from physiologically controlled influences. If you are looking at intraspeaker differences, the task is relatively easy: all you have to do is to compare the individual's mean F_0 in the different speaking styles or situations.

Interspeaker differences are more complicated. If your sample is large enough (more than 30 or so speakers in each cell) and if you control for age and sex of speakers, you can compare mean values of different groups. For smaller samples, you will have to resort to other methods. One way is to compute the difference between mean and median F_0 values (in ERB) for each speaker and then to compare those subtracted values among the groups you're analysing. This technique can work because F_0 values typically show a skewed, not a normal, distribution, and changes in F_0 register will affect the shape of the skewing. Another method is to compute the difference between each speaker's mean F_0 value and their lowest F_0 value in ERB.

Phonation

Phonation is commonly thought of as a continuum of breathy, modal and creaky voicing. There is more to it than that, though. What often passes for 'creakiness' includes a number of recognizably distinct states. 'Roughness' is another factor that is related to creakiness. Some definitions are in order. First, *modal* phonation is what is considered to be 'normal'. A waveform and spectrogram of the word *bed* spoken in modal phonation are shown in Figure 7.1. Note that the glottal pulses are well defined in the waveform and don't show much variation in frequency or amplitude from one pulse to the next.

Breathy voicing, or simply *breathiness*, is a state in which much of the length of the vocal folds is open while they are vibrating. As a result, considerable air escapes through the hole during voicing, producing aspiration. Female voices are typically slightly breathier than male voices (Van Borsel et al. 2009) though, as Henton and Bladon (1985) note, the difference can be exaggerated and serve to index femininity in some locales.[1] When the opening is narrowed so that the vocal folds are open at only one end, *whispery voicing* results. Whispery voicing sounds similar to breathy voicing and there is a continuum between them, even though the muscular activities resulting in the two differ markedly (Laver 1980:133–4). Figure 7.2 shows a waveform and spectrogram of *bed* spoken with breathy voicing. In the waveform, the pulses seem better defined than for modal voicing because the first harmonic (F_0) dominates the spectrum. On the spectrogram, though, the glottal pulses have a fuzzy appearance because of the failure of the vocal folds to close.

Roughness, or *harshness*, is voicing that sounds 'scratchy'. It is characterized by irregularity in the frequency and amplitude of glottal pulses. It can be effected in order to signify toughness or anger. Figure 7.3 shows a waveform and spectrogram of *bed* uttered with rough voicing. The effects of roughness are particularly evident in the waveform, where the uneven spacing and amplitude of the glottal pulses can be seen clearly. Closely connected to roughness is *hoarseness*. For the most part, hoarseness occurs as a pathological condition, such as from nodules on the vocal folds or when somebody has a headcold and has been coughing a lot. Kreiman and Gerratt (2000) note that hoarseness is generally regarded as roughness and breathiness together, though they also note that roughness typically shows levels of noise similar to those that typify breathiness.

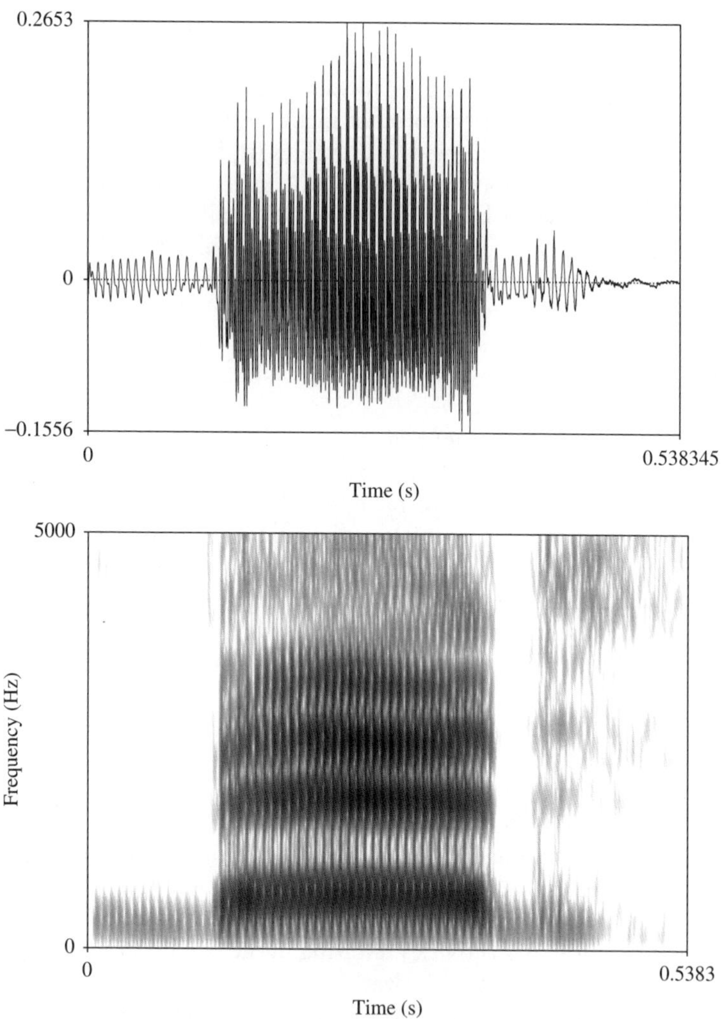

Figure 7.1 Waveform and spectrogram of the word *bed* spoken with modal phonation. The glottal pulses are well defined and relatively even.

Non-specialists often use the term *creaky voicing,* or *creakiness,* to refer to various conditions involving slow vocal fold vibrations. Creakiness may involve merely marked slowing of glottal pulses, as shown in the waveform and spectrogram of *bed* produced with creaky voicing in Figure 7.4. The mean F_0 of the vowel in Figure 7.4 is 57 Hz, as compared with the mean F_0 of 134 Hz for the vowel in Figure 7.1. Another common condition occurs when the amplitude of pulses varies, often alternating between high and low amplitudes. Such a configuration appears in parts of both syllables in the utterance of *bothered* in Figure 7.5. This alternating pattern frequently appears when the speaker is transitioning between modal and creaky phonation. Irregular glottal pulse frequency, which is to say roughness, also ordinarily involves slowing of the

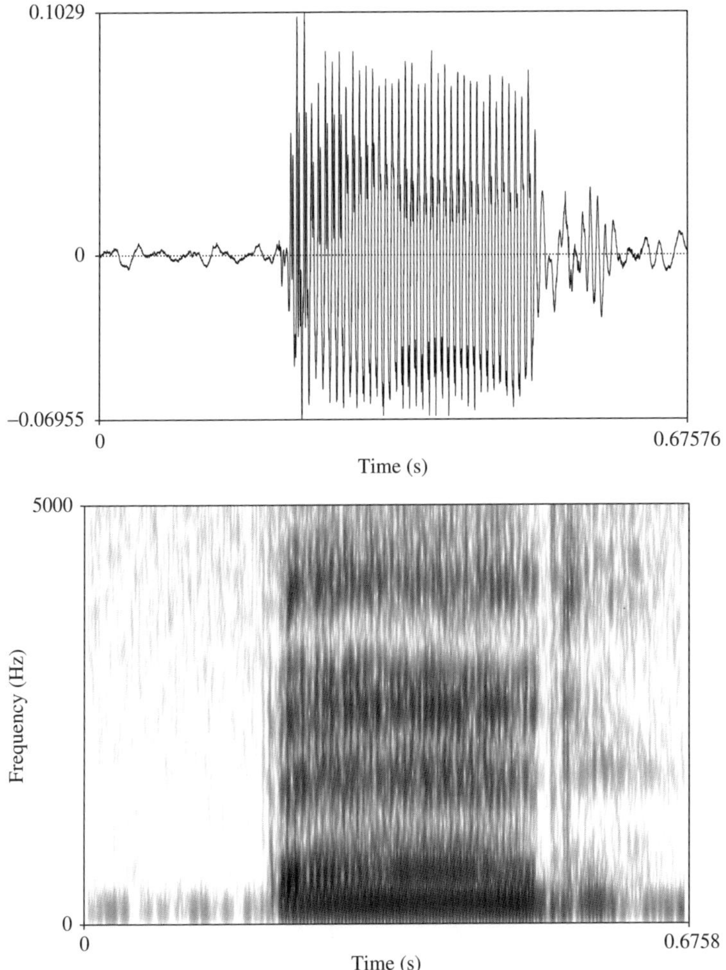

Figure 7.2 Waveform and spectrogram of the word *bed* spoken with breathy phonation. The glottal pulses appear well defined in the waveform but fuzzy in the spectrogram.

vibration. Creakiness, like breathiness and roughness, can be controlled by speakers to index particular social meanings.

A number of different techniques are used to measure phonation. The methods used to measure breathiness aren't always the same as those used for creakiness and roughness, though measures of spectral tilt can be used for both.

Fundamental frequency

A seemingly simple way of testing for creakiness is to look at F_0. Since creakiness is characterized by slowed glottal pulses, markedly low F_0 can indicate creakiness. There are some complications to beware of. First, what is a markedly low F_0 for one speaker (e.g. a female) won't be markedly low for another

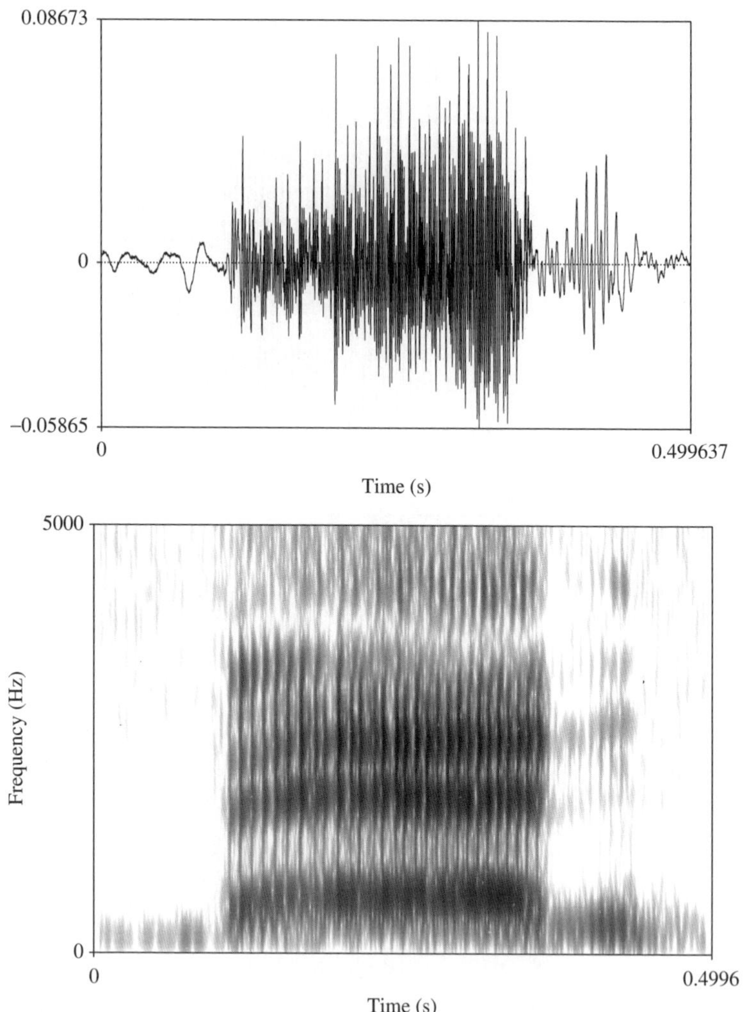

Figure 7.3 Waveform and spectrogram of the word *bed* spoken with rough phonation. The spacing and amplitude of glottal pulses is uneven, which is especially evident in the waveform.

speaker (e.g. an adult male), so you have to compare measurements of F_0 for putatively creaky areas to average or median F_0 values for the speaker. Another problem is that F_0 in creaky voicing can be hard to measure with pitch tracking programs because there is usually at least a little irregularity in the frequency of glottal pulses.

Long-term average spectra (LTAS)

You recall that a spectrum shows frequency on the x-axis and amplitude on the y-axis. A *long-term average spectrum*, or *LTAS*, shows energy (represented as amplitude) over a period of time instead of at one instant. It's useful for gauging phonation because different phonations show distinct patterns of *spectral tilt*.

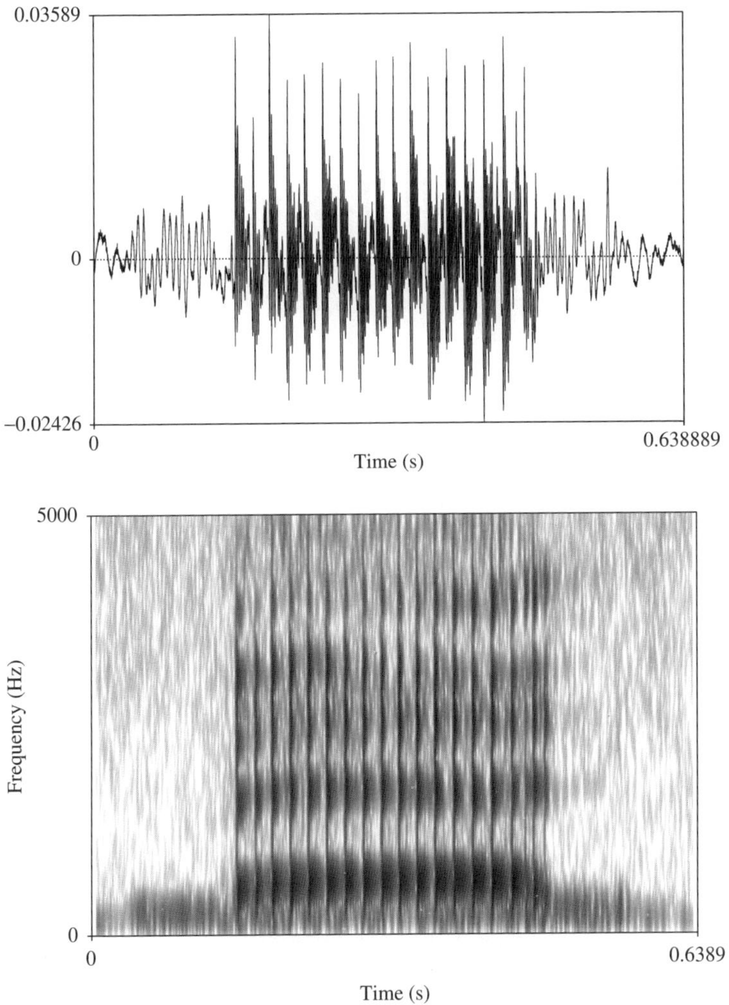

Figure 7.4 Waveform and spectrogram of the word *bed* spoken with creaky phonation. The most obvious feature is the wide spacing of glottal pulses.

Spectral tilt is the flatness of the overall spectrum – that is, whether higher-frequency parts of a spectrum show much lower amplitude than lower-frequency parts, only slightly lower amplitude, or even greater amplitude. Spectral tilt is a relative term. For low frequencies, i.e. those below 1 kHz, it can mean the degree to which successive harmonics decrease in amplitude. That is, before resonances in the oral tract shape the signal, the first harmonic (the fundamental frequency) has the highest amplitude, the second harmonic has the next highest amplitude, the third harmonic has the third-highest amplitude, and so on. The degree to which the amplitude falls off varies considerably.

Creaky, modal and breathy voicing show well-known patterns for spectral tilt. Figure 7.6 shows LTAS for the vowels in Figures 7.1, 7.2 and 7.4. LTAS

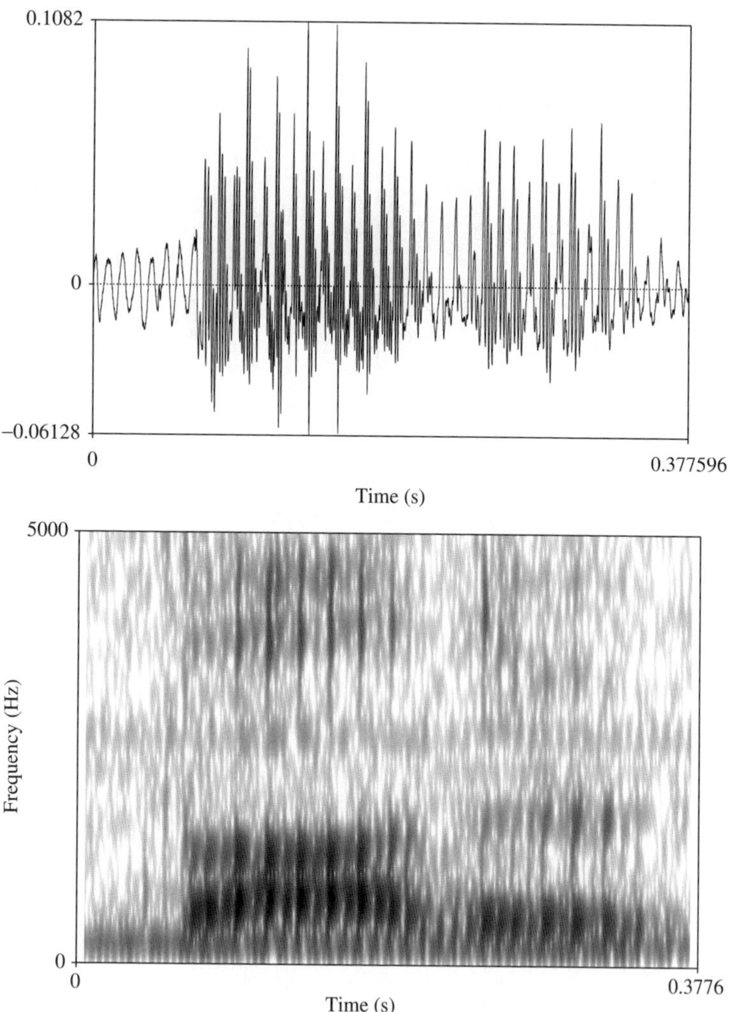

Figure 7.5 Waveform and spectrogram of the word *bothered* spoken with glottal pulses alternating in amplitude.

is commonly used for longer utterances, but I am applying it to single vowels here to illustrate the different phonation types. Amplitude falls off rapidly for breathy voicing – the highest-amplitude point is between 100 and 200 Hz, corresponding to F_0, and from there the amplitude drops quickly, with a lower-amplitude spike corresponding to F_1 at around 550 Hz. In contrast, for modal and creaky voicing, the point of highest amplitude is the spike for a harmonic close to F_1. On the other hand, at higher frequencies, the amplitude for breathy voicing rebounds. The breathy voicing contour in Figure 7.6 shows a mound in its amplitude between 5.5 and 8 kHz. This amplitude peak results from the presence of aperiodic noise in breathy voicing caused by the escape of air through the vocal folds.

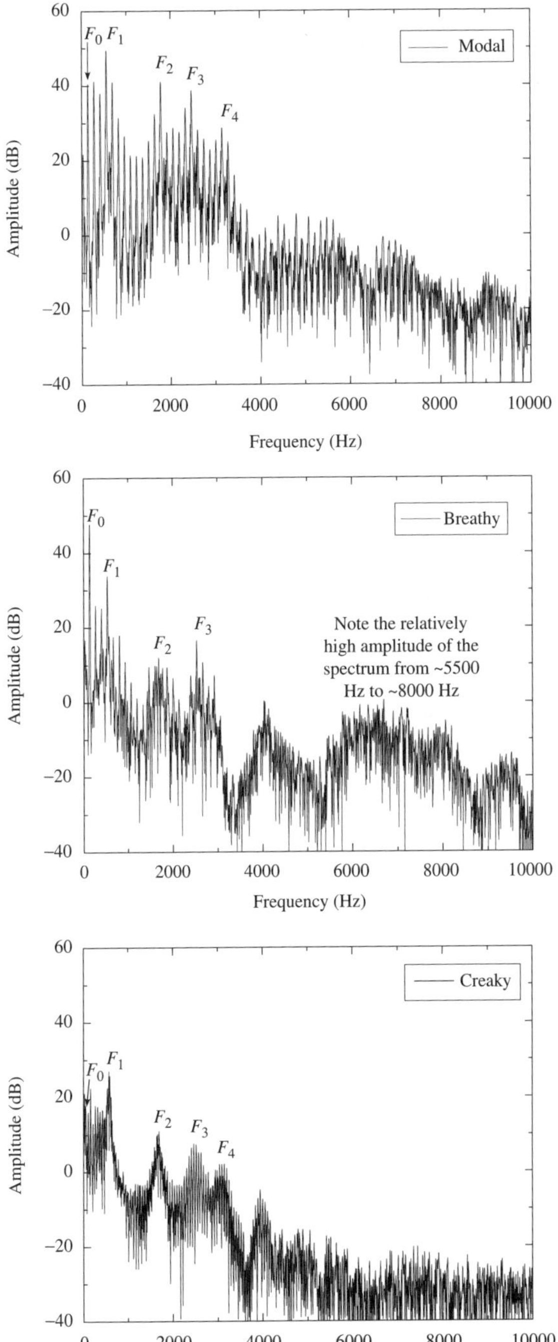

Figure 7.6 LTAS for modal, breathy and creaky utterances of the vowel in *bed*.

LTAS can be used as a metric for phonation by comparison of amplitudes in different parts of the spectrum. Amplitudes of lower- and higher-frequency parts of the whole spectrum are compared: e.g. the amplitude for frequencies under 500 Hz can be compared with those of frequencies between 500 and 1000 Hz, or amplitudes of frequencies from 0 to 1.5 kHz with those from 1.5 to 5 kHz, or 0 to 5 kHz with 5 to 10 kHz, or whatever division seems most appropriate.

Ratios of harmonic amplitudes

Spectral tilt can be measured in another way. Using LTAS or a narrowband power spectrum, you can compute the ratio of the amplitude of the first harmonic (H1, equivalent to F_0) to that of another low harmonic. Ordinarily, you would compare the amplitudes of H1 and H2, the next harmonic. However, because the filters imposed by different vowels shape the spectrum and thus affect harmonic amplitudes, you may find it more suitable to use a different harmonic. For example, it may work better if you compare H1 with the strongest harmonic associated with the first formant. At any rate, breathy voicing should show a greater difference between H1 amplitude and the amplitude of other harmonics than other phonation types do.

For creaky voicing, H1 ordinarily isn't the harmonic of highest amplitude. Instead, the second or, less commonly, the third or even fourth harmonics show the highest amplitudes. The amplitude of H1 usually significantly exceeds those of H2, H3 and H4 for breathy voicing and on average (depending on vowel quality) slightly exceeds them for modal voicing. However, the amplitude of H1 is normally lower than one of the next three harmonics for creaky voicing.

Figures 7.7–7.9 show power spectra of the same vowels as in Figures 7.1, 7.2, 7.4 and 7.6, but for frequencies below 2 kHz. The first three harmonics are labelled in each spectrum. For modal phonation, H2 has a slightly higher amplitude – by about 1 dB – than H1. For breathy phonation, the amplitude of H2 is much lower than that of H1, by about 20 dB. For the example of creaky phonation featured here, H3 has a higher amplitude than H1 or H2; note that there is some noise at frequencies slightly lower than H1 whose amplitude is greater than that of H1 in the creaky example. The acoustic skirt of that noise may inflate the measured amplitude of H1.

Jitter

Jitter is the degree of local variation in F_0 frequency. For a perfectly monotonal voice, the amount of jitter would be zero. Conversely, rough voicing would yield a high degree of jitter because the pitch periods have irregular durations. Of course, only a synthetic voice could be perfectly monotonal, and a certain amount of irregularity in F_0 is necessary to make a voice sound authentic. Acoustic analysis packages designed for use on human voices usually have a function for measuring jitter.

Measures of jitter depend heavily on their ability to identify pitch periods, i.e. the time between each glottal pulse. One method of doing so is *peak picking*, which, as Buder (2000:126) describes, involves autocorrelation followed

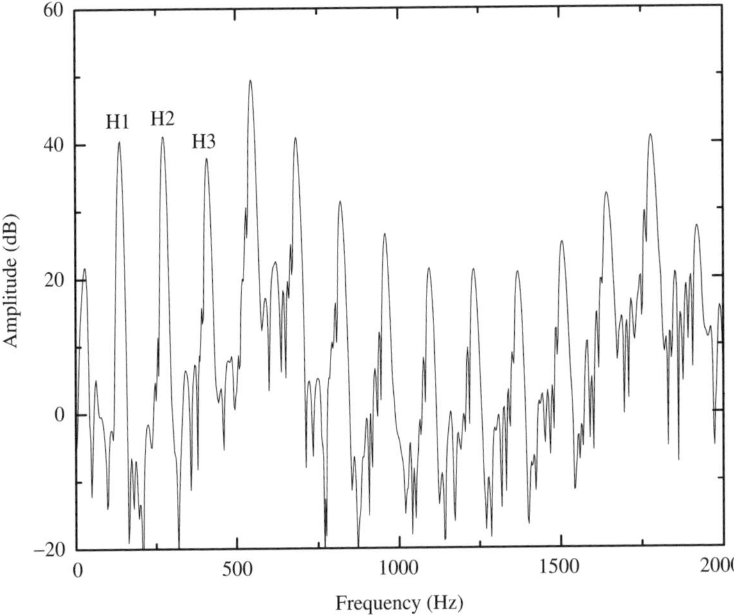

Figure 7.7 LTAS of the vowel in *bed* produced with modal phonation, with the three lowest harmonics labelled. The peak to the left of H1 is noise, perhaps from the speaker's (my) exhalation or introduced by the connection between the microphone and the recorder.

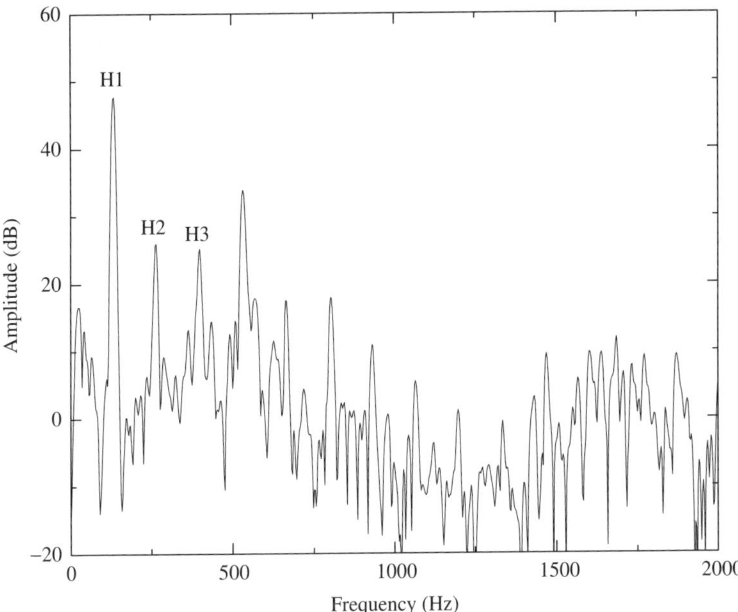

Figure 7.8 LTAS of the vowel in *bed* produced with breathy phonation, with the three lowest harmonics labelled

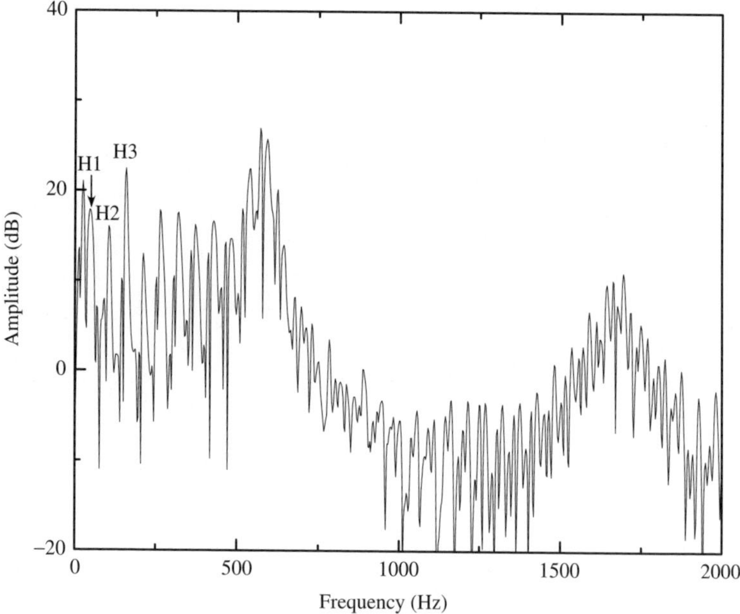

Figure 7.9 LTAS of the vowel in *bed* produced with creaky phonation, with the three lowest harmonics labelled.

by location of the highest peaks in the waveform within a frame length assumed to be less than two pitch periods – the pitch period is equated with the duration between the peaks. Peak picking seems to be adversely affected by noise. Other methods of identifying pitch periods involve matching similar waveform patterns, much like autocorrelation, and analysing zero-crossing points. Once the pitch periods have been determined, the degree of variation in their length is then analysed. Today, one of the most common ways of quantifying this variation is the *relative average perturbation* (RAP) method, first developed by Koike (1973). In RAP, jitter is computed as the mean duration of three consecutive pitch periods divided by the length of the middle pitch period. Another method is to compare only two consecutive pitch periods.

Shimmer

Shimmer is the degree of local variation in amplitude, i.e. between successive vocal fold vibrations. It is often considered together with jitter because the two co-vary much of the time. Like jitter, shimmer can be measured by most acoustic analysis packages for human voices.

The issues of pitch period determination that affect jitter measurement also apply to shimmer measurement. However, measures of shimmer tend to involve averages of more pitch periods than measures of jitter. For example, the *amplitude perturbation quotient* (APQ) method of Koike et al. (1977) averages together amplitudes of up to 11 consecutive pitch periods before dividing by the amplitude of the middle one.

Harmonics-to-noise ratio

The *harmonics-to-noise ratio* (HNR), which for speech is functionally equivalent to the *signal-to-noise ratio*, measures the ratio of periodic components to aperiodic components within a voice sample. It is often used as a measure of hoarseness. For a modal voice, the ratio is relatively high, while for a rough or hoarse voice, it is lower. Breathy voicing often shows a high HNR because F_0 dominates its spectrum. Creakiness frequently shows a relatively low HNR. HNR is measured in decibels. Its basic formula is

$$\text{HNR} = 10(\log_{10}(\text{periodic component/aperiodic component}))$$

However, you have to start with actual sound signals before you can calculate HNR. That is, you have to determine what's periodic and what's not in the signal. For that, there are several formulas involving differences in how long the analysis windows are, how the signal is sampled, and whether cepstral analysis (described below) is involved. See, e.g., Yumoto et al. (1982), Boersma (1993) and de Krom (1993) for discussion of some of those formulas. HNR includes all aperiodic noise as part of its aperiodic component. As a result, any noise, whether from the speaker's voice or from the background of the recording, figures into it. This makes HNR hard to use on field recordings, where background noise is ubiquitous.

Cepstral peak prominence (CPP)

Cepstral peak prominence, or CPP, is used to gauge breathiness, and it can also be used for hoarseness. It involves the creation of something called a *cepstrum*. 'Cepstrum' is simply 'spectrum' with the first syllable spelled backwards (the *c* is pronounced like a *k*), and cepstra are made somewhat analogously. Cepstral analysis starts with a power spectrum of a signal, which, as you'll recall, is extracted using Fourier analysis. The logarithm of the spectrum is computed, and then a spectrum of the logarithmic function is created, again with a Fourier transform. In the display that the process yields, the x-axis, measured in milliseconds, is called the *quefrency* and the y-axis, measured in dB, is the *cepstral magnitude*. The most prominent feature of a cepstral analysis is a spike at the lower quefrencies that corresponds to F_0. This spike is the second peak visible in each of the two cepstra in Figure 7.10. The upper window shows a raw cepstrum, and the lower window shows a smoothed cepstrum (see Hillenbrand and Houde 1996). The earliest application of cepstra to speech was as a means of estimating F_0 (Noll 1967), though they have mostly been superceded by autocorrelation for F_0 measurement because they work poorly when there's noise in the signal. The quefrency of the spike represents the pitch period, which is divided into 1 sec or 1,000 msec to obtain F_0. A series of cepstra at intervals in the original signal may be averaged to produce a mean cepstrum for the whole time period.

Although cepstral analysis isn't used as often to determine F_0 as it once was, it has found a new application in gauging breathy and rough voicing. Hillenbrand et al. (1994) expound on this method, which is designed to find the prominence of the spike representing F_0 compared to the rest of the cepstrum. The

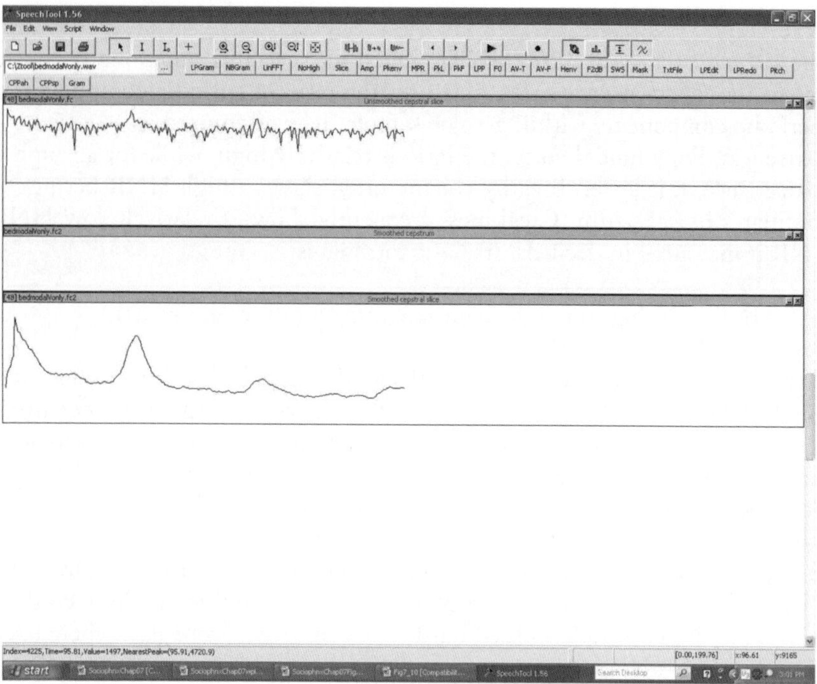

Figure 7.10 Screenshot of the SpeechTool analysis of the vowel from the utterance in Figure 7.1, showing the cepstrum (upper) and smoothed ceptstrum (lower) windows. The leftmost peak in each window is ignored, and CPP and CPPS analyses are based on the next major peak, which is more clearly demarcated in the smoothed cepstrum window.

signal is subjected to cepstral analysis, as described above. Quefrencies below 1 msec are excluded because they aren't determined by F_0. For the rest of the cepstrum – from 1 msec to the maximum quefrency – a linear regression line of the cepstral magnitude is extracted. Then the distance in dB between the cepstral peak – i.e. the spike – and the regression line is calculated, and this distance is the CPP. The linear regression line should be determined using a program called SpeechTool available for free on James Hillenbrand's website (http://homepages.wmich.edu/~hillenbr/). Be sure to download the version of SpeechTool that includes CPP scripts.

The program has different settings depending on whether a single vowel (CPPV) or any speech (CPPCS) is being analysed. Smaller CPP values indicate greater breathiness, greater values indicate less breathiness. Hillenbrand et al. (1994) found that CPP was correlated with auditory ratings of breathiness better than any other acoustic method. Hillenbrand and Houde (1996) stated that analysis of smoothed cepstra (CPPS) such as the one shown in Figure 7.10 gave more reliable values than raw cepstra. To give you an idea of what sorts of values to expect, here are the CPP and CPPS values for the vowels in figures 7.1–7.4. For CPP: modal, 21.14 dB; breathy, 12.72 dB; creaky, 9.05 dB; and rough, 12.21 dB (same for both CPPV and CPPCS options). For CPPS, CPPV option:

modal, 8.77 dB; breathy, 5.12 dB; creaky, –1.00 dB; and rough, 1.31 dB. For CPPS, CPPCS option: modal, 9.42 dB; breathy, 5.59 dB; creaky, 0.91 dB; and rough, 3.48 dB. Because cepstral analysis is adversely affected by background noise, the CPP and CPPS measures may be affected as well. The numbers you obtain from noisy recordings should be lower than those for Figures 7.1–7.4.

7.4 Supralaryngeal settings

Larynx height

Speakers regularly move their larynges up and down during speech. For example, lowering of the larynx characterizes voiced consonants. However, larynx height can also function as a voice quality setting. For example, men's larynges are normally lower than women's, but speakers could potentially exaggerate the difference to project a gender identity. Exactly how much speakers index gender identity by exaggerating or counteracting physiological larynx height differences needs to be investigated.

Vertical movement of the larynx changes the length of the pharyngeal cavity, so it changes the resonances of any formant associated with the pharynx. Lowering the larynx will lower those resonances, while raising the larynx will raise them. Because F_1 is associated with the back cavity, it is predictably affected by larynx movement. F_2 can be affected when there's no constriction and hence a single cavity from the pharynx to the lips, as with [ə], or if F_2 is affiliated with the back cavity. Lindblom and Sundberg (1971) provide measurements of modal and lowered-larynx formant values for a male producing Swedish vowels. Their measurements show that F_1 falls consistently by about 5 per cent when the larynx is lowered. F_2 falls by over 100 Hz for all the front vowels but barely falls at all for back vowels, which Lindblom and Sundberg attribute to a back cavity affiliation for F_2 for the front vowels. F_3 usually shows only slight declines in frequency because it is a front cavity resonance. F_4, however, falls by approximately 5 per cent, bringing it relatively closer to F_3, as Lindblom and Sundberg point out. Presumably, these effects would be the opposite for larynx raising. Changes in the relative distances between F_1 and F_2 and between F_3 and F_4 could be used to detect larynx height settings. Table 7.1 shows F_1–F_4 for modal vs lowered-larynx values of some English vowels in *hVd* frames, as spoken by my daughter (at age nine) and me. The juxtaposition of adult male and nine-year-old-girl values is intended to give you an idea of how formant values are affected for speakers with differently proportioned oral tracts. In general, the results are similar to those of Lindblom and Sundberg, with consistent drops in F_1 values, though occasionally certain formant values increase in the lowered-larynx condition.

Tongue settings

In certain pathological cases, speakers articulate speech sounds – most noticeably, vowels – with the tongue body shifted backward, forward, up or a combination from its 'normal' position. Laver (1980:48) notes that such settings of

Table 7.1 Modal and lowered-larynx values of F_1–F_4 for me (adult male) and my daughter (at age nine) of various vowels.

Adult male

Word	*Modal*				*Lowered larynx*			
	F_1	F_2	F_3	F_4	F_1	F_2	F_3	F_4
heed (centre of vowel)	327	2134	2626	3144	260	2016	2903	3272
hid (centre)	510	1795	2442	3106	367	1703	2317	3089
hayed (35 ms after onset)	500	1820	2514	3339	392	1662	2277	3118
hayed (35 ms before offset)	383	2104	2625	3163	313	1812	2378	3057
head (centre)	537	1745	2421	3178	474	1579	2258	2985
had (centre)	744	1644	2274	2937	555	1612	2306	3079
hod (centre)	724	1155	2341	3515	585	1106	2398	2676
HUD (centre)	566	1380	2363	3442	487	1265	2227	2909
hoed (35 ms after onset)	561	1449	2123	2891	471	1290	2201	2864
hoed (35 ms before offset)	417	1301	2140	2875	318	1386	2055	2987
hood (centre)	527	1450	2347	3077	425	1295	2263	3021
who'd (centre)	401	1658	2043	2828	340	1439	2105	3017
hold (centre)	432	602	2216	3542	457	770	2422	2669
hauled (35 ms after onset)	529	786	2687	3266	468	818	2489	2705
hauled (35 ms before offset)	414	649	2667	3698	375	908	2515	2884
heard (centre)	478	1288	1446	2832	351	1282	1503	2813

Nine-year-old girl

Word	*Modal*				*Lowered larynx*			
	F_1	F_2	F_3	F_4	F_1	F_2	F_3	F_4
heed (centre of vowel)	349	3203	3508	5115	324	3001	3444	4603
hid (centre)	560	2663	3421	5062	368	2356	3390	4896
hayed (35 ms after onset)	453	2758	3411	4719	523	2444	3352	4765
hayed (35 ms before offset)	466	3090	3623	5006	322	2919	3323	4796
head (centre)	703	2538	3529	5397	584	2309	3325	4983
had (centre)	1146	2346	3433	?	802	2557	3280	4835
hod (centre)	1260	1932	3259	5449	1060	1666	3280	4707
HUD (centre)	1138	2458	3452	4603	924	2153	3577	5018
hoed (35 ms after onset)	759	2229	3741	4924	519	2324	3128	4702
hoed (35 ms before offset)	663	2254	4014	5033	?	?	?	?
hood (centre)	680	2331	3424	5078	511	2166	3339	4404
who'd (centre)	558	2423	3639	5052	428	2476	3221	4659
hold (centre)	674	1218	4285	5254	381	1340	3568	4484
hauled (35 ms after onset)	1182	1579	2648	?	1082	1682	3582	4445
hauled (35 ms before offset)	711	1383	2774	4644	880	1644	3459	4248
heard (centre)	729	2247	2711	3957	482	2304	2957	4183

Note: Cells marked with '?' indicate the formant was too indistinct to measure.

the tongue are not always pathological, however, but can also characterize certain dialects. Stuart-Smith (1999) corroborated Laver's assertion in her study in Glasgow. In fact, she found rich interactions of tongue setting (among other voice quality features) with social class, age group and sex.

Stuart-Smith's study was based on auditory ratings of voice quality. However, acoustic means of assessing tongue settings are also available. They involve looking at measurements of vowel formants for the vowel system as a whole. For vocal settings, the important thing is to get measurements of the first three formants for vowels representing a range of a speaker's vowels. Non-modal lingual settings don't seem to slide a speaker's entire vowel envelope into a new space with the same proportions. Instead, as Laver (1980:44) states, lingual settings squeeze 'vowel articulations such that they are constrained to fall only in a restricted zone within the vowel area'. The articulatory restriction that Laver describes is reflected in the acoustics.

The acoustic effects of lingual settings mirror those of consonantal places of articulation, which we saw in Chapter 4. In fact, lingual settings are described with names corresponding to consonantal articulations, such as alveolarization, palatalization and pharyngealization. They are named depending on which way the tongue is shifted – e.g. for a palatal lingual setting, the tongue is shifted towards the (hard) palate. Nolan (1983) provides mean formant values for speech impersonated by John Laver with various supralaryngeal settings. The effects on formants for lingual settings, based on Nolan's data, are summarized in general terms in Table 7.2. As a whole, fronting of the tongue results in a general raising of F_2 values; raising of the tongue leads to a fall in F_1 and a rise in F_2; and retraction of the tongue causes a rise in F_1 and a fall in F_2.

Detecting lingual settings requires comparison with a point of reference. One way to do that would be to compare mean values and variances or standard deviations with those for speakers who are deemed to be modal. This method is hard to implement because it's hard to distinguish objectively speakers whose formant values are shifted because of a lingual setting from those whose formant values are shifted simply because their mouths are different sizes. An easier

Table 7.2 Generalized effects of lingual settings on the first three formants, interpreted from data in Nolan (1983).

Lingual setting	*General effect on:*		
	F_1	F_2	F_3
Dentalized	Little/no effect	Raised	Little/no effect
Alveolarized	Little/no effect	Raised	Little/no effect
Retroflexed	Raised	Lowered	Strongly lowered
Palato-alveolarized	Little/no effect	Raised	Raised
Palatalized	Lowered	Strongly raised	Little/no effect
Velarized	Lowered	Strongly raised	Raised
Uvularized	Little/no effect	Lowered	Little/no effect
Pharyngealized	Raised	Strongly lowered	Strongly lowered
Laryngo-pharyngealized	Raised	Strongly lowered	Effect unclear

method is to apply normalization to the formant values. The normalization should be a vowel-intrinsic method, which isn't based on a mean value for a speaker, so differences in lingual settings will show up as an overall shifting of the vowel envelope – or at least of most vowel values – in plots of normalized values, as compared with 'modal' speakers.

Labial settings

In speech, the lips may be moved from a relaxed position so that they are constricted, protruded or spread. Constriction and protrusion can be thought of as forms of rounding and as having the same acoustic effect: lowering of all formants. The degree of formant lowering varies proportionally with the degree of rounding. Lip spreading raises formants slightly, with perhaps a stronger effect on F_3, according to the figures given in Nolan (1983) (see also Lindblom and Sundberg 1971). As with lingual settings, a vowel-internal normalization technique will reveal labial settings. For the Bark-difference metrics described in Chapter 5, all values will be lower with lip constriction and protrusion than they would be for a neutral setting. With lip spreading, values will be somewhat higher than for a neutral setting.

Nasality

Nasality is among the most commonly recognized voice quality settings by the general public. It is readily apparent in certain cartoon voices, such as Bugs Bunny's. Nevertheless, it isn't always easy to measure or to define. Nasality is often thought of as a particular voice quality associated with lowering of the velum and concomitant opening of the nasopharyngeal port during speech, when such opening isn't required for the segments being produced. Opening the nasopharyngeal port makes the nasal cavity into a side chamber that produces extra resonances as well as antiformants (antiresonances or 'zeroes') that cancel resonances from the oral and/or pharyngeal cavities at specified frequencies. As Laver (1980) points out, however, there are some problems with this definition. The root of the problem is that 'nasality' is a perceptual impression, while lowering of the velum is an articulatory gesture. The two don't coincide entirely. First, Laver (1980:78 ff.) notes that the nasopharyngeal port is, for most speakers, slightly open during speech that sounds 'non-nasal'. It turns out that, to produce an impression of nasality, the nasopharyngeal port has to be wider than the velopharyngeal port (the opening to the oral cavity). Second, Laver reports that, for a few speakers, the side chamber that produces the resonances resulting in the impression of nasality isn't the nasal cavity at all – instead, it seems to be a cavity in the lower pharynx.

As with measurement of other aspects of voice quality, measurement of nasal voice quality focuses on vowels. One problem that makes nasality hard to measure is that, for some techniques to gauge it, the different vowels have to be considered separately. That is, for measures involving ratios of oral to nasal formant properties, the scale will differ depending on the values of the oral formants. What numbers constitute nasal and non-nasal values on the scale of nasality for [ɔ] won't be the same as those for [i]. A possible solution for this problem would be to normalize for vowel quality, as Chen (1995) does for her A1-P1 method.

A1–H1

An older method of gauging nasality is to subtract the amplitude of the first harmonic, H1 – i.e. the harmonic whose frequency is F_0 – from the amplitude of F_1, called A1. F_1 is understood to be the first *oral* formant. This value will be greater for non-nasal vowels than for nasal vowels because nasalization increases the bandwidth of F_1, thereby decreasing its amplitude. This method has largely been superseded by other methods.

A1–P1 and A1–P0

Chen (1995, 1996) developed two formulas for gauging nasality that involve comparing amplitudes of the first oral formant with those of nasal formants. Narrowband spectrograms are used for this method. In a nasalized vowel, there is a nasal formant with a frequency close to that of F_1 of an upper-mid vowel, and another nasal formant that lies between the first two oral formants. There is also a nasal antiformant that is often close to the value of the first oral formant. Higher nasal formants and antiformants also exist, but they aren't part of the method.

Figure 7.11 shows a spectrogram of *bed* produced with a nasal setting. Compared to the modal voicing example in Figure 7.1, F_1 appears to show lower amplitude. Other differences can be seen in Figure 7.12, which shows superimposed power spectra of the centres of the vowels from Figures 7.1 and 7.11. The nasal spectrum shows two valleys – antiformants – that the modal spectrum lacks, one at 425 Hz and the other at 2,675 Hz.

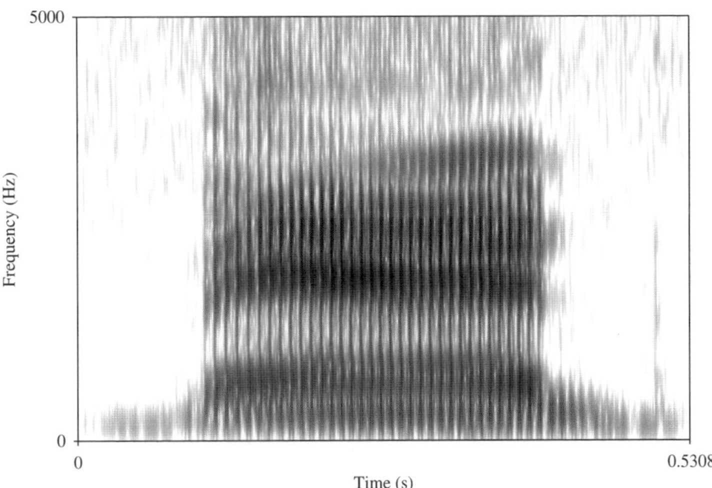

Figure 7.11 Spectrogram of *bed* spoken with a nasal setting. The oral F_1 and F_3 seem to be split into two or three formants for part of the vowel, and the oral F_4 disappears in the first half of the vowel.

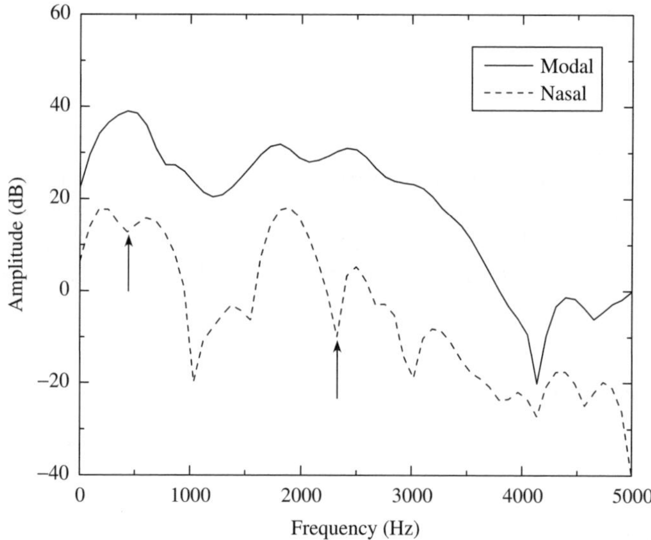

Figure 7.12 Wideband spectra of the centres of modal (solid line) and nasal (dotted line) utterances of the vowel in *bed*. Arrows indicate the locations of antiformants.

Because nasality decreases the amplitude of the oral F_1, its amplitude can be compared with those of the two lowest nasal formants. The amplitudes of the two lowest nasal formants were referred to by Chen as *P0* and *P1*, respectively, while the amplitude of the first oral formant was called *A1*. Hence the two formulas are: $A1 - P1$ (i.e. the amplitude of the oral F_1 minus the amplitude of the second nasal formant – the one that lies between the oral F_1 and oral F_2) and $A1 - P0$ (i.e. the amplitude of the oral F_1 minus the amplitude of the first nasal formant). The larger the subtracted values are, the less nasal the sample is. The $A1 - P1$ method tends to be easier to use than the $A1 - P0$ method, partly because the low nasal formant can be hard to distinguish from the oral F_1 for higher vowels.

It may seem that these formulas should work only for nasal vowels because a non-nasal vowel isn't supposed to have any nasal formants. Nevertheless, 'non-nasal' vowels quite often do have vestigial nasal formants, perhaps because the nasopharyngeal port isn't usually completely closed during speech. To find them, you have to know where to look. Just remember that the first nasal formant usually lies at about 200–500 Hz, while the second is just a little higher than the highest oral F_1 value for a speaker, generally at about 800–1,300 Hz. A single individual's nasal formants don't vary much, regardless of what the vowel is, so you can often compare different vowels to figure out where the speaker's nasal formants are.[2]

An individual's oral formants do vary quite a lot, however, and that's where complications arise. Depending on its value, the oral F_1 may lie close to a nasal formant, raising the amplitude of the nasal formant because it is riding on the skirt of the oral formant, or farther from nasal formants. A resulting artefact is that the $A1 - P0$ formula can make high vowels appear to be more nasal than they are. When the oral F_2 is low, as for back vowels, its skirt can also increase the amplitude of the second nasal formant. To counteract these effects, Chen (1995, 1996) developed correction formulas to normalize the amplitudes of the second nasal formant. The correction factors for the effects of the two oral formants are called *T1* and *T2*, respectively. Simplified formulas for computing the correction factors, which Chen (1995:2452) states work if the bandwidths 'are much less than the formant frequencies', are:

$$T1_{approx} = F_1^2/[(950 - F_1)(F_1 + 950)]$$
$$T2_{approx} = F_2^2/[(950 - F_2)(F_2 + 950)]$$

where F_1 and F_2 represent the frequencies, in hertz, of the first two oral formants. *P'1*, the corrected amplitude of the second nasal formant, is then computed as

$$P'1 = P1 - T1 - T2$$

The formulas assume that the second nasal formant has a value of 950 Hz; you should adjust this number in the correction formulas to match a given speaker's second nasal formant frequency. Chen provides longer formulas for cases where the formant bandwidths aren't much smaller than the formant frequencies.

Let's work through a couple of examples to see how to implement Chen's formulas. Figure 7.13 shows a power spectrum for the vowel from Figure 7.11, but this time for the entire vowel. The peaks from which the amplitudes *P0*

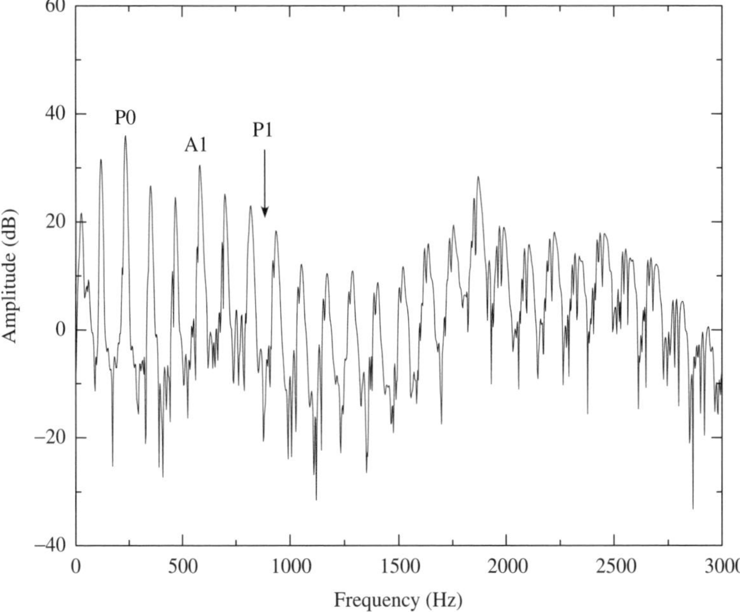

Figure 7.13 LTAS of the vowel in *bed* spoken in a nasal setting, showing where to take P0, A1 and P1 measurements.

and *A1* are taken are marked. The second nasal formant is harder to see, but there is a modest bump in the spectrum around the seventh and eighth harmonics. The formant falls somewhere between those two harmonics, as indicated by the arrow underneath the *P1* label, so we use the harmonic with the higher amplitude, the seventh, for the *P1* measurement. *P0*, *A1* and *P1* are 35.9, 30.5 and 23.0 dB, respectively. To apply the correction formulas, we need the frequencies of F_1, the second nasal formant and F_2, which are 584, 818 and 1,871 Hz, respectively. $T1_{approx}$ is then calculated to be 0.6 and $T2_{approx}$ to be –1.3, so $P'1 = 23.0 - 0.6 - (-1.3)$, or 23.7 dB. Then, $A1 - P0 = -5.4$ dB and $A1 - P'1 = 6.8$ dB. Figure 7.14 shows the power spectra for the vowel uttered with a modal setting from Figure 7.1. *A1* is quite hard to discern for this vowel, but there is a slight rise around the seventh harmonic, indicating that it lies between the sixth and seventh harmonics, which puts it at the same frequency as for the nasal setting, as it should be. *P0*, *A1* and *P1* are 41.1, 48.5 and 31.4 dB, respectively. Since the frequencies of F_1, the second nasal formant, and F_2 are 544, 821 and 1,779 Hz, in that order, $P'1 = 32.3$ dB (you can check the maths). $A1 - P0$ then becomes 7.4 dB and $A1 - P'1$ becomes 16.2 dB. Note how much higher the $A1 - P0$ and $A1 - P'1$ values are for the modal setting than for the nasal setting.

Because a large fraction of sociophonetic recordings are obtained in the field, some precautions are needed for using the $A1 - P1$ and $A1 - P0$ formulas. First, background noise during recording should be minimized, especially at frequencies near those of F_1 and the first two nasal resonances. Second, the type of microphone can make a significant impact on relative amplitudes of

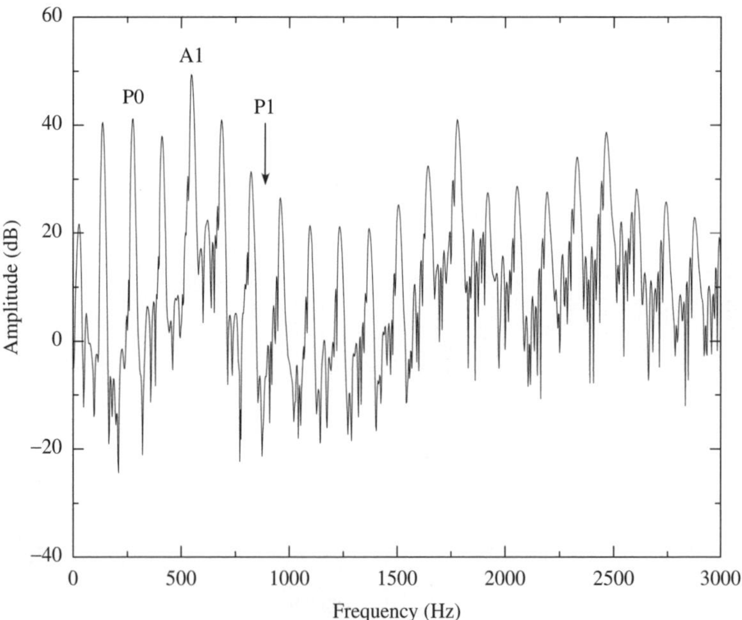

Figure 7.14 LTAS of the vowel in *bed* spoken in a modal setting, showing where to take P0, A1 and P1 measurements.

different frequencies in the signal. For this reason, all recordings that are analysed should be made with the same model of microphone. Third, placement of the microphone can have a detectable effect, so it should be located at about the same distance and direction from speakers in all recording sessions.

A battery of acoustic parameters

Recently, Tarun Pruthi has developed a new way of analysing nasality that builds on the earlier techniques but adds additional ones (Pruthi 2007; Pruthi and Espy-Wilson 2007). The resulting battery includes nine acoustic parameters that fall into five groups. These parameters are listed in Table 7.3. See Pruthi (2007) for details of how some parameters were computed: e.g. for the first three, formant peaks were located using a combination of types of spectra. Pruthi combined the nine parameters by training a support vector machine classifier to distinguish oral and nasal vowels of Hindi. While you may not wish to use the entire battery the way Pruthi did, the method provides additional acoustic properties that you can use to gauge nasality.

Nasometry devices

There are devices that can measure the amount of airflow out of the nostrils or through the nasopharyngeal port during speech, but they are invasive and hard to apply for variationist work. As an alternative, devices are commercially available that separate voice signals into nasal and oral components. They are designed for clinical applications, such as for cleft palate patients, people with hearing impairments and others who may exhibit excess vocal nasality. However, they can also be used for people without clinical problems. They usually provide a gauge of *nasalance*, which is defined either as the ratio of acoustic output of the nasal cavity to that of the oral cavity (the 'nasalance ratio') or as the percentage of nasal acoustic output out of the total of both nasal and oral output ('percentage nasalance').

Although I'm avoiding discussion of particular equipment models in this book because equipment changes so quickly, I am making an exception here in order to explain how nasometry devices work. Two currently used nasometry devices are the Nasometer (Kummer 2001), produced by Kay Elemetrics, and the OroNasal system (Rothenberg n.d.), by Glottal Enterprises. They differ in two key respects. The Nasometer consists of a headset and focuses on frequencies close to F_1, while the OroNasal system consists of a mask that fits over the subject's mouth and nose and focuses on frequencies close to F_0. Both use two microphones, one for the mouth and one for the nose, that are separated by a plate that fits against the subject's upper lip. As Kummer (2001) notes, the plate doesn't separate the oral and nasal sound outputs perfectly. Both devices are designed for clinical use, and the Nasometer has to be attached to a desktop computer. They certainly aren't suitable for studying casual conversations. Nevertheless, they can be used for dialectal investigations in which subjects are asked to read or repeat items. Kummer (2001:322) acknowledges that some nasalance differences are due to dialectal differences and even cites a study by Santos-Terron et al. (1990) showing a cross-linguistic difference in nasalance.

Table 7.3 Acoustic parameters for gauging nasality used by Pruthi (2007) and Pruthi and Espy-Wilson (2007).

General acoustic property	*Name of parameter*	*Description of parameter*	*Effect of nasality on parameter*
Relative amplitudes of low-frequency formants	sgA1 – P0	Amplitude of (oral) F_1 minus amplitude of extra formant below F_1	Lowers
	sgA1 – P1	Amplitude of (oral) F_1 minus amplitude of extra formant above F_1 (same as Chen's *A1 – P1*)	Lowers
	sgF1 – F_{P0}	Amplitude of (oral) F_1 minus amplitude of extra formant below F_1 (same as Chen's *A1 – P0*)	Lowers
	teF1	Correlation of energy in a narrowband filter (100 Hz bandwidth) and a wideband filter (1,000 Hz bandwidth) around F_1	Lowers
Presence of extra formants (across spectrum)	nPeaks40dB	For one frame of the spectrum, the number of formants with amplitudes within 40 dB of the formant with highest amplitude	Raises
F_1 amplitude	a1 – h1max800	Amplitude of (oral) F_1 minus amplitude of H1 (first harmonic)	Lowers
	a1 – h1fmt	Amplitude of (oral) F_1 minus amplitude of harmonic closest to F_1	Lowers
Bandwidth of F_1 (see section 2.5 for measurement)	F1BW	Bandwidth of F_1	Raises
Spectral flatness (low frequencies)	std0 – 1K	Standard deviation of centre of spectral mass for portions ≤1,000 Hz	Raises

7.5 Tenseness

The terms *tense* and *lax* are applied to voice quality. Be careful not to confuse this usage with that of *tense* and *lax* for vowel quality, which have completely different meanings. In voice quality, *tense* and *lax* refer to overall muscular tension of the entire vocal tract, including both laryngeal and supralaryngeal regions. According to Laver (1980), a tense voice quality setting is characterized by relatively creaky or harsh phonation, little vowel reduction and often higher F_0; and it is frequently louder. A lax setting, conversely, is characterized by relatively breathy phonation, greater vowel reduction, wider formant bandwidths and a moderate degree of nasality.

EXERCISES

For the following exercises, you can download practice samples from http://ncslaap.lib.ncsu.edu/sociophonetics/.

1. Compare mean and median F_0 values, in ERB, for at least ten seconds of speech by any two speakers.
2. Compute LTAS for the vowels of several syllables and compare them.
3. Record yourself saying the same word in modal and breathy phonation. Then compute H2–H1 in dB. Do you get a larger H1–H2 value for breathy voicing? If not, you're probably not producing the two phonation types correctly! Compare measurements of your own voice with measurements of downloaded examples.
4. Record yourself saying a vowel with creaky phonation or download a practice example and then make a power spectrum of the vowel. How many harmonics show higher amplitudes than H1?
5. Download Hillenbrand's 'SpeechTool with CPP scripts' program and measure CPP and CPPS for several syllables. Note that it's designed for a PC with Windows and may or may not function properly on a Macintosh. You'll need to save SpeechTool and the sound files to the same drive in order to get the CPP scripts to work. In SpeechTool, CPPV is used for files that consist only of the vowel portion of a signal, while CPPCS is used for signals with both vowel and non-vowel portions. What range of values do you obtain, both for CPP and for CPPS?
6. Record yourself saying the words *bud* and *bun* or download a practice example. Then, using the A1–P1 and A1–P0 methods, compare the degree of nasality in the vowels of the two words.
7. How would you design a study to test whether speakers show stylistic variation in vocal settings? How would you compare larynx height setting or lingual setting in a speaker's interactions with friends, interactions at work and interview speech?
8. Outline how you would plan a survey to test whether different social class groups or different communities of practice tend towards distinct phonation settings. How would you test how gender interacts with other social factors, given that physiology naturally renders average male voices a little less breathy than average female voices?

FURTHER READING

Laver, John. 1980. *The Phonetic Description of Voice Quality*. Cambridge: Cambridge University Press.

Lindblom, Björn E.F. and John E.F. Sundberg. 1971. Acoustical consequences of lip, tongue, jaw, and larynx movement. *Journal of the Acoustical Society of America* 50:1166–79.

Nolan, Francis. 1983. *The Phonetic Bases of Speaker Recognition*. Cambridge: Cambridge University Press.

8 Combinations of Different Types of Variables

This short chapter leads us from issues of measurement and experimental technique to theoretical linguistic matters. It is also a plea for sociophoneticians to take a broader approach to investigating variation than is usually done. Studies tend to focus on a single variable, such as VOT or intonational boundary tones, or a few variables from the same domain, such as vowels. This result can be reminiscent of the fable of the blind men and the elephant, in which each man felt one part of the elephant and thought he understood the whole animal. More emphasis needs to be placed on examining a wide suite of variables in the same study. A holistic approach will provide more complete answers to the questions that sociophoneticians ask about language.

From a sociological perspective, it's hard to get a representative idea of how social identity is indexed by linguistic variation when only one or a few variables are examined. Each variable may be correlated differently with identity. Moreover, it's quite possible that variables may fall into groups that are indexed in different ways. Let's create a hypothetical example. Let's say that, in some community, consonantal variables index speaking style, vocalic variables index social class and cliques, prosodic variables index gender identity, and voice quality indexes individual identity. If the researcher examines only consonantal variables, he or she will get one view of the sociolinguistic structure of the community. However, if the researcher concentrates on vocalic variables, or prosody, or voice quality, a decidedly different sociolinguistic image will emerge. This example is oversimplified, of course, but the point is that only a holistic approach will provide a full view of the sociolinguistics of a community. I don't mean to exclude non-phonetic variables, either – morphosyntactic, lexical and discourse style variables should also be included. If enough variables are examined, a comparison of which linguistic variables index more or fewer social factors can be conducted. At that point, it may become clearer what the most important social factors are that cleave the community.

In terms of how linguistic change occurs, a focus on only a few kinds of variables or on one type of variable doesn't provide a well-rounded picture. The mechanisms responsible for vowel shifting, for example – either the origin or the propagation of the change – most likely differ significantly from those responsible for intonational change. The constraints that determine what kinds of vowel shifts are common, infrequent or impossible certainly aren't applicable to other domains of variables. When intonational change, or consonantal change, or any other kind is examined, it is necessary to formulate a completely new set of constraints. The interactions that voice quality has with physiological differences may make constraints on dialectal change in voice quality especially different from other domains. We can't understand linguistic change if we don't gain a broad-based perspective of it.

Studies that focus on a single feature typify phonetic research. The single-feature approach makes it easy to focus an experiment. However, it is also important to examine how phonetic processes operate across phonetic domains. One example is phonetic undershoot. As we've seen, it applies readily to vowel quality and has garnered considerable attention from phoneticians with regard to vowels. It could be applied to intonation, as with Grabe et al.'s (2000) work on compression vs truncation of intonational contours. It might be utilized to explain some tonal processes as well, such as the mechanism of the tonal merger described by Bauer et al. (2003). A unified approach to undershoot that can cover vowel quality, prosody, consonantal weakening and perhaps voice quality features, too, is needed to tie the lines of research together. Another example is perceptual similarity. Various phonetic work, as described by Johnson (2003), has determined that speakers of different languages perceive specific consonants or vowels as more or less similar to each other, depending on the segmental inventories of their first language. Experiments on perceptual similarity work well when the phonological structure is easily definable, as it is for segments. How does perceptual similarity apply to other domains, particularly prosodic qualities such as intonation and rhythm, though? Are there principles of perceptual similarity that pertain to all domains? Yet another example has to do with theories of how listeners perceive speech sounds accurately when there's so much variability caused by coarticulation. The *Motor Theory* (e.g. Liberman and Mattingly 1985), for instance, states that listeners interpret speech by relating what they hear to how they would articulate speech sounds and that a special speech module is used to do that. Other theories place primary importance on the acoustic signal. Most of the discussion has centred on segments, and more attention should be given to applying them to prosody. In addition, much work remains on how these theories can account for interspeaker variability.

The links between variation and cognitive processing should also be explored in a holistic fashion. One current controversy in phonetics and phonology is the degree of distinctness between phonological and phonetic encoding. Language variation could shed light on the problem because how speakers produce and perceive variant forms ought to be connected with how deep the structures are – i.e. at what stage of encoding the variant forms are specified. However, a range of variables needs to be examined, including phonological distinctions, phonetic forms of segments, different aspects of prosody and voice quality. According to Indefrey and Levelt (2004), segmental specification seems to precede prosodic specification in the assembly of utterances in the brain. It would be informative to see whether language variation exerts any effect on the processing order or processing speed, and whether any such effects differ for different kinds of variables. Social indexing of variables could interact with cognitive processing in complex ways. If a range of variables can be identified in a community, and if they are found to show different kinds of social indexing, will the varying social indices be reflected in neurological connections with different parts of the brain during speech production and perception? Labov (1972: 178–80) divided linguistic variants into three categories. Indicators are correlated with different groups but apparently not recognized because they don't show stylistic conditioning. Markers are recognized at some level because they exhibit stylistic conditioning. Stereotypes are stigmatized, remarked upon by speakers and actively avoided by some members of the community. How is each kind of variant processed cognitively? You might expect that, during speech perception, stereotypes would activate more areas of the brain than indicators because they are associated with social meanings while indicators are not. Will this kind of difference in activation actually play out, though?

8.1 Combining variables in production studies

Examining a variety of phonetic variables in a sociolinguistic survey is ordinarily a straightforward affair. Because the interviews in such surveys usually contain a conversational component, there are plenty of phonetic variables available. Most or all of the vowels and consonants are present, and, if the interview is long enough (say, close to an hour), the majority will occur in ample numbers for studying such factors as coarticulatory effects and undershoot. Most prosodic variables are well-represented, with the possible exception of question intonation because often the interviewer asks all the questions. Voice quality is pervasive. The main limiting factors are the investigator's available time and knowledge of how to measure variables, and perhaps the recording quality.

Surveys that involve only read speech may have fewer options. If the reading involves stories or sentences instead of just words in isolation, however, a range of variables will still be present. Combinations of read and spontaneous speech in a survey provide researchers with the greatest flexibility. Read speech can allow researchers to elicit less common vowels or consonants, such as the CHOICE vowel or the /ʒ/ consonant in English, and to place controls on variables so that utterances can be compared directly among different speakers. Spontaneous speech, as from conversations, can fill in variables such as discourse-specific prosody or voice quality and undershoot forms that are difficult to elicit in read speech. It doesn't take extensive planning to design a survey so that it provides data on broad suites of variables.

Analysis of such data involves determining how different variables are correlated with each other. Statistical procedures designed for multiple dependent variables, such as multivariate analysis of variance (MANOVA), can be applied to them. However, it's important not to lose sight of the larger linguistic issues. Knowing which linguistic variables are correlated with each other can illuminate both how linguistic changes occur and how language is processed cognitively.

8.2 Combining variables in perception studies

Perception studies differ from production studies because there are limits to how many variables can be examined in a single experiment. If a perception experiment involves a matrix format, the number of stimuli multiples quickly. For example, in an experiment on which features are diagnostic for distinguishing two dialects, you might test a vocalic variable, a consonantal variable, an intonational variable and a voice quality variable. Assuming that you set up the experiment so that the character states for each variable are presence or absence of the variable, the result is $2 \times 2 \times 2 \times 2 = 16$ combinations. For each of the 16 combinations, you will need several stimuli, perhaps including both male and female voices. The number of stimuli quickly grows to over a hundred and the experiment will reach the ten- to fifteen-minute limit that you can expect from respondents' attention spans. But what if you have more than one intonational variable to investigate, or several vocalic and consonantal variables? To investigate more than three or four variables – which is necessary in order to investigate language variation holistically – you will need to carry out a series of experiments, not just one.

Using a speech synthesizer makes it easier to create arrays of stimuli that test multiple variables. With unsynthesized stimuli, you are often limited to stimuli in which the variable is either present or absent. Synthesis, on the other hand, allows you to create stimuli that contain variants of different variables that don't usually occur together. If you're comparing the speech of two groups in the experiment, and a variable is highly correlated with membership in the two groups, it may be hard to find good tokens of a variant that's infrequent in one group. Synthesis allows you to circumvent that problem. If a particular variant is rare among one of the groups you're comparing, you can synthetically modify utterances so that your stimuli do have it. Then you can test whether the presence of the rarer variant affects listeners' judgements. This sort of design can be equally useful in experiments that examine listeners' judgements of speakers' personality traits or emotional states. For example, you can vary voice quality features, prosodic features and segmental features independently to see which variants or which combinations of variants elicit particular stereotypes.

Timing listeners' reactions could be especially effective in a perception experiment in which different variables are tested against each other. Timing allows you to compare which variants or combinations of variants confuse listeners more and which ones they tend to access the most when they make identifications or judgements. If, for example, two otherwise unrelated variables are both highly correlated with a particular dialectal division, mixing the variables so that a stimulus shows one variant from one of the dialects and another variant from the other dialect should slow listeners' identifications of speakers.

8.3 Links between sociophonetics and abstract linguistic issues

It should be clear by now that a full application of sociophonetics, whether to sociolinguistic structure, to phonetic processes or to cognition, requires examination of a diverse range of linguistic variables. A view of language in terms of interconnectedness is essential to sociophonetics. In the remaining chapters we will explore other kinds of interconnectedness. We will examine what language variation can say about the cognitive organization of speech sounds, how sociophonetic variation informs us about historical linguistic change, and how social organization is intertwined with the cognition of language. The recurring theme is that it's not enough to examine the different components of language, social structure and cognition. Their interfaces should also be a major focus.

EXERCISES

1. What would be necessary for you to carry out a holistic study of speech production in a community if you're familiar with which segmental variables are salient in the community but you don't know which prosodic or voice quality features are?
2. Explain how you would set up a perception test comparing the importance of several variables on identification of two ethnic groups – say, ancestral English and south Asian English speakers in London? Would you use spontaneous or read speech as the basis for the stimuli, and why?
3. How can comparison of phonetic variables of different types – segmental, prosodic and voice quality – improve our understanding of the cognitive processing of language?

9 Variation and the Cognitive Processing of Sounds

9.1 Phonetic processes aren't always automatic

The cognitive organization of speech sounds has been a primary object of inquiry among phoneticians and phonologists for decades, and sociolinguists could have more input in it. The traditional understanding of the relationship between phonetics and phonology, exemplified by Chomsky and Halle (1968), was that phonology includes phenomena that are discrete, such as phonemes, phonological features, syllable structure and rules predicting positional allophones, while phonetics includes phenomena that are gradient. Furthermore, phonological phenomena were assumed to be language-specific and thus cognitively represented. Phonetic phenomena, conversely, were assumed to be universal and automatic consequences of articulatory mechanisms, and hence not cognitively represented. This understanding has been assailed by the discovery of a subclass of what Keating (1985, 1988, 1990) called *phonetic rules*. These are processes that take phonological specifications to their surface realizations. This subclass is language- or dialect-specific – under a speaker's control – but not discrete. As we'll see in this chapter, they can involve a variety of factors, including the cues used for phonological contrasts, the relative timing of articulatory gestures and interactions between timing and articulation.

The discovery that phonology and phonetics can't be differentiated as easily as once thought has influenced theories about how each is constituted. Phonologists have increasingly incorporated phonetics into phonology. In Optimality Theory, a large fraction of the proposed constraints are phonetic properties (see, e.g., various papers in Hayes et al. 2004). The laboratory phonology movement uses phonetic analyses extensively. Phoneticians have presented various opinions about where the boundary between phonetics and phonology lies. Fourakis and Port (1986) assign language-specific phonetic rules to a level between phonetics and phonology. Kingston and Diehl (1994) limit phonology to contrastiveness and assign language-specific phonetic rules, along with automatic processes, to phonetics. Ohala (1990) rejects any distinction between phonetics and phonology, arguing that all proposals about speech sounds should be testable by comparable empirical methods. Purnell

(2009) dismisses Ohala's approach on the grounds that it doesn't account for *invariance*. Invariance is the notion that tokens of a phonological category – e.g. /t/ or a [+high, –back, –tense] vowel – all share some phonetic property or are all the same at some psychological level. Invariance has its limits as a construct, though. For example, locus equations have been largely, but not completely, successful at revealing putative invariant properties of stop consonants. Furthermore, languages sometimes have loose ends whose assignment to phonemes is uncertain. Guenter (2000), for example, found that subjects had great difficulty identifying pre-/r/, pre-/l/ and pre-/ŋ/ vowels in English with a particular phoneme consistently. In essence, English phonemes are not invariant because these vowels show unstable assignments, even for the same speaker. Lotto and Holt (2000) present other experimental evidence for rejecting the phoneme as a cognitive entity. Perhaps phonological entities should best be seen as probabilistic, not absolute, systems. And after all, how could sound changes involving phonological assignment occur if phonological categories were absolutely predictive?

Probabilistic approaches to phonology bring us to a larger cognitive issue, that of how phonological categories as a whole are acquired, encoded and accessed. The traditional assumption of invariance led generative phonologists to assume that phonological categories are stored cognitively as discrete entities. Schemes involving more active and malleable storage have steadily gained traction among phoneticians and psychologists, however. These proposals have crystallized in the form of exemplar models. Coincidentally, language variationists have long argued that language users have detailed knowledge about indexical properties of variants. Variationists have also produced voluminous evidence that language users access multiple variants for indexical reasons, and the traditional response that the different variants represent different grammars (Fries and Pike 1949) hasn't satisfied variationists. Exemplar models and the variationist evidence are now coming together. Testing and refining these new models should be the central programme for sociophonetics in the future.

9.2 Variability in cues used for contrasts

At various points in earlier chapters, we noted how contrasts could be signified by suites of phonetic cues, not just the property that the contrast is named after. The voicing contrast among consonants, for example, is signalled not just by vibration of the vocal folds, but also by the duration of the consonant, the duration of the preceding vowel, the F_0 contours in the transitions between the vowel and consonant, the F_1 contours in the transitions, and sometimes other cues as well (see, e.g., Lisker 1986; Kingston and Diehl 1994). Table 4.4 summarized the main cues for the [±voice] feature. These cues have a mix-and-match quality to them, which is to say they are in trading relations, since it isn't necessary for all of them to be present in order to cue the phonological distinction. Various languages and dialects omit some of them or use the cues in different ways.

As noted in Chapter 4 for the voicing contrast among consonants, the mixing and matching are far from random. Certain cues tend to co-occur for various reasons. Sometimes there is a physiological factor that links them, and sometimes there is a perceptual reason. For example, in the tense/lax vowel distinction, tense vowels tend to be longer, more peripheral and more diphthongal. These attributes co-occur readily because the greater length of tense vowels allows the articulators (the tongue and, for rounded vowels, the lips) to reach more extreme positions and it provides sufficient time for diphthongal movement. However, the co-occurrence of those attributes isn't immutable. Diphthongization of tense vowels doesn't appear in German, in most dialects of Scandinavian languages or in certain dialects of English, such as Scottish and most Caribbean varieties. However, it does occur in most dialects of English and Dutch. Clearly, the diphthongization isn't automatic – it is controlled by the speaker and it is part of the speaker's grammar at some level.[1] Even so, diphthongization not only is facilitated by the greater length of tense vowels, it also reinforces length distinctions perceptually.

On occasion, phonetic cues can actually go the opposite of the expected way. For example, across a large number of languages, vowels are longer before a voiced obstruent than before a voiceless one (Chen 1970). This length distinction serves as a perceptual cue as to whether the obstruent is voiced or voiceless. However, as we saw in Chapter 4, Purnell et al. (2005b) found that the oldest generations in German-American communities in Wisconsin showed longer vowel durations before voiceless obstruents. In German, all final obstruents are devoiced, and the unusual configuration in Wisconsin seems to have been due to first-generation speakers accommodating to English by lengthening voiceless obstruents instead of shortening the preceding vowel. Lengthening voiceless obstruents served to simulate the ratio of consonant duration to preceding vowel duration found in other varieties of English.

Sociophonetic studies can shed more light on the operation of such phonetic cues. Which phonetic attributes are automatic consequences of articulator configurations, and which ones can speakers control? The most definitive way to find that out is to look for differences among dialects, speakers and speaking styles in the realizations of these attributes.

Nearly every phonological contrast is realized by multiple phonetic cues. The tense/lax distinction has just been discussed. Similarly, height distinctions in vowels are typically realized not just by F_1 values. Compared to lower vowels, higher vowels on average tend to be shorter (Peterson and Lehiste 1960; Crystal and House 1988) and to have a higher F_0 (see the review in Hoemeke and Diehl 1994:661), though prosody can impact on the realization of those cues. Velar consonants are distinguished not just by the 'velar pinch' – the convergence of F_2 and F_3 in their transitions – but also by the fact that they tend to have long transitions and two bursts instead of one. Nasal consonants are differentiated from oral consonants by the number, amplitude and bandwidth of formants, the presence of antiformants and the spread of those properties to adjacent vowels. The best-studied suite of phonetic cues, however, is that of the [±voice] feature.

There is plenty of room in the discussion on variability in phonetic cues – concerning both [±voice] and other distinctions – for contributions by sociophoneticians. Kingston and Diehl (1994) discussed variations in phonetic realization of cues for [±voice] across several languages and concluded that the F_0 contour was the only consistent cue; but then Purnell et al. (2005a) found F_0 variation to be absent in some Wisconsin English. For intralinguistic comparisons, language contact situations are especially fertile grounds for variation in cues. For example, in Thomas (2000), I compared Anglo and Mexican American English. Using a combination of production and perception analysis, I determined that the realization of diphthongal glides could serve as a cue to the /t/–/d/ distinction in English. Low F_1 and high F_2 were associated with a following /t/, and higher F_1 and lower F_2 with a following /d/. However, the robustness of this cue was much greater in Anglo English than in Mexican American English. A more extensive example is the work on Wisconsin English by Purnell et al. (2005a, 2005b). In this German–English contact situation, as discussed in Chapter 4, the cues for the [±voice] feature in word-final position seemed to be in continuous flux. We noted above that the oldest German-American generations, attempting to accommodate English, acquired vocal fold vibration in final obstruents, though they lengthened voiceless obstruents instead of shortening the preceding vowel to attain the proper ratio of vowel duration to closure duration. Then the generation born between the World Wars began to show preceding vowel duration patterns more like speakers of mainstream English varieties, with shorter durations before voiceless obstruents than before voiced obstruents. They maintained strong glottal vibration for voiced obstruents, though, and they failed to acquire the typical F_0 and F_1 patterns noted in Table 4.4. Subsequent generations have shown less differentiation as a whole between voiced and voiceless obstruents.

9.3 Phasing of gestures

Articulatory gestures are typically associated with particular segments. However, gestures aren't necessarily aligned perfectly with each other. When gestures from different segments overlap, the result is coarticulation. Browman and Goldstein (1991) discuss overlapping of gestures extensively. Much of their discussion covers rapid speech. This increases both misalignment of gestures associated with the same segments and overlapping of gestures from different segments.

Misalignment and overlapping of gestures are not entirely automatic consequences of articulation. Speakers have some control over them. Browman and Goldstein (1991) focus on the role of gestural realignment in historical change. A contemporary example is reported by Fourakis and Port (1986). They observed that American English inserts an epenthetic [t] in words such as *prince* [pʰɹĩnts] and *dense* [dɛ̃nts], while South African English doesn't ([pʰɹĩns], [dɛ̃ns]). However, the epenthetic [t] isn't identical to the underlying [t] in words such as *prints* and *dents*: it averages a little shorter. Because the epenthetic [t] doesn't occur in all dialects, it isn't an inevitable consequence of articulatory processes. However, since it's not the same as an underlying [t],

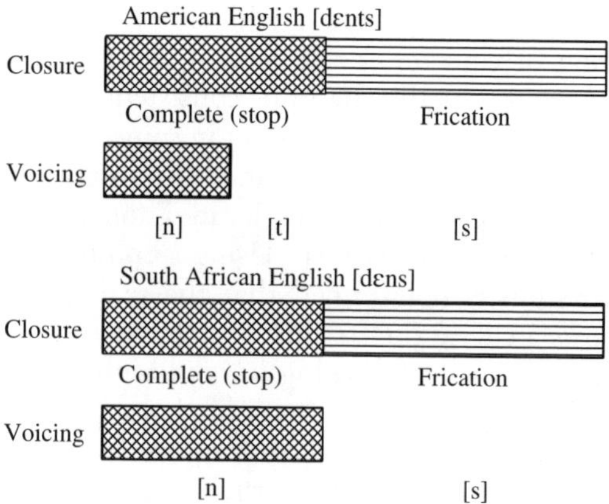

Figure 9.1 Phasing of gestures in American and South African pronunciations of *dense*.

it's not produced by a phonological rule in the traditional sense. It's another one of those in-between processes. Fourakis and Port described it as a difference in the relative timing of gestures. That is, American English shuts off the voicing before switching to a fricative articulation, while South African English performs both gestural shifts simultaneously, as shown in Figure 9.1. Fourakis and Port called the control of relative timing *phase rules* and suggested that variations in them are quite common.

9.4 Variations in undershoot

We've already discussed methods of measuring undershoot and related processes such as truncation and coarticulation: for vowels in Chapter 5 and for prosodic phenomena, including lexical tone and intonation, in Chapter 6. Undershoot also affects consonants, not surprisingly. For approximants, the effects are often similar to those of vowels and can be measured with the same techniques. For other consonants, undershoot tends to be manifested as the apparent deletion of the consonant, even when a weak articulatory gesture is present. Browman and Goldstein (1989, 1990) present some examples, such as the acoustic camouflaging of the [t] between the [k] and [m] in the phrase *perfect memory*.

What is important about undershoot-related processes for the status of phonetics and phonology is that speakers exert some control over the degree of undershoot that they exhibit. Lindblom (1990) discusses experimental evidence and presents a model, the 'H&H Theory' (for 'hyperspeech' and 'hypospeech'), for how speakers attain different degrees of undershoot. According to the H&H model, speakers enunciate more carefully when necessary, such as when speaking to a non-native speaker of the language or somebody with a hearing impairment, but also when the content might be ambiguous, such as with infrequently used words. At other times, when ambiguity is less likely – such as when speaking to a familiar person about mundane topics – they revert

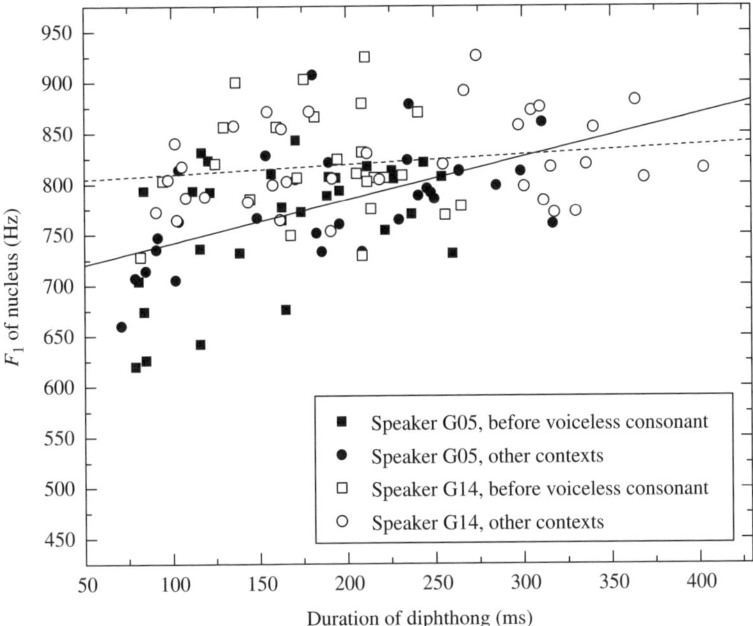

Figure 9.2 Duration of diphthong vs F_1 of nucleus for tokens of the PRICE/PRIZE diphthong uttered by two high school girls, G05 and G14, who had been close friends a few years before the recordings were made. The solid regression line pertains to G05 and the dashed line to G14. The different slopes of the lines reflect the fact that G05 tends to truncate the diphthong, bringing the nucleus closer to the glide, when the diphthong's duration is short, while G14 mainly compresses the diphthong. The difference isn't due to whether the following consonant is voiceless.

to the lower-cost behaviour of enunciating less carefully. The result is more undershoot.

An example of variation in degree of truncation is shown in Figure 9.2. These figures show F_2 realizations in the nucleus of the PRICE diphthong for two girls, G05 and G14, from the same community (Johnstown, Ohio) who had been close friends. In spite of their close association with each other, one girl exhibits more differentiation between tokens with long durations and tokens with short durations than the other girl. Both girls seem to have essentially the same target values, which the tokens with long durations represent. However, at shorter durations, G14 tends to compress the diphthong, while G05 tends to truncate it, thereby bringing the nucleus closer to the realization of the glide. We saw in Chapter 6 that dialects can also differ in whether they compress or truncate intonational contours. Truncation vs compression is clearly a factor that speakers can manipulate, as opposed to being an automatic phonetic process. As such, it represents another factor that blurs the distinction between phonetics and phonology, and another topic on which sociophonetic research can contribute to understanding the cognition of speech.

9.5 Prototype Theory and Exemplar Theory

The nature of phonological representations of sounds has been a long-standing research issue in phonetics. Some issues related to it are old, such as questions about the Motor Theory (e.g. Liberman and Mattingly 1985) – the notion that speech perception proceeds by listeners matching speech they hear to the articulatory commands they would use to produce speech sounds. Other issues are more recent. One that has attracted a fair amount of attention from phoneticians, and which sociophonetics could address, is the controversy over the status of prototypes, exemplars and related concepts.[2]

In psychology and other fields, a *prototype* is generally defined as a form that is rated as most typical of a category (Lotto and Holt 2000). Being 'typical' of a category can mean different things, however. As Medin and Barsalou (1987) note, a prototype can represent the central tendency of a category – i.e. an average value – or it can represent a form with the most ideal or diagnostic features of the category, which is often the most extreme form, not the average form. Among linguists, the term is used most widely in semantics, but it is also applied in phonology and phonetics to units approximating the notion of the phoneme.

The status of phonemes has been a subject of dispute for many years, as we've already seen. To a great extent, phonological features and then autosegmental specifications and Optimality Theory constraints have superseded them in phonology, though the phoneme has remained a useful construct. Regardless, the problem of whether prototypes or some other conceptualization best fits phonemes also applies to phonological features and to autosegmental and Optimality specifications.

According to Medin and Barsalou (1987), there are several such conceptualizations by which exemplars could be classified. One is by rules or ideal standards: i.e. there is a set of criteria for membership in a particular category, and an exemplar has to meet all of them to belong to the category. The flexibility in phonetic cues used for phonological categories and the effects of undershoot make rules/ideals unrealistic for phonology. Another means of classification is by prototypes. That is, exemplars are classified according to their similarity to the prototype. They don't have to have everything in common with the prototype, but they have to be more like it than the prototype for any other phonological category. A third way is classification by boundaries. Listeners have a preconceived notion of where the boundary between two phonological categories is. Any exemplar with, e.g., a normalized F_1/F_2 distance above the threshold will be interpreted as a member of one category, and one that falls below the threshold will be interpreted as a member of another category. A fourth way is classification by exemplars. A new exemplar is compared with memories of previously heard exemplars that were judged as belonging to one category or another. Each category consists of a cloud of remembered exemplars. The new exemplar is assigned to the cloud of exemplars that it is most similar to.

The different conceptualizations are normally investigated using perception experiments, often by use of stimuli that form a continuum. However, it

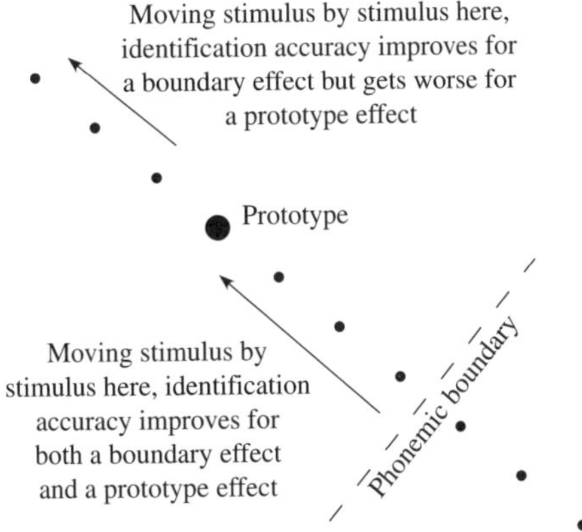
Moving stimulus by stimulus here, identification accuracy improves for a boundary effect but gets worse for a prototype effect
Prototype
Moving stimulus by stimulus here, identification accuracy improves for both a boundary effect and a prototype effect
Phonemic boundary

Figure 9.3 Schematic diagram of the kind of continuum that could be used to distinguish prototype effects from boundary effects. The dots represent stimuli lying along a continuum.

can be hard to find the right experimental technique to show which conceptualization best matches a particular perceptual phenomenon. For example, Medin and Barsalou (1987:478) note that neither accuracy rate nor reaction time can distinguish prototype effects from boundary effects when subjects are asked to classify stimuli. They suggest one method that would distinguish them, though. If a continuum of stimuli is used, as depicted in Figure 9.3, that includes both a prototype and a category boundary, a boundary effect will yield different results than a prototype effect for stimuli that lie on the opposite side of the prototype from the boundary. For a boundary effect, subjects' accuracy should steadily improve as stimuli get farther away from the boundary. However, for a prototype effect, accuracy should improve as stimuli get closer to the prototype, but then it should worsen for stimuli beyond the prototype.

Prototype effects are quite difficult to tell from exemplar effects. The problem is that an exemplar effect involves a sort of average of the exemplars a subject has heard, which isn't too much different from a prototype. A possible way to tell them apart is to present subjects with new exemplars that differ from the prototype. In an exemplar model, such exemplars should shift the cloud of recently experienced exemplars and thereby shift subjects' notions of the category. Prototypes are relatively stable and shouldn't be affected by new exemplars. See Knapp and Anderson (1984) for further discussion.

The Perceptual Magnet Effect

One reported phenomenon that seems to support a prototype account is the *Perceptual Magnet Effect*, as described in Kuhl (1991) and several other papers, e.g. Iverson and Kuhl (1995). The Perceptual Magnet Effect is the apparent shrinking of perceptual space around the 'prototype', used by Kuhl to mean the most typical quality of a particular sound. That is, phones are

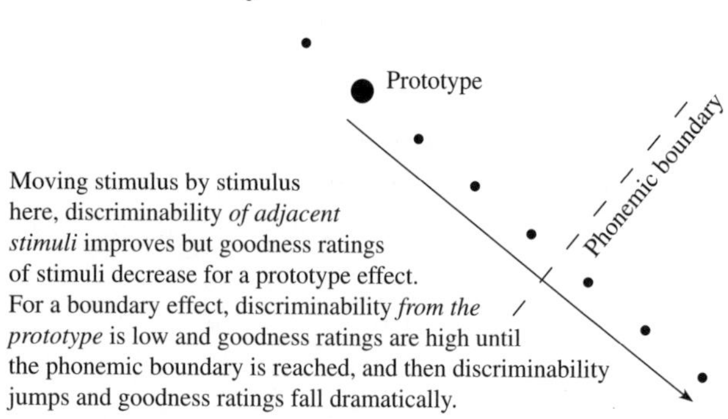

Prototype
Phonemic boundary
Moving stimulus by stimulus here, discriminability *of adjacent stimuli* improves but goodness ratings of stimuli decrease for a prototype effect.
For a boundary effect, discriminability *from the prototype* is low and goodness ratings are high until the phonemic boundary is reached, and then discriminability jumps and goodness ratings fall dramatically.

Figure 9.4 A schematic diagram of how discriminability and goodness ratings can be used to differentiate a prototype effect, as reflected in the Perceptual Magnet Effect, from a boundary effect. The dots represent stimuli lying along a continuum.

harder to discriminate when they are very like the prototype than when they are not. Kuhl and her associates conducted several experiments investigating whether listeners showed poorer discriminatory abilities near a postulated prototype than near a stimulus selected as the 'non-prototype'. In Kuhl (1991), for example, listeners first rated the goodness of an array of stimuli representing an [i] vowel. Then a different set of subjects was tested to see if their ability to discriminate slight variations in formant values was reduced near the prototype compared to the non-prototype, which it was. Figure 9.4 shows how goodness ratings and discriminability of adjacent stimuli should be related for the Perceptual Magnet Effect vs a boundary effect. Iverson and Kuhl (1995) took the process a step further by comparing goodness ratings of stimuli against discriminability using a statistical technique: multidimensional scaling.

A number of other researchers, e.g. Lotto et al. (1998), argued that what had been reported as the Perceptual Magnet Effect was actually a boundary effect. That is, some of the stimuli used by Kuhl (1991) were different enough from [i] that subjects would hear them as the FACE vowel instead of the FLEECE vowel. Lotto et al. (1998) presented stimuli in pairs, one of the members of each pair being either the prototype or a non-prototype. They asked different groups of subjects to identify one member of each pair and to rate its goodness. The identification of stimuli as [i] or [e] and their goodness ratings shifted depending on whether a stimulus was paired with the prototype or the non-prototype. They attributed this shift to a boundary effect. Iverson and Kuhl (2000) countered with experimental evidence that goodness ratings and discriminability showed a tight inverse relationship and that identification of adjacent stimuli as different phonemes didn't coincide with discriminability.

Dialectal variation could be useful for further comparison of boundary effects and prototype effects related to the Perceptual Magnet Effect. An informative test would be to examine how speakers of different dialects that have different realizations of a particular phoneme react to stimuli. For example, the DRESS vowel is raised in New Zealand and South Africa, but it is lowered in the Great Lakes region (on both the United States and Canadian sides) and in some Scottish and Northern Irish varieties. How much differently would subjects from such dialects rate stimuli representing front vowels? Would they show different prototypes, different boundaries, or both? Would they show the same relationship between goodness ratings and discriminability, especially if they were familiar with other dialects? Another experiment would be to pair test stimuli with other words representing a pronunciation diagnostic for a dialect different from the subjects' own. When the two stimuli are played together, does it affect the relationship between goodness and discriminability for stimuli? For example, lowered, central KIT vowels are diagnostic of New Zealand English. If front vowel stimuli are played together with a KIT word with a New Zealand realization, would it affect how Australians (who might be familiar with New Zealand English) place the prototype and boundary of the DRESS vowel, since DRESS is raised to high front position in New Zealand?

Exemplar Theory

In recent years, a new conception of phonology and its relation to phonetics called *Exemplar Theory* has been proposed. Exemplar Theory differs significantly from traditional generative conceptions of phonology. One of the biggest differences has to do with the amount of memory proposed to be devoted to phonology. Generative phonology theories of the 1960s assumed that the amount of memory available to phonology and other domains of language was limited, and that therefore the system worked by having a relatively small number of underlying forms and phonological rules. In subsequent years, it has become clear that memory space is not that restricted and that people store surface forms (see, e.g., Jaeger 1986). Exemplar Theory takes an approach completely opposite to that of generativism. Language users are assumed to have a vast store of accumulated memories of words, phrases and other linguistic chunks (Johnson 1997). The memories are not merely of linguistic entities, but of utterances by individual people. That is, listeners have detailed memories of particular utterances by particular individuals in particular situations. In early conceptions of Exemplar Theory, the listeners were thought to construct their own utterances from these memories, not from phonological abstractions (Coleman 2002:126).

At first glance, Exemplar Theory might seem rather unreasonable. How could anybody possibly remember every utterance they'd ever heard? Exemplar theorists don't actually think that listeners remember that much information. Instead, they posit that listeners develop a statistical understanding of the speech that they're exposed to. Children acquiring language gradually recognize that the speech they hear isn't randomly distributed over the entire range of possible speech sounds, but is clustered at certain points. They extract 'average' values of each cluster, and the values that they settle upon become the phones of their speech. Johnson (1997) proposed that language users attach something like factor weights – attention weights and association weights – to the variants they're familiar with.

Pierrehumbert (2003a, 2003b) suggested that language users don't learn phonemes per se, but instead learn the positional allophones. These allophones can be acquired because, unlike the traditional conception of phonemes, tokens within allophones are similar enough that the allophones fall out into separate categories. For example, in English, most exemplars of aspirated [t^h] are acoustically similar enough that children acquiring English, after accumulating a large enough store of exemplars that the differences from other phones become apparent, will group them into a category. Exemplars of unaspirated [t] will emerge as another category. This sorting-out process occurs statistically and is possible if the input occurs as a discernible bimodal distribution, with one pile for [t^h] and the other for unaspirated [t]. If the input lacked such a bimodal distribution, children wouldn't acquire separate [t^h] and [t] forms. Eventually, language learners associate each allophone with particular words. This scenario by itself doesn't account for the fact that speakers get the appropriate allophone in novel words that they utter. However, only a little elaboration of Exemplar Theory is necessary to do so. Perhaps language users can piece together syllable onsets and rhymes from words already in their exemplar store when they need to utter a new word.

Exemplar Theory was developed as a better way to explain certain aspects of linguistic behaviour than generative models could. It accounts for frequency effects, such as the fact that more common words are recognized and produced more quickly than less common ones. It also explains how language users are able to handle variation so adeptly. Whereas generative models tend to be antagonistic to variation, exemplar models are built on variation, both phonetically motivated and socially motivated. There are some other advantages, too. For instance, Exemplar Theory doesn't require matching of heard speech to abstract categories, which would slow down speech perception.

Applications of Exemplar Theory

Exemplar Theory is applied to several linguistic phenomena. It is proposed as a mechanism for child language acquisition. In addition, however, it is used to model a number of processes by adult speakers. It has been cited as a mechanism of speech perception and, in particular, speaker normalization. As we saw in Chapter 5, there has been a lot of discussion among phoneticians about how listeners are able to normalize the vowels (and, by extension, consonants and F_0-related properties) of speakers with differing mouth sizes: e.g. whether it is vowel-intrinsic or vowel-extrinsic, and what mathematical formula models it best. Exemplar Theory dispenses with the whole problem by proposing that listeners don't normalize voices they hear at all. Instead, they match up voices with their store of exemplars (Johnson 1997; Pisoni 1997). In support of this notion is evidence that 'typical' male and female speakers are easier to understand than those with mixed voice characteristics.

Exemplar Theory has also been used as a model for speech production. Earlier versions of it held that language users lack, as Johnson (1997:146) put it, 'abstract category prototypes'. They determine some sort of 'average' value for phonological categories, and often for entire morphemes, words or phrases, from their exemplar store and then simply string them together. Pierrehumbert's

(2003b, 2006) less extreme position makes use of some abstract phonological categories.

Finally, Exemplar Theory provides a powerful means of accounting for how linguistic variables emerge as indices of social identity. Language users are exposed to a wide variety of other speakers, and if this exposure induces them to add new exemplars to their stores constantly, it would explain why some users' speech continues to change well into young adulthood or later. All that is still needed is a mechanism allowing language users to index the right social identity, which Exemplar Theory also provides.

Problems with Exemplar Theory

A number of objections have been raised to Exemplar Theory. In each case, there is an answer. First, Johnson (1997) anticipated that objections about memory saturation, or what he called the 'head-filling-up problem', could be raised. That is, can language users really remember all the exemplars needed to make Exemplar Theory plausible? He argued that storage space in memory isn't anywhere near as big a problem as is often supposed and that exemplars could be mapped onto auditory space. Pierrehumbert (2006:525) acknowledged that language users can't remember everything, but she contended that exemplars that are salient to a listener are easily remembered because salient events are more memorable than everyday ones.

Another problem was the total rejection of phonological abstractions by early exemplar models. Pierrehumbert (2003b:178) noted that all languages possess certain clearly demonstrable abstract phonological entities, such as a consonant/vowel distinction, syllables or morae.[3] Pierrehumbert (2006:523) added that speakers can learn nonce words quickly, implying some phonological structure. Yet Pierrehumbert also staunchly defended some aspects of Exemplar Theory, such as its reliance on statistical modelling by language learners. The solution, according to Pierrehumbert, is to posit a combined theory – a revised version of Exemplar Theory that retains the store of exemplars and the statistically based learning of language but allows for some phonological abstractions. Of course, Exemplar Theory has always provided a means for acquiring 'average' values of phones, which, as Pierrehumbert argued, can be thought of as corresponding to positional allophones.

A third problem, raised by Labov (2006), is that empirical evidence from vowel shifting didn't seem to support Exemplar Theory. He asserted that the Theory should produce lexical diffusion (word-by-word spread) of sound changes of the sort proposed by Wang (e.g. 1977), but that no shifting clearly attributable to lexical effects could be found in results from Labov et al. (2006). One potential example he examined had to do with certain words with the GOAT vowel, such as *home*, which don't show as much fronting as other GOAT words in some U.S. dialects. The normalized formant values for *home* averaged across a large number of speakers were intermediate between those of non-pre-liquid GOAT words and pre-/l/ GOAT words such as *pole*. He attributed the intermediate values to phonetic factors, mostly coarticulation with neighbouring segments. However, averaging obscures the values of individuals, and individuals can be found who show clearly fronted or clearly backed values

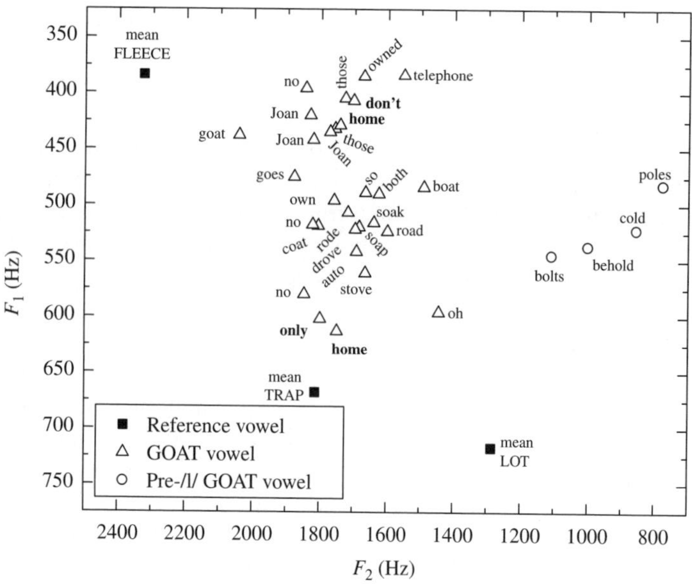

Figure 9.5 Formant plot with tokens for a speaker from Johnstown, Ohio, who groups *home*, *don't* and *only* with non-pre-/l/ tokens of the GOAT vowel. F_1 values for prenasal tokens are influenced by nasality, so little importance should be placed on F_1.

for *home*, as shown in Figures 9.5 and 9.6. Other cases of idiosyncratic words also occur, such as the common occurrence in African American English of *sister* with the FOOT vowel (see Figure 9.7). One likely reason Labov didn't find more such cases is that his subject pool was literate. In traditional folk dialects, however, words that jumped phonological categories used to be a lot more common. For example, there are a number of words in which the DRESS vowel was replaced in folk dialects by the KIT vowel after palatal consonants, notably *kettle*, *get*, *chest*, *Chevy* and, even in dialects without pre-nasal merger of DRESS and KIT, *again(st)* and *general* (see Krapp 1925:92).[4] Other examples are *bristle* with the STRUT vowel; *crop* and *drop* with the TRAP vowel; and the TRAP/LOT alternation in *stamp/stomp*, *tramp/tromp*. These cases are odds and ends that switched categories, not necessarily when the vowels were shifting, but often when they were otherwise stable. That is exactly what you would expect from an exemplar model: most lexical items end up in the 'right' pile when a child learns language, but a few don't. Without the normative influence of literacy, a few of the words that got into the 'wrong' pile persisted as children got older and became dialectal variants. It would be worthwhile seeing how often children today make such switches as they acquire language.[5] This process is sometimes called sporadic sound change. It is definitely not regular, Neogrammarian (exceptionless) sound shifting. However, it is not the same as Wang's (1977) lexical diffusion because it affects only a few words and then stops. Exemplar Theory probably does have a role in explaining regular sound change, though.

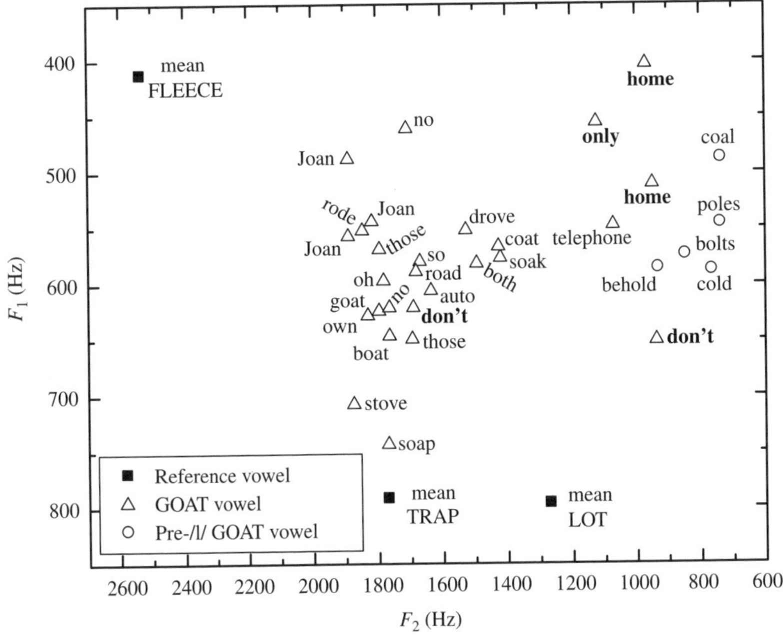

Figure 9.6 Formant plot with tokens for a speaker from Johnstown, Ohio, who groups *home*, *don't* and *only* with pre-/l/ tokens of the GOAT vowel. Note that she varies in her pronunciation of *don't*. F_1 values for prenasal tokens are influenced by nasality. The difference in F_2 values between her and the preceding speaker show that the difference is not a phonetic effect.

Implications for sociophonetics

Exemplar Theory fits well with sociolinguistic thought because the detailed memories of exemplars include information about who uttered the exemplar and when. Listeners can thus contextualize the utterances. Sociolinguistic findings since Labov (1966) have shown that language users have considerable awareness of what forms are associated with particular kinds of speakers and particular situations. As Foulkes and Docherty (2006:426) noted, generative models of phonology lack a mechanism to account for indexical meaning, but indexicality is inherent to Exemplar Theory. In fact, it provides a means by which children can acquire linguistic and sociolinguistic knowledge at the same time (ibid.:429; Hay et al. 2006), and sociolinguistic findings suggest that children do learn sociolinguistic distributions from an early age. Moreover, the constant additions to a speaker's exemplar store explain how children's speech can continue to change through adolescence. They also explain how sudden changes in a child's life, such as moving or beginning schooling, are quickly reflected in a child's speech (Foulkes and Docherty 2006:431). Children constantly internalize new information about the social indexing of variants. We will explore a lot more about what kinds of things social indexing entails in Chapter 11.

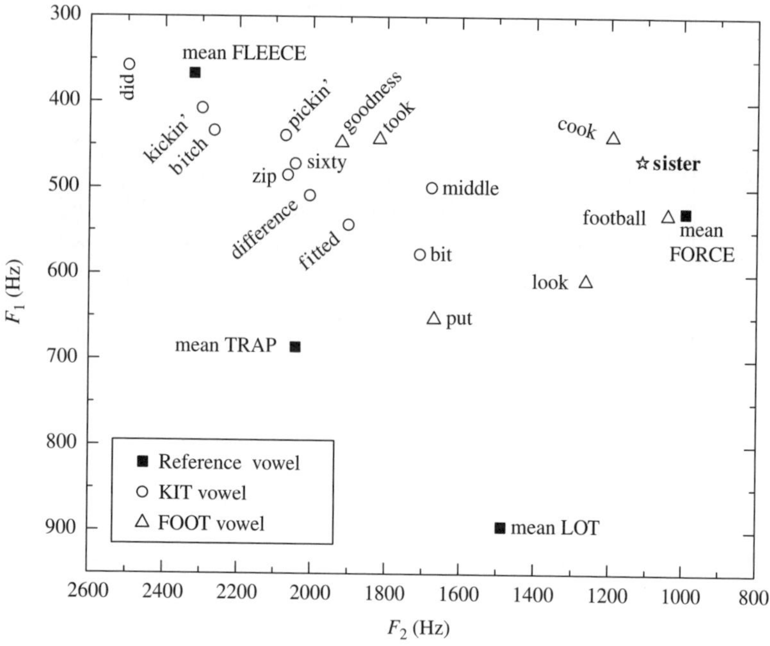

Figure 9.7 Formant plot with tokens uttered by an African American speaker who groups *sister* with the FOOT vowel. Two of her FOOT tokens are fronted because of coarticulation with adjacent consonants.

If the exemplar store includes all kinds of speech a person has heard, how do children acquire some variants that they hear while rejecting others? The model of Exemplar Theory promoted by Pierrehumbert (2006:525) holds that some exemplars are more salient than others to language users. By extension, children may have more active memories of exemplars collected from interactions with people and groups that they want to emulate. This scenario is essentially the issue to be presented in Chapter 10 concerning whether Ohala's model of linguistic change as misperception can be applied to the spread of linguistic variants within, for example, communities of practice (for which see Chapter 11). Testing the sociolinguistic salience of different kinds of encounters that children have – how they can be more linguistically influenced by some encounters than others – represents a crucial issue for future sociophonetic research.

Another sociophonetic outlet for Exemplar Theory is investigating how it can permit regular, Neogrammarian sound change. The conception of Exemplar Theory advanced by Pierrehumbert (2006) actually lends itself to regular sound change. In her view, language learners sort speech sounds they hear into categories. This process can be somewhat haphazard, though, and the norm or target value that one individual settles on may differ slightly from that of another individual. It allows sounds to drift, particularly when it interacts with other factors, such as dispersion of sounds in acoustic space or coarticulation effects. Yu (2007) proposed just such a model to explain how two lexical tones in Cantonese could drift so close together that listeners couldn't distinguish them, even though they remained slightly distinct, on average, in production. Sociophonetic investigations of how language learners acquire their norms and how they react to new exemplars that differ from the variants that they usually hear (e.g. from a different dialect) could be quite useful.

Hay and Sudbury (2005:818–19) provided an example of how an exemplar model readily accounts for the progression of a sound change. They describe the development of non-rhoticity in New Zealand English, with preservation of [ɹ] in hiatus positions: e.g. [foɹ æpəɫz] 'four apples' vs [foə p^{h}eəz] 'four pears'. Archival recordings demonstrate that New Zealanders were once more rhotic – i.e. [foɹ p^{h}eɹz] was a possible pronunciation at one time over much of New Zealand. As Hay and Sudbury explain, the current configuration emerged after a long period of variability in which speakers were exposed to both rhotic and non-rhotic exemplars. Rhotic pronunciations gradually became associated with hiatus contexts or, in pre-consonantal or pre-pausal contexts, with older speakers as rhoticity declined. In support of the Exemplar Model, they note that common collocations such as *for instance* showed higher rates of rhoticity in hiatus than word combinations that aren't common. The frequency effect is predicted by Exemplar Theory because common collocations are remembered.

Exemplar Theory is still an unproven theory. Sociophonetic investigation can contribute to testing it, however. One possibility is the one suggested by Medin and Barsalou (1987), in which listeners are played recordings of a particular variant that differs from their own 'average' value. Their articulation is checked before and after hearing the stimuli to see whether it's changed. This kind of experiment might be most effective with children, and actually occurring dialectal variants would make ideal stimuli.

Prototype Theory could probably be adapted to include associations with indexical information. However, Foulkes and Docherty (2006:428–9) argue that Exemplar Theory would predict that 'awareness of some types of indexical knowledge could emerge more readily than others' and that increasing transparency between phonetic forms and social categories should speed learning of the link. These hypotheses suggest further ways of testing Exemplar Theory. Child language learners could be tested for their knowledge of social constraints to see whether, for example, they find gender associations of variants easier to learn than stylistic associations. The amount of exposure language users have to different regional or ethnic dialects could be compared with their ability to recognize them or even to imitate them. Experiments might be set up in which subjects listen to a highly unfamiliar dialect and the rates of comprehension that they show at different degrees of exposure are compared. To get at social information, subjects might listen to speakers of different dialects talking about different subjects, after which they hear other recordings with the same dialects and answer questions on their subjective evaluation of each speaker in the second group of recordings.

EXERCISES

1. What do language- or dialect-specific phonetic rules indicate about the cognitive organization of speech sounds? Why does cross-dialectal variation in phonetic rules provide such valuable information?
2. Where might you look for variation in phonetic rules – i.e. what sorts of dialectal, sociolectal or stylistic situations might be especially fertile grounds for such phenomena?
3. Explain how boundary effects can be distinguished from prototype effects and the Perceptual Magnet Effect.
4. Compare and contrast the main tenets of Prototype Theory and Exemplar Theory. Are the two completely incompatible or are there ways that both could operate simultaneously? Is it plausible that each could predominate at different stages of a person's life, and, if so, how could you test for that? Might they have different degrees of influence on production versus perception – e.g. when somebody gets used to hearing a dialect different from his or her own?
5. What advantages and disadvantages does Exemplar Theory have in terms of (a) its compatibility with sociolinguistic and phonetic theory and (b) testing it empirically?

FURTHER READING

Foulkes, Paul and Gerard Docherty. 2006. The social life of phonetics and phonology. *Journal of Phonetics* 34:409–38.

Fourakis, Marios and Robert Port. 1986. Stop epenthesis in English. *Journal of Phonetics* 14:197–221.

Johnson, Keith. 1997. Speech perception without speaker normalization: An exemplar model. In Keith Johnson and John W. Mullennix (eds), *Talker Variability in Speech Processing*. San Diego, CA: Academic, 145–65.

Knapp, Andrew G. and James A. Anderson. 1984. Theory of categorization based on distributed memory storage. *Journal of Experimental Psychology* 10:616–37.

Medin, Douglas L. and Lawrence W. Barsalou. 1987. Categorization processes and categorical perception. In Stevan Harnad (ed.), *Categorical Perception: The Groundwork of Cognition*. Cambridge, UK: Cambridge University Press, 455–90.

Pierrehumbert, Janet B. 2006. The next toolkit. *Journal of Phonetics* 34:516–30.

Sound Change 10

10.1 (In)separability of linguistic and social factors

How and why languages vary and change was presented in Chapter 1 as one of the two major theoretical thrusts of linguistics. Historical linguists have addressed this issue for two centuries, and phonologists and phoneticians for a much shorter period. It has also been part of sociophonetics from the beginning. With such diverse scholars investigating it, it is not surprising that some of the resulting answers differ, at times diametrically.

Two assumptions held by some that have impacted on how sound change has been studied are that linguistic and social factors can be distinguished and that they perform different functions. Ohala (1993b) and to some extent Blevins (2004:269–70) contended that linguistic factors account for the origin of changes, while social factors account for their spread. Labov (1972:277) argued against this separability. In his view, a change isn't a change until it begins to spread – an innovation used by only one speaker isn't a true change. Weinreich et al. (1968) listed five issues that a theory of linguistic change should explain, and the way they presented these issues underlies Labov's position on the inseparability of linguistic and social factors. *Constraints* involve what changes are possible and impossible. *Transition* asks what the intervening states are when a sound change takes place. *Embedding* has to do with how a change is connected with other linguistic and social changes. *Evaluation* involves the consequences of a change on the linguistic structure, communicative efficiency and social standing of speakers. *Actuation* asks why a change happens where and when it does. Each one of these issues includes both linguistic and social aspects.

10.2 Approaches to the causes of sound change from phonetics

Several scholars have addressed sound change from a phonetic or phonological/phonetic perspective. The body of work they have produced has shed considerable light on the process and generated a few controversies. It has been heavily weighted towards investigation of the origin of changes, as opposed to their propagation. For this reason, together with the fact that most of these scholars accept the notion that linguistic factors are responsible for the origin of changes and social factors are responsible for their spread, their research has focused on linguistic explanations.

Teleology and change

Among the most enduring controversies in the study of sound change concerns whether sound change is teleological – that is, whether it serves a (phonological or phonetic) purpose. A teleological concept dating from the nineteenth century is *ease of articulation*, or economy of effort. That is, sound changes that make things easier to say should be favoured. Without doubt, certain kinds of sound changes do yield ease of articulation. The vast majority of conditioned changes, such as assimilation and most deletions, do. For example, palatalization of a velar before a front vowel results in less tongue movement and hence less effort, and obviously deletion of a sound eliminates the expenditure of effort to pronounce it. Lenitions of consonants, such as weakening a stop to a fricative, also appear to require less energy. The same could be said for monophthongization of a diphthong. Using less energy to express a meaning would represent an increase in efficiency. In a competitive system, such as one in which quick expression of concepts is desirable, increased efficiency should be favoured.

Nevertheless, many other kinds of sound changes, called fortitions, have the opposite result – they create a sound that is more difficult to utter. Aspiration or affrication of a stop requires greater airflow than lack of aspiration or frication; frication of an approximant requires more precision in placement of articulators; and diphthongization of a monophthong involves more manoeuvres for the tongue and/or lips.[1] In response, the notion of the need for clarity was developed. The need for clarity works in opposition to economy of effort. The idea is that speakers hyperarticulate in order to make their meanings clearer to addressees. This hyperarticulation can then lead to sound changes of its own. Under this conceptualization, economy of effort and the need for clarity operate as a kind of yin and yang, balancing each other. Blevins (2004:72–3) suggests that the notion of these processes as opposing forces was most fully developed by Grammont (1933).

A more recent offshoot of the need for clarity construct is *maximal dispersion*. According to this, contrastive sounds tend to become located as far apart as possible in perceptual space, as if they repel each other like the same pole of two magnets. Contrastive sounds do generally become maximally dispersed – to a point. There is ample evidence that vowels take full advantage of F_1/F_2 space. Moulton (1962) demonstrated how local dialects of Swiss German maximize the distances between vowels. When a dialect had an /æː/ vowel but not an /ɔː/, the /aː/ vowel usually shifted backward, away from /æː/, and when a dialect had /ɔː/ but not /æː/, /aː/ showed some tendency to shift frontward. Liljencrants and Lindblom (1972) and Lindblom (1986) had partial success using maximal dispersion to predict the configuration of vowel systems. For example, the predicted most common three-vowel system was /i, a, u/, not /i, e, ɨ/. Consonants likewise show some propensity towards maximizing their distances from each other. For instance, many languages contrast labial, coronal and dorsal stops, but none contrast stops at two coronal places of articulation without also showing either labial or dorsal stops. Maximal dispersion offers an explanation for chain shifts: when one sound shifts, other sounds can move out of its way (a *push chain*) or fill in behind it (a *pull chain*). Martinet (1952) provided a mechanism for how that happens. He spoke of the 'margin of security' of a phoneme. If phoneme 'A started to shift away from [phoneme] B, chance deviations out of the normal range of B and in the direction of the receding A would no longer conflict with communicative needs' (ibid.:6). That is, phoneme B is free to fill the vacated space because no perceptual confusion would result. Stray tokens of B may do just that, eventually pulling B's centre of gravity in that direction when no ill (i.e. perceptual confusion with A) comes from it.

There are some weaknesses with maximal dispersion theory, though. First, mergers occur. A merger is the ultimate violation of maximal dispersion because the dispersion between two sounds shrinks to zero. Mergers seem to be most favoured when speakers with different phonological systems mix, as with language contact or dialect mixture (e.g. Herold 1997), or when shifts between phonological categories, such as vocalization of a consonant, disrupt the system. However, they can still happen without such events. A second problem is that languages sometimes exhibit contrasts with rather minimal dispersion, such as /f/ and /θ/ in English. Sounds in such contrasts, admittedly, are highly susceptible to changes. A third problem is that languages never maximize contrasts to the fullest extent possible. As Lindblom et al. (1995:22) note, theoretically a language could use a different secondary articulation, such as breathiness, creakiness, nasalization or pharyngealization, for each of its vowels, but none does. Languages have a certain number of phonetic cues in their repertoires and they seldom expand that repertoire for just one sound. Instead, they rely on sufficient, not truly maximal, differentiation of phonemes.

Those who have studied carefully the problem of how to apply ease of articulation and the need for clarity to sound change have noted a logical problem with doing so. Paul (1898:55; my translation) stated, 'it is also totally backwards always to attribute the occurrence of a sound change to a particular laziness, carelessness or inattentiveness and to blame the absence of the same [change] elsewhere on a particular carefulness and attentiveness'.[2] Over a hundred years later, Blevins (2004:293) pointed out, 'the principle of maximal perceptual contrast suffers the same general weakness as that of articulatory ease: it is too strong, since complete mergers and contextual neutralizations are quite common; and it is too weak, since it does not account for the fact that sound change results in maximizing perception only where it has a clear source'. Essentially, there don't seem to be any predictive constraints on when articulatory ease controls the course of sound change versus when the need for clarity does. This fact in itself doesn't disqualify these two forces as underlying causes of specific sound changes. As Ohala (1989, 1993b) has noted, it's a mistake to assume that sound change is absolutely predictable. Instead, it is a probabilistic phenomenon.

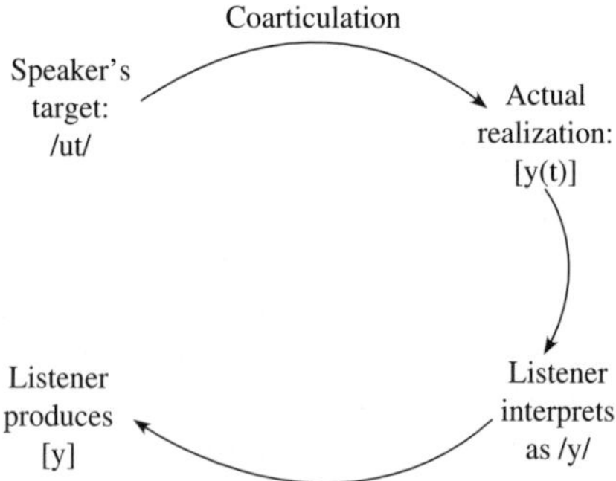

Figure 10.1 A model for how misperception could lead to a sound change, using the example of /ut/>/yt/, from Ohala (1981b, 1986). This change is attested in, e.g., Lhasa Tibetan and, for /tu/, the GOOSE vowel in American English.

Phonetic models of sound change

The debate over whether sound change serves some adaptive purpose for language has spawned further theorizing about the causes of sound change. In a series of papers, John J. Ohala (see especially Ohala 1974a, 1981b, 1986, 1989, 1993b) developed a model based on misperception to account for it. Certain changes, Ohala (1981a, 1993b) noted, are motivated by articulation. For instance, the loss of a voicing distinction among consonants can lead to tonogenesis: the lowered F_0 near a previously voiced consonant becomes a low tone, and the elevated F_0 near a previously voiceless consonant becomes a high tone (Hombert et al. 1979). Nonetheless, most of Ohala's work on sound change dealt with the mechanism behind misperception, which is inherently unintentional, and some sound changes are clearly due to perceptual confusion. For example, /θ/ has shifted to [f] in quite a few English dialects. [θ] and [f] are not articulatorily similar beyond both being voiceless fricatives, but they are quite similar acoustically. Ohala (1989, 1993b) found numerous other examples, such as the widespread tendency of [kʷ] to shift to [p] or for [kʲ] and [pʲ] to shift to [t]. Perception experiments involving confusion matrices of different sounds, such as those in Miller and Nicely (1955) and Guion (1998), can predict which sound changes are most likely. An example that Ohala (1981b, 1986) cited to show how the process might play out is the fronting of back vowels before coronals. As Figure 10.1 shows, in the sequence /ut/, the coronal [t] raises the F_2 of the vowel, making it come out as [yt]. Ordinarily, a listener can filter out this coarticulatory effect by means of 'corrective rules'. However, under certain circumstances – Ohala (1989, 1993b) specifically mentioned language acquisition – the listener fails to filter out the coarticulation. In this case, the listener interprets the target as /yt/ and may then learn the sequence as /yt/. One other aspect of Ohala's model is the notion of misperception as a 'two-way street'. That is, assimilatory changes such as /ut/→/yt/ can occur if the listener doesn't filter out the contextual effects, but dissimilation such as /yt/→/ut/ can also occur if the listener assumes a greater contextual effect than there actually is. Ohala (1981b, 1986, 1993b) cited numerous cases of dissimilation taken from historical linguistics.

Ohala has staunchly opposed any teleological approach to the origin of sound changes. In his view, sound change cannot originate for purposes such as making articulation or perception easier. It happens strictly as accidents. In contrast, Lindblom (1990) proposed that speakers vacillate between enunciating less clearly ('hypospeech') when it doesn't impede communication and enunciating more clearly ('hyperspeech') when it is needed. A variety of situations call for hyperspeech, or what Moon and Lindblom (1994) call 'clear speech'. Among the more common are uttering an unfamiliar word, speaking to a second-language learner with a weak command of the language or to very young children ('motherese' or 'parentese'), speaking to somebody who's hard of hearing, and speaking in a noisy environment or from a distance. As a result, variations are always present in natural speech. Lindblom et al. (1995) extended this theory to the origin of sound change. According to them, language users have separate modes for focusing on semantic content and for focusing on phonetic aspects of what they hear. From the latter mode, they evaluate variations for their communicative value. They thus have some choice in what variants they acquire. When they adopt an unusual variant as their norm, a sound change occurs. The main differences between Ohala's views and those of Lindblom et al. are outlined in Table 10.1.

Boersma (1998) took issue with Ohala's approach on different grounds. He argued that there are both teleological and non-teleological aspects to sound change. He discussed evidence that sound changes quite often follow patterns that would increase the perceptual similarity between sounds, not those that would be predicted from perceptual similarity. For example, the shorter back cavity makes it harder to sustain vocal pulsing for [g] than for [b], thus making [g] more similar to [k] than [b] is to [p]. Mergers of /g/ and /k/ should therefore be common, but they're not. Instead, /g/ tends to palatalize or shift to [ɣ], making it less like [k]. This is a teleological process because it increases perceptual distance between /g/ and /k/. In Boersma's view, what is not teleological is the ranking of phonological constraints. He contended, using an Optimality Theory approach, that sound changes occur when languages change the ranking of constraints and that altering of the rankings themselves isn't goal-oriented.

Other variations on these theories have also appeared. Browman and Goldstein (1991) stressed the relative timing of articulatory gestures. In their conception, gestures can become phased differently over time. They discussed the shift of Middle English /x/ to Modern English /f/ after back rounded vowels, as in *tough* /tɔux/>/tʌf/ and *laugh* /laux/>/læf/. The lip-rounding gesture shifted from being aligned with the vowel to being aligned with the fricative, resulting in the loss of the [u] glide and the emergence of [f]. Their emphasis on speech production agreed with Lindblom et al. (1995), but in contrast they considered the process accidental, like Ohala.

More recently, Blevins (2004) proposed a more elaborated theory that takes Ohala's misperception model as a starting point but incorporates ideas similar to those of Lindblom et al. (1995). She called her model CCC, after its three components: CHANGE, CHANCE and CHOICE. CHANGE represents Ohala-style misperception. CHANCE involves cases in which 'the phonetic signal is accurately perceived by the listener but is intrinsically phonologically ambiguous'

Table 10.1 Comparison of the conceptions of sound change advanced in Ohala (1993b) and Lindblom et al. (1995)

Issue	*Stance of Ohala (1993b)*	*Stance of Lindblom et al. (1995)*
Why does variation occur in the first place?	Variations are always present because of coarticulation and numerous other phonetic factors.	Variations are always present because speakers adjust their own articulation according to the communicative needs of listeners, enunciating more carefully (hyperspeech) or less carefully (hypospeech).
How do sound changes originate?	Many (not all) sound changes originate by misperceptions: listeners (usually language learners) make mistakes in reconstructing the target pronunciation of a sound.	Variations originate teleologically – for a purpose. (They maintain, though, that hypospeech is not teleological.)
What's the purpose of sound change?	The origin of sound changes is non-teleological – i.e. it is not purpose-driven. Speakers don't intend (even subconsciously) to make speech easier to pronounce or easier to understand, or to make the grammar simpler.	Speaker/listeners test natural variations for their communicative value.
How are sound changes propagated?	Sound changes may *spread* teleologically because social factors such as prestige provide a motivation.	Speaker/listeners deliberately take advantage of variations and *select* certain variants to use as social symbols.

and the listener simply picks the wrong phonological form (Blevins 2004:32). Her example was a word phonologically represented as /aʔ/ but consistently realized as [ʔa̰ʔ]. There are quite a few ways that a listener could interpret that signal, and perhaps the listener settles on /ʔa/ instead of /aʔ/. CHOICE consists of cases in which undershoot/hyperspeech or other processes result in multiple realizations of a given phonological form, and the listener perceives all of them accurately, but settles on a prototype or phonological form different from the speaker's. For example, the English words *off* and *of* were originally the same word, but during the Middle English period a cline of variants [ɔf~ɔv̥~əv̥~ə] developed. In some semantic contexts ('he spoke of love', 'a loaf of bread'), reduced forms were reinterpreted as the phonological form, while in others ('he fell off the chair'), the original unreduced form survived.

While these theories have advanced our understanding of sound change, they share a shortcoming. They all have a weak treatment of sociolinguistics. Ohala relegated sociolinguistic processes to the propagation of change, effectively excluding them from his scheme. The Lindblom et al. model involved evaluation of variations for their communicative value, leaving the door open to sociolinguistic choice of variants, but they focused instead on the consequences of clear versus reduced speech. In Blevins's model, CHOICE is compatible with sociolinguistic focusing on particular variants, but she didn't elaborate on the sociolinguistics. The avoidance of sociolinguistic effects has much to do with the assumption that the origin, or actuation, of change is distinct from its propagation.

It's not really clear that the two can be separated so easily, however. As noted above, Labov (1972) argued that they can't on the grounds that an innovation used by only a single person isn't a sound change. I find that stipulation too restrictive, and Romaine (1982a:258) objects for a different reason, stating that 'the conflation of selection and origin obscures the exact point of spatio-temporal actuation of a change'. Nevertheless, there's another reason to reject a clear split between the origin and spread of an innovation. Phonetic processes such as undershoot and misperception mean that there's always variation present and a community of speakers will never be completely uniform, not just in their performance in a given utterance but in their target values for sounds. These small, often individual differences are outgrowths of what Ohala (1993b) called 'mini sound changes', which he defined as occurring in a single conversational interaction. Because of this inherent community variation, whenever an innovation takes on social meaning, allowing it to spread, it will already have a constituency of speakers because many speakers will have acquired the same innovation independently.

It would seem at this point that the Lindblom et al. scheme and Blevins's CHOICE are the only mechanisms that can be reconciled with sociolinguistic findings about the role of prestige and identity in sound change. We shouldn't write misperception off as incompatible with sociolinguistic processes, however. It's possible that a misperception model could be extended to account for sociolinguistic progressions. That is, it's conceivable that individuals may try to identify with some group, yet misperceive the phonetic variants that serve as symbols of identity for that group. In one respect, such a model might actually fit sociolinguistic findings better than a model like Blevins's CHOICE. Individuals sometimes exaggerate linguistic group identity markers, which is how sound changes get pushed to ever more extreme realizations: e.g. raising of the TRAP vowel in the Great Lakes region of the United States, which has progressed as [æ]>[ɛæ̱]>[eæ̱]>[iæ̱]. Although this exaggeration could be explained as a deliberate choice, it might be explained more easily as a misperception. Regardless of which explanation is simpler, the problem of choice versus accidental misperception presents a research problem. Network-based studies, including experiments on perception and subjective reactions, may be necessary to resolve it.

10.3 Approaches to the causes of sound change from sociolinguistics

Sociolinguists who have addressed the causes of sound change have designed theories for compatibility with social factors. How identity and prestige play out has been a crucial issue, and we'll discuss some approaches to it in Chapter 11.

Here we'll focus mainly on what sociolinguists have had to say about linguistic factors, with a little discussion of how linguistic and social factors interface on a macrolevel. One sociolinguist in particular, William Labov, has led inquiry into linguistic factors behind sound change. His work has focused in large part on three issues: constraints on chain shifting of vowels, vowel mergers, and testing the Neogrammarian Hypothesis.

Labov's principles of vowel shifting

Chain shifting of sounds cannot be accounted for by the principle of least effort, though vowel dispersion theory helps to explain it in part. Labov et al. (1972) addressed the motivations for chain shifting by conducting both a review of historical vowel chain shifts across a large number of languages and an acoustic analysis of ongoing vowel chain shifts in various dialects of English. They identified several recurrent trends, proposed two shifting patterns to account for shifting in many dialects of English, and formulated a set of principles to account for the patterns. In later work (Labov 1991, 1994; Labov et al. 2006), these findings have been refined.

A key element of Labov's theorizing, based on his acoustic work, is the notion that there are *peripheral* and *non-peripheral* sections of the vowel envelope. As the names suggest, the peripheral section lies on the margins and the non-peripheral section lies to the inside. This division is illustrated in Figure 10.2. Peripheral vowels are usually tense or long and non-peripheral vowels are normally lax or short. There are exceptions, though, such as the NURSE vowel of non-rhotic dialects of English ([ɜː]), which is long and presumably tense (whatever 'tense' means) but non-peripheral.

Labov's principles of vowel shifting are stated as follows:

- Principle I. In chain shifts, tense nuclei rise along a peripheral track (Labov 1994:176); reformulated from 'in chain shifts, long vowels rise' (ibid.:116).
- Principle II. In chain shifts, lax nuclei fall along a non-peripheral track (ibid.:176); reformulated from 'in chain shifts, short vowels fall' (ibid.:116).

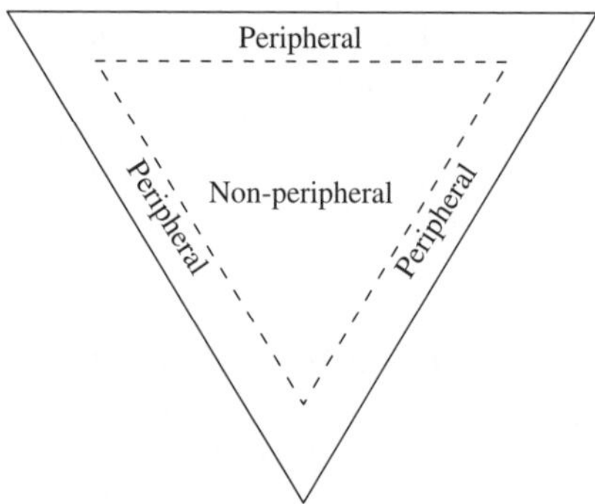

Figure 10.2 The peripheral and non-peripheral tracks in the vowel envelope, as per Labov (1991, 1994).

- Principle IIA. In chain shifts, the nuclei of upgliding diphthongs fall (ibid.). This principle accounts, e.g., for the lowering of Middle English and Middle High German /uː/, after diphthongization to [ʊu], through the stages [o̟u>ʌ̠u>ɐu>au].
- Principle III. In chain shifts, tense vowels move to the front along peripheral paths, and lax vowels move to the back along non-peripheral paths (ibid.:200).
- Principle IV. In chain shifting, low non-peripheral vowels become peripheral (the 'lower exit principle'; ibid.:280). That is, a vowel that falls will eventually hit bottom and enter the peripheral space when it reaches an [a] value.
- Principle V. In chain shifting, one of two high peripheral morae becomes non-peripheral (ibid.:281). This principle accounts for the diphthongization of long high vowels – e.g. /uː/ shifting to [ʊu].
- Principle VI. In chain shifts, peripheral vowels rising from mid to high position develop inglides (ibid.:284). This accounts for shifts such as /oː/ becoming [uə].
- Principle VII. Peripherality is defined relative to the vowel system as a whole (ibid.:285).
- Principle VIII. In chain shifts, elements of the marked system are unmarked (ibid.:288). This principle is designed for languages that have a series of creaky or nasal vowels, which count as the 'marked' system. By Principle VIII, such vowels tend to lose the secondary articulation.

A few objections have been raised to these principles. One is that the first two appear to apply only to languages with a long/short or tense/lax distinction. In response, Labov contends that, in systems without such a distinction, all the vowels behave like long or tense vowels (ibid.:121), and that in languages with a 'marked' series of vowels, the marked system can possibly function like tense vowels (ibid.:290). More examinations of non-Indo-European languages are warranted to substantiate those contentions. Another objection, by Cox (1999), is that there are exceptions to some of the rules. She cites the raising of the LOT vowel in Australian English, in which LOT is phonologically short. However, LOT is peripheral in Australian English, and Principle I states that vowels rise on peripheral paths. Moreover, Labov (1994) noted some exceptions to various principles and stated that the principles were tendencies, not inviolable rules. A third objection that I've raised is that peripherality may be only an incidental effect of shifting, not a controlling factor. Principle IIA predicts that diphthongal nuclei should fall along a non-peripheral path. That is, they would have to become non-peripheral before falling. Because peripherality of one vowel is defined relative to other vowels (Principle VII), the FACE nucleus would be non-peripheral if it's more backed than the DRESS nucleus. However, comparison of the FACE and DRESS nuclei for a substantial sample of speakers showed that deperipheralization of the FACE nucleus happened simultaneously with lowering, not before it (Thomas 2003:156–62).

Another problem is the motivations behind the principles. Labov (1994) argued that Principle III is motivated by articulatory asymmetry, in that the back vowel space is more crowded than the front vowel space. Principle IV seems self-evident, and Principle VII is something of a metaprinciple. The others have been harder to explain. Gussenhoven (2007) suggested that shifts described by Principles I and II may arise from a perceptual factor. That is, higher vowels sound longer than lower vowels – in compensation for the fact that they're actually shorter on average – and lowering a short vowel or raising a long vowel could enhance the effect. See Thomas (2003:162) for a possible explanation for Principle V related to aspiration.

Labov (1994) identified four chain shift patterns that recurred in various languages. Pattern 1 was a combination of Principles I and II in which a long high vowel diphthongized and another vowel rose to take its place. Pattern 2 was a combination of Principles I, II and III in which fronting and raising of long vowels was accompanied by falling of short vowels. Pattern 3 exhibited Principles I and III, with fronting of back vowels and raising of vowels to fill the vacated spaces. Pattern 4 involves the reversal of peripherality of vowels – i.e. one that had been peripheral becomes non-peripheral and vice versa. Labov also applied the principles to shifting patterns found in various dialects of English. Figures 10.3 and 10.4 show the Northern Cities Shift, found in the Great Lakes region of the United States, and the Southern Shift, found in southern England, Southern Hemisphere English and the southern

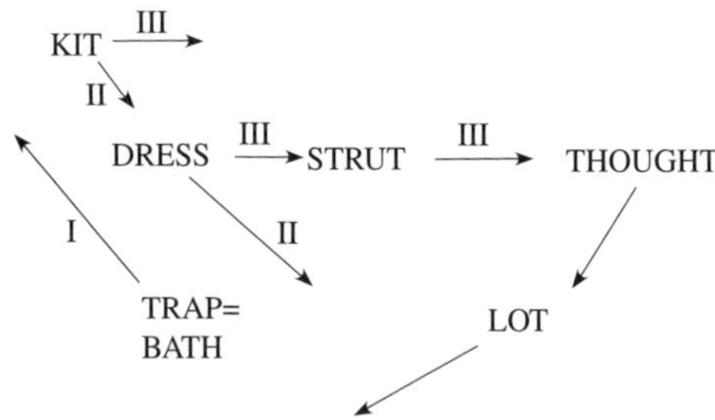

Figure 10.3 The Northern Cities Shift, which affects English in the Great Lakes section of the United States. Arrows indicate the direction of each diachronic shift. Operation of Labov's Principles is indicated with Roman numerals.

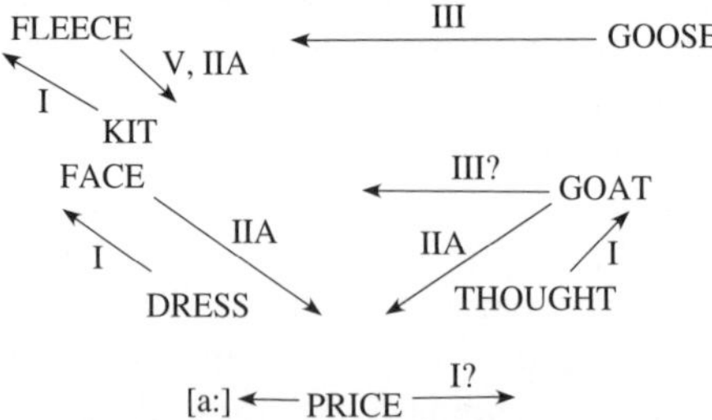

Figure 10.4 The Southern Shift, which affects English in southern England, the Southern Hemisphere and the southern United States. Arrows indicate the direction of each diachronic shift. Operation of Labov's Principles is indicated with Roman numerals.

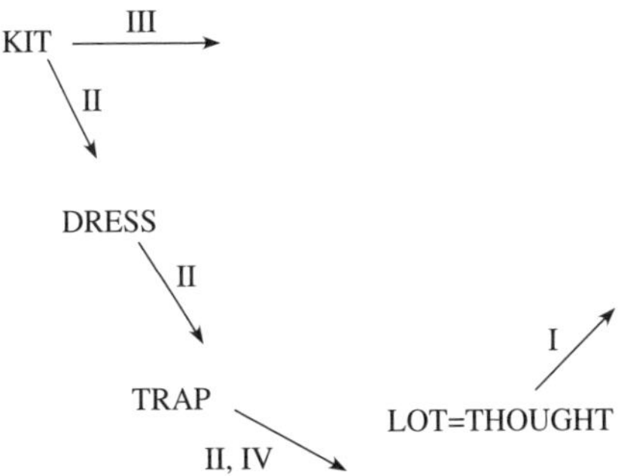

Figure 10.5 The Canadian Shift, which affects English in Canada and to some extent in western and southern Midwestern parts of the United States. Arrows indicate the direction of each diachronic shift. Operation of Labov's Principles is indicated with Roman numerals.

United States in various forms. Figure 10.5 shows the 'Canadian Shift', first described by Clarke et al. (1995).

No sociophonetician has formulated a similar set of principles for consonantal chain shifts, let alone shifts in intonational contours or tones. Historical linguists and phonologists have certainly noticed trends in consonantal shifts. For example, aspirated stops and voiceless fricatives often shift to [h], but the usual change affecting [h] is for it to disappear. Unifying principles have been elusive, though, perhaps because consonants are more diverse than vowels. Efforts to explain one kind of consonantal change at a time have been more popular. Hock (1991) divided sound changes, mostly of consonants, into categories – dissimilation, epenthesis and metathesis, for instance – and explained how each one of them works. Most of these kinds of changes aren't typical of chain shifts, though Hock (1991:83) showed how weakening might occur in a chain. That is, liquids or fricatives may shift to semivowels, single stops might shift to liquids or fricatives, and geminate stops may shift to single stops. Other authors have employed similar divisions. Blevins (2004) focused on a few kinds of changes. For instance, she enumerated seven kinds of processes that can create geminate consonants, such as assimilation in which C_1C_2>C_2C_2. She argued that perceptual similarity is necessary for a consonantal change of place, such as /θ/>[f] or [t]>[k]. Similarly, Lavoie (2001) concentrated on the weakening and strengthening of consonants. She surveyed known fortition and lenition processes across languages, most of which were conditioned, and performed acoustic and electropalatogram (EPG) analyses on these processes in English and Spanish. Lenition was most consistently tied to decreased duration.

Mergers

Phonological mergers present some special problems. The biggest is determining whether a speaker has a merger. One way is to analyse tokens of the possibly merged sounds uttered by a speaker and determine whether there is any acoustic differentiation of them. Larger samples are better – with only a few tokens, incidental factors such as prosody can make it look like there's a difference even when there isn't. Moreover, you have to be careful that you have comparable phonetic contexts for the two sounds in order to eliminate skewing caused by coarticulation. Another method is to ask speakers for their judgements about the two sounds (usually by asking them about minimal pairs of words). This technique usually works, but there are troublesome exceptions. Sometimes, mostly when two sounds are very similar, speakers aren't consciously aware of a distinction that they produce. This situation is called a *near-merger* (see e.g. Labov 1994). In other cases spelling can make speakers think that two homophonous words are pronounced differently. A final method, more reliable but harder to implement, is to use one of the various cognitive perception experiments described in Chapter 3 that can show whether speakers differentiate sounds. Even these experiments can yield ambiguous results at times, though.

Like other sound changes, mergers can be conditioned or unconditioned. Chain shifts are usually unconditioned or nearly so. Additionally, it is common for a sound to split into two conditioned allophones, after which one of them merges with another sound (Hoenigswald 1946).

Labov (1994) listed two related principles that affect the status of mergers:

1. mergers are irreversible by linguistic means (ibid.:311 – *Garde's Principle*);
2. mergers expand at the expense of distinctions (ibid.:313 – *Herzog's Principle*).

Garde's Principle can be violated by social factors, such as swamping of a community by immigrants. For example, the NEAR and SQUARE vowels were once merged in the South Carolina Low Country, but this merger is disappearing there because of outsiders moving in (O'Cain 1977; Baranowski 2007). Otherwise, without special training, speakers don't learn distinctions they didn't learn as young children. Herzog's Principle refers to the geographical and social spread of a merger – i.e. a larger and larger number of speakers will have the merger as time goes by. It works because, apparently, language learners exposed to speakers with and without the merger most often go with the cognitively easier configuration, which is to have just one contrastive sound, not two.

Another research issue related to mergers is the mechanism by which the merger progresses. Trudgill and Foxcroft (1978) proposed two mechanisms, *merger-by-approximation* and *merger-by-transfer*. Merger-by-approximation, schematized in Figure 10.6, occurs when two sounds get closer and closer together over time until they finally fall together. Merger of certain vowels before /l/ – e.g. in western Pennsylvania English – probably happened this way. Fronting of the GOOSE and FOOT vowels in non-pre-/l/ contexts left the pre-/l/ allophones, as in *pool* and *pull*, stranded in the back vowel space, and vocalization of coda /l/ made the POOL and PULL classes into very similar diphthongs whose realizations overlapped. Merger was an easy next step.

In merger-by-transfer, represented in Figure 10.7, either words or phonetic contexts are moved individually from one category to the other. An example

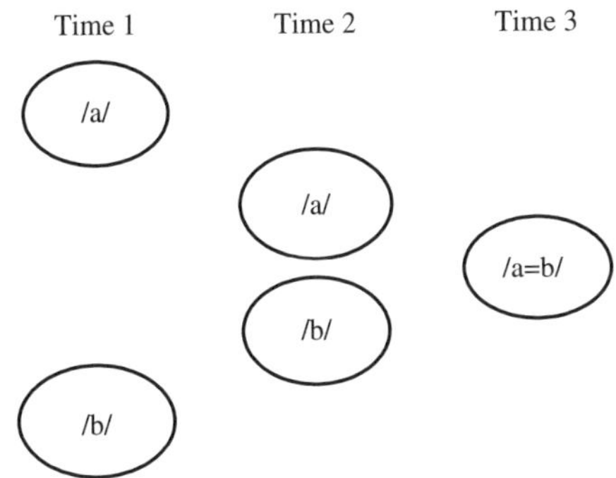

Figure 10.6 A schematized depiction of merger-by-approximation.

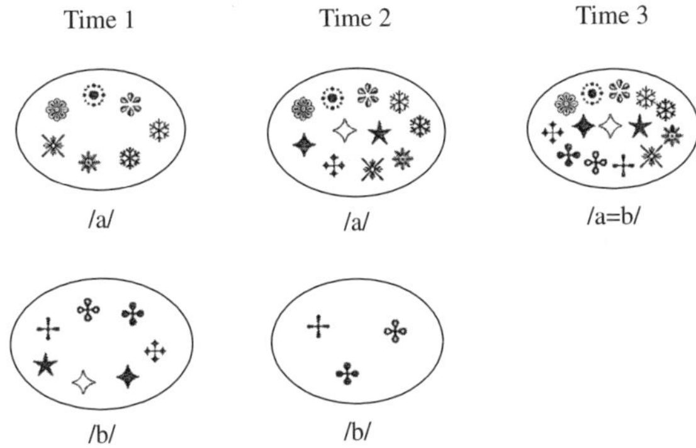

Figure 10.7 A schematized depiction of merger-by-transfer.

is the absorption of the BATH vowel into the TRAP vowel in North Carolina English. At one time, BATH was produced as [æɛ] and TRAP variably as monophthongal [æ] or triphthongal [æɛæ]. However, the two sets began to merge and, as they did, some speakers showed a reduced BATH set. One speaker I analysed, for instance, had [æɛ] in *last* and *half* but [æ] in *ask* and *after*.

A third mechanism, *merger-by-expansion*, was proposed by Herold (1990, 1997). In merger-by-expansion, the two sounds don't converge. Instead, the phonic space formerly divided between the two sounds is combined and the result is one sound with an exceptionally wide range of variation, as depicted in Figure 10.8.

Neogrammarian change versus lexical diffusion

As noted in Chapter 1, the *Neogrammarian Hypothesis* stated that sound changes were exceptionless and that they could be conditioned only by phonetic factors. In recent years, the major challenge to this notion has been *lexical diffusion*, the notion that sound changes spread word by word through a language instead of affecting all words at once. The main proponents of lexical diffusion have been William S.-Y. Wang and his associates (e.g. Wang 1977). Neogrammarians

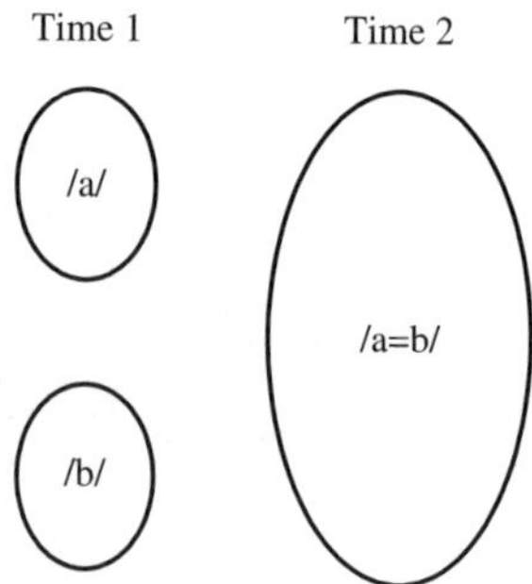

Figure 10.8 A schematized depiction of merger-by-expansion.

never denied that lexical properties affected sound change, but they ascribed those effects to analogy and dialect mixture. Lexical diffusionists, conversely, argued that lexical effects were the vehicle of sound change.

Labov (1981, 1994) devoted considerable attention to sorting out the controversy. He saw it as a crucial part of the transition issue raised in Weinreich et al. (1968). He focused on the unique constituency of the TRAP and BATH classes in Philadelphia, which shows partial lexical conditioning – e.g. *bad*, *mad* and *glad* are in the BATH class, but *sad*, *pad* and *clad* are in the TRAP class. In Labov (1981), he cautioned that apparent lexical affects can be artefacts of small datasets, particularly for words that occur infrequently in conversation and words that vacillate between two variants. Based on his acoustic analyses of vowel shifts and his review of historical changes, he suggested that Neogrammarian change affects low-level shifts, such as the movement of a vowel, while lexical diffusion drives shifts between abstract classes (i.e. phonemes). He made more detailed predictions in Labov (1994:543). For instance, he stated that vowel shifts in place of articulation, vocalization of liquids, deletions of vowels and semivowels, and changes in consonantal manner of articulation were more likely to result from Neogrammarian change. He predicted that shortening and lengthening, deletions of obstruents, stop/liquid metathesis, and changes in consonantal place of articulation were more likely to stem from lexical diffusion.

Propagation of changes

Linguistic changes are often described as being either *internally motivated* or *externally motivated*. Internally motivated changes are those that originate within a dialect because of phonetic factors such as coarticulation, phonological restructuring, lexical obsolescence or a need for a new term, morphological or syntactic structures, or semantic factors. External motivations include language contact, in which a change spreads into one language from another; innovations that spread from one dialect to another; and prestige-related changes that spread from privileged groups to those with less power.

Each kind of externally motivated change has been the subject of linguistic research. Language transfer is the subject of much linguistic research (see e.g. Weinreich 1953; Lehiste 1988; Odlin 1989) and a pervasive influence on linguistic change. In fact, study of the most extreme form of language transfer – pidgin and creole formation – is a field of its own with numerous outlets, such as the *Journal of Pidgin and Creole Languages*. Thomason and Kaufman (1988) developed an influential and useful theory of language contact. By their reckoning, there are two kinds of contact situations. In a *borrowing* situation, a group doesn't shift its language. Lexicon is affected most strongly as the group borrows words from other groups. Morphosyntax and phonology may or may not be affected, and if they are it is to a lesser extent. In an *interference* situation, the affected group undergoes language shift. Phonology and phonetics are strongly affected – this is the 'foreign accent' of L2 learners – as is morphosyntax. Lexicon is affected least. When these influences persist after the source language disappears, they are often called *substrate* influences, with the source language called the *substrate language*. The degree of substrate influence depends on such factors as the speed of the language shift, the relative power of the groups in contact and – to a lesser extent – similarities in the structures of the languages in contact.

Related to language contact is dialect contact. This occurs when new settlements are created – in earlier times from colonialization and currently from the creation of new suburbs – or when an older community is swamped by newcomers. The result is often dialect levelling (Trudgill 1986; Kerswill 1994; Thomas 1997; Williams and Kerswill 1999; Kerswill and Williams 2000; Mattheier 2000). Trudgill (1986) treats levelling as part of the process of koineization, which consists of the mixing of speakers, levelling and simplification as younger members of the community develop a new dialect. Typically, stigmatized regional features and phonologically complex features (i.e. allophonic variations) are lost, though some variations in the source dialects may become social variations in the new community.

Spread of changes across dialects is associated with the *Wellentheorie*, or *wave theory*, of linguistic change. First proposed by Schmidt (1872), the wave theory is the notion that an innovation can spread outward from its point of origin, crossing dialectal and even linguistic boundaries in the process. It explains patterns that the older genetic theory of linguistic change can't. The *genetic*, or *Stammbaum*, *theory*, set forth by Schleicher (1853), is the view of language as consisting of lineages that develop independently once they diverge from each other. The genetic approach closely resembles traditional Darwinian notions of how biological evolution operates. Subsequent Wellentheorie-oriented research has focused on the importance of focal areas, usually influential cities, from which innovations spread (e.g. Trudgill 1974a). Other patterns, such as contrahierarchical diffusion – from outlying areas to focal centres – and contagious diffusion that is blind to focal areas, have also been demonstrated, however (Bailey et al. 1993).

Maps are frequently used to illustrate the geographical spread of sound changes (see e.g. Kirk 1994). Such maps can show data from each subject in the study, as in Anderson (1987) or Labov et al. (2006). Alternatively, they can average data from subjects by geographical locality following predetermined geographical regions (e.g. Bailey et al. 1993; Pederson et al. 1986–92) or in

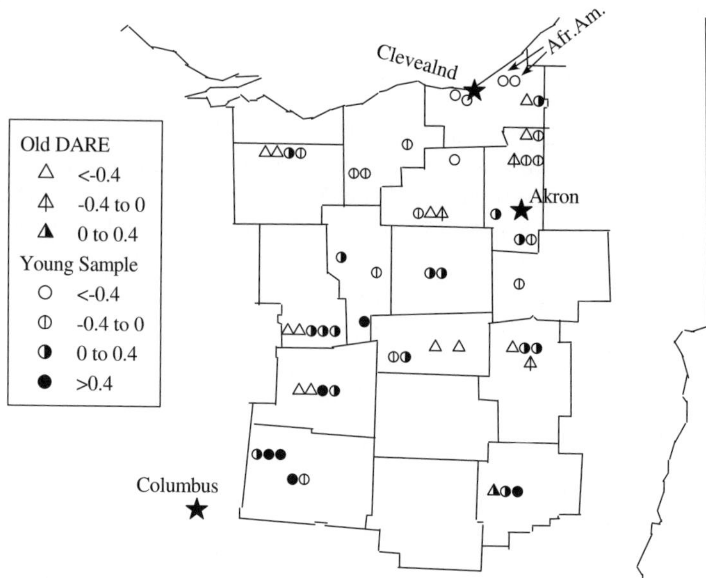

Figure 10.9 A map showing the spread of fronting of the GOAT vowel over part of Ohio, comparing subjects from the *Dictionary of American Regional English* (DARE) born in 1907 or earlier and subjects from a recent survey who were born in 1970 or later. The numbers represent mean Lobanov-normalized F_2 values of the nucleus. Higher numbers and darker symbols indicate greater fronting.

contour intervals that follow the data values (Trudgill 1974a). Acoustic data lend themselves to mapping, as Labov et al. (2006) demonstrate. An example of mapping applied to acoustically derived data appears in Figure 10.9. It illustrates the spread of fronting of the GOAT vowel in the area between Cleveland and Columbus, Ohio and shows data for individual subjects. Triangles represent speakers interviewed for the *Dictionary of American Regional English* survey in 1967 who were at least 60 years old when interviewed. Circles represent speakers born in 1970 or later, who were interviewed for a more recent survey. Darker symbols indicate greater fronting. The older speakers show little evidence of fronting. For the younger sample, fronting is greatest in areas near Columbus, suggesting hierarchical diffusion from Columbus. However, to the north, fronting is more advanced in rural areas than areas close to Cleveland, suggesting contrahierarchical diffusion there.

Prestige-related change is dubbed *change from above* by Labov (1972). Speakers normally have some awareness of these changes. Labov opposed change from above to *change from below*, which speakers usually aren't aware of until the change has advanced somewhat. Change from above is associated with *overt prestige*, promulgated by authorities such as social elites, teachers and authors of usage guides. Trudgill (1972) noted that change from below has its own kind of prestige. It is associated with *covert prestige*. Covert prestige rests on expression of solidarity within disempowered groups, such as the working classes, ethnic minorities and minors. One fairly consistent finding in sociolinguistic studies, though, is that changes don't usually spread early on within either the top or the bottom of society. The middle classes, not the upper class, are typically most concerned with overt prestige, while changes from below ordinarily take hold fastest among the lower middle and upper working classes, not the lower working class. As is well known in sociolinguistics, females ordinarily lead in changes from above but also, perhaps nine times out of ten, lead in changes from below (see Labov 2001). Chapter 11 will examine the spread of sound changes through local institutions such as communities and social networks.

EXERCISES

1. How would you go about tracking potential sound changes before they take on social identity functions?
2. What are some experimental ways you could test whether speakers deliberately innovate or innovate by misperception? Does your choice of method depend on the kind of variable you're examining?
3. How does the opposition of least effort vs clarity relate to the controversy over the Neogrammarian Hypothesis vs lexical diffusion?
4. What methods could be used to test Labov's principles of vowel shifting?

FURTHER READING

Blevins, Juliette. 2004. *Evolutionary Phonology: The Emergence of Sound Patterns.* Cambridge, UK: Cambridge University Press.

Labov, William. 1994. *Principles of Linguistic Change. Volume 1: Internal Factors.* Language in Society 20. Oxford, UK: Blackwell.

Lindblom, Björn, Susan Guion, Susan Hura, Seung-Jae Moon and Raquel Willerman. 1995. Is sound change adaptive? *Rivista di Linguistica* 7:5–37.

Ohala, John J. 1993b. The phonetics of sound change. In Charles Jones (ed.), *Historical Linguistics: Problems and Perspectives.* London: Longman, 237–78.

Social Factors and Phonetics

11

11.1 Socio… linguistics

Sociolinguistics has benefited from an infusion of theories and analysis techniques – such as density and multiplexity of networks, the community of practice concept, and sociometric analysis – from sociology. Studies incorporating these innovations have often involved phonetic variables, though only a few have utilized acoustic analysis. The time is certainly ripe for studies that take full advantage of both the new kinds of social analyses and fine-grained acoustic analyses. In this chapter, we'll cover the main points of social analyses, how they relate to phonetics and how both relate to cognition. For more depth on sociolinguistic analysis, you should consult a standard sociolinguistics text such as Chambers (1995), Mesthrie et al. (2000), Meyerhoff (2006) or Wardhaugh (2010).

In contrast to the increasing use of sociological analyses, only a few areas of sociolinguistics have addressed cognition directly, though discourse analysis and pragmatics have, as evidenced by publications such as the journal *Pragmatics & Cognition*. However, as we saw in Chapter 9, areas of sociolinguistics that deal with pronunciation are only beginning to engage cognition. A fully developed sociophonetics should explore how phonological/phonetic processing is cognitively and neurologically linked to social indexing.

We've mentioned *social indexing* several times earlier in this book. This is the linking of linguistic variables to social categories, which can range from large entities such as languages, regional dialects, gender or ethnic groups to small entities such as specific cliques of friends. Language users may be aware of the indexing, but they don't have to be.

The quantitative sociolinguistic framework

The approach taken in most of the prominent older quantitative sociolinguistic studies was coarse-grained. A survey of a community was conducted. Then linguistic variables were coded and correlated against general demographic factors. Variables were transcribed auditorily and coded as discrete variants in order to facilitate certain kinds of statistical analysis. The demographic factors were treated as independent variables and the linguistic variables as dependent variables. Demographic factors could include social class or caste, educational level, housing type, age group or birth cohort, length of residency in the community, sex, and ethnicity, among others. This protocol was pioneered in Labov (1966). Among the other key early studies that used this method for pronunciation variables are Wolfram (1969), Trudgill (1974b) and Macauley (1977). Pederson et al. (1986–92) followed the same method in trying to adapt dialect geography to sociolinguistic standards, treating region as another demographic factor.

Unfortunately, any of the demographic variables can be problematic. For example, the difficulties created by using the biological entity of sex to get at the social correlates of sex – i.e. gender – are well known (e.g. Eckert 1989b). Concerning the relationship sex/gender and linguistic change, Labov (2001) generalizes that females usually lead in both changes from above and changes from below, though it isn't necessarily the same females who lead in the two types of change. My impression, based on numerous studies that have been conducted, is that female leadership in sound changes might hold for nine out of ten changes. For age groups, it's impossible to tell whether generational differences represent real changes over time or age-grading (changes that occur in a person's speech over his or her lifetime) unless longitudinal data are available (see e.g. Bailey et al. 1991). Social class is especially hard to quantify because any scale to rate it will be subjective – do you base it on income, education, occupation, domicile, neighbourhood, family background, leisure activities or some combination of these? How do you decide the relative status of different occupations or domiciles, and how do you weight different class indicators against each other? Moreover, different members of a community have different ways of viewing class and status. Each study has had to find and justify ways to quantify criteria that it uses to gauge class. Sociolinguists have used a variety of scales to do so, though all are necessarily artificial in their own ways (see Wardhaugh 2010:150 ff.). Sometimes, researchers focus on one particular social class or they reduce the strata in quantitative comparisons to as few as two classes. Some studies substitute one key correlate of class, such as education level, for a more general social class scale. These kinds of reductions are often reasonable and defensible. However, you have to be careful not to misrepresent them as full depictions of social class structure or to suppose that finer-grained scaling wouldn't reveal anything new. Much research in the Labovian tradition has pointed to the lower-middle and upper-working classes as the most innovative groups in sound changes (see Labov 2001), though a few exceptions have emerged: Baranowski (2007), for instance, found that the highest social class led in the fronting of the GOAT vowel in Charleston, South Carolina.

The quantitative sociolinguistic approach is a somewhat roundabout way of getting at social meanings. It tells you the degree to which different groups use particular variants. By itself, however, it doesn't tell you how salient each of the variants is in the community. Nor does it tell you how aware language users are of the association between variants and social groups. The coding process can also introduce artificial distinctions that community members don't recognize. In spite of these complexities, people often show robust indexing of linguistic variants with factors such as class, gender, age group and ethnicity and hence show strong cognitive associations between the variants and the demographic groups.

As we saw in Chapter 8, Labov (1972:178–80) proposed a classification of variants according to their salience within a community. Young variants are normally least salient. Such variants tend to be typical of some segments of society but do not show stylistic conditioning because they are 'below the level of social awareness' (ibid.:178). Labov called variants that meet those two criteria *indicators*. He added that changes from below start as indicators. When a variant begins to show stylistic conditioning, meaning that people show some level of awareness of it, it is called a *marker*. At that point, people develop a negative evaluation of the variant. Finally, when people become so aware of a variant that they make overt remarks about it, it becomes a *stereotype*.

11.2 Intraspeaker variation

Style and register

In sociolinguistics, speaking style, or just *style*, is used to refer to any differences in the way of speaking that a speaker exhibits at different times. Another term, *register*, is used to refer to speech in particular situations, such as with specialists in one's field of work, but because it is largely differentiated by special lexicon – *jargon* – it's not as important here. The simplest way of classifying styles is by formality, as Labov (1966) and other early sociolinguistic studies did. In his study of the Lower East Side of Manhattan, Labov elicited five kinds of speaking styles – casual speech, interview speech, reading passage speech, word list speech and minimal pair speech, in increasing level of formality. He regarded the amount of self-monitoring as the primary factor translating the formality of the situation into actual speech differences (Labov 1972:208). This perspective became known as the *attention-to-speech model*.

Although Labov's taxonomy remains a useful device, it has become clear in the years since then that formality and self-monitoring are only two of several factors that influence style. For example, let's say that you have a grandmother whose speech is quite vernacular.[1] When you're speaking with her, your speech will probably be at its most vernacular and casual, too. However, it still won't be the same as your casual speech with your peers. For example, you may use taboo words such as swearing with your peers, but not with your grandmother. You might even exaggerate such features in casual conversations with peers. The differences can carry over to other realms: e.g. in deference to your grandmother, you may avoid prosodic patterns associated with aggressive or competitive speech acts, but with peers you may be induced to magnify them. The amount of self-monitoring is about the same in both cases, involving deliberate avoidance of certain features with your grandmother and deliberate emphasis of them with your peers.

Stylistic variation has become the object of a blossoming field of inquiry in its own right. Bell (1984) played an important role in this growth. He was highly critical of the attention-to-speech model. Instead, he proposed an *audience design model*, in which speakers tailor their speaking style according to their audience. In this model, speakers shift their speech depending on their addressees, other people who might be part of the conversation but aren't being addressed directly, and sometimes other people who are outside the conversation. Speakers have to make some assumptions about their audience based on their prior knowledge of the audience, and if the audience is unfamiliar to the speaker, the speaker may tend to speak in a less vernacular or colloquial manner. However, increasing familiarity can cause speakers to shed their assumptions and make their speech more like that of the audience. In support of that notion, Bell discussed some experiments in which interviewees' speech shifted depending on the speech of the interviewer.

Other ideas on what controls style-shifting have been presented as well. Schilling-Estes (1998) noted that speakers can sometimes style-shift as a performance, in an attempt to create a persona for themselves. Wolfram and Schilling-Estes (2006:286 ff.) developed this notion into a *speaker design model* for style-shifting. This model holds that speakers can shift their speech in order to fill roles. Bell (2001) incorporated such role playing in which the speaker initiates a style into the audience design model. Lindblom's (1990) *H&H model* takes a phonetically motivated stance, arguing that style-shifting may occur for the purpose of communication. That is, sometimes more clearly enunciated speech ('hyperspeech') is necessary, such as when you're speaking to somebody who's hard of hearing or to a non-native speaker or when you're uttering an unfamiliar word or phrase. At other times, speakers fall back on less clearly enunciated speech ('hypospeech') because it takes less effort, thereby saving energy. Lindblom's position doesn't account for sociolinguistic factors, but it could be considered one of the several factors influencing speaking style.

Phonetic aspects of style shifting bring up another issue. You have to be careful about attributing variants directly to stylistic variation. As we saw in Chapters 5 and 6, undershoot and associated phenomena such as coarticulation can greatly affect how segments and F_0 contours are realized. In certain styles, particularly some reading styles, the rate of speech is slowed down. As a result, there will be less phonetic undershoot in those styles. It might look like the undershot variants are the stylistically specified forms and that formality is directly responsible for the more canonical speech, but actually the causality is that style leads to a slower rate of speech, which leads to less undershot variants. What is really being specified in that speaking style is the rate of speech, not the segmental or F_0 contour variants. To avoid spuriousness, you should always look for a mechanical explanation such as undershoot before you move on to a fancier explanation such as speaking style.

Accommodation

One important facet of style shifting is *accommodation*. This occurs when one or more interlocutors in a conversation shift their speech to make it more like that of the others (convergence), or sometimes less like it (divergence or 'disaccommodation'). Giles and Smith (1979:46) and Giles et al. (1991:7) describe how accommodation has been demonstrated for a number of linguistic and non-linguistic features. The linguistic features include, besides code-switching in bilingual contexts, several prosodic factors. Among them are length and duration of pauses, vocal intensity, speech rate and utterance length. Segmental features may also be subject to accommodation, as the results in Giles (1973) hint.

Much of what is known as Communication Accommodation Theory concerns how much accommodation occurs in a particular situation and the amount that leads addressees to react favourably or unfavourably (see Giles and Smith 1979:47; Giles et al. 1991). Another question, however, is the degree to which accommodation is deliberate by a speaker. The evidence that accommodation is usually viewed favourably by addressees suggests that speakers benefit from accommodating deliberately. At the same time, Exemplar Theory, as discussed in Chapter 9, suggests that some accommodation might be involuntary. Experimentation could clarify the degree to which accommodation is voluntary or not and whether various kinds of linguistic variables differ in how voluntary accommodation of them is.

Giles et al. (1979) and Thakerar et al. (1982) introduced a model in which accommodation is affected by two factors. One is cognitive, involving how speakers make sense of and organize their social environments. That is, they need to know how to behave, linguistically and otherwise, depending on the situation they're in. The other has to do with identity. Individuals speak in a manner that allows them to project an identity. Both factors lead individuals to slip into particular speech styles, and both can cause them to speak more like or less like addressees.

11.3 Clustering of subjects

The speech community

Delineation of the *speech community* that is being studied has usually been a central concern to sociolinguists because it circumscribes a study. However, defining what a speech community is has proved controversial. The starting point for sociolinguistic uses of the term *speech community* is often regarded as the one Labov (1972) formulated based on his findings in Labov (1966). Labov (1972:120–1) stated, 'the speech community is not defined by any marked agreement in the use of language elements, so much as by participation in a set of shared norms; these norms may be observed in overt types of evaluative behavior, and by the uniformity of abstract patterns of variation which are invariant in respect to particular levels of usage'. That is, different speakers within a speech community don't all speak alike, but they regard the same variants as prestigious or unprestigious and their stylistic variation will reflect that.

At about the same time, however, Gumperz (1971) gave a less specific definition. He stated that any groups of any size 'may be treated as speech communities, provided they show linguistic peculiarities that warrant special study' (1971:114).

Labov's definition certainly fits within Gumperz's definition, though. Romaine's (1982b) critique of Labov's notion accepted his definition but argued that it is an idealization. She added that individual variation means that, even when different members of a speech community share the same norms, their usage patterns still are not all likely to obey the same quantitative rules. This latter point was a reaction to the variable rules that Labov and others had posited at the time. Variable rules mathematically specified proportions of competing variants that different groups of speakers within a community would use in different speaking styles.

For sociophonetic research, a speech community is, practically speaking, an area that you can recruit subjects from without compromising the research. Hence, depending on the phenomenon that you're examining, you might consider a speech community to be anything from speakers of a particular language to members of a specific group of friends or relatives. It all depends on whether they share linguistic variants or behaviour regarding the variants. Nevertheless, speech communities aren't the only way to circumscribe the population to be studied, as the next two sections illustrate. According to Holmes and Meyerhoff (1999:178–9), certain factors distinguish the speech community approach from other ways of defining a study population. First, norms are critical: members of a speech community acquire norms – not ordinarily ones that an individual member has a say in creating – and they behave similarly towards the norms, as in showing similar stylistic conditioning. Second, a member's individual identity isn't important in defining the community. Third, members don't become part of the community for a specific purpose, and their membership may be defined by non-members – perhaps even by the researcher.

Social network analysis

A second approach to defining the study population is *social network analysis*. In this, individuals are asked who they associate with or, better yet, are observed interacting with other people. Then their networks of associates can be mapped *sociometrically*, as in the hypothetical example in Figure 11.1. The observed networks reflect individuals' social identities. In social network analysis, according to Holmes and Meyerhoff (1999:179–80), shared identifications, not shared norms, are essential. Membership in the group is determined by means of contrast with other groups. As with the speech community approach, attainment of membership doesn't necessarily serve a purpose for an individual.

The simplest linguistic analysis involving networks examines whether linguistic variables are correlated with particular networks or with non-membership. An early application in sociolinguistics that analysed several consonantal and some non-phonetic variables was Labov et al.'s (1968) examination of three cliques called the Jets, the Cobras and the Thunderbirds. Certain speakers called 'Lames' who were poorly tied to any of the cliques showed lower rates of variants associated with African American Vernacular English than clique members. However, more derivative kinds of analyses have also been productive. The best-known such study is the survey of three neighbourhoods in Belfast, Northern Ireland, conducted by James and Leslie Milroy (e.g. Milroy 1987). The Milroys popularized among sociolinguists measures of *network*

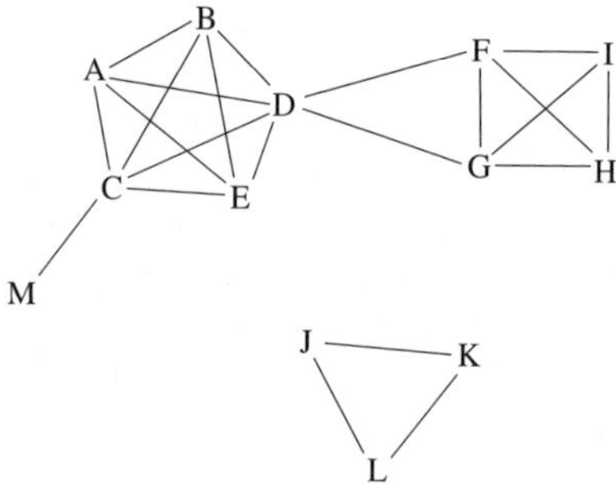

Figure 11.1 A hypothetical network analysis. Note that speakers A–E form one network, F–I form another and J–L form yet another. Speaker D, however, has connections with speakers F and G, and speaker C has a link to speaker M, who is otherwise outside the network structure.

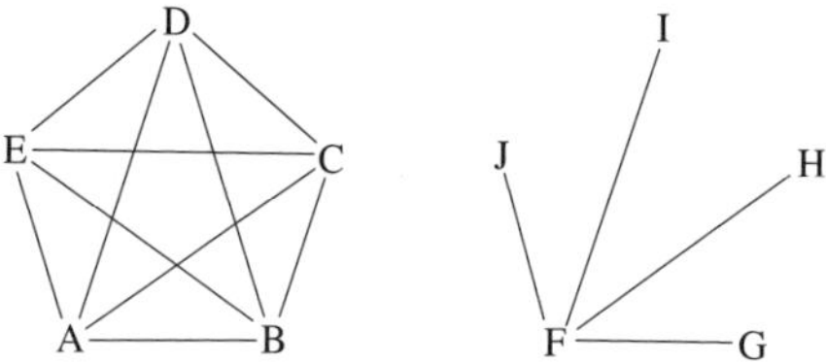

Figure 11.2 A hypothetical example illustrating network density. In the network on the left, speakers A–E are all linked with each other, creating a high-density network. In the network on the right, speaker F is linked to speakers G, H, I and J, but speakers G–J have no connections with each other, creating a low-density network.

density and *network multiplexity*. Density has to do with how many of an individual's associates also associate with each other. Density can be high or low. Its formula, given in Milroy (1987:50), is

$$D = (100\%)(\text{actual links})/(\text{possible links})$$

where D is density and possible links are all the possible connections between an individual's associates, as shown in Figure 11.2.

For example, if an individual is linked to five other people, there are $4 + 3 + 2 + 1 = 10$ possible links among those five people, but if there are only three actual links among them, then the density is $(100\%)(3)/(10) = 30\%$. Multiplexity, in contrast, is the number of different contexts that two individuals are in contact – e.g. as neighbours, as relatives, at work, at religious services, and in other organizations. Ties can be multiplex or uniplex. Multiplexity (M) is given by the formula from Milroy (1987:51):

$$M = (100\%)(\text{total contexts})/(\text{actual links})$$

As an example, if an individual is linked to five other people, but sees one person in four contexts, three people in two contexts and the other person in one context, the multiplexity is $(100\%)(4 + 2 + 2 + 2 + 1)/(5) = 220\%$.

The Milroys examined several vowel and one consonantal variable in Belfast in light of levels of network density and multiplexity by different speakers. It turned out that the network measures were correlated with the linguistic variables in one neighbourhood where both men and women showed high density and multiplexity, but not in the two neighbourhoods where men showed low density and multiplexity. A similar study was conducted in a German-speaking community in Austria by Lippi-Green (1989), who found that men with greater network density were more likely to use a local dialectal variant of one vowel.

Labov (2001) used sociometric analysis differently in a study of Philadelphia. He constructed scales indicating how many close friends a speaker had and how localized the friends were. Then he correlated these scales with various sound changes. People with more friends and higher degrees of locality of friends tended to show more advanced sound changes. Principle components analysis revealed that individuals who were most advanced in the sound changes as a whole were mostly people who were more central in the social networks.

Communities of practice

A *community of practice* (COP) is a more specific group than a speech community or a demographic division within a speech community such as social class. The term was originally defined to describe patterns of learning (Lave and Wenger 1991; Wenger 1998). It has been adapted for sociolinguistic use, however. A COP, according to Eckert and McConnell-Ginet (1992:464), is a group of people whose reason for associating with each other is to participate in some activity together. Holmes and Meyerhoff (1999:175–6) and Meyerhoff (2002:527–8), following Wenger (1998), elaborate, naming three features of COPs. Members not only (a) participate in an activity together, but also (b) have to agree on the rules for and goals of conducting the activity and (c) have to share resources such as memories of past events or jargon used for the activity. For linguistic variables, point (b) means that members negotiate the social meanings of the variables. Holmes and Meyerhoff (1999:179) note that shared *practices*, not shared norms or identifications, set COPs off from speech communities or social networks. Furthermore, members, not circumstances, decide who belongs to the COP, and the COP exists to facilitate the practice that is shared, such as playing a sport or engaging in regular conversation sessions.

COPs can be identified once a researcher is familiar enough with a group of people and how they live. Ethnographic research is usually necessary to get that level of familiarity, though sometimes you can use the shortcut of asking people who they associate with. The trick is to find linguistic variants, particularly non-lexical forms, that are correlated with the COPs. Most individuals belong to numerous COPs, and the majority of them aren't likely to show much correlation with phonetic properties of the individual's speech. A few studies have had some success finding such correlations by looking at the use of vocalic variants by adolescents in locales where vowel shifting is occurring. An early attempt, long before the term *community of practice* was even introduced, was by Habick (1980), who correlated the fronting of the GOOSE and GOAT vowels with social groups in a rural Illinois high school. Better known is the work by Eckert (e.g. 1989a), who discussed in depth how social groups constituted

COPs in a high school in a suburb of Detroit. The two groups were the 'Jocks', who identified with school activities and were largely middle-class, and the 'Burnouts', who identified with extracurricular – sometimes delinquent – activities, partly in reaction to the 'Jocks', and who were largely working-class. She found that backward shifting of the DRESS and STRUT vowels, raising of the PRICE nucleus and glide weakening of the PRIZE diphthong, all new processes in the community, were highly correlated with the COPs. Speakers called the 'Burned-out Burnouts', who showed the strongest identification with the 'Burnouts', also pushed the vowel shifts the furthest. Other recent studies that found correlations between phonetic variables and COPs are Bucholtz (1998) and Dodsworth (2005), both in high schools, and Mallinson (2006), among adults in a rural community.

An example of how a COP approach can be applied to a community study comes from a survey of Johnstown, Ohio. A class of sixth-graders, their parents and a few elderly natives of the community were interviewed and asked to read a story (see Thomas 1996). Vowels from the story were measured. One particular clique of eight girls constituted a COP: they sat together in the cafeteria and other places when possible, they all named each other as their main friends, and they'd been friends since starting elementary school. Two important vowel variables were the degree of fronting of the GOAT vowel and the lowering and retraction of the TRAP vowel. Figure 11.3 illustrates results for these two vowels.

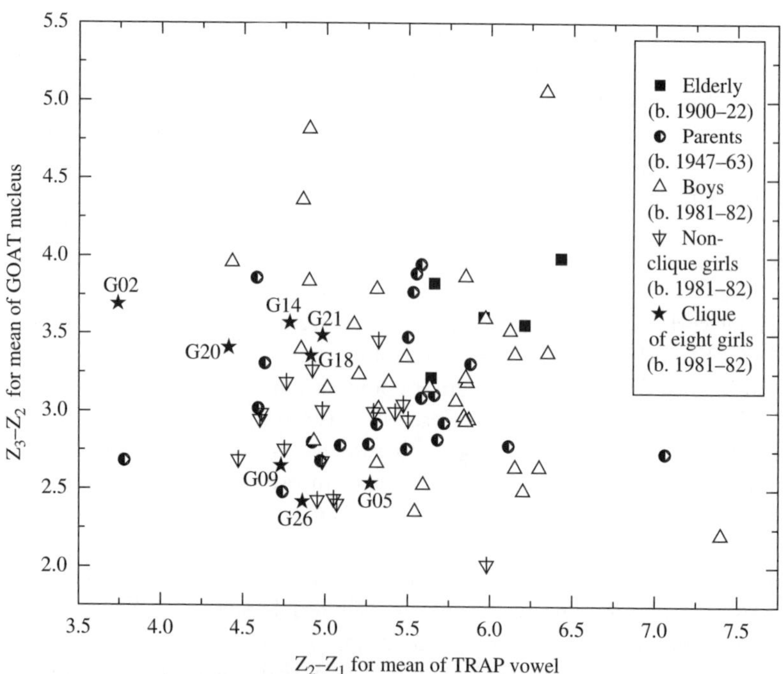

Figure 11.3 Normalized values of the mean values of the TRAP and GOAT vowels for the Johnstown, Ohio, subjects. Note that lower values for the TRAP nucleus indicate more lowering and retraction, while lower values for the GOAT nucleus indicate more fronting.

Members of the clique, denoted by stars, are labelled with code numbers. Compared to the rest of the corpus of subjects, most girls in the clique showed low TRAP scores, indicating lowering/retraction. The clique showed a curious bimodal distribution for the GOAT nucleus. Three of them, G05, G09 and G26, produced strongly fronted GOAT nuclei, while the other five produced much less fronted forms. In fact, the only other girl in the class with such a low fronting score as those five was a newcomer to Johnstown. What does this result mean? Most likely, lack of fronting bore meaning for some members of the clique, but not all the members had agreed on the interpretation – the meaning was still being negotiated.[2]

One obstacle to implementing the COP approach on a wide scale is that the way one COP uses language isn't necessarily how any other COP uses language. Because each COP negotiates its own meanings for linguistic variables, you can't generalize from one COP to society as a whole. As a result, COP studies can often look like case studies, especially if they focus on the linguistic behaviour of just a few individuals. That doesn't detract from the accuracy of COP findings – after all, the evaluation of variables starts on such a local scale. Moreover, as Bucholtz's (1998) analysis of 'geek girls' shows, some COPs deliberately set up norms diametrically opposed to those of the larger community. However, researchers need to explain how a norm can make the leap from a COP to the larger society.

Individual variation

One of the appeals of COP theory is that it focuses attention on individual speakers. Individuals decide what groups they want to associate with and what features from each group they incorporate in constructing their own identity. Together with the rest of a group, they deliberate how they want to fashion the group identity. In other approaches, identity features are thrust upon speakers simply because of their social circumstances. Even in the COP approach, however, identity is still tightly linked to social groups. Individuals negotiate features of their identity, but they do so within the groups they identify with. What isn't accounted for is the potential for originality by individuals. To what extent can an individual construct an identity independently of social groups? Can linguistic variables be constructed and indexed by an individual?

Sociolinguistics has usually avoided these questions. Even though the field may pay lip service to the importance of individuals, 'the individual is often anywhere but in the center of interest in practice' (Johnstone 1996:14). The dogma from Weinreich et al. (1968) that a linguistic change is a change only when it starts to spread through a community, not when one individual takes it on, was discussed in Chapter 10. That dogma has discouraged sociolinguists from examining individual variation. Dorian's (1994) study of morphological and phonological variation in a dying language and Johnstone's (1996) study of discourse variation demonstrate that individuals can and do display originality in language, however. It seems that they can construct unique identities in most realms of language, including phonology and phonetics. The main difficulty is that it's harder to prove that a phonetic variant represents originality by a speaker because there's less room for variation. A unique discourse variant is easy to recognize because there are so many words in a language that novel combinations are possible. For phonetics, though, one person's innovation – say, an unusually front variant of some vowel or an unusually strongly aspirated variant of a stop – is probably somebody else's innovation, too. Or, to cite a hypothetical scenario, what if one network of speakers tended to raise a certain vowel more than other members of a community, but within the network one individual distinguished herself by raising the vowel less than other network members? Even though her behaviour would stem from her own originality, it would look to a linguist as if she'd acquired it from speakers outside the network. Thus it is quite difficult to verify that a speaker innovates independently.

One means of doing so is to show that a certain speaker has pushed an ongoing sound shift further than the speaker's associates. Labov (2001), as discussed above, took this tack. His principle components analysis of several vowel shifts showed that the speakers who pushed sound changes the furthest in Philadelphia were typically social leaders, central in their social networks. Nevertheless, he also noted that his model didn't apply to a suburban neighbourhood with looser social networks the way it worked in established urban neighbourhoods with dense, multiplex networks. Moreover, it is not clear that speakers who extend any specific sound shift, as opposed to all sound shifts operating in a community, have to be social leaders.

One other potential problem with individual variation is its motivation. Once you've identified individual variation, how do you tell whether it's due to a speaker deliberately moulding a personal identity or merely a fortuitous, unintentional development? It may be possible to ask the speaker, but it may also be necessary to create an experiment testing the speaker's attitudes towards the variant.

11.4 Cognitive sociolinguistics

As we've seen, linguistic variables can be correlated with lots of factors: demographic characteristics of individuals, membership in particular social groups and speaking styles. An important question arises from these correlations: how strongly are linguistic representations cognitively linked to knowledge about social and stylistic categories? People have varying degrees of awareness of these linguistic correlations. In fact, Labov's (1972) division of variables into indicators, markers and stereotypes implies just that: individuals have little or no awareness of the relationship of indicators to social categories, but their awareness increases as variants become markers and ultimately stereotypes. It should be remembered that conscious awareness is only part of the story because listeners often possess latent, subliminal associations of linguistic variants with groups of speakers or with speaking styles.

Recently, this issue has begun to be addressed by the new subfield of *cognitive sociolinguistics*. Linguistics as a whole needs this contribution from sociolinguistics. Kristiansen (2003:112), for example, argues that 'a cognitive account of phonology would be incomplete if it did not consider socially motivated variation'. Much of the literature on cognitive sociolinguistics has focused on pragmatics and discourse variation. That's not surprising, considering that cognitive linguistics as a whole has focused mainly on semantics, pragmatics and syntax (e.g. Lakoff 1987; Langacker 2008). Nevertheless, phonetic and phonological variants should constitute a crucial part of it. Cognitive sociolinguistics rests on the twin notions that people associate variants with social and demographic categories and that speakers use language to project their desired identity (Kristiansen 2008). Of course, both of those notions are basic tenets of sociolinguistics as a whole. Cognitive sociolinguistics, however, invites us to examine the psychological associations between linguistic variants and social categorizations. Ultimately, examination of these cognitive associations could be complemented with examination of neurological connections between language and social knowledge.

Kristiansen (2008) speaks of these associations in terms of 'receptive competence'. By that, she means that people acquire, often subconsciously, the ability to associate linguistic variants with speaking styles, social groups and larger demographic categories. This sort of knowledge is deeper than the kind of identifications elicited by 'perceptual dialectology' or 'folk dialectology' (e.g. Preston 1999). The latter often taps language users' overt knowledge of popular stereotypes more than their full receptive competence. For example, subjects may be asked to draw lines on a map showing where they think people have noticeable accents. To investigate the full extent of receptive competence of language users, however, true perception experiments are necessary. We need empirical evidence that people cognitively associate linguistic variants with social categories ranging from regional dialects and gender to COPs, as well as with situational speaking styles.[3]

We discussed designs for such social psychology experiments in Chapter 3. For example, recordings of different accents or speaking styles could be played to subjects, who then identify how recognizably different the speaker sounds to them. Asking subjects whether a speaker belongs to a certain regional, age, ethnic or other group can be effective. Related kinds of questions, such as asking subjects where they'd expect to encounter such a speaker or how the speaker would respond to certain questions (e.g. on political issues), can be helpful. Eliciting attitudes towards accents can also reveal whether a subject has some latent awareness of the social associations of linguistic variants. These attitudes can be tapped by asking subjects to rate voices on various scales, such as intelligence, friendliness, trustworthiness or suitability for particular jobs.

EXERCISES

1. How could perception experiments that explore cognitive processing be used to differentiate gender associations from correlations of variables with sex? Or, when variables are correlated with age groups, how could such experiments help distinguish actual diachronic change from age-grading?

EXERCISES

2. Attention to speech, audience design, speaker design and H&H may all be factors that contribute to style shifting. How can you distinguish their effects in a study? To what degree do their effects overlap?
3. What kinds of experiments and elicitation of speech can reveal normative attitudes towards particular linguistic variants within a speech community?
4. In a COP study, how much can you learn from the speakers' production and how much from perception experiments about their attitudes towards variables?
5. Design a perception experiment that taps subjects' subliminal cognitive associations between some linguistic variant and knowledge of which groups use that variant.

FURTHER READING

Bell, Allan. 2001. Back in style: Reworking audience design. In Penelope Eckert and John R. Rickford (eds), *Style and Sociolinguistic Variation*. Cambridge, UK: Cambridge University Press, 139–69.

Giles, Howard, Nikolas Coupland and Justine Coupland. 1991. Accommodation theory: Communication, context, and consequence. In Howard Giles, Nikolas Coupland and Justine Coupland (eds), *Contexts of Accommodation: Developments in Applied Sociolinguistics*. Cambridge, UK: Cambridge University Press, 1–68.

Holmes, Janet and Miriam Meyerhoff. 1999. The community of practice: Theories and methodologies in language and gender research. *Language in Society* 28:173–83.

Kristiansen, Gitte. 2003. How to do things with allophones: Linguistic stereotypes as cognitive reference points in social cognition. In René Dirven, Roslyn Frank and Martin Pütz (eds), *Cognitive Models in Language and Thought: Ideology, Metaphors and Meanings*. Berlin: Mouton de Gruyter, 69–120.

12 Lateral Transfer

Assumptions of modularity make concepts simple and easy to package. Linguists have certainly taken advantage of these properties. Modularity pervades linguistic constructs, from the notion of a language or a dialect or a speech community to Chomsky's (1965) famous 'ideal speaker-listener' to the concept of a phoneme to many approaches to neurolinguistic organization. While modularity has proved quite useful in many respects and is a necessary component of linguistic description, its limitations inevitably come to light whenever the object of the construct is examined long enough. By itself, it can't account for language, either descriptively or cognitively.

Among the clearest cases of modularity is the Stammbaum or family tree model of language change developed by August Schleicher, mentioned in Chapter 10. This approach treats linguistic evolution as if each language were on an independent course once it diverges from sister languages. That is, each language becomes a module. The concept is quite old: Percival (1987) observed that the terms *mother* and *daughter* for languages date from the Renaissance. Schleicher's ideas appear to be derived partly from the textual studies of his teacher, Friedrich Ritschl, and partly from biological ideas of his day (Maher 1966; Koerner 1982; Wells 1987). He conceived of a language as an 'organism' – though he meant something like a species, not an individual – that grew, matured and then decayed. His trees illustrating his hypotheses about Indo-European language relationships owed something to the hierarchical biological classification system of Linnaeus and something to the evolutionary ideas of Lamarck.[1] Towards the end of his life, when he read Darwin's *Origin of Species*, he welcomed it as a corroboration of his own ideas (Koerner 1982:18), though there were differences between Darwin's and his conceptions of evolution. Darwin (1874), in turn, noted the parallels between biological and linguistic evolution.

Historical linguistics and biological systematics have key points in common, such as the emphasis placed on shared innovations and parsimony in determining relatedness (Wiener 1987). Hence, analogies between the two fields can be quite instructive. At the same time, it's no secret that application of biological models of evolution, whether Lamarckian or Darwinian, to language change has been problematic. Wiener (1987), for example, noted that while features that a species exhibits determine its survival, the survival of a language isn't decided by its features but by the social standing of its speakers. Another stumbling block is that languages – even unrelated ones – influence each other extensively, whereas only closely related species can hybridize. Many historical linguists, such as Lehmann (1962), consider Schleicher's Stammbaum model hopelessly outdated for that reason. Substratum, superstratum and adstratum effects – all incorporated into the borrowing and interference model of Thomason and Kaufman (1988) – and Schmidt's (1872) Wellentheorie or wave theory have been formulated to address the pervasive hybridity of languages, as we saw in Chapter 10. Although historical linguists still rely on family tree models for constructing relationships among languages, particularly when the language family is poorly known, it would seem that analogies between linguistic change and biological evolution have limited usefulness.

As it turns out, however, nineteenth-century models don't provide an adequate explanation for biological evolution any more than they do for linguistic evolution. Lamarck, Darwin and others based their theories on what they observed from organisms they were able to see – namely, multicellular eukaryotes, nearly all of which reproduce sexually. For such organisms, a tree-like model of evolutionary radiation works well because sexual reproduction can occur only between organisms that are closely related. Once two populations reach a certain threshold, they can no longer interbreed and hence are on independent evolutionary paths. Over the past several decades, however, it has been found that this kind of reproduction isn't the only way or even the main way that deoxyribonucleic acid (DNA) is propagated. Studies of microbes have shown that DNA is passed extensively among organisms with only the most distant relationships. There are various mechanisms, as Bushman (2002) describes. Conjugation, in which one bacterium injects DNA into another, usually occurs between members of the same species, but can take place between different kinds of bacteria. Bacteria can also undergo what is called transformation, in which a bacterium takes up free-floating DNA from its environment and incorporates the DNA into its genome. The free-floating DNA can come from dead microbes, often of a different species, or other sources. Two other common vehicles for DNA movement are retroviruses and retrotransposons. Retroviruses are unusual because they contain ribonucleic acid (RNA), from which they produce DNA – the opposite of the pathway of most organisms. Their DNA is readily integrated into the genome of their host. Retrotransposons are similar but lack an extracellular phase. It is thought that viruses may carry them to new cells. Collectively, these processes are called *lateral DNA transfer*. They have played a crucial role in the evolution of bacteria and archaeans, the two other divisions of life besides eukaryotes.[2] They are so prominent that bacterial and archaean evolution is now seen as web of interconnected branches with evolutionary lineages that are barely discernable (Doolittle 2004). It doesn't stop there, though. Even eukaryotes are affected by lateral DNA transfer. They have taken over some of the DNA that originally belonged to chloroplasts and mitochondria, both of which evolved from free-living bacteria that became integrated commensally into eukaryote cells. Eukaryote genomes, including the human genome, are also full of retrovirus and retrotransposon remnants. Most of them are genetic junk, but sometimes they prove useful – our immune system apparently started out as a retrotransposon. 'Much of our genetic heritage was contributed by genomic "parasites", a point that Darwin could never have anticipated' (Bushman 2002:170).

Thus linguistic evolution operates much like biological evolution after all. Language change behaves more like evolution among microbes, with its extensive dependence on lateral DNA transfer and its reticulated interrelationships, than like nineteenth-century notions of biological evolution, based as they were on sexually reproducing eukaryotes. The problem isn't inappropriateness of the analogy but instead that it took the genomic revolution in biology to show how apt the analogy is. Figure 12.1 depicts the difference between a traditional Stammbaum tree and a reticulated tree. Perhaps what we need to do is to stop taking family tree relationships and modules as our starting point, filling in the interconnections after we determine the Stammbaum or modular pattern, and instead place interconnectedness on an equal footing with modularity. I will refer to such interconnections as *lateral transfer*.

Lateral transfer can be applied productively to linguistic study on numerous levels. An individual's linguistic development, with influences from many other people and groups, can look much like the reticulation of the right tree in Figure 12.1. On the level of linguistic structure, we discussed several cases

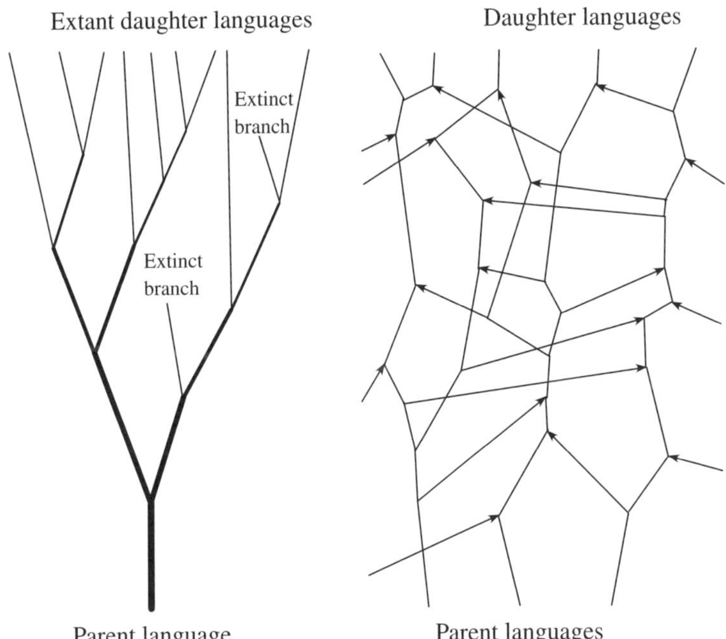

Figure 12.1 A comparison of a traditional Stammbaum tree (left) and a tree with extensive reticulation caused by lateral transfer (right). Arrows indicate lateral transfer between lineages, some of it from languages besides the three at the bottom of the right tree.

in Chapter 9 in which a modular approach fails to give a full or even accurate picture. We looked at several phenomena that lie between the traditionally constituted domains of phonetics and phonology. Such phenomena illustrate how a strict division of labour between phonetics and phonology is untenable. The two domains aren't easily separable into distinct modules, and processes can transfer between them readily.

We also touched on some problems with the concept of the phoneme in Chapter 9. Whether phonemes are actual cognitive entities or just descriptive conveniences has been debated a lot. Lotto and Holt (2000:191) point out that 'structure and organization in behavior need not imply that this structure and organization is present in mental representation'. That is, perception tests may yield results in which phoneme-like categories emerge clearly, but that doesn't mean that phonemes are part of a language user's cognitive structures. Following Pierrehumbert (2003a, 2003b), positional allophones may make better cognitive structures than phonemes. It would seem that this solution only pushes the categorization from phonemes to allophones and still doesn't leave room for lateral transfer. Allophones, though, are more flexible than phonemes. They can evolve rapidly. They can also switch their affiliation with other entities readily. For example, pre-Latin *s developed an allophone *z between vowels, as in **mus* 'mouse, nominative singular', **muzes* 'mice, nominative plural'. Then, however, *z merged into *r, resulting in the classical Latin forms *mus*, *mures*. Moreover, the affiliations of allophones can be unclear. In English, for instance, there is debate over whether the identification of the unaspirated [t] of *steer* should be with the [tʰ] of *tier* or the [d] of *deer*. Another example is that speakers of American English are often unsure whether the vowel in words such as *big* and *think* is the same as the KIT vowel or the FLEECE vowel.

A third issue discussed in Chapter 9 for which a lateral transfer model has advantages over a purely modular model has to do with indexical marking of linguistic forms. One of the biggest advantages of Exemplar Theory is that it assumes simultaneous acquisition of linguistic specifications and social indexical information, along with links between them. That is, every remembered exemplar comes with information about not only how it was pronounced, but also where and by whom. There is no need to propose a separate mechanism for learning social indexicality because it is inherent in the exemplar. The transfer of information between linguistic and social realms is robust and constantly updated. Of course, lateral transfer of phonetic and social information shouldn't be an exclusive property of Exemplar Theory. Prototype Theory can and should be reformulated so that it allows for lateral transfer of social information, too. The mixed model proposed by Pierrehumbert (2006) is one way to do that, but not the only way. You might consider how you could reformulate Prototype Theory to include social indexing.

The connectedness of linguistic and social information brings us to the issues discussed in Chapter 11. Social indexical information involves what people 'know', even latently, about the associations between linguistic forms and demographic groups, speech communities, networks, communities of practice, and individuals. It also includes what language users know about the associations between speaking styles and situations. Speakers use this knowledge to construct and project their identities. A linguistic theory should provide a mechanism for explaining acquisition of such associations for all of this information. Sociolinguistics and cognitive linguistics thus have to be integrated, which is the aim of the cognitive sociolinguistics movement (e.g. Kristiansen 2003, 2008).

A lateral transfer approach to language moves sociolinguistic theory from the margins of linguistic theory as a whole to the centre. Cognitive connections between different kinds of information become crucial. It integrates Saussure's concept of *parole*, which sociolinguistics and the ethnography of speaking first emerged to address, into the heart of grammar. It has often been pointed out that Labov (1972:xiii) stated, 'I have resisted the term *sociolinguistics* for many years, since it implies that there can be a successful linguistic theory or practice which is not social'. He envisioned his work as encompassing both *parole*, the social uses of language and aspects of linguistic structure itself. Linguistic structure appears variously in Saussure's notion of *langue* and in Chomsky's concept of competence, though Chomsky excluded social uses from linguistic structure. Labov (1966:v–vi) explained:

> My own intention was to solve linguistic problems, bearing in mind that these are ultimately problems in the analysis of social behavior: the description of continuous variation, of overlapping and multi-layered phonemic systems; the subjective correlates of linguistic variation; the causes of linguistic differentiation and the mechanism of linguistic change.

That is, the social and structural sides of language are so tightly interwoven, so subject to lateral transfer, that you can't study one without encountering the other. Sociophonetics is a further development of this idea that the social and the structural not only are both integral parts of language, but are in constant communication with each other. Social indexing becomes a cognitive linguistic process, inherent in grammar and in the neurological connections associated with language.

Sociophonetics, with the lateral transfer model, shares with generativism an emphasis on cognition. However, it conceives of cognition much differently. Generativism assumed a modular conception of language. Furthermore, it assumed that the idealization of language as a static system was necessary to discern the cognitive organization of grammar. It isn't the nature of language to be a static system, though. Instead it is to exhibit flexibility and constant flux. Lateral transfer mediates its cognitive connectivity with the ever-changing structures of communities. A view of language incorporating lateral transfer assumes that every aspect of language is psychologically associated both with its linguistic specifications and with the circumstances of its use. Sociophonetics, then, considers specification of social indexing to be every bit as much a part of grammar as specifications for whether a segment is coronal or [±voice]. The constant lateral transfer of new information gives language its flexibility. Modularity is only one part of an adequate theory of language.

Application of lateral transfer between sociolinguistic 'knowledge' and other aspects of language should be applied both to speech production and to speech perception. Harley (2008) argues that speech perception is modular in the sense advanced by Fodor (1983), which is to say that it involves reflexive processes that are necessary because of the fleeting nature of speech signals. Harley contends that speech production isn't reflexive in that sense because it requires more careful planning. Hence it is necessary to approach cognition of production and cognition of perception separately. Two models of speech production are illustrated in Figure 12.2. The model on the left is an older version in which information from a circumscribed semantic conception function moves to the syntactic and lexical/morphological functions, with syntactic specifications also travelling to the lexical/morphological function, and then from the lexicon information passes to a phonology processor, where segments, syllabification and prosody are filled in.[3] The model on the right is much more integrative. There is feedback between different functions, and there are feedback loops within functions (see Harley 2008). Moreover, sociolinguistic information infiltrates the production chain at every step. That is to say, speakers have a sense of the appropriateness of alternative linguistic forms within their repertoires for different situations, and they choose forms that are best for the situation. These choices aren't necessarily conscious decisions. They may occur at a deeper cognitive level, and they can be influenced both by past memories and by accommodation to the interlocutor(s).

Because of its reflexive nature, speech perception operates differently. A number of models for speech perception have been advanced. They differ on various points. One issue has been whether the reflex-like modules are inborn, as Fodor (1983) advocated, or learned. Ingram (2007:127) said that the evidence now available favours acquired modules. Probably the most elementary disagreement concerns symbolic versus connectionist models. Symbolic models

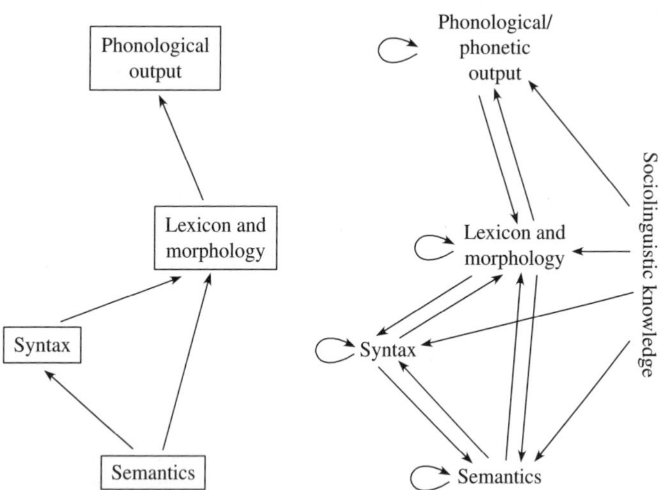

Figure 12.2 Models of speech production without (left) and with (right) extensive feedback, including lateral transfer from sociolinguistic knowledge. The boxes around modules in the left diagram indicate their self-contained nature in that model, in contrast with the feedback in the right model.

have information being coded by the brain into symbols, which are then stored at addresses, where they can be accessed when needed and transported to machinery that can read them (Gallistel and King 2009). The mechanism resembles the way a computer works and is favoured by many generativists. Connectionist models, conversely, have the information contained in the way neurons are wired – that is, how they're connected to each other. Information travels through arrays of neurons, ordinarily in parallel networks. Connectionist models hold sway at present, in part because currently there is no known physiological structure that could host a symbolic mechanism, while connectionist models match what is known about neural networks. The construction of connectionist models has differed. The older TRACE model of McClelland and Elman (1986) featured bidirectional processing – both top-down (that is, word recognition was influenced by the sentence context) and bottom-up (based on phonetic features) – a sequence by which phonetic features were used to identify phonemes, which were then used to identify words, and a localist network of neural connections. More recent models have backed away from top-down processing, eliminated the phonemic identification stage and replaced the localist network with a distributed network (Ingram 2007; Harley 2008). Exemplar Theory, as discussed in Chapter 9, is strongly connectionist. As you recall, it includes extensive specification about phonetic features and about both the speaker and the setting of the exemplar.

The evidence against much top-down (context-dependent) processing that has accumulated and the reflexive nature of speech perception disfavour much influence of sociolinguistic factors on word-level perception. However, the problems with top-down processing are based on a sentential context, and sociophonetic experiments on the effects of sociolinguistic context on perception could be informative. Nevertheless, lateral transfer of information between sociolinguistic knowledge and speech perception undoubtedly occurs in other ways. First, higher-level semantic meanings may be influenced by sociolinguistic context. Second, there is transfer of information from speech perception to sociolinguistic knowledge as the listener absorbs the experiences of hearing speech in a myriad of settings from a wide assortment of people. The means by which listeners internalize this information should be a focus of sociophonetic experimentation. Figure 12.3 contrasts an old model of speech perception with a new model incorporating parallel processing and lateral transfer.[4]

Constituted in this way, sociophonetics offers a couple of advances over earlier sociolinguistic approaches. One is an intensified focus on cognition, which many sociolinguists other than Labov have abandoned, with an eye towards eventual neurolinguistic investigation. The second is a more modern view of phonological structure, incorporating current theories from phonetics and laboratory phonology. Phonetics provides something that can be measured physically and behaviourally, but it also contributes a rich store of its own cognitive theories and evidence for the close binding of social indexicality and linguistic structure.

Sociophonetic studies have often perpetuated a reliance on modularity in that many studies focus on a single variable. The point of Chapter 8 was that a complete sociophonetic study should compare different variables and examine

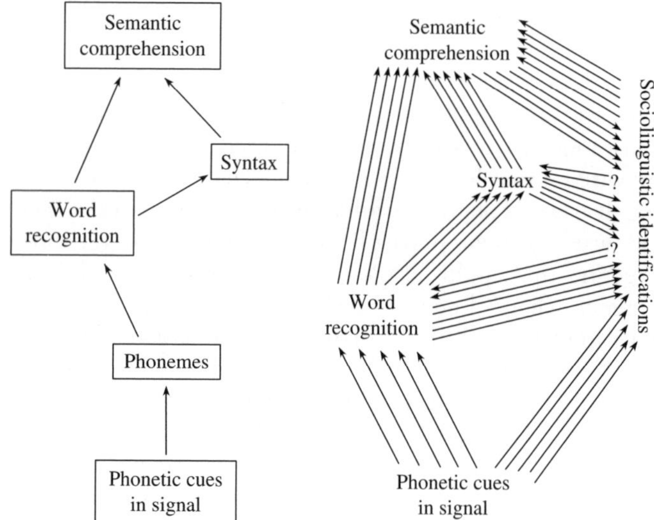

Figure 12.3 Models of speech perception without (left) and with (right) extensive parallel processing. In the right model, a distributed network is assumed, and, in line with distributive models, the phonemic identification stage is eliminated. Lateral transfer to and from sociolinguistic identifications, representing information about both the situation and the speaker, is included.

how they interact, both with each other and with social factors. Chapters 2–7 were intended to give you the tools to examine a range of phonetic variables – not that you should neglect non-phonetic variables, either – so that you have a more complete picture. The very name *sociophonetics* implies that this field ties two seemingly disparate elements, social structure and phonetics, together. Its empirical bases from both sociolinguistics and phonetics allow it to do so. It should not be a vehicle for further partitioning of the object of our study. Integration of these elements will allow us to explore lateral transfer of information connected to language. This integration has been used productively in explaining how and why languages vary and change. It now needs to be brought to bear on the other major question of linguistics, how language is structured in the brain/mind, and in examining how those two overarching questions are themselves related. Sociophonetics is the prime vehicle for this integration.

EXERCISES

1. We saw in Chapter 9 how lateral transfer is inherent in Exemplar Theory. How could Prototype Theory be adapted so that it incorporates lateral transfer of social information as well?

EXERCISES

2. If you were conducting a linguistic study of a community of practice, analysing a variety of linguistic variables, how many ways could lateral transfer be said to affect what you were studying?
3. Outline the major ways that sociophonetics differs from (a) other sociolinguistic approaches and (b) generativism. How does it incorporate phonetic theories?
4. How, from a cognitive perspective, is sociolinguistic knowledge about indexicality integrated into speech production?
5. Construct an experiment that would investigate how lateral transfer of information between word recognition and social indexing works in speech perception. Is it easier to show whether social indexing influences word recognition or vice versa?

FURTHER READING

Harley, Trevor A. 2008. *The Psychology of Language: From Data to Theory*, 3rd edn. Hove, UK/New York: Psychology Press. (See especially Chapters 9 and 15.)

Ingram, John C.L. 2007. *Neurolinguistics: An Introduction to Spoken Language Processing and its Disorders*. Cambridge, UK/New York: Cambridge University Press. (See especially Chapters 4–7.)

Wiener, Linda F. 1987. Of phonetics and genetics: A comparison of classification in linguistic and organic systems. In Henry M. Hoenigswald and Linda F. Wiener (eds), *Biological Metaphor and Cladistic Classification: An Interdisciplinary Perspective*. Philadelphia, PA: University of Pennsylvania Press, 217–26.

Notes

2 Production

1. Some analysis programs, instead of giving you window length settings to modify, will allow you to set the number of 'points' or 'samples': 1,024 points is appropriate for a narrowband spectrogram and 100 points for a wideband spectrogram.

3 Perception

1. The phoneme names used in this chapter, NEAR, SQUARE and MOUTH, are from the system initiated by Wells (1982). They are used more extensively in Chapter 5 and subsequent chapters.

4 Consonants

1. I've borrowed some of the ideas in this section from Foulkes (2005).
2. I'm indebted to Warren Maguire for providing me with the recordings from which Figures 4.31, 4.33, 4.34 and 4.35 were taken.

5 Vowels

1. These speakers are those who show a stage of the 'Northern Cities Shift' (see Chapter 10) in which the vowel of *bad* has not yet become diphthongized. In the fully developed Northern Cities Shift dialect, *bad* shows a clear downglide, but many speakers show earlier stages without the downglide.
2. Thanks to Margaret Maclagan for providing me with the recording of the Cardinal Vowels. I have grouped all the rounded vowels together and all the unrounded vowels together in order to emphasize how rounding affects vowel formant values, even though that's not the conventional way of depicting the Cardinal Vowels.
3. I thank Jaclyn Ocumpaugh for the recording of the Oregon speaker. Whether TRAP and LOT = THOUGHT are tense or lax is debatable. My opinion is that tense and lax don't apply to them because the feature isn't needed for any phonological contrasts for low vowels. In addition, some authors regard THOUGHT as the lax counterpart to GOAT. I think that's a mistaken notion. It's based mostly on the traditional use of /ɔ/, or 'open o', for THOUGHT and of /o/, or 'closed o', for GOAT, much like /ɛ/, or 'open e', is used for DRESS and /e/, or 'closed e', for FACE. It ignores the relationship of STRUT and GOAT as mid non-front vowels that differ in terms of length and degree of diphthongization, the

same way that DRESS and FACE differ from each other. THOUGHT, conversely, is normally about as long as GOAT.

4. The formula for Euclidean distance is

$$\sqrt{(F_{1a} - F_{1b})^2 + (F_{2a} - F_{2b})^2}$$

where F_{1a} is F_1 of point a, F_{1b} is F_1 of point b, F_{2a} is F_2 of point a, and F_{2b} is F_2 of point b. Point a would be the mean value and point b the measurement of the individual token. Euclidean distance can be useful for other things besides finding outliers. For example, it can be used to gauge diphthongal dynamics in F_1/F_2 space or to determine the distance between two vowels or allophones, though normalization is also needed for some such uses.
5. Watt and Fabricius are still working on improvements to their technique, so the formula presented here won't be their final version.
6. I thank Warren Maguire for the recording of the Northern Ireland speaker.

6 Prosody

1. Of course, during the late-nineteenth century, there was a period when there were competing systems for segmental transcription before the IPA became the standard.

7 Voice Quality

1. Henton and Bladon (1985) obtained this result for British English. In North American English, it's worth investigating whether the opposite is happening – that is, has creakiness come to index femininity? Yuasa (2010) found that it has.
2. Actually, nasal formants and antiformants do vary somewhat depending on how open the nasopharyngeal port is. It's just that they don't vary much depending on the particular vowel being produced.

9 Variation and the Cognitive Processing of Sounds

1. Diphthongization of the FACE and GOAT classes in English and of the corresponding long mid-vowels of Dutch is often treated as an underlying phonological property. Nonetheless, it might be best viewed as one of several phonetic cues to the identity of the vowel class.
2. I thank Tom Purnell for introducing me to this controversy.
3. See McLennan et al. (2003) for an experimental study defending abstract phonological levels. Pitt (2009) suggests, like Pierrehumbert, that both lexical and abstract phonological processes are involved.
4. For two other words, *yet* and *yesterday*, forms with the KIT vowel were derived from variants in Old English.
5. As a child, I acquired *am* with a pronunciation that rhymes (when stressed) with *stem*. I was surprised to learn as an adult that almost everybody else rhymes it with *ham*.

10 Sound Change

1. Affrication isn't always considered a fortition. However, intraoral airflow is probably greater for an affricate than for an analogous unaspirated stop.
2. Ganz verkehrt ist es auch, das Eintreten eines Lautwandels immer auf eine besondere Trägheit, Lässigkeit oder Unachtsamkeit zurückzuführen und das Unterbleiben desselben anderswo einer besondern Sorgfalt und Aufmerksamkeit zuzuschreiben.

11 Social Factors and Phonetics

1. I'm thinking of my own grandmothers, who were both rather vernacular.
2. The impasse was ultimately resolved by the fragmentation of the group when they reached high school.
3. Some perceptual dialectology work has involved perception experiments. Preston's (1993) experiment in which subjects heard voices representing a transect from Michigan to Alabama and divided them into categories is an example, as is Williams et al.'s (1999) experiment in which judges rated the Welshness and likability of different voices.

12 Lateral Transfer

1. Jean-Baptiste de Lamarck proposed a model for biological evolution half a century before Charles Darwin. However, he lacked a plausible mechanism for evolution. He proposed that organisms pass on to their offspring traits that they acquire during their lifetimes, which even his own experiments disproved. Darwin's contributions were (a) his proposal that mutations, not acquired traits, are the raw material for evolution and (b) considerable evidence to back that proposal up.
2. The old division of life forms into plants and animals went out of the window a long time ago. Today, plants, animals, fungi, 'protozoa' and other groups that have cell nuclei are recognized as mere branches within one of the major divisions of life, the eukaryotes. Bacteria form another major division, and the less well-known archaeans form the third division.
3. Lexicon and morphology are grouped in Figure 12.2 for convenience. They could easily be separated as well.
4. See Sumner and Samuel (2009) for an experimental study on the perception and cognition of dialectal variants that seems to support an exemplar (and thus connectionist) model.

References

Abercrombie, David. 1967. *Elements of General Phonetics*. Edinburgh: Edinburgh University Press.

Adank, Patti, Roel Smits and Roeland van Hout. 2004. A comparison of vowel normalization procedures for language variation research. *Journal of the Acoustical Society of America* 116:3009–107.

Adank, Patti, Roeland van Hout and Hans van de Velde. 2007. An acoustic description of the vowels of northern and southern standard Dutch II: Regional varieties. *Journal of the Acoustical Society of America* 121:1130–41.

Addington, David W. 1968. The relationship of selected vocal characteristics to personality perception. *Speech Monographs* 35:492–503.

Anderson, Peter M. 1987. *A Structural Atlas of the English Dialects*. London: Croom Helm.

Arvaniti, Amalia and Gina Garding. 2007. Dialectal variation in the rising accents of American English. In Jennifer Cole and José Ignacio Hualde (eds), *Laboratory Phonology 9*. Berlin/New York: Mouton de Gruyter, 547–75.

Arvaniti, Amalia, D. Robert Ladd and Ineke Mennen. 1998. Stability of tonal alignment: The case of Greek prenuclear accents. *Journal of Phonetics* 26:3–25.

Ash, Sharon. 1988. Speaker identification in sociolinguistics and criminal law. In Kathleen Ferrara, Becky Brown, Keith Walters and John Baugh (eds), *Linguistic Change and Contact (Proceedings of the Sixteenth Annual Conference on New Ways of Analyzing Variation in Language)*. Texas linguistic forum 30. Austin: Department of Linguistics, University of Texas, 25–33.

Asu, Eva Liina and Francis Nolan. 2006. Estonian and English rhythm: A two-dimensional quantification based on syllables and feet. In *Proceedings of Speech Prosody 2006, Dresden, Germany*. http://aune.lpl.univ-aix.fr/~sprosig/sp2006/

Atal, B.S. and Suzanne L. Hanauer. 1971. Speech analysis and synthesis by linear predictive coding of the speech wave. *Journal of the Acoustical Society of America* 50:637–55.

Atterer, Michaela and D. Robert Ladd. 2004. On the phonetics and phonology of 'segmental anchoring' of *F0*: Evidence from German. *Journal of Phonetics* 32:177–97.

Baayen, R.H. 2008. *Analyzing Linguistic Data: A Practical Introduction to Statistics Using R*. Cambridge, UK: Cambridge University Press.

Bailey, Guy, Tom Wikle, Jan Tillery and Lori Sand. 1991. The apparent time construct. *Language Variation and Change* 3:241–64.

Bailey, Guy, Tom Wikle, Jan Tillery and Lori Sand. 1993. Some patterns of linguistic diffusion. *Language Variation and Change* 5:359–90.

Ball, Peter and Howard Giles. 1988. Speech style and employment selection: The matched guise technique. In Glynis M. Breakwell, Hugh Foot and Robin Gilmour (eds), *Doing Social Psychology: Laboratory and Field Exercises*. Cambridge: Cambridge University Press, 121–49.

Baranowski, Maciej. 2007. *Phonological Variation and Change in the Dialect of Charleston, South Carolina*. Publication of the American Dialect Society 92. Durham, NC: Duke University Press.

Bauer, Matt and Frank Parker. 2008. /æ/-raising in Wisconsin English. *American Speech* 83:403–31.

Bauer, Robert S., Cheung Kwan-Hin and Cheung Pak-Man. 2003. Variation and merger of the rising tones in Hong Kong Cantonese. *Language Variation and Change* 15:211–25.

Beckman, Mary E. and Gayle Ayers Elam. 1997. Guidelines for ToBI labelling. Version 3.0. http://www.ling.ohio-state.edu/~tobi/ame_tobi/labelling_guide_v3.pdf

Beckman, Mary E. and Julia Hirschberg. 1994. The ToBI annotation conventions. Online typescript. http://www.ling.ohio-state.edu/~tobi/ame_tobi/annotation_conventions.html

Beckman, Mary E., Manuel Díaz-Campos, Julia Tevis McGory and Terrell A. Morgan. 2002. Intonation across Spanish, in the Tone and Break Indices framework. *Probus* 14:9–36.

Beckman, Mary E., Julia Hirschberg and Stephanie Shattuck-Hufnagel. 2005. The original ToBI system and the evolution of the ToBI framework. In Sun-Ah Jun (ed.), *Prosodic Typology: The Phonology of Intonation and Phrasing*. Oxford, UK: Oxford University Press, 9–54.

Bell, Allan. 1984. Language style as audience design. *Language in Society* 13:145–204.

Bell, Allan. 2001. Back in style: Reworking audience design. In Penelope Eckert and John R. Rickford (eds), *Style and Sociolinguistic Variation*. Cambridge, UK: Cambridge University Press, 139–69.

Bezooijen, Renée van. 1988. The relative importance of pronunciation, prosody and voice quality for the attribution of social status and personality characteristics. In Roeland van Hout and Uus Knops (eds), *Language Attitudes in the Dutch Language Area*. Dordrecht: Foris, 85–103.

Bezooijen, Renée van and Rob van den Berg. 1999. Word intelligibility of language varieties in the Netherlands and Flanders under minimal conditions. In René Kager and Renée van Bezooijen (eds), *Linguistics in the Netherlands 1999*. Amsterdam: John Benjamins, 1–12.

Bezooijen, Renée van and Charlotte Gooskens. 1999. Identification of language varieties: The contribution of different linguistic levels. *Journal of Language and Social Psychology* 18:31–48.

Birkner, Karin. 2004. List intonation of German and Portuguese bilinguals in South Brazil. In Peter Gilles and Jörg Peters (eds), *Regional Variation in Intonation*. Linguistische Arbeiten 492. Tübingen: Max Niemeyer Verlag, 123–44.

Bladon, R. Anthony W., Catherine G. Henton and J.B. Pickering. 1984. Towards an auditory theory of speaker normalization. *Language and Communication* 4:59–69.

Blevins, Juliette. 2004. *Evolutionary Phonology: The Emergence of Sound Patterns*. Cambridge, UK/New York: Cambridge University Press.

Bloomfield, Leonard. 1933. *Language*. New York: Holt, Rinehart, and Winston.

Boersma, Paul. 1993. Accurate short-term analysis of the fundamental frequency and the harmonics-to-noise ratio of a sampled sound. *Proceedings of the Institute of Phonetic Sciences* 17:97–110.

Boersma, Paul. 1998. Functional phonology: Formalizing the interactions between articulatory and perceptual drives. Ph.D. dissertation, University of Amsterdam.

Boersma, Paul and David Weenink. 2009. Praat: Doing phonetics by computer (Version 5.1.04). Retrieved 29 April 2009 from http://www.praat.org/.

Borzone de Manrique, Ana Maria and Angela Signorini. 1983. Segmental duration and rhythm in Spanish. *Journal of Phonetics* 11:117–28.

Britain, David. 1992. Linguistic change in intonation: The use of high rising terminals in New Zealand English. *Language Variation and Change* 4:77–104.

Browman, Catherine P. and Louis Goldstein. 1989. Articulatory gestures as phonological units. *Phonology* 6:201–51.

Browman, Catherine P. and Louis Goldstein. 1990. Tiers in articulatory phonology, with some implications for casual speech. In John Kingston and Mary E. Beckman (eds), *Papers in Laboratory Phonology I: Beyond the Grammar and Physics of Speech.* Cambridge, UK: Cambridge University Press, 341–76.

Browman, Catherine P. and Louis Goldstein. 1991. Gestural structures: Distinctiveness, phonological processes, and historical change. In Ignatius G. Mattingly and Michael Studdert-Kennedy (eds), *Modularity and the Motor Theory of Speech Perception.* Hillsdale, NJ: Lawrence Erlbaum, 313–38.

Brown, Bruce L., William J. Strong and Alvin C. Rencher. 1972. Acoustic determinants of perceptions of personality from speech. *International Journal of the Sociology of Language* 6:11–32.

Brown, Bruce L., William J. Strong and Alvin C. Rencher. 1974. Fifty-four voices from two: The effects of simultaneous manipulations of rate, mean fundamental frequency and variance of fundamental frequency on ratings of personality from speech. *Journal of the Acoustical Society of America* 55:313–18.

Bucholtz, Mary. 1998. Geek the girl: Language, femininity, and female nerds. In Natasha Warner, Jocelyn Ahlers, Leela Bilmes, Monica Oliver, Suzanne Wertheim and Melinda Chen (eds), *Gender and Belief Systems: Proceedings of the Fourth Berkeley Women and Language Conference, April 19, 20, and 21, 1996*, 119–31. Berkeley, CA: Berkeley Women and Language Group.

Buder, Eugene H. 2000. Acoustic analysis of voice quality: A tabulation of algorithms 1902–1990. In Raymond D. Kent and Martin J. Ball (eds), *Voice Quality Measurement.* San Diego: Thomson Learning Singular, 119–244.

Bush, Clara N. 1967. Some acoustic parameters of speech and their relationships to the perception of dialect differences. *TESOL Quarterly* 1(3):20–30.

Bushman, Frederic. 2002. *Lateral DNA Transfer: Mechanisms and Consequences.* Cold Spring Harbor, NY: Cold Spring Harbor Laboratory Press.

Campione, Estelle and Jean Véronis. 2002. A large-scale multilingual study of silent pause duration. In Bernard Bel and Isabelle Marlien (eds), *Proceedings of Speech Prosody 2002, Aix-en-Provence.* Aix-en-Provence: Laboratoire Parole et Langage, 199–202. http://aune.lpl.univ-aix.fr/sp2002/

Carlson, Rolf and Björn Grandström. 1997. Speech synthesis. In William J. Hardcastle and John Laver (eds), *The Handbook of Phonetic Sciences.* Oxford: Blackwell, 768–88.

Carter, Paul and John Local. 2007. F2 variation in Newcastle and Leeds English liquid systems. *Journal of the International Phonetic Association* 37:183–199.

Cedergren, Henrietta J. 1973. The interplay of social and linguistic factors in Panama. Ph.D. dissertation, Cornell University.

Cedergren, Henrietta J. and David Sankoff. 1974. Variable rules: Performance as a statistical reflection of competence. *Language* 50:333–55.

Chambers, J.K. 1995. *Sociolinguistic Theory: Linguistic Variation and Its Social Significance.* Language in society 22. Oxford, UK/Malden, MA: Blackwell.

Chen, Marilyn Y. 1995. Acoustic parameters of nasalized vowels in hearing-impaired and normal-hearing speakers. *Journal of the Acoustical Society of America* 98:2443–53.

Chen, Marilyn Y. 1996. Acoustic correlates of nasality in speech. Ph.D. dissertation, Massachusetts Institute of Technology.

Chen, Matthew. 1970. Vowel length variation as a function of the voicing of the consonant environment. *Phonetica* 22:129–59.

Cho, Taehong and Peter Ladefoged. 1999. Variations and universals in VOT: Evidence from 18 languages. *Journal of Phonetics* 27:207–29.

Cho, Taehong and James M. McQueen. 2005. Prosodic influences on consonant production in Dutch: Effects of prosodic boundaries, phrasal accent and lexical stress. *Journal of Phonetics* 33:121–57.

Chomsky, Noam. 1965. *Aspects of the Theory of Syntax.* Cambridge, MA: MIT Press.

Chomsky, Noam. 1980. *Rules and Representations.* New York: Columbia University Press.

Chomsky, Noam. 1988. *Language and Problems of Knowledge: The Managua Lectures.* Cambridge, MA: MIT Press.

Chomsky, Noam and Morris Halle. 1968. *The Sound Pattern of English.* New York: Harper and Row.

Clark, Herbert H. and Jean E. Fox Tree. 2002. Using *uh* and *um* in spontaneous speaking. *Cognition* 84:73–111.

Clarke, Sandra, Ford Elms and Amani Youssef. 1995. The third dialect of English: Some Canadian evidence. *Language Variation and Change* 7:209–28.

Clopper, Cynthia G. 2008. Auditory free classification: Methods and analysis. *Behavior Research Methods* 40:575–81.

Clopper, Cynthia G. 2009. Computational methods for normalizing acoustic vowel data for talker differences. *Language and Linguistics Compass* 3:1430–42.

Clopper, Cynthia G. and David B. Pisoni. 2007. Free classification of regional dialects of American English. *Journal of Phonetics* 35:421–38.

Clopper, Cynthia G., David B. Pisoni and Kenneth de Jong. 2005. Acoustic characteristics of the vowel systems of six regional varieties of American English. *Journal of the Acoustical Society of America* 118:1661–76.

Cohen, Antonie, René Collier and Johan 't Hart. 1982. Declination: Construct or intrinsic feature of speech pitch? *Phonetica* 39:254–73.

Colantoni, Laura. 2004. Reinterpreting the CV transition: Emergence of the glide as an allophone of the palatal lateral. In Julie Auger, J. Clancy Clements and Barbara Vance (eds), *Contemporary Approaches to Romance Linguistics: Selected Papers from the 33rd Linguistic Symposium on Romance Languages (LSRL), Bloomington, Indiana, April 2003.* Amsterdam/Philadelphia: John Benjamins, 83–102.

Cole, Jennifer and José Ignacio Hualde (eds). 2007. *Laboratory Phonology 9.* Berlin/New York: Mouton de Gruyter.

Coleman, John. 2002. Phonetic representations in the mental lexicon. In Jacques Durand and Bernard Laks (eds), *Phonetics, Phonology, and Cognition.* Oxford, UK/ New York: Oxford University Press, 96–130.

Cox, Felicity. 1999. Vowel change in Australian English. *Phonetica* 56:1–27.

Cruttenden, Alan. 1997. *Intonation.* Cambridge, UK: Cambridge University Press.

Crystal, Thomas H. and Arthur S. House. 1988. The duration of American-English vowels: An overview. *Journal of Phonetics* 16:263–84.

Cummins, Fred. 2002. Speech rhythm and rhythmic taxonomy. In Bernard Bel and Isabelle Marlien (eds), *Proceedings of Speech Prosody 2002, Aix-en-Provence.* Aix-en-Provence: Laboratoire Parole et Langage, 121–6. http://aune.lpl.univ-aix.fr/sp2002/

Darnell, Michael, Edith Moravcsik, Frederick J. Newmeyer, Michael Noonan and Kathleen M. Wheatley (eds). 1999. *Functionalism and Formalism in Linguistics.* 2 vols. Amsterdam/Philadelphia: John Benjamins.

Darwin, Charles. 1874. *The Descent of Man, and Selection in Relation to Sex*, 2nd edn. New York: A. L. Burt.

Dauer, R.M. 1983. Stress-timing and syllable-timing reanalyzed. *Journal of Phonetics* 11:51–62.

Delattre, Pierre. 1969. An acoustic and articulatory study of vowel reduction in four languages. *International Review of Applied Linguistics in Language Teaching* 7:295–325.

Delattre, Pierre C. and Donald C. Freeman. 1968. A dialect study of American *r*'s by x-ray motion picture. *Linguistics* 44:29–68.

Delattre, Pierre C., Alvin M. Liberman and Franklin S. Cooper. 1955. Acoustic loci and transitional cues for consonants. *Journal of the Acoustical Society of America* 27:769–73.

Dellwo, Volker. 2006. Rhythm and speech rate: A variation coefficient for ΔC. In Pawel Karnowski and Imre Szigeti (eds), *Proceedings of the 38th Linguistic Colloquium, Budapest.* Frankfurt: Peter Lang, 231–41.

Demolin, Didier. 2001. Some phonetic and phonological observations concerning /ʀ/ in Belgian French. In Hans Van de Velde and Roeland van Hout (eds), *'r-atics: Sociolinguistic, Phonetic and Phonological Characteristics of /r/.* Brussels: Etudes & Travaux, 63–73.

Denes, Peter B. 1955. Effect of duration on the perception of voicing. *Journal of the Acoustical Society of America* 27:761–4.

Deschaies-Lafontaine, Denise. 1974. A socio-phonetic study of a Québec French community: Trois-Riviéres. Ph.D. dissertation, University College London.

Deterding, David. 2001. The measurement of rhythm: A comparison of Singapore and British English. *Journal of Phonetics* 29:217–230.

Deterding, David. 2003. An instrumental study of the monophthong vowels of Singapore English. *English World-Wide* 24:1–16.

Dickens, Milton and Granville M. Sawyer. 1952. An experimental comparison of vocal quality among mixed groups of Whites and Negroes. *Southern Speech Journal* 17:178–85.

Di Paolo, Marianna. 1992. Hypercorrection in response to the apparent merger of (ɔ) and (ɑ) in Utah English. *Language and Communication* 12:267–92.

Di Paolo, Marianna and Alice Faber. 1990. Phonation differences and the phonetic content of the tense-lax contrast in Utah English. *Language Variation and Change* 2:155–204.

Disner, Sandra Ferrari. 1980. Evaluation of vowel normalization procedures. *Journal of the Acoustical Society of America* 67:253–61.

Docherty, Gerard J. and Paul Foulkes. 1999. Derby and Newcastle: Instrumental phonetics and variationist studies. In Paul Foulkes and Gerard J. Docherty (eds), *Urban Voices: Accent Studies in the British Isles.* London: Arnold, 47–71.

Docherty, Gerard J. and Paul Foulkes. 2001. Variability in (r) production—instrumental perspectives. In Hans Van de Velde and Roeland van Hout (eds) *'r-atics: Sociolinguistic, phonetic and phonological characteristics of /r/.* Brussels: Etudes & Travaux, 173–84.

Docherty, Gerard J., Paul Foulkes, James Milroy, Leslie Milroy and David Walshaw. 1997. Descriptive adequacy in phonology: A variationist perspective. *Journal of Linguistics* 33:275–310.

Dodsworth, Robin M. 2005. Linguistic variation and sociological consciousness. Ph.D. dissertation, The Ohio State University.

Doolittle, W. Ford. 2004. Bacteria and Archaea. In Joel Cracraft and Michael J. Donoghue (eds), *Assembling the Tree of Life*. Oxford, UK: Oxford University Press, 86–94.

Dorian, Nancy. 1994. Varieties of variation in a very small place: Social homogeneity, prestige norms, and linguistic variation. *Language* 70:631–96.

Dumas, Denis. 1987. *Nos Façons des Parler*. Sillery, Québec: Presses de l'Université du Québec.

Eckert, Penelope. 1989a. *Jocks and Burnouts: Social Identity in the High School*. New York: Teachers College Press.

Eckert, Penelope. 1989b. The whole woman: Sex and gender differences in variation. *Language Variation and Change* 1:245–67.

Eckert, Penelope. 2005. Variation, convention, and social meaning. Paper presented at the annual meeting of the Linguistic Society of America, Oakland, CA, 7 January. Accessed 9 January 2008 from http://www.stanford.edu/~eckert/

Eckert, Penelope and Sally McConnell-Ginet. 1992. Think practically and look locally: Language and gender as community-based practice. *Annual Review of Anthropology* 21:461–90.

Engstrand, Olle. 1988. Articulatory correlates of stress and speaking rate in Swedish VCV utterances. *Journal of the Acoustical Society of America* 83:1863–75.

Esling, John H. 1978. The identification of features of voice quality in social groups. *Journal of the International Phonetic Association* 7:18–23.

Esling, John H. 2000. Crosslinguistic aspects of voice quality. In Raymond D. Kent and Martin J. Ball (eds), *Voice Quality Measurement*. San Diego: Thomson Learning Singular, 25–35.

Esling, John H. and Henry J. Warkentyne. 1993. Retracting of /æ/ in Vancouver English. In Sandra Clarke (ed.), *Focus on Canada*. Varieties of English around the world, General series 11. Amsterdam/Philadelphia: John Benjamins, 229–46.

Espy-Wilson, Carol Y. 1992. Acoustic measures for linguistic features distinguishing the semivowels /w j r l/ in American English. *Journal of the Acoustical Society of America* 92:736–57.

Espy-Wilson, Carol Y., Suzanne E. Boyce, Michael Jackson, Shrikanth Narayanan and Abeer Alwan. 2000. Acoustic modeling of American English /r/. *Journal of the Acoustical Society of America* 108:343–56.

Faber, Alice. 1992. Articulatory variability, categorical perception, and the inevitability of sound change. In G.W. Davis and G.W. Iverson (eds), *Explanation in Historical Linguistics*. Amsterdam/Philadelphia: John Benjamins, 59–75.

Faber, Alice and Marianna Di Paolo. 1995. The discriminability of nearly merged sounds. *Language Variation and Change* 7:35–78.

Fabiani, Monica, Gabriele Gratton and Kara D. Federmeier. 2007. Event-related brain potentials: Methods, theory, and applications. In John T. Cacioppo, Louis G. Tassinary and Gary G. Berntson (eds), *Handbook of Psychophysiology*, 3rd edn. Cambridge: Cambridge University Press, 85–119.

Fabricius, Anne. 2002. Weak vowels in modern RP: An acoustic study of happY-tensing and KIT/schwa shift. *Language Variation and Change* 14:211–37.

Flege, James Emil. 1988. Effects of the speaking rate on tongue position and velocity of movement in vowel production. *Journal of the Acoustical Society of America* 84:901–16.

Flege, James Emil. 1991. Age of learning affects the authenticity of voice-onset time (VOT) in stop consonants produced in a second language. *Journal of the Acoustical Society of America* 89:395–411.

Flege, James Emil and James Hillenbrand. 1984. Limits on phonetic accuracy in foreign language speech production. *Journal of the Acoustical Society of America* 76:708–21.

Fodor, Jerry A. 1983. *The Modularity of Mind: An Essay on Faculty Psychology*. Cambridge, MA: MIT Press.

Forrest, Karen, Gary Weismer, Paul Milenkovic and Ronald N. Dougall. 1988. Statistical analysis of word-initial voiceless obstruents: Preliminary data. *Journal of the Acoustical Society of America* 84:115–23.

Fought, Carmen. 1999. A majority sound change in a minority community: /u/-fronting in Chicano English. *Journal of Sociolinguistics* 3:5–23.

Foulkes, Paul. 2005. Best practices in sociophonetics: Stops. Workshop presented at New Ways of Analyzing Variation 34, New York, 20 October.

Foulkes, Paul and Gerard J. Docherty. 1999. Urban voices: Overview. In Paul Foulkes and Gerard J. Docherty (eds), *Urban Voices: Accent Studies in the British Isles*. London: Arnold, 1–24.

Foulkes, Paul and Gerard J. Docherty. 2000. Another chapter in the story of /r/: 'Labiodental' variants in British English. *Journal of Sociolinguistics* 4:30–59.

Foulkes, Paul and Gerard J. Docherty. 2006. The social life of phonetics and phonology. *Journal of Phonetics* 34:409–38.

Foulkes, Paul and Gerard J. Docherty. 2007. Phonological variation in the English of England. In David Britain (ed.), *Language in the British Isles*, 2nd edn. Cambridge, UK: Cambridge University Press, 52–74.

Fourakis, Marios and Robert Port. 1986. Stop epenthesis in English. *Journal of Phonetics* 14:197–221.

Frazer, Timothy C. 1987. Attitudes toward regional pronunciation. *Journal of English Linguistics* 20:89–100.

Fridland, Valerie. 2000. The Southern Shift in Memphis, Tennessee. *Language Variation and Change* 11:267–85.

Fridland, Valerie. 2003. Network strength and the realization of the Southern Vowel Shift among African Americans in Memphis, Tennessee. *American Speech* 78:3–30.

Fries, Charles C. and Kenneth L. Pike 1949. Coexistent phonemic systems. *Language* 25:29–50.

Gallistel, C.R. and Adam Philip King. 2009. *Memory and the Computational Brain: Why Cognitive Science Will Transform Neuroscience*. Oxford, UK/Malden, MA: Wiley-Blackwell.

Gerstman, Louis J. 1968. Classification of self-normalized vowels. *IEEE Transactions of Audio Electroacoustics* AU-16:78–80.

Gick, Bryan. 2002. The American intrusive *l*. *American Speech* 77:167–83.

Giles, Howard. 1973. Accent mobility: A model and some data. *Anthropological Linguistics* 15:87–105.

Giles, Howard and Philip Smith. 1979. Accommodation theory: Optimal levels of convergence. In Howard Giles and Robert N. St. Clair (eds), *Language and Social Psychology*. Baltimore: University Park Press, 45–65.

Giles, Howard, Klaus R. Scherer and Donald M. Taylor. 1979. Speech markers in social interaction. In Klaus R. Scherer and Howard Giles (eds), *Social Markers in Speech*. Cambridge: Cambridge University Press, 343–88.

Giles, Howard, Nikolas Coupland and Justine Coupland. 1991. Accommodation theory: Communication, context, and consequence. In Howard Giles, Nikolas Coupland and Justine Coupland (eds), *Contexts of Accommodation: Developments in Applied Sociolinguistics*. Cambridge, UK/New York: Cambridge University Press, 1–68.

Giles, S.B. and K.L. Moll. 1975. Cinefluorographic study of selected allophones of /l/. *Phonetica* 31:206–27.

Godinez, Manuel, Jr. 1984. Chicano English phonology: Norms vs. interference phenomena. In Jacob Ornstein-Galicia (ed.), *Form and Function in Chicano English*. Rowley, MA: Newberry, 42–8.

Gordon, Matthew. 2008. Pitch accent timing and scaling in Chickasaw. *Journal of Phonetics* 36:521–35.

Grabe, Esther. 1998. Pitch accent realization in English and German. *Journal of Phonetics* 26:129–43.

Grabe, Esther. 2004. Intonational variation in urban dialects of English spoken in the British Isles. In Peter Gilles and Jörg Peters (eds), *'r-atics: Sociolinguistic, phonetic and phonological characteristics of /r/*. Brussels: Etudes & Travaux, 9–31.

Grabe, Esther, Brechtje Post, Francis Nolan and Kimberley Farrar. 2000. Pitch accent realization in four varieties of British English. *Journal of Phonetics* 28:161–85.

Graff, David, William Labov and Wendell A. Harris. 1986. Testing listeners' reactions to phonological markers of ethic identity: A new method for sociolinguistic research. In David Sankoff (ed.), *Diversity and Diachrony*. Amsterdam studies in the theory and history of linguistic science, series 4: Current issues in linguistic theory 53. Amsterdam/Philadelphia: John Benjamins, 45–58.

Grammont, Maurice. 1933. *Traité de Phonétique*. Paris: Librairie Delgrave.

Greenwood, Donald D. 1961. Critical bandwidth and the frequency coordinates of the basilar membrane. *Journal of the Acoustical Society of America* 33:1344–56.

Grice, Martine, Stefan Baumann and Ralf Benzmüller. 2005a. German intonation in autosegmental-metrical phonology. In Sun-Ah un (ed.), *Prosodic Typology: The Phonology of Intonation and Phrasing*. Oxford, UK: Oxford University Press, 55–83.

Grice, Martine, Mariapaola D'Imperio, Michelina Savino and Cinzia Avesani. 2005b. Strategies for intonation labelling across varieties of Italian. In Sun-Ah Jun (ed.), *Prosodic Typology: The Phonology of Intonation and Phrasing*. Oxford, UK: Oxford University Press, 362–89.

Gries, Stephan Thomas. 2009. *Statistics for Linguistics with R: A Practical Introduction*. Berlin: Mouton de Gruyter.

Grosjean, François. 1980. Comparative studies of temporal variables in spoken and sign languages: Studies in pause distribution. In Hans Dechert and Manfred Raupach (eds), *Temporal Variables in Speech: Studies in Honour of Frieda Goldman-Eisler*. The Hague: Mouton, 307–12.

Guenter, Joshua. 2000. Vowels of California English before /r/, /l/, and /ŋ/. Ph.D. dissertation, University of California at Berkeley.

Guion, Susan Guignard. 1998. The role of perception in the sound change of velar palatalization. *Phonetica* 55:18–52.

Gumperz, John J. 1971. The speech community. In Anwar Dil (ed.), *Language in Social Groups: Essays by John J. Gumperz*. Palo Alto, CA: Stanford University Press, 114–27.

Gussenhoven, Carlos. 2005. Transcription of Dutch Intonation. In Sun-Ah Jun (ed.), *Prosodic Typology: The Phonology of Intonation and Phrasing*. Oxford, UK: Oxford University Press, 118–45.

Gussenhoven, Carlos. 2007. A vowel height split explained: Compensatory listening and speaker control. In Jennifer Cole and José Ignacio Hualde, *Laboratory Phonology 9*. Berlin/New York: Mouton de Gruyter, 145–72.

Gussenhoven, Carlos and Peter van der Vliet. 1999. The phonology of tone and intonation in the Dutch dialect of Venlo. *Journal of Linguistics* 35:99–135.

Gut, Ulrike, Eno-Abasi Urua, Sandrine Adouakou and Dafydd Gibbon. 2002. Rhythm in West African tone languages: A study of Ibibio, Anyi and Ega. In Ulrike Gut and Dafydd Gibbon (eds), *Typology of African Prosodic Systems*. Bielefeld: Bielefeld University, 159–65.

Guy, Gregory, Barbara Horvath, Julia Vonweiler, Elaine Daisley and Inge Rogers. 1986. An intonational change in progress in Australian English. *Language in Society* 15:23–52.

Habick, Timothy. 1980. Sound change in Farmer City: A sociolinguistic study based on acoustic data. Ph.D. dissertation, University of Illinois at Urbana-Champaign.

Hagiwara, Robert. 1995. Acoustic realizations of American /r/ as produced by women and men. UCLA working papers in phonetics 90. Los Angeles: Department of Linguistics, UCLA.

Harley, Trevor A. 2008. *The Psychology of Language: From Data to Theory*, 3rd edn. Hove, UK/ New York: Psychology Press.

Hawkins, Sarah and Noël Nguyen. 2004. Influence of syllable-coda voicing on the acoustic properties of syllable-onset /l/ in English. *Journal of Phonetics* 32:199–231.

Hay, Jennifer and Andrea Sudbury. 2005. How rhoticity became /r/-sandhi. *Language* 81:799–823.

Hay, Jennifer, Paul Warren and Katie Drager. 2006. Factors influencing speech perception in the context of a merger-in-progress. *Journal of Phonetics* 34:458–84.

Hayes, Bruce, Robert Kirchner and Donca Steriade (eds). 2004. *Phonetically Based Phonology*. Cambridge, UK: Cambridge University Press.

Henderson, Alan, Frieda Goldman-Eisler and Andrew Skarbek. 1966. Sequential temporal patterns in spontaneous speech. *Language and Speech* 8:236–42.

Henton, Caroline G. 1988. Creak as a sociophonetic marker. In Larry M. Hyman and Charles N. Li (eds), *Language, Speech, and Mind: Studies in Honour of Victoria A. Fromkin*. London: Croom Helm, 3–29.

Henton, Caroline G. and R. Anthony W. Bladon. 1985. Breathiness in a normal female speaker: Inefficiency versus desirability. *Language and Communication* 5:221–27.

Herold, Ruth. 1990. Mechanisms of merger: The implementation and distribution of the low back merger in eastern Pennsylvania. Ph.D. dissertation, University of Pennsylvania.

Herold, Ruth. 1997. Solving the actuation problem: Merger and immigration in eastern Pennsylvania. *Language Variation and Change* 9:165–89.

Heselwood, Barry and Louise McChrystal. 1999. The effect of age-group and place of L1 acquisition on the realisation of Panjabi stop consonants in Bradford: An acoustic sociophonetic study. *Leeds Working Papers in Linguistics and Phonetics* 7:49–69.

Hewlett, Nigel and Janet Mackenzie Beck. 2006. *An Introduction to the Science of Phonetics*. London: Routledge/Mahwah, NJ: Erlbaum.

Hewlett, Nigel and Monica Rendall. 1998. Rural versus urban accent as an influence on the rate of speech. *Journal of the International Phonetic Association* 28:63–71.

Hillenbrand, James and Robert A. Houde. 1996. Acoustic correlates of breathy vocal quality: Dysphonic voices and continuous speech. *Journal of Speech and Hearing Research* 39:311–21.

Hillenbrand, James, Ronald A. Cleveland and Robert L. Erickson. 1994. Acoustic correlates of breathy vocal quality. *Journal of Speech and Hearing Research* 37:769–78.

Hindle, Donald. 1978. Approaches to vowel normalization in the study of natural speech. In David Sankoff (ed.), *Linguistic Variation: Models and Methods*. New York: Academic, 161–71.

Hindle, Donald. 1980. The social and structural conditioning of vowel variation. Ph.D. dissertation, University of Pennsylvania.

Hirst, Daniel and Albert Di Cristo. 1998. *Intonation Systems: A Survey of Twenty Languages.* Cambridge, UK: Cambridge University Press.

Hock, Hans Henrich. 1991. *Principles of Historical Linguistics,* 2nd edn. Berlin/New York: Mouton de Gruyter.

Hoemeke, Kathryn A. and Randy L. Diehl. 1994. Perception of vowel height: The role of *F1-F0* distance. *Journal of the Acoustical Society of America* 96:661–74.

Hoenigswald, Henry M. 1946. Sound change and linguistic structure. *Language* 22:238–43.

Holmes, Janet and Miriam Meyerhoff. 1999. The community of practice: Theories and methodologies in language and gender research. *Language in Society* 28:173–83.

Hombert, Jean-Marie, John J. Ohala and William G. Ewan. 1979. Phonetic explanations for the development of tones. *Language* 55:37–58.

House, Arthur M. and Grant Fairbanks. 1953. The influence of consonant environment upon the secondary acoustical characteristics of vowels. *Journal of Speech and Hearing Research* 5:38–58.

Hughes, George W. and Morris Halle. 1956. Spectral properties of fricative consonants. *Journal of the Acoustical Society of America* 28:303–10.

Hymes, Dell. 1974. *Foundations in Sociolinguistics: An Ethnographic Approach.* Philadelphia: University of Pennsylvania Press.

Indefrey, Peter and Willem J.M. Levelt. 2004. The spatial and temporal signatures of word production components. *Cognition* 20:101–44.

Ingram, John C.L. 2007. *Neurolinguistics: An Introduction to Spoken Language Processing and Its Disorders.* Cambridge, UK/New York: Cambridge University Press.

International Phonetic Association. 1999. *Handbook of the International Phonetic Association: A Guide to the Use of the International Phonetic Alphabet.* Cambridge, UK: Cambridge University Press.

Iri, Masao. 1959. A mathematical method in phonetics with a special reference to the acoustical structure of Japanese vowels. *Gengo Kenkyu* 35:23–30.

Ito, Rika and Dennis R. Preston. 1998. Identity, discourse, and language variation. *Journal of Language and Social Psychology* 17:465–83.

Iverson, Gregory K. and Joseph C. Salmons. 1995. Aspiration and laryngeal representation in Germanic. *Phonology* 12:369–96.

Iverson, Paul and Patricia K. Kuhl. 1995. Mapping the perceptual magnet effect for speech using signal detection theory and multidimensional scaling. *Journal of the Acoustical Society of America* 97:553–62.

Iverson, Paul and Patricia K. Kuhl. 2000. Perceptual magnet and phoneme boundary effects in speech perception: Do they arise from a common phenomenon? *Perception & Psychophysics* 62:874–86.

Jacewicz, Ewa, Joseph Salmons and Robert A. Fox. 2007. Vowel duration in three American English dialects. *American Speech* 82:367–85.

Jacobi, Irene, Louis C.W. Pols and Jan Stroop. 2007. Dutch diphthong and long vowel realizations as changing socio-economic markers. In Jürgen Trouvain and William J. Barry (eds), *ICPhS XVI, Saarbrücken, Germany, 6–10 August 2007. 16th International Congress of Phonetic Sciences: Book of Abstracts.* Saarbrücken: International Congress of Phonetic Sciences. www.icphs2007.de., 1481–84.

Jaeger, Jeri J. 1986. On the acquisition of abstract representations for English vowels. *Phonology Yearbook* 3:71–97.

Jakobson, Roman. 1962. Kindersprache, Aphasie und allgemeine Lautgesetze. In *Roman Jakobson: Selected Writings, vol. 1: Phonological Studies.* The Hague: Mouton, 328–401.

Janson, Tore. 1983. Sound change in perception and production. *Language* 59:18–34.

Jesus, Luis M.T. and Christine H. Shadle. 2002. A parametric study of the spectral characteristics of European Portuguese fricatives. *Journal of Phonetics* 30:437–64.

Johnson, Keith. 1997. Speech perception without speaker normalization: An exemplar model. In Keith Johnson and John W. Mullennix (eds), *Talker Variability in Speech Processing.* San Diego: Academic, 145–65.

Johnson, Keith. 2003. *Acoustic and Auditory Phonetics*, 2nd edn. Oxford, UK/Malden, MA: Blackwell.

Johnson, Keith. 2008. *Quantitative Methods in Linguistics.* Oxford, UK/Malden, MA: Blackwell.

Johnson, Keith, Elizabeth A. Strand and Mariapaola D'Imperio. 1999. Auditory-visual integration of talker gender in vowel perception. *Journal of Phonetics* 27:359–84.

Johnstone, Barbara. 1996. *The Linguistic Individual: Self-Expression in Language and Linguistics.* Oxford/New York: Oxford University Press.

Jonasson, Jan. 1971. Perceptual similarity and articulatory reinterpretation as a source of phonological innovation. *Papers from the Institute of Linguistics, University of Stockholm (STL-QPSR)* 8:30–42.

Jones, Daniel. 1966. *The Pronunciation of English*, 4th edn. Cambridge, UK: Cambridge University Press.

Jongman, Allard, Sheila E. Blumstein and Aditi Lahiri. 1985. Acoustic properties for dental and alveolar stop consonants: A cross-language study. *Journal of Phonetics* 13:235–51.

Jongman, Allard, Ratree Wayland and Serena Wong. 2000. Acoustic characteristics of English fricatives. *Journal of the Acoustical Society of America* 108:1252–63.

Jun, Sun-Ah. 2005a. Korean intonational phonology and prosodic transcription. In Sun-Ah Jun (ed.), *Prosodic Typology: The Phonology of Intonation and Phrasing.* Oxford, UK: Oxford University Press, 201–29.

Jun, Sun-Ah. 2005b. Prosodic typology. In Sun-Ah Jun (ed.), *Prosodic Typology: The Phonology of Intonation and Phrasing.* Oxford, UK: Oxford University Press, 430–58.

Jun, Sun-Ah (ed.). 2005c. *Prosodic Typology: The Phonology of Intonation and Phrasing.* Oxford, UK: Oxford University Press.

Jun, Sun-Ah and C. Fougeron. 2002. Realizations of accentual phrase in French intonation. *Probus* 14:147–72.

Kalton, Graham. 1983. *Introduction to Survey Sampling.* Quantitative Applications in the Social Sciences 35. Newberry Park, CA/London: Sage Publications.

Keating, Patricia A. 1985. Universal phonetics and the organization of grammars. In Victoria A. Fromkin (ed.), *Phonetic Linguistics: Essays in Honor of Peter Ladefoged.* Orlando, FL: Academic Press, 115–32.

Keating, Patricia A. 1988. The phonology-phonetics interface. In Frederick J. Newmeyer (ed.), *Linguistics: The Cambridge Survey, vol. I. Linguistic Theory: Foundations.* Cambridge, UK: Cambridge University Press, 281–302.

Keating, Patricia A. 1990. Phonetic representations in a generative grammar. *Journal of Phonetics* 18:321–34.

Kendall, Tyler S. 2008. On the history and future of sociolinguistic data. *Language and Linguistics Compass* 2:332–51.

Kendall, Tyler S. 2009. Speech rate, pause, and sociolinguistic variation: An examination through the sociolinguistic archive and analysis project. Ph.D. dissertation, Duke University.

Kent, Ray D. and Charles Read. 2002. *The Acoustic Analysis of Speech*, 2nd edn. Albany, NY: Thomson Learning.

Kerswill, Paul. 1994. *Dialects Converging: Rural Speech in Urban Norway*. Oxford, UK: Clarendon Press.

Kerswill, Paul and Ann Williams. 2000. Mobility versus social class in dialect levelling: New and old towns in England. In Klaus Mattheier (ed.), *Dialect and Migration in a Changing Europe*. Frankfurt am Main: Peter Lang, 3–13.

Kingston, John and Randy L. Diehl. 1994. Phonetic knowledge. *Language* 70:419–54.

Kirk, John M. 1994. Maps: Dialect and language. In *Encyclopedia of Language and Linguistics, vol. 5*, 1st edn. Amsterdam: Elsevier, 2363–77.

Klatt, Dennis H. 1975. Voice onset time, frication, and aspiration in word-initial consonant clusters. *Journal of Speech and Hearing Research* 18:686–706.

Klatt, Dennis R. 1987. Review of text-to-speech conversion for English. *Journal of the Acoustical Society of America* 82:737–93.

Knapp, Andrew G. and James A. Anderson. 1984. Theory of categorization based on distributed memory storage. *Journal of Experimental Psychology* 10:616–37.

Kochanski, Greg, Esther Grabe, John S. Coleman and B.S. Rosner. 2005. Loudness predicts prominence: Fundamental frequency lends little. *Journal of the Acoustical Society of America* 118:1038–54.

Koerner, E.F. Konrad. 1982. The Schleicherian paradigm in linguistics. *General Linguistics* 22:1–39.

Koike, Yasuo. 1973. Application of some acoustic measures for the evaluation of laryngeal dysfunction. *Studia Phonologica* 7:17–23.

Koike, Yasuo, H. Takahashi and T.C. Calcaterra. 1977. Acoustic measures for detecting laryngeal pathology. *Acta Otolaryngologica* 84:105–17.

Komatsu, Masahiko. 2007. Reviewing human language identification. In Christian Müller (ed.), *Speaker Classification II: Selected Projects*. Berlin: Springer-Verlag, 206–28.

Komatsu, Masahiko, Kazuya Mori, Takayuki Arai, Makiko Aoyagi and Yuji Murahara. 2002. Human language identification with reduced segmental information. *Acoustical Science and Technology* 23:143–53.

Kowal, Sabine, Daniel O'Connell and Edward Sabin. 1975. Development of temporal patterning and vocal hesitations in spontaneous narratives. *Journal of Psycholinguistic Research* 4:195–207.

Krapp, George Phillip. 1925. *The English Language in America*, 2 vols. New York: Ungar.

Kreiman, Jody and Bruce Gerratt. 2000. Measuring vocal quality. In Raymond D. Kent and Martin J. Ball (eds), *Voice Quality Measurement*. San Diego: Thomson Learning Singular, 73–101.

Kristiansen, Gitte. 2003. How to do things with allophones: Linguistic stereotypes as cognitive reference points in social cognition. In René Dirven, Roslyn Frank and Martin Pütz (eds), *Cognitive Models in Language and Thought: Ideology, Metaphors and Meanings*. Berlin/New York: Mouton de Gruyter, 69–120.

Kristiansen, Gitte. 2008. Style-shifting and shifting styles: A socio-cognitive approach to lectal variation. In Gitte Kristiansen and René Dirven (eds), *Cognitive Sociolinguistics: Language Variation, Cultural Models, Social Systems*. Berlin/New York: Mouton de Gruyter, 45–88.

Krom, Guus de. 1993. A cepstrum-based technique for determining a harmonics-to-noise ratio in speech signals. *Journal of Speech and Hearing Research* 36:254–66.

Kügler, Frank. 2004. The phonology and phonetics of nuclear rises in Swabian German. In Peter Gilles and Jörg Peters (eds), *Regional Variation in Intonation*. Linguistische Arbeiten 492. Tübingen: Max Niemeyer Verlag, 75–98.

Kuhl, Patricia K. 1991. Human adults and human infants show a 'perceptual magnet effect' for the prototypes of speech categories, monkeys do not. *Perception & Psychophysics* 50:93–107.

Kummer, Ann W. 2001. *Cleft Palate and Craniofacial Anomalies: The Effects on Speech and Resonance.* San Diego, CA: Singular Thomson Learning.

Kutas, Marta, Kara D. Federmeier, Jenny Staab and Robert Kluender. 2007. Language. In John T. Cacioppo, Louis G. Tassinary and Gary G. Berntson (eds), *Handbook of Psychophysiology*, 3rd edn. Cambridge: Cambridge University Press, 555–80.

Labov, William. 1963. The social motivation of a sound change. *Word* 19:273–309.

Labov, William. 1966. *The Social Stratification of English in New York City.* Washington, DC: Center for Applied Linguistics.

Labov, William. 1969. Contraction, deletion, and inherent variability of the English copula. *Language* 45:715–62.

Labov, William. 1972. *Sociolinguistic Patterns.* Conduct and Communication 4. Philadelphia: University of Pennsylvania Press.

Labov, William. 1975. On the use of the present to explain the past. In Luigi Heilmann (ed.), *Proceedings of the Eleventh International Congress of Linguists, Bologna-Florence, August 28–September 2, 1972, vol. 2.* Bologna: Il Mulino, 825–51.

Labov, William. 1980. The social origins of sound change. In William Labov (ed.), *Locating Language in Time and Space.* New York: Academic, 251–65.

Labov, William. 1981. Resolving the Neogrammarian controversy. *Language* 57:267–308.

Labov, William. 1991. The three dialects of English. In Penelope Eckert (ed.), *NewWays of Analyzing Sound Change.* New York: Academic, 1–44.

Labov, William. 1994. *Principles of Linguistic Change, vol. 1: Internal Factors.* Language in Society 20. Oxford, UK/Malden, MA: Blackwell.

Labov, William. 2001. *Principles of Linguistic Change, vol. 2: Social Factors.* Language in Society 29. Oxford, UK/Malden, MA: Blackwell.

Labov, William. 2006. A sociolinguistic perspective on sociophonetic research. *Journal of Phonetics* 34:500–15.

Labov, William and Sharon Ash. 1997. Understanding Birmingham. In Cynthia Bernstein, Thomas Nunnally and Robin Sabino (eds), *Language Variety in the South Revisited.* Tuscaloosa/London: University of Alabama Press, 508–73.

Labov, William, Paul Cohen, Clarence Robins and John Lewis. 1968. *A Study of the Non-Standard English of Negro and Puerto Rican Speakers in New York City.* Report on Cooperative Research Project 3288. New York: Columbia University.

Labov, William, Malcah Yaeger and Richard Steiner. 1972. *A Quantitative Study of Sound Change in Progress.* Philadelphia: U.S. Regional Survey.

Labov, William, Mark Karen and Corey Miller. 1991. Near-mergers and the suspension of phonemic contrast. *Language Variation and Change* 3:33–74.

Labov, William, Sharon Ash and Charles Boberg. 2006. *The Atlas of North American English: Phonetics, Phonology and Sound Change. A Multimedia Reference Tool.* Berlin: Mouton de Gruyter.

Ladd, D. Robert, Dan Faulkner, Hanneke Faulkner and Astrid Schepman. 1999. Constant 'segmental anchoring' of F_0 movements under changes in speech rate. *Journal of the Acoustical Society of America* 106:1543–54.

Ladd, D. Robert, Astrid Schepman, Laurence White, Louise May Quarmby and Rebekah Stackhouse. 2009. Structural and dialectal effects on pitch peak alignment in two varieties of British English. *Journal of Phonetics* 37:145–61.

Ladefoged, Peter. 2001. *A Course in Phonetics*, 4th edn. New York/ Orlando: Harcourt Brace.

Ladefoged, Peter and Ian Maddieson. 1996. *The Sounds of the World's Languages*. Oxford, UK/Malden, MA: Blackwell.

Laeufer, Christiane. 1992. Patterns of voicing-conditioned vowel duration in French and English. *Journal of Phonetics* 20:411–40.

Lakoff, George. 1987. *Women, Fire, and Dangerous Things: What Categories Reveal about the Mind*. Chicago/London: University of Chicago Press.

Lambert, Wallace E., R.C. Hodgsen, R.D. Gardner and S. Fillenbaum. 1960. Evaluational reaction to spoken language. *Journal of Abnormal and Social Psychology* 60:44–51.

Langacker, Ronald W. 2008. *Cognitive Grammar: A Basic Introduction*. Oxford, UK: Oxford University Press.

Lass, Norman J., Pamela J. Mertz and Karen L. Kimmel. 1978. The effect of temporal speech alterations on speaker race and sex identifications. *Language and Speech* 21:279–90.

Lave, Jean and Etienne Wenger. 1991. *Situated Learning: Legitimate Peripheral Participation*. Cambridge/New York: Cambridge University Press.

Laver, John. 1980. *The Phonetic Description of Voice Quality*. Cambridge: Cambridge University Press.

Lavoie, Lisa M. 2001. *Consonant Strength: Phonological Patterns and Phonetic Manifestations*. New York/London: Garland Publishing.

Lehiste, Ilse. 1988. *Lectures on Language Contact*. Cambridge, MA/London: MIT Press.

Lehiste, Ilse and Gordon E. Peterson. 1961. Transitions, glides, and diphthongs. *Journal of the Acoustical Society of America* 33:268–77.

Lehmann, Winfred P. 1962. *Historical Linguistics: An Introduction*. New York: Holt, Rinehart, and Winston.

Lemmetty, Sami. 1999. Review of speech synthesis technology. Master's thesis, Helsinki University of Technology. http://acoustics.hut.fi/publications/files/theses/lemmetty_mst/thesis.pdf

Liberman, Alvin M. and Ignatius G. Mattingly. 1985. The motor theory of speech perception revised. *Cognition* 21:1–36.

Lickley, Robin J., Astrid Schepman and D. Robert Ladd. 2005. Alignment of 'phrase accent' lows in Dutch falling rising questions: Theoretical and methodological implications. *Language and Speech* 48:157–83.

Lieberman, Philip and Sheila E. Blumstein. 1988. *Speech Physiology, Speech Perception, and Acoustic Phonetics*. Cambridge, UK/New York: Cambridge University Press.

Liljencrants, Johan and Björn Lindblom. 1972. Numerical simulation of vowel quality systems: The role of perceptual contrast. *Language* 48:839–62.

Lindau, Mona. 1978. Vowel features. *Language* 54:541–63.

Lindau, Mona. 1985. The story of /r/. In Victoria Fromkin (ed.), *Phonetic Linguistics: Essays in Honor of Peter Ladefoged*. Orlando, FL: Academic Press, 157–68.

Lindblom, Björn. 1963. Spectrographic study of vowel reduction. *Journal of the Acoustical Society of America* 35:1773–81.

Lindblom, Björn. 1986. Phonetic universals in vowel systems. In John J. Ohala and Jeri J. Jaeger (eds), *Experimental Phonology* Orlando, FL: Academic Press, 13–44.

Lindblom, Björn. 1990. Explaining phonetic variation: A sketch of the H&H theory. In William J. Hardcastle and Alain Marchal (eds), *Speech Production and Speech Modelling*. Dordrecht: Kluwer, 403–39.

Lindblom, Björn E.F. and Michael Studdert-Kennedy. 1967. On the role of formant transitions in vowel recognition. *Journal of the Acoustical Society of America* 42:830–43.

Lindblom, Björn E.F. and John E.F. Sundberg. 1971. Acoustical consequences of lip, tongue, jaw, and larynx movement. *Journal of the Acoustical Society of America* 50:1166–79.

Lindblom, Björn E.F., Susan Guion, Susan Hura, Seung-Jae Moon and Raquel Willerman. 1995. Is sound change adaptive? *Rivista di Linguistica* 7:5–37.

Lippi-Green, Rosina L. 1989. Social network integration and language change in progress in a rural Alpine village. *Language in Society* 18:213–34.

Lisker, Leigh. 1986. 'Voicing' in English: A catalogue of acoustic features signaling /b/ versus /p/ in trochees. *Language and Speech* 29:3–11.

Lisker, Leigh and Arthur Abramson. 1964. A cross-language study of voicing in initial stops. *Word* 20:384–422.

Lloyd James, Arthur. 1940. *Speech Signals in Telephony.* London: Pitman.

Lobonov, B.M. 1971. Classification of Russian vowels spoken by different listeners. *Journal of the Acoustical Society of America* 49:606–08.

Loman, Bengt. 1975. Prosodic patterns in a Negro American dialect. In Håkan Ringbom, Alfhild Ingberg, Ralf Norrman, Kurt Nyholm, Rolf Westman and Kay Wikberg (eds), *Style and text: Studies presented to Nils Erik Enkvist.* Stockholm: Språkförlaget Skriptor AB, 219–42.

Lotto, Andrew J. and Lori L. Holt. 2000. The illusion of the phoneme. In S.J. Billings, J.P. Boyle and A.M. Griffith (eds), *Chicago Linguistic Society, Volume 35: The Panels.* Chicago: Chicago Linguistic Society, 191–204.

Lotto, Andrew J., Keith R. Kluender and Lori L. Holt. 1998. Depolarizing the perceptual magnet effect. *Journal of the Acoustical Society of America* 103:3648–54.

Low, Ee Ling and Esther Grabe. 1995. Prosodic patterns in Singapore English. In Kjell Elenius and Peter Branderud (eds), *Proceedings of the XIIIth International Congress of Phonetic Sciences, vol. 3.*. Stockholm: KTH and Stockholm University, 636–39.

Low, Ee Ling, Esther Grabe and Francis Nolan. 2000. Quantitative characterizations of speech rhythm: Syllable-timing in Singapore English. *Language and Speech* 43:377–401.

Macauley, Ronald K.S. 1977. *Language, Social Class, and Education: A Glasgow Study.* Edinburgh: Edinburgh University Press.

Maclagan, Margaret A. 1982. An acoustic study of New Zealand English vowels. *New Zealand Speech Therapists' Journal* 37:20–26.

Maclagan, Margaret A., Catherine I. Watson, Ray Harlow, Jeanette King and Peter Keegan. 2009. /u/ fronting and /t/ aspiration in Māori and New Zealand English. *Language Variation and Change* 21:175–92.

Maher, John P. 1966. More on the history of the comparative method: The tradition of Darwinism in August Schleicher's work. *Anthropological Linguistics* 8(3):1–12.

Mallinson, Christine. 2006. The dynamic construction of race, class, and gender through linguistic practice among women in a Black Appalachian community. Ph.D. dissertation, North Carolina State University.

Maniwa, Kazumi, Allard Jongman and Travis Wade. 2009. Acoustic characteristics of clearly spoken English fricatives. *Journal of the Acoustical Society of America* 125:3962–73.

Markel, John D. and Augustine H. Gray, Jr. 1976. *Linear Prediction of Speech.* New York: Springer-Verlag.

Martinet, André. 1952. Function, structure, and sound change. *Word* 8:1–32.

Mattheier, Klaus (ed.). 2000. *Dialect and Migration in a Changing Europe.* Vario Lingua 12. Frankfurt am main: Peterlang.

Mayo, Catherine J. 1996. Prosodic transcription of Glasgow English: An evaluation study of GlaToBI. Master's thesis, University of Edinburgh.

McClelland, James L. and Jeffrey L. Elman. 1986. The TRACE model of speech perception. *Cognitive Psychology* 18:1–86.

McClure, J. Derrick. 1995. The vowels of Scottish English: Formants and features. In Jack Windsor Lewis (ed.), *Studies in General and English Phonetics: Essays in Honour of Professor J. D. O'Connor*. London/New York: Routledge, 367–78.

McGurk, Harry and John McDonald. 1976. Hearing lips and seeing voices. *Nature* 264:746–48.

McLennan, Conor T., Paul A. Luce and Jan Charles-Luce. 2003. Representation of lexical form. *Journal of Experimental Psychology: Learning, Memory, and Cognition* 29:539–53.

Medin, Douglas L. and Lawrence W. Barsalou. 1987. Categorization processes and categorical perception. In Stevan Harnad (ed.), *Categorical Perception: The Groundwork of Cognition*. Cambridge, UK: Cambridge University Press, 455–90.

Mesthrie, Rajend, Joan Swann, Andrea Deumert and William L. Leap. 2000. *Introducing Sociolinguistics*. Amsterdam/Philadelphia: John Benjamins.

Meyerhoff, Miriam. 2002. Communities of practice. In J.K. Chambers, Peter Trudgill and Natalie Schilling-Estes (eds), *The Handbook of Language Variation and Change*. Oxford, UK/Malden, MA: Blackwell, 526–48.

Meyerhoff, Miriam. 2006. *Introducing Sociolinguistics*. London: Routledge.

Mielke, Jeff, Adam Baker and Diana Archangeli. 2005. Tracing the tongue with GLoSsatron. Paper presented at Ultrafest 3, Tucson, AZ. http://aix1.uottawa.ca/~jmielke/

Miller, George A. and Patricia E. Nicely. 1955. An analysis of perceptual confusions among some English consonants. *Journal of the Acoustical Society of America* 27:338–52.

Miller, James D. 1989. Auditory-perceptual interpretation of the vowel. *Journal of the Acoustical Society of America* 85:2114–34.

Miller, M. 1984. On the perception of rhythm. *Journal of Phonetics* 19:231–48.

Milroy, Lesley. 1980. *Language and Social Networks*. Oxford, UK/Malden, MA: Blackwell.

Milroy, Lesley. 1987. *Language and Social Networks*, 2nd edn. Language in Society series 2. Oxford, UK/Malden, MA: Blackwell.

Mochizuki-Sudo, Michiko and Shigeri Kiritani. 1991. Production and perception of stress-related durational patterns in Japanese learners of English. *Journal of Phonetics* 19:231–48.

Moon, Seung-Jae and Björn Lindblom. 1994. Interaction between duration, context, and speaking style in English stressed vowels. *Journal of the Acoustical Society of America* 96:40–55.

Moulton, William G. 1962. Dialect geography and the concept of phonological space. *Word* 18:23–32.

Mukherjee, Joybrato. 2000. Speech is silver, but silence is golden: Some remarks on the function(s) of pauses. *Anglia* 118:571–84.

Munro, Murray J., Tracey M. Derwing and James E. Flege. 1999. Canadians in Alabama: A perceptual study of dialect acquisition in adults. *Journal of Phonetics* 27:385–403.

Myers, Scott. 1999. Tone association and F_0 timing in Chichewa. *Studies in African Linguistics* 28:215–239.

Nagy, Naomi and Bill Reynolds. 1997. Optimality Theory and variable word-final deletion in Faetar. *Language Variation and Change* 9:37–55.

Narayanan, Shrikanth S., Abeer A. Alwan and Katherine Haker. 1997. Toward articulatory-acoustic models for liquid approximants based on MRI and EPG data. Part I. The laterals. *Journal of the Acoustical Society of America* 101:1064–77.

Nearey, Terrance M. 1977. Phonetic Feature Systems for Vowels. Ph.D. dissertation, University of Alberta. Reprinted 1978 by the Indiana University Linguistics Club.

Nearey, Terrance M. and Peter F. Assmann. 1986. Modeling the role of inherent spectral change in vowel identification. *Journal of the Acoustical Society of America* 80:1297–1308.

Nguyen, Thi Anh Thu. 2003. Prosodic transfer: The tonal constraints on Vietnamese acquisition of English stress and rhythm. Unpublished Ph.D. dissertation, University of Queensland.

Niedzielski, Nancy. 1999. The effect of social information on the perception of sociolinguistic variables. *Journal of Language and Social Psychology* 18:62–85.

Nittrouer, Susan. 2004. The role of temporal and dynamic signal components in the perception of syllable-final stop voicing by children an adults. *Journal of the Acoustical Society of America* 115:1777–90.

Nolan, Francis. 1983. *The Phonetic Bases of Speaker Recognition*. Cambridge, UK/New York: Cambridge University Press.

Noll, A. Michael. 1967. Cepstral pitch determination. *Journal of the Acoustical Society of America* 41:293–309.

O'Cain, Raymond K. 1977. A diachronic view of the speech of Charleston, South Carolina. In David L. Shores and Carole P. Hinds (eds), *Papers in Language Variation: SAMLA-ADS Collection.*Tuscaloosa: University of Alabama Press, 135–50.

Ocumpaugh, Jaclyn. 2001. The variable chapter in the story of R: An acoustic analysis of a shift in final and pre-consonantal instances of American /r/ production in Louisburg, North Carolina. Unpublished M.A. thesis, North Carolina State University.

Odlin, Terence. 1989. *Language Transfer: Cross-Linguistic Influence in Language Learning.* Cambridge, UK/New York: Cambridge University Press.

Ohala, John J. 1974a. Experimental historical phonology. In J.M. Anderson and Charles Jones (eds), *Historical Linguistics II: Theory and Description in Phonology. Proceedings of the First International Conference on Historical Linguistics, Edinburgh, 2–7 September 1973*, 353–89.

Ohala, John J. 1974b. Phonetic explanation in phonology. In Anthony Bruck, Robert Allen Fox and Michael W. LaGaly (eds), *Papers from the Parasession on Natural Phonology, April 18, 1974*. Chicago: Chicago Linguistics Society, 251–74.

Ohala, John J. 1981a. Articulatory constraints on the cognitive representation of speech. In Terry Meyers, John Laver and John Anderson (eds), *The Coginitive Representation of Speech*. Amsterdam/New York: North-Holland, 111–27.

Ohala, John J. 1981b. The listener as a source of sound change. In Carrie S. Masek, Roberta A. Hendrick and Mary Frances Miller (eds), *Papers from the Parasession on Language and Behavior. Chicago Linguistic Society, May 1–2, 1981*. Chicago: Chicago Linguistic Society, 178–203.

Ohala, John J. 1986. Phonological evidence for top-down processing in speech perception. In Joseph S. Perkell and Dennis H. Klatt (eds), *Invariance and Variability in Speech Processes*. Hillsdale, NJ: Lawrence Erlbaum, 386–401.

Ohala, John J. 1989. Sound change is drawn from a pool of synchronic variation. In Leiv Egil Breivik and Ernst Håkon Jahr (eds), *Language Change: Contributions to the Study of Its Causes*. Berlin/New York: Mouton de Gruyter, 173–98.

Ohala, John J. 1990. There is no interface between phonology and phonetics: A personal view. *Journal of Phonetics* 18:153–71.

Ohala, John J. 1993a. Coarticulation and phonology. *Language and Speech* 36:155–70.

Ohala, John J. 1993b. The phonetics of sound change. In Charles Jones (ed.), *Historical Linguistics: Problems and Perspectives*. London: Longman, 237–78.

Ohala, John J. and Deborah Feder. 1994. Listeners' normalization of vowel quality is influenced by 'restored' consonantal context. *Phonetica* 51:111–18.

Osthoff, Hermann and Karl Brugmann. 1967. Morphologische Untersuchungen auf den Gebiete der indogermanischen Sprachen, I. In Winfred P. Lehmann (ed. and tr.), *A Reader in Nineteenth-Century Historical Indo-European Linguistics*. Bloomington: Indiana University Press. Originally published 1878 as *Morphologische Untersuchungen auf dem Gebiete der indogermanischen Sprachen*. Leipzig: S. Hirzel.

Parker, Ellen M., Randy L. Diehl and Keith R. Kleunder. 1986. Trading relations in speech and nonspeech. *Perception & Psychophysics* 39:129–42.

Parthasarathy, Vijay, Jerry L. Prince, Maureen Stone, Emi Z. Murano and Moriel NessAiver. 2007. Measuring tongue motion from tagged cine-MRI using harmonic phase (HARP) processing. *Journal of the Acoustical Society of America* 121:491–504.

Paul, Hermann. 1898. *Prinzipien der Sprachgeschichte*, 3rd edn. Tübingen: Max Niemeyer.

Pederson, Lee A., Susan Leas McDaniel, Guy Bailey, Marvin H. Basset, Carol M. Adams, Caisheng Liao and Michael B. Montgomery (eds). 1986–92. *The Linguistic Atlas of the Gulf States*. 7 vols. Athens: University of Georgia Press.

Peeters, Wilhelmus Johannes Maria. 1991. Diphthong dynamics: A cross-linguistic perceptual analysis of temporal patterns in Dutch, English, and German. Ph.D. dissertation, Rijksuniversiteit te Utrecht.

Percival, W. Keith. 1987. Biological analogy in the study of language before the advent of comparative grammar. In Henry M. Hoenigswald and Linda F. Wiener (eds), *Biological Metaphor and Cladistic Classification: An Interdisciplinary Perspective*. Philadelphia: University of Pennsylvania Press, 3–38.

Peterson, Gordon E. and Harold L. Barney. 1952. Control methods used in a study of vowels. *Journal of the Acoustical Society of America* 24:175–84.

Peterson, Gordon E. and Ilse Lehiste. 1960. Duration of syllable nuclei in English. *Journal of the Acoustical Society of America* 32:693–703.

Pierrehumbert, Janet B. 2003a. Phonetic diversity, statistical learning, and acquisition of phonology. *Language and Speech* 46:115–54.

Pierrehumbert, Janet B. 2003b. Probabilistic phonology: Discrimination and robustness. In Rens Bod, Jennifer Hay and Stefanie Jannedy (eds), *Probabilistic Linguistics*. Cambridge, MA: MIT Press, 177–228.

Pierrehumbert, Janet B. 2006. The next toolkit. *Journal of Phonetics* 34:516–30.

Pike, Kenneth L. 1945. *The Intonation of American English*. Ann Arbor: University of Michigan Press.

Pisoni, David B. 1997. Some thoughts on 'normalization' in speech perception. In Keith Johnson and John W. Mullenix (eds), *Talker Variability in Speech Processing*. San Diego: Academic, 9–32.

Pitt, Mark A. 2009. How are pronunciation variants of spoken words recognized? A test of generalization to newly learned words. *Journal of Memory and Language* 61:19–36.

Podesva, Robert J., Sarah J. Roberts and Kathryn Campbell-Kibler. 2002. Sharing resources and indexing meanings in the production of gay styles. In Kathryn Campbell-Kibler,

Robert J. Podesva, Sarah J. Roberts and Andrew Wong (eds), *Language and Sexuality: Contesting Meaning in Theory and Practice*. Stanford, CA: CSLI Publications, 175–89.

Popperwell, R.G. 1963. *The Pronunciation of Norwegian*. Cambridge, UK: Cambridge University Press/Oslo: Oslo University Press.

Preston, Dennis R. 1993. Folk dialectology. In Dennis R. Preston (ed.), *American Dialect Research*. Amsterdam/Philadelphia: John Benjamins, 333–77.

Preston, Dennis R. (ed.). 1999. *Handbook of Perceptual Dialectology, vol. 1*. Amsterdam/ Philadelphia: John Benjamins.

Prieto, Pilar, Jan van Santen and Julia Hirschberg. 1995. Tonal alignment patterns in Spanish. *Journal of Phonetics* 23:429–51.

Pruthi, Tarun. 2007. Analysis, vocal-tract modeling and automatic detection of vowel nasalization. Ph.D. dissertation, University of Maryland at College Park.

Pruthi, Tarun and Carol Y. Espy-Wilson. 2007. Acoustic parameters for the automatic detection of vowel nasalization. In *Proceedings of Interspeech 2007*. Antwerp, Belgium, 1925–8.

Purnell, Thomas C. 2008. Prevelar raising and phonetic conditioning: Role of labial and anterior tongue gestures. *American Speech* 83:373–402.

Purnell, Thomas C. 2009. Phonetic influence on phonological operations. In Eric Raimy and Charles Cairns (eds), *Contemporary Views on Architecture and Representations in Phonological Theory*. Cambridge, MA: MIT Press, 337–54.

Purnell, Thomas, William Idsardi and John Baugh. 1999. Perceptual and phonetic experiments on American English dialect identification. *Journal of Language and Social Psychology* 18:10–30.

Purnell, Thomas, Joseph Salmons and Dilara Tepeli. 2005a. German substrate effects in Wisconsin English: Evidence for final fortition. *American Speech* 80:135–64.

Purnell, Thomas, Joseph Salmons, Dilara Tepeli and Jennifer Mercer. 2005b. Structured heterogeneity and change in laryngeal phonetics: Upper Midwestern final obstruents. *Journal of English Linguistics* 33:307–38.

Queen, Robin M. 2001. Bilingual intonation patterns: Evidence of language change from Turkish-German bilingual children. *Language in Society* 30:55–80.

Quené, Hugo. 2008. Multilevel modeling of between-speaker and within-speaker variation in spontaneous speech tempo. *Journal of the Acoustical Society of America* 123:1104–13.

Rae, Megan and Paul Warren. 2002. Goldilocks and the three beers: Sound merger and word recognition in NZE. *New Zealand English Journal* 16:33–41.

Ramus, Franck. 2002. Acoustic correlates of linguistic rhythm: Perspectives. In Bernard Bel and Isabelle Marlien (eds), *Proceedings of Speech Prosody 2002, Aix-en-Provence*. Aix-en-Provence: Laboratoire Parole et Langage, 115–20. http://aune.lpl.univ–aix.fr/ sp2002/

Ramus, Franck, Marina Nespor and Jacques Mehler. 1999. Correlates of linguistic rhythm in the speech signal. *Cognition* 73:265–92.

Ray, George B. and Christopher J. Zahn. 1990. Regional speech rates in the United States: A preliminary analysis. *Communication Speech Reports* 7:34–7.

Recasens, Daniel. 1996. An articulatory-perceptual account of vocalization and elision of dark /l/ in the Romance languages. *Language and Speech* 39:63–89.

Recasens, Daniel and Aina Espinosa. 2005. Articulatory, positional and coarticulatory characteristics for clear /l/ and dark /l/: Evidence from two Catalan dialects. *Journal of the International Phonetic Association* 35:1–25.

Recasens, Daniel, Jordi Fontdevila and Maria Dolors Pallarés. 1995. Velarization degree and coarticulatory resistance for /l/ in Catalan and German. *Journal of Phonetics* 23:37–52.

Reetz, Henning and Allard Jongman. 2009. *Phonetics: Transcription, Production, Acoustics, and Perception*. Blackwell Textbooks in Linguistics 22. Oxford, UK/Malden, MA: Blackwell.

Repp, Bruno H. 1982. Phonetic trading relations and context effects: New experimental evidence for a speech mode of perception. *Psychological Bulletin* 92:81–110.

Rietveld, Toni and Rouland van Hout. 2005. *Statistics in Language Research: Analysis of Variance*. Berlin: Mouton de Gruyter.

Roach, Peter. 1982. On the distinction between 'stress-timed' and 'syllable-timed' languages. In David Crystal (ed.), *Linguistic Controversies: Essays in Linguistic Theory and Practice in Honour of F. R. Palmer*. London: Edward Arnold, 73–79.

Robb, Michael P., Margaret A. Maclagan and Yang Chen. 2004. Speaking rates of American and New Zealand varieties of English. *Clinical Linguistics & Phonetics* 18:1–15.

Romaine, Suzanne. 1982a. *Sociohistorical Linguistics: Its Status and Methodology*. Cambridge, UK/New York: Cambridge University Press.

Romaine, Suzanne. 1982b. What is a speech community? In Suzanne Romaine (ed.), *Sociolinguistic Variation in Speech Communities*. London: Edward Arnold, 13–24.

Rosner, B.S. and J.B. Pickering. 1994. *Vowel Perception and Production*. Oxford, UK/ New York: Oxford University Press.

Rothenberg, Martin. n.d. A new method for measurement of nasalance. http://www.rothenberg.org/Nasalance/Nasalance.htm

Sangster, Catherine M. 2001. Lenition of alveolar stops in Liverpool English. *Journal of Sociolinguistics* 5:401–12.

Santos-Terron, M.J., G. Gonzalez-Linda and I. Sanchez-Ruiz. 1990. Nasometric patterns in the speech of normal child speakers of Castillian Spanish. *Revista Española de Foniatrica* 4:71–75.

Saussure, Ferdinand de. 1983. *Course in General Linguistics*, Charles Bally and Albert Sechehaye (eds) Roy Harris (tr). La Salle, IL: Open Court.

Schilling-Estes, Natalie. 1998. Investigating 'self-conscious' speech: The performance register in Ocracoke English. *Language in Society* 27:53–83.

Schleicher, August. 1853. Die ersten Spaltungen des indogermanischen Urvolkes. *Allgemeine Monatsschrift für Wissenschaft und Literatur* (vol. not numbered):786–7.

Schmidt, Johannes. 1872. *Die Verwandtschaftsverhältnisse der indogermanischen Sprachen*. Weimar: Hermann Böhlau.

Scobbie, James M. 2006. Flexibility in the face of incompatible English VOT systems. In Louis Goldstein, D.H. Whalen and Catherine T. Best (eds), *Laboratory Phonology 8*. Phonology and phonetics 4–2. Berlin/New York: Mouton de Gruyter.

Selting, Margret. 2003. Treppenkonturen im Dresdenerischen. *Zeitschrift für Germanistische Linguistik* 31:1–43.

Sharbawi, Salbrina Haji. 2006. The vowels of Brunei English: An acoustic investigation. *English World-Wide* 27:247–64.

Son, R.J.J.H. van and Louis C.W. Pols. 1990. Formant structure of Dutch vowels in a text, read at normal and fast rate. *Journal of the Acoustical Society of America* 88:1683–93.

Sproat, Richard and Osamu Fujimura. 1993. Allophonic variation in English /l/ and its implications for phonetic implementation. *Journal of Phonetics* 21:291–311.

Stanford, James N. 2008. A sociotonetic analysis of Sui dialect contact. *Language Variation and Change* 20:409–50.

Stevens, Kenneth N. 1998. *Acoustic Phonetics*. Current studies in linguistics 30. Cambridge, MA/London: MIT Press.

Stevens, Kenneth N. and Sheila E. Blumstein. 1994. Attributes of lateral consonants. *Journal of the Acoustical Society of America* 95:2875.

Strand, Elizabeth A. 1999. Uncovering the role of gender stereotypes in speech perception. *Journal of Language and Social Psychology* 18:86–100.

Strange, Winifred. 1989. Evolving theories of vowel perception. *Journal of the Acoustical Society of America* 85:2081–7.

Stuart-Smith, Jane. 1999. Glasgow: Accent and voice quality. In Paul Foulkes and Gerard J. Docherty (eds), *Urban Voices*. London: Arnold, 203–22.

Stuart-Smith, Jane. 2007. Empirical evidence for gendered speech production: /s/ in Glaswegian. In Jennifer Cole and José Ignacio Hualde (eds), *Laboratory Phonology 9*. Berlin/New York: Mouton de Gruyter, 65–86.

Sumner, Meghan and Arthur G. Samuel. 2009. The effect of experience on the perception and representation of dialect variants. *Journal of Memory and Language* 60:487–501.

Sussman, Harvey M., Helen A. McCaffrey and Sandra A. Matthews. 1991. An investigation of locus equations as a source of relational invariance for stop place categorization. *Journal of the Acoustical Society of America* 90:1309–25.

Sussman, Harvey M., Kathryn A. Hoemeke and Farhan S. Ahmed. 1993. A cross-linguistic investigation of locus equations as a phonetic descriptor for place of articulation. *Journal of the Acoustical Society of America* 94:1256–68.

Swerts, Marc, Eva Stranger and Mattias Heldner. 1996. F_0 declination in read-aloud and spontaneous speech. In *Proceedings of the Fourth International Conference on Spoken Language Processing, Philadelphia, October 1996, vol. 3*. Piscataway, NJ: IEEE, 1501–4.

Syrdal, Ann K. and H.S. Gopal. 1986. A perceptual model of vowel recognition based on the auditory representation of American English vowels. *Journal of the Acoustical Society of America* 79:1086–100.

Syrdal, Ann K., Julia Hirschberg, Julie McGory and Mary Beckman. 2001. Automatic ToBI prediction and alignment to speed manual labeling of prosody. ftp://ftp.cis.upenn.edu/pub/sb/sact/syrdal/syrdal.pdf

Takada, Mieko and Nobuo Tomimori. 2006. The relationship between VOT in initial voiced plosives and the phenomenon of word-medial plosives in Nigata and Shikoku. In Yuji Kawaguchi, Susumu Zaima and Toshihiro Takagaki (eds), *Spoken Language Corpus and Linguistic Informatics*. Usage-based linguistic informatics 5. Amsterdam/Philadelphia: John Benjamins, 365–79.

Tang, Chaoju and Vincent J. van Heuven. 2008. Mutual intelligibility of Chinese dialects tested functionally. In Marjo van Koppen and Bert Botma (eds), *Linguistics in the Netherlands 2008*. Amsterdam: John Benjamins, 145–56.

Tannen, Deborah and Muriel Saville-Troike (eds). 1985. *Perspectives on Silence*. Norwood, NJ: Ablex.

Tarone, Elaine E. 1973. Aspects of intonation in Black English. *American Speech* 48:29–36.

Thakerar, Jitendra N., Howard Giles and Jenny Cheshire. 1982. Psychological and linguistic parameters of speech accommodation theory. In Colin Fraser and Klaus R. Scherer (eds), *Advances in the Social Psychology of Language*. Cambridge, UK: Cambridge University Press, 205–55.

Thomas, Erik R. 1996. A Comparison of variation patterns of variables among sixth-graders in an Ohio community. In Edgar W. Schneider (ed.), *Focus on the USA*, 149–68.

Varieties of English around the world, General series 16. Amsterdam/Philadelphia: John Benjamins.

Thomas, Erik R. 1997. A rural/metropolitan split in the speech of Texas Anglos. *Language Variation and Change* 9:309–32.

Thomas, Erik R. 2000. Spectral differences in /ai/ offsets conditioned by voicing of the following consonant. *Journal of Phonetics* 28:1–25.

Thomas, Erik R. 2001. *An Acoustic Analysis of Vowel Variation in New World English*. Publication of the American Dialect Society 85. Durham, NC: Duke University Press.

Thomas, Erik R. 2002a. Instrumental phonetics. In J.K. Chambers, Peter Trudgill and Natalie Schilling-Estes (eds), *The Handbook of Language Variation and Change*. Oxford, UK/Malden, MA: Blackwell, 168–200.

Thomas, Erik R. 2002b. Sociophonetic applications of speech perception experiments. *American Speech* 77:115–47.

Thomas, Erik R. 2003. Secrets revealed by Southern vowel shifting. *American Speech* 78:150–70.

Thomas, Erik R. and Guy Bailey. 1992. A case of competing mergers and their resolution. *The SECOL Review* 16:179–200.

Thomas, Erik R. and Phillip M. Carter. 2006. Rhythm and African American English. *English World-Wide* 27:331–55.

Thomas, Erik R. and Jeffrey Reaser. 2004. Delimiting perceptual cues used for the ethnic labeling of African American and European American voices. *Journal of Sociolinguistics* 8:54–86.

Thomas, Erik R., Norman J. Lass and Jeannine Carpenter. 2010. Identification of African American speech. In Dennis R. Preston and Nancy Niedzielski (eds), *A Reader in Sociophonetics*. Trends in Linguistics: Studies and Monographs 219. New York: De Gruyter Mouton, 265–85.

Thomason, Sarah Grey and Terrence Kaufman. 1988. *Language Contact, Creolization, and Genetic Linguistics*. Berkeley: University of California Press.

Torgersen, Eivind and Paul Kerswill. 2004. Internal and external motivation in phonetic change: Dialect levelling outcomes for an English vowel shift. *Journal of Sociolinguistics* 8:23–53.

Torp, Arne. 2001. Retroflex consonants and dorsal /r/: Mutually excluding innovations? On the diffusion of dorsal /r/ in Scandinavian. In Hans Van de Velde and Roeland van Hout (eds), *'r-atics: Sociolinguistic, phonetic and phonological characteristics of /r/*. Brussels: Etudes & Travaux, Institut des Langues Vivantes et de Phonétique, Université Libre de Bruxelles, 75–90.

Trager, George L. and Henry Lee Smith. 1951. *An Outline of English Structure*. Norman, OK: Battenburg Press.

Traill, Anthony, Martin J. Ball and Nicole Müller. 1995. Perceptual confusion between South African and British English vowels. In Kjell Elenius and Peter Branderud (eds), *Proceedings of the 13th International Conference of Phonetic Sciences, ICPhS 95: Stockholm, Sweden, 13–19 August 1995*. Stockholm: Royal Institute of Technology and Stockholm University, 620–23.

Traunmüller, Hartmut. 1990. Analytical expressions for the tonotopic sensory scale. *Journal of the Acoustical Society of America* 88:97–100.

Traunmüller, Hartmut. 1997. Auditory scales of frequency representation. http://www2.ling.su.se/staff/hartmut/bark.htm

Trudgill, Peter. 1972. Sex, covert prestige, and linguistic change in the urban British English of Norwich. *Language in Society* 1:179–95.

Trudgill, Peter. 1974a. Linguistic change and diffusion: Description and explanation in sociolinguistic dialect geography. *Language in Society* 2:215–246.

Trudgill, Peter. 1974b. *The Social Differentiation of English in Norwich*. Cambridge: Cambridge University Press.

Trudgill, Peter. 1978. Introduction: Sociolinguistics and sociolinguistics. In Peter Trudgill (ed.), *Sociolinguistic Patterns in British English*. London: Edward Arnold/Baltimore: University Park Press, 1–18.

Trudgill, Peter. 1986. *Dialects in Contact*. Oxford, UK/New York: Blackwell.

Trudgill, Peter. 1988. Norwich revisited. *English World-Wide* 9:33–49.

Trudgill, Peter and Tina Foxcroft. 1978. On the sociolinguistics of vocalic mergers: Transfer and accommodation in East Anglia. In Peter Trudgill (ed.), *Sociolinguistic Patterns in British English*. London: Edward Arnold/Baltimore: University Park Press, 69–79.

Tsao, Ying Chiao and Gary Weismer. 1997. Interspeaker variation in habitual speaking rate: Evidence for a neuromuscular component. *Journal of Speech, Language & Hearing Research* 40:858–66.

Tukey, John W. 1977. *Exploratory Data Analysis*. Reading, MA: Addison-Wesley.

Ulbrich, Christiane. 2004. A comparative study of declarative intonation in Swiss and German standard varieties. In Peter Gilles and Jörg Peters (eds), *Regional Variation in Intonation*. Tübingen: Max Niemeyer Verlag, 99–122.

Van Borsel, John, Joke Janssens and Marc De Bodt. 2009. Breathiness as a feminine voice characteristic: A perceptual approach. *Journal of Voice* 23:291–4.

Van Heuven, Vincent J., Loulou Edelman and Renée van Bezooijen. 2002. The pronunciation of /ɛi/ by male and female speakers of avant-garde Dutch. In Hans Broekhuis and Paula Fikkert (eds), *Linguistics in the Netherlands 2002*. Amsterdam/ Philadelphia: John Benjamins, 61–72.

Van Hofwegen, Janneke. 2009. The apparent-time evolution of /l/ in one African American community. M.A. capstone report, North Carolina State University.

Veatch, Thomas Clark. 1991. English vowels: Their surface phonology and phonetic implementation in vernacular dialects. Ph.D. dissertation, University of Pennsylvania.

Venditti, Jennifer J. 2005. The J_ToBI model of Japanese intonation. In Sun-Ah Jun (ed.), *Prosodic Typology: The Phonology of Intonation and Phrasing*. Oxford, UK: Oxford University Press, 172–200.

Verbrugge, Robert R., Winifred Strange, Donald P. Shankweiler and Thomas R. Edman. 1976. What information enables a listener to map a talker's vowel space? *Journal of the Acoustical Society of America* 60:198–212.

Verhoeven, Jo, Guy De Pauw and Hanne Kloots. 2004. Speech rate in a pluricentric language: A comparison between Dutch in Belgium and the Netherlands. *Language and Speech* 47:297–308.

Wager, Tor D., Luis Hernandez, John Jonides and Martin Lindquist. 2007. Elements of functional neuroimaging. In John T. Cacioppo, Louis G. Tassinary and Gary G. Berntson (eds), *Handbook of Psychophysiology*, 3rd edn. Cambridge: Cambridge University Press, 19–55.

Walton, Julie H. and Robert F. Orlikoff. 1994. Speaker race identification from acoustic cues in the vocal signal. *Journal of Speech and Hearing Research* 37:738–45.

Wang, William S.-Y. (ed.). 1977. *The Lexicon in Phonological Change*. Monographs on linguistic analysis, no. 5. The Hague/Paris: Mouton de Gruyter.

Wardhaugh, Ronald. 2010. *An Introduction to Sociolinguistics*, 6th edn. Oxford, UK/ Malden, MA: Blackwell.

Warren, Paul. 2005. Patterns of late rising in New Zealand English: Intonational variation or intonational change? *Language Variation and Change* 17:209–30.

Wassink, Alicia Beckford. 2006. A geometric representation of spectral and temporal vowel features: Quantification of vowel overlap in three linguistic varieties. *Journal of the Acoustical Society of America* 119:2334–50.

Watt, Dominic and Anne Fabricius. 2002. Evaluation of a technique for improving the mapping of multiple speakers' vowel spaces in the F1 ~ F2 plane. *Leeds Working Papers in Linguistics and Phonetics* 9:159–73.

Watt, Dominic and Jennifer Tillotson. 2001. A spectrographic analysis of vowel fronting in Bradford English. *English World-Wide* 22:269–302.

Weinreich, Uriel. 1953. *Languages in Contact: Findings and Problems.* Publications of the Linguistic Circle of New York, no. 1. New York: Linguistic Circle of New York.

Weinreich, Uriel, William Labov and Marvin Herzog. 1968. Empirical Foundations for a Theory of Language Change. In Winfred P. Lehmann and Yakov Malkiel (eds), *Directions for Historical Linguistics: A Symposium.* Austin: University of Texas Press, 95–188.

Wells, J. C. 1982. *Accents of English*, 3 vols. Cambridge, UK: Cambridge University Press.

Wells, Rulon S. 1987. The life and growth of language: metaphors in biology and linguistics. In Henry M. Hoenigswald and Linda F. Wiener (eds), *Biological Metaphor and Cladistic Classification: An Interdisciplinary Perspective.* Philadelphia: University of Pennsylvania Press, 39–80.

Wenger, Etienne. 1998. *Communities of Practice: Learning, Meaning, and Identity.* Cambridge/New York: Cambridge University Press.

Wenk, Brian J. and François Wiolland. 1982. Is French really syllable-timed? *Journal of Phonetics* 10:193–216.

Westbury, John R., Michiko Hashi and Mary J. Lindstrom. 1998. Differences in lingual articulation for American English /ɹ/. *Speech Communication* 26:203–26.

White, Laurence and Sven L. Mattys. 2007. Rhythmic typology and variation in first and second languages. In Pilar Prieto, Joan Mascaró and Maria-Josep Solé (eds), *Segmental and Prosodic Issues in Romance Phonology.* Current issues in linguistic theory series. Amsterdam/Philadelphia: John Benjamins, 237–57.

Wiener, Linda F. 1987. Of phonetics and genetics: A comparison of classification in linguistic and organic systems. In Henry M. Hoenigswald and Linda F. Wiener (eds), *Biological Metaphor and Cladistic Classification: An Interdisciplinary Perspective.* Philadelphia: University of Pennsylvania Press, 217–26.

Wiese, Richard. 2001. The unity and variation of (German) /r/. In Hans Van de Velde and Roeland van Hout (eds), *'r-atics: Sociolinguistic, phonetic and phonological characteristics of /r/.* Brussels: Etudes & Travaux, Institut des Langues Vivantes et de Phonétique, Université Libre de Bruxelles, 11–26.

Wightman, Colin W., Stefanie Shattuck-Hufnagel, Mari Ostendorf and Patti J. Price. 1992. Segmental durations in the vicinity of prosodic phrase boundaries. *Journal of the Acoustical Society of America* 91:1707–17.

Williams, Ann and Paul Kerswill. 1999. Dialect levelling: Change and continuity in Milton Keynes, Reading and Hull. In Paul Foulkes and Gerard Docherty (eds), *Urban Voices: Accent Studies in the British Isles.* London: Arnold, 141–62.

Williams, Angie, Peter Garrett and Nikolas Coupland. 1999. Dialect recognition. In Dennis R. Preston (ed.), *Handbook of Perceptual Dialectology, vol. 1.* Amsterdam: John Benjamins, 345–58.

Willis, Clodius. 1972. Perception of vowel phonemes in Fort Erie, Ontario, Canada, and Buffalo, New York: An application of synthetic vowel categorization tests to dialectology. *Journal of Speech and Hearing Research* 15:246–55.

Wolfram, Walter A. 1969. *A Sociolinguistic Description of Detroit Negro Speech*. Urban language series 5. Washington, DC: Center for Applied Linguistics.

Wolfram, Walt and Natalie Schilling-Estes. 2006. *American English*, 2nd edn. Oxford, UK/Malden, MA: Blackwell.

Wolfram, Walt, Kirk Hazen and Natalie Schilling-Estes. 1999. *Dialect Change and Maintenance on the Outer Banks*. Publication of the American Dialect Society 81. Durham: Duke University Press.

Xu, Yi. 1999. Effects of tone and focus on the formation and alignment of f_0 contours. *Journal of Phonetics* 27:55–105.

Xu, Yi. 2001. Fundamental frequency peak delay in Mandarin. *Phonetica* 58:26–52.

Xu, Yi and Q. Emily Wang. 2001. Pitch targets and their realization: Evidence from Mandarin Chinese. *Speech Communication* 33:319–37.

Yu, Alan C.L. 2007. Understanding near mergers: The case of morphological tone in Cantonese. *Phonology* 24:187–214.

Yuan, Jiahong, Mark Liberman and Christopher Cieri. 2006. Towards an integrated understanding of speaking rate in conversation. *Proceedings of INTERSPEECH 2006, Pittsburgh, PA*, 541–4. http://www.ling.upenn.edu/~jiahong/

Yuasa, Ikuko Patricia. 2010. Creaky voice: A new feminine voice quality for young urban-oriented upwardly mobile American woman? *American Speech* 85:315–37.

Yumoto, Eiji, Wilbur J. Gould and Thomas Baer. 1982. Harmonics-to-noise ratio as an index to the degree of hoarseness. *Journal of the Acoustical Society of America* 71:1544–50.

Zawadzki, Paul A. and David P. Kuehn. 1980. A cineradiographic study of static and dynamic aspects of American English /r/. *Phonetica* 37:253–66.

Zhou, Xinhui, Carol Y. Espy-Wilson, Suzanne Boyce, Mark Tiede, Christy Holland and Ann Choe. 2008. A magnetic resonance imaging-based articulatory and acoustic study of 'retroflex' and 'bunched' American English /r/. *Journal of the Acoustical Society of America* 123:4466–81.

Zwicker, E., G. Flottorp and S.S. Stevens. 1957. Critical band width in loudness summation. *Journal of the Acoustical Society of America* 29:548–57.

Zwicker, E. and E. Terhardt. 1980. Analytical expressions for critical-band rate and critical bandwidth as a function of frequency. *Journal of the Acoustical Society of America* 68:1523–25.

Index